NATION AND IDEOLOGY
ESSAYS IN HONOR OF
WAYNE S. VUCINICH

Edited by

Ivo Banac, John G. Ackerman,
and
Roman Szporluk

EAST EUROPEAN MONOGRAPHS, BOULDER
DISTRIBUTED BY COLUMBIA UNIVERSITY PRESS
NEW YORK

1981

82-673

EAST EUROPEAN MONOGRAPHS, NO. LCV

FOREWORD AND ACKNOWLEDGMENTS

The jacket of this *Festschrift* contains Pavao Ritter Vitezović's rendition of Hercegovina's coat of arms and his accompanying explanatory poem as they both appeared in the original 1700 Vienna edition of this Croat polyhistor's famous *Stemmatographia* and in the subsequent 1741 Slavo-Serbian version by Hristofor Žefarović and Thomas Messmer. The editors feel that these images suggest both the ancestral land of Wayne S. Vucinich, whose lifework we celebrate with this volume, and the theme of Eurasian national ideologies, ever close to his scholarly interest, which we have chosen to unify the array of interests and styles characteristic of Vucinich's former students. During the course of work on this book, the editors were frequently reminded that Ritter opened a poem on Bileća Rudine, an area of Hercegovina which is Professor Vucinich's most immediate *patria,* with a line that begins, *"Rudina, in mala dura fatis."* Our joy at the successful completion of this *Festschrift* and our pride in finding this vehicle to honor our mentor and dear friend are, however, ample awards for the long ordeal.

Wayne Vucinich is one of the most distinguished pioneers of Slavic and Middle Eastern studies in the United States: a member of a small band of scholars who made American historical studies truly international, he has made indelible contributions to the study of the Balkan lands under the Ottomans and in the more recent past. He is, moreover, one of the first American scholars who appreciated the vast national variety of the Soviet Union and who contributed to and promoted the research of the non-Russian, especially Caucasian and Central Asian, nationalities of the USSR. The span of his research interests has included the history of European diplomacy, developments in East European historiography, the effects of Marxist socialism on the political culture of Russia and East Europe, as well as the history of East European minorities in this country. And, if that were not enough for a single scholarly career, Vucinich continues as a tireless promoter of all of these areas, with scores of already formed scholars in his debt.

In honoring Wayne Vucinich, the editors and the contributors of this volume wished to focus on a theme that united most of Vucinich's concerns. The question of national ideologies and their role in the history of

Southern and Eastern Europe and the Middle East was the obvious choice. Indeed, the growth of national sentiment, the defense of ethnic and religious uniqueness, and the rise of nationalism informed the majority of Vucinich's writings and was faithfully transmitted to his students. This shared interest is expressed on these pages.

The preparatory work on this *Festschrift* would have been impossible without the kind encouragement and assistance of Professor Peter D. Stansky, chairman of the Department of History at Stanford. Assistants at the department, notably Nancy J. Ray, Loraine E. Sinclair, and Elise M. Johnson, helped us in compiling the long list of Professor Vucinich's doctoral students and other Stanford historians who were prominent in Vucinich's undergraduate and graduate seminars. The copy-editing and the publication of the *Festschrift* were assisted by generous donations from several Stanford graduates to whom we are extremely grateful.

I.B.

J.G.A.

R.S.

3 February 1981

DONORS

CONTENTS

A TRIBUTE TO WAYNE S. VUCINICH: SCHOLAR, TEACHER, AND UNCLE*

Reginald E. Zelnik
University of California–Berkeley

Vartan Gregorian
University of Pennsylvania

To his students Wayne S. Vucinich has been many things: the author of the acclaimed *Serbia between East and West*, awarded the American Historical Association's George Louis Beer Prize in 1955, and other important works; a scholar who has organized and contributed to major conferences and publications on topics as wide-ranging as Russia and Asia, contemporary Yugoslavia, and the peasant in nineteenth-century Russia; a leader within such professional associations as the American Historical Association and the American Association for the Advancement of Slavic Studies; a vigorous champion of Balkan, Slavic, East European, and Near Eastern studies. Moreover, to many of us who have grown accustomed to thinking of scholarship and teaching as conflicting choices in an academic career, Wayne Vucinich has been living proof that it need not be that way: a scholar, a man whose breadth of learning and depth of historical understanding are manifested in his books and articles, can at the same time be an outstanding teacher sharing with students his contagious sensibility, knowledge, and, above all, his spontaneous enthusiasm for history and historical discourse. And, we hasten to add, giving of his time, as personal and academic adviser.

---

* The following remarks are said to have been delivered in unison by Professors Gregorian and Zelnik at a banquet in honor of Professor Vucinich's retirement. However, the editors have been unable to ascertain the date and location of this event.

One of Wayne Vucinich's favorite subjects is the South Slavic *zadruga* (extended family). The authors of the rich and diverse articles contained in this *Festschrift* have many ties, but they have one trait in common. They were all "nephews" and "nieces" of "Uncle Wayne."* They all belong to the Vucinich *zadruga*. For Wayne Vucinich has created and sustained a community of students and a community of scholars. That adult men and women—some of us already middle-aged and greying professors, others well advanced along that road, dispersed throughout the United States and the world—can continue to employ this unique and sentimental designation without embarrassment and with warm affection, even commit it, perhaps for the first time, to print, is indisputable evidence of this man's impact on all of us. He has made us into cousins, some collateral, some once, twice, even many times removed, but intellectual and even spir-'IT-ual (his emphasis) cousins nonetheless. The "nephews" and "nieces" of Uncle Wayne have always been one of his central preoccupations. He has always looked after them, no matter how young, or how old, no matter how "successful," or how "unsuccessful" they have been. He has done this unabashedly as a patriarch, as a teacher, and as a friend, and, we might add, to the regret of none of us. . . .

(Of course, membership in the Vucinich *zadruga* is not without its obligations. For example, when Vucinich chairs a program committee or a conference, you can be sure that his widely dispersed nephews and nieces will be well represented. [Accordingly, the program is consistently outstanding!] And if a nephew or a niece is delivering a paper, he or she can always be assured of a friendly and familiar audience.)

What secret can account for the invisible web of intellectual and spiritual solidarity that Vucinich has spun among his students over the decades? Is it his personality? His intellect? His humanity? His enthusiasm? Alas, there is no single key, no single factor. It has been all these things and more. Perhaps some insight into W. S. V. the man can be gained by recalling some of our experiences as members of Uncle's seminars.

The one we remember the best, but typical of many others, is the Vucinich seminar on Nazi Germany's penetration of Eastern Europe and the Balkans (essentially the Habsburg successor states). The course was very demanding. It required a good command of German and

---

* Hereafter cited in its more commonly used short form: "Uncle."

knowledge of an East European language would have provided additional help. Among the participants—and this kind of cosmopolitan atmosphere was typical of the Vucinich entourage—were an exchange student from Poland and a recent refugee from Hungary, soon magically transformed into American nephews. The discussion was always lively, as both instructor and students peppered their historical analyses with personal anecdotes and reminiscences. Indeed, Vucinich has always been an unsurpassed master of the illustrative anecdote (sometimes embodied in the stories of Nasreddin Hoca), used not only to infuse academic history with the humor it so often lacks, but also as a mnemonic device; for him, history could be fun, yet the fun had a serious purpose.

Like all of Vucinich's seminars, this one was organized around a theme of common interest—one that lent itself to a series of different but parallel research projects. Working in this way, the students were encouraged to raise similar questions about comparable problems, to assist each other in their formulation and resolution, to chat about them informally outside the classroom. Which "elements" (a favorite Vucinich expression) in Yugoslavia, Czechoslovakia, or Hungary were most likely to collaborate with the Germans? Was ethnicity or class the more decisive consideration —today we would say "variable"—in determining the likelihood—today, "propensity"—of collaboration? These and a variety of related questions were discussed in an intense but friendly atmosphere. Uncle always set the tone which we at first would imitate—some of us to the point where we began to drop our definite articles and imagine we were speaking in Serbian. But gradually, with his encouragement, we began to find our individual styles and idioms, though we have observed moments of recidivism even to the present.

Amazingly, we cannot remember a deadline that was not met: first draft, second draft, final draft. Our alacrity was not the result of pressure from an iron hand; rather, it reflected the enthusiasm that Vucinich's teaching engendered and our own desire to share the results of our research with one another and with him. Though his criticism was always sharp, we cannot recall a single instance of a student who was rebuked or admonished. Avuncular, but not authoritarian.

Mutatis mutandis, the same warm atmosphere obtained in Uncle's undergraduate lecture courses (always regularly attened by a coterie of graduate students). Of course even a *zadruga* has its limits, and it would be misleading to suggest that the sixty, eighty, or one hundred rosey-cheeked lads and lasses who crowded into the lecture hall in Stanford's "History Corner"—to listen to *our* Uncle hold forth on the Battle of Klokotnitsa, the Bogumils, János Hunyadi and Skenderbeg, Koraïs and Karadjordje, Ban Jelačić and Nikita of Montenegro, or the Treaty of Hünkar Iskelesi—could possibly be part of our extended family. *We* were the privileged stratum; our special privileges included ready access to the scholarly wisdom of Uncle's colleagues in the Hoover Institution coffee room, as well as many kind invitations to Sally Vucinich's friendly home (a dinner after passing one's Ph.D. orals was *de rigeur*). These were further examples of the advantages of "nepotism" that we regret not at all. Of course, our younger colleagues did not even notice these gaps in their lives, and profit from Uncle's lectures nonetheless, many becoming budding experts on Mustafa Kemal before they had even heard of Maximilien Robespierre, on the Serbian epic before the *Divine Comedy*, on the battle of Kosovo before Trafalgar. And they knew all about Muhammad Ali *avant la parole*. . . .

A recent issue of Stanford University's paper for faculty and staff contains an essay, part of its "series on notable Stanford teachers," bearing the title: "Wayne Vucinich has played role [notice the ubiquitous missing article!] of father and advisor to all."[1] Informative as it is, the essay overlooks certain nuances. The title itself misses the subtle distinction between the paternal and avuncular (though "Uncle" gets its due in the text) and the word "all" is clearly a journalistic exaggeration, stretching the boundaries of family life beyond recognition. The opening paragraph on young Vojo's historic emigration from the mountains of Hercegovina neglects the historically vital fact that no genuine, patriotic niece or nephew would fail to reveal at the outset: little Vojo's virtually mythic birth in the ranges of Montana.[2] The author's judicious account of Vucinich's academic and military career—his studies at Berkeley with the formidable yet venerable Robert J. Kerner, his sojourn at "Prague University" (*sic,* or is it *sich*?), his outstanding service in intelligence work during the Second World War with the Office of Strategic Services, his participation in the United States Contingent of the Allied Control Council in Bulgaria, and his swift rise to academic stardom—is accurate and unexceptionable, though a true nephew longs to flesh it out with stories absorbed over wine in the wee hours of the morning. But the high point of the article is a rare, introspective account of Vucinich's approach to teaching by the master himself. We quote:

> Some elements [again those elements!] in good teaching are basic: know your subject, avoid the impression of being authoritarian and a disciplinarian, be kind and receptive, be organized and articulate. If you heed these basic principle, you will be a good teacher. To be a superior teacher takes more than a mastery of pedagogical techniques. *Infectious enthusiasm for the subject and complete mastery of it* are the most essential qualities.[3]

Nothing could better capture what was unique in Vucinich's teachings than the italicized words. A hard act to follow!

Yes, we have all reaped benefits from being Uncle's nephews and nieces. Our scholarship, our teaching, our decisions to pursue this or that language and field of specialization, our sense of responsibility to our students and our colleagues, and, not to be forgotten, our original "placement" (always one of Uncle's prime concerns, accompanied by reminders of the days of the Depression and the requirements of "marketability")—all bear the mark of his influence. But we also like to think that the nieces and nephews did something for him, as well. We have in mind not only such memorable moments as when Gabor Vermes, almost fresh from Budapest, rescued a faculty party at the Vucinich's by tending bar and almost put some stones in a drink when someone ordered Scotch-on-the-rocks. More seriously, we like to think that we—the contributors to this *Festschrift* and others as well—have helped to keep the *zadruga* alive for Wayne, have made it possible for a piece of old country to survive with him here, just as his summer home in Sea Ranch, his "Villino Bilecha," evokes for him the memory of his ancestral homeland. Neither, of course, can replace the reality, any more than ferrying down the Danube every summer can take the place of the river trips of Uncle's boyhood. But Uncle Wayne, at heart, is a romantic, and so are most of his nephews and nieces. No apologies, no regrets.

NOTES

1. *Campus Report,* 28 November 1979, pp. 3-4. The author is Donald Stokes.
2. Fortunately, this point is clarified later in the article.
3. *Campus Report* (our emphasis).

COUNT MARCELLINUS AND DALMATIAN AUTONOMY: A STUDY IN THE CONTINUITY OF THE ROMAN TRADITION

Frank E. Wozniak
University of New Mexico

The Roman province of Dalmatia received its final geographical delineation in the reign of Diocletian, a native Dalmatian emperor who organized the southern portions of principate Dalmatia into the province of Praevalitana, which developed along lines similar to most of old Dalmatia.[1] Even though stripped of the more primitive mountain regions that in the Middle Ages became the nucleus of the Slavic kingdom of Doclea, Diocletian Dalmatia was not a homogeneous province, but an area that comprised several distinct geographical regions. The most obvious topographical distinction was that between the coastal region and the interior. Though the densely wooded and mountainous interior of Dalmatia was difficult to penetrate, the Romans had managed to drive several important roads into the region, first in their efforts to subdue the province in the early principate and then as part of their attempt to exploit the interior's considerable mineral wealth.[2] But even this Dalmatian interior was divided into two regions; the northern, which was oriented toward the Sava Valley, and an eastern section focused on the valley of the Drina. Both of these areas were linked with the coast and the outside but not with each other.

After the conquest the Romans were attracted to the interior primarily because of its mineral wealth. The mining industry was concentrated in two separate areas corresponding to the interor's topographical divisions. The Sana Valley, which lay in northwestern Dalmatia near the Sava River, had rich deposits of iron which were mined into the sixth century.[3] Like much of interior Dalmatia, the Sana Valley mining district was linked more naturally to another Roman province, in this case Savia, than with its own administrative region. The Domavia mining area, rich in argentiferous lead, was located in the Drina Valley,[4] and its most logical communications route led down the Drina to Pannonia secunda and the capital of the Illyrian diocese, Sirmium. The Romans, however, with considerable effort built a satisfactory network of roads that linked these disparate regions with Salona, the administrative capital of the province. Administrative imperatives prevailed over geographical realities and the province of Dalmatia was knit together by a road system that centralized the political activities of the province at Salona on the coast.

The integration between coast and interior was, however, only administrative; the interior of Dalmatia was never more than partially Romanized.[5] The settlement patterns of the Latin-speaking colonists segregated them from the more superficially Romanized Illyrian population. The Romans were concentrated in the mining areas and the coastal plain because of these regions' economic potential. Roman garrisons were scattered throughout the interior but their numbers were small and relatively unimportant away from the two or three major road axes. Other than the Sana Valley and the Domavia district the politically and economically important parts of Dalmatia were not in the interior.

Despite the system of roads, the coast and the interior were not even closely knit in an economic sense. While the mining districts attracted Roman settlers and became important settlements and markets, they seem to have remained largely isolated and insulated from the coast. The volume of trade between the coast and the interior was relatively small, especially as most of the mineral wealth of northern and eastern Dalmatia was mined under a government monopoly and shipped outside the province; consequently, this wealth tended to be only an indirect factor in the coastal economy. Even the large-scale recruitment of soldiers into the Roman army from among the partially Romanized Illyrian population of the interior, a practice that lasted from the third to the late sixth century, did not break down the isolation of the interior. The several regions of Dalmatia were administratively part of the same province but the divisions between the coastal plain and the inland regions were deep and tended to persist not only until the collapse of the Imperial system in the early seventh century but for centuries beyond.

Though this essay will be concerned with the whole of Dalmatia, it will focus largely on the coastal area and its immediate hinterland. In part this emphasis is necessitated by the nature of the sources, but more so by the fact that it was the coastal region with its Romanized population and urban traditions which encompassed and perpetuated the Roman ideals of government and society.[6] The coastal plain, its hinterland, and the islands were oriented not toward the Balkan interior but toward the Adriatic and Italy. The road system that radiated from Salona facilitated access to the interior and some of the resources of the interior were probably used to supply the state factories at Salona and Spalatum. Nonetheless, the mountains were not only a physical but also a psychological barrier. Once over the mountains, even on the excellent Roman roads, the traveler found himself beyond the Mediterranean region and in the midst of an only partially Romanized population, at least until that person reached the mining districts or the great interior river valleys.

From the Roman perspective, except for its exploitable mineral wealth and its abundance of sturdy recruits, the interior was not nearly so important as the coastal region and the islands. Here was the locus of the urban and commercial life that made for civilization. The climate, the soil, and the sea attracted settlers and led directly to the Romanization of coastal Dalmatia before the fourth century A. D.[7] The sea made life possible for the Romanized population of Dalmatia. The Adriatic gave fish and salt but even more importantly it provided trade. The abundance of good harbors and the protected waters of the Dalmatian littoral encouraged maritime activity. The mountains provided timber for ships; the land and the sea supplied goods for commerce. As a result, the cities of Dalmatia prospered. The close ties between Dalmatia and Italy were strengthened, and Roman traditions and the Roman system were firmly entrenched on the eastern side of the Adriatic below the Dinaric Alps.

Their isolation from the interior was to prove immensely beneficial to the cities of the littoral during the barbarian invsions. The whole of Dalmatia was little affected by the wars and invasions of the third century and, because it was off the main lines of communication in the Balkans, Dalmatia was not much involved in the civil wars of the early and mid-fourth century. Although continued recruitment of Illyrian peasants into the Roman army perpetuated contacts on a military and political level, the modest economic links that had existed between the littoral and the interior began to disintegrate. The roads from the coast fell into disuse during the fourth century[8] and, by the end of that century, the interior, particularly the north, had suffered a devastating and irreversible setback.[9] All of these changes were related to the onset of a decade of serious barbarian invasions that affected the whole of the Balkans following the death in 395 of the emperor Theodosius the Great.

In the ultimate settlement between Theodosius's heirs, Dalmatia was alloted as part of the diocese of Illyricum (western Illyricum) to the praetorian prefecture of Italy, while Praevalitana (which included former parts of Dalmatia) became part of the diocese of Dacia under the praetorian prefect of Illyricum (eastern Illyricum).[10] Consequently, Dalmatia was on the border between the eastern and western halves of the Roman Empire and, as a result, became involved in the administrative wrangling of the next half century over the disposition of the whole of Illyricum.

In the aftermath of the death of Theodosius, the Visigoths under Alaric, a former federate of Theodosius, left their assigned regions in the northern parts of Illyricum and broke into rebellion. They sacked northern Dalmatia in late 395 and reached Salona in the same year before proceeding south into Epirus and Thessalia.[11] Although none of the coastal cities seems to have been adversely affected, the cities and towns of the northern interior near the Sava Valley were badly damaged. In their wake, the Goths drew other barbarians into northern though not littoral Dalmatia.[12] After some lapse of time, the combined Roman forces under Stilicho landed at Salona and pursued the Goths down the coastal road into Epirus. It appears that the well-fortified but ungarrisoned cities of coastal Dalmatia probably received some small garrisons at this time.

The northern regions of Dalmatia were afflicted by barbarian attacks again in 397. Then with Alaric commissioned as *magister militum per Illyricum* alternately by the eastern and western Roman governments, the Visigoths pillaged the area legally and illegally from 398 to 408.[13] Few of the Roman settlements in northern Dalmatia were defensible, and many of them were destroyed by the barbarians or abandoned by their population during the decade after 395. The consequent decline in urban life further reinforced the split between the littoral and the island districts.

When the local population escaped immediate destruction, its best option was flight either to hill forts (the principal destination of the partially Romanized Illyrian peasants) or to the Dalmatian coast and Italy.

The fortifications of the Dalmatian littoral provided some measure of security for those who did not attempt the extra step of crossing the Adriatic.[14] In either case the refugees had put a substantial though not impenetrable mountain range between themselves and the barbarians and placed themselves directly in contact with the Roman world. The mountainous terrain between the Sava Valley and the littoral tended to discourage and weaken attacks from the north; in fact, after the invasion of 395, coastal Dalmatia was free from attack by barbarians from the north for more than fifty years.

Not only people but whole factories found refuge on the coast. Salona, already the site of an Imperial arms factory, was the recipient of an Imperial textile factory that was moved from Bassiana, an area that bore the brunt of contemporary barbarian attacks.[15] At the same time the Imperial mint at Siscia in the province of Savia was closed.[16] (The possibility exists that it was also moved to Salona.)

From a certain perspective the refugees presented a serious policing problem, and in 415 Imperial officials in Dalmatia and the diocese of Illyricum were ordered to address the situation.[17] Still, the continuation of barbarian devastations in the regions beyond the Dinaric Alps perpetuated the influx of refugees whose movements government officials were not able to supervise. The *Notitia Dignitatum* and other contemporary sources provide evidence that the refugees found a fully elaborated and functioning Roman administration in coastal Dalmatia.[18] While to a certain extent an administrative incumbrance, the refugees constituted an important addition to the population of the coastal cities and reinforced not only the numbers but also the Roman character of this part of Dalmatia. Perceiving themselves as the preservers of Roman tradition in an increasingly unstable and non-Roman world, the refugees and the native littoral population developed an intense commitment to their Roman identity. Though firmly committed to the empire, the Romans of littoral Dalmatia found themselves at the center of an administrative quarrel between Ravenna and Constantinople which was not of their own making but which for nearly a half a century left the area under West Roman sovereignty.[19]

During much of the wrangling between the two parts of the empire, which lasted until 437, Dalmatia was only indirectly affected by events in either Italy or the rest of the Balkans. Protected by their geographical position, the cities of coastal Dalmatia did not attract the attention of the barbarians, as did their neighbors to the east and the west, and were drawn into higher govenmental affairs only on rare occasions, as in 425 when Salona was the base for an Eastern-financed and militarily supported effort that successfully reestablished Valentianian III as emperor in the West.[20] But this intrusion only briefly and temporarily affected coastal Dalmatia. Even the transfer of the Illyrian diocese to Constantinople in 437 seems to have left coastal Dalmatia to the Italian government and thus to its traditional West Roman orientation. For the most part littoral Dalmatia lived in isolation from the events of the day, but all this was changed after 454. From this point Dalmatia enjoyed virtual autonomy under the administrations of Count Marcellinus and Julius Nepos but at the same time it became deeply involved in the complex of political and military problems which beset the West Roman government in the last quarter century of its existence.

The presence of Marcellinus as the military commander in Dalmatia attests to the fact that coastal Dalmatia continued to be administered under the prefecture of Italy and the Western Empire after 437.[21] Marcellinus was apparently a pagan from the Gallo-Roman nobility. His father, also named Marcellinus, was probably the *comes rerum privatorum* in the eastern part of the empire who was mentioned in the Novel of Theodosius II for October 438.[22] Like many of his fellow Gallo-Roman aristocrats, Marcellinus seems to have accepted the necessity of cooperating with the *magister militum* for the Western Empire, Aetius, in the defense of those territories.[23] This cooperation between the Gallo-Romans and Aetius culminated in the defeat of the Huns in Gaul in 451.

Aetius probably appointed Marcellinus as *comes rei militaris* for Dalmatia in the mid or late 440s. That Marcellinus's father had probably been the *comes rerum privatorum* in Constantinople points to the lingering ties between the two parts of the empire but does not indicate any special ties between the family of Marcellinus and the Constantinopolitan government.[24] Though Marcellinus himself would eventually develop a close relationship with the East Roman Emperor Leo, he was, nonetheless, initally the appointee of the Western Roman government in its only remaining Balkan territories.

Marcellinus's administration seems at first to have encompassed the Dalmatian coast, its immediate hinterland, and the East Adriatic islands, though it is possible that the surviving Roman communities of the interior were included, especially those in the region of the Sana Valley iron mines. As we have seen, coastal Dalmatia's geographic isolation had protected it from the raids and other travails that afflicted the interior in the fifth century. Given the region's limited trade with the interior, the economic losses were not severe; and, in addition, the flight of refugees from the interior had reinforced the Roman population of coastal Dalmatia in both physical and cultural terms. It was thus a prosperous and easily defended province that Marcellinus received, a province as Roman as Italy itself and an important source of potential support for the West Roman government new ensconced at Ravenna.[25]

All of the sources assert that Marcellinus was a friend of Aetius, and it seems to have been that closeness that prompted Marcellinus in 454 to break with the government of Valentinian III because of the latter's complicity in Aetius's murder.[26] The militarily isolated location of Dalmatia encouraged this separatist effort by Marcellinus. While neither separating Dalmatia from the Roman world nor seeking the protection of the Eastern emperor, Marcellinus established an autonomous regime in Dalmatia which with some lapses and vicissitudes lasted until 480/481, when the province was reincorporated into the prefecture of Italy.

As *comes rei militaris,* Marcellinus seems to have exercised authority over both the military and the civil administration of Dalmatia. Marcellinus's government controlled the coastal area of Dalmatia from Liburnia south to Epidaros and beyond, and until 459 the coast of Praevalitana and Epirus nova with Dyrrachium. The sources do not reveal how or why he acquired the coastal region south of Dalmatia to Dyrrachium; we know only that in 459 these areas were Marcellinus's and that they were subsequently lost to the Ostrogoths and shortly thereafter absorbed back into the Eastern Roman administration.[27] It seems possible, however, that Marcellinus acquired the west Balkan littoral down to Dyrrachium in order to protect the region from the Vandals after the sack of Rome in 455 and the expansion of the Vandal activities throughout the central Mediterranean. Since the Imperial government of Marcian at Constantinople did not have the means or the inclination to become involved in west Balkan or Adriatic naval affairs, Marcellinus seems to have stepped in and met the defensive emergency with his own resources. He was the head of a neighboring Roman administration that had the

means and the will to resist the Vandals, and the threatened Roman populations of the region would surely have welcomed his initiative. It is
possible that Marcian's government called upon Marcellinus, as the nearest
available Roman general, to defend the region.

It remains impossible to define precisely how far into the Dalmatian
interior Marcellinus's writ ran. His presence on the coast south of Dalmatia
was too brief to have permitted any move into that interior, but we
can be confident that he controlled the Dalmatian islands, the coastal
plain of Dalmatia, and the immediate hinterland with the interior valleys
around the cities of Scardona, Narona, and Trebinje—all of which were
easily accessible from the coast and located west of the main interior
plateau. The effectiveness of his government beyond the Dinaric Alps
is uncertain. Marcellinus's control surely extended some way up the Roman
roads into the interior but at any great distance from the coast, his control
probably became nominal. The semi-Romanized Illyrian peasants were
a source of recruits for Marcellinus's army as they were to be for Justinian's in the sixth century. It would seem that some residual authority
or tradition enabled him to attract these recruits, but perhaps it was
only the prospect of good wages and regular employment which lured
the Illyrians down from the mountains. Some scattered pockets of Roman
population survived in the interior along the road network and in areas
such as the Sana Valley. Later in the century the Ostrogoths found some
important residual Roman elements that survived the turmoil of war
and invasion until the early sixth century, when the Ostrogoths asserted
their authority in the interior of Dalmatia and western Illyricum, south
of the Drava River.

If Marcellinus's authority did extend into the interior, he does not
seem to have been able to reopen the Domavia mines, which had been
abandoned in the late fourth or early fifth century, but he may have
been able to reopen or keep open the Sana Valley iron mines.[28] Though
they were probably disrupted in the latter part of the century and reorganized by the Ostrogoths in the early sixth century, these mines at
Sana appear to have been in continuous operation during much of the
fifth century.[29] The Dalmatian government of Marcellinus and those
of his predecessors and successors do not seem to have suffered from a
shortage of iron to supply the Imperial arms factory that functioned continually at Salona.[30] While it was possible that the Dalmatians imported

their iron by sea (they had the commercial and maritime capacity to do this), it appears more likely that their iron came from the Sana Valley. The mining and smelting operations in that region were not so sophisticated that they could not be revived readily even if temporarily disrupted.[31] Furthermore, since fifth-century Dalmatia as a whole seems to have been spared much of the attention of the barbarians, it is possible, indeed likely, that the province's needs for iron were met by the Sana Valley mines.

At least in coastal Dalmatia, Marcellinus inherited a fully functioning provincial administration.[32] Until 454 this administration was subordinate to the prefecture of Italy in civil affairs and the *magister militum* of the West in military affairs.[33] Marcellinus, in breaking with the emperor, must have assumed the fiscal administration that had previously been under the centralized control of either the Italian prefecture or the diocese of Illyricum. In order to sustain this newly autonomous position, he needed the sole disposition of the revenue of the province; he could not afford to continue the dispersal of funds from Dalmatia to the central government with which he had now broken. Most if not all of the civil provincial administration as defined by the *Notitia Dignitatum* probably continued to function under Marcellinus, who now made the administrative appointments formerly controlled by the central administration at Ravenna. Only by controlling these appointments could Marcellinus assure his control of the province, secure its autonomy, and at the same time deter any subversion initiated by the government at Ravenna.

The geographical position of Dalmatia was the first element that facilitated separatism, but it was the province's commercial prosperity, economic autonomy, and military immunity that enabled Marcellinus not only to carry out his defiance of the emperor Valentinian, but also to become a feared and important factor in the politics of the Western Empire. Dalmatia had a self-sustaining commercial economy that brought prosperity to the province and revenues to the *comes* and his administration.[34] The wealth of Dalmatia was founded on the Adriatic maritime trade. The merchant marine of littoral and insular Dalmatia sustained this commercial position and also provided Marcellinus with a virtual monopoly on regional shipping in the Adriatic. In addition, the demise of the Imperial fleet in the West meant that Dalmatia was nearly immune from naval attack except from the Imperial fleet at Constantinople or the Vandals' piratical fleet at Carthage.[35]

Marcellinus was in a position similar to that of Geiseric, the king of the Vandals.[36] He controlled a prosperous maritime region with a hinterland adequate to provide raw materials, food, and revenues to support an autonomous regime. An additional similarity was his ability to maintain a naval capacity that insured the autonomy of his government against the Ravenna regime. Unlike Geiseric, Marcellinus never faced a challenge from the only regular battle fleet in the Mediterranean, that of the Eastern Empire. At the crucial junctures of Constantinopolitan intervention in the West, Marcellinus was a friend and ally of the East Romans. At Salona, Marcellinus was able to equip a fleet of converted merchant ships to serve as warships and transports which gave him control of the Adriatic.[37] From this base in Dalmatia, Marcellinus secured the timber reserves of the Dalmatian coast and the ready supply of sailors from the Dalmatian population with its maritime traditions. This naval monopoly in the Adriatic sustained the autonomy of Dalmatia and made Marcellinus a powerful factor in West Roman politics. In addition, the maritime trade of the Adriatic was not seriously affected by the disorders of the mid- and late fifth century. While the Vandals raided and controlled much of the Mediterranean, their presence in the Adriatic was sporadic and the regional trade in the Adriatic seems to have remained consistently good during the fifth and into the sixth centuries.[38]

In military as opposed to naval matters, Marcellinus was also in an excellent position. Two Imperial textile factories at Salona and Spalatum provided uniforms and revenue.[39] Even more important was the Imperial arsenal at Salona which made Dalmatia self-sufficient in the production of a wide range of weaponry.[40] With a secure source of weapons and revenues, Marcellinus seems to have recruited some numbers of Illyrian peasants into the provincial army, though most of his army was composed of Hunnic mercenaries (federates?). The availability of these soldiers, who had been of great worth to Aetius, was enhanced by the contemporaneous breakup of the Hunnic Empire, which allowed the *comes* to draw upon significant supplies of manpower from the regions to the north of Dalmatia. The *comes rei militaris* had, in Dalmatia, the means to sustain his autonomy and the potential to act in a wide expanse of the central Mediterranean and Adriatic.

The several years of anarchy within the West Roman government after the deaths of Aetius and Valentinian III had given him the opportunity to consolidate his position in Dalmatia.[41] After a few years, no one seems to have considered suppressing Marcellinus's separatist venture; even the East Romans only sought to influence his actions and not to displace him. Marcellinus now had all of the requisite resources and credentials to consider a bid for the much disputed West Roman throne. In the immediate aftermath of 454 the question was how far Marcellinus would push the separatism of his province and what role he would play in West Roman affairs.

After Valentinian III was murdered in March 455, there was no male heir of the Western emperor nor was there any powerful military leader, such as Aetius had been, to dispose of the throne;[42] the result was civil war. The brief reign of Maximus was followed by that of Avitus, recently appointed *magister militum* for Gaul. Avitus had also been a close friend of Aetius and had persuaded Theoderic II, king of the Visigoths, to fulfill his *foedus* with the empire and to march against the Huns in 451. In his bid for the emperorship, Avitus had the encouragement of Theoderic and the support of the Gallo-Roman nobility who had resented, for more than half a century, the preponderant influence of the Italian aristocracy in the central government at Ravenna. Avitus was proclaimed emperor by the Visigoths in July 455 and invested with the Imperial insignia at Arles (August 455) with the support of the fiercely chauvinistic Gallo-Roman nobility. Avitus crossed the Alps to assert his authority in Italy, and in September 455 the Italo-Roman aristocrats and the Roman army in Italy grudgingly but finally accepted the Gallic contender as emperor.[43]

Avitus brought peace to the prefecture of Gaul and the promise of a war of extermination against the Vandals.[44] When the Vandals attacked Sicily in 456, *comes* Ricimer repulsed them at Agrigento and destroyed their naval expedition to Corsica in the waters off that island. Using his newly won prestige, playing on popular discontent, and conspiring with the dissident Italo-Roman nobility, Ricimer (now *magister militum praesentalis*) set out to undermine the authority of Avitus. In this endeavor Ricimer had the support of Majorian, the *comes domesticorum,* who served as his intermediary with the senatorial aristocracy in Italy. Confronted with the powerful coalition of Ricimer, Majorian, and the senatorial nobility, Avitus fled Rome in September 456 and made one attempt to rally support from the Gallo-Romans and Visigoths. When the emperor and his modest forces recrossed the Alps in October 456, they were crushed by the rebels and Avitus himself was captured. Ricimer and his allies deposed Avitus and installed him as bishop of Placentia. Still fearing for his life, Avitus attempted a winter escape to the safety of his native Gaul but died on the journey. We do not know whether his death was natural or the result of a criminal act, but given Ricimer's later treatment of those who held the Imperial throne, we must suspect the latter.

The response of the Gallo-Roman nobility was two-fold: on the one hand, they momentarily detached the prefecture of Gaul from the empire and refused to submit to the murderers of Avitus; on the other hand, a faction of the Gallo-Roman aristocracy, insisting on Roman unity, wished to proclaim *comes* Marcellinus of Dalmatia as emperor.[45] The choice was the most logical one for the Imperial party of the Gallo-Roman leadership. Marcellinus was a Gallo-Roman and a pagan who controlled a substantial fleet and had access to large numbers of mercenaries in the anarchic world of the Danubian Valley. His promotion to emperor would trap the Italian prefecture, Ricimer, and the whole murderous conspiracy in a vise between Gaul and Dalmatia. The only possible impediment to the scheme of the Imperial party was the apparent separatist tendencies that Marcellinus had displayed in refusing to recognize any Western emperor since the death of Aetius.

If Marcellinus had any inclination to become emperor, he did not accept the offer of the Gallo-Roman aristocrats but rather preserved his own independence and the autonomy of his province.[46] It is possible that he had absorbed the strong separatist tendencies of one part of the Gallo-Roman nobility.[47] At the same time, however, Marcellinus did not withdraw himself from affairs in the West. He seems to have intended to maintain his unchallenged position as the separatist ruler of an autonomous Dalmatia who would threaten the Roman government at Ravenna by retaining his ability to intervene in Western Imperial affairs. He was much too powerful to be ignored by the Ravenna government, but he was perspicacious enough to avoid the Imperial office itself. His decision must have been helped by the inability of Gallo-Roman nobility to maintain their previous candidates on the throne for very long and by his recognition, given the career of Aetius, that the emperorship was obviously not the office that gave one control of Western Roman affairs.[48]

The power vacuum left by the deposition of Avitus had meanwhile been filled in April 457, when Majorian was proclaimed emperor by his own soldiers and those of Ricimer, but this same act precipitated a crisis with Eastern Rome. Since there was no constitutional monarch in the West, Leo I, the senior and undeniably legitimate emperor, had now assumed responsibility for the whole of the empire. He had already enhanced the positions of both Majorian and Ricimer, appointing them *magister militum* and patrician respectively, but he refused to recognize Majorian as emperor, viewing the proclamation as an unconstitutional act. Because of Leo's persistence in politely but firmly refusing to accept Majorian as more than *magister militum* in the West, Majorian finally in exasperation had himself installed as emperor in December 457 with the consent of the Roman Senate. Not only had Leo not recognized Majorian as emperor, he had also not responded to Majorian's request for military assistance and cooperation against the Vandals.[49]

At least temporarily isolated from the East Romans, Majorian decided to save the state with his forces alone. After subjugating Gaul (458-59) as a prelude to an attack on the Vandals, Majorian advanced into the Iberian peninsula, which he planned to use as his base of operations against Vandalic North Africa. During his military operations in Gaul, Majorian had inaugurated fiscal reforms that supplied him with the means to construct a fleet for transporting his army to North Africa and the wherewithal to recruit that army from among the disparate tribal elements in the Danuabian lands. Next, the emperor gained the Burgundians as federates and secured the acquiesence of the Visigoths to his march along the coast of Spain.[50] The final step in Marjorian's preparations was to secure the support of *comes* Marcellinus.

As a former tentative candidate for the throne and the ruler of an autonomous province, Marcellinus had ample reason to distrust Majorian, especially given the new emperor's obvious centralist tendencies. Still, Majorian was able to win Marcellinus's support both through his own diplomacy and as a result of some unexpected assistance from the emperor Leo at Constantinople. The expansion of Vandal raids to the Adriatic and Ionian Seas in the late 450s directly threatened Marcellinus's own territories and helped to change Leo's attitude toward Majorian. Since Leo claimed to rule as the sole legitimate emperor, he saw the need for a common effort against the Vandals and relented in his opposition to Majorian by recognizing him as de facto emperor in the West. At the same time, ca. 459, Leo was able to maneuver Marcellinus into the service of East Rome as a participant in the common cause against the Vandals.[51] In 458 Leo had suspended the East Roman subsidy to the Ostrogoths in the diocese of Pannonia, an action that led to Ostrogoth raids on Roman territories in the Balkans. Marcellinus's possessions on the western Balkan littoral bore the brunt of these attacks, and indeed, this seems to have been Leo's underlying aim. The devastations, which included the loss of Dyrrachium and the coast of Praevalitana and Epirus, induced Marcellinus to cooperate with Constantinople and even enter Leo's service by assisting Majorian in Sicily. As a result, Marcellinus contributed directly to Leo's efforts to aid the West Romans.

Leo's decision to intervene vigorously in the West and to crush the Vandals had enhanced Constantinopolitan claims of sovereignty over the West, yet the East Romans still needed to reassert their presence in coastal western Illyricum. They therefore secured Dyrrachium from the Ostrogoths by renewing their *foedus* with the latter and inducing them to return to Pannonia. Leo had maneuvered Marcellinus into the service of East Roman interests in the West, curbed the apparent expansionism of Marcellinus on the west Balkan littoral, and recovered Dyrrachium, the vital western terminus of the Via Egnatia and the essential naval base for future East Roman operations in the central Mediterranean. As for Marcellinus, while formally submitting to the Emperor Leo and probably even receiving a title of office from Constantinople, he had preserved the autonomy of Dalmatia. Leo apparently had no intention of interfering with the de facto administrative autonomy of Dalmatia so long as Marcellinus cooperated with the East Roman plans to assist the Ravenna government. The Vandal threat had served to provide a community of interests between Ravenna, Constantinople, and Salona. As a result, in aiding Majorian, Marcellinus should be seen as protecting the immediate local interests of Dalmatia, furthering the plans of the emperors, and fulfilling his patriotic duty as a Roman citizen.

As part of Majorian's plan to divide Vandal defenses and take them from two directions at once, Marcellinus was assigned to command the second prong of the naval assault, which was to originate in Sicily.[52] Majorian himself would open the war against the Vandals in Mauretania with his own barbarian army and the fleet that he had had constructed at Cartegena. In Sicily Marcellinus commanded a force of Hunnic mercenaries, whether his own or not remains unclear. In addition, the Dalmatian fleet seems to have accompanied the *comes*, for it was essential to any invasion of North Africa. As the commander in Sicily, Marcellinus not only served Imperial interests (East and West), but also protected his own province of Dalmatia.

Though able to defend Sicily against the Vandals, Marcellinus never was called upon to initiate an invasion of North Africa. The whole of Majorian's preparations (ca. 460) were aborted when Geiseric's fleet made a surprise descent on Cartegena, capturing the greater part of the Roman fleet and destroying the rest. The Vandal war was over. All that was needed to bring it to a formal conclusion was a treaty between Majorian and Geiseric. The peace (ca. 460) between the Vandals and the emperor humiliated the West Romans and confirmed the Vandals in their naval supremacy in the western Mediterranean by formally ceding them North Africa, the Belearics, Sardinia, and Corsica.[53]

The peace did not put an end to Vandalic raids against Roman territories, and Marcellinus seems to have remained in Sicily for another year, apparently to protect the island from further Vandal attacks. He soon found himself subject to the intrigues of the increasingly ambitious patrician Ricimer. Evidently fearing the potential influence on Marjorian of this independent Gallo-Roman aristocrat, Ricimer suborned the Hunnic troops under Marcellinus to desert the *comes* and join Ricimer's growing army of barbarians. Although he remained secretive in his hostile intentions toward Majorian, Ricimer obviously intended to control the West Roman government. To do so, he had to eliminate all potential rivals, gradually isolating and then eliminating the all too indpendent-minded Majorian himself. When Marcellinus found that his position in Sicily was being undermined, he returned to Dalmatia where he was at least safe from the hostile intrigues of Ricimer.[54] If Marcellinus had any intentions of becoming the power behind the throne and the indispensible adviser of the West Roman emperor, he had evidently concluded that the time was not opportune.

Though in a sense of leaving Majorian to his fate, the *comes* preserved his freedom of action by retiring to his base in Dalmatia. In August 461 the Emperor Majorian was murdered on orders from Ricimer, who now succeeded to the position previously held by Stilicho and Aetius.[55] Still needing an emperor in whose name he could act, the all-powerful patrician selected Libius Severus, who was elected by the Senate and proclaimed emperor in November 461. It was soon apparent, however, that it was one thing to force the Senate to elect an emperor and to get him installed but quite another to have his legitimacy recognized outside of Italy. Severus was thus only a figurehead and Ricimer was the real ruler, at least of the prefecture of Italy; outside of Italy, Libius Severus was not recognized by any regime.[56]

Aegidius, the *magister militum* in Gaul, had established a semi-independent regime that was preoccupied with the region's defense. A friend of the murdered Majorian (who had appointed Aegidius to his position in Gaul), Aegidius refused to acknowledge Ricimer's choice of a successor as emperor. The other Roman government in the West, that of Marcellinus in Dalmatia, not only did not recognize Severus but also displayed outright hostility toward the Italo-Roman regime of Ricimer and Severus.[57] Until his death in 464 Aegidius was preoccupied by local affairs, but Marcellinus, recently returned from Sicily, was free to pursue a course of action which appeared threatening to the government in Italy.[58] The ties previously established between the *comes* and the government of Leo I only amplified Marcellinus's potential threat to Ricimer.

When he assumed the rights of sole legitimate Roman emperor after the death of Valentinian III, Leo I had not intended to rule the entire empire directly, but he was determined that Imperial policy reflect his wishes and the interests of Constantinople. He was therefore not prepared to accept any Western emperor in whose installation he had not at least been consulted. Consequently, he had never formally accepted Majorian as emperor, but did acquiesce in his reign when their interests coincided in the struggle against the Vandals. The regime of Ricimer and Severus represented an even more blatant usurpation of power, and Leo viewed it as a serious abridgement of his own rights as senior emperor.

Military intervention by the East Romans in the West was not unknown before the 460s, and from the point of view of Ricimer there was a real danger that Leo might mount an expedition to establish some candidate that Constantinople could recognize as legitimate. Between 461 and 464, it appeared that such an expedition was exactly what Leo intended. At some time between 459 and 464 Leo appointed Marcellinus *magister militum Dalmatiae*.[59] Whether this appointment was made before or after

461 cannot be ascertained, but clearly Marcellinus had now accepted the sovereignty of the East Roman government and recognized the emperor Leo as the legitimate emperor. Although this new development apparently ended the separatist tendencies of Dalmatia, the rights of Constantinople in Dalmatia were in fact nominal and the provincial government remained essentially autonomous. The same appointment also suggested that the East might be preparing to capitalize on Marcellinus's hostility toward Ricimer in order to mount an intervention against Italy from the naval base at Salona. Salona had been the base for several East Roman military expeditions against the West before the time of Marcellinus, and Ricimer correctly recognized the danger that this alliance between Dalmatia and Constantinople presented to his government.

In addition to the threat of hostilities with Marcellinus and Leo, the Italian-Roman regime faced continued attacks from the Vandals—attacks that Ricimer was unable to counter.[60] Italy was very vulnerable to naval attacks, for the Roman government had no fleet while its enemies in North Africa and Dalmatia did. In addition the government of Ricimer did not have sufficient military forces to garrison all of the coastal cities of Italy and Sicily. Ricimer himself would not leave Ravenna to lead the defense against the Vandals, for he feared that in his absence he would be overthrown. Among those Ricimer suspected as likely candidates to his position, the most obvious was the hostile *magister* Marcellinus, the man who to all appearances was now Leo's agent in the West. After several years of impotence in the face of the Vandals, during which the Italian and Sicilian coasts were constantly plundered, Ricimer attempted to mend his fences with Constantinople and convince Leo to intervene on his behalf with Marcellinus and Geiseric.[61]

For a considerable time the representations from Italy had little effect on the emperor Leo I. Before 464/65, the only real results for Ricimer from his embassies to Leo were some rather weak East Roman protests to Geiseric about the Vandals' continued attacks and one tangible intervention with Marcellinus. As the result of the requests of a West Roman delegation in 463, Phylarchus, an East Roman envoy, made representations to Marcellinus which terminated the *magister's* hostilities toward the Italo-Roman regime.[62] We are not apprised of the exact nature of those hostilities, but they must have included some naval demonstrations against the usurper across the Adriatic or at least serious military preparations and threats that looked as if they might come to fruition. This armistice between Marcellinus and Ricimer, mediated by the representatives of the emperor Leo, was probably concluded in 464; there even exists the possibility that Marcellinus went further in his cessation of hostilities and came to the assistance of the Sicilians in that same year.[63]

Following the death of Libius Severus in November 465, Ricimer found it possible to initiate a full rapprochement with the East Roman regime. In return for reconciliation and military aid, Ricimer accepted the legal fiction that Leo was the sole legitimate emperor and the constitutional fiction of the sovereignty of East Rome over the whole of the empire. After negotiations, Ricimer also agreed to accept Leo's appointment of a caesar for the West; the choice was Anthemius, *magister militum per Illyricum* and a relative of Marcian, Leo's predecessor.[64]

Leo provided Anthemius with an army that would given him military independence from Ricimer and form the nucleus of a West Roman expedition against the Vandals. Anthemius seems to have marched into Dalmatia from where he sailed to Italy. Concurrently, Marcellinus had been raised to the office of *magister militum utriusque militiae et patricius* by Leo, which gave Marcellinus command of the Western Roman forces against the Vandals.[65] The newly appointed *magister praesentalis* for the West provided the fleet that transported Anthemius across the Adriatic; this naval force was Marcellinus's own navy from Dalmatia. Initially, Leo seems to have anticipated providing only indirect military assistance through Marcellinus to the West Romans as he had in 460. However, a Vandal raid against the Ionian coast of Greece in 467 prompted Leo to escalate his aid to include a powerful East Roman naval expedition that would cooperate with Anthemius and Marcellinus to crush the Vandals in North Africa. No longer content with simply blunting Vandal raids against Roman territory, Leo was determined to eradicate the Vandal threat at its source.[66]

In his intervention to aid the West and to sustain Anthemius as his candidate, Leo needed the support of Marcellinus. While amenable to diplomatic interventions from his nominal sovereign, Marcellinus had maintained the autonomy of Dalmatia even while he served as *magister militum Dalmatiae* for Leo. Several years of hostility toward Ricimer (ca. 461-64) had apparently not given Marcellinus any real advantage over his rival; the upshot was the reconciliation and the patriotic service of bringing aid to Sicily in 464. Once again the Vandal threat had produced a community of interests among the Roman regimes.

In 466-67 then, Marcellinus had placed before him the opportunity to assume one of the chief military commands in the West (Ricimer still held the other and similar position). Anthemius was the representative of Leo in the West, his caesar and subordinate, but Marcellinus had command of the western expeditionary forces against the Vandals, including the East Roman troops delegated to accompany Anthemius. His own naval forces now constituted the West Roman battle fleet. Marcellinus thus possessed all the requisite military assets to become the next all-powerful minister of the Western emperor, the real power behind the throne.

While marching to Rome to take power, Anthemius was proclaimed emperor in April 467. Backed by the evidence of powerful support from the East and the naval forces of Marcellinus, he was accepted as emperor in Italy and Gaul by the West Roman aristocracy.[67] Sometime in the summer of 467, Marcellinus made a naval demonstration in the Tyrrhenian Sea.[68] The accompanying seizure of Sardinia from the Vandals reinforced the impression in the West that the government of Anthemius had renewed the vigor of Imperial policy. Ricimer was in no position to remonstrate but had to accept quietly his at least temporary demotion and displacement from control of West Roman affairs. With Marcellinus as Ricimer's coequal and with the Eastern forces that Anthemius himself had brought to Italy, the new emperor was free from the machinations of the barbarian patrician. Nor was Anthemius at the mercy of whatever ambitions Marcellinus might have harbored, for Ricimer retained his offices and his control of part of the West Roman army. In fact a balance had been struck in Western Roman affairs, one that guaranteed Anthemius considerable power as long as he could keep the two patricians in harness and himself preserve the prestige and influence of the Imperial office.[69] Still, Marcellinus had gained significantly, and if the opportunities were favorable, he could eventually hope to become the controlling figure in Western Roman affairs.

When Leo revealed his intention to send a major expedition against the Vandals, he required Anthemius to provide the military assistance from the West, a task that he and Marcellinus undertook willingly. Here was the

opportunity to crush the Vandals and remove the threat that had sapped
the strength of the Western Empire, defying and discrediting several
emperors and their ministers. Victory would constitute the brilliant
military achievement that would secure the throne for Anthemius and
greatly increase the power and prestige of Marcellinus, the leader of
the Western expeditionary forces. When the great expedition departed
Constantinople in the spring of 468, Marcellinus took his position in
Sicily to cover the flank of Basiliscus's forces.[70] But this phase of the
Vandal war was over before Marcellinus made any direct contribution,
and as the remnants of the expedition struggled into Sicily, he was murdered.[71] The assassination probably occurred on the order of Ricimer,
who had the most to gain by the removal of Marcellinus. At one blow
Anthemius was deprived of his most competent general and firmest
supporter against Ricimer. With Marcellinus dead, the army in Sicily
broke up and the Dalmatian fleet seems to have returned to Salona; there
is no mention of its activities again until 473-74. Because of his own
difficulties Leo was unable to provide any further assistance to his co-
emperor in the West. Ricimer quickly asserted his position and in 472,
secured the assassination of Anthemius, dying himself shortly thereafter.[72]

For fourteen years Dalmatia had been the locus for an autonomous
government under Marcellinus. Though its ruler had been nominally
subordinate to the East Roman emperor for half that time, the province
itself remained virtually independent. That autonomy was preserved
under Julius Nepos, Marcellinus's successor (ca. 468-80), who was the
recognized but largely ineffectual ruler of the West Roman Empire from
June 474 until his death in 480. His successor, Odovacer, reintegrated
the province into the central administration at Ravenna, though he was
careful to obscure this loss of autonomy by making the province fiscally
part of the *res privatae*.[73] Such an administrative arrangement seems to
have been a continuation of the government provided recently by Julius
Nepos. The latter had kept Dalmatia under his personal and direct control,
even while emperor, rather than subordinating it to diocesan or prefectural
officers whom he could not control.

Following the defeat and murder of Odovacer (489-93), the Ostrogoths
under Theoderic assumed control of Dalmatia.[74] Since the province
had traditionally strong economic and cultural ties with Italy, it almost

naturally feel to the rulers of Italy, especially as no native Roman of the stature of Marcellinus emerged to lead it. Because Theoderic and Athalaric preserved peace and order in Dalmatia for more than forty years, the change in government in the 490s did not disrupt the lives of the native Roman population. The administrative ties between Dalmatia and Italy were strengthened by the Ostrogoths and the province came under the relatively close supervision of the central administration at Ravenna, which preserved the governmental traditions of Rome.[75] The native Romans in Dalmatia were thus governed by the Roman administrators of the Ostrogothic king.[76] This Roman administration subordinated to and appointed from Ravenna controlled the civil, economic, and legal life of the Dalmatian Romans while military affairs were left to the Ostrogoths.

Theoderic and Athalaric provided a competent administration for Dalmatia, but they had terminated the autonomy of the province. Under the Ostrogoths, Dalmatia prospered with an economy closely regulated from Ravenna. This circumstance continued even during the Gothic war, initiated by the Emperor Justinian in 535 in Dalmatia itself. During the East Roman liberation of Italy, Dalmatia, especially Salona, served as a supply base and transit point for Roman reinforcements on their way to the war. More fortunate than the lands across the Adriatic, the province largely escaped the devastations wrought by the Gothic war.[77]

Dalmatia was liberated by the East Romans at the beginning of the war against the Goths (535-37), and was firmly reabsorbed into the empire. As in all of the reconquered provinces, Justinian seems to have restored—or in the case of Dalmatia sustained—the Roman administration that had flourished in the period of autonomy and Gothic occupation. While Salona and Dalmatia were a staging area for the war in Italy, Dalmatia seems to have been subordinated to the military administration of the *magister militum per Illyricum* and the praetorian prefect of Illyricum. With the pragmatic sanction of 554, which reestablished a regular civil administration in Italy, Dalmatia seems to have been placed under the supervision of the Imperial administration at Ravenna, thus perpetuating the Ostrogothic arrangements arrived at fifty years earlier.[78] Though we have no direct information, the prosperity of Dalmatia seems to have continued throughout the sixth century as a result of the traditional maritime trade. We are unaware to what extent the Romans reasserted a formal administration in the interior of Dalmatia, though when needed Roman military forces did intervene in the interior.

In 600 A. D. as around 400 A. D., the coastal cities (especially Salona), the mountain fortress of Clusium near Salona, and the islands became refuges for the Roman population fleeing the Slavic invasions. These invasions seem to have forced many of the last remnants of the Roman population out of the interior and down to the coast, thus reinforcing the Roman population of the cities and islands and beginning the distinction between Romans and Slavs in Dalmatia. The Romanized Illyrians retreated into the mountains.

The pressure of the Slavic migrations seems to have increased dramatically after 600. Between 612 and 614, during the rule of the last Byzantine proconsul Marcellinus, Salona was taken and destroyed. The last pre-invasion bishop of Salona seems to have fled across the Adriatic and part of the surviving population took refuge on the neighboring islands and in the palace of Diocletian at Spalatum, which had not been abandoned after the fourth or fifth century. Ultimately a considerable portion of the Salonitan refugees moved to Spalatum, which was easily defended against the Slavs. There they resumed the Roman traditions that they were to preserve intact for the next several centuries. Shortly after the disaster at Salona, the other cities of coastal Dalmatia (except Trojir and Dubrovnik) fell to the Slavs. Their populations retired to the islands, which had been the "ager" of the coastal cities, or to other coastal cities, as did the population of Epidauros, which moved to Dubrovnik. Once the initial invasions had spent their force, the Romans relocated to easily fortified or already fortified positions along the Dalmatian coast.[79]

The new Roman Dalmatia that emerged by the late seventh century or early eighth century was in some ways similar to the old: the pivotal parts of the province were the cities and the islands, and the economy was oriented toward the sea with Adriatic shipping and commerce as its mainstay. The society of the cities and islands was still predominantly Roman in culture and the inhabitants were still firmly bound by their loyalties to the empire at Constantinople. But there were also changes that hinted at future developments: all of the interior and much of the coastal hinterland had been lost, Roman Dalmatia was divided into separate and incontiguous urban enclaves, the Slavs were present in the interstices in overwhelming if peaceful numbers. The history of Dalmatia from the mid-seventh/early eighth to the fifteenth centuries was one of gradual transition, assimilation, and fusion of the various cultural elements in coastal and insular Dalmatia.

For the Romans, Dalmatia remained an urban society until that Roman cultural element faded away. The life of the province had been controlled by the cities in the fifth and sixth centuries; the domination of the cities would continue throughout the whole history of the province. The cities controlled the islands and their own hinterlands before 600 and with modifications this pattern was to continue at least until the seventeenth or eighteenth century. Politically the urban, Roman Dalmatians remained part of the empire as they had been before 600 (after the Justinianic annexation). The separatist or particularist tendencies within the province reemerged as the Dalmatians were largely left to their own by the government at Constantinople. The identification with the East Roman state represented more a conscious cultural response from the Dalmatians than any real effort by the East Romans/Byzantines to preserve their sovereignty in the Adriatic.

Whereas Salona had dominated Dalmatia before 600, after the seventh century no one city overshadowed the others; Spalatum, Zadar, Dubrovnik, and Trojir were equally important and virtually independent of each other. The Roman population of these cities and the islands continued to have a common identity as Romans which distinguished them linguistically and culturally from the Slavs. In internal affairs, each city seems to have been administered as a late Roman city with individualistic modifications suited to local circumstances. The traditions of Roman municipal organization and administration persisted, modified but never submerged.

From the days of *comes* Marcellinus in the fifth century, the Dalmatians of the coastal cities had clung as closely as possible to the political and cultural traditions of Rome. This Romanism had sustained them in autonomy, subjugation to the Ostrogoths, reintegration into the Roman state, and the long era of independence of the early middle ages. In the end, the insistence of the ruling Dalmatian patricians on their Roman heritage and descent was more than a cultural veneer: it represented a clear effort to preserve their distinction from those whom they ruled, just as the inhabitants of old Roman Dalmatia had distinguished themselves from invaders or conquerors by clinging to their Roman culture.

30 Nation and Ideology

NOTES

1. B. Saria, "Praevalitana," *Real-Encyclopädie der classischen Alter-tumswissenschaft* (henceforth, *R. E.*) eds. A. F. Pauly, G. Wissowa, and W. Kroll, 22:2 (Stuttgart, 1954), col. 1675.

2. Philipp Baillif and Karl Patsch, *Romische Strassen In Bosnien und Hercegovina* (Vienna, 1893), pp. 12-43.

3. Oliver Davies, *Roman Mines in Europe* (Oxford, 1935), pp. 183-85.

4. Davies, *Roman Mines,* pp. 189-97.

5. J. J. Wilkes, *Dalmatia* (Cambridge, 1969), p. 415.

6. Constantin Jireček, *Die Romanen in der Städten Dalmatiens während des Mittelalters* (Vienna, 1902), and Jadran Ferluga, "Les iles dalmates dans l'empire byzantine," in his *Byzantium on the Balkans* (Amsterdam, 1976), pp. 97-130.

7. Wilkes, *Dalmatia,* pp. 262-78, 396-409.

8. Ibid., p. 417.

9. Ernst Stein, *Histoire du Bas Empire,* I (Paris, 1959), 228-31, and B. Saria, "Dalmatia," *R. E.,* suppl. 8 (1956), 28.

10. *Notitia Dignitatum,* ed. Otto Seeck (Berlin, 1876) *pars Occidentis,* ii, 31; *Pars Orientis,* iii, 19.

11. Claudian, *In Rufinum,* ed. M. G. Birt, *Monumenta Germaniae Historica, Auctores Antiquiores* (henceforth, *MGH, AA*) 10 (Berlin, 1892), II, 37.

12. Ludwig Schmidt, *Die Ostgermanen,* 2d. ed. (Munich, 1934), p. 190.

13. Alan Cameron, *Poetry and Propaganda at the Court of Honorius* (Oxford, 1970), pp. 156-88, and Stein, *Histoire du Bas Empire,* I, 231, 247-51.

14. Saria, "Dalmatia," col. 29.

15. *Notitia Dignitatum, pars Occ.,* xi, 46.

16. Jaroslav Šašel, "Siscia," *R. E.,* suppl. 14 (1974), col. 739, and *Notitia Dignitatum, pars Occ.,* xi, 39.

17. *Codex Theodosianus,* ed. Th. Mommsen (Berlin, 1905), VI, 29, 12.

18. *Notitia Dignitatum, pars Occ.,* xlv, 1-15.

19. Ernst Stein, "Zur Geschichte von Illyricum im V-VII Jahrhundert," *Rheinische Museum für Philologie,* 74 (1925), 354-64.

20. Stein, *Histoire du Bas Empire,* I, 282-85.

21. Wilhelm Ensslin, "Marcellinus," *R. E.,* 14:2 (1930), col. 1446.

22. *Novellae Theodosii II* (collected with *Codex Theodosianus*) nov. XVII, Oct. 20, 439.

23. Stein, *Histoire du Bas Empire,* I, 317-42; Francois Paschoud, *Roma aeterna, études sur le patriotisme romain dans l'occident latin à l'époque des grandes invasions* (Rome, 1967); and John Matthews, *Western Aristocracies and Imperial Court 364-425* (Oxford, 1975).

24. See above notes 21 and 22.

25. Wilkes, *Dalmatia,* p. 420.

26. Procopius, *Bellum Vandalicum,* ed. J. Haury (Leipzig, 1905) I, 6, 7-8.

27. Gerald E. Max, "Political Intrigue during the Reigns of the Western Emperors Avitus and Majorian," *Historia,* 28 (1979), 235.

28. Davies, *Roman Mines,* p. 191.

29. Ibid., p. 191.

30. *Notitia Dignitatum, pars Occ.,* ix, 22.

31. See Davies, *Roman Mines,* pp. 182-97.

32. *Notitia Dignitatum, pars Occ.,* xlv, 1-15, and Cassiodorus, *Variae,* ed. Th. Mommsen, *MGH, AA.* 12 (Berlin, 1894), I, 2; II, 16; III, 23-26; IV, 9; VI, 7-9; VIII, 1, 3, 8, 24; IX, 8-9.

33. Stein, "Zur Geschichte von Illyricum im V-VII Jahrhundret," pp. 354-59, and Saria, "Dalmatia," cols. 43-45.

34. On the commercial and economic prosperity of Dalmatia, see Ivanka Nikolajević, "Veliki posed u Dalmaciju u V-VI veku u svetlosti archeoloških nalaza," *Zbornik radova, Srpska akademija nauka i umetnosti, Vizantološki Institut,* 13 (1971), 277-91; and Francis W. Carter, *Dubrovnik (Ragusa): A Classical City State* (London, 1972), passim.

35. For naval affairs in the late empire, see Ch. Courtois, "Les politiques navales de l'empire romain," *Revue historique,* 186 (1939), 225-59.

36. On the Vandals and Geiseric, see Ch. Courtois, *Les Vandales et l'Afrique* (Paris, 1955), pp. 185-214.

37. Ensslin, "Marcellinus," col. 1447.

38. See Nikolajević, "Veliki posed u Dalmaciju u V-VI veku," pp. 277-91, on the continuing prosperity of Dalmatia in the fifth century A.D.

39. *Notitia Dignitatum, pars Occ.,* xi, 46, 48.

40. *Notitia Dignitatum, pars Occ.,* ix, 22.

41. Procopius, *Bellum Vandalicum,* I, 6, 8.

42. Stein, *Historie du Bas Empire*, I, 365-67.

43. C. E. Stevens, *Sidonius Apollinaris and his Age* (Oxford, 1933), pp. 25-30.

44. Stevens, *Sidonius Apollinaris*, pp. 35, 37; and Stein, *Histoire du Bas Empire*, I, 371-73.

45. For the reaction of the Gallo-Romans, see Stevens, *Sidonius Apollinaris*, pp. 41-43.

46. Ensslin, "Marcellinus," col. 1447.

47. See John Matthews, *Western Aristocracies and Imperial Court, A. D. 364-425*, (Oxford, 1975), pp. 329-51, for separatist tendencies within the Gallo-Roman aristocracy.

48. Stein, *Histoire du Bas Empire*, I, 367-74, and Matthews, *Western Aristocracies*, pp. 308-14.

49. Johannes Antiochenus, *Fragmenta*, ed. K. Müller, *Fragmenta Historicorum Graecorum* (henceforth *F.H.G.*) 4 (Paris, 1868) frg. 202; Stevens, *Sidonius Apollinaris*, pp. 43-44.

50. Priscus, *F.H.G.*, 4, frg. 27.

51. Priscus, *F.H.G.*, 4 frg. 30; Stein, *Histoire du Bas Empire*, I, 379; Ensslin, "Marcellinus," col. 1447; see also Gerald E. Max, "Political Intrigue during the Reigns of the Western Emperors Avitus and Majorian," *Historia*, 28 (1979), 235-37.

52. Stein, *Histoire du Bas Empire*, I, 379.

53. Johannes Antiochenus, *F.H.G.*, 4, frg. 203, and Stevens, *Sidonius Apollinaris*, p. 51.

54. Priscus, *F.H.G.*, 4, frg. 29.

55. Johannes Antiochenus, *F.H.G.*, 4, frg. 203.

56. Stein, *Histoire du Bas Empire*, I, 380.

57. Priscus, *F.H.G.*, 4, frg. 30.

58. Priscus, *F.H.G.*, 4, frg. 30.

59. Ensslin, "Marcellinus," col. 1447, and Saria, "Dalmatia," col. 30.

60. Stein, *Histoire du Bas Empire*, I, 386-87.

61. Priscus, *F.H.G.*, 4, frg. 30.

62. Priscus, *F.H.G.*, 4, frg. 30; it seems likely that the Emperor Leo had used or even induced the hostility of Marcellinus toward Ricimer to bring pressure on the latter to submit to the Constantinopolitan government.

63. Wilkes, *Dalmatia*, p. 420; Ensslin, "Marcellinus," col. 1447.

64.   Marcellinus comes, *Chronicon*, ed. Th. Mommson, *MGH, AA*, 11 (Berlin, 1894) a. 467; Stein, *Histoire du Bas Empire*, I, 387-88; Stevens, *Sidonius Apollinaris*, pp. 92-94.

65.   Marcellinus comes, a. 468; Cassiodorus, *Chronicon*, a. 468; Stein, *Histoire du Bas Empire*, I, 388; Ensslin, "Marcellinus," col. 1447.

66.   Priscus, *F.H.G.*, 4, frgs. 40 and 42, and Stein, *Histoire du Bas Empire*, I, 359-60, 390-91.

67.   Procopius, *Bellum Vandalicum*, I, 6, 5; and Stevens, *Sidonius Apollinaris*, p. 94.

68.   Procopius, *Bellum Vandalicum*, I, 6, 8.

69.   Stein, *Histoire du Bas Empire*, I, 389-90.

70.   Marcellinus comes, a. 468; Cassiodorus, *Chronicon*, a. 468; Stein, *Histoire du Bas Empire*, I, 359-60; 390-91.

71.   Procopius, *Bellum Vandalicum*, I, 7, 75; Marcellinus comes, a. 468; Ensslin, "Marcellinus," col. 1447.

72.   Procopius, *Bellum Vandalicum*, I, 7, 1; and Johannes Antiochenus, *F.H.G.*, 4, frg. 209.

73.   Nikolajević, "Veliki posed u Dalmaciji u V-VI veku," pp. 277-82.

74.   Stein, *Histoire du Bas Empire*, II, 54-58; Wm. Ensslin, *Theoderich der Grosse* (Munich, 1947), pp. 66-77.

75.   Cassiodorus, *Variae*, ed. Th. Mommsen, *MGH, AA*, 12 (Berlin, 1894), I, 2, 40; III, 23-26; IV, 9; VI, 7; VII, 1, 3, 8, 24; IX, 8, 9; XII, 24.

76.   John Moorhead, "Boethius and Romans in Ostrogothic Service," *Historia*, 27 (1978), 604-12; P. Courcelle, *Les grandes invasions germaniques* (Paris, 1948), pp. 170-79; A. Momigliano, "Cassiodorus and Italian Culture of his Time," *Proceedings of the British Academy*, 41 (1955) 207-45; Ensslin, *Theoderich der Grosse*, pp. 84-96, 157-84; James J. O'Donnell, *Cassiodorus* (Berkeley and Los Angeles, 1979), pp. 1-102.

77.   Wilkes, *Dalmatia*, pp. 425-27, and Saria, "Dalmatia," cols. 35-37.

78.   D. Mandić, "Dalmatia in the Exarchate of Ravenna from the Middle of the VIII Century," *Byzantion*, 34 (1964), 351-58; see also Saria, "Dalmatia," col. 44, and Stein, "Zur Geschichte von Illyricum im V-VIII Jahrhundert," pp. 360-64, who disagree with Mandić.

79.   Wilkes, *Dalmatia*, p. 436; Ferluga, "Les îles dalmates dans l'empire byzantin," pp. 103-15; Jireček, *Die Romanen in den Städten Dalmatiens*, p. 27.

BALKAN FOREIGN LEGIONS
IN EIGHTEENTH-CENTURY ITALY :
THE *REGGIMENTO REAL MACEDONE*
AND ITS SUCCESSORS

Nicholas C. Pappas
Stanford University

During the four centuries of Ottoman domination in the Balkans, many Christian warriors found refuge and served in the armed forces of the surrounding Christian powers. In Central Europe, *Grenzer* regiments composed of South Slavs provided the backbone of the border defences in the Habsburg crownlands, while in Dalmatia the South Slavic *Schiavoni, Oltramarini,* and *Croati a Cavallo* units served the Venetian Republic.[1] Likewise, military companies of Greeks and Christian Albanians served Venice and Spain in the Balkans and Italy. During the Turco-Venetian wars of the fifteenth century, large numbers of soldiers who had served the last Christian states in the Balkans found employment in the Venetian holdings in Greece and Dalmatia. Known as *stradioti* (from the Byzantine term stratiōtēs, meaning soldier or wayfarer), these troops were light cavalrymen who used the spear, long saber, and mace as weapons and were attired in a mixture of oriental and Byzantine martial garb.[2]

Throughout the sixteenth century *stradioti* served in the armies of Venice, Genoa, France, England, and the Holy Roman Empire. A number of contemporary memoirists and historians described the activities of the *stradioti* in Western Europe and have attributed the reintroduction of light cavalry tactics to them. As their clients began forming native light cavalry units, such as the later hussars and dragoons, the employment opportunities of the *stradioti* became limited to Italy and the Near East. They continued to be garrisoned in the Levant and took part in the sixteenth- and seventeenth-century wars against the Ottomans. Their main stations of service were the Venetian-held areas of Nauplion, Korone, Methone, and Monemvasia in the Peloponnesus; such towns as Trogir, Sibenik, Herceg Novi, and Zadar in Dalmatia; and the island possessions in the Ionian and Aegean seas.[3]

Naples, under both the Spanish Habsburgs and the Bourbons, remained another center of military activity and colonization for Balkan peoples abroad. In the fifteenth century, large numbers of Christian Albanians, refugees from Skenderbeg's wars, were settled in Calabria and Sicily, and in both the fifteenth and sixteenth centuries, many Greek and Albanian *stradioti* and their families from the Peloponnesus settled in Neapolitan lands. Later refugees from the autonomous warrior communities of Cheimarra and Mani formed colonies in Apulia and elsewhere. Most of these settlements had military privileges and responsibilities, but by the eighteenth century these conventions had fallen into decline.[4]

As they became hereditary units, the military prowess of these older *stradioti* companies declined, but in the eighteenth century new military institutions arose which prolonged the tradition of Balkan legions in Venice and Naples. The two major formations comprised of Balkan troops were the Venetian *Reggimento Cimarrioto* and the Neapolitan *Reggimento Real Macedone*. The *Reggimento Cimarrioto* was organized during the Candian and Morean wars by the Venetians, while the *Reggimento Real Macedone* was formed soon after the founding of the independent Kingdom of Naples in 1734.

These new troops were armed in what was known as the "Albanian" manner. Their chief firearm was a long musket known as a *toupheki*, or *karyophyli*. A set of pistols supplemented the rifle, and a powder case (*patrona*) with shot (*phousekia*) was carried for all firearms. Hand weapons included a sword, either a large oriental saber known as a *yatagan* or a traditional Balkan long-knife of archaic style known as a *pala*, which had a shape similar to a gurhka knife. These arms were complemented by a least one dagger.[5] The distinctive costume of these troops consisted of a white pleated kilt (*phoustanella*) or a long, dark colored tunic (*phermelē*), long stockings (*kaltses*), moccasins (*tsarouchia*), and a shepherd's cloak (*kapa*). This attire was based upon peasant dress and was decorated with embroidery and silvered arms, symbols of the warrior's profession. Because of their long tunics or kilts, those troops in Neapolitan service were nicknamed *camiciotti* by Italians.[6]

Like the *klephtes* and *hajduks,* these Balkan troops practiced a style of fighting which entailed swift movements, sharpshooting, and hand-to-hand fighting. Ambushes and skirmishes were the rule in their combat, and due to their ability as marksmen, the Balkan recruits were often used as marine riflemen in naval campaigns.[7]

The area of Cheimarra (Himarë) provided the bulk of the manpower for the *Reggimento Cimarrioto* and a major component of the *Reggimento Real Macedone.*[8] Like Mani, Montenegro, and Souli, Cheimarra was one of those Balkan regions whose inhabitants were able to maintain their self-rule by virtue of their tribal or clan organization, the inaccessibility of their mountainous homelands, their proximity to Venetian controlled areas, and the prowess of their arms. Located along the coastal promontories of the Acroceraunian mountains between Agia Saranta (Sarandë) and Avlona (Vlorë) in present-day southern Albania, the warrior society known as Cheimarra arose during the fifteenth and sixteenth centuries. Initially this group of about fifty villages was a center of resistance to Ottoman conquest during the wars of Skenderbeg. It became a refuge not only for remnants of Skenderbeg's forces under his son John Kastriotes, but also for Peloponnesian Greeks and Albanians under Korkodeilos Kladas in the 1470s.[9] In the ensuing years Cheimarra participated in the wars of Venice and of other western powers against the Porte.

In 1537 the Ottomans mounted an expedition that destroyed or captured many of the villages of Cheimarra, but did not totally subdue the area. Indeed, the victors found it necessary to compromise with the inhabitants of Cheimarra by granting them the following privileges: local self-government, local administration of justice, the right to bear arms, and exemption from the *harac* and *dzizije* ("head tax") in exchange for a yearly tribute. These conditions were negotiated in 1519 through the offices of Liaz (Elias) Pasha, an Islamized local figure representing Sultan Selim I.[10] When renewed during the sultanates of Murad IV and Suleiman II, these conventions were modified to provide that the Cheimarriotes render service in time of war and to expend the maritime privileges of Cheimarra.

In spite of these privileges, the Cheimarriotes rose against Ottoman authority on a number of occasions, notably during the third Turco-Venetian War (1537-40), the War of the Holy League (1571), and the Morean Wars (1684). Ottoman reprisals somewhat depopulated the region and led to a certain amount of forced Islamization which, coupled with voluntary conversions to Islam, limited the area's Christian population by the eighteenth century to the town of Cheimarra and six other large villages.[11] Despite the diminution of its size, the community of Cheimarra retained its privileges into the twentieth century, although these were often violated by local Muslim officials.

In the meantime, the strategic position of Cheimarra near the Straits of Otranto (separating Italy from the Balkans and the Adriatic from the Ionian Sea), along with its proximity to Italy (100 kilometers from Apuglia) and to Venice's Ionian possessions (35 kilometers from Corfu), had attracted the interest of the Venetian Republic and the Kingdom of Spain (later Naples). These powers saw strategic advantage in the preservation of Cheimarra's autonomy and the maintainance of their influence in the region. Through the use of trade, military aid, arms shipments, missionaries, and agents, Venice and Naples derived, in turn, two important assets from Cheimarra. Besides its uprisings during the western powers' wars against the Ottoman Empire, Cheimarra provided soldiers for the armies of Venice and Naples. During the earlier centuries of Ottoman rule, it had been a recruiting ground for *stradioti,* whereas by the eighteenth century it was supplying the aforementioned light-infantry bodies for Naples and Venice.[12]

Following the 1685 uprising, many Cheimarriotes joined Venetian ranks and were later organized into a two-thousand man *Reggimento Cimarrioto.* This regiment distinguished itself in the last years of the Morean wars, and in the ensuing years of peace its companies were deployed in the Ionian Islands and other garrisons in the Levant. The regiment was mustered in full only for infrequent inspections by Venetian authorities.[13]

The gross irregularities that plagued the *Reggimento Cimarrioto* are evidence that the Venetians and the Neapolitans were rivals in the recruitment of the Cheimarriotes. In an inspection of the fortress at Corfu in 1745, Venetian officials found that the two companies of the *Reggimento Cimarrioto* serving in the Corfiote garrison were absent en masse.

Two of their officers, a Major Bitsilēs and a Captain Polimeros, were present only to collect pay for their troops. The bulk of the soldiers were in Cheimarra and received their pay there. Some, indeed, were collecting pay from both the Venetian Republic and the Kingdom of Naples, as they were also in active duty with the *Reggimento Real Macedone.*[14]

This latter unit had its antecedents in a military unit founded soon after the Neapolitan kingdom became independent under its own branch of the house of Bourbon. Initial organization and recruitment were directed by Athanasios Glykēs, an Epirote merchant living in Naples, and Count Stratēs Gkikas, a veteran *stradioto* from Cheimarra in Neapolitan service. In 1735 these two men organized a small unit of troops, no doubt Cheimarriotes, for service as guards for King Carlos. This unit had increased to battalion size by 1738, but in that same year problems erupted within the ranks, supposedly due to the intrigues of Venetian agents. The Venetian interference was probably a consequence of the recruitment competition mentioned above.[15]

As a result of this discord, the Neapolitan unit was reorganized under a new command in 1739. The new commander was the Cephalonian Count Geōrgios Choraphas, a former officer in the Venetian army. Under his leadership, the battalion-sized unit was eventually expanded into a full regiment that, in 1754, comprised two battalions of thirteen companies each. The initial commander, Stratēs Gkikas, had the rank of lieutenant colonel and was second in command. This organization, known as the *Reggimento Real Macedone,* remained basically intact until the 1790s.[16] Choraphas exercised command over the regiment until 1775, when he died with the rank of lieutenant general. Stratēs Gkikas succeeded him as regimental leader until his death in 1784 when he, in turn, was provisionally replaced by a Colonel Vlasēs. Soon afterward, Athanasios Gkikas, the son of Stratēs, assumed command and led the regiment until the eve of the French invasion of Italy in 1798.[17]

The *Reggimento Real Macedone* was one of the most highly regarded units in the Neapolitan army.[18] The record of the regiment and its later sister units was, according to their historians, quite distinguished. In the War of the Austrian Succession the regiment acquitted itself well against Habsburg forces, taking over four hundred of the enemy prisoner. It continued campaigning in 1745 and 1746 with other Neapolitan regiments that were consolidated into a Macedonian brigade in the regiment's honor. Although its men were taken prisoner as a result of the general defeat of Neapolitan forces, the regiment maintained one of the best reputations in the campaign.[19]

Later, detachments from the *Reggimento Real Macedone* served as marines aboard vessels of the Neapolitan navy in expeditions against the Barbary pirates. Since marine service then entailed sniping from atop the rigging against the crews of enemy warships, as well as amphibious operations, the troops of the regiment, with their renowned marksmanship, were well suited for this duty. The Tripolitanian operations of the 1750s, for example, found over three hundred of the regiment's men involved in marine service.[20]

In peacetime, the Macedonian troops were often used in the suppression of brigandage and uprisings in southern Italy and Sicily. Their mode of fighting, being similar to that employed by the bandits of the Balkans, made them ideal for dealing with Italian outlaws, while their foreign origin kept them aloof from any local sympathies in the quelling of insurrections.[21]

In 1793 the advent of revolutionary France as a threat to the European status quo marked the beginning of a new chapter in the history of the regiment. The Kingdom of Naples joined England and other allies in an attempt to stifle the burgeoning power of France, employing one battalion of the Macedonian regiment as marines in an abortive expedition against the French at Toulon.[22] As the French military involvement in Italy grew in the 1790s, there were moves to augment the regiment with new units.

In 1786, the eve of a new recruiting effort in Epirus under the officer Kōnstantinos Kasnetsēs, the regiment had a numerical strength of 2,012 officers and men.[23] After the Toulon campaign, recruits appeared in such numbers that it was necessary to form a second regiment, which together with the original *Reggimento Real Macedone* was consolidated into a new, homogeneous Macedonian brigade (*Brigata Macedone*) under the command of Prince Ludwig Adolf of Saxony.[24] In 1797-98, when the Kingdom of the Two Sicilies was desperate for troops in the face of an impending French invasion, another active recruitment campaign in Epirus mustered a new six hundred-man force. This unit was organized into the *Battaglione dei Cacciatori Albanesi* under the command of Kōnstantinos Kasnetsēs, who was chiefly responsible for its recruitment.[25]

In the 1798 campaign against the French in the Papal States, the *Brigata Macedone* and the *Battaglione dei Cacciatori Albanesi* took part in the actions in and around Rome. In battles and skirmishes at Civita-Castellana, Caiazzo, San Giovanni Laterano, and Capua, the two Balkan forces put up a resistance to French forces which was more effective than that of the other Neapolitan units and thus distinguished themselves in an otherwise disgraceful campaign.[26]

Following the defeat of Naples's forces at the hands of the French, the Balkan units were the main contributors to the two-day defence of Fort Carmine and other sections of Naples. The *Battaglione dei Cacciatori Albanesi* and elements of the *Brigata Macedone* were eventually holed up in the Carmine fortress and negotiated a surrender. This agreement was not respected by the French, who held the troops prisoner in the San Francesco prison and gave them small rations. The imprisoned troops received necessary foodstuffs from Greek merchants and Neapolitans.[27] While the troops of the *Battaglione dei Cacciatori Albanesi* remained prisoners of war, the two Macedonian regiments were disbanded. Their personnel either scattered to the homes of friends and to the neighboring islands of Procida and Ischia, or returned to their homelands by obtaining passports under assumed names from the Ottoman consul.[28] Under the short-lived Republic of Naples, some Balkan officers entered the service of the French and two of them attained the rank of brigadier general.[29]

Within six months of the French victory, the Neapolitan republic fell and the kingdom was restored by Anglo-Russian forces and the military movement of Cardinal Ruffo. Two reconstituted units were formed under the titles *Battaglione dei Cacciatori Macedoni* and *Reggimento Albania*. With the return of the French in 1805, these units were transferred to Sicily and served together with allied forces in the exile army of the Neapolitan kingdom.[30] These diminished forces were maintained on Sicily until 1812, when both were discharged. A number of officers accepted positions in other military units or assumed Neapolitan consular or intelligence posts in the Levant.[31]

After a five-year hiatus the tradition of Macedonian forces was revived in 1817 by Lieutenant General Richard Church, military commander of Apulia. Previous to his accepting a Neapolitan commission, Church had seen service as an English officer in Egypt, Italy, and the Ionian Islands.

He had acquired the reputation of being an expert at training and commanding foreign troops in British service. In 1805 he made a study of the military uses of Calabrian brigands, and from 1805 to 1808 he led a unit of Corsican Rangers on reconnaissance missions in French-occupied Italy. From 1809 to 1814, he was organizer and a commander of the Duke of York's two Greek Light Infantry Regiments on the Ionian Islands.[32]

Following the defeat of Napoleon, the Greek regiments were dissolved and Church transferred to the Kingdom of Naples. As military governor of Apulia, he was able to organize a new *Battaglione dei Cacciatori Macedoni* that included not only veterans of the old Neapolitan units but also former members of the Ionian Islands regiments.[33] This battalion participated actively in Church's internal campaigns against brigandage and popular uprisings until June 1820, when it was disbanded after less than three years of service. This was the last Balkan unit to serve the Kingdom of Naples.[34]

In the eighty odd years during which Naples employed light infantry from the Balkans, the troops of the regiment and its successors were known popularly under three names in addition to the aforementioned *camiciotti*: the seemingly national names of *Greci, Albanesi,* and *Macedoni.* These names did not, however, have their later ethnic connotations but were instead stylized terms that described the soldiers' general origins or mode of fighting. The term *Greci* was religious, denoting Orthodox faith and not necessarily Greek nationality. The term *Albanesi* was used because that nation had achieved fame for its style of fighting as mercenaries of the Ottoman Empire. Muslim Albanians had become a mainstay of the sultan's armies and were given the nickname "the Swiss of the Near East" by Europeans. The third epithet, *Macedoni*, which was used in the title of the regiment, indicated not only inhabitants of the area of Macedonia (as understood in either ancient or modern terms) but also applied to all peoples living in the areas once under the sway of Alexander the Great. This usage in effect made virtually all of the Balkan peninsula, as well as the Near East, a potential recruiting ground for these troops.[35]

Recruiting records from the 1740s and 1750s indicate that Naples levied men for the *Reggimento Real Macedone* from such distant centers as Tinos, Dubrovnik, Smyrna, Constantinople, Messolongi, Mani, the

Peloponnesus, and Montenegro.[36] Another source cites recruitments from the Peloponnesus and the islands of the Aegean and Ionian Seas.[37]

Recruitment among the South Slavs caused friction with the Venetian Republic. Venetian authorities maintained intelligence on the recruiting activities of agents and officers from Naples, not only among Venetian subjects in Dalmatia, but also among Montenegrins and other Turkish subjects.[38] They attempted to restrict the Neapolitan recruitment activities in Dalmatia and Montenegro (along with Cheimarra) because these areas were also recruiting grounds for Venetian *schiavoni, morlachi,* and *Cimarrioti* troops.[39] Recruitment of South Slavs for the Macedonian regiment continued nonetheless, particularly among Serbs from Montenegro, Bocca di Cattaro, and Paštrovići.[40]

In the 1760s, a dispute concerning the South Slavic troops arose between the Neapolitan general staff and the commander of the regiment, Geōrgios Choraphas. The polemic was over whether "Illyrians" (Slavs) could serve in the *Reggimento Real Macedone* along with "Greeks" (Greeks and Christian Albanians). At various inspections the regiment had been found to include categories of men which had been excluded by the recruitment agreements of 1739 and 1754—agreements that forbade the levying of troops from areas of the Venetian Republic.[41] These strictures had been violated both with regard to the Cheimarriotes serving on the Ionian Islands (1740s) and the Serbs in Venetian-held Bocca.[42] In addition, it was found that a number of former *Grenzer* troops from Austrian service had been serving in the *Reggimento Real Macedone* since the 1740s. Initally these men were deserters from the Habsburg army that fought against Naples in the War of the Austrian Succession. Between 1744 and 1768 these troops numbered between 50 and 200 of the regiment's men.[43]

There were instances when Italians joined the regiment, as well. One attraction was that the pay of the *camiciotti* was considerably higher than that of other units in the Neapolitan army, although the former troops had to provide their own uniforms, accouterments, and weapons.[44] According to an English observer, the pay of Macedonians was twice that of Italian troops.[45]

The inclusion of troops in the Macedonian regiment from areas not included in its recruitment regulations was basically a jurisdictional problem. The commander of the regiment, in defending his recruitment policies, used not only jurisdictional evidence, but also cited historical and ethnic reasons for maintaining the "Illyrian" troops. Colonel Choraphas argued in favor of their inclusion on the historical grounds that their homelands had been in Alexander the Great's realm. Although this argument is tendentious in light of modern scholarship, it was persuasive in a period when ancient claims still took historical precedence.[46]

More significant were the points that Choraphas made regarding the ethnic composition of the regiment. He distinguished the troops of the regiment by their native language and area, calling them Illyrians and Greeks. Among troops of these two "nations" he made regional distinctions but affirmed their attachment to their respective "nations." He thus considered Dalmatian, Montenegrin, and *Grenzer* troops generically Illyrians, and argued for their inclusion in the regiment on these grounds. Also, he emphasized that in religion, customs, dress, and modes of fighting "the Illyrians were related to the Greeks."[47]

Colonel Choraphas also cited language as a criterion for maintaining Illyrians in the regiment. He recounted the case of an Italian, Giovanni Bonifacio, who was allowed to remain in the regiment because he knew the Greek and Illyrian languages.[48] This precedent indicates that the commander considered language a basic prerequisite for service in the regiment. It also implies that a certain number of men, probably commissioned and noncommissioned officers, were obliged to know both Greek and Serbo-Croatian and that bilingualism or even multilingualism (if one includes Italian or Albanian) existed in the regiment. It is clear that Choraphas's view regarding the Illyrians prevailed, for South Slavs served in the *Reggimento Real Macedone* and its successors into the nineteenth century, as is seen by a number of Serb and Croat officers and men cited for distinguished service.[49]

Cheimarra remained the chief source for the manpower needs of the regiment, over and above other regions, as is evidenced by the great number of officers from notable Cheimarriote families such as: Andrōutses, Dōules, Gkikas, Gkinēs, Kōstas, Lekas, Mēlios, Panos, Vlasēs, and Zachos, as well as other sources listed below.[50] This participation was no doubt due to Cheimarra's proximity to the Neapolitan state and to the special relations maintained between them over the years.

An indication of the extent to which Cheimarriotes served the Macedonian regiment and its successors is given in the account of William

Leake, who traveled to Cheimarra in 1805. There he found about one hundred veterans of Neapolitan service living on pensions, several soldiers on leave, and three or four officers recruiting their countrymen for service in Naples.[51]

Since Cheimarra has been part of the disputed border region of Greece and Albania in this century, the question of the nationality of the Cheimarriotes has prompted much discussion. From a lingusitic standpoint, the issue is not clear, but there is some trend toward the Greek language. William Leake observed in 1805 that the male population of Cheimarra spoke Greek as well as Albanian, while most women spoke only the latter language. This observation, if correct, would indicate that Hellenization had occurred either as a result of their mercenary service with Greek speakers or through the work of a school that had operated in Cheimarra since the seventeenth century. A number of scholars, however, maintain that Greek is the autochthonous language of the area, some claiming that the dialect spoken there is akin to the Greek of the southen Peloponnesus or to that of the Greek-speaking villages of Apulia in southern Italy.[52] In an ethnological gazetteer of 1857, a Greek author claimed that both Greek and Albanian were spoken in all of the villages of Cheimarra. An Italian scholar, who visited the area at the turn of this century, observed that five of the seven villages were bilingual and commented that the population, although of "pure Albanian origin," was of Greek sentiment.[53] A German geographer and a British archeologist, who both visited Cheimarra in the interwar period, came to the conclusion that most of the area's villages were Greek-speaking.[54] Finally, a Soviet study of the Albanian language and its dialects published in 1968 reported that three of the seven villages, including the town of Cheimarra, were wholly Greek-speaking but "considered themselves Albanians."[55]

Leaving conflicting linguistic evidence aside and using the modern criteria of nationality, one cannot label the Cheimarriotes as either Greeks or Albanians. In a narrow sense their allegiances were to their respective clans and areas, and in a broader sense to their religious and cultural heritage. This latter allegiance to Orthodox Christianity would seem to indicate closer ties to their Greek coreligionists than to the Muslim Albanians.[56] These ties are seen in the participation of many Cheimarriotes, including a number of veterans of Neapolitan service, in the Greek War of Independence. Their contributions in that conflict, although less well known, can be compared to those of the Souliotes on land and the Hydriotes and Spetsiotes at sea. These people, like the Cheimarriotes, were known to be Albanian-speaking or bilingual, yet they identified themselves wholly with the Greek national cause.[57]

In the decade following the disbandment of Naples's last Macedonian military formation, Cheimarriote veterans played a significant role in the Greek War of Independence, 1821-1830. Among those who became officers in the Greek insurrectionary forces were: Lt. General Kostas Kaznezēs, Chieftain Giannēs Kōstas, Colonel Nikolaos Mēlios, General Spyros Mēlios (Spyromēlios), Colonel Zachos Mēlios, Lt. General Chrēstos Mpekas, Colonel Georgios Mpenas, Major P. Strakēs, Major Chrēstos Varphēs, and Lt. Colonel Spyros Varphēs.[58] The most notable of these officers was General Spyromēlios. In the course of more than fifty years he served in the Light Infantry Battalions of the Greek state, as the commandant of the National Military Academy, and had a political career first as minister of war and then as both deputy and president of the parliament.[59]

Aside from these and other chieftains, many Cheimarriotes came to fight in insurgent Greece via Hellenic committees on the Ionian Islands.[60] They served both in several Epirote corps and in units made up of Cheimarriotes alone. One Cheimarriote unit of 250 men under the Mēlios brothers participated in the famed defense and sortie of Messolongi and came out with ten survivors.[61] Another Cheimarriote unit later served in the last campaigns in West Central Greece in 1828-29.[62] In addition to these Cheimarriote contributions, there were other significant ways in which the *Reggimento Real Macedone* and its successors had an impact on the development of the Greek movement for independence.

In the late eighteenth century, the *Reggimento Real Macedone* began to be supplanted and overshadowed by new formations recruited and organized by the major European powers that were becoming involved in the Mediterranean. In the founding of some of these Russian, French, and British units, the Neapolitan regiment's traditional manpower sources were tapped and its organization used as a paradigm. These later legions provided much of the rank and file of the Greek War of Independence.

As early as 1759, negotiations between the Cheimarriotes and the Russian Empire were undertaken for the raising of one to two regiments.[63]

These contacts did not bear fruit, but during the Russo-Turkish Wars of 1769-74 over three thousand Greeks and Orthodox Albanians served as marines on the ships of the Russian fleet that operated in the Eastern Mediterranean after the uprisings in Cheimarra, Mani, and other areas of Greece. In the Russo-Turkish War of 1787-92, over eight hundred warriors were again recruited by Russian agents for marine service in the privateer flotillas of Lampros Katsonēs and Guilielmo Lorenzi. Veterans of both these wars emigrated to Russia and formed the basis of two regular units in the Southern Ukraine: the *Grecheskii pekhotnyi polk* (later the *Balaklavskii grecheskii pekhotnyi batal'on*), formed in the Crimea in 1775, and the *Odesskii grecheskii division,* founded in Odessa in 1795.[65]

It is significant to note that two of the most active recruiting agents for these troops had some connection with the older Balkan military units of Venice and Naples. Major Panos Bitsilēs, the main recruiter in Cheimarra and later Russian consul in Albania and Cheimarra, was the scion of a well-known Cheimarriote family that had provided officers for the *Reggimento Cimarrioto* of Venice and was the first Cheimarriote clan to offer its services to the Russian Empire. Another member of this family, Kōnstantinos Bitsilēs, was the initial commander of the *Odesskii grecheskii division*. There is evidence that Panos Bitsēlēs or a later namesake was a member of the secret Greek revolutionary society, *Philikē Hetaireia*.[65] The other important recruiter, Major Ludovikos Sōtērēs, who was instrumental in recruiting many troops from Epirus and Central Greece during both Russo-Turkish wars, was a Lefkadian Greek who was a doctor in Naples for a number of years and no doubt had contact with many members of the *Reggimento Real Macedone* during his stay there. This experience, together with his residence in Ioannina, made him an effective recruiter for Russia. Indicative of his contact with Balkan troops in Naples is the fact that he called the troops that he recruited *Makedones*.[66]

The Napoleonic wars brought about a proliferation of Greek units serving European powers which included veterans of the Neapolitan armed forces. During their occupation of the Ionian Islands, the Russians organized units of Greek mainlanders, either under the sovereignty of the Septinsular Republic (*Pichetti Albanesi, Corpo Macedone*), or under direct Russian control (*Legion legkikh strelkov, Osobyi grecheskii korpus*).[67] During the French occupation of the Ionian Islands, these units were transformed into *Le Régiment Albanaise* and *Les Chasseurs à pied Greces*.[68] Later, the English, struggling with the French over the Ionian Islands (1809 to 1814), organized two Greek Light Infantry Regiments from the earlier Russian and French formations.[69]

All of the above Russian, French, and English formations had some elements that had previously been in Neapolitan forces. There is evidence that whole companies transferred their service from Naples to the Septinsular Republic in the early years of the Russian occupation. For example, there was a Major Stratēs Gkikas, probably a descendant of one of the founders of the *Reggimento Real Macedone,* commanding a company on Zakynthos for the Ionian Republic in 1802. This company still bore the nomenclature of its former Neapolitan service, being the first company of the Macedonian regiment (*Reggimento Macedonia –Piedalista–Prima Compagnia*).[70] Major Gkikas later held a commission in the Russian *Legion legkikh strelkov* and was subsequently an officer in French and British service as well. During the Greek War of Independence, he served as an officer in the revolutionary forces of Western Greece.[71]

Another individual from the Neapolitan officer corps was Kōnstantios Androutsēs, who entered the service of the French during their occupation of Naples in 1799. He acted as commander and instructor of one of the Neapolitan Republic's civic guard regiments in that year, but the allied restoration of the Kingdom of Naples forced him to return clandestinely to his homeland of Cheimarra. He remained in Cheimarra until 1806, when he was assigned by the French to scout out the Russian *Legion legkikh strelkov* and to recruit Cheimarriotes and others for French service instead. While on this mission on Corfu, he was arrested and imprisoned by Septinsular authorities in November 1806 for pro-French activities, but was able to escape to Cheimarra. With the cession of the Ionian Islands to the French he was given the command of one of the battalions, of the *Régiment Albanaise*. He later became native adjutant commander of the regiment with the rank of lieutenant colonel.[72]

The English, in organizing the Duke of York's Greek Light Infantry, recruited not only from among those men who had served in previous Russian and French sponsored organizations, but also from the veterans of the *Reggimento Real Macedone*.[73] Indeed, each of the three powers maintained a section of the Greek regiments with Cheimarriotes, many of whom were no doubt Neapolitan veterans. The Russians, in their *Legion legkikh strelkov*, had a Cheimarriote legion of four companies on Corfu, while the French later had a battalion of six Cheimarriote companies in the *Régiment Albanaise*.[74]

In the initial organization of these units, the precedent of the *Reggimento Real Macedone* was kept in mind. In 1802, when the Septinsular Republic institutionalized the irregular *Pichetti Albanesi* ("Albanian detachments") into a single unit, the named the five hundred-man unit the *Corpo Macedone*. Among the officers and men of the corps who later served in the Greek War of Independence were: Georgakes Grivas, Velisarios Kalogeros, Giannes Kavadias, and Theodoros Grivas.[75]

It is also evident that the founding of the *Legion legkikh strelkov* was effected by the *Reggimento Real Macedone*, since the first men to offer their services to the Russians on the Ionian Islands in 1804 were Cheimarriotes, who wanted conditions of service similar to those they had enjoyed in Neapolitan service.[76] Likewise, the French, one year before the organizing of the *Régiment Albanaise*, had considered the feasibility of raising a new *Reggimento Real Macedone* for the French sponsored Kingdom of Naples, ruled by Joseph Murat.[77] There is also little doubt that Richard Church had encountered Macedonian troops in Italy before he had organized the Greek Light Infantry on the Ionian Islands.

After the defeat of Napoleon and the cession of the Ionian Islands to England, the Duke of York's Greek Light Infantry Regiments were fully disbanded in 1817. Some of the discharged warriors were able to find service in the *Battaglione dei Cacciatori Macedone* with their old commander, Richard Church, and there is evidence that he recruited from among his most trusted officers.[78] Others went to Russia and sought patents of commission for service with the tsar, but were turned down. Russian Foreign Minister Iōannēs Kapodistrias, who knew these troops well from his service in the Septinsular Republic, feared that their unemployment would lead them into the ranks of the secret Greek revolutionary society, *Philikē Hetaireia*. He attempted, through letters to the Neapolitan ambassador in St. Petersburg, to persuade the king of Naples to reactivate the *Reggimento Real Macedone* with the bulk of these Ionian veterans as its rank and file. His efforts did not produce the expected results and the Neapolitan Balkan forces were limited to the one battalion under Richard Church.[79]

Those officers that had gone to Russia (Anagnostēs Papageōrgiou, Ēlias Chrysospathēs, Christophoros Perraivos, and others) did join the *Philikē Hetaireia* and became among its most active members, initiating their former comrades-in-arms from service in the Ionian Islands.[80] The leadership of the *Philikē Hetaireia* had taken the Neapolitan forces into account in its plans for the Greek struggle. It was planned that Christophoros Priniarēs, a member residing in Italy, would arrange for the recruitment and transport of the Macedonian troops to Sparta.[81]

Although this particular plan was never realized, a number of veterans of the last *Battaglione dei Cacciatori Macedoni,* including Souliotes and others, were involved in the rebellion of Ali Pasha in 1820-21 and later made their marks in the Greek campaigns in Central Greece.[82]

Besides these Cheimarriotes and other former soldiers of Neapolitan service who participated in the Greek War of Independence, the members of those Ionian formations that rivaled the *Reggimento Real Macedone* in its last years constituted a significant part of the forces of independent Greece.[83]

The legacy of the *Reggimento Real Macedone* and its successors was of two-fold importance for the development of modern Greece. The units provided an important number of trained officers and seasoned troops for the forces of the Greek Revolution. Indirectly, the Neapolitan formations acted as models and as recruiting grounds for later Russian, French, and English units on the Ionian Islands that likewise provided an even greater number of chieftains and soldiers for independent Greece.

This study, based upon published sources, has only briefly recounted the history of the Balkan forces of the Kingdom of Naples and their impact upon the formation of their foreign counterparts and upon the Greek national movement. It has also touched upon the ethnic and regional composition of these units. Nevertheless, these and other subjects need further systematic study, using available archival materials in Italy and elsewhere. Investigation into the recruitment policies and the internal

organization of Naples's Balkan legions, along with their relation to Vene-
tain and Russian rivals, may provide further insights into the development
of Balkan military institutions in the eighteenth and early nineteenth
centuries.

NOTES

1. Two important studies of Austrian units in English are Gunther
E. Rothenberg's *The Austrian Military Border in Croatia: 1522-1747* (Urbana, Illinois, 1960), and *The Military Border in Croatia, 1740-1881*
(Chicago, 1966). Information on units in Dalmatia are found in Grga
Novak, *Prošlost Dalmacije*, 2 pts. (Zagreb, 1944), pp. 193-95, 208-12,
221-34, 248-49; Miloš Milošević, "Pokusaj mletačkog osvajanja Ulsinja
1718. godine," *Godišnjak Pomorskog Muzeja u Kotoru*, vol. 20 (Kotor,
1972), 41-64; Gligor Stanojević, *Jugoslovenske zemlje u Mletačko-turskim
ratovima XVI-XVIII vijeka* (Belgrade, 1970); and in the various documents published in the series *Commissiones et Relationes Venetae*, vols.
1-7 (1433-1676). *Monumenta spetantia historiam Slavorum Meridionalum*,
vols. 6, 8, 11, 47-50 (Zagreb, 1876, 1877, 1880, 1963-1972).

2. Kōnstantinos Sathas, *Hellēnes stratiōtai en tēi dysēi kai hē ana-
gennēsis tēs hellēnikēs taktikēs* (Athens, 1885), pp. 11-13.

3. Sathas, pp. 13-14, 43. For accounts of the activities of the
stradioti, see F. Babinger, "Albanischen stradioten im dienst Venedigs
im ausgehenden Mittelalter," *Studia Albanica*, vol. 1 (Tirana, 1964), 162-
82; Kōstas Mpirēs, *Hoi Arvanites, hoi Dorieis tou neoterou Hellēnismou*
(Athens, 1960), pp. 162-82; Aleko Rapo, "Stratiotet shqiptare gjate she-
kujve XV-XVI," *Studimë Historikë*, vol. 4 (Tirana, 1965), 88-96; Apostolos Vakalopoulos, *Historia tou Neou Hellēnismou*, vol. 3 (Thessalonikē,
1968), 88-96; and Giannes Vlachogiannes, "Vouzikios," in *Hapanta
Gianne Vlachogianne*, vol. 5 (Athens, 1970), 107-11. Sources and documents on the *stradioti* are found in *Mnēmeia Hellenikēs Historias: Documents inédits à l'histoire de la Grèce au Moyen Âge*, Kōnstantinos Sathas,
ed., vols. 1, 4, 7, 9 (Paris, 1880-90) and *Historika anekdota*, K. Sathas,
ed., vol. 1 (Athens, 1867).

4. I. K. Chasiōtēs, "Hellēnikoi epoikismoi sto Basileio tēs Neapolēs
kata ton dekato ebdomo aiona," *Hellēnika*, vol. 22 (Thessalonikē, 1969),

134-35; I. K. Chasiōtēs, "La comunità greca di Napoli et i moti insurres-tionali nella penisola Balcanica meridionale durante la seconda metà del XVI secolo," *Balkan Studies*, vol. 10 (Thessalonikē, 1969), 285-86; I. K. Chasiōtēs, *Scheseis hellēnōn kai hispanōn sta chronia tēs Tourkokratias* (Thessalonikē, 1969), pp. 42-44; and S. P. Lampros, "Metanasteusis hellēnōn, idiōs Peloponnēsiōn apoikōn eis ton Basileion tēs Neapoleos," *Neos Hellēnomnēmōn*, vol. 8 (Athens, 1911), 377-461.

5.   Takēs Lappas, "Hē phoresia kai ta armata tōn agōnistōn," in *Gyro ap' to Eikosiena* (Athens, 1971), pp. 28-43; Periklēs Rodakēs, *Klephtes Kai armatoloi*, 1 (Athens, 1975), 223; and Apostolos Vakalo-poulos, *Ta hellēnika strateumata tou 1821* (Thessalonikē, 1948), p. 172.

6.   Lappas, pp. 8-28; Rodakēs, vol. 1, 224-25; Attanasio Lehasca, *Cenno storico dei servigi militari prestati nel Regno delle Due Sicilie dai Greci, Epiroti, Albanesi e Macedoni in epoche diverse* (Corfu, 1843), p. 46; Raul Manselli, "Il Reggimento Albanese Real Macedone durante il Regno di Carlo di Borbone," *Archivio Storico per le Provincie Napolet-ane*, n.s., vol. 32 (Naples, 1950-51), 147: Matteo Sciambra, "Prime vi-cende della Communità greco-albanese di Palermo e suoi rapporti con l'Oriente bizantino," *Bolletino della Badia Greca di Grottaferrata*, n.s., vol. 16 (Rome, 1962), 101-2.

7.   Vakalopoulos, *Ta hellēnika strateumata tou 1821*, pp. 139-46.

8.   Vittorio Buti, "Albanesi al servizio de Regno delle Due Sicilie," La Rassegna *Italiana Politica Letteraria ed Artistica*, 3d series, vol. 51, no. 259 (Rome, 1939), 152-53; Giovanni Jacopo Casanova de Seingalt (Casa-nova), *Memoires*, vol. 1 (Paris, 1924), 133-35; Instituti i Historise dhe i Gjuherisë, *Burime të zgjedhura për historinë e Shqiperisë*, vol. 3 (Tirana, 1961), 238-39; Petraq Pepo, "Materiale për   historinë e krahinës se Himarës në vitet 1785-1788," *Studimë Historikë*, no. 3 (Tirana, 1964), 129-30, 132-33; Petraq Pepo, "Materiale për krahinat e Himarës dhe te Shkodrës në vitet 1787-88," *Studimë Historikë*, no. 4 (Tirana, 1964), 135-36, 139-40, 143-44; Mēlios Spyromēlios, *Apom-nēmōneumata tēs deuteras poliorkias tou Mēsolongiou 1825-1826*, intro-duction by I. Vlachogiannēs, in *Apomnēmōneumata agōnistōn tou Eiko-siena*, vol. 19 (Athens, 1957), 95; and Lampros P. Spyrou, *Hē Cheimarra: Toponymia, laographia, historia* (Athens, 1966), pp. 76-77.

9.   Kōnstantinos Sathas, *Tourkokratoumenē Hellas* (Athens, 1869), pp. 45-46.

10. P. Aravantinos, *Chronographia tēs Ēpeirou tōn te homorōn hellēnikōn kai Illyrikōn chōrōn diatrechousa kata seiran ta en autais symbanta apo tou Sotēriou etous mechri tou 1854,* vol. 1 (Athens, 1856), 191; I. K. Chasiōtēs, "Hē epanastasē tōn Chimariōtōn (*sic*) sta 1570 kai hē alōsē tou Sopotou," *Ēpeirotikē Hestia,* vol. 16 (Iōnnina, 1969), 265-76; Mpirēs, p. 298. On the privileges of Cheimarra, consult A. Petridēs, "Hē Cheimarra kai ta archaia pronomia autēs," *Ho Hellēnismos,* vol. 2 (Athens, 1899), 497-505, and Miltiadēs Spyromēlios, "Ta pronomia tēs Cheimarras," *Ēpeirōtikon Hēmerologion* (Athens, 1914), 275-78.

11. Kōstas Dedes, *Drymades Cheimarra* (Athens, 1978), pp. 20-26; Mpirēs, p. 299; and Spyrou, pp. 74-75.

12. Chasiōtēs, "La comunità greca di Napoli," 285-86; Chasiōtēs, *Scheseis hellēnōn kai hispanōn,* pp. 44-45; Instituti i Historisë dhe i Gjuherisë, *Burime të zgejedhura për historinë e Shqiperisë,* vol. 3, 237-38; Vladimir Lamansky, *Secrets d'état de Venise* (St. Petersburg, 1884), pp. 801-3; and Lehasca, pp. 1-14.

13. Casanova, *Memoires,* vol. 1, 133-35; and Spyrou, pp. 76-77.

14. Buti, 152-55; *Dissertazione istorico-cronologico del Reggimento Real Macedone nella quale si tratta sua origine, formazione e progressi, e delle vicissitudini, che gli sono accadute fino all' anno 1767,* 2d ed. (Bologna, 1768), pp. 205-9; and Fabio Mutinelli, *Memorie storiche degli ultimi cinquant' anni della Repubblica Veneta* (Venice, 1854), pp. 159-60.

15. Buti, pp. 152-53; Mariano D'Ayala, *Napoli Militare* (Naples, 1847), p. 71; Lehasca, pp. 15-16; Manselli, pp. 143-45; and Spyromēlios, *Apomnēmōneumata,* p. 95.

16. Lehasca, pp. 16-18; and Manselli, pp. 157-58.

17. Buti, p. 155; and Lehasca, pp. 30, 32.

18. Chasiōtēs, *Scheseis hellēnōn kai hispanōn,* p. 45, n. 1.

19. Buti, pp. 153-54; *Dissertazione,* pp. 65-150; Lehasca, pp. 19-27; and Manselli, pp. 151-57.

20. Buti, pp. 153-54; *Dissertazione,* pp. 152-53; Lehasca, pp. 28-29; and Manselli, p. 157.

21. Buti, pp. 153-54; Lehasca, pp. 28, 31; and "Zapiski Grafa Ioanna Kapodistriia o ego sluzhebnoi deiatel'nosti," *Sbornik russkago istoricheskago obshchestva,* vol. 3 (St. Petersburg, 1868), 226.

22. Buti, p. 155; and Lehasca, p. 32.

23. G. L. Arsh, *Albaniia i Epir v kontse XVIII-nachale XIX v.* (Moscow, 1960), p. 37; and Spyromēlios, *Apomnēmōneumata*, p. 95.

24. D'Ayala, p. 75; and Lehasca, p. 33.

25. D'Ayala, p. 77; and Lehasca, pp. 35-36.

26. Lehasca, pp. 40-42.

27. Lehasca, pp. 40-42; and Ferdinando Nunziante, "Il generale Vito Nunziante (1775-1836)," *Archivio Storico per le Provincie Napoletane*, 4th series, vol. 2, (Naples, 1963), pp. 144-45.

28. Lehasca, p. 45.

29. Ibid., pp. 47-48.

30. Ibid., pp. 48-49.

31. Ibid., pp. 55-56.

32. E. M. Church, *Sir Richard Church in Italy and Greece* (London, 1895), pp. 1-20; Douglas Dakin, *British and American Philhellenes during the Greek War of Independence, 1821-1833* (Thessalonikē, 1955), pp. 10-16; and Stanley Lane-Poole, *Sir Richard Church* (London, 1890), pp. 9-30.

33. D'Ayala, pp. 32-33; Lane-Poole, p. 40; and Lehasca, pp. 58-59.

34. Buti, p. 157; and Lehasca, p. 59.

35. *Dissertazione*, pp. 213-15. For discussion on the term "Albanian" in the nomenclature of that era, see G. L. Arsh, "Grecheskaia emigratsiia v Rossiiu v kontse XVIII-nachale XIX v.," *Sovetskaia etnografiia*, no. 3 (Moscow, 1969), 86, n. 3; and Konstantinos Rados, "Hoi Souliōtai kai armatōloi en Heptanēsōi," *Epetēris Philologikou Syllogou Parnassou*, vol. 12 (Athens, 1916), 54-55.

36. *Dissertazione*, pp. 230-32, 265-74.

37. Chasiōtēs, *Scheseis hellēnōn kai hispanōn*, p. 45.

38. On Neapolitan recruitment of Montenegrins, see: *Dissertazione*, pp. 266-72; Gligor Stanojević and Milan Vasić, *Istorija Crne Gore*, vol. 3, pt. 1 (Titograd, 1975), 299-300, 311-12, 359-60; and Stanojević, "Seoba crnogoracu u Kraljevinu Dveju Sicilija sredinom XVIII vijeka," *Glasnik Etnografskog Instituta Srpske Akademije Nauke i Umjetnosti*, vol. 9/10 (Belgrade, 1960-61), 171-77.

39. *Dissertazione*, pp. 201-3, 205-9; and Stanojević, "Seoba crnogoraca u Kraljevinu Dveju Sicilija," pp. 173-74.

40. Stanojević and Vasić, *Istorija Crne Gore*, vol. 3, pt. 1, 359-60.

41. *Dissertazione*, pp. 201-3, 262.

42. On the rivalry between Venice and Naples over recruitment of Cheimarriotes, see: Buti, pp. 152-53; *Dissertazione,* pp. 205-9; Manselli, pp. 144-47; and Mutinelli, pp. 159-60.

43. *Dissertazione,* pp. 216, 233; and Lehasca, p. 22.

44. *Dissertazione,* pp. 190-95.

45. William M. Leake, *Travels in Northern Greece,* vol. 1 (London, 1835), 87.

46. *Dissertazione,* pp. 213-15, 256-60, 273-76.

47. Ibid., pp. 261-63.

48. Ibid., p. 265.

49. Lehasca, pp. 38-39. In addition, a list of 41 veterans who received last rites in the Greek church in Palermo, Sicily, indicates that two were South Slavs—Jovan Gravic (*ex Illyrico delle Boche di Cattaro*) in 1810, and Jovan Markovic (*Illyricus Dalmatinus*). Sciambra, p. 104.

50. Spyromelios, *Apomnemoneumata,* p. 95.

51. Leake, vol. 1, 86-87.

52. Leake, vol. 1, 88. On the Greek spoken in Cheimarra, see: G. P. Anagnōstopoulos, "Peri tou rēmatos en tē en Ēpeirōi omiloumenē," *Athēna,* vol. 36 (Athens, 1924), 62-63; "Chimaras (*sic*) kai Ēpeirou glōssaria," *Lexikographikon Archeion tēs mesēs kai neas hellēnikēs,* vol. 5, appendix to *Athēna,* vol. 30 (Athens, 1920), 358, 395; Dēmetrios Evangelidēs and Spyridōn Lampros, "Hai archaiotētes kai ta Byzantina mnēmeia tēs Boreiodytikēs Ēpeirou," *Neos Hellēnomnēmon,* vol. 10 (Athens, 1913), 283; Michael Dendias, "Apoulia kai Chimara (*sic*)," *Athena,* vol. 38 (Athens, 1926), 75-82; and Carsten Höeg, "Paratērēsis sta 'Glōssika analekta' tou k. G. P. Anagnostopoulou," *Athēna,* vol. 36 (Athens, 1925), 289-96. On the Albanian spoken in areas around Cheimarra, see: A. V. Desnitskaia, *Albanskii iazyk i ego dialekty* (Leningrad, 1968), pp. 351-58; and Menella Totoni, "Efolmja e Bregdetit të Poshtëm(skicë), " *Studimë Filologjikë,* vol. 1 (Tirana, 1964), no. 1, 129-58, and no. 2, 121-39.

53. Aravantios, vol. 2, 358; and Antonio Baldacci, *Itinerari Albanesi (1892-1902)* (Rome, 1917), pp. 166, 501-2.

54. N. G. L. Hammond, *Epirus* (Oxford, 1967), pp. 20-21 (map 2), 27, 29-32, 122-25; and Alfred Philippson, *Die Griechischen Landschaften,* vol. 2, pt. 1, *Epirus und Pindos* (Frankfurt-am-Main, 1953), p. 59, and folding map 2.

55. Desnitskaia, pp. 353-54.

56. On the impact of Greek language and culture upon Orthodox Albanians and Vlachs, see Trajan Stoianovich, "The Conquering Balkan Orthodox Merchant," *Journal of Economic History,* vol. 20 (1960), 280.

57. For a discussion of this phenomenon, see the study by Giannēs Vlachogiannēs, "Souliōtēs-Arvanitēs," *Mnēmē Souliou,* Vasilēs Krapsitēs, ed., vol. 3 (Athens, 1976), 171-83.

58. Angelos Papakōstas, *Agones kai thysies Boreioēpeirōtōn sto Eikosiena* (Athens, 1945), pp. 23-27; Nikolaos V. Patselēs, *Hē Boreios Ēpeiros kai ta physike tēs synora* (Athens, 1946), pp. 100-1; Spyrou, p. 78. On Cheimarra during the Greek War of Independence, see Spyros Stoupēs, "Hai diekdikēsis mas en Epeirō kai hē stasis tēs Cheimarras kata tēn Epanastasin," *Ēpeirōtikē Hestia,* vol. 6 (Ioannina, 1958), 269-73.

59. Spyromēlios, *Apomnēmōneumata,* pp. 92-108; Spyrou, pp. 78-85.

60. L. I. Vranousēs, *Athanasios Psalidas, ho didaskalos tou genous (1767-1829)* (Iōannina, 1952), pp. 78-85, 109, 130-31, 134-35.

61. Spyromēlios, *Apomnēmōneumata,* pp. 97-100.

62. Domna Dontas, *The Last Phase of the War of Independence in Western Greece* (Thessalonikē, 1966), p. 134.

63. Peter Bartl, "Albanien—ein Randgebiet der russischen Balkan politik 18. Jahrhundert (1711-1807)," *Saeculum,* vol. 17 (1966), 386; Aleks Buda, "Traditsii druzhby mezhdu albanskim i russkim narodami," ANSSSR. Istoricheskii Inst. *Doklady i soobshcheniia* (Moscow, 1954), p. 81; and Instituti i Historisë dhe i Gjuherisë, *Burime të zgjedhura për historinë e Shqiperisë,* vol. 3 (Tirana, 1961), 233-39.

64. On these units, consult: "Albanskoe voisko," *Voennyi entsiklopedicheskii leksikon,* vol. 1 (St. Petersburg, 1911), 239-41; Arsh, *Eteristskoe dvizhenie v Rossii* (Moscow, 1972), pp. 130-32, 135-38, 144-45; Arsh, "Grecheskaia emigratsiia v Rossiiu," pp. 85-91; Alan W. Fisher, *The Russian Annexation of the Crimea 1772-1783* (Cambridge, Eng., 1970), pp. 90-92, 100-1, 111, 147; G. L(ampisēs), *Peri tōn hellenōn tēs Mesēmbrinēs Rōsias* (Athens, 1853), pp. 47-57; K. A. Palaiologos, "Ho en Notiōi Rōsiai Hellēnismos," *Parnassos,* vol. 5 (Athens, 1881), 535-42, 544, 549, 602-4; S. Safonov, "Ostatki grecheskikh legionov v Rossii ili nyneshnee naselenie Balaklavy: Istoricheskii ocherk," *Zapiski odesskago obshchestva istorii i drevnostei,* vol. 1 (Odessa, 1844), 205-38; T. I.

Teokharidi (T. I. Theocharides), "Hrets'ka viys'kova kolonizatsiia na pini Ukrainy na prykinsti XVIII ta pochatku XIX stol." ("Ho hellenikos stratiotikos apoikismos sten notio Oukrainia. Apoikies sta perichora tes Odesas"), *Visnyk Odes'koi komysii Kraeznavstva pri Ukrainskoi Akademii nauk,* no. 4/5, *Sektsiia dlia vyvcheniia hrets'koi natsmenshosty,* 1 (Odessa, 1930), 1-47 (reviewed by A. N. Diamantopoulos in *Hellēnika,* vol. 3 [Athens, 1930], 263-66).

65. Arsh, *Albaniia i Epir,* pp. 5, 140-41; Arsh, *Eteristskoe dvizhenie,* p. 136; Arsh, "Rusko-Albanskie sviazi v period Russko-Turetskoi voiny 1787-1791 gg.," *Istoricheskie zapiski,* vol. 63 (Leningrad, 1958), 260-61; A. N. Petrov, *Vtoraia Turetskaia voina v tsarstvovanie Imperatritsi Ekateriny II, 1787-1791 gg.,* vol. 1 (St. Petersburg, 1880), appendices, pp. 20, 28; Iōannēs Philēmōn, *Dokimion historikon peri tēs Hellēnikēs Epanastaseōs,* vol. 1 (Athens, 1859), 401; and Emmanouēl Prōtopsaltēs, "He epanastatikē kinēsis tōn Hellēnōn kata ton deuteron epi Aikaterinēs B' Rōsotourkikon polemon (1787-1792). Loudovikos Sōtōrēs," *Deltion tēs Historikēs kai Ethnologikēs Hetaireias tēs Hellados,* vol. 14 (Athens, 1960), 55-62.

66. "Arkhipelazhskie korsary v russkoi sluzhbe," *Arkhiv grafov Mordvinovykh,* V. A. Bil'basov, ed., vol. 2 (St. Petersburg, 1901), 415-16; Arsh, *Albaniia i Epir,* pp. 140-41; Arsh, "Russko-Albanskie sviazi," pp. 260-61, 263; and Prōtopsaltēs, pp. 59-62.

67. On these Septinsular and Russian units, consult: Arsh, *Albanjia i Epir,* pp. 235-36; Rados, pp. 34-38, 41-54, 62-63; A. M. Stanislavskaia, *Rossiia i Gretsiia v kontse XVII-nachale XIX veka* (Moscow, 1976), pp. 307-18, 337-47; and this writer's doctoral dissertation, entitled "Greeks in Russian Military Service on the Ionian Islands, 1798-1807," (Stanford University, 1981).

68. On these French units, see August Boppe, "Le Régiment Albanaise (1807-1814)," in *L'Albanie et Napoléon (1797-1814),* (Paris, 1914), pp. 219-69; Rados, pp. 54-64; and Jean Savant, "Soldats grecs de la Révolution et de l'Empire et héros de l'indépendnece," *Les Balkans,* vol. 11 (Athens, 1939), 375-76.

69. On the Duke of York's Light Greek Infantry Regiments, see E. M. Church, pp. 17-20; "Copy of Extracts from any Correspondence which may have taken place between the commander of forces during the occupation of Sicily by the British forces and the Home Government, relative

to the Attack which led to the Capture and Subsequent Occupation of the Ionian Islands," Great Britain, Parliament, House of Commons, *Sessional Papers,* 1864, vol. 66, no. 3, enclosures 1-15, pp. 1-28; Dakin, pp. 1-28; Lane-Poole, pp. 9-25; Rados, pp. 81-96.

70. Roll call for the Macedonian Regiment-Infantry-First Company-Zante, November 1802, Genika Archeia tou Kratous (General State Archives), Athens, Greece. Vlachogiannēs Collection, folio G37 (1802). Gkikas and his troops were not the only veterans of Neapolitan service to join the Ionian armed forces. Other former veterans of the Macedonian regiments were: Colonel Nikolaos Pierēs, commander of Septinsular regular forces on Corfu and Cephalonia from 1800; Colonel Lavrentios Pierēs, Stepinsular Battalion Commander from 1803; and Colonel Andreas Garzonēs, Garrison Commander on Zante from 1802. Nikolaos Pierēs later served in the Greek War of Independence as a commander of artillery and regular infantry. Roll of Officers not only company rolls on Zante, n.d., Genika Archeia tou Kratous, Vlachogiannēs Collection, folio G37, nos. 42-44 (1802); Gerasimos Mavrogiannes, *Historia ton Ioniōn Nēsōn archomenē to 1797 kai lēgousa to 1815,* vol. 1 (Athens, 1889), 379; E. R. Rhangave, *Livre d'or de la noblesse ionienne,* vol. 1 (Athens, 1925), 136-37; Savant, "Soldats grecs," pp. 285-86, 376-77; Savant, *Sous les aigles impériales: Napoléon et les Grecs* (Paris, 1946), pp. 317-18; Chrestos Vyzantios, *Historia tōn kata tēn Hellēnikēn Epanastasin ekstrateiōn kai machōn ōn symmeteschen ho taktikos stratos apo tou 1821 mechri tou 1833,* in *Apomnēmōneumata agōnistōn tou Eikosiena,* vol. 10 (Athens, 1956), 291, n. 27; and Leonidas Zōēs, *Lexikon historikōn kai laographikōn Zakynthou,* vol. 1 (Athens, 1963), 116-17.

71. Philemon, vol. 1, 131-32; Petimezas manuscript (1809-1812), Genika Archeia tou Kratous, Vlachogiannēs Collection, folio G15; and Alexandros Mavrokordatos to Kostakes Karatzas, 7 October 1821, in *Historikon Archeion Alexandrou Mavrokordatou,* Emmanouel Protopsaltes, ed., vol. 1, Akademia Athenon, *Mnemeia tes Hellenikes historias,* vol. 5 (Athens, 1963), 65-67.

72. Boppe, pp. 239, 242, 251-53; Savant, "Soldats grecs," pp. 150-51; and Savant, *Sous les Aigles Impériales,* pp. 19-30.

73. Major Oswald to Lt. General Lord William Bentinck, 3 January 1813, in "Ionian Islands," *Sessional Papers,* 1864, vol. 66, no. 3, enclosure 1, no. 12, p. 24.

74. Boppe, p. 242; and Stanislavskaia, p. 314.

75. Report of the Senate on the Macedonia troops, 23 January 1803, Genika Archeia tou Kratous, Vlachogiannēs Collection, folio G37 (1803).

76. Arsh, *Albaniia i Epir,* pp. 214-15.

77. Boppe, p. 232.

78. William Meyer to Lord Castlereagh, 15 March 1821, in Eleutherios Prevelakes, "Hē Philikē Hetaireia, ho Alē Pasas kai hoi Souliōtēs (dyo ektheseis tou William Meyer)," *Meletēmata stē mnēmē tou Vasileiou Laourda* (Thessalonikē, 1975), p. 455; Theodōros Kolokotrōnēs, *Diegēsis tōn symbatōn tēs Hellēnikēs phylēs* (Athens, 1971), p. 57; and F. C. H. L. Pouqueville, *Voyage dans la Grèce,* vol. 5 (Paris, 1821), 197.

79. I. A. Kapodistrias to Alexander I, January 1818, in Arsh, *I. Kapodistriia i grecheskoe natsional'no-osvoboditel'noe dvizhenie 1809-1822 gg.* (Moscow, 1976), pp. 275-82; and "Zapiski Grafa Ioanna Kapodistriia o ego sluzhebnoi deiatel'nosti," pp. 226-27.

80. George D. Frangos, "The Philike Etaireia, 1814-1821: A Social and Historical Analysis" (Columbia University Doctoral Dissertation, 1971), pp. 111-12, 166, 176, 232; Ioannes Philemon, *Dokimion historikon peri tēs Philikēs Hetaireias* (Nauplion, 1834, reprint, n.d.), pp. 184-85, 199-203; Emmanouel Zanthos, *Apomnēmōneumata peri tēs Philikēs Hetaireias* (Athens, 1971), pp. 38, 40-41.

81. Philēmon, *Dokimion historikon peri tēs Hellēnikēs Epanastaseōs,* vol. 1, 56.

82. Prevelakes, p. 455; and Dennis N. Skiotis, "Mountain Warriors and the Greek Revolution," *War, Technology and Society in the Middle East,* V. J. Parry and M. E. Yapp, eds. (London, 1975), pp. 324-29.

83. Boppe, p. 219, and Rados, pp. 31-33, 113.

KOSOVO: DEVELOPMENT AND IMPACT
OF A NATIONAL ETHIC

Thomas A. Emmert
Gustavus Adolphus College

On 28 June 1389 an alliance of Serbian and Bosnian forces engaged a large Ottoman army on the plain of Kosovo in southern Serbia. When the battle was over, Prince Lazar, the commander of the Christian army, and Murad, the ruler of the Ottomans, lay dead. In the years that followed, the battle and the martyred Prince Lazar became the subjects of a rich literature of popular legend and epic poetry that has profoundly influenced the Serbian historical consciousness. The bard, the storyteller, and, eventually, the traditionalist historian depicted the battle of Kosovo as the catastrophic turning point in the life of Serbia; it marked the end of an independent, united Serbia and the beginning of five hundred years of oppressive Ottoman rule. The legend of the battle became the core of what we may call the Kosovo ethic, and the poetry that developed around the defeat contained themes that were to sustain the Serbian people during the long centuries of foreign rule.

That generations of Serbs should develop a national cult of the battle of Kosovo which served as a reservoir of spiritual strength, inspiring them through the long period of Ottoman rule, is a phenomenon that emerged in response to psychological needs and specific national and confessional circumstances. It has been said that the essence of the Kosovo ethic and cult is a basic attitude of the Serb toward the state and life itself.[1] With the dawning of the nineteenth century and the beginning of the century-long struggle for independence and unification of Serbian lands, the cult of Kosovo was further refined and generously utilized in the service of the Serbian national renaissance. It is the intent of this short study to shed some light on the development of the Kosovo legend

61

and ethic and to consider some manifestations of the emotional appeal of the cult of Kosovo in the nineteenth and twentieth centuries.

The collapse of medieval Serbia was certainly not the result of one day-long battle on the field of Kosovo.[2] Serbia had actually ceased to exist as a strong and unified state thirty-four years earlier with the untimely death in 1355 of her most powerful ruler, Stefan Dušan. Between the date of his death and 1389, the Ottoman Turks had continued their advance into the Balkans. The Nemanjić dynasty died out in 1371; and by 1389, Prince Lazar, who governed the lands which today constitute northern and central Serbia, was the only still-independent Serbian lord who could possibly withstand a strong Ottoman attack. Even the battle of Kosovo itself, however, was not the final end of medieval Serbia. Lazar's widow, Milica, did not agree to pay tribute to the Ottomans until the following year; and for almost seventy years thereafter the Serbs enjoyed a relative autonomy within the Ottoman orbit. The final subjugation of Serbia occurred only in 1459. Nevertheless, in the popular consciousness of the Serbs, Kosovo was the singular event that signified the end of Serbia's greatness and independence. To struggle and even to die in order to avenge Kosovo became the common goal of generations. The roots of this fierce commitment are found in Serbian literature written not long after the battle itself.

A feeling of despair permeated Lazar's lands after the prince's death and his wife's surrender to the Ottomans the following year. Conscious of the need to combat pessimism in Serbia and to provide hope for a bright future, religious figures wrote eulogies and sermons in praise of Lazar in which they interpreted the events of this troubled period for their own contemporaries.[3] In their writings Lazar is portrayed as God's favored servant and the Serbian people as the chosen people of the New Testament—the "new Israel." Like the Hebrews in Babylonian captivity the Serbs would be led out of slavery to freedom. Lazar's death is depicted as the triumph of good over evil—a martyrdom for the faith and the symbol of a new beginning. Serbia and her people would live. Responding to contemporary needs, the medieval writers transformed the defeat into a kind of moral victory for the Serbs and an inspiration for the future. The development of the Serbian epic tradition only developed these ideas further and established them soundly in the consciousness of the Serbian people.

Lazar's hagiographers also endeavored to legitimate Lazar's rule in Serbia. If Prince Lazar could be viewed as part of a continuous line of authority that had begun with the' Nemanjići and that would continue after Lazar, it might be possible to overcome the sense of disorder and chaos which had characterized the troubled years 1355-89. These religious writers wanted to see their own society as an integral part of the Nemanjić tradition. In giving legitimacy to Lazar, they sought to identify Lazar's Serbia and Nemanjić Serbia as one and the same entity.

These medieval writers did more than simply identify Lazar as the successor to the Nemanjići through genealogical fabrications; they also fundamentally altered contemporary political ideology. In the political ideology of the Nemanjić kingdom there had been a complete identity between land and dynasty, and this equation now had to be eliminated so that the fate of the Serbian land could be considered separately from the fate of the ruling dynasty. The medieval writers' solution was to interpret the ruler's right to authority as an appointment from God and a gift of His blessing—not as the privilege of inheritance.

According to a sermon by Patriarch Danilo III, for example, Lazar had been designated as God's chosen one even before Stefan Dušan's death. The patriarch develops the theory that Emperor Stefan Dušan and Pribac, Lazar's father, were twins bound by an alliance of love as if they were a single soul. This was not a blood relationship, however, but one established according to the will of God. Stefan Dušan recognized God's providence at work in Lazar, for he was gifted with all the virtues and talents of the ideal ruler. He treated him like a son and prepared him for the throne. Therefore, even before Stefan Dušan's son, Uroš, began to rule, Lazar was destined by God to shepherd the Serbian flock. Other contemporary writers used different images to establish Lazar's legitimacy, but all of them emphasized the importance of God's providence in providing a peaceful transference of authority during those troubled years.

After establishing this continuity of leadership, the medieval writers had to deal with the battle of Kosovo itself. Varied as their accounts are in style, length, and content, the central theme in each is the death of the Serbian prince. In the view of his eulogists, he sacrificed himself so that Serbia might live. One anonymous author expresses this theme in his introduction:

The head of the new Lazar was cut off in June on the fifteenth day, clearly for the sake of the devout.[5]

In Patriarch Danilo's sermon, Lazar speaks to his soldiers of the glory which accompanies a righteous struggle for the faith:

It is better to die in battle than to live in shame. Better it is for us to accept death from the sword in battle than to offer our shoulders to the enemy. We have lived a long time for the world; in the end we seek to accept the martyr's struggle and to live forever in heaven.[6]

Another anonymous eulogist views Lazar almost as though he were Christ Himself. He is the "unsleeping eye," "the unfaltering pillar of the church," "the most lustrous of all the stars," "a strong *vojvoda* against the devil," and "a savior."[7] Throughout the work the writer celebrates Lazar's martrydom and prays that the prince will continue to protect his flock:

You are the good shepherd who offered his soul for us. With what praise shall we praise you? O praiseworthy martyr, Lazar, come unseen to us and stand in our midst. Show us the songs of praise so that we will not be like sheep who have no shepherd. You are our shepherd; you cared for your flock which Christ the Lord gave to you. Do not surrender us to a shepherd whom we do not know. Do not scatter your flock which you gathered and for whose sake you shed your holy blood.[8]

The most important emphasis in these early post-Kosovo writings, therefore, is the death of the Serbian prince. The battle itself is dealt with in little detail, and its outcome is interpreted very differently in these several accounts. Some writers indicate that the battle was a victory for the Serbs:

Armed with their prayers [those of St. Simeon and St. Sava] they went off to meet those evil ones and won a shining victory.[9]

> When the pagan horde lunged at you,
> . . . .
> You, holy, new David opposed them
> And defeated that Goliath
> With his multitude of heathen
> And as a martyr because of blood
> > [which you shed]
> You are crowned with the victor's wreath.[10]

Other authors do not credit either side with victory in the battle:

> Again the word was given to rise up in battle. Both sides became
> exhausted and the battle ended. A countless multitude of both
> were killed—I am speaking of Serbs and of the enemy.[11]

If the battle of Kosovo were indeed the decisive defeat that delivered
Serbia into Ottoman hands, such an interpretation is not found in the
writings of Serbian contemporaries or even in works written decades
later. The Serbs had sustained substantial losses in the battle, and yet
Murad and a multitude of his troops had been killed and Bayezid and
his army had retreated in haste to Edirne. Serbian writers did not consider the battle to be an Ottoman victory. What they *were* conscious of
was the fact that the battle robbed Lazar's principality of its strength
and leadership.

Lazar's death paralyzed Serbian society. He had been the strongest
territorial lord in Serbia, and his principality enjoyed a certain prosperity
and stability after three decades of disorder and polarization had wracked
the lands of the former Serbian Empire. He represented the last and only
hope against the Ottomans, and it is for this reason that his death was
seen as the great tragedy of Kosovo. When the enemy returned again,
there was no one to oppose them, and Serbia's fate was sealed.

Fifteenth-century Serbian writings about the battle, writings which
incorporated several new nuances of interpretation, shed considerable
light on the emerging epic tradition of Kosovo. One of the fifteenth-
century Serbian chronicles does not mention victory for either the Serbs
or the Ottomans, but it does offer the possibility that Lazar was betrayed
by one of his own men:

And toward the end of this battle—I do not know what to say
in truth about this, whether he was betrayed by one of his own
or whether God's judgment was fulfilled in this—he [Bayezid]
took him [Lazar] in his hands, and after much torture he himself cut off his venerable, God-fearing head.[12]

Betrayal was to become a dominant theme in subsequent accounts
and in the Serbian epic poetry about Kosovo. At the end of the fifteenth
century Konstantin Mihailović, an Ottoman Janissary of Serbian origin,
included this observation about the battle in his memoirs:

Lords who supported Prince Lazar fought bravely, loyally, and
honorably at his side; others, however, observed the battle looking through their fingers. Because of this disloyalty and dissension and the jealousies of evil and wicked people, the battle was
lost on Friday at noon.
     And here Miloš Kobila, Prince Lazar's knight, killed Emperor
Murad.[13]

The idea of betrayal is very clear here. Moreover, the account includes
the information that Murad was assassinated by a Serbian knight.
     Konstantin Mihailović was not the first to mention the assassination
of Murad. It appears in West European sources at the end of the fourteenth century, and it is found in all fifteenth-century Ottoman accounts
of the battle. The first Serbian account of Murad's assassination appears
in Constantine the Philosopher's *Život Stefana Lazarevića despota srpskoga*, (Life of Despot Stefan Lazarević), written in either 1431 or 1432.[14]
It is interesting that this account of the assassination ties it closely to the
theme of betrayal:

Among the soldiers who were fighting in the front lines was one
of very noble birth who was slandered before his lord by certain
jealous ones and marked as disloyal. In order to demonstrate his
loyalty as well as his bravery, this one found the favorable time
and rushed to the great leader himself as though he were a deserter
and they opened the way to him. And when he was near, he dash-
ed forward at once and thrust a sword into that very haughty and
terrible autocrat, and then he himself fell there at their hands.[15]

In the Kosovo epic this soldier of very noble birth (Miloš Obilić in the epic) becomes the ideal of the courageous man who dares to strike out against tyranny. We can perhaps find the inspiration for this heroic archetype in the earlier sermon of Patriarch Danilo III, mentioned above. According to Danilo, after Lazar admonished his soldiers to "accept the martyr's struggle," his soldiers responded:

> Is it so much for us to die for you, for godliness, and for our homeland? We do not spare ourselves because we know that after all this we must depart and become one with the dust. We die so that we may live forever. We bring ourselves before God as a living sacrifice—not as earlier with delusive feasting for our own enjoyment but in the good fight with our own blood. We give our lives freely so that after this we will be a vivid example to others. . . . O comrades and fellow soldiers, in order to praise Christ we assume the burdens of former soldiers who are now with Christ. We are one humanity, subject to the same passions. And a single grave will be ours. And a single field will receive our bodies and bones so that the colony of heaven will receive us in glory.[16]

Self-sacrifice in the struggle against tyranny and as an example to others was to become the central theme in the Kosovo epic.

The epic tradition of Kosovo would develop much more detail and many more themes and characters during the centuries of Ottoman rule in Serbia. In the one hundred years after Kosovo, however, we can discern the origins of the major themes that were to give shape to the cult of Kosovo: the glory of pre-Kosovo Serbia; the necessity of struggle against tyranny; and the essential link between the Kosovo ethic and Christianity, which was expressed most clearly in the heroic ideal of self-sacrifice for the faith and for Serbia, the futility of betrayal, and the assuredness of resurrection.

With the establishment of Ottoman rule in the Balkans, those Serbs who remained in the mountains or who fled there to find refuge preserved the ancient tribal traditions of that remote, mountain life. The mountains became the protector of the cultural and ethnic characteristics of this patriarchal society. Moreover, encouraged by the Serbian church, this patriarchal society carried on memories of an independent Serbian state. The church romanticized the Nemanjić tradition for the masses and, removing any negative feudal connotations, helped to create the image of a once glorious state.[17] Lazar's death on Kosovo was the atonement for all of Serbia's sins—sins that had called the wrath of God upon them in the first place and caused them to lose their state.

When these mountain Serbs began to colonize other parts of the Balkan peninsula, they brought with them both these patriarchal, democratic ideas and their memories of an independent Serbia. From this tribal society came the understanding that there can be no free state without a struggle. Serbian patriarchal society encouraged a feeling for justice and social equality. According to the argument of Vaso Čubrilović, it was the democratic, patriarchal aspirations of the Serbian village which gave a social-revolutionary tone to the eventual wars for Serbian national liberation.[18]

These democratic, patriarchal ideas are seen most clearly in the oral epic poetry that is an expression of the Serbian patriarchal society during the centuries of Turkish rule. The epic poem is a chronicle in verse through which the Serbs expressed their past at a time when they had no state of their own and when most of them were illiterate. Only those events that were important for them and for their fate became subjects of the epic tradition. The result is that the epic contains a perculiar periodization of history in which events that were viewd as turning points in the history of the Serbs became so important that earlier developments were all but forgotten.

It should come as no surprise, therefore, that the Serbs viewed the collapse of the medieval Serbian state as the central event in their history and sought an explanation for it in the battle of Kosovo. Indeed, the epic cycle of Kosovo became the longest, the most beautiful, and the most important of all the Serbian epics. The roots of such a development were clearly established soon after the battle in those early religious eulogies and sermons composed in memory of Prince Lazar. The church nourished the ideas in these writings during the centuries of Turkish rule, and the patriarchal society of the Serbs accepted them and added its own visions, attitudes, and experiences to create the epic tradition of Kosovo.

The highly moralistic society of the Serbian village is clearly reflected in the epic tradition. Such virtues as courage, honor, justice, and respect for tradition were fundamental to the ethos of the village and the epic.

This was a society which refused to accept the right of any man to rule another; thus we discover in the epic the glorification of those brave men who fought against tyranny. Miloš Obilić, the supposed assassin of Murad, became the ideal hero who sacrifices himself in order to strike a blow against tyranny. The epic interpreted sacrifice for the good of society as the noblest of virtues and inspired the Serbs to countless struggles and sacrifices in the cause of liberation. The epic of Kosovo inspired brigandry and revolutionary acts against the Ottomans throughout the sixteenth, seventeenth, and eighteenth centuries; it continued to be a powerful psychological factor in the wars for liberation and unification in the nineteenth and twentieth centuries.

Perhaps the best examplar of this Kosovo revolutionary spirit and one of the greatest interpreters of the Kosovo ethic was the prince and poet Petar Petrović Njegoš, ruler of Montenegro during the second quarter of the nineteenth century. For Njegoš life was war against the Turks, and the spirit and memory of Kosovo dominated his actions and writings. In his most important work, the epic poem *Gorski vijenac* ("Mountain Wreath"), the word "Kosovo" (along with "God") is mentioned most often, and Miloš Obilić is referred to no fewer than twelve times.[19] It was this epic poem, in fact, that helped to create the image of Obilić as the pure, Christian hero—the symbol of freedom. Njegoš's message was clear. Encouraged by the long centuries of Ottoman rule and the spirit of the Kosovo epic, Serbians were to understand that the noblest of acts was to kill the foreign tyrants. Njegoš's "Mountain Wreath" in itself had an enormous influence on the Serbian national movement in the decades following its publication in 1847, and was of special importance among those Serbs who remained rural and uneducated.

Destroying tyranny, liberating the land of all foreign control, and reuniting all Serbs in one strong state were primary goals among Serbs in the nineteenth century. The Serbian Revolution of 1804-15 created a new Serbian society and was a partial fulfillment of that agelong dream of avenging Kosovo and liberating Serbia. Many of the Serbian lands, however, including Kosovo, remained under foreign control during most of the nineteenth century. Prince Njegoš certainly reflected the impatience and the desires of many in his constant demands for vigilance and con- tinued sacrifice against the Ottomans. Fifty years after the Serbian Revolu- tion an article in the Vojvodina newspaper *Napredak* expressed frustration over the relative lack of progress in the unification of Serbia and hinted that the problem resulted from a lack of understanding of the spirit of Kosovo:

> Our successes have been small. Half of the Serbian nation still remains in Kosovo chains. An indifference toward our basic responsibilities is the main shortcoming and the most harmful sickness of our people. Even the most powerful and bloody examples cannot cure us from this disease . . . and today we put little effort into knowing our Miloš.[20]

Twelve years after his comment was made, Serbia found herself at war with the Porte on behalf of her fellow Slavs in Bosnia and Hercegovina. Soundly defeated, she existed at the mercy of the big powers for the rest of the century. By the time of the five-hundredth anniversary of the battle of Kosovo in 1889, Serbia was under Austrian influence and her plans for unification were necessarily thwarted.

The first suggestion for a five-hundredth anniversary celebration had been made in 1886 in the Novi Sad newspaper *Zastava*. Nothing came of it, however, and near the end of 1888 *Zastava* suggested that the Serbs in Ruma should organize a celebration since Ruma was near Vrdnik where Prince Lazar's bones were preserved. On 1 January 1889, *Zastava* announced that a committee had been organized in Ruma for the Kosovo commemoration.[21]

Belgrade newspapers immediately protested this development and demanded that any celebration be held in liberated Serbia. On 6 February 1889, *Male novine* argued that the commemoration should be observed in Kruševac, Lazar's medieval capital. The Serbian government accepted this idea and submitted a set of suggestions for the celebration to the regency: (1) it should be commemorated in all parts of Serbia; (2) a foundation should be laid in Kruševac for a monument to the heroes of Kosovo; (3) the state should support the printing of new editions of the Kosovo epic; (4) a new Order of Prince Lazar should be established which would be awarded only to the Serbian ruler and his heir apparent; and (5) Aleksandar Obrenović should be crowned King of Serbia in the monastery of Žiča as a part of the celebration.[22] On 12 April 1889, it was announced in Belgrade that a commission of fifteen had begun to organize a commemoration to be held in Kruševac. Both Ruma and Belgrade, therefore, had commissions for official celebrations; their plans progressed simultaneously.

The prospect of a five-hundredth anniversary celebration excited the imagination of the Slavs throughout Eastern Europe. To many South Slavs who still lived under foreign rule the Kosovo ethic sounded a note of hope. A Slavophile newspaper in Russia termed Kosovo the "Serbian Troy" and called on all Russians to recognize it as such. "Not to praise the memory of Kosovo in Russia," the article argued, "means treason to Slavic ethnic feeling."[23]

As the day of the commemoration drew near, tensions began to mount in those South Slavic areas controlled by Austria-Hungary. As of April 1889, no one was permitted to travel in the empire without a Great Passport, and no Serbs were given such passports for travel in any southerly and easterly directions. Imperial police began to guard all roads which faced Serbia, and any Serb who wished to travel during the two or three days before the actual celebration was deterred.[24]

Croats everywhere were encouraged to celebrate the Serbian holiday, even though Khuen-Héderváry, the Budapest-appointed Ban of Croatia had prohibited all commemorations in his jurisdiction. He succeeded in preventing a large, public memorial, but he was unable to stop a requiem mass in Zagreb's Orthodox church and a commemorative session of the Yugoslav Academy of Arts and Sciences. The Ban confiscated the committee's funds for the celebration in Ruma, and in Novi Sad two thousand commemorative medallions were seized. Although continually banned during this period, the newspaper *Obzor* managed to put out an issue on the day of Kosovo, which included the following:

> Whenever the Serbs rose up to lead whatever part of their people
> to freedom, they always appeared with the wreath of Kosovo
> around their heads to say in unison: This, o people, is what we
> are, what we want, and what we can do. And we Croatians—
> brothers by blood and by desire with the Serbs—today sing:
> Praise to the eternal Kosovo heroes who with their blood made
> certain that the desire for freedom and glory would never die.
> Glory to them and to that people who gave them birth.[25]

In spite of the incredible efforts to prevent the commemoration from becoming a symbol for all South Slavs, fifteen thousand people made their way to Vrdnik for the celebration that had been organized by the commission in Ruma. In Vienna, South Slav youths gathered in their respective ethnic clubs, churches, and in outdoor parties to remember the heroes of Kosovo. And midnight prayers were sung in the Serbian monastery of Peć, Dečani, and Gračanica in the heart of Ottoman Serbia.[26]

The Serbian Royal Academy of Arts and Sciences opened the period of celebration in Serbia with a commemorative session in Belgrade on 11 June 1889. Čedomil Mijatović, Serbia's minister of foreign affairs, began the festivities with an emotional, romantic address on the meaning of Kosovo:

> An inexhaustible source of national pride was discovered on Kosovo. More important than language and stronger than the Church, this pride unites all Serbs in a single nation. . . . The glory of the Kosovo heroes shone like a radiant star in that dark night of almost five hundred years. . . . Our people continued the battle in the sixteenth, seventeenth, and eighteenth centuries when they tried to recover their freedom through countless uprisings. There was never a war for freedom—and when was there no war?—in which the spirit of the Kosovo heroes did not participate. The new history of Serbia begins with Kosovo—a history of valiant efforts, long suffering, endless wars, and unquenchable glory. . . . Karadjordje breathed with the breath of Kosovo, and the Obrenovići placed Kosovo in the coat of arms of their dynasty. We bless Kosovo because the memory of the Kosovo heroes upheld us, encouraged us, taught us, and guided us.[27]

These sentiments were echoed later that month in Kruševac where the most important of the Serbian memorials to Kosovo was held. Arsa Pajević, a writer from Novi Sad, attended the events in Kruševac and left us a typically romantic chronicle of the festivities. For Pajević the first day was one of intense emotion—even the mountains seemed to raise their heads higher, straining as if to see that day five hundred years before. The commemoration began with a service in the Church of Lazarica followed by an outdoor service of prayer for the souls of those who died on Kosovo. The metropolitan of the Serbian church delivered the sermon, which was inspired primarily by the epic tradition of Kosovo. He concluded his brief remarks with the prayer that Lazar and all the martyrs of Kosovo intercede with God to seek his help in restoring the Serbian Empire and unifying the whole Serbian nation.[28]

In the evening after vespers a large procession led by Aleksandar wound its way through Kruševac to the center of the city where a foundation stone was laid for a monument to honor the heroes of Kosovo. The site was covered with wreaths, and one of them in particular impressed the crowd. Sent to Kruševac by a Czech organization in Prague, it was made of two thousand laurel leaves, on each of which was sown a card with the wishes and signatures of individual Czech sympathizers. On the silk sash across the wreath were written the words: "The Czech Nation. 1389. +27/6 1889. From Ashes to Greatness."[29]

The five-hundredth anniversary commemorations were more successful than anyone could have imagined. On 1 July 1889, although banned three times that day, *Obzor* managed to publish the following:

> Opponents of the national idea must recognize that two accomplishments were made in this beautiful celebration. It brought Serbs and Croats closer together, and it ignited the smoldering embers on Lazar's grave into full flames, which will not be easy to extinguish.[30]

One thing that was not accomplished in time for the 1889 celebration (something that would probably have prevented the competition between Ruma and Belgrade) was the transfer of Lazar's bones from Vrdnik to Lazar's monastery of Ravanica near Kruševac. Čedomil Mijatović got the idea for the transfer of Lazar's remains while he was on a tour of Serbia with Prince Milan in 1874. Because of the possibility of conflict with the monks of Vrdnik and with the Hungarian government, Milan was not particularly interested in the idea. In 1880, however, the Hungarian government indicated that it would not oppose the transfer if the Serbian government first secured the approval of the Vrdnik monks. Mijatović sent the Serbian poet Milorad Popović Šapčanin to Vrdnik with an offer of a yearly payment amounting to twice the revenue generated in Vrdnik from an average year of pilgrims. This idea was criticized openly in a letter to the Serbian press from Danilo Medaković, an interpreter with the Russian legation, who argued that the removal of Lazar's bones from Vrdnik would lead to the Magyarization of those Serbs living in Hungary. He believed that the presence of Lazar's remains sustained the Vojvodina Serbs in their patriotism. The Belgrade newspapers, which were subsidized by the Russians, sided with Medaković, and Mijatović was convinced to give up his idea at that time.[31]

A decade later Mijatović argued again for the transfer of Lazar's remains and suggested that such an act might give Serbia a renewed sense of unity and bring an end to her political problems:

> If the interests of our people are what is in question, then it is far more important that thousands of Serbs from Montenegro, Dalmatia, Hercegovina, Bosnia, Old Serbia, and Macedonia come to the center of Serbia on Vidovdan than go to the Kingdom of Hungary. . . . Gathered around the body of the Kosovo martyr, we might be ashamed of our political disorder. We might feel that the ties which bind us together as one and the same people are older, more important, and more sacred than the ties of party.[32]

Nothing came of Mijatović's appeal. Throughout the late nineteenth century, the spirit of Kosovo was evoked on each anniversary of the battle, and priests and politicians alike reminded their people of the obligation to avenge Kosovo and unify Serbia. Until the beginning of the twentieth century, however, any hope that Serbia would play the role of a "South-Slavic Piedmont" was frustrated by the actions of the big powers.

The turn of the century seemed to bring with it a new, more intense desire to alter the status quo not only in Serbia but throughout the Balkans. Many young people living under Habsburg or Ottoman rule were especially frustrated by the factionalism, chauvinism, and narrow-mindedness of their fathers and leaders, which made unity and effective action against foreign tyranny impossible. One such youth who channeled these concerns into the works of his creative genius was Ivan Meštrović, the most important Croat and South Slav sculptor of the twentieth century.

Meštrović tended sheep as a teenager in Dalmatia where he learned to read the epic poetry of the Serbs in Cyrillic and was profoundly influenced by the ideas of freedom and liberation expressed in the epic of Kosovo. The centuries-long struggle of the South Slavs against foreign oppression became a dominant theme in his early sculpture.[33] Between 1905 and 1910, he studied sculpture in Vienna and Paris and spent his summers on the Dalmatian coast in Split. One summer night Meštrović sat with some intellectuals and artists in the People's Square in Split and listened to the dramatist Ivo Vojnović read from his recent play on the tragedy of Kosovo, *Smrt majke Jugovića* (The Death of the Mother of the Jugovići). Soon after that Meštrović developed the idea for a monumental temple in honor of the Kosovo heroes:

> What I had in mind was an attempt to create a synthesis of popular national ideals and their development, to express in stone and building how deeply buried in each one of use are the memories of the great and decisive moments in our history . . . . I wanted at the same time to create a focus of hope in the future, standing out in the countryside and under the free sky.[34]

Meštrović hoped that the monument would serve as a symbol of the suffering and hopes of all South Slavs. He envisioned a monumental gate with triumphal arches, a central building with a cupola, and a belfry whose columns would be representations of the Kosovo heroes. Under the cupola was to stand an enormous statue of Miloš Obilić. He anticipated that like the medieval cathedrals, this monument would involve the collective efforts of several generations.[35]

Meštrović's obsession with the Kosovo temple continued until World War I. Several of the Kosovo figures were completed, and the emotional impact of his work encouraged the art historian Josef Strzygowski to suggest that there could certainly be trouble for the Hsbsburg Empire if "Meštrović's fellow nationals understand his message and if his art awakes in them new ideas of unity."[36]

After the turn of the century the youth of Serbia were offered more aggressive outlets for their passions and idealism. The return of the Karadjordjević dynasty to the Serbian throne in 1903 signalled a new period of independence vis-à-vis Austria-Hungary. Within a decade Serbia was at war.

In the Balkan Wars of 1912-13 examples of self-sacrifice were abundant among Serbian soldiers. The realization that Kosovo could finally be liberated after more than five hundred years fired the imaginations and the emotions of young Serbs. Consider the recollections of one of these young patriots as he was told that his unit was heading for Kosovo:

> The single sound of that word—Kosovo—caused an indescribable excitement. This one word pointed to the black past—five centuries. In it exists the whole of our sad past—the tragedy of Prince Lazar and the entire Serbian people. . . .
>
> Each of us created for himself a picture of Kosovo while we were still in the cradle. Our mothers lulled us to sleep with the songs of Kosovo, and in our schools our teachers never ceased in their stories of Lazar and Miloš. . . .
>
> My God, what awaited us! To see a liberated Kosovo. The words of the commander were like music to us and soothed our souls like the miraculous balsam.
>
> When we arrived on Kosovo and the battalions were placed in order, our commander spoke: "Brothers, my children, my sons!" His voice breaks. "This place on which we stand is the graveyard of our glory. We bow to the shadows of fallen ancestors and pray God for the salvation of their souls." His voice gives out and tears flow in streams down his cheeks and grey beard and fall to the ground. He actually shakes from some kind of inner pain and excitement.
>
> The spirits of Lazar, Miloš, and all the Kosovo martyrs gaze on us. We feel strong and proud, for we are the generation which will realize the centuries-old dream of the whole nation: that we with the sword will regain the freedom that was lost with the sword.[37]

When Kosovo was finally liberated in the Balkan War of 1912, King Peter I Karadjordjević was on the throne. The liberation guaranteed that Peter would be remembered by some as the romantic fulfillment of Miloš's legacy:

> He was not an ordinary king. Rather he was the incarnation of the idea of Great Serbia, the symbol of Serbian liberty and the

Serbian epic, the dream of centuries, and the hope of all generations. He was the synthesis of national feelings, the soul of the
Serbian people, a gentle balm and solace for those who suffer.[38]

Less than two years after the liberation of Kosovo, Gavrilo Princip
waited on the streets of Sarajevo to assassinate the heir to the Habsburg
throne. A teenager who knew Njegoš's "Mountain Wreath" by heart,
Princip had certainly been inspired by Njegoš's characterization of Miloš
Obilić as the ideal examplar of the philosophy that the murder of a tyrant
is no murder.[39]

World War I encouraged many to view the epic of Kosovo as a theme
which inspired all South Slavs. The implication was that Serbs, Croats,
and Slovenes were fighting for a unified state and that all of them viewed
the creation of this state as the final vindication of the fourteenth-century
battle. Serbs actively encouraged this interpretation. Tihomir Djordjević,
a Serbian professor of ethnography who wrote for the English public
during the war, argued that Yugoslav unity had been the ultimate goal
of Emperor Stefan Dušan, and had it not been for Kosovo, "a great,
powerful, and free Jugoslav Empire would have grown."[40] Kosovo was,
therefore, a tragedy for all the South Slavs and necessarily became a
symbol for the freedom of them all as well. Obviously, this was a view
of the medieval world molded by contemporary concerns.

During the war Serbia was the "darling" of both the English and French
publics, which interpreted her determination to fight and secure her freedom as an expression of the Kosovo spirit. In 1916 a nation-wide tribute
to Serbia was arranged in Britain to celebrate the anniversary of Kosovo.
Information about Serbia was disseminated throughout the country. A
shop opened in London in order to sell literature about Serbia, which
British publishing houses had printed in tens of thousands of copies.
Posters created from a *Punch* cartoon, "Heroic Serbia," were displayed
conspciuously throughout the country. Schools and churches arranged
special lectures and services in commemoration of the Serbian holiday.
Cinemas showed films about Serbia, and the Serbian national anthem
was played in some theaters. The English press publicized all the activities
with more than four hundred articles and news items.[41]

R. W. Seton-Watson, who helped organize the celebration, prepared
an address on Serbia for the schools of Great Britain. Entitled "Serbia:
Yesterday, Today, and Tomorrow," the address was read aloud in whole

or in part in almost twelve thousand schools and helped to acquaint the
youth of Great Britain with Serbia's history. In his brief remarks Seton-
Watson characterized the battle of Kosovo as one of the decisive events
in the history of Southeast Europe. He wanted his listeners to understand
"how completely the story of Kosovo is bound up with the daily life of
the whole Serbian nation."[42]

In June 1918, five months before the end of the war, the United States
recognized the anniversary of Kosovo as a day of special commemoration
in honor of Serbia and all other oppressed peoples who were fighting in
the Great War. The meaning of Kosovo was the subject of countless sermons, lectures, and addresses throughout the United States. In a special
service in New York City's Cathedral of St. John the Divine, the Reverend
Howard C. Robbins compared Serbs to the people of Israel and observed
that Serbia "voices its suffering through patience far longer than Israel's
and it voices a hope that has kept burning through five centuries."[43]

The primary commemoration was held at the Waldorf-Astoria on the
evening of 17 June 1918. James M. Beck, former Assistant Attorney General of the United States, endeavored in his address to draw a relationship
between the ethic of Kosovo and the tragedy of the Great War:

> It is true that we commemorate a defeat, but military defeats
> are . . . often moral victories. If Serbia is now temporarily de-
> feated, she has triumphed at the great bar of public opinion,
> and she stands in the eye of the nations as justified in her quarrel.
> Serbia was not only the innocent, precipitating cause of this
> world war, but it is the greatest martyr, and I am inclined to
> think in many respects its greatest hero.[44]

He then related the legend of the angel who came to Lazar on Kosovo
and offered him a choice between the Kingdom of Heaven and the kingdom of this earth. Lazar, of course, chose the Kingdom of Heaven, and Mr.
Beck considered this the revelation of a great truth:

> Running through recorded history as the golden thread of a di-
> vine purpose is this truth, that the nation which condones a
> felony against the moral order sooner or later suffers. . . . Each
> nation which took part in that Congress of 1878 had reason to

regret the compounding of the felony that first started on the plains of Kossovo in 1389 . . . . The war is a great expiation for the failure of civilized nations for centuries to recognize the duty that . . . Lazar assumed on the eve of Kossovo.[45]

With the end of the war and the establishment of a Yugoslav state the centuries-long ordeal was apparently over. If Kosovo had become a symbol for all South Slavs in their quest for freedom and unity, then it was reasonable for many to expect that the new state would honor the basic principles of the Kosovo ethic: social justice, equality, liberty, and a disdain for tyranny. Such was not to be the case. In the intense struggle of the postwar years between Great Serbian advocates of centralism and the proponents of a federal system, the victory of the centralists guaranteed that the individual rights of some nationalities would be denied. The Kosovo ethic was often invoked during the turbulent interwar years as the epitome of Yugoslav unity; in fact it was being manipulated to serve the purposes of the Serbian hegemonists.

The last year in which Kosovo was given elaborate attention was 1939, the 550th anniversary of the battle and a moment when the clouds of war again loomed on the horizon. The commission for the celebration of the anniversary announced to all Yugoslavs that the Kosovo ethic was, indeed, a Yugoslav ethic:

> Kosovo gave us Vidovdan from whose faith, ethic, and symbols we remained alive . . . until this very day. The Vidovdan mystique was that magical lever for all our unprecedented undertakings and accomplishments in history. It was the foundation of our national, spiritual image, our heroism, and our Christian view of man. It was the greatest and most difficult test of the Serbian people, and it remained as an example not only to them but to all Yugoslavs. . . .
>
> Vidovdan is the torch of our spirit which is stronger than all other factors in anything we do. It is our deepest sign and warning not to forget our national duties and honor, but to be like those perfect soldiers who fell alongside the righteous prince on Kosovo for his unified nation, its happy future, for honor and national ideals.[46]

Yugoslavs everywhere were reminded that Kosovo belonged to them all. To the Croats, who were less than enthusiastic about celebrating a Serbian holiday, the message was direct:

> Prince Lazar integrated the national and religious ideals. The Kosovo myth gave the Serbian people strength and created a collective consciousness.
>
> This should be a lesson to the Croatian public. On the crossroads of the world where so many interests are in conflict, collective consciousness is necessary. Without it there is no strength, no self-sacrifice, no future.[47]

In Slovenia the message was also an appeal to unity:

> What does this national holiday mean to us today in these extraordinary circumstances? Nothing less than our national consciousness and our strong desire to remain united, free, and independent.[48]

The Serbs were reminded to remember Kosovo as the source of their strength:

> Today when all of Europe—including our own fatherland—is covered with the darkest clouds, we again return to Kosovo, the Serbian Jerusalem, the eternal source of our life force in order to breathe its air, scented with the aroma of red poppies and the spirit of Miloš's bravery.[49]

Since Kosovo was proclaimed a symbol of Yugoslav unity, opponents of Great Serbian centralism were labeled betrayers of the Kosovo ideal. A 1939 article in *Slobodna Misao,* entitled "The Kosovo Religion," demonstrated that the Kosovo epic could be exploited by some to judge those whose political positions were not popular. Using the examples of Stojan Protić and Velja Vukičević, the author suggested that after World War I, in a period of increasing decadence, some new leaders followed ideas which were not inspired by the religion of Kosovo.[50] Apparently there were many ways to interpret this old "religion."

It is clear today that these appeals for unity in 1939 were eleventh-hour alarms. Three months after the anniversary of Kosovo, Europe was at war again. In less than two years the fragile unity of Yugoslavia would be destroyed. On 25 March 1941, representatives of the Yugoslav goverrnment signed the Tripartite Pact. Two days later widespread dissatifaction with this capitulation to the Axis powers led to a coup d'etat in Belgrade. Patriarch Gavrilo of the Serbian church saw the capitulation as a betrayal of the Kosovo ethic. Lazar had faced the enemy and accepted his fate for the sake of the Serbian people. In an address on Belgrade radio Patriarch Gavrilo interpreted the coup in the spirit of the Kosovo ethic and argued that the contemporary situation demanded the same sacrifice:

> Before our nation in these days the question of our fate again presents itself. This morning at dawn the question received its answer. We chose the heavenly kingdom—the kingdom of truth, justice, national strength, and freedom. That eternal ideal is carried in the hearts of all Serbs, preserved in the shrines of our churches, and written on our banners.[51]

Ten days later the Axis invasion began. Yugoslavia was dismembered, and puppet states were established in Croatia and Serbia. Within weeks of the occupation the resistance struggle began. On the anniversary of Kosovo in 1942, in an article in Belgrade's *Naše Borba,* an organ of the puppet government, it was argued that everything the Communist resistance movement represented was in direct opposition to the spirit, ideals, and legacy of the heroes of Kosovo:

> It is not dangerous to lose a battle. It is not even that dangerous to lose a state. . . . Such losses can be made up. It is dangerous, however, when one begins to distort the truth, warp principles, corrupt ideals, and poison traditions. Then the spirit suffers, craziness overcomes it, and self-destruction crushes it. . . .
>
> Can the discord be greater? Can the blunder be worse? It can if the eel is exchanged for the snake, the heavenly sower for the sower of corn cockles. . . if truth is replaced with lies, wisdom with foolishness, beauty with ugliness, patriotism with hatred of country, the church with the synagogue, blessing with damnation, St. Lazar of Kosovo with the Zionist Simović of London.

The defeat of a nation is either a tragedy or a comedy, depending on whether the blow comes from outside or from inside, from Providence or from a crazy mind. Our Kosovo is a tragedy. The "Kosovo without Kosovo" is a comedy—a comedy as a symbol of Njegoš's curse:
"Lords, damn their souls . . .
They threw away the government and the state
Lords, ugly cowards
They became traitors of the land."[52]

This incredible distortion of the Kosovo ethic contains its own irony, for Njegoš's curse was the sentiment of many others in their attacks on the puppets in Belgrade.

With the establishment of a socialist society in Yugoslavia after World War II, the impact of Kosovo has become markedly less visible. Commemorations of the anniversary of the battle are essentially confined to services of the Serbian church; and it is the church that continues to remind the faithful of the basic religious and humanistic qualities of the Kosovo ethic:

One of the main characteristics of Kosovo is the idea of a conscious, willing sacrifice for noble ideals, a sacrifice of one individual for the benefit of the rest, a sacrifice now for the sake of a better future. According to popular understanding which developed in our folk literature, the battle of Kosovo was not an event in which it was possible to win or lose. It was rather a conscious, heroic sacrifice. A slave is only half a man; a freeman is similar to God.[53]

Such an expression of the essential meaning of Kosovo is certainly not incompatible with the aspirations of a socialist society. As recently as 1970, one finds an even more "acceptable" statement of the basic idea of the Kosovo spirit. Miloslav Stojadinović, in the preface to his *Kosovska trilogija* (Kosovo Trilogy), argues that the Kosovo spirit is the "revolutionary spirit of justice, humanity, equity, equality of rights, with a noticeably democratic and progressive quality for respect for the rights of all other peoples."[54]

Stojadinović expresses the contemporary sounding, yet timeless quality of the ethic. As we have noted, the ethic of Kosovo was nourished in that patriarchal society of the Serbian peasant during the centuries of Ottoman domination. That ethic expressed a basic attitude toward life itself: democratic, anti-feudal, with a love for justice and social equality. The emotional impact of the Kosovo ethic was exploited by many individuals and movements in the quest for freedom and independence. Sometimes, in contradiction to the ethic itself, it was manipulated for purely narrow, selfish concerns. Whatever its uses and abuses, however, it was always an essential ingredient in the historical consciousness of the Serbian people. Stripped of any particular national reference, the ethic does have a timeless quality. Perhaps that in itself explains its strength and its impact.

NOTES

1. Vaso Čubrilović, *Istorija političke misli u Srbiji XIX veka* (Belgrade, 1958), p. 35.

2. A new study of the end of the Serbian Empire has been published recently in Belgrade. See Rade Mihaljčić, *Kraj Srpskog Carstva* (Belgrade, 1975). See also Thomas Allan Emmert, "The Battle of Kosovo: A Reconsideration of its Significance in the Decline of Medieval Serbia," (unpublished Ph.D. dissertation, Department of History, Stanford University, 1973).

3. These early post-Kosovo writings can be found in the following editions. The writings themselves are listed in approximately chronological order:

a. *Prološko žitije kneza Lazara* (Anonymous), in Dj. Radojičić, "Pohvala knezu Lazaru sa stihovima," *Istorijski časopis,* 5 (1955), 251-53.

b. *Slovo o knezu Lazaru* (Patriarch Danilo III), in V. Ćorović, "Siluan i Danilo II, srpski pisci XIV-XV veka," *Glas srpske kraljevske akademije,* 136 (1929), 83-103.

c. *Žitije kneza Lazara* (Anonymous), in S. Novaković, "Nešto o knezu Lazaru," *Glasnik srpskog učenog društva,* 21 (1867), 159-64.

d. *Slovo o knezu Lazaru* (Anonymous), in A. Vukomanović, "O knezu Lazaru," *Glasnik društva srbske slovesnosti,* 11 (1859), 108-18.

e. *Pohvala knezu Lazaru* (Jefimija), in L. Mirković, "Monahinja Jefimija," *Hrišćanski život*, 1, 9-10 (1922), 539-40.

f. *Služba knezu Lazaru* (Anonymous), in *Srbljak*, 2 (Belgrade, 1970), 143-99.

g. *Pohvalno slovo knezu Lazaru* (Anonymous), in Dj. Daničić, "Pohvala knezu Lazaru," *Glasnik društva srbske slovesnosti*, 13 (1861), 358-68.

h. *Natpis na mramornom stubu na Kosovu* (Anonymous or Stefan Lazarević), in Dj. Sp. Radojičić, "Svetovna pohvala knezu Lazaru i kosovskim junacima," *Južnoslovenskii filolog*, 20 (1953-54), 140-41.

i. *Vrše mislni knezu Lazaru* (Andonius Raphael of Lepanto), in Lj. Stojanović, "Stari srpski hrisovulji, akti, biografije, letopit i, tipici, pomenici, zapisi, i drugi," Spomenik, 3 (1890), 81-88. Corrections made by V. V. Kachanovskii, *Istoriia Serbii s' poloviny XIV do kontsa XV v.* (Kiev, 1899), pp. 349-59.

These writings in honor of Lazar received their most scholarly analysis as purely literary works in a relatively recent study by Djordje Trifunović: *Srpski srednjovekovni spisi o knezu Lazaru i Kosovskom boju* (Kruševac, 1968).

4. V. Ćorović, "Siluan i Danilo II," pp. 85-86.

5. Trifunović, *Srpski srednjovekovni*, p. 93. Trifunović presents this introduction to the anonymous *Žitije kneza Lazara*, as it was omitted in Novaković's edition of the text.

6. Ćorović, "Siluan i Danilo II," pp. 89-90.

7. Daničić, "Pohvala knezu Lazaru," p. 367.

8. Ibid., p. 360.

9. Radojičić, "Pohvala knezu Lazaru sa stihovima," p. 252.

10. Trifunović, ed., *Srbljak*, 2, 148-49. Trifunović argues that any mention of victory in these laudatory works must be interpreted as a spiritual victory and not as an actual victory on the battlefield. Certainly the idea of martyrdom implies a spiritual victory for the individual who sacrifices himself for his faith. That theme is central to these texts of Lazar's cult; it does not, however, preclude the possibility that real, temporal victory over the Turks is also expressed in these works. In the passage from *Služba knezu Lazaru* cited above, Lazar is plainly the victor in both a real and spiritual sense. See Trifunović, *Srpski srednjovekovni*, pp. 34-36.

11. Ćorović, "Siluan i Danilo II," p. 94.

12. Stojanović, "Stari srpski hrisovulji," p. 96.

13. Konstantin Mihailović iz Ostrovice, *Janičarove uspomene ili Turska hronika,* ed. Djordje Živanović (Belgrade, 1966), p. 105.

14. V. Jagić, "Konstantin Filosof i njegov Život Stefana Lazarevića despota srpskoga," *Glasnik srpskog učenog društva,* 42 (1875), 223-328. Cf. M. Braun, *Lebensbeschreibung des Despoten Stefan Lazarević von Konstantin dem Philosophen* (The Hague, 1956).

15. V. Jagić, "Konstantin Filosof," pp. 260-61.

16. Ćorović, "Siluan i Danilo II," p. 90.

17. See Čurbilović, *Istorija političke misli,* pp. 26-27.

18. Ibid., p. 34.

19. *Gorski vijenac* (Belgrade, 1947); *The Mountain Wreath of P. P. Nyegosh,* tr. James W. Wiles (Westport, Ct.: Greenwood Press, 1970). See also Ivo Andrić, *Njegoš kao tragični junak kosovske misli* (Belgrade, 1935), p. 5; and Vladimir Dedijer, *Sarajevo 1914* (Belgrade, 1966), p. 421 *(The Road to Sarajevo* [New York: Simon and Schuster, 1966]).

20. "Na Vidovdan," *Napredak,* 17, 70 (16 June 1864), 1.

21. Veljko Petrović, "Petstogodišnjica Kosova pre pedeset godina," *Politika,* 36, 11160 (28 June 1939), 3-4.

22. Budimka Kovbasko, "Petstogodišnjica Kosovske Bitke," *Bagdala,* 2, 14-15 (May-June, 1960), 1-2.

23. Petrović, "Petstogodišnjica," p. 4.

24. Ibid.

25. Viktor Novak, "Kako su Hrvati proslavili petstotu godišnkicu kosovske tragedije," *Politika,* 36, 11160 (28 June 1939), 5.

26. Petrović, "Petsogodišnjica," p. 4.

27. Čedomil Mijatović, "Kosovo: Beseda Čedomila Mijatovića u svečanoj sednici kraljevske akademije 11-og. juna, 1889," *Otadžbina,* 22, (1889), pp. xiv-xv.

28. Branko Peruničić, *Kruševac u jednom veku* (Kruševac, 1971), pp. 33-37.

29. Ibid., pp. 38-40.

30. Novak, "Kako su Hrvati proslavili," p. 5.

31. Chedomille Mijatovich, *Memoirs of a Balkan Diplomatist* (London, 1917), pp. 224-26.

32. Čedomil Mijatović, "Prenos kostiju knezu Lazara," *Branik,* 7, 69 (27 June 1891), 2. Two years before he died, Mijatović still exhibited

a naïve romanticism about the Kosovo epic. He suggested that Lazar's wife, Milica, and the legendary "maiden of Kosovo" who brought water to the dying and wounded Serbian soldiers after the battle should be proclaimed saints. See Č. Mijatović, "Ko je kosovska devojka," *Vreme*, 10,2910 (1 February 1930), 3; Mijatović, "Caricu i kosovsku devojku treba proglasiti svetiteljkama," *Vreme*, 10, 2889 (2 January 1930), 1.

33.   Duško Kečkemet, *Ivan Meštrović* (Zagreb, 1970), pp. 1-3.

34.   Ibid., p. 12.

35.   Ibid., p. 13.

36.   Ibid., p. 18.

37.   P. M., "Prvi na Kosovu," *Vojnički Glasnik*, 13, 12 (28 June 1932), 186-87.

38.   Dušan Sijački, ed., *Vidov-dan: Ilustrovana Istorija Srpskih Ratova* (Belgrade, 1926), 4, 54.

39.   Dedijer, *Sarajevo 1914*, pp. 423, 432.

40.   Tihomir Georgevitch, "Kosovo, 1389," *Kosovo Day* (London, 1916), p. 7.

41.   "Report of 'Kosovo Day' Celebrations," *Kosovo Day* (London, 1916), pp. 11-25.

42.   R. W. Seton-Watson, *Serbia: Yesterday, Today, and Tomorrow* (London, 1916), p. 6.

43.   Serbian National Defense League of America, *Kosovo Day in America: 1389-1918* (New York, 1918), p. 9.

44.   Ibid., pp. 15-17.

45.   Ibid., pp. 18-20.

46.   *Vrbaske Novine*, 10, 1599, (28 June 1939), 1.

47.   "Hrvati o Kosovu," *Slobodna Misao*, 17, 24 (2 July 1939), 5.

48.   "Slovenački listovi povodom vidovdanske proslave," *Politika*, 36, 11160 (28 June 1939), 10.

49.   Milan Nedić, "Kosovo, izvor nesalomljivih nada i životne snage našeg naroda," *Politika*, 36, 11160 (28 June 1939), 1-2.

50.   "Kosovska religija," *Slobodna Misao*, 18, 24 (2 July 1939), 1-2.

51.   D. Stranjaković, "Vidovdan," *Glasnik službenog lista Srpske pravoslavne crkve*, 6 (1953), p. 16.

52.   D. Najdanović, "O Kosovu onda i sad," *Naša Borba*, 2, 43 (28 June 1942), 4.

53.   Stranjaković, "Vidovdan," p. 8.

54.   Miloslav Stojadinović, *Kosovoska Trilogija* (Belgrade, 1970), p. 5.

NATIONALISM AND COLONIZATION
IN THE
BANAT OF TEMESVÁR, 1718-1778

Karl A. Roider, Jr.
Louisiana State University

In the continuing debate concerning nationalism and national ideologies in the Habsburg Empire, one of the areas that has received a good deal of scholarly attention is the Banat of Temesvár.[1] An intriguing land bordered on three sides by the Danube, Tisza, and Maros rivers and on the fourth by a traditional overland boundary, the Banat was won by the Habsburgs from the Turks at the conclusion of the Austro-Turkish War of 1716-18. Although the Banat traditionally had belonged to Hungary before it fell to the Ottomans in the sixteenth century, Charles VI, now refused to return it to Hungarian administration. Instead, following the advice of his foremost military officer, Prince Eugene of Savoy, the emperor declared it *neoacquisita*—newly-acquired rather than reconquered—and subjected it to the administration of a specially-created joint commission in Vienna.[2]

The new commission believed its first task was the repopulation of a land laid waste by years of war and neglect. To find inhabitants for the Banat, the government sent agents to the western regions of the Holy Roman Empire. There they recruited German colonists for settlement and, in doing so, established a precedent for the periodic influx of Germans that was to continue for the remainder of the eighteenth century.

By adopting this policy, the government unwittingly planted the seeds of the subsequent historical controversy over the Habsburg motive for importing these German populations to settle the Banat. Historians who have investigated this German colonization have advanced three different explanations of Austrian intentions. Some argue that the settling of large German populations represented a conscious attempt to Germanize the Banat. Others, still focusing on the German colonists, conclude that Vienna sought to Catholicize the province. A third group of historians believes that the wholesale importation of Germans was an aspect of a Habsburg attempt to Westernize the Banat, raising its cultural and economic level and thereby transforming it into a formidable barrier to Ottoman influences and incursions. This paper re-examines the colonization of the Banat during the Carolinian and Theresian periods in an attempt to ascertain more clearly the intentions of the Habsburg administration.

To examine Austrian motives in this matter, we must begin by questioning the joint commission's fundamental assumption that the Banat was indeed depopulated. Austrian and German historians who have studied the problem have generally agreed with the commission that it was. Citing a census conducted by the *Hofkriegsrat* in the late autumn of 1718, they have noted that the Banat's approximately 11,150 square miles contained only 85,000 inhabitants, thus placing the population density at an extremely low 7.62 people per square mile.[3] More recently, however, the Romanian historian Aurel Tinta has mustered evidence to show that the Banat possessed not 85,000 but 300,000 inhabitants in 1718, or slightly more than 26 people per square mile.[4] His figures imply that repopulation by foreigners may not have been necessary and that the Habsburgs could have introduced improvements and avoided many difficulties by working with the people already there.

Whatever their implications, Tinta's figures are undoubtedly closer to the actual population total than the earlier estimate, a fact that seems to be confirmed by the research of some German historians working on later periods. In his leading work on colonization in the Theresian period (1745-78), Konrad Schünemann has estimated that the population of the Banat was 400,000 in 1760, before the most intensive period of German settlement began.[5] If Schünemann's figure is correct, the population in 1718 must have exceeded the *Hofkriegsrat's* figures. The population could not have increased from 85,000 to 400,000 between 1718 and 1760, even with a sizeable influx of Germans. In fact, most Germans who settled during the Carolinian period (1718-40) were either driven out by the Turkish war and Romanian uprising (1737-39) or died from the plague that accompanied and followed the war.[6] Another historian has argued, however, that the total population in 1760 cannot be ascertained. "One knows only that around 1760 there lived in the Banat 32,981 Catholics, of whom about 24,000 were Germans."[7] But even if the population in

1760 were 400,000, Schünemann points out that the density was still below every other Habsburg province except Croatia-Slavonia.[8] Thus, even if its figures were wrong, the administration in Vienna was justified in regarding the Banat as underpopulated.

Since it believed that the Banat needed people, the government set out to find colonists willing to establish homes there. The most likely place to find such recruits was the Holy Roman Empire, whose western lands, in the eighteenth century, were the traditional recruiting ground for all states intent upon increasing their populations. England sought Germans for settlement in North America and Ireland, France for colonizing French Guiana, Russia for peopling the Black Sea and Volga regions, and Spain for inhabiting the Sierra Morena. And many Germans were eager to go. In the Carolinian period, as Tinta points out, the intensifying exploitation by their lords, the ruination of many farms during the War of the Spanish Succession, and the imposition of higher taxes by the petty princes combined to make emigration to the Banat and other lands attractive to the Germans.[9] The 1760s, the decade in which the largest number of western colonists moved to the Banat, were hunger years in western Germany. Consequently, many people were willing to emigrate to this new land, especially after the agents portrayed in such glowing terms the opportunities one could find there.[10]

It appears, however, that the Habsburgs did not settle Germans as part of a conscious policy to establish a loyal national bloc in that part of the empire. Indeed, throughout the periods of colonization the Habsburg administrators also settled Serbs, Romanians, Italians, Frenchmen, Albanians, Bulgarians, and Spaniards in the Banat. German colonists were recruited most actively, but that was in part the consequence of severe restrictions placed on recruiting in areas inhabited by some of these other populations. In France, for example, people caught leaving their homes to settle outside the country were sentenced to the galleys, a prospect that undoubtedly discouraged potential colonists and recruiters alike. Agents entering the Ottoman Empire to recruit Balkan peoples might themselves be arrested and sold into slavery. Nonetheless, the sheer variety of peoples recruited makes it clear that the Habsburgs were not attempting to Germanize the Banat. As the German historian Fritz Valjevac has put it, "Such national goals were simply not known in the eighteenth century."[11] Instead it appears that the administration sought Germans because they were the easiest people to attract.

Another author has suggested that the Habsburg objective was not to Germanize but instead to Catholicize the Banat.[12] In the thinking of the eighteenth-century Habsburg monarchs, religion, not nationality, determined a man's political loyalty. Because the Banat was crucial to the defense of Hungary, a loyal Catholic population was essential in that province, and, since the Holy Roman Empire possessed a large number of Catholics willing to emigrate, it was logical for the Habsburgs to encourage those people to move to the Banat. Protestants were strictly forbidden. Viennese officials clearly believed that they would be loyal to a Protestant ruler, most likely a hostile king of Prussia.[13] If Catholicization and not Germanization were the objective, then non-German Catholics should have been welcomed in the Banat, and indeed they were. In the 1730s the governor, Count John Andreas Hamilton, found homes for five hundred Catholic Albanian families and encouraged "many thousand" Catholic Bulgarians to join them.[14] In the Theresian period Vienna encouraged French, Italian, Hungarian, Bulgarian, and even a few Turkish Catholics to emigrate, allowing them to be served by native-speaking priests and guaranteeing them linguistic autonomy.[15]

Despite the effort to import Catholics, Orthodox Romanians and Serbs continued to constitute the bulk of the population of the eighteenth-century Banat. If the Habsburgs really intended to Catholicize the Banat, then they should have tried to convert these people if not to Catholicism, at least to the Uniate church. Instead, the administration, especially the *Hofkriegsrat,* discouraged the efforts of Catholic proselytizers because it feared that religious pressure would alienate the Orthodox Serbian *Grenzer,* who were essential to the defense of the Habsburg-Ottoman frontier. In fact, one of the principle functions of the *Kommission* (later *Hofdeputation*) *in Banaticis, Transylvanicis, et Illyricis* established in 1745 was to defend the interests of the Orthodox.[16] Whereas the rights of the Orthodox were protected primarily to insure the loyalty of the *Grenzer,* the government also refrained from attempts to Catholicize the Romanians. In 1774 when some advisers recommended using schools to convert Orthodox children, the *Hofkammer* officials in charge rejected the suggestion, arguing that schools should not be used to force children to change their religions but "to broaden their education in general as much as possible."[17] Consequently, one can assume that the importation of Germans could not have been exclusively to Catholicize the Banat, for they never reached a figure that approached the Orthodox in total numbers.

If the importation of Germans were not necessarily to Germanize or to Catholicize the Banat, then perhaps the Austrian government hoped these people would raise the land's cultural and economic levels. Indeed, Friedrich Lotz has argued that the Germans entered the Banat not to change its ethnic or religious nature but to Westernize it, to make it less like the Ottoman Empire.[18] Agreeing with Lotz, Valjevac noted that the Germans were to serve as "teachers in economic and cultural affairs."[19] The government recruited Germans because they possessed the knowledge most needed in the Banat, notably of modern agriculture and mining. Living in the same land as the Romanians and Serbs, the Germans would presumably pass on their skills to the more backward natives.[20] Like the Germans, the other nationalities were recruited by the authorities for their skills in certain fields. The government sought Italians for their ability to manufacture silk, paper, and olive oil and to grow vegetables and rice; Armenians for their making of corduan leather; and even Turks for their weaving of *abatuches,* an uncolored woolen cloth.[21]

Diffusing these skills among the indigenous population posed something of a problem. At least after 1740 the colonists remained in villages of their own instead of mixing with the natives. Some Italians, however, were sent out in groups of one or two families to both German and Romanian villages to teach the people how to grow silkworms. In fact, the administration was so anxious to encourage silk production that it decreed the death penalty for anyone harming mulberry trees.[22] Nonetheless, the settling of families of one nationality in villages of another was not a common practice, even though there was no prohibition against it.[23]

If the Habsburg government truly intended to uplift the Banat cultur-ally and economically—to Westernize it as Lotz suggests—then it must have allowed only those Germans and others who possessed the required skills and virtues to become colonists. In fact, Vienna looked upon the Banat as a dumping ground for all kinds of people, not just those who would contribute to its economic and cultural improvement. In the early Theres-ian period, the authorities sent criminals to the Banat, including convicted prostitutes who went as "wives" to those areas short of females. By and large, those sentenced to the Banat were not perpetrators of serious crimes like robbery or murder, but those convicted of such offenses as begging, desertion from debts, and poaching. It was sometimes suggested that even these people bore a certain virtue. Thus, one *Staatsrat* document of 1771 described them as "hard-working people experienced in farming whose crimes resulted not from a vicious heart or from unmitigated wickedness, but from unfortunate prejudice and obstinacy."[24] But despite the petty nature of their offenses, neither the administration at Temesvár nor the other colonists welcomed them, precisely because of their questionable past.[25]

A substantially larger group of colonists of uncertain quality included the soldiers mustered out of the army at the end of the Seven Year' War. In the colonization patent of 1763, Maria Theresia announced her intention to settle ex-soldiers in Hungary, Transylvania, and the Banat in order "to win the army personnel for the crown" and at the same time to protect the other crownlands from a flood of unemployed.[26] The head of the administration at Temesvár, Count Vilana Perlas-Rialp, objected to the influx of such people. He argued that the very fact that they had served in the army indicated that they must have been and probably still were "unvirtuous people and vagabonds."[27] His assessment seems to have been correct. In 1764 the Temesvár administration informed the *Hofkammer* that the ex-soldiers were not at all inclined to work but instead to "drunkenness, indolence, and an evil life. . . . There appears to be no hope left of any of them [becoming] good subjects in the future."[28] The *Staatsrat* even tried to settle Prussian prisoners of war in the Banat by arguing that they would be loyal to any monarch who offered them inducements. Such optimism proved ill founded, for shortly after arriving in the Banat virtually all of these men fled for their original homes.[29]

Whereas the administration might have anticipated that ex-soldiers and criminals would be poor exponents of western virtues, it soon discovered that the supposedly industrious farmer-settlers also included an unreliable element. During both the Carolinian and Theresian periods, many sold the materials and livestock given to them, using the money to buy strong drink and to gamble, while others abandoned the lands they worked in order to escape their creditors.[30] In 1766, for example, forty-six families fled the German community of Mercysdorf, leaving behind six thousand florins in unpaid bills.[31]

Even those colonists who wished to Westernize the Banat faced serious obstacles. Probably the most enduring problem was disease, especially malaria, plague, and smallpox. Ever since the Carolinian period, many western Europeans had labeled the Banat the "graveyard of Germans," and for good reason. In 1728 the Temesvár administration recorded fifty-one baptisms and 484 deaths within the community.[32] When Joseph II visited the Banat on his first inspection tour in 1768, he was horrified to learn that, of all the Germans born in Temesvár, only three had reached the age of thirty. In response to Joseph's discovery, the *Hofkammer* tried to improve medical services by establishing a central medical office in Temesvár to dispatch surgeons and their assistants to each district. As a further measure the *Hofkriegsrat* in 1770 strengthened the *Pestkordon* along the Turkish border, establishing the regulations and procedures that would remain in effect until the cordon's abolition in 1871.[33] A shortage of trained personnel limited the effectiveness of these measures, however, and the people of the Banat—regardless of nationality— did not always understand or appreciate them. Many "saw the *Pestkordon* and most of the other measures designed to hinder the plague as a greater evil than the plague itself."[34]

Disease was not the only obstacle to the success of the serious German colonists. Things were not cheap in the Banat, and there seemed to be a chronic shortage of certain essential items, especially draft animals and dairy cattle. Even when a colonist established his home and procured the necessary tools and livestock, all his efforts could be washed away by flooding, a common danger in the low-lying areas. The administrations in Temesvár and Vienna tried to alleviate flooding, even hiring a famous Dutch hydraulic engineer to advise them on how to control rising water.[35] The government made modest progress, but the rivers were not effectively controlled until the next century.

Despite their praiseworthy efforts to control illness and floods, the authorities in Temesvár often obstructed progress. Many officials were of low quality, willing to accept bribes and to ignore crimes. In fact, in 1768 Joseph sharply criticized the bureaucrats for using their offices for private gain, and, to do away with such graft, suggested establishing estates for the Banat and then finding a way to sell the province to them.[36] The administration always lacked qualified personnel. When the major period of colonization ended in 1773, the *Hofkammer* decided to replace the colonization officials with *Wirtschaftsbeamten,* specialists in agriculture who would help the farmers improve production. This posed two questions. What could be done with the colonization officers? And where could one find *Wirtschaftsbeamten?* The answer to both was obvious though unsatisfactory: train the colonization officials to be *Wirtschaftsbeamten.* Although this was done, the new *Wirtschaftsbeamten* knew as little about their duties as the old colonization officials has known about theirs.[37]

If the Habsburgs had hoped to Westernize the Banat through the transmission of western skills by German nationals, they must have been surprised by the hostile reaction of the indigenous Romanians, the supposed beneficiaries of their efforts. The Romanians often harassed these German interlopers, usually by stealing their livestock and driving it across the Maros River to sell in Hungary.[38] Such activities elicited an outpouring of German slurs on the Romanian character. A 1769 document described the Romanians as "inconstant, disloyal, rebellious, lazy, and barbaric," while a memorandum from the *Hofkriegsrat* in 1763 portrayed them as "hardly distinguishable from cattle."[39] In his work on the Banat written in the 1770s, Francesco Griselini wrote of the Romanians: "The carefree, leisurely shepherd's life, which they practice in their early years, develops in them the aptitude for the burdens which are unique to the shepherd's life: that is, they never lack for thieves and robbers." He added, "Today they have sunk to the worst barbarism—coarse and ignorant, full of physical and moral weaknesses."[40]

It appears, then, that the major purpose of the Habsburgs was not to Germanize, Catholicize, or Westernize the Banat, but simply to fill the region with people—virtually any kind of people. Since the mercantilist thought of the time stated that people constituted a state's wealth, the Habsburg government sought recruits wherever they could get them. The traditional and most accessible area of recruitment being the Holy Roman Empire, the government sought settlers there, insisting only that they be Catholic. As mentioned before, this was not because Vienna envisioned an exclusively Catholic Banat, but because the Habsburgs viewed Protestant Germans as potential adherents of the king of Prussia. Unfortunately, these colonization efforts, which failed to consider in any serious way the quality of the settlers, succeeded only in increasing the quantity of people in the Banat.[41]

Following his 1768 tour, Joseph harshly criticized the Vienna and Temesvár administrations for thinking only to increase the population and failing to consider how to improve the lives of the people. On one page of his report he remarked in exasperation, "Never had 900,000 florins been spent worse, more uselessly, or unwisely as in this colonization business."[42]

Joseph's criticism coincided with more intensive efforts by such government officials as Joseph von Sonnenfels to analyze population theory and internal improvements. Soon this combination of criticism and initiative had its effect. After 1768 the Viennese administration began to focus its efforts on improving the conditions of the people who already resided in the Banat, giving primary attention to the education of the indigenous Orthodox. As early as 1764 the *Hofkammer* had announced its intention to establish schools primarily to instill Christian virtues in the Romanians and to purge them of the "liabilities of cattle-stealing, murder, and bigamy."[43] Although endorsed by the Orthodox bishop of Temesvár, the *Hofkammer's* proposal was rejected by the administration of that same city on the grounds that "guilt for the depravity of the nationalities is not the fault of a lack of schools but of malice that can only be fought through punishment." If the *Hofkammer* really intended to end wickedness among the Orthodox population, the provincial authorities argued, then it should "support the priests and use hussars to force the people to church and to confession."[44]

Joseph's criticisms prevailed over such objections, and after 1768 *Hofkammer* investigators submitted various proposals for the creation of an educational system.[45] Finally in 1774, six months before Maria Theresia's general order regulating schools throughout the monarchy, the *Hofkammer* issued *Regulae Directivae,* the instructions for establishing elementary schools in the Banat.[46]

Rather than pursue the development of the Banat schools, which has been discussed extensively in other works, we should ask whether these new schools became the vehicles for Germanization, Catholicization, or Westernization. While not conscious of these concepts in the first half of the eighteenth century, perhaps the Habsburgs came to recognize their usefulness in the latter half. As to Germanization, some *Hofkammer* officials did recommend that the language of instruction be German, largely because they believed that the ultimate purpose of educating Serbian and Romanian children was to provide recruits for the Habsburg army and administration. Their suggestion was rejected however, for the majority of *Hofkammer* authorities believed that education was first and foremost a means to uplift local culture and thereby to eradicate banditry. Consequently, they decided to use Serbian and Romanian as the primary languages of instruction and to reserve the study of German for later, reasoning that only after students learned their own languages, "could one think of beginning instruction in the German tongue."[47]

Similarly, when some *Hofräte* proposed using the schools to persuade children to become Catholics or at least Uniates, the majority of officials rejected this suggestion. They argued that "in those schools furnished with Catholic teachers, when the hour for religious studies comes, the non-Uniate children will run away."[48] Since the *Hofkammer* believed that religion in general served to inculcate virtue, the schools provided religious instruction in Orthodoxy and no attempt was made to change the students' faith. The *Hofkammer* did rule, however, that since the Orthodox priests "show no enthusiasm for education," instruction must be the preserve of secular teachers who would teach that personal virtue and loyalty to the state were common to all religions, including Orthodoxy.[49]

Did the *Hofkammer* then envision Westernization as the purpose of education? If the belief that a people can be dissuaded from lawlessness by learning to read and write in its own language can be called western, then Westernization was indeed the purpose of the reforms. However, education in the eighteenth-century Banat did not go much beyond that. The *Regulae Directivae* did authorize the use of a small book on agriculture, animal husbandry, and beekeeping for students in larger villages, but no *Fachschulen* appeared until the nineteenth century.[50]

Essentially, nationalism in its modern sense played little or no role in the improvement of the Banat beyond the Habsburg government's recognition that different nationalities lived or could live there. Prior to 1768, the policy to fill the Banat with people represented a rather simplistic interpretation of the population theories of eighteenth-century mercantilism. When Joseph II made it known after his first tour that this policy by itself was not leading to an improved Banat, the administration turned primarily to educating the youth to seek that improvement. And the purpose of the education was not to transform the children into Germans, Catholics, or West Europeans, but to improve social attitudes, a policy that reflected another of the common beliefs of the eighteenth century, that of the Enlightenment. Only through schooling that taught the virtues of honest behavior and loyalty to the state could the people of the Banat serve the monarchy as the authorities wished. Such policies were neither particularly forward-looking nor particularly reactionary; they reflected instead the common beliefs of Europe at that time.

NOTES

1. A convenient discussion of published books on the Banat can be found in Aurel Tinta, *Colonizarile habsburgice in Banat, 1716-1740* [Habsburg Colonization in the Banat, 1716-1740] (Temesvár, 1972), pp. 7-16. Since the *Hofkammerarchiv* in Vienna contains a great number of documents in its *Banater Akten,* many students have written doctoral dissertations concerning various aspects of colonization, economics, and culture in the Banat. For a list see Alexander Krischan, "Dissertation über das Banat (1897-1967)," *Südostdeutsches Archiv,* 13 (1970), 203-21.

2. The *Hofkammer* recommended this course of action and Prince Eugene endorsed it. Prince Eugene to *Hofkriegsrat,* 21 June 1717, in *Feldzüge des Prinzen Eugens* (Vienna, 1891), XVII, supplement, 70-72. The joint commission in fact could implement no decisions on its own; it could only advise the *Hofkammer* and *Hofkriegsrat.*

3. Sonja Jordan, *Die kaiserliche Wirtschaftspolitik im Banat im 18. Jahrhundert* (Munich, 1967), p. 17; and Josef Kallbrunner, *Das kaiserliche Banat; Einrichtung und Entwicklung des Banats bis 1739* (Munich, 1958), pp. 26-60.

4. Tinta, *Colonizarile habsburgice,* p. 82.

5. Konrad Schünemann, *Oesterreichs Bevölkerungspolitik unter Maria Theresia* (Berlin, 1935), p. 73.

6. Scholarly estimates of the total number of Germans settled between 1718 and 1739 vary between ten and twenty thousand. See Kallbrunner, *Kaiserliche Banat,* p. 35; Jordan, *Kaiserliche Wirtschaftspolitik,* p. 22; and Peter Gaenger, "Graf Mercy als Governeur des Temescher Banats," *Österreichische Begegnung,* 6 (1966), vol. 3-4, p. 49.

7. Ernst Schimscha, *Technik und Methoden der Theresianischen Besiedlung des Banats* (Baden bei Wien, 1939), p. 13.

8. Schünemann, *Oesterreichs Bevölkerungspolitik,* p. 73.

9. Tinta, *Colonizarile habsburgice,* pp. 24-29.

10. Schünemann, *Oesterreichs Bevölkerungspolitik,* pp. 303-16.

11. Fritz Valjevac, *Geschichte der deutschen Kulturbeziehungen zu Südosteuropa* (Munich, 1958), III, 79.

12. Schimscha, *Technik und Methoden,* p. 176.

13. Ernst Nowotny, *Die Transmigration ober- und innerösterreichischer Protestanten nach Siebenburgen im 18. Jahrhundert* (Jena, 1931), p. 46. See point three of the copy of an advertisement to be sent to German newspapers in the empire to recruit settlers in Schünemann, *Oesterreiches Bevölkerungspolitik,* p. 280.

14. Kallbrunner, *Kaiserliche Banat,* p. 37. From 1739 to 1750 one of the principal Catholic officials in the land was Bishop Stanislavich, himself a Bulgarian.

15. Schimscha, *Technik und Methoden,* p. 177.

16. Gunther Rothenberg, *The Military Border in Croatia, 1740-1881* (Chicago, 1966), pp. 32-33.

17. Quoted from the *Regulae Directivae* of 1774 in Herta Tietz, "Die Einrichtung eines Schulwesens für Rumänen und Serben im kaiserlichen Banat (1718-1778)," *Südostdeutsches Archiv,* 9 (1966), 195.

18. Friedrich Lotz, "Die frühtheresianische Kolonisation des Banats (1740-1762)," in *Gedenkschrift für Harold Steinacker* (Munich, 1966), p. 153.

19. Valjevac, *Geschichte der deutschen Kulturbeziehungen,* III, 101.

20. Valjevac wrote that the German colonists introduced the potato to the Romanians and that a few German agricultural terms passed into the Romanian language. Ibid., III, 102.

21. Jordan, *Kaiserliche Wirtschaftspolitik,* pp. 24-26.

22. Ernst Joseph Görlich and Felix Romanik, *Geschichte Österreichs* (Innsbruck, 1970), p. 283.

23.   Schimscha noted that Maria Theresia had nothing against the intermarriage of Germans, Romanians, and Serbs so long as the weddings took place in Catholic churches and the parents raised their children as Catholics. Schimscha, *Technik und Methoden,* p. 178.

24.   Quoted in Schünemann, *Oesterreichs Bevölkerungspolitik,* p. 78.

25.   Lotz, "Frühtheresianische Kolonisation," p. 162. Between 1752 and 1768, 3,130 criminals were transported to the Banat.

26.   Alexander Krischan, "Das Kolonisationspatent Maria Theresias von 25 II 1763 als Beitrag zur Besiedlungsgeschichte des altungarischen Raumes," *Deutsches Archiv für Landes- und Volksforschung,* 7 (1943), p. 101.

27.   Quoted in Schünemann, *Oesterreichs Bevölkerungspolitik,* pp. 160-61.

28.   Quoted in Ibid., p. 164. The settlement of invalid soldiers in the Banat Military Border proved to be more successful. Felix Milleker, *Geschichte der Banater Militärgrenze, 1764-1783* (Pančevo, 1926), pp. 41-42.

29.   Josef Kallbrunner, "Deutsche Wanderungen nach Siebenburgen in neuerer Zeit," *Deutsches Archiv für Landes- und Volksforschung,* 2 (1938), 678; Irene Binder, "Die Urheimat der 1763-76 in des Temescher Banat abgegangenen Kolonisten," *Deutsche Hefte für Volks- und Kulturbodenforschung,* 1 (1931), vol. 5, p. 306.

30.   One author wrote of few virtuous people and much rabble among the Germans coming to Belgrade after its acquisition in 1718 and noted that the most common commercial establishment in the German city was the saloon. Theodore von Stefanovich-Volovsky, *Belgrad unter der Regierung Kaiser Karls VI, 1717-1739* (Vienna, 1908), pp. 31-34.

31.   Schmischa, *Technik und Methoden,* pp. 123, 126.

32.   Johann Schwicker, *Geschichte des Temeser Banats* (Grosz-Becskerek, 1861), p. 317.

33.   Gunther Rothenberg, "The Austrian Sanitary Cordon and the Control of the Bubonic Plague, 1710-1871," *Journal of the History of Medicine and the Allied Sciences,* 28 (1973), 18.

34.   Valjevac, *Geschichte der deutschen Kulturbeziehungen,* III, 32.

35.   Francesco Griselini, *Versuch einer politischen und natürlichen Geschichte des Banats in Briefen an Standespersonen und Gelehrte* (Vienna, 1780), I, 182-83. For a study of the efforts to alleviate the water problem, see Herman von Guettler, "Die Wasserbauarbeiten im Banat 1717-79 und die Kultivierung und deutsche Besiedlung des Landes" (Doctoral dissertation, University of Vienna, 1936).

36.   Sieglinde Neidenbach, "Die Reisen Kaiser Josephs II ins Banat" (Doctoral dissertation, University of Vienna, 1967), pp. 55-63.

37.   Schimscha, *Technik und Methoden,* pp. 128-29.

38.   Ibid., 100-101. The penatly for stealing livestock was death, but it apparently did not deter the thieves.

39.   Quoted in Ibid., 38-39; and Mathias Bernath, "Die Einrichtung der Siebenbürgischen Militärgrenze und die Wiener Romänenpolitik in der frühjosephinischen Zeit," *Südostforschungen,* 19 (1960), 168.

40.   Griselini, *Versuch,* I, 214-15.

41.   The population figures most often cited for the Banat in the 1770s are Griselini's: 181,639 Romanians; 78,780 Serbs; 43,201 Germans, French, and Italians; 8,683 Bulgarians; 5,272 Gypsies; and 353 Jews. These figures total 317,928 for the Central Banat to which Griselini added 142,000 from the Military Border which brings the total to 460,000, an increase of 160,000, or 53.33 percent, from Tinta's figure of 300,000 in 1718. Ibid., I, 196.

42.   Quoted in Konrad Schünemann, "Die Wirtschaftspolitik Josephs in der Zeit seiner Mitregenschaft," *Mitteilungen des Instituts für österreichische Geschichtsforschung,* 47 (1934), 30. For Joseph's particular criticisms of the administration see Neidenbach, "Die Reisen Kaiser Josephs II," pp. 31-63.

43.   Quoted from the Orthodox Bishop of Temesvár, Vinzentius Joannovich Viedek, in Tietz, "Einrichtung des Schulwesens," p. 188.

44.   Quoted in Ibid., p. 188.

45.   See Hans Wolf, *Das Schulwesen des Temesvarer Banats im 18. Jahrhundert* (Vienna, 1935), passim.

46.   The Banat Military Border was not included in the regulations because it remained under the administration of the *Hofkriegsrat.*

47.   Quoted in Tietz, "Einrichtung des Schulwesens," pp. 194-95. One could argue that there were some evidences of a conscious nationalism in the school texts. Serbian primers were printed in the Cyrillic alphabet but Romanian materials appeared in Latin letters. It was explained that this was necessary to tear the people away from the influence of their "Russophile princes." Ibid., p. 210.

48.   Quoted in Ibid., p. 195.

49.   A *Hofrat* Kress argued against religious instruction in the Orthodox schools because it would make the Orthodox more intelligent in matters of their faith than the Roman Catholics were in theirs. Ibid., p. 196.

50.   Valjevac, *Geschichte der deutschen Kulturbeziehungen,* III, 274.

IDENTITY AND CONSCIOUSNESS: CULTURE AND POLITICS AMONG THE HABSBURG SERBS IN THE EIGHTEENTH CENTURY*

Roger V. Paxton
University of Utah

An analysis of the psychological, cultural, social, and political processes that infuse a given national community with a sense of cultural identity and of national consciousness illustrates the complexities that confront the student of nationalism. As I have discussed elsewhere,[1] the terms "cultural identity" and "national consciousness" are inextricably linked. While association with a particular culture does not inevitably lead to an attachment to a particular nationality, frequently the two terms represent phases of a single psychological process. During this process, an individual first establishes a sense of identification with a given culture and then gradually strives to protect it from external onslaughts against it integrity. When the rulers and the ruled do not share common cultural values, a political struggle often ensues with an attendant rise of national consciousness. Ultimately, members of this politicized nationality aspire to construct an autonomous or independent government that can guarantee cultural and national survival. Due to regional, occupational, economic, educational, and personal dissimilarities, however, members of a national community at any particular point in time may develop different perceptions of the "national interest." Consequently, disagreement over the issue of cultural and national preservation manifests itself in a variety of attitudes, objectives, and tactics.

* The author is grateful for the financial assistance provided by the Research Committee of the University of Utah which made possible the travel necessary to complete the research of this study.

101

Several scholars have asserted that the "progressive middle class" and the Serbian Orthodox church were responsible for generating and sustaining a sense of national consciousness among eighteenth-century Habsburg Serbs. According to some writers, prosperous merchants single-handedly promoted the nationalist cause when they became embroiled in a civil rights struggle with Austrian and Hungarian authorities. During the last quarter of the century, the "progressive middle class" subsidized the publications of the intelligentsia.[2] Other specialists have recognized the role that the Serbian Orthodox church played in maintaining a sense of cultural identity. In the absence of indigenous political institutions, the church represented the only organization that strove to protect Serbian national interests.[3] Acknowledging that traders and clerics fostered national consciousness, one historian has suggested that other sectors of society engaged in the "struggle against denationalization and unionism."[4] We as yet have no study that analyzes the role of these leading elements within the context of significant eighteenth-century developments.

This essay intends to identify the social actors and to analyze the cultural and political factors that perpetuated, stimulated, and transformed Serbian cultural identity and national consciousness from 1690 until 1790. Since this process must be examined within a framework that is both international and institutional, particular attention is devoted to the interaction between foreign and indigenous elements in the evolution of Serbian identity and consciousness. Russian, German, and French influences as well as the roles of education, language, religion, social customs, the press, and literature will be treated in a synthetic approach to the issues raised.

Throughout the eighteenth century, Serbian society in Habsburg lands experienced substantial demographic growth, underwent considerable social stratification, witnessed a steady improvement in living standards, and benefited from an impressive expansion of educational facilities. According to one historian, there were approximately 667,247 Serbs residing in the empire by 1797. The size of the Serbian population swelled as waves of emigrants from Ottoman territories traversed the Danube in the aftermath of periodic Austro-Turkish wars. Inhabiting numerous urban and rural communities in Hungary, Croatia, and the Military Frontier, these Serbs were occupied as traders and craftsmen, served the crown in military and administrative capacities, formed a thin layer of the aristocracy, toiled the land as serfs, day laborers, lease-holders, and state peasants, filled the clerical ranks of the Serbian Orthodox church, and participated in a wide range of literary and artistic endeavors. Vienna's establishment of an elementary school system for the Serbs and the Serbian merchants' financial support of educational and cultural activities fostered a modest increase in literacy levels and provided for a measure of public enlightenment.[5]

From the beginning of the "Great Migration" in 1690 to the convocation of the Assembly of Temesvár in 1790, a cross-section of Serbian society exhibited a sense of belonging to and identification with a cultural community that transcended its own place of habitat. Throughout the eighteenth century Serbian religious and lay leaders frequently alluded to the special Austro-Serbian relationship established during and after the "Great Migration" of 1690. At that time, the Habsburg emperor Leopold I guaranteed his newly acquired subjects freedom of religion, exemption from taxation, and the right to elect their own military commanders. Immensely significant for the maintenance of Serbian identity and consciousness was the establishment of an Orthodox church on Habsburg territory.[6] This privilege provided an institutional foundation for Serbian religous self-rule and served as an organizational means by which a measure of public opinion could be channeled to imperial authorities.

While the historical significance of the privileges granted between 1690 and 1695 should not be minimized, the granting of those privileges represented a continuation of the well-established Austrian administrative policy of extending limited self-rule to the Serbian inhabitants of the Habsburg Empire. From 1578 until 1659, the Serbs had obtained certain civil, judicial, and political rights from Austrian officials. During the eighteenth century, Joseph I, Charles VI, Maria Theresia, Joseph II, and Leopold II confirmed and extended the rights affecting their Serbian subjects.[7]

One additional forum of communication for Serbian public opinion throughout the eighteenth century was the national-religious assembly, or *sabor*.[8] Convened irregularly between 1708 and 1790, the assembly's periodic meetings provided secular and religious dignitaries with an opportunity to air their grievances and to express current aspirations. Although Vienna refused to permit the Serbs to assemble on a regular basis, its tolerance of such an institution inevitably fostered the spread of Serbian national consciousness. Representatives from Buda and Pest discussed common problems with their brethren from the imperial cities, the Military Frontier, and southern Hungary. The mere fact that the assembly debated the resolution of issues affecting the welfare and concerns of all Habsburg Serbs diluted the countervailing forces of regional parochialism and individual self-interest.

As noted above, several Serbian and Yugoslav scholars have maintained that the Serbian "progressive middle class" assumed the leadership of a struggle designed to maintain and expand national liberties.[9] According to Mita Kostić, Serbian merchants and craftsmen developed a "civic consciousness" and a sense of class self-respect based on their economic well-being and an aggressive, competitive spirit. The most vigorous spokesmen of this particular element appeared in the free royal cities that possessed some form of self-rule: Buda, Pest, Esztergom, Székesfehérvár, and Szeged. As early as 1696, Vienna gave the Serbian residents of Buda the right to elect their own judges, police officials, and tax collectors; and two years later Arsenije III, the Serbian patriarch, bestowed upon the Serbs of Buda and Pest the privilege of electing their own priests.[10] Thus with the end of the seventeenth century, Austrian secular and Serbian religious authorities permitted the Serbs a degree of public participation in municipal and church government.

After acquiring this relatively privileged status, this most economically advanced sector of the Serbian populace became involved in a series of confrontations with Hungarian governmental and Serbian church officials. Urban leaders occasionally criticized Hungarian magistrates for violations of their civil rights and castigated Serbian clerics for a variety of financial misdeeds. During the assemblies of 1708 and 1726, they called for increased representation in local and provincial government (including membership in the prestigious Hungarian Royal Chancellery), civil freedoms equal to those which the Germans and the Hungarians enjoyed, the popular election of bishops, and the establishment of a lay-clerical system of national church governance. Though these requests were denied, Hungarian and Austrian municipal, provincial, and imperial authorities were induced to reaffirm previously granted privileges in a series of pronouncements issued between 1724 and 1752.[11] However, these periodic assurances of Hungarian and Austrian fidelity to past concessions failed to allay the fears and fulfill the needs of Serbian spokesmen.

Central to our comprehension of these apprehensions and aspirations was the Serbs' overriding concern—securing the legal codification of their privileges from Austrian and Hungarian authorities. Repeated violations of their civil rights and persistent threats to their cultural identity fostered widespread Serbian distrust of Austrian and Hungarian intentions. In some instances, Serbs sought to redress their grievances by demanding a legal foundation for their status within the empire. They reasoned that the legalization of Serbian privileges was the most efficacious way of guaranteeing their right to an autonomous cultural existence. It was the frequent example of the Magyar leaders vigorously defending their national rights against Austrian violations which proved crucial to the political education of these Serbs. Both Serbian lawyers trained at the universities of Vienna and Pest and those Serbs who were members of the imperial bureaucracy witnessed the legal process by which Hungarians challenged alleged Austrian infringements upon their privileges. Observing that occasionally these efforts led to productive results, politically conscious Serbs adopted similar tactics in an attempt to protect existing and secure additional rights.[12]

Despite arguments to the contrary, the "progressive middle class" was not the sole champion of Serbian national rights. Other sectors of Serbian society shared similar experiences with their brethren in the free imperial municipalities. Those Serbs who settled in military communities along the Austro-Turkish border in the 1520s were granted modest land parcels, exemption from manorial dues, the right to elect their own military and judicial officials, and freedom of religion. As the Austrian frontier advanced southward into the Balkans, additional Serbian settlers joined the ranks of the military colonists and thus acquired a privileged status within the Habsburg Empire.[13]

The Roman Catholic clergy and the Hungarian aristocracy posed serious threats to the frontiersmen's (graničari) cultural identity and national liberties. While the former desired to convert the "schismatics," the latter aspired to subject these Serbs to Magyar political and economic domination. To defend themselves against persistent clerical and aristocratic assaults upon their freedoms, the frontiersmen occasionally petitioned Vienna and frequently resorted to acts of violence. When neither of these measures proved effective, some disgruntled frontiersmen and their families migrated to the Ottoman and Russian empires. All three reactions were manifested in the crisis precipitated by the abolition of two military districts during the late 1740s and 1750s.

Adverse military conditions induced Empress Maria Theresia to promise the Hungarians in 1741 that she would place the Maros and Tisa border districts (*krajine*) under Hungarian civil jurisdiction. Fearful of losing their social status, property, and civil rights, dissatisfied Serbian frontiersmen in 1748-50 repeatedly petitioned the empress calling for a halt to the demilitarization of the two districts and asking that they not be transferred to Hungarian authorities. The petitioners alluded to the privileges granted by Leopold I, reminding the empress of their most recent reaffirmation, and recalled the numerous examples of Serbian military contributions in protecting the empire against its foreign and domestic enemies. Protest meetings were held and clandestine contacts were established between Serbian military commanders and the Russian ambassador in Vienna. Empress Elizabeth I's offers of officer promotions, land grants, and resettlement assistance enticed 1,800 residents of the Habsburg frontier to migrate to Russia in 1751-52. When the wave of emigration subsided at the end of the decade, some 2,200 Serbian border families had become Russian subjects.[14]

Emigration was not the only way in which the frontiersmen responded to the abolition of the two districts. Approximately 40 percent of the Maros and Tisa officers (50 of a total of 122) accepted Austrian and Hungarian offers of ennoblement and landed estates as the "price" for becoming Hungarian civilians. Other officers and soldiers retained their military status and moved into the frontier districts located in the Banat. Although occupational opportunities, economic inducements, and political alienation influenced the behavior of these Serbian frontiersmen, cultural and national concerns were also crucial factors in their behavior. Serbian petitioners had expressed anti-Hungarian sentiment and the migrants to both Russia and the Banat strove to maintain their distinctive cultural and national identity. Their determination was particularly evident in the names selected for the two newly created Russian frontier provinces, "New Serbia" and "Slavoserbia," and in the abortive attempt to establish a Serbian Orthodox episcopate on Russian soil. Ironically, the very threat that had impelled them to emigrate from Austria befell them in Russia. In 1764 St. Petersburg renamed the two military colonies "New Russia" and "Catherine's Province" and combined Serbian regiments with Cossack contingents, thus marking the beginning of a long and complex process of acculturation.[15]

Russian cultural and political influence upon the Habsburg Serbs extended far beyond those few thousand military colonists in southern Russia. Indeed, it was deeply rooted in the public mind, and had a particularly strong impact in the Orthodox church, the schools, and the realm of literature. Although they had accepted Russian influence for a variety of reasons, folk poets, clerics, educators, and intellectuals endeavored to employ it as a means of promoting Serbian cultural and political interests.

From the years immediately following the Great Migration, many Serbs began to look to Russia as an alternative to the inhospitable conditions that they encountered in the Habsburg Empire. Religious intolerance and a hostile political atmosphere created discord in the Serbs' new homeland. In 1702, 1,000 families returned to the Ottoman Empire and two years later several Serbian militia officers expressed a desire to migrate to Russia. As dissatisfaction with Austrian rule grew, an increasing number of Serbs commenced to regard Peter the Great as a defender of their faith and as their tsar. Peter's 1711 appeal to the Balkan Christians for an insurrection against the Turks seemed to confirm the Russian emperor's image as the liberator of the South Slavs. Peter soon became a popular topic for folk poets, and throughout the eighteenth century Serbs living in Hungary sang these songs of liberation.[16]

While the "cult of Peter the Great" developed as one clear expression of the aspirations of the Serbian populace, the hierarchs of the Orthodox church fostered the spread of Russification, thereby underscoring the church's political disenchantment with the Habsburg state. Vienna's failure to restrain belligerent Catholics and Uniates from infringing upon the Orthodox religious right of coexistence created a "credibility gap" in the minds of church leaders. Austrian cultural policies and attitudes also were regarded as inimical to the survival of Serbian culture and the Orthodox church.

Religious leaders endeavored to preserve the cultural heritage of the Serbian people and to fulfill the liturgical and pedagogical needs of the Orthodox church. After the Great Migration of 1690, Serbian patriarchs, metropolitans, and assemblies had petitioned the crown for permission to establish church schools and a Cyrillic printing press. When an imperial rescript of 1727 approved the opening of Orthodox schools, Russian instructors immediately arrived in Karlovci and Belgrade to train neophyte clerics and teachers. Recognizing a continuing need for qualified teachers and for instructional materials, several metropolitans enthusiastically welcomed the arrival of the learned "Muscovites" and eagerly awaited the influx of Russian religious literature, grammars, dictionaries, and primers.[17]

Russian instructors speaking in their native tongue and teaching from books published in the Russo-Slavonic language made a tremendous cultural and linguistic impact upon their Serbian audience. Two generations of Habsburg Serbs learned to read, write, and speak Russo-Slavonic, and during the metropolitanate of Pavle Nenadović (1749-68), Russo-Slavonic became the official language of the Serbian Orthodox church. The metropolitan's missives to both clergy and laity were written in Russo-Slavonic. Serbian literati also published their works in Russo-Slavonic and, according to Skerlić, many clerics, writers, and townsmen characterized themselves as having become "slavicized."[18]

Confronted with the problem of a Serbian gravitation toward St. Petersburg, Vienna launched a vigorous cultural and political offensive aimed at uprooting Russian influence among the Habsburg Serbs. The establishment of a Cyrillic printing press in Vienna reduced the demand for a massive importation of Russian books, and Empress Maria Theresia's educational reforms destroyed the monopolistic position of Russo-Slavonic as the language of instruction in Serbian schools. Although Austrian efforts achieved a modicum of success, they unintentionally contributed to a heightening of Serbian cultural identity and national consciousness.

Habsburg bureaucrats recognized the necessity and the desirability of founding a Cyrillic press for Austria's Orthodox subjects. During a session of the Royal Chamber for the Banat held on 23 May 1769, officials admitted that a new school system for the frontiersmen would require an appropriate publishing house. In an 23 October 1769 memorandum addressed to the empress, Philipides de Gaya stressed the multiple benefits that would accrue to the regime if it established such a printing press. This highly respected crown adviser argued that an Orthodox printing establishment in Vienna would eliminate the need for the Serbs to import books from "schismatic lands," thereby stemming the flow of money from the country and interrupting the "dangerous" relations that the Orthodox inhabitants of the empire maintained with their co-religionists abroad (i.e., with the Russians). De Gaya also claimed that through government-controlled schools and state-censored books the enlightened schismatics eventually would unite with the Uniate church and consequently become more loyal towards the Habsburg court. Ostensibly impressed with the cogency of her councilor's arguments, Maria Theresia immediately decided to approve the proposal to establish a Cyrillic press in the capital.[19]

Military, political, economic, and foreign policy considerations had prompted Maria Theresia to initiate a series of educational and cultural reforms during the 1770s. Prussia's defeat of Austria during the Seven Years' War convinced the Royal War Council that there was a correlation between a nation's military strength and the nature of its schools. The councilors believed that a secularized and enlarged educational system would remedy the situation and thus, they advised the empress to undertake decisive action in that direction. The government was also concerned with maintaining the security and the stability of the existing political and social order, and reasoned that if the schools were brought under state control, they could serve these purposes. Written for the newly created state educational facilities, the Austro-Serbian teacher's manual of 1776 identified the teachers' primary pedagogical responsibilities as instructing the students to remain loyal to the fatherland and teaching them to be obedient to the will of their feudal lord.[20] Steps were also taken to de-Russify Serbian education. According to the School Constitution of 1776, Russian teachers and Russian books were excluded from Serbian secular elementary schools. Henceforth, Serbian instructors trained in Austrian pedagogical methods taught classes in their native tongue and used textbooks published in the Serbo-Slavonic language.[21]

Even as this program of de-Russification was implemented, the regime of Maria Theresia introduced a Germanization policy affecting a wide range of public services, including the empire's educational system. In order to make governmental operations more efficient, the newly established, centralized administrative and military apparatus required that all forms of communications be conducted in a common language. It has been argued that the choice of German as the official state language was not based upon German nationalistic considerations and did not signify that Vienna opposed the use of non-Germanic tongues. Nonetheless, the Habsburg court's desire that German become the "national language" of Hungary and the declaration that all elementary students learn the official state language represented the beginning of an acculturation process.[22]

Some members of the Serbian community welcomed the opportunity to study German. For those Serbs who aspired to enter the imperial bureaucracy, serve in the army, or engage in commerce, a knowledge of German was imperative. Instruction in the elementary schools of the Military Frontier was Germanized as early as 1776, while German language classes were offered to primary pupils in other Serbian communities on a voluntary basis. German also became the language of instruction in all secondary schools and in most universities. A German grammar in Serbo-Slavonic was printed in 1772 and in 1790 a two-volume German-Serbian dictionary appeared—both reflected a widespread usage of German among the Habsburg Serbs. Even the unschooled populace was exposed to the official state language when German colonists settled in Hungary during the last decades of the eighteenth century.[23]

As Germanization proceeded slowly, the Viennese government tried to Latinize the Serbian alphabet and took steps to create a common literary language for all of the crown's "Illyrian-speaking" subjects. The rationale for Vienna's efforts to Latinize and Illyrianize the Serbs, Kostić has suggested, was linked with the monarchy's conviction that the translation of German pedagogical literature into the vernacular would be facilitated if there were a uniform language for all Habsburg South Slavs. The eminent Serbian historian has also asserted that the centralizing tendencies of the regime demanded the establishment of linguistic uniformity for all of the empire's nationalities.[24] One should add, however, that the proposed alphabet and language reforms ostensibly were designed to deprive the Serbs of part of their cultural distinctiveness, thereby accelerating their Western acculturation and de-Russification.

From 1779 until 1785 Austrian and Hungarian officials strove to restrict the usage of Cyrillic and Serbo-Slavonic to religious publications and church services. An imperial commission for education demanded in 1782 that all Serbian secular materials use the Latin alphabet and conform linguistically with the "Illyrian" dialect taught in Croatian schools.

Two years later Hungarian authorities argued that since Serbo-Slavonic was unintelligible to the ordinary people, it should be eliminated as the language of instruction in Serbian elementary schools.[25]

Serbian educational and religious authorities effectively resisted these measures. Teodor Janković Mirijevski, one of the three inspectors of the empire's Serbian schools, opposed the formation of an "Illyrian" language. In a memorandum written in 1781, Mirijevski predicted that if the proposed linguistic reforms were introduced, Austrian political and economic interests would be impaired. Ottoman Serbs, retaining their alphabet and language, would become estranged from the Habsburg monarchy and from their ethnic brethren north of the Danube. Linguistic differences would also hamper commercial relations among the South Slavic merchants of the two empires.[26]

Metropolitan Mojsije Putnik's staunch opposition to language reform proposals surfaced frequently during the duration of the controversy. Writing to Emperor Joseph II on 9 November 1784, the head of the church alleged that the removal of Cyrillic from Serbian and Romanian schools would produce repercussions unfavorable to Habsburg interests. Orthodox Serbs and Romanians in the Austrian and Ottoman empires would regard such an act as a violation of religious freedom and as a restriction of educational rights. How could students ignorant of the Cyrillic alphabet comprehend religious instructors teaching with Cyrillic catechisms in the lay schools? Would Orthodox pupils be deprived of formal instruction in their faith? To protest this injustice, Putnik contended that church leaders would disavow the government's policy and that parents would refuse to send their children to latinized schools. Other sectors of the Orthodox community lodged similar complaints. Subsequently, in early 1785, Joseph II removed the ban on the publication of Cyrillic books and rescinded previous measures calling for the removal of Serbo-Slavonic from elementary education and the construction of a common South Slavic literary language.[27]

Abortive linguistic reform was not the only governmental policy that elicited negative reactions from Serbian society. Additional controversies stemmed from alterations of the calendar, burial customs, and the catechism. Economic and political reasons motivated Vienna to reduce drastically the number of Serbian holidays. Including Sundays, the Orthodox church calendar for 1769 had listed 170 non-working days! Russian as well as Serbian saints were commemorated with their own holidays. The first revision of the calendar occurred when the government pressured the Synod of the Orthodox church to abolish fifty-six holidays on 31 December 1769. Vienna justified its action on economic and social grounds, asserting that more workdays would promote productivity and eliminate the vices fostered by idleness.

A political rationale for a further reduction of Orthodox holidays was advanced in the 1771 writings of Vasilije Božičković, a Uniate vicar. Božičković averred that the repeated commemoration of medieval rulers and hierarchs evoked memories of the Serbs' past, thereby nurturing in the Serbs a desire to recapture their former glory; similarly, he felt that the periodic honoring of Russian saints strengthened the feeling of Serbian kinship with the Russians. Debate on this topic within Habsburg administrative and clerical circles continued until early 1775, by which time Orthodox church officials had agreed to annul thirty additional holidays. When the new Serbian calendar appeared in 1776, only one national holiday remained and all Russian saints' days had been eliminated.[28] Thus, another step towards the de-Russification of Serbian cultural life had been taken.

While revisions of the Orthodox calendar were being implemented, imperial authorities sought to effect certain spiritual and social reforms directed towards promoting acculturation. Informing the papacy that it was assisting the Uniate church in its endeavors to Catholicize the Orthodox community, Maria Theresia's administration in 1774 urged the Serbian Orthodox Synod to adopt a catechism used in the empire's Catholic schools. When it abandoned this effort because of synodal hostility, the regime tried to insert Roman Catholic doctrine into a recently written Orthodox catechism. Although this move was also thwarted, reports of Catholic machinations reached the Serbian public and intensified its distrust of the Habsburg government. Animosity surfaced when burial regulations issued in 1775 and 1777 attempted to change the traditional Serbian funeral service. Because of public health concerns, monarchial officials prohibited the Serbs from carrying the deceased in an open casket into the church. To the officials' chagrin, Serbian mourners openly defied the law and practiced their time-honored burial customs.[29]

Tolerance of Austrian attacks upon Serbian cultural traditions reached a breaking point in the autumn of 1777 and the winter of 1778, the catalyst being a governmental attempt to compel the Serbs to obey the state's new burial regulations. Since local church authorities were responsible for supervising the enforcement of this law, the public's ire was directed against them in a wave of unrest which cut across class and regional lines. On three occasions between 19 October and 6 November 1777, angry crowds confronted the metropolitan and the bishops of Novi Sad, Temesvár, and Vršac with a list of charges. The demonstrators condemned the church leaders for acquiescing in the introduction of the Theresian reforms and alleged that the prelates had betrayed the Orthodox faith. The reduction of holidays, the new burial law, the falsified Germano-Serbian catechism, and the distribution of German books among the faithful were seen as parts of a concerted move to convert the Orthodox laity to the Uniate church. When the Vršac protesters refused to disperse and seemingly threatened the bishop's life, a squadron of hussars was summoned to the episcopal residence. The cavalrymen attacked the civilians, killing six and wounding twenty-six. After news of this incident spread throughout Vojvodina, local security forces were placed on the alert.[30]

Though the use of violence perhaps deterred other Serbs from participating in demonstrations, lay members of parish organizations in Buda, Pančevo, and Vukovar threatened to boycott church services and to condemn openly the Orthodox hierarchy if the latter accepted the Theresian reforms without submitting them to public scrutiny. They also informed the empress that their loyalty to the regime was contingent upon a Habsburg guarantee of religious freedom. Convinced that their faith was being jeopardized, the townsmen and frontiersmen pledged their readiness to die for the sake of protecting the Orthodox religion. They expressed their hostility to recent burial, calendar, and catechism changes, as well as their criticism of the government's ban on Russian teachers and books.[31]

Contemporaneous with this mounting opposition to Vienna's treatment of Serbian affairs, there arose the specter of an Austro-Prussian war. Prussia's manpower advantage, the absence of reliable Austrian allies, and the possibility of a defection of Serbian frontiersmen from the empire's forces compelled the regime to adopt a conciliatory attitude towards its Serbian critics. Between 19 February and 23 April 1778, governmental decisions nullified or modified previous actions. Authorities revoked the law prohibiting the Serbs from practicing their traditional burial customs, a Russian catechism replaced the German-Serbian religious primer, and a revised Orthodox calendar appeared. Although the abolished holidays were not restored, the names of saints removed from earlier editions were printed on the new copies.[32]

Another issue that generated discontent and discussion among members of the Serbian community concerned the activities of the Cyrillic printing press. Established in 1770 and housed in Vienna, the German-owned, private publishing firm of Joseph von Kurzböck received from the government exclusive publication rights for all Cyrillic printed materials. An official ban was placed upon the importation of Cyrillic literature from Russia, Poland, Venice, and Wallachia. Censorship regulations for Orthodox books required censors to prevent the publishing of any statement hostile to the Christian religion, monarchial principles, and the ruling monarch. When in 1778 Kurzböck was granted permission to import Russian church and school publications, he was instructed to excise all references, including those in prayers to members of the Romanov dynasty and to substitute the names of Habsburg rulers in their place.[33] During the twenty-two year history of the Kurzböck press, 151 publications were issued for the empire's Orthodox and Uniate populations. Among the items published were church books, school materials, governmental acts, panegyrics honoring Habsburg dynasts, and literary works.[34]

Serbian clerics and teachers were unquestionably thankful for the availability of materials printed in Church Slavonic and Serbo-Slavonic, but despite its contribution to the fields of religious and secular education, the Kurzböck press failed to attract public acclaim. Indeed, the Orthodox church, a leading beneficiary of the press's activities, became a critic of the publishing house. In a 5 February 1778 letter submitted to imperial authorities in Vienna, Metropolitan Vidak complained that Kurzböck's books were too expensive, replete with errors, and unpopular. Recently revised Kurzböck editions of the Orthodox calendar and catechism, Vidak correctly observed, were responsible for the press's unpopularity. Townsmen and frontiersmen from Buda, Pančevo, and Vukovar believed that the Kurzböck publishing efforts represented a thinly disguised attempt to lure the Orthodox faithful into the fold of the Uniate church. Before these public expressions of animosity, an unofficial boycott of Kurzböck's publications had created serious financial problems for the Vienna publisher and, in an attempt to alleviate this situation, the state had purchased the unsold books and distributed them free of charge to its Orthodox subjects. The metropolitan claimed that all of these problems could be eliminated if the press were moved to the church's headquarters in Karlovci and placed under his supervision. Although the government declined to follow Vidak's advice, it approved in 1792 the sale of the press to Stefan Novaković, a former secretary of the metropolitan.[35]

A composite portrayal of Serbian cultural life would be incomplete without mention of French influence upon the Habsburg Serbs. The impact of French culture upon Serbian society was limited in nature and scope. In social terms, only a small minority, comprising *graničari* officers, prosperous merchants, intellectuals, aristocrats, and upper clergy, was exposed to the French language and culture. These members of the Serbian community were exposed to French cultural influence from a variety of sources. Well-to-do Serbian families hired private tutors to teach French to their sons and daughters or sent their young children to Slovak secondary schools where the language was taught. Serbian students attending universities in Vienna, Budapest, Leipzig, Halle, and Göttingen acquired a knowledge of the French language and the French Enlightenment. Although the Austrian government in 1759 announced a prohibition on the importation and distribution of the works of Voltaire, Rousseau, and certain other foreign authors, Serbian frontiersmen returning from the campaigns of the Seven Years' War and writers reentering their homeland illegally transported numerous copies of French books that had been placed on the government index. Politically innocuous French literature, including a few translated novels, was published by the Kurzböck press and also imported into the country. Gradually, Serbian private and public libraries accumulated a large quantity of French material. Metropolitan Stevan Stratimirović, elected to his post in 1790, possessed many examples of French literature in his library, and Bishop Petar Petrović owned almost four hundred French publications.[36]

As the preceding discussion and analysis demonstrate, the cultural and political history of the Habsburg Serbs in the eighteenth century attests to the complexity of the factors contributing to the perpetuation, stimulation, and transformation of cultural identity and national consciousness.

Commencing with the civil rights struggle in the early eighteenth century, continuing throughout the turmoil surrounding the abolition of the military districts at mid-century, and culminating in the Theresian acculturation campaign of the 1770s, merchants, artisans, frontiersmen, bureaucrats, clerics, and lawyers from Hungary, the imperial cities, and the Military Frontier engaged in confrontations with secular and religious authorities. No one occupation or region monopolized the vigilant efforts to preserve Serbian cultural integrity and to prevent a diminution of national privileges. A sense of belonging to a national community whose interests transcended those of the individual or one's village or city was shared by an ever-widening stratum of Serbian society.

Although Hungarian leaders steadfastly refused to recognize the Serbs as a nation with legal rights, Austrian authorities periodically acknowledged the Serbs' special status as a privileged national minority within the empire. Serbian spokesmen based their arguments for the retention, expansion, and codification of their cultural and political rights upon these Austrian declarations. Participation in local government, the proceedings of the national-religious assembly, and petition campaigns stimulated the political consciousness of Serbian activists.

Throughout the period, the external threat to Serbian national rights and cultural integrity was the most important factor in the intensification of national consciousness. By the last decade of the eighteenth century, the Serbs had blunted or negated several Habsburg policies that had attempted a religious, linguistic, and cultural integration of the Orthodox community with that of the dominant Germano-Catholic culture. Entering the era of the French Revolution, the Serbs were neither Germanized nor Illyrianized, nor had they been de-Russified. Whereas Russian influence among the Serbs had diminished, Russian books were legally imported as well as smuggled into the Habsburg Monarchy where some were translated into Serbo-Slavonic and others were read in the original. The cult of Peter the Great persisted (as evidenced in Zaharija Orfelin's idealized biography of the Romanov emperor), and during the second half of the century many Serbian writers lived and wrote in Russia, later returning to Austria.[37] As children of the European Enlightenment and members of the intelligentsia, these literati advocated the development of a more eclectic and less traditional national culture. The eighteenth century had witnessed a heightening of national consciousness among the Habsburg Serbs; they now stood on the threshold of an era of even greater political and cultural changes.

NOTES

1. Roger Viers Paxton, "Nationalism and Revolution: A Re-examination of the Origins of the First Serbian Insurrection 1804-1807," *East European Quarterly,* 6:3 (Sept. 1972), 337-38.

2. Vladimir Stojančević, "Šezdeseta godišnjica naučnog rada i osamdeset i pet godina života akademika Mite Kostića," *Zbornik za istoriju,* No. 4 (Novi Sad, 1971), 15, 19.

3. Wayne S. Vucinich, "The Serbs in Austria-Hungary," *Austrian History Yearbook,* 3:2 (1967), 34. Ivo J. Lederer, "Nationalism and the Yugoslavs," in Peter F. Sugar and Ivo J. Lederer, eds., *Nationalism in Eastern Europe* (Seattle, 1969), pp. 407-8.

4. Nikola Petrović, "O nekim specifičnostima razvitka srpske nacije u Habsburškoj Imperiji," *Jugoslovenski istorijski časopis,* No. 1-2 (Belgrade, 1970), 45-48.

5. Dušan J. Popović, *Srbi u Vojvodini* (Novi Sad, 1963), III, 7. B. Vranešević, "Ekonomski i društveni razvitak," in Edib Hasanagić, ed., *Istorija škola i obrazovanja kod Srba* (Belgrade, 1974), pp. 94-95.

6. Privileges of 6 April 1690, in Jovan Radonić and Mita Kostić, *Srpske privilegije od 1690 do 1792* (Belgrade, 1954), pp. 89-90. Privileges of Leopold I of 21 August 1690, in ibid., pp. 91-92. Privileges of Leopold I of 4 March 1695, in ibid., pp. 92-95.

7. Ibid., pp. 1-5.

8. B. Vranešević, "Položaj srpskog naroda u okviru Habzburške Monarhije," in Hasanagić, *Istorija škola,* p. 92.

9. Jovan Skerlić, *Istorija nove srpske književnosti* (Belgrade, 1967), pp. 29-30. Mita Kostić, *Dositej Obradović u istoriskoj perspektivi XVIII i XIX veka* (Belgrade, 1952), p. 243.

10. Ibid., pp. 243-46.

11. Ibid., pp. 244-51.

12. Jovan Muskatirović to Metropolitan Putnik, 14 February 1790. Slavko Gavrilović and Nikola Petrović, eds., *Temišvarski sabor 1790* (Novi

118 Nation and Ideology

Sad, 1972), pp. 5-6. Slavko Gavrilović, "Srbi u Habsburškoj Monarhiji pred ugarski sabor 1790," *Jugoslovenski istorijski časopis,* No. 4 (Belgrade, 1965), 18, 22-27. Kostić, *Dositej Obradović,* pp. 233-25, 248.

13. Gunther Rothenberg, *The Military Border in Croatia 1740-1881: A Study of an Imperial Institution* (Chicago, 1966), pp. 6-12. Vucinich, "The Serbs in Austria-Hungary," pp. 8-12.

14. Mita Kostić, *Srpska naselja u Rusiji: Nova Srbija i Slavenosrbija* (Belgrade, 1923), pp. 25, 30-34, 40-50, 53-54, 93, 110-11.

15. Ibid., pp. 31, 33-38, 45, 82-84, 92-94, 125-28.

16. Mita Kostić, "Kult Petra Velikog kod Rusa, Srba i Hrvata u XVIII veku," *Istoriski časopis,* 8 (Belgrade, 1959), 88-95. Skerlić, *Istorija nove srpske književnosti,* pp. 49-50.

17. Mita Kostić, *Grof Koler kao kulturnoprosvetni reformator kod Srba u Ugarskoj u XVIII veku* (Belgrade, 1932), pp. 23-24. R. Čurić, "Srpsko-slovenske osnovne škole 1690-1726," in Hasanagić, *Istorija škola,* pp. 100-101. Nikola Gavrilović, *Istorija ćirilskih štamparija u Habzburškoj monarhiji u XVIII veku* (Novi Sad, 1974), pp. 13-16.

18. Skerlić, *Istorija nove srpske književnosti,* pp. 52-54. Kostić, *Grof Koler,* pp. 26-30. Within the metropolitanate's jurisdiction in 1769, there were 211 schools (142 in Hungary and 69 in the Military Frontier) located in 1,651 Serbian-inhabited localities. Thus, approximately one-eighth of all such localities possessed an educational facility. N. Gavrilović, "Škole u Vojnoj granici," in Hasanagić, *Istorija škola,* p. 149.

19. Gavrilović, *Istorija ćirilskih štamparija,* pp. 128, 134-38.

20. Ibid., p. 117. S. Kostić, "Srpske osnovne škole u Banatu," in Hasanagić, *Istorija škola,* pp. 169-70.

21. Mita Kostić, "Pokušaji Bečke vlade oko uvodjenja narodnog jezika i pravopisa u srpske, hrvatske i slovenačke škole krajem 18. veka," *Prilozi za književnost, jezik, istoriju i folklor,* 17:2 (Belgrade, 1937), 255, 259. Kostić, *Grof Koler,* pp. 103-18.

22. C. A. Macartney, *The Habsburg Empire, 1790-1918* (New York, 1969), pp. 99-100, 113-14, 123. Oscar Jaszi, *The Dissolution of the Habsburg Monarchy* (Chicago, 1961), pp. 63-64.

23. Georgije Mihailović, *Srpska bibliografija XVIII veka* (Belgrade, 1964), pp. 101-2, 212. Kostić, "Pokušaja," pp. 255, 259. Kostić, *Grof Koler,* pp. 88-90, 97, 110, 114, 118.

24. Kostić, "Pokušaji," pp. 253-54, 256.

25. Gavrilović, *Istorija ćirilskih štamparija,* pp. 175-76. Kostić, "Pokušaji," pp. 258-59.

26. Milorad Pavić, *Istorija srpske književnosti klasicizma i predromantizma: klasicizam* (Belgrade, 1979), p. 143.

27. Gavrilović, *Istorija ćirilskih štamparija,* pp. 175-80. Kostić, "Pokušaji," p. 260.

28. Kostić, *Grof Koler,* pp. 131-37, 143-50.

29. Ibid., pp. 152-61, 165.

30. Ibid., pp. 166-68.

31. Ibid., pp. 180-82.

32. Ibid., pp. 187-93.

33. Gavrilović, *Istorija ćirilskih štamparija,* pp. 167-68, 171-72, 181.

34. Mihailović, *Srpska bibliografija,* pp. 90-241.

35. Kostić, *Grof Koler,* pp. 181-82, 184-86. Gavrolović, *Istorija ćirilskih štamparija,* pp. 196-97, 200-201.

36. Mita Kostić, *Prve pojave francuske kulture u srpskom društvu* (Sremski Karlovci, 1929), pp. 5-14. Mita Kostić, "Volter kod Srba," *Glas,* 240:5 (Belgrade, 1960), pp. 57-63. Pavić, *Istorija srpske književnosti,* pp. 53-59.

37. Tihomir Ostojić, *Zaharija Orfelin: zivot i rad mu* (Belgrade, 1923), pp. 137-80. Pavić, *Istorija srpske književnosti,* pp. 61-62.

LOYALTY AND LEGALITY:
AUSTRIA AND THE WESTERN BALKANS, 1848-1853*

Kenneth W. Rock
Colorado State University

From the late eighteenth to the early twentieth centuries one of the central issues of international affairs was the manysided struggle in which various states and peoples sought to gain influence and territory in the Balkan peninsula from the retreating Ottoman Empire. While Europe's major powers, particularly Great Britain and Imperial Russia, hoped to achieve political hegemony, the native Christian peoples, primarily the Greeks, Serbs, Romanians, and Bulgarians, struggled to acquire territory for national fatherlands.

The Habsburg Monarchy, with kingdoms and lands bordering the Romanov and Ottoman empires, as well as the Danubian, Serbian, and Montenegrin principalities, was directly involved in and affected by the development of this so-called Eastern Question. Still, ever since the extensive territorial acquisitions ratified by the 1699 Treaty of Karlowitz, Habsburg statesmen had seemed almost indifferent to developments in southeastern Europe. Empress Maria Theresia in 1772 warned of the dangers that would issue from the partitioning of the Ottoman Empire

* The research for this essay was conducted in the Haus- Hof- und Staats-archiv in Vienna, Austria, during 1972-1973 under the auspices of a National Endowment for the Humanities Younger Humanist Fellowship and at the University of Virginia in Charlottesville during a National Endowment for the Humanities 1978 Summer Seminar for College Teachers.

121

and, consonant with this admonition, the long tutelage of Chancellor Prince Clemens von Metternich had directed the Monarchy's attention primarily to Central and Western Europe. The growing national consciousness of the Danubian and Balkan peoples was conceived as an internal problem, only incidentally related to foreign policy.[1]

The Revolutions of 1848 shattered Habsburg complacency and "almost completely inverted the premises on which Austrian policy had been based for two generations."[2] The events of that year and their continuing aftershocks were a powerful stimulus to the further development of national aspirations among the Danubian and Balkan peoples; henceforward nationalism was to be "at every critical juncture the main determinant of Austrian diplomacy."[3]

After November 1848 Minister President and Foreign Minister *Feldmarschall Leutnant* Prince Felix zu Schwarzenberg presided over the "rejuvenation" of the Habsburg Empire, inaugurating an era of energetic liberal-centralism that by 31 December 1851 had metamorphosed into the neo-absolutism associated with Baron Karl von Kübeck and Dr. Alexander Bach. Standing before the Kremsier (Kroměříž) *Reichstag* on 27 November 1848, Schwarzenberg pledged that the equality of all Danubian nationalities (*Volkstämme*) and the "foundation of a new bond that would unite all lands and peoples (*Stämme*) of the Monarchy into one great body politic" were integral to Austria's recovery.[4] The promises, reasserted in the imperial constitution of 4 March 1849, were partial recognition of the transformation in Austrian assumptions wrought by the 1848 revolutions. Schwarzenberg's ensuing eastern policy has received little attention from historians, largely because he devoted most of his energy to the pressing Italian, German, and Hungarian questions.[5] But in southeastern Europe, Vienna confronted a region where rising national consciousness everywhere conflicted with political frontiers, and after 1848 the Habsburg government could not ignore the Balkan princes and peoples from the perspective of either foreign or domestic affairs. An analysis of Schwarzenberg's policy toward the western Balkans —Serbia, Bosnia, and Montenegro—thus illustrates not only the birthpangs of Balkan nationalism but also the determination of Vienna, confronted by internal and external upheaval, to maintain Habsburg influence and authority throughout the *Gesamtmonarchie* and along its southern frontiers.

The Principality of Serbia, its autonomy within the Ottoman Empire guaranteed by Imperial Russia since the 1829 Treaty of Adrianople, lay directly adjacent to the Habsburg Monarchy's Croatian-Slavonian, southern Hungarian, and military frontier districts. In March 1848 these Habsburg regions had exploded as competing constitutional, national, and socioeconomic claims engulfed the region from Zagreb to Sremski Karlovci to Temesvár. From the onset of the "Hungarian disorders" in the spring of 1848 and throughout 1849, the Habsburg consulate general at Belgrade functioned as a pivotal link in Vienna's tenuous communications network of Habsburg agents in southern Hungary, the western Balkans, and eastward to the Danubian Principalities and Constantinople itself.

Lieutenant Colonel Baron Ferdinand von Mayerhofer, *kaisertreu* Austro-German soldier and Habsburg consul general at Belgrade, insisted upon the Monarchy's tutelary position vis-à-vis Serbia. He unflinchingly voiced his opinions concerning the policies the imperial government should adopt toward both Serbia proper and the Monarchy's Croatian and Serbian populations. Mayerhofer's repeated recrossing of the Danube from his post at Belgrade to Habsburg soil at Zemun expressed his recognition that nationalist fervor among the Serbs and Croats by no means ceased at the Habsburg-Ottoman frontier. In early May 1848 a Serbian National Assembly convened at Karlovci to "restore" the Vojvodina (principality) and the Serbian patriarchate as territorial and spiritual expressions of the Serbian nation. The assembly simultaneously divorced the region from Hungary and proclaimed its unity with Croatia; at the same time Serbs from Serbia proper, Bosnia, and Hercegovina made common cause with Habsburg Serbs and Croats. Although Britain's sagacious envoy at Constantinople, Stratford Canning, doubted that anything tangible would issue form this "mountain in labour," the growing animosity toward Lajos Kossuth's Hungary sparked a sense of Slavic unity along the valleys of the Una, Sava, Drava, and Danube. "Each people sees in each a brother, And all acclaim their one Slav mother!" ran a folksong of the time.[6]

Ironically, the Habsburg crown proved to be the immediate beneficiary of this first genuine pan-South Slav nationalist movement. By September 1848, *Feldmarschall Leutnant* Josip Jelačić, the popular *Kaisertreu* officer of the *Grenzer* regiments whom the emperor had installed as

Ban of Croatia, summoned all Croats, Serbs, Slovenes, Bosnians, and Bulgarians in the name of the Austrian emperor *and* Slavic unity to a crusade against Kossuth's Hungary. Further evidence of Habsburg pre-eminence occurred in December 1848, when Emperor Franz Joseph appointed the energetic consul general Meyerhofer as first provisional commander of the Serbian military force sanctioned by Vienna in the newly established Vojvodina.[7]

Faced with this turmoil to the north, the Serbian government of Prince Aleksandar Karadjordjević vacillated over the extent to which it should involve itself on behalf of its conationals. Prince Aleksandar's chief advisor, Interior Minister Ilija Garašanin, sought to exploit the situation to advance the South Slavic mission he had outlined for Serbia in his 1844 *Načertanije* memorandum.[8] In 1848, his agents created links among Slavs in Serbia, Croatia, Slavonia, Bosnia, and Montenegro, while Garašanin personally campaigned for and provided money, weapons, and ammunition for 8,000 Serbian volunteers. Gathered from Serbia proper, Bosnia, Hercegovina, Montenegro, and Bulgaria, and led by Serbian State Councilor Stevan Petrović Knićanin, the volunteers joined the Habsburg colors in the Vojvodina where they fought against the Magyars in 1848 and 1849.[9]

Vienna could appreciate Serbs "voluntarily" assisting the hard-pressed imperial soldiers in southern Hungary, but it would be quite another matter if the Serbian government should intervene officially in the conflict upon Habsburg soil. Habsburg authorities did not want any other ruler to arouse South Slavic popular enthusiasm and thus detract from the emperor's prestige; Serbia's prince should therefore remain benevolently neutral toward the Habsburg cause. Garašanin's efforts were doubly suspect because Mayerhofer had learned of a Belgrade secret society that sought to unite the South Slavs of both the Habsburg and Ottoman empires. As early as 2 March 1848, Mayerhofer had characterized the group as "a democratic pan-Slavic club whose center is the Serbian Council."[10] Austria's consul charged that on the evening of 24 March 1848 the society had posted inflammatory placards in Belgrade calling on all South Slavs "to liberate themselves completely from the Ottoman Empire and to create, since Austria is in agony, a Yugoslav Kingdom under the banner of Prince Aleksandar Karadjordjević, consisting of Serbia, Bosnia, Bulgaria, Croatia, Slavonia, Srem, Dalmatia, and Southern

Hungary."[11] While warfare raged in the Vojvodina, Mayerhofer vigorously added his voice to those of the Russian and Turkish representatives in Belgrade who discouraged official Serbian intervention in this eruption of South Slavic national enthusiasm which would shortly be curtailed by Habsburg authority.

In January 1849 the Schwarzenberg government, hastening to tighten the reins of policy which had slackened since March 1848, commended Mayerhofer's actions on both banks of the Danube and urged him to "continue working assiduously" to maintain Habsburg authority and maximum "loyalty" toward the emperor's government among all Serbs domiciled upon Habsburg, Hungarian, Turkish, and Serbian soil.[12] Although Austrian agents in Belgrade repeatedly noted that elements of the Serbian populace were extremely aroused and that the Turkish frontier authorities sympathized with the Magyar cause, the Russian, Austrian, and Ottoman governments collectively opposed official Serbian intervention north of the Danube. Impressed by such firmness, Aleksandar Karadjordjević, precarious on his Belgrade throne, remained neutral. Pleased with Aleksandar's "good neighborly" attitude, Vienna in March 1849 bestowed on him the great cross of Austria's Leopold Order. Aleksandar's inaction, subsequently rewarded by the Romanovs as well, embarrassed the Serbian ruler and lessened his prestige in the eyes of his more fervently nationalistic subjects.[13]

As the Habsburg military reasserted imperial authority in Hungary during the summer of 1849, Vienna reemphasized its approval of the "legal order in Serbia" but required reciprocal "loyal" behavior. To bolster the tremulous Aleksandar, Austria promised to prevent Serbia's exiled former prince, Miloš Obrenović, from approaching the country's frontiers. At the same time, however, Vienna insisted that the Karadjordjević regime terminate the intrigues of Belgrade's British, French, and Sardinian consuls which could create "unpleasant misunderstandings" between the Habsburg and Serbian states.[14] Such plotting was endemic, Mayerhofer asserted, because the consuls in question were "notorious emissaries" for Polish and Italian propaganda. Furthermore, the Ottoman pashas of Belgrade and Orsova had behaved "disgracefully" toward the Magyar "insurgents."[15] Schwarzenberg instructed Mayerhofer to furnish precise details regarding the Turkish functionaries' Magyarophile sentiments "in order to give his complaints more weight," but later dismissed

the consul general's alarms as Habsburg and Romanov legions overwhelm-
ed Hungary. The Habsburg government markedly commended, however,
the Serbian volunteers led by State Councilor Knićanin.[16]

After the capitulation of the major Hungarian nationalist army at
Világos on 13 August 1849 and the flight of approximately 3,600 Hungarian and 800 Polish refugees across the Turkish border (among them
such luminaries as Governor-President Lajos Kossuth and the Polish
general Jósef Bem), Vienna charged its Balkan agents to be alert for
"important Hungarian refugees." Mayerhofer discounted the presence
of such personages on Serbian territory, for Kossuth's party had crossed
the Danube to the east at Orsova and had been taken by Turkish frontier
authorities to Vidin in northwestern Bulgaria.[17] The status of the Hungarian refugees abruptly became the dominant issue of contention between
the Habsburg Monarchy, the Ottoman Empire, and the powers of Europe.

As Vienna's pursuit of the Hungarian refugees quickened, acrimony
intensified within Belgrade's consular community. The Habsburg-Romanov
suppression of Hungary's bid for liberation had produced a fluid situation
in which passionate recrimination replaced rational policy. Serbs, Turks,
Magyars, and the West European consuls unanimously expressed dislike
for the arrogant Austro-German military officer and Habsburg consul
general. Mayerhofer countered that the British consul, Julian Fonblanque,
and even the Russian consul, Major General Levshin, appeared determined
to "paralyze" Habsburg influence south of the Danube in the bitter aftermath of the Hungarian insurrection. Austrophile Serbs urged Vienna to
establish a newspaper in the Serbian language to influence local opinion
favorably toward the Habsburg Monarchy.[18] In Vienna a once again confident Schwarzenberg could disregard both consular bickering and appeals
to Serbian public opinion because by October 1849, Habsburg and Romanov arms had mastered the Hungarian insurrection. Since the Karadjordjević regime had neither intervened nor embarked upon a South Slavic
nationalist policy antagonistic to Habsburg interests, Vienna professed
satisfaction with the Serbian court's official neutrality and inactivity.
Even if Habsburg policy were not blessed with popular South Slavic
approval, Austria's cause had emerged victorious: its Sava and Danube
frontier remained intact, legality and loyalty prevailed on the empire's
western Balkan borders.

When the Ottoman government declined an Austro-Russian demand to extradite the leading Magyar and Polish refugees (among them Governor-President Lajos Kossuth, Prime Minister Bertalan Szemere, Generals Jósef Bem and Count Henryk Dembinsky), the Russian and Austrian ministers at Constantinople suspended diplomatic relations on 17 September 1849. A major diplomatic crisis rapidly overshadowed the Near East.[19] British and French naval squadrons sailed to Levantine waters to bolster the Porte's resistance to Austro-Russian refugee demands. Even if Russian Ambassador V. P. Titov, Austrian Internuncio Bartholomaeus Count Stürmer, British Ambassador Canning, and Admiral Sir William Parker exceeded their respective governments' explicit instructions, the specter of great-power conflict in the Levant, following months of revolutionary tension, preoccupied Europe's chancelleries from October to December 1849. The preemptory nature of the Habsburg-Romanov demands branded the Russian and Austrian emperors as despotic tyrants in the eyes of the broad public, both in Europe and America, which was fascinated with the plight of the illustrious refugees.[20]

Although Vienna never contemplated resorting to arms over the Hungarian refugees, Schwarzenberg insisted upon Ottoman acknowledgment of Austria's treaty rights and deference to revitalized Habsburg authority throughout southeastern Europe. Behind such legal arguments lay Vienna's antagonism to popular insurrection and nationalist fervor. By the spring of 1850, when rational diplomacy and diplomatic restraint had diffused the Near Eastern crisis, Schwarzenberg directed Austria's Balkan representatives to forestall additional apostacies to Islam and to render "harmless" (in any of the regions of their jurisdiction) any Ottoman-protected refugees from Hungary.[21] With the 1848-49 crises surmounted, a good neighborly stance rather than the utilization of overbearing diplomatic or military force could prove advantageous to the Monarchy's interests south of its borders.

As "rejuvenated" Austria consolidated its authority in the early 1850s, Habsburg policymakers consciously focused more attention upon Balkan peoples and problems. Under Schwarzenberg's guidance the Ballhausplatz sought to augment Habsburg surveillance and political influence in these restless areas. The new Ministry of Commerce, under the dynamic direction of Karl Ludwig Freiherr von Bruck, began to reorganize Austria's

consular system in order to expand Austria's share of Danubian and
Levantine trade. New, better trained, salaried Habsburg consuls general established residence in 1850 in the Serbian and Danubian principalities. Austria's consular network expanded into Bosnia-Hercegovina,
while vice-consulates and consular agencies (*Starostien*) multiplied from
Moldavia to Albania. Although political surveillance and religious patronage initially overshadowed the promotion of commerce, Vienna desired
that Habsburg consuls vigorously champion the civil and legal actions
of Austrian shipping and commercial interests, Austrian citizens abroad,
and Balkan Roman Catholics. Austrian agents insisted that Ottoman, as
well as local Balkan authorities, honor Austria's economic and political
rights guaranteed by the treaties.[22]

In February 1850, Colonel Theodor von Radosavljević, a zealous
Habsburg official of Serbian extraction eager to "sacrifice everything"
to serve the emperor and "my government," replaced Mayerhofer as
Habsburg consul general in Belgrade. His mission was to improve Austria's
position at the Serbian court. Although Ilija Garašanin declined Austria's
Order of the Iron Crown (offered in appreciation for Knićanin's volunteer
force), Radosavljević found Prince Aleksandar cordial.[23] Serbia's prince
faced his own rebel and refugee problem. In May 1850 he confided to
Radosavljević that a conspiracy led by the popular Serbian military leader
Toma Vučić-Perišić and endorsed by Russian consul Levshin sought
to place Mihailo Obrenović, exiled son of the former Prince Miloš, on
the Serbian throne.[24] Schwarzenberg at once reaffirmed Austria's support
of the malleable Aleksandar's efforts to maintain "law and order" and
specifically commended Radosavljević's "good neighborly stance" toward
the Karadjordjević prince. Discounting Aleksandar's fears of an Obrenović
coup as "nothing new," Vienna urged the prince to practice "a strong
neutrality" in Balkan politics, and to act in accord with Austrian, Russian,
and Ottoman advice. Radosavljević should not display the prince's trust
too openly, however, but should warily observe all activities of the British
consul and the Magyarophile Pasha of Belgrade. As evidence of Vienna's
neighborly regard for Prince Aleksandar, Schwarzenberg instructed General Mayerhofer, now military commander in the Vojvodina, and General
Count Johann Coronini, Habsburg commander in the Banat, to patrol
the Austro-Serbian border for suspicious Serbs. For good measure Vienna
promised to maintain former Prince Miloš under strict supervision whenever he traveled across Habsburg territory from his estates in Wallachia.[25]

Suspicious of Garašanin and wary of the rival influence of the British, French, and even Russian consuls, Radosavljević spent the summer of 1850 tactfully ingratiating himself with Prince Aleksandar by capitalizing upon a quarrel between the British consul general and the prince's court. Radosavljević feared that the incident could enable either Britain or Turkey to reassert its influence over Serbia, a possibility Austria's consul sought to prevent.[26] Alarmed at the intensity of Belgrade's current intrigue, Avram Petronijević, Serbia's experienced foreign minister, declared to Radosavljević that if he resigned under British or Russian pressure, Garašanin would assume control of Serbia's foreign as well as domestic policy, whereas Petronijević's presence in Prince Aleksandar's government would retard Garašanin's Austrophobe endeavors. Branding Garašanin a "liberal" who desired to transfer the entire Magyar emigration to Serbia, thereby rekindling insurrection on Austria's southern frontier, Radosavljević advised that Vienna resolutely support Petronijević and Serbia's prince.[27] Not only must Austria counter the schemes of Garašanin, Fonblanque, and Levshin, but also the growing influence of the French consul, Theodore de Goëpp. Radosavljević termed the French consul a "socialist" and confidant of Garašanin who accorded "Hungarian refugees" and "other revolutionary demagogues a protection so manifest one could believe it was motivated by order of his government. To date he has neither offered proof of his devotion to the cause of order nor to conservative principles." Radosavljević begged Vienna to demand that Paris discipline its Belgrade consul or better, "recall him from his post."[28]

Although Schwarzenberg strongly supported the Serbian regime at Constantinople, consular rivalry continued in Belgrade. Fonblanque resumed relations with the Serbian government in September, Radosavljević remained intimate with Prince Aleksandar, and French influence grew within Garašanin's ministry. By 1850 the national struggle at Belgrade appeared transformed from one of submerged peoples against foreign rule to a Machiavellian contest among the European consuls, each of whom sought to mold Serbian institutions and policies to his respective state's purpose. Keen in this role, Radosavljević apprised Vienna that Prince Aleksandar heeded Habsburg counsel and that General Knićanin, now Serbian army commander at Kragujevac, had requested permission to accompany the Austrian army in the anticipated military campaign against Prussia.[29] No sooner had the threat of war in Central Europe been diffused by the Austro-Prussian accord at Olmütz on 29

November, than tension reerupted in the Balkans. In October 1850, the conservative Muslim beys of Bosnia rose against the tepid Tanzimat reform efforts of the Ottoman Empire. Vienna now confronted not simply consular intrigues but a "general insurrection" along its Croatian, Slavonian, and Dalmatian borders.[30]

Eager to localize the revolt, Schwarzenberg turned directly to Constantinople, instructing Chargé d'affaires Eduard von Klezl to impress the Porte with the "urgent necessity" of pacifying its rebellious provinces by instituting "indispensible administrative reforms." Vienna immediately ordered military precautions along its Croatian and Dalmatian frontiers, and urged the Ottoman government to display reciprocal "proof" of its professed "sincere attitude" toward the Habsburg Monarchy by restoring order in Bosnia as rapidly as possible.[31]

The Ottoman Empire did share a community of interest with Austria in reestablishing order in its Balkan Christian provinces. In April 1850 Constantinople recalled from Wallachia its vigorous military commander, Omer Pasha, placed him at the head of an 8,000-man army, and entrusted him to quell Bulgarian Christian peasant unrest around Vidin and Niš. Omer accomplished his mission with clemency and dispatch. By August 1850 the Porte had armed him with a *firman* to implement Tanzimat reforms in Bosnia to ameliorate the conditions of the Muslim-dominated Christian peasantry.[32] Keenly aware that instability in Bosnia endangered not only the Ottoman but also the Habsburg Empire, Schwarzenberg sought detailed intelligence about the number of "Hungarian, Polish, and German renegades" serving in Omer's army who could transform the Bosnian insurrection into a Danubian conflagration. Vienna desired cordial relations with Ottoman authorities, but reasons of state demanded that Austrian agents vigilantly observe all refugees from Hungary and "represent our treaty rights with firmness and energy."[33]

Dr. Atanasije Atanacković, Austria's new consul in Bosnia, kept watch on the explosive situation for months. He informed Vienna that South Slavic propaganda was in circulation, that the Hungarian refugees in Omer's army (primarily Magyar and Polish officers but also common soldiers) were unpaid and desired to return to their homes, that Bosnia's populace objected to Ottoman conscription and military requisitioning, and that "very slow progress" was being made toward meaningful administrative reform. By 18 October the Muslim populace of Mostar, Hercegovina, revolted precisely against the Ottoman recruitment and the Tanzimat civil regulations.[34] Omer Pasha, accompanied by four Turkish battalions, the Albanian militia, and a Magyar refugee battalion, at once left Sarajevo to quell the revolt.

The viciousness of the fighting prompted Atanacković to comment repeatedly on the oppression of the Christian and Muslim peasantry and the sorry state of the provinces under their current rulers. Aware of the Habsburg consul's patronizing, skeptical, and acquisitive attitude, and with his troubles compounded since the Posavina region of northeastern Bosnia adjacent to Austria's frontier had also risen in revolt, Omer Pasha complained bitterly to Atanacković that Austria did not sympathize with Ottoman authorities.[35] Omer was not far from the mark, for Atanacković reported that Sarajevo would have risen even if the rural insurgents had been more successful and if the Turks had not kept twelve of the town's leading citizens hostage each night in their camp. Reform, Austria's consul asserted, was impossible since the local Ottoman dignitaries intimidated the populace while the soldiery terrorized and plundered the "poor *rayah.*"[36]

Although sporadic fighting continued throughout the winter and spring of 1850-51 in mountainous Hercegovina, in Bosnia's forested northwestern Krajina, and in the Sava valley, Omer Pasha ruthlessly crushed the insurrection. He executed rebel beys, dispatched them in chains to Constantinople, liquidated their fortunes, and disarmed both bitter Muslims and resigned Christians. A new Ottoman civil governor, Hayreddin Pasha, and his staff arrived to assist Turkey's resolute general since, as Atanacković reported, "there are few loyal Turks for the Porte to count on or to serve Constantinople here."[37]

"Pacification" promoted Habsburg visibility in Bosnia. On Epiphany, 6 January 1851, Atanacković presided proudly at flag-raising ceremonies over the consulate general in Sarajevo, henceforth the seat of Bosnia's government. Since it was a Roman Catholic as well as an Eastern Orthodox holiday, the large crowd demonstrated Christian "jubilation" at Austria's presence. According to the Austrian consul, only the "fanatical Muslims" among the Ottoman officials in attendance were displeased. In the days of the janissaries, Atanacković reflected, neither the French nor Austrian consulates at Travnik had dared display flags or coats of arms.[38] Atanacković continued to badger Omer Pasha about the number and activities of Hungarian refugees in his army, but voiced Austria's approval when Omer razed the mountaintop fortresses recently held by the insurgents in the Krajina districts along the Croatian frontier. At Omer's request, Austria proved its good neighborliness by refusing the suspect vizier of Hercegovina permission to purchase munitions in Dubrovnik.[39]

While Austria profited by Antanacković's promoting the religious, commercial, and educational interests of Bosnia's Christians, Vienna insisted upon the sanctity of its own frontiers. Schwarzenberg countenanced neither Ottoman military nor commercial activity that would bisect Habsburg Dalmatia via Klek and Sutorina, two enclaves of Hercegovina that penetrated to the Adriatic coast, a possibility that Omer Pasha had raised in his conversations with Atanacković. Austria *"can in no case sanction"* the transit of Ottoman troops across Habsburg territory. "Our border officials are authorized to grant the Turks all possible good neighborly considerations, but are strongly charged to do their utmost to avoid any incursion against the territory this side of the frontier."[40] Doubly sensitive of the border issue given the upheavals of 1849, Schwarzenberg remained adamant about Habsburg sovereignty, determined to consolidate the *Gesamtmonarchie's* domains, and insisted upon exerting Austrian influence along the Monarchy's borders. Schwarzenberg's stance was arrogant although characteristically Austrian. It was also essentially defensive in nature. Nevertheless, he expected immediate deference from the Turks.

When pressed by Atanacković, Omer Pasha admitted that approximately ninety Hungarian refugees served with his army, demurred on the matter of transit rights through Dalmatia, but raised a further issue that was destined to provoke more serious Austro-Turkish conflict. "Commercial interests" in Klek and Sutorina were "only secondary," Omer said. "What is most important to us is the shortest and most comfortable way to procure additional troops into Hercegovina, for I must tell you frankly that we can no longer tolerate the status quo in Montenegro. This country must come once more under the suzerainty of the Porte."[41] Omer's resolve to move against the Prince-Bishopric of Montenegro augured ill for Habsburg-Ottoman cordiality. Just as Vienna urged Prince

Aleksandar to rule firmly and practice a strong neutrality in Serbia, so she sanctioned and indeed encouraged Ottoman pacification of Bosnia and Hercegovina in accord with a good neighborly and counterrevolutionary imperial policy. But an Ottoman military campaign to conquer Christian Montenegro was another matter. Vienna could not remain disinterested in an issue that transcended border politics and civil disobedience and constituted a direct challenge to Austria's domination of the Adriatic.

If diverging Austrian and Ottoman ambitions pointed to a clash in the western Balkans, Habsburg policy concentrated on strengthening its position in Serbia where intrigue and insecurity flourished throughout 1851. In February and August Consul General Radosavljević noted Prince Aleksandar's customary uneasiness when Prince Miloš and Mihailo Obrenović traversed Hungary enroute from their Wallachian estates. The Habsburg gendarmerie escorted the princely travelers on both occasions, to serve Vienna's own interests and to cement cordial relations with the Karadjordjević court.[42] Austria's consul assiduously sought to bolster Serbian Foreign Minister Petronijević, despite the latter's failing health, and to lessen the influence of Interior Minister Garašnin and his deputy, "the pan-Slavist and Austrophobe" Jovan Marinović.[43] Given the prince's timidity and the "intrigues" of Belgrade's Austrophobe faction, Radosavljević prediced that Serbia was "marching toward catastrophe" that would terminate with Prince Aleksandar's fall.[44]

On 27 June 1851, excited by the anniversary of Kosovo and agitated over Omer Pasha's proceedings in Bosnia, a youthful Interior Ministry official and adherent of Garašanin's "national-liberty party" spoke heatedly against the Turks at a Belgrade student dinner urging his "brothers" to "take the path of the battlefield of Kosovo." "Stormy applause" greeted the speech, according to Austria's consul, whereupon a Serbian soldier murdered a local Turk. "At last," Radosavljević exalted, the Ottoman pasha in Belgrade's Kalemegdan fortress expressed concern about the dangers of a Garašanin ministry, the perils of which Austria's consul had ceaselessly foretold.[45] Apprehensive of Vienna's reaction to Belgrade's alleged call for an anti-Ottoman insurrection, Prince Aleksandar nervously wrote to Schwarzenberg that Radosavljević had "misrepresented" the Kosovo sppech and emphasized that the persons involved were "not" in the government. Aleksandar insisted that Serbia desired only to be Austria's good neighbor and, in a counterstroke, criticized Radosavljević for appearing too cordial with Belgrade's Serbophobe and Magyarophile Sardinian consul.[46] Schwarzenberg lent no credence to Aleksandar's alarms but charged Radosavljević to do his utmost to separate the prince from the "vile influence" of Garašanin, to capitalize upon every provocation of the "party inimical to us," and to practice correct diplomatic conduct to avoid criticism.[47]

Intrigue in Belgrade paled before the intensifying crisis in Bosnia. Throughout 1851 Atanacković reported Muslim resistance and Christian resignation to Tanzimat measures. The Turks would never grant the Christians true "equality" (Gleichberechtigung), the Habsburg consul asserted.[48] He labeled Travnik a "great penitentiary," where quarreling officials, multiple arrests, and prisoners abounded. Omer Pasha was "proceeding, as they call it," to create a flotilla, modeled after Austria's, on the Sava River. Omer's actions impeded Austrian subjects from obtaining lumber and potash from Bosnia as prescribed by the treaties. When Atanacković protested Turkish curtailment of Austrian subjects' prerogatives, Omer Pasha replied with "anti-Austrian sentiments," and alleged that every Austrian subject who crossed the border only spread pan-Slavic propaganda.[49]

Behind Atanacković's complaints and Omer's allegations lay the fact that the Ottoman general's vigorous methods in Bosnia curtailed Austrian commercial exploitation of Bosnia's economy. Tanzimat regulations had imposed 12 percent duties on Bosnian exports, but Austrian merchants paid only 3 percent. A profitable trade in the legal exploitation of Bosnia's timber, potash, and iron had grown up alongside an even more profitable smuggling operation. But Omer's repression of brigandage, his construction of a road from Travnik to Sarajevo, his attempt to launch steamers on the Sava's Bosnian tributaries, his closure of the Croatian and Dalmatian frontiers, and his establishment of border patrols—all combined to make smuggling difficult. Furthermore, his proclamation that Bosnia's forests were the property of the Ottoman crown cancelled Austria's profitable timber concessions. His plans for a transit route from the Adriatic coast at Klek or Sutorina to the interior contained both economic and political implications. Disorder along the Habsburg-Ottoman border had traditionally offered multiple opportunities for Austrian interference in Bosnia. Omer's vigorous pacification thus annoyed both legitimate and illegitimate commercial interests in Croatia and Dalmatia, as well as Habsburg army officers who periodically harbored throughts of strategic border rectification. In addition, although Omer stopped trade on the border, his measures drove refugees across it. This situation agitated Slavic Christians on both sides and created precisely the instability that Vienna was determined to prevent.[50]

In truth, Austria did not desire the significant improvement of the Porte's Bosnian position. Schwarzenberg would "not allow.... in either a political or military sense" the establishment of a Turkish military camp in the upper Krajina at Novi, "that is five hundred steps from our borders."[51] When pressed by Atanacković, Omer Pasha spoke nonchalantly about a commercial rather than a military route to Bosnia's interior via Klek, and discounted the significance of the Novi camp, although he stressed that it would facilitate Ottoman suppression of disturbances along the Habsburg frontier. To demonstrate his independence from Habsburg pressures, Omer prohibited the importation of Austrian newspapers into Bosnia and deliberately accelerated Tanzimat reforms.[52] Skeptical of Turkish assurances and reforms, Atanacković reported mounting Christian discontent and publicly displayed greater solicitude for Bosnia's Christians.

Throughout the fall and winter of 1851-52 relations between Vienna's consul and the Porte's general deteriorated. By mid-September Omer Pasha forbade Bosnian Christians to visit the premises of the Habsburg consulate general. The two officials exchanged insults daily. Furious at Austria's persistent Turcophobia, Omer quipped that Kossuth was not worth so much trouble.[53] By October the Turkish commander denounced Bosnia's Christian populace as "mutinous" because of the "malevolent Austrian influence" exercised by the consul general and the Eastern Orthodox and Roman Catholic clergy.[54] By late November Atanacković reported that the Ottoman general's anti-Christian sentiments had become public knowledge. Sarajevo's Christians were anxious as well as angry since the Turks were mishandling Christians in Mostar and Sarajevo and were proving unnecessarily deliberate in permitting construction of a Catholic church in Sarajevo. When queried, Omer responded that Constantinople, not he, was the cause of the delay.[55]

Believing the local controversy to be fruitless and seeking to prepare a brief against the difficult pasha, Schwarzenberg instructed Atanacković to apprise Vienna "with your most exact knowledge" of all "political incidents." He also authorized the Ministry of Commerce and the Internuntiatur to negotiate directly with the Porte concerning the disputed coastal facilities, customs duties, border closings, and religious disharmony.[56] Schwarzenberg's direct diplomacy prompted the Porte to lecture its Bosnian commander that Constantinople had "grounds to doubt the mutinous sentiments he had described," since the Christian populace of Bosnia and Hercegovina "nowhere" had joined the rebellious Muslims in the "recent disturbances," but had willingly subjected itself to Ottoman authority. "As for the alleged Austrian infringements, they would—in case they were true—have no results," Constantinople stated, "because the Christian populace of Bosnia does not sympathize with Austria."[57] Behind this frank exchange lay the desire of the two imperial governments to maintain correct relations despite the antagonisms of local officials.

Persecution and unrest among the Christians of Bosnia, even if "exaggerated," as Radosavljević believed from his Belgrade perspective, catalyzed the Serbian government to support its Slavic brothers. Revealing that he too was sensitive to nationalist emotions, Prince Aleksandar dispatched an emissary to Bosnia despite Austria's insistence on neutrality. Serbia's prince "could not understand why the Christian powers, especially the neighboring and powerful Austrian government, should not intervene enegetically to protect Bosnia's religious cobelievers. He and his people were prepared to rush to assist the oppressed"[58] Both Radosavljević and Charles Alison (the Oriental Secretary of the British Embassy in Constantinople dispatched by Stratford Canning to mediate yet another breach between Fonblanque and the Serbian government) sought to prevent Aleksandar from taking any hastily considered action. The upsurge of Slavic national feeling from Cetinje to Belgrade nonetheless prompted Schwarzenberg to send Radosavljević detailed instructions emphasizing Vienna's support for Constantinople's measures to redress the grievances of Bosnian Christians. Radosavljević should marshal this evidence to placate and bolster Austria's good neighbor, Prince Aleksandar, then confronted by mounting pressure to intervene from an aroused public and council.[59] Austria desired to improve the status of Bosnia's Christians but only via the Ottoman government's program of legal reform. Vienna would tolerate neither South Slavic popular action nor official Serbian intervention, which could spawn a chain of events along its borders and conceivably obliterate existing frontiers.

By 1852 Bosnia-Hercegovina had become the major arena on Austria's Balkan periphery where official efforts at post-revolutionary "pacification" were not proceeding smoothly and where Austrian agents were encountering difficulty influencing the local authorities toward a "firm" policy that Vienna could construe as "loyal." When Atanacković, no longer on speaking terms with Omer Pasha, sent his interpreter to present a letter "in the Illyrian language" from the Bosnian clergyman Pavao Tvertković (then a refugee in Zagreb), Omer responded that he would arrest the cleric if he appeared on Bosnian soil, despite the fact that Tvertković professed his loyalty to the Ottoman sultan and admonished his flock to do likewise. Refusing to answer the letter, Omer stated that he would demand the priest's removal from the Austro-Turkish border provinces. The Habsburg spokesman replied that by so doing the Pasha would lose Austria's trust, whereupon Omer "insolently" remarked that he did not need it![60]

Nothing could hide the fact that the Bosnian imbroglio was embittering already tense Austro-Turkish relations. In March 1852 Vienna presented its grievances directly to Ottoman Foreign Minister Ali Pasha in Constantinople. Schwarzenberg charged Klezl to make the strongest remonstrances and ultimately to threaten that Austria would mobilize its border forces if Omer's "hostile" (*feindselige*) actions against Habsburg prerogatives, Bosnia's Christians, and Consul Akanacković did not cease.[61] The borders must be reopened and the "barbarous" treatment of Roman Catholic and Eastern Orthodox Christians must terminate, since the disruption of trade and inhumane treatment greatly excited the inhabitants of Austria's border provinces who shared "the same religion and nationality" (*gleichen Religion und Nationalität*).[62] Ali Pasha listened patiently to Austrian reproaches, ventured to suggest that Vienna's charges were exaggerated, but nonetheless promised to dispatch "categorical orders" charging Omer to mend his ways, to remove the border cordon, to respect Austrian subjects and their interests, and to implement a general disarmament of Muslims as well as Christians.[63] Austria demanded "deeds" (*Thatsachen*), however, not promises. If the Porte sincerely desired reform, Ottoman officials must cease persecuting the Christian populace since such "barbarous" treatment was keeping Bosnia in a state of "permanent agitation" (*permanenten Aufruhr*)[64] that Vienna found intolerable.

As 1852 progressed, Austro-Turkish dissonance and South Slavic agitation expanded from Bosnia to encompass Montenegro, as the miniscule state's fundamental relationship with the Ottoman Empire become entangled with the other simmering west Balkan issues. After the death of Prince-Bishop Petar II Petrović Njegoš on 31 October 1851, his nephew and heir, Danilo II Petrović, desired to marry. With Russia's agreement and Austria's tacit consent, Danilo in 1852 secularized the principality and proceeded to conduct his activities as if Montenegro were independent from the Porte, a condition long established in fact but not by law.[65] Constantinople ordered Omer Pasha to crush such insubordination. By 29 December 1851 Sarajevo's Turkish garrison had departed *en masse* for Montenegro, against which the Porte had declared a "holy war." Prince Danilo immediately appealed for Austrian and Russian assistance.[66]

Count Karl Ferdinand von Buol-Schauenstein, who became Habsburg foreign minister after Schwarzenberg's sudden death on 5 April 1852, followed Viennese precedent by resorting to direct diplomacy at Constantinople. Demanding political stability along its South Slavic borders, Vienna would sanction neither insurrection nor a war that could spread from Montenegro to Bosnia, provoke Serbian volunteer and official intervention, and electrify South Slavs north and south of Habsburg frontiers. At the same time, Vienna could countenance neither an assertive Ottoman nor Russian presence in the western Balkans. Since thousands of refugees were streaming from Bosnia and Montenegro onto Dalmatian and Croatian soil, Vienna had to terminate the conflict before additional complications developed. In sum, having consolidated the Monarchy's dominions and revived Habsburg prestige throughout Central Europe only to encounter frustration in the western Balkans, Austria's rulers, exasperated by Turkish tergiversations, demanded a favorable political settlement resting upon "deeds" (*Thatsachen*) not "doubts" (*Zweifel*) or "difficulties" (*Schwierigkeiten*).[67]

To reinforce Chargé Klezl's representations at the Porte, Vienna dispatched a special envoy, *Feldmarschall Leutnant* Count Christian Franz von Leiningen, to the Ottoman capital in late January 1853. Leiningen's mission, seconded by a formidable military display along the Croatian, Dalmatian, and Bosnian borders, plus the tsar's indication that Russia would support Austria by arms if necessary, forestalled the Ottoman drive on Montenegro.[68] When Vienna firmly asserted its prerogatives and

restricted its demands to Montenegro, Bosnia, and the Adriatic coast—
and threatened neither Ottoman sovereignty nor the sultan's honor as it
had in the Hungarian refugee demands of 1849—Constantinople yielded.
Leiningen achieved agreement with the Porte by 12 February. The Montenegrin campaign was halted, and peace was made between the Porte and
Montenegro by 3 March 1853. Austria gained, fleetingly, another client
Balkan Slavic prince, for Constantinople recognized Danilo's claim to
sovereignty as stipulated by Austria's envoy. Omer Pasha was dismissed.
Thus Austria was rid of an obstreperous Ottoman general whose personal
vigor had frustrated Habsburg privileges and designs in Bosnia and who
had associated too flagrantly with Hungarian refugees. The termination
of hostilities eased the Bosnian Christian refugee exodus and forestalled
wider South Slavic intervention. Austria had achieved a striking diplomatic victory.

The fundamental issues underlying Austria's relationship to the Balkans
and its peoples had not, however, been resolved. A policy of legality,
loyalty, and firmness to prevent national insurrection called for imposing
strength, public support, and skilled political action that could simultaneously inspire popular allegiance and respect. Habsburg policy in the
western Balkan borderlands lacked these prerequisites for long-term success. Its strength was instead in short-term palliatives: consular intrigue
against suspected opponents, the ingratiation of princes sympathetic to
Habsburg arguments that they wield centralized authority over restless
peoples, and periodic intimidation to compel deference to the "good
neighbor" north of the Danube. In an age of national awakening, Habsburg policies under Schwarzenberg's guidance remained dynastic and
counterrevolutionary. It was an approach that assumed that all national
affinities were immaterial since all nationalities were "equal" in rejuvenated Austria.

Always imperial, often preemptory, occasionally arrogant, Austria's
Balkan policy under Schwarzenberg's direction was thus essentially defensive. Preoccupied with Hungarian refugees, suspicious of British subversion, and opposed to nationalist agitation, his policy was more reactive
than active. Schwarzenberg's emphasis upon the legality of Balkan partic-
ularism nonetheless masked Vienna's determination to prevent South
Slavic nationalism from acquiring a regional, and therefore more dangerous,
political character, for Austrian authorities were clearly conscious that
Balkan political borders nowhere corresponded with ethnic frontiers.

Despite occasional bluster, Schwarzenberg's Eastern policy rested upon neither territorial acquisitiveness nor militant bellicosity, but rather upon favorable treaty prerogatives, legality, firm governmental authority, and Habsburg imperial prestige. Both diplomat and soldier, Schwarzenberg recognized that legal arguments in the Metternichian tradition, boldly employed in the tense post-1848 atmosphere, could enhance Austria's case wherever force proved insufficient. From the Danube to Dalmatia, Habsburg agents labored to manipulate conservative officials and to exploit radical nationalism to secure the emperor's cause. Vienna resolutely supported its consuls since it believed that Austria's prestige could be enhanced by a more visible Habsburg presence in the Balkans, by the promotion of commerce, and by fostering religious patronage.

In the end, however, Habsburg influence proved strongest where Vienna could deploy military force in addition to diplomatic persuasion. As Maria Theresia had long ago pointed out, Austria's position was essentially more favorable in the western Balkans, in Serbia and the Adriatic littoral, than to the east in Wallachia and Moldavia. Under Schwarzenberg's direction, Austria had by 1852 achieved gratifying, if limited, success in Prince Aleksandar's Serbia, but had encountered resistance in Bosnia from a surprisingly resolute Omer Pasha. By 1853, Buol had won a striking diplomatic victory over Montenegro which reverberated favorably throughout Bosnia. Despite consular acrimony and nationalist agitation, Habsburg imperial frontiers remained intact. No changes had occurred to benefit either South Slav nationalism or the Ottoman Turks. Still, Austria's achievement in the western Balkans remained negative rather than positive. In the wider Near Eastern realm Habsburg statesmen could reflect that Imperial Russia and Great Britain cast longer shadows over the Ottoman Balkans than did the Habsburg double eagle. Before many months had elapsed, Austria's perennial quest for stability and the maintenance of its Balkan prerogatives would be challenged and eclipsed by issues of general European conflict as the continuing Eastern Question erupted into the Crimean War.

NOTES

1. See M. S. Anderson, *The Eastern Question 1774-1923* (London, 1966), and the classic J. A. R. Marriott, *The Eastern Question, An Historical Study in European Diplomacy* (4th ed., Oxford, 1940). On Austrian Eastern policy see Adolf Beer, *Die orientalische Politik Österreich seit 1774* (Prague, 1883), and Maria Theresia, "Second Memorandum" (February, 1772), in C. A. Macartney, ed., *The Habsburg and Hohenzollern Dynasties in the Seventeenth and Eighteenth Centuries* (New York, 1970), pp. 190-91.

2. Enno E. Kraehe, "Foreign Policy and the Nationality Problem in the Habsburg Monarchy, 1800-1867," *Austrian History Yearbook, 3* (1967), Pt. 3, 22.

3. Ibid., p. 23.

4. Rudolf Kiszling, *Fürst Felix zu Schwarzenberg, der Erzieher Kaiser Franz Josephs* (Graz, 1952), pp. 52-53.

5. On Schwarzenberg's foreign policies see especially Eduard Heller, *Fürst Felix zu Schwarzenberg, Mitteleuropas Vorkämpfer* (Vienna, 1933); Erzsébet Andics, *Das Bündnis Habsburg-Romanow: Vorgeschichte der zaristischen Intervention in Ungarn im Jahre 1848* (Budapest, 1963); and Waltraud Heindl, *Graf Buol-Schauenstein in St. Petersburg and London, 1848-1852* (Vienna, 1970). On Schwarzenberg's Eastern policy see Heinrich Friedjung, *Der Krimkrieg und die österreichische Politik* (Stuttgart, 1907); Bernhard Unckel, *österreich und der Krimkrieg: Studien zur Politik der Donaumonarchie in den Jahren 1854-1856* (Lübeck, 1969); and Johanna Haugwitz, "Die Beziehungen Österreichs zur Turkei unter Felix Schwarzenberg," (Unpublished doctoral dissertation, University of Vienna, 1970).

6. Canning's comment is in E. F. Malcolm-Smith, *The Life of Stratford Canning* (London, 1933), p. 215. The folksong is cited by Harold Temperley, *England and the Near East: The Crimea* (London, 1936), p. 212. For discussions of the expressions of hitherto fragmented Croatian and Serbian national aspirations during the upheavals of 1848-49, see in addition to the standard German and English volumes on nationalism and the 1848 revolutionary movements: Vladimir Dedijer, Ivan Božić, Sima Ćirković, and Milorad Ekmečić, *History of Yugoslavia* (New York, 1974), pp. 310-21; Dimitrije Djordjević, *Revolutions nationales des peuples*

balkaniques 1804-1914 (Belgrade, 1965), pp. 77-85; R. W. Seton-Watson, *Racial Problems in Hungary* (London, 1908), pp. 90-116; and Gunther E. Rothenburg, *The Military Border in Croatia, 1740-1881: A Study of an Imperial Institution* (Chicago, 1966), pp. 57-85; as well as the articles devoted to the South Slavs in the *Austrian History Yearbook,* 3 (1967), Pt. 2.

7.   Josef Karl Mayr, ed., *Das Tagebuch des Polizeiministers Kempen von 1848 bis 1859* (Vienna, 1931), p. 102. See also Dedijer, *History of Yugoslavia,* p. 315.

8.   Michael Boro Petrovich, *A History of Modern Serbia 1804-1918* (New York, 1976), I, 244. Garašanin's *Načertanije* declared that "the unification of Serbia with all the other subject peoples must be considered a fundamental law of the state." Cited by L. S. Stavrianos, *The Balkans since 1453* (New York, 1961), p. 255. The *Načertanije* suggested that a Bosnian insurrection against Ottoman rule would provoke Serbian intervention and pressure the Habsburg *Grenzer* regiments to furnish armed support to their fellow Slavs. This could convert a local revolt into a liberation movement of all South Slavs against both Ottoman and Austrian rule. Such ideas incubated for twenty years after 1844 and became politically significant in the 1860s.

9.   Petrovich, *Modern Serbia,* I, 244-45. See also Djordjević, "The Serbs as an Integrating and Disintegrating Factor," *Austrian History Yearbook,* 3 (1967), Pt. 2, 62; and Dedijer, *History of Yugoslavia,* p. 318.

10.   Petrovich, *Modern Serbia,* I, 244. See also Fran Zwitter, *Les problems nationaux dans la Monarchie des Habsbourg* [*sic*] (Belgrade, 1960), p. 69.

11.   Cited in Stavrianos, *The Balkans since 1453,* p. 255. See also Petrovich, *Modern Serbia,* I, 244-45; Dedijer, *History of Yugoslavia,* pp. 319-20; and Djordjević, *Revolutions nationales,* pp. 79-80.

12.   Schwarzenberg to Mayerhofer in Pansova, Olmütz, 7 January 1849, Haus- Hof- und Staatsarchiv, Vienna, Politisches Archiv (henceforth PA) XXXVIII (Konsulate) 90.

13.   Schwarzenberg to Prince Aleksandar, Vienna, 23 March, 1849, PA XXXVIII 90.

14.   Schwarzenberg to Jaurisch, Vienna, 1 June 1849, PA XXXVIII 90.

15.   Mayerhofer to Schwarzenberg, Zemun. 18 July 1849, PA XXXVIII 90.

16. Schwarzenberg to Mayerhofer, Vienna, 31 July, 1849; Mayerhofer to Schwarzenberg, Zemun, 25 July and 2 Sept., 1849, PA XXXVIII 90.

17. Rescript, Vienna, 1 Sept. 1849; Mayerhofer to Schwarzenberg, Zemun. 5 Sept. 1849, PA XXXVIII 90.

18. Correspondence from Belgrade, 21 Oct. and 2 Dec. 1849, PA XXXVIII 90.

19. Austria's demand for extradition rested upon the 1739 Treaty of Belgrade and the Russians upon the 1774 Treaty of Küçük Kaynarca.

20. See especially Edmond Bapst, *Les Origines de la guerre de Crimée* (Paris, 1912), pp. 91-118; Vernon John Puryear, *England, Russia, and the Straits Question 1844-1856* (Berkeley, 1931), pp. 153-80, and R. W. Seton-Watson, *Britain 1789-1914: A Survey of Foreign Policy* (Cambridge, 1955), pp. 259-89.

21. Schwarzenberg to Timoni, Vienna, 4 Mar. 1850, PA XXXVIII 93. Restraint by Britain and Russia diffused the international crisis. Nicholas I (angered by Austria's execution of Magyar officers in Hungary, impressed by the British public's vociferous support of Turkey, and pleased by Palmerston's apology that the British fleet had transgressed the 1841 Straits Convention) yielded to an appeal from the sultan, dropped his demand to extradite the major Polish refugees, and reestablished Russo-Turkish relations on 31 December 1849. Although some 3,000 Hungarian common soldiers accepted a Habsburg amnesty, Austria and Turkey did not reach agreement about the major political refugees until 5 April 1850, when Vienna acquiesced to Constantinople's interning the Hungarian leaders remote from Habsburg frontiers in the Anatolian city of Kütahya. See Istvan Deak, *The Lawful Revolution: Louis Kossuth and the Hungarians 1848-1849* (New York, 1979), pp. 340-42.

22. Karl Krabicka, "Das österreichische Konsularwesen zwischen 1848 und 1859," (Unpublished doctoral dissertation, University of Vienna, 1953).

23. Radosavljević to Schwarzenberg, Belgrade, 11 Feb. 1850, PA XXXVIII 93 (in documents the Habsburg consul general's name appears as "Radossavlievié"). Garašanin had viewed Knićanin's volunteer army as part of Serbia's mission to aid its fellow Slavs and posited the eventual dissolution of the Habsburg Empire. Embarrassed by the proffered Habsburg decoration, Garašanin refused and remarked that he could never recall having done anything to deserve the honor. Petrovich, *Modern Serbia,* I, 246.

24. Radosavljević to Schwarzenberg, Belgrade, 12, 13, 18, and 30 May 1850, PA XXXVIII 93. The unlettered, charismatic warrior, Vučić-Perišić, was among the "defenders of the Serbian constitution" of 1838 who deposed both Miloš and Mihailo Obrenović and in 1842 called Aleksandar Karadjordjević to power. He broke with Aleksandar in 1844 (over military issues) and with the other "constitutionalists" (Garašanin and Petronijević, who strove for a state administration guided by an educated bureaucratic elite) and became leader of the Russian party opposed to both Garašanin's Council and the Karadjordjević camarilla. A superb demagogue and vehement Austrophobe, he reembraced the Obrenović cause to gain a wider popular following and intrigued with the Russian consul as a means to power. See Petrovich, *Modern Serbia,* I, 223-24, 237-38, 247.

25. Schwarzenberg to Radosavljević, Vienna, 24 May 1850, PA XXXVIII 93. An additional reason for Austria favoring the pliant Aleksandar was the fact that the Obrenovićes from their Wallachian exile and in two spectacular appearances at Zagreb and Novi Sad in 1848, had openly supported the Habsburg Serbs against the Magyars while Aleksandar Karadjordjević, in accord with Vienna's wishes, had remained neutral.

26. Radosavljević to Schwarzenberg, Belgrade, 14, 16, 19, 24 June and 4 and 18 July 1850, PA XXXVIII 93. When the Belgrade police administered corporal punishment to one of Fonblanque's servants, the British consul general officially protested, demanded compensation, and referred the incident to the British ambassador at Constantinople and the Pasha of Belgrade.

27. Radosavljević to Schwarzenberg, Belgrade, 9 August 1850, PA XXXVIII 93.

28. Radosavljević to Schwarzenberg, Belgrade, 17 August 1850, PA XXXVIII 93. Garašanin and the Serbian Council, in the early 1850s often at odds with Prince Aleksandar and the court camarilla, were supported by the French consul who, in accord with Parisian Polish émigrés, encouraged France to lessen Russian influence in the Balkans. Garašanin opposed all undue foreign influence, thus winning the approval of Serbian students and intellectuals, but also the enmity of the Russian and Austrian consuls. Petrovich, *Modern Serbia,* I, 247.

29. Radosavljević to Schwarzenberg, Belgrade, 19 November 1850, PA XXXVIII 93.

30. Radosavljević to Schwarzenberg, Belgrade, 26 October 1850, PA XXXVIII 93. Temperley asserted that the ramifications of 1848 in Bosnia

were unique. "Elsewhere the people revolted against kings or nobles. In Bosnia Mohammedan nobles revolted against the Sultan to prevent him from improving the lot of the peasants." Temperley, *The Crimea,* p. 214.

31.   Schwarzenberg to Klezl, Vienna, 5 Nov. 1850, PA XXXVIII 94.

32.   Omer Pasha, born Mihajlo Latas, a Habsburg Croat from Lika, had converted to Islam after fleeing to Bosnia to escape punishment while a military cadet. Stern, resolute, and cunning, he became one of the most able military commanders in the Ottoman Empire.

33.   Schwarzenberg to Atanacković, Vienna, 24 Sept. 1850, PA XXX-VIII 94.

34.   Atanacković to Schwarzenberg, Travnik, 31 Aug., and Sarajevo, 26 Sept., 18 and 24 Oct. 1850, PA XXXVIII 94.

35.   Atanacković to Schwarzenberg, Sarajevo, 24 and 29 Oct., and 7 Nov. 1850, PA XXXVIII 94.

36.   Atanacković to Schwarzenberg, Sarajevo, 7 and 28 Nov. 1850, PA XXXVIII 94. Atanacković's solicitude for Bosnia's Christians and skepticism of Ottoman reform reflected Habsburg economic as well as political and religious interests. Austrian merchants engaged in a profitable trade in Bosnian timber and iron by paying customs duties some 9 percent less than those the Tanzimat imposed on native merchants. The only way Bosnian merchants could circumvent the Tanzimat's 12 percent import and export duties was by illicit trade across the Austrian border. Such smuggling was a highly profitable means for Austrian commercial penetration of Bosnia, a charge Atanacković was instructed to advance. See Temperley, *The Crimea,* pp. 212-13.

37.   Atanacković to Schwarzenberg, Sarajevo, 2 Jan. 1851, PA XXXV-III 95.

38.   Atanacković to Schwarzenberg, Sarajevo, 9 Jan. 1851, PA XXXV-III 95.

39.   Schwarzenberg to Atanacković, Vienna, 4 Feb. 1851, No. 1, PA XXXVIII 95.

40.   Schwarzenberg to Atanacković, Vienna, 4 Feb. 1851, No. 2, PA XXXVIII 95. Italics in the original.

41.   Atanacković to Schwarzenberg, Sarajevo, 20 Feb. 1851, PA XXX-VIII 95.

42.   Schwarzenberg to Radosavljević, Vienna, 25 Feb. and 24 Aug. 1851, PA XXXVIII 95.

43.   Radosavljević to Schwarzenberg, Belgrade, 15 Mar. 1851, PA XXXVIII 95. Cordiality was so intense among Austria, Russia, and Serbia in the early 1850s that Petronijević journeyed to Constantinople to allay Turkish fears. He died in the Ottoman capital on 22 April 1852, whereupon Garašanin became foreign minister. Wary of both Romanov and Habsburg domination, Garašanin's Francophile sympathies antagonized both imperial courts. At Russia's demand, and to Austria's delight, Garašanin was dismissed in March 1853 as head of the Serbian ministry. Petrovich, *Modern Serbia,* I, 247-48.

44.   Radosavljević to Schwarzenberg, Belgrade, 27 April 1851, PA XXXVIII 95.

45.   Radosavljević to Schwarzenberg, Belgrade, 14 July 1851, PA XXXVIII 95.

46.   Aleksandar to Schwarzenberg, Belgrade, 14 July 1851, transmitted in Radosavljević to Schwarzenberg, Belgrade, 16 July 1851, PA XXXVIII 95.

47.   Schwarzenberg to Radosavljević, Vienna, 2 Sept. 1851, PA XXXVIII 95.

48.   Atanacković to Schwarzenberg, Travnik, 3 April 1851, PA XXXVIII 95.

49.   Atanacković to Schwarzenberg, Sarajevo, 5 and 19 June 1851, PA XXXVIII 95.

50.   See Temperley, *The Crimea,* pp. 219-20, and Unckel, *Österreich und der Krimkrieg,* pp. 58-59.

51.   Schwarzenberg to Atanacković and FML Count Grünne, Vienna, 17 July 1851, PA XXXVIII 95.

52.   Atanacković to Schwarzenberg, Sarajevo, 7 and 21 Aug. 1851, PA XXXVIII 95.

53.   Atanacković to Schwarzenberg, Sarajevo, 4, 11, and 18 Sept. 1851, PA XXXVIII 95. The Bosnian acrimony occurred simultaneously with West European exhilaration over Kossuth's release, for on 1 September 1851, Kossuth, his wife, and 55 aides ended their interment at Kütahya. Despite Austrian protests, Kossuth began a triumphal tour of Western Europe and America which further blackened Austria's reputation as a tyrannical suppressor of popular liberties. See Klezl to Schwarzenberg, Büjükdere, 3 and 13 Sept. 1851, PA XII (Turkey) 44, and John H. Komlos, *Louis Kossuth in America, 1851-1852* (Buffalo, N.Y., 1973), pp. 49-72.

54. Atanacković to Schwarzenberg, Sarajevo, 2 and 16 Oct. 1851, PA XXXVIII 95. After 1849 religion was well as refugees became integral to Austria's Balkan policy, for both Vienna and Paris claimed to protect Roman Catholics in the Ottoman Empire. Austria established funds to educate Catholic clergy and to construct Catholic churches from Moldavia to Montenegro. It doubled its annual grants to Bosnian and Albanian bishops who were requested to conduct services on 18 August, Franz Joseph's birthday. In March 1851 Vienna considered sponsoring an Orthodox patriarchate on Habsburg soil, analogous to the patriarchate in Eastern Orthodoxy, to influence Serbian and Romanian Christians. After the October 1851 death of Montenegro's prince-bishop, Vienna sought to subordinate the Montenegrin church to the Dalmatian diocese of Zadar and to educate Montenegrin priests as it hoped to educate Bosnia's clergy. Religion too could be utilized to inspire devotion and loyalty to the neighboring Christian power. See Schwarzenberg to Klezl, Vienna, 21 Jan. and 11 Mar. 1851, PA XII 44.

55. Atanacković to Schwarzenberg, Sarajevo, 2 and 27 Nov. and 11 Dec. 1851, PA XXXVIII 95.

56. Schwarzenberg to Atanacković, Vienna, 11 Oct. 1851, PA XXXVIII 95.

57. Atanocković to Schwarzenberg, Sarajevo, 6 Nov. 1851, PA XXXVIII 95.

58. Radosavljević to Schwarzenberg, Belgrade, 7 Mar. 1852, PA XXXVIII 96.

59. Schwarzenberg to Radosavljević, Vienna, 16 Mar. 1852, PA XXXVIII 96.

60. Atanacković to Schwarzenberg, Sarajevo, 22 Jan. 1852, PA XXXVIII 97.

61. Schwarzenberg to Klezl, Vienna, 24 Feb. 1852, PA XII 44.

62. Klezl to Schwarzenberg, Constantinople, 7 April 1852, PA XII 45.

63. Klezl to Schwarzenberg, Constantinople, 6, 10, and 13 Mar. 1852, PA XII 45; Schwarzenberg to Klezl, Vienna, 23 Mar. 1852, PA XII 44.

64. Schwarzenberg to Klezl, Vienna, 3 Feb. and 16 Mar. 1852; Buol to Klezl, Vienna, 13 April and 7 June 1852, PA XII 44.

65. On Austrian policy toward Montenegro see Schwarzenberg to Klezl, Vienna, 6 Jan. and 2 Mar. 1852, PA XII 44; Klezl to Schwarzenberg, Constantinople, 13 Mar. 1852, PA XII 45; and Buol to Klezl, Vienna, 2 Aug. 1852, PA XII 44. See also Milovan Djilas, *Njegoš. Poet Prince Bishop* (New York, 1966), pp. 166-68, 446-47, 453-58.

66. Atanacković to Buol, Sarajevo, 30 Dec. 1852, PA XXXVIII 97.

67. Schwarzenberg to Klezl, Vienna, 3 Feb. and 16 Mar. 1852; Buol to Klezl, Vienna, 13 April, 5 July, and 27 Dec. 1852, PA XII 42.

68. On the Leiningen mission see Beer, *Die orientalische Politik Österreichs,* pp. 433-37; Mayr, *Kempens Tagebuch,* pp. 270, 274-77, 281; Paul W. Schroeder, *Austria, Great Britain and the Crimean War* (Ithaca, 1972), pp. 25-27; and Unckel, *Österreich und der Krimkrieg,* pp. 57-80.

MINISTRATION AND DESECRATION:
THE PLACE OF DUBROVNIK IN MODERN CROAT NATIONAL IDEOLOGY AND POLITICAL CULTURE

Ivo Banac
Yale University

The singular importance of the tiny Republic of Dubrovnik (Ragusa) in the history of Croat culture is well known and has provoked numerous studies. The course of Dubrovnik's crepuscular decline after the loss of state independence in 1808 is much less familiar. Recalling Lytton Strachey's hunch that the history of the Victorian age will never be written because we know too much about it, we might fairly say that, for students of Dubrovnik, the nineteenth- and twentieth-century history of this astonishing polity will never be written because we do not wish to know too much about it. It need not appear paradoxical that whereas we have practical understanding of Dubrovnik's splendid fifteenth and sixteenth centuries and are well acquainted with its troubled seventeenth century, our knowledge of the city's most recent past is almost negligible. Historians are simply more attracted to the periods of economic and cultural prestige. In the nineteenth and twentieth centuries Dubrovnik was anything but a leader. Quite the contrary; during that long period the clocks stopped and the city became little more than an elegant if tarnished symbol which was alternately admired and reviled. This study is an effort to reconstruct the ideas and qualities that a city of chiseled stones and generations of eminences came to represent in the course of modern Croat integrations.

The Republic of Dubrovnik ceased to be a political protagonist in the aftermath of Napoleonic occupation. European powers chose not to resurrect it at the Congress of Vienna and turned it over to Austria, which then relegated the city to the backwaters of Dalmatia, one of the Monarchy's most wretched provinces. Though Dubrovnik's fortunes had been built on its role as intermediary in the Balkan and Levantine trade, as early as the eighteenth century the importance of the city as a trade center was declining, partly because native Christian merchants exploited the disarray of central authority in Ottoman Bosnia and Serbia to squeeze the Ragusans out of Balkan commerce and also because products from the hinterland were no longer competitive. As a result, Dubrovnik's still impressive merchant fleet increasingly bypassed the native shores, carrying on the growing foreign trade between Mediterranean and Atlantic ports. Habsburg policies, especially the efforts to attract Ottoman trade toward the Monarchy's central Danubian provinces, made Dubrovnik's decline all the more evident and acute.

The Ragusan elite, fiercely proud of the role that its small republic had played in the history of Slavic letters, was especially discouraged by the decline of learning and the steady penetration of Italian national consciousness at the hands of educators and civil servants imported from Habsburg Lombardy and Venetia. The higher the level of education in the inferior Ragusan schools, the greater was the predominance of Italian. During the first thirty years of Habsburg rule more than five hundred books, including scholarly and literary works of a high level, were published in the Italian language throughout Dalmatia. During the same period only sixty-seven works, mainly prayer books and diocesan circulars, were published in Croatian.[1] Petar Frano Martecchini's 1826 edition of the works of Ivan Gundulić (1589-1638), Dubrovnik's greatest Baroque poet, was the sole exception to this dreary literary record. Small wonder that the mood of the portion of the nobility that maintained republican traditions deteriorated from one of impotent rage, to sullen silence, and passive resignation. These same attitudes also shaped the disposition of a formerly affluent merchant bourgeoisie, which mourned the passing of the republic only a shade less ardently than the nobility.

By the middle of the nineteenth century the Ragusans increasingly thought of themselves as sentinels at the tomb of their city. Ivan Stojanović (1829-1900), a priest, amateur historian, and moralist, divided his history of nineteenth-century Dubrovnik into three epochs: "first, the fall and death of Dubrovnik; second, the state of that moral body after death; third, the present age [the turn of the twentieth century], when it has completely decomposed and the stink commences."[2] Indeed, the achievements of Dubrovnik's nineteenth- and twentieth-century notables cannot be compared with those of the previous generation. With the exception of Ivo Vojnović (1857-1929) in drama, Vlaho Bukavoc (1855-1922) and Celestin Medović (1857-1920)—and to a lesser extent the trio of Ivo Dulčić, Antun Masle, and Djuro Pulitika, all active after 1945—in painting, and Frano Supilo (1870-1917) in politics, the Ragusans have played relatively insignificant roles in Croat national cultural and political life during the last two centuries. And it is characteristic that, except for the activist Supilo, all these notables were in one way or another preoccupied with Dubrovnik's golden past.

The veneration of old Dubrovnik was not, however, simply a local phenomenon. It was in a very decided way one of the cornerstones and great affections of the Croat Revival. By the mid-eighteenth century the question of a Croat linguistic standard had on the whole been solved in favor of Latin script and štokavian dialect, spoken by most Croats. Though the exact scriptory and orthographic norms for all the Croat lands were not fully settled until the time of the Illyrian movement of the 1830s and 1840s, it was clear that the čakavian and kajkavian dialects, spoken by the Croats of the northeastern Adriatic littoral and northwestern Croatia, respectively, had no prospects of directing the course of Croat linguistic standardization. The emerging Croatian standard was to be based on the štokavian idioms of central Dalmatia, western Hercegovina, and Slavonia, which received their literary expression in the poetry of Antun Kanižlić (1700-1777), Andrija Kačić Miošić (1704-60), and Matija Antun Relković (1732-98).[3]

These writers, however, were themselves to a great degree dependent on the štokavian literary tradition of Dubrovnik. During the Baroque period especially, the influence of Ragusan poetry reached its apex in the works of Gundulić, Junije (Džono) Palmotić (1606-57), and Ignjat Djurdjević (1675-1737), who were, each in his own way, poets of ecstatic Catholic reform, Slavic cultural and religious unity, and Ragusan patriotism. Their writings were transmitted to the libraries and tiny reading public throughout Slavonia, Bosnia-Hercegovina, and Dalmatia largely through the intermediacy of Franciscan friars, who alone ministered to the religious needs of Catholics under Ottoman rule. As a result, Baroque Ragusan models exerted their thematic, stylistic, and linguistic influence far beyond Dubrovnik's borders. Kanižlić, for example, credited Djurdjević with the impulse to pursue the cultivation of "Illyrian language." In due course, Ragusan literary influence was also felt in kajkavian Croatia.

Under ordinary circumstances, the growing importance of štokavian in Croat linguistic standardization would have created grave problems for the established kajkavian literature. Centered on Zagreb, which despite its location was increasingly the political hub of the Croat lands, kajkavian writers created a literary tradition of their own, which was dialectal only from the point of view of subsequent Croat integrations. Their idiom was a sophisticated linguistic medium with its share of impressive dictionaries and skillful poetical, religious, historical, and dramatic works. Nevertheless, the political urgency, engendered first by Habsburg centralism and then by the growth of expansive Magyar national sentiment, worked against kajkavian self-centeredness. External pressures could be resisted only if northwestern Croatia encouraged and undertook to lead Croat—and indeed South Slavic—national integrations. Since this could be accomplished only on the štokavian basis, through the maintenance of a process of linguistic standardization already in effect among the Croats of Slavonia, Bosnia-Hercegovina, most of Dalmatia, and Lika, the intellectual elite of northwestern Croatia increasingly contemplated the abandonment of its effective kajkavian standard in favor of štokavian.

The prestige of Ragusan literature helped to remove the lingering doubts about the acceptance of štokavian. By the turn of the eighteenth century, in the twilight of Ragusan independence, Dubrovnik's Baroque classics were the rage of Zagreb. Gundulić, Palmotić, and Djurdjević were read, recited, and imitated. Franjo Fancev calls this great vogue a peculiar "Dubrovnik-štokavian orientation."[4] Indeed, the highest praise that one could bestow on a poet was to compare him to the Ragusans, *"quorum merita,"* in the words of Adam Alojzije Baričević, *"in rempublicam litterariam celebratissima sunt."*[5] Moreover, the writers from Zagreb and Dubrovnik were increasingly corresponding and establishing personal ties.

All these tendencies were extended and deepened during the Illyrian phase of the Croat revival. The circle of Ljudevit Gaj (1808-72), the dominant figure of the Illyrian movement, was a product of a Raguseophile upbringing. Its principals had been raised with the image of golden Dubrovnik, the distant and once free homeland of the Slavonic muses, whose past belied the cultural poverty of their race. In the words of the ode to Dubrovnik by Petar Preradović (1818-72):

Jer nam prošast nejasnog je raza,
Jednolična pustara velika:
U njoj nigdje sačuvanih staza
Našem svietu, nigdje spomenika,
Ti jedini—zelena oaza—
U pustoši toj si naša dika,
Ter na tebi jedinom počine
Trudni putnik, koji onud gine.[6]

Because our past is of uncertain rank,
A vast, monotonous wasteland
In which there are no well-marked paths,
No monument to our folk and kind,
You alone—as a green oasis—
Our only pride in this desert;
You alone can give a haven
To weary pilgrims who limp along.

Dubrovnik's geographical remoteness only inflamed the devotion. A pilgrimage to the city became a great fashion. Preradović regretted that he visited it only twice and Ivan Trnski, an early hadji, who was so taken with Dubrovnik that he rhapsodized even over the crude folk songs (*ojkanje*) that kept him awake at night.[7] Nor could he restrain his joy at seeing the house of the "immortal Gundulić," in the city where Gundulićes still lived. Gundulić personified the idealized vision of "Illyrian Athens," and his reputation accurately measured Dubrovnik's standing in Croat cultural and political life.

The legend of Gundulić was a key element in the ideology of the Illyrian movement. And since his stature bestowed unquestionable dignity upon "Illyrian" language, his opus dominated the Ragusan orientation of the Illyrian awakeners. The best visual expression of this theme is certainly the grand curtain of the Croat National Theater, which Bukovac painted in 1895. This famous work, now as much a patriotic cliché as any number of Géricaults and Groses, depicts Gundulić receiving the homage of the Illyrian leaders. The bewigged poet, clad in the crimson tunic of a republican councillor and attended by a muse, sits enthroned in a flag-decorated neoclassical temple, surrounded by satyrs, nymphs, and peasants tossing flowers. Gaj approaches him bearing a golden laurel wreath, followed by a reverent procession of all the Illyrian greats, major and minor: Antun Mihanović (1796-1861), the author of the Croat national anthem, who hoped to publish a Zagreb edition of Gundulić's works as early as 1818; Janko Drašković (1770-1856), the senior Illyrian statesman; poets Ivan Mažuranić (1814-90) and Preradović; the historian Ivan Kukuljević-Sakcinski (1816-89), and numerous others. In the background, partly hidden by the Doric capitals of the temple, lie the misty Dubrovnik harbor and Zagreb, united symbolically as the Croat north and south were seen to be united in a new center that would carry on the ancient artistic and political glories of the Republic of Dubrovnik.

Bukovac's vision was perhaps not so heady as the baroque exaggeration implies. Even those critics who question the pervasiveness of Gundulić's impact—Mihovil Kombol, for example—admit that though his influence was not as lasting as that of Shakespeare and Cervantes on the romanticist writers, it was similar in kind and, within the limits of Croatian literature, significant and fruitful.[8] Other scholars claim a great deal more. Ivo Frangeš, for example, has underlined the parallels between Gundulić's pastoral play *Dubravka* (written in 1627), with its running apotheosis of Dubrovnik's liberty, and the literature of the Illyrian movement: "The whole literature of [Croat] Illyrians does nothing but sing Gundulić's [theme], which afforded them a rapturous vision of a better, freer life."[9] And even if one does not know to what extent Antun Mihanović worshiped Gundulić, Frangeš's dramatic counterposing of a stanza that appears in both *Dubravka* and *Osman,* Gundulić's great unfinished heroic epic that he started in the 1620s, to a section from Mihanović's *Horvatska domovina* (Croat Homeland, 1835) illustrates the links between the two:

Skladni puci, mirna sela,	*Vedro nebo, vedro čelo,*
travna polja, doba ugodna,	*Blaga persa, blage noći,*
rojne pčele, stada cijela,	*Toplo lěto, toplo dělo,*
žitne njive, dubja plodna.	*Bistre vode, bistre oči:*
Tranquil folk, peaceful hamlets,	*Vele gore, veli ljudi,*
Grassy meadows, pleasant times,	*Rujna lica, rujna vina,*
Swarming bees, wholesome flocks,	*Silni gromi, silni udi;–*
Fertile fields, teeming groves.	*To je nasa domovina!*
(Gundulić)	

Bright skies, bright faces,
Tender hearts, tender nights,
Warm summers, warm deeds,
Clear waters, clear eyes!

Bold mountains, bold men,
Tender faces, deep red wine,
Mighty thunder, mighty limbs—
That is our fatherland!

(Mihanović)

Since the 1940s Gundulić's reputation as the star of pre-Revivalist Croat literature has been overshadowed by that of Marin Držić. Držić (1510-67), the great Ragusan comic dramatist, was almost unknown to the Illyrian generation. The Illyrians were attracted by Gundulić's solemnity, his love of bucolic settings, and his cult of Ragusan liberty, which they understood in the most literal sense. Most of all, they saw in Gundulić a great native genius who did not hesitate to use—and in that way enrich—the unjustly slighted "Illyrian" language, and they unabashedly compared his work with the greatest classics of the Western world. "Rejoice, oh glorious Illyria," wrote Dimitrije Demeter (1811-72) at the bicentennial of Gundulić's death in 1838, "for you can be proud of your Gundulić no less than Greece of its Homer and Italy of Dante."[10]

The bicentennial of 1838 was the occasion for the most lavish homage that the Illyrians paid to any poet. They erected a catafalque in the Jesuit Church of Saint Catherine in Zagreb's Old Town, mounted it with Gundulić's mementos, and encircled it with a hundred candles.[11] Pavao Stoós (1806-62) read a long eulogy in which he lauded Gundulić as the "greatest spirit of our lands," and, in a slight departure from historical fact, delighted in noting that Ferdinand II, the Grand Duke of Tuscany, learned the "Illyrian" language in order that he might read Gundulić.[12]

The highest honor paid to Gundulić was, however, the determination of the Illyrians to canonize his opus. The historical epopee *Osman*, Gundulić's greatest work, was not published in his lifetime and indeed not until Martecchini's edition of 1826. Many reasons have been suggested to try and explain how it was that this work, so enormously successful, it seems, in copies circulated by hand, was never brought out in a printed version. The usual explanation, improbable but still widely held, is that it was suppressed by Ragusan authorities because of its anti-Ottoman bias. An ever greater mystery is what happened to the fourteenth and fifteenth out of twenty cantos. A number of Croat poets, including some natives of Dubrovnik, have tried their hand at filling the gap—most successfully Ivan Mažuranić, the best poet of the Illyrian movement. He completed the two cantos in 1844, two years before the publication of his classic *Smrt Smail-age Čengijića* (The Death of Smail-aga Čengijić), which was written in the manner of folk epic poetry. Gundulić and folk epic indeed represented the two poles of Illyrian inspiration, blending the Croat literary tradition with the rugged authenticity of folk expression. It was a considerable accomplishment for Mažuranić to master both the štokavian dialect of Gundulić's Dubrovnik and the Dinaric folk poetry since he was himself a native of Vinodol, a čakavian dialect area on the northern Croatian littoral.

Mažuranić's supplement to Gundulić's *Osman* was commissioned by Matica Ilirska, the cultural foundation that Drašković and Gaj had founded in 1842. Gundulić's great poem was the first publication of this exceptionally meritorious society—better known under the name it took in 1874, Matica Hrvatska.[13] The men of Matica, all of them prominent Illyrian leaders, approached their undertaking with much seriousness. Ivo Frangeš has demonstrated the depth of their feeling that the publication of a completed *Osman* discharged an outstanding obligation to the foremost work of older Croat literature.[14] Only the most respected artists were entrusted with work relating to the Gundulić canon—such as the musical scores for the *Dubravka* (done by Ivan Zajc in the 1880s and more recently but in the same high tradition by Jakov Gotovac). In the context of the Revival, the scandal of Ivica Kunčević's 1973 adaptation of *Dubravka* would have been impossible, as would, for different reasons, his all too contemporary attitude that "when anybody so persistently and repetitiously makes references to liberty, as Gundulić does in his *Dubravka,* then such a practice becomes suspect."[15]

The respect for Gundulić was indeed almost excessive. In the course of fifteen years his assorted verses were used no less than eighty-three times in the changing motto in the masthead of *Danica* (Morning Star), Gaj's weekly literary supplement. But though the cult of Gundulić overshadowed that of the other Ragusans, notably Palmotić and Djurdjević, it did not extinguish it, because the Illyrians worshiped everything

Ragusan, not just the major poets, nor the poets alone. The familiarity of Illyrian leaders (most of them from northwestern Croatia) with the writings of bygone Dubrovnik authors was quite impressive. The historians Ludovik Crijević Tubero, Frano Lukarević Burina, and Mavro Orbin were quoted by Gaj, Kukuljević, and Ivan Frano Jukić. Gaj based his belief that the ancient Illyrians were Slavs at least in part on his reading of Orbin and used the works of more recent Ragusan lexicographers Joakim Stulli (1729-1817) and Frano Marija Appendini (1768-1837) to substantiate some of his linguistic arguments. Kukuljević, Vjekoslav Babukić, Šime Ljubić, and Ivan Rukavina Ljubički did the same. And though one finds no references to Ragusan artists and architects in Illyrian journals, Gaj was provoked by an irritated mathematician, who resented *Danica's* slighting of the natural sciences, to express his admiration for Rudje Bošković (1717-87), an outstanding eighteenth-century physicist, who is nowadays regarded as old Dubrovnik's greatest intellect.[16]

The ministration at the altar of Dubrovnik's gilded past also had its immediate practical side. The Illyrian awakeners wished to unite all the Croats (and South Slavs) behind the common, though artificial, Illyrian appellation. Though they recognized the differences between the Croats, Serbs, and Slovenes, and indeed hoped to maintain a separate Croat official nationality (the only legitimist, and therefore effective, weapon against Magyar nationalism), they nevertheless fostered a common Illyrian culture based on a common language and orthography. To accomplish this aim Gaj advanced a new Latin scriptory system, based on Czech diacritical marks, and a štokavian idiom enriched by the elements of čakavian and kajkavian. In short, the philological school of Zagreb, founded by Gaj and Babukić, completed, perfected, and codified the practical results of centuries-old Croat linguistic standardization outside kajkavian Croatia and introduced this linguistic medium to the kajkavian northwest. But despite his high hopes and best efforts, Gaj failed to attract the Serbs and Slovenes to his Illyrian supranationhood and common culture. The Serbs and Slovenes went their separate ways, underlining the strict Croat significance of the Illyrian experiment. As a result, the first modern Croat national integration was unwittingly accomplished under the Illyrian name.

The course of linguistic standardization was not always straightforward, but at every turn the choices maintained the normative character of the

Ragusan literary tradition. In 1836, when Gaj abandoned kajkavian and introduced the štokavian dialect into his newspapers, he justified his decision in part by the "priceless literary treasury of forty and more classical writers from the *Illyrian Parnassus–Dubrovnik* . . . and by other important literary accomplishments, which by inherent right we again assumed as our ancient heritage."[17] Štokavian, however, is divided into three basic subdialects (ijekavian, ikavian, ekavian), depending on the reflexes of Church Slavonic ѣ (e.g., *mlijeko, mliko, mleko* = milk). The choice of subdivision adopted by the Illyrians was certainly one of the movement's most extensive determinations. Had they gone by numbers, territory, and recent literary accomplishments (Kačić and Relković), Gaj and his associates would have chosen ikavian. Instead, they opted for ijekavian, the idiom of Dubrovnik's great literary tradition and a subdialect that was otherwise, with the exception of early eighteenth-century Bosnian Franciscan authors, hardly present in Croat letters.

It has been argued that the choice of ijekavian represented another attempt at linguistic unity with the Serbs. As early as 1818, Vuk Stefanović Karadžić (1787-1864) chose the ijekavian speech of eastern Hercegovina as the basis for his Serbian linguistic reform. Pavle Ivić has suggested that the predominance of ijekavian among the Orthodox or Serb population of Croatia paradoxically made this subdialect all the more attractive to the Illyrians. Had they chosen ikavian, an exclusively Croat idiom, they presumably would have risked a nationality-based linguistic division.[18] These interpretations cannot be discounted, but among the arguments in favor of ijekavian, its Ragusan connection was certainly primary.

This fact was certainly stressed by the partisans of integral ikavian, represented by a circle of awakeners associated with *Zora dalmatinska* (Dalmatian Dawn), a journal started in Zadar in 1844. Ante Kuzmanić (1807-79), the leading figure of this group, was opposed to the abandonment of ikavian, even in deference to Dubrovnik's ijekavian tradition. He dated the adoption of ijekavian from 1841, the year when Gaj and Mažuranić made their pilgrimage to Dubrovnik: as he says, "Their hearts danced after Dubrovnik."[19] Long before this, while Gaj was but a child, Šime Starčević (1784-1859), an old grammarian, Catholic priest, and Kuzmanić's principal associate, had taken a firm stand against ijekavian on account of its supposed foreign impurities. In his *Nova ricsoslovica iliricska* (New Illyrian Grammar, Trieste, 1812) Starčević argued that the

"Illyrian" language was not "glued to a small patch of land" and that the emulation of Ragusan models would inevitably transform Croatian into an "Italian monkey."[20] He believed that Italian borrowings made the Ragusan idiom too foreign and that the ijekavian reflex of ѣ derived from the Church Slavonic used by the Orthodox church.

In some ways, Kuzmanić and Starčević were closer to Karadžić than to the school of Zagreb. Like the Serbian reformer, they also sanctified the popular idiom, in this case štokavian ikavian, and as a result objected to any tampering with Croat linguistic practice. They refused to accept the Ragusan tradition, however distinguished, as the only yardstick in linguistic standardization. Nor could they accept Gaj's simple premise, expressed in an editorial comment on a contested orthographic question, that "in our opinion, the names of Ranjina, Zlatarić, Gundulić, Palmotić, and [Djurdjević] alone, among the majority of other most esteemed Ragusans, outweigh [the usage] of all other authors ten times over."[21] They did not regard Croatian as being above all the language of Croat literary tradition. Though part of their objection to ijekavian was that it was a concession to the Serbs, some of their arguments against it were remarkably similar to those of Karadžić's Croat followers. For example, Andrija Torkvat Brlić contended that the epic poetry of Gundulić and Palmotić was inferior because it was based on foreign models and should be rejected in favor of native folk poetry: "We have our heroic [epic] meter which is much more beautiful than the one which the Ragusans followed in this business."[22] These were also the sentiments of Kuzmanić and Starčević, though for slightly different reasons.

Dubrovnik the symbol was not of course completely above criticism even by the Illyrian awakeners. But their criticism was very selective and had the purpose of refining the ideal and making it more worthy of its unique place in Illyrian ideology, as well as pointing the way to modern-day Ragusans. Gaj, for example, regretted that the eighteenth-century Ragusans so often "sacrificed to the muses in Latin, instead of in their own popular idiom."[23] Kukuljević thought it a great loss that Bošković wrote nothing in his mother tongue (though that was not entirely true).[24] And Preradović unjustly blamed the "black seed of Loyola" for the rise of foreign influences in modern Dubrovnik and predicted its spiritual renaissance only "when Giorgi, Gondola, and others again become Djurdjevićes and Gundulićes."[25]

Such criticisms could not have been very palatable to Ragusans who were convinced that in Dalmatia and indeed throughout the South Slavic lands Dubrovnik alone was awake "when many others did not even know the meaning of the word,"[26] but these chastisements were allayed by the lasting determination of the Illyrians to maintain "that fairyland palace, which the Ragusans built with the stones from Helicon."[27]

The edifice in question was the linguistic standard that the Illyrian movement hoped to extend to all the South Slavs. By 1849, following the return of absolutism and harsh Germanization, it was evident to the Illyrian leaders that their "Illyrian dialect" was only the Croat choice. Had an integral Croat national ideology prevailed in their ranks, the Illyrians would have recognized this achievement as their preeminent contribution. Instead, the very accomplishment seemed to dampen their self-confidence. To be sure, the Illyrian mainstream, best represented after 1860 by Bishop Josip Juraj Strossmayer (1815-1905) and Franjo Rački (1828-94), continued to uphold South Slavic reciprocity in politics. And in the questions of literary standard, Illyrian tradition was faithfully expressed by Adolfo Veber Tkalčević (1825-89) and his generation of the Zagreb philological school, which maintained an altered štokavian idiom, enriched by elements of other Croat dialects and built on the foundations of Croat literary monuments, notably the heritage of Dubrovnik.

Nevertheless, some former Illyrians, such as Ante Starčević (1823-96) and his followers, thought that after 1849 the time had come to assert one's own interests in plain Croat colors. Starčević believed that the Illyrian preoccupation with South Slavic unity weakened the Croat struggle against absolutism. Instead of trying to win favor with the Serbs and Slovenes on the basis of a supranational Illyrian category, he wanted to incorporate them within Croat political nationhood. When he went so far as to consider them "genetically"(= ethnically) Croat, the circle of his integralist reasoning was complete. Starčević's ideology dominated the thinking of his Party of (Croat State) Right, formed in the 1860s. This ideology was a reaction to the failures of Illyrianism among the Serbs and Slovenes and a protest against the diminution of Croatia's constitutional prerogatives under the successive Habsburg regimes. After the unfavorable Croat-Hungarian agreement, the Nagodba of 1867, which in effect made Croatia-Slavonia the ward of Hungary and ended all chance of unification with Austrian Dalmatia, Starčević's party captured the allegiance of radical urban youth. Every significant Croat politician of the turn-of-the-century period, including Dubrovnik's Supilo, passed through Starčević's school.

Some Croat intellectuals, among them an influential group of linguists who were followers of Vuk Karadžić, saw the decline of Illyrianism as an opportunity to bring about linguistic unity with the Serbs, but on an anti-Illyrian basis. They favored a wholesale adoption of Karadžić's neoštokavian ijekavian, which was based on popular neoštokavian idioms, spoken mainly by the Serbs, rather than on any tradition of Croat regional literature, including that of Dubrovnik. But in accepting Karadžić's linguistic orientation they all too often accepted his national ideology, including his teaching that the štokavian dialect defined Serbian nationhood. This doctrine was explicitly assimilationist; it meant to claim for the Serbs all native štokavians, even in purely Croat areas. One of the consequences of Karadžić's theories, and the great prize, was the claim that Dubrovnik was in fact an ancient Serb city.

To a considerable degree the conflict between Croat and Serb national ideologies was a matter of the Ragusan inheritance. Dubrovnik's high and unique place in Illyrian thought made it all the more seductive to the Serbs. Karadžić's linguistic Serbianism, however, permitted him to advance an entirely novel idea whereby Orthodox dispensation was not the prerequisite for Serbian nationality. As a result, his followers in the Dalmatian Orthodox community, notably Božidar Petranović and Djordje Nikolajević, the latter an Orthodox parish priest in Dubrovnik, laid Serb claims to the city as early as 1838, and mainly by virtue of its štokavian usage. Though this contrivance brushed aside the overwhelmingly Catholic stature of the Dubrovnik region, as well as its residual Croat national consciousness, the theory nonetheless attracted a considerable following among Ragusan intelligentsia and in the 1840s brought about a "Serb-Catholic" circle under the inspiration of Matija Ban (1818-1903) and Medo Pucić (1821-82), the latter a scion of an ancient Ragusan aristocratic family.

During the age of Illyrianism, the "Serb-Catholic" group supported common action with the Croats. In 1848-49, as well as after the promulgation of the October Diploma in 1860, the group's principals fought for the unification of Dalmatia with Croatia-Slavonia. The continuers of this tendency, however, entered into a sharp conflict with the leaders of Ragusan Croats in the 1880s and thereafter, in coalition with the pro-Italian autonomists, sought to frustrate the conjoining of the Croat lands. The "Serb-Catholics" never assembled a modicum of a following among the common people, but even in their benign early days they provoked a great deal of controversy. It is not an exaggeration to say that Ante Starčević began his struggle against Karadžić's Serb national ideology over the very issue of Dubrovnik. In 1851 Starčević evaluated the second volume of *Dubrovnik,* Matija Ban's literary annual, and concluded that although the quality of the journal was high, the editor should "in the future refrain from missionary activity and proselytism, of which [Ban's] volume mightily reek[ed]." As for each fellow countryman, Starčević added, "Everyone knows and ought to know what he is. The spirit will bend to no force and history will tell who we are and where we came from."[28]

At that point, though Starčević still preferred to think in Illyrian rather than purely Croat terms, he was hardly indifferent to the gains of Serb propaganda in Dubrovnik, as we see from the tone of his infrequent comments on Ragusan concerns. Starčević was a cultivated, indeed impressive, thinker and writer, but on the whole coldly intellectual when it came to aesthetic questions. Though Dubrovnik's literary heritage mattered to him, there was nevertheless a certain detachment in his feelings on the subject, possibly something that he inherited from Šime Starčević, his uncle and first mentor.

It is entirely characteristic that Ante Starčević saw Gundulić and Kačić as the two most representative voices of the Croat spirit. He observed that the educated preferred Gundulić, whose language and manner were alien to the people. He himself favored Kačić more and believed that the Franciscan bard of the Biokovo littoral expressed the popular spirit in its totality. As Mirjana Gross has remarked, Starčević evidently planned to reconcile the heritages of these two giants.[29] Starčević was quite aware that such a reconciliation would mean a lowering of the influence of the Ragusans, but Dubrovnik's literary tradition was not part of Starčević's linguistic ideas, which were in any case undeveloped.

Starčević's inability to come forward with an attractive alternative to the teachings of Karadžić's Croat followers certainly contributed to their steady gains, which were consolidated in the last two decades of the nineteenth century. Curiously, though the Croat division of Karadžić's school completely ignored the entire Croat pre-Revival literature, finding its inspiration almost exclusively in Karadžić's collection of folk songs, its prestige in Croatia was enhanced through the support of such Ragusan Slavicists as Pero Budmani (1835-1914) and Milan Rešetar (1860-1942).

Before the turn of the century and the rise of such scholars as Pavle Popović (1868-1939), the continuers of Karadžić's reforms in Serbia were also essentially uninterested in the Ragusan heritage; they routinely claimed it, but it was culturally alien to them. The local "Serb-Catholics" advanced the Serb assertions of a right to Dubrovnik in a far more compelling way, since, though differing from the Dubrovnik Croats in national orientation, they shared much the same cultural outlook and moreover also belonged to the Illyrian tradition. (Matija Ban, for example, believed that Gaj's linguistic reforms were superior to Karadžić's precisely because the Illyrians avoided Karadžić's infatuation with the plainness of folk expression.)[30] The "Serb-Catholics" simply attempted to transplant the Illyrian preoccupation with Gundulić and the rest to the Serb cultural diapason, to which they thought they belonged.

"The past to Dubrovnik, the future to Belgrade," cried Matija Ban in 1887 at a commemorative session of Belgrade's Serbian Royal Academy on the occasion of what was then thought to be Gundulić's tricentennial.[31] And six years later, in 1893, the commune of Dubrovnik, then under a "Serb-Catholic" management, attempted to convert the unveiling of a monument to Gundulić into a Serb manifestation. The effort failed. Mutually unfriendly Croat factions, the followers of Starčević and Strossmayer, acted in unison to subvert "Serb-Catholic" intentions.[32] The usually mild-mannered Strossmayer was discomfited by these events. He observed, in a letter to Rački, that the Croats were the first "to publish the Ragusan and Dalmatian authors, and as a result should have impressed a Croat stamp [on Gundulić's festivity] from the very beginning."[33] But that was just the point: the activities of "Serb-Catholics" in Dubrovnik were at odds with the understandable indifference to Gundulić in Serbia proper.

In the changed circumstances of the turn-of-the-century Croat politics, the Illyrian emphasis on cultural affirmation was no longer the foremost Croat concern. Croat culture limped along even under the Magyarizing regime of Ban Károly Khuen-Héderváry, who oversaw the "pacification" of Croatia-Slavonia in the two decades 1883-1903. The Croat opposition, whether the Independent Populists of Strossmayer or Starčević's Party of Right, was far more concerned with national independence and political liberties than with questions of cultural policy. Under the circumstances, Dubrovnik's attraction lay not so much in its past cultural leadership as in its history as a republic that had been politically independent and whose citizens, it was thought, had been politically free. Starčević himself long believed that the Republic of Dubrovnik represented the Croat state tradition only in part, but in his review of Ban's second literary annual in 1851 he recongnized that the republic represented the Croats who inhabited its territory—implying that it was therefore a suitable carrier of a part of Croat statehood. Starčević's followers dispensed with such legalistic quibbling. The writers associated with the Party of Right excelled in praising Dubrovnik, but unlike the Illyrians, to whom the liberty of the old republic was only one—and not the most important —of the elements that kindled their devotion, Starčević's *stekliši* (lit., mad dogs) were almost exclusively preoccupied with Ragusan liberty.

August Harambašić (1861-1911), the bard of Starčević's party, inspired by the Dubrovnik of Gundulić's period, wrote rapturously of those days of glory:

> *Krasno li je onda vrieme bilo,*
> *Dok je Hrvat bio svoj na svome;*
> *Divno l' se je onda pjevat dalo,*
> *A sad samo plakati se mora!*

> Were not the times wonderful then,
> When the Croat was his own on his land;
> Was it not lovely to sing then,
> When weeping is nowadays our sole command![34]

Similarly, but in characteristically solemn tones, Silvije Strahimir Kranjčević (1865-1908) suggested that "Gundulić's hymn: 'Oh beautiful, oh dear, oh sweet liberty,' resounded through the centuries" of Croat literature.[35] And in a poem written in honor of Gundulić "in Lijevno in Bosnia 1877," he evoked the day, three hundred years earlier, "when the Croat spirit fell on the [Ragusan] strands / and summoned a child from the ordinary world." Kranjčević urged his countrymen to come together at the cradle of the infant Gundulić:

> *Zakunimo se kletvom do nebesa,*
> *Da složni ljudi protiv starog bijesa*
> *Ne damo svoje pravde povijesne!*
>
> Let us swear an oath to the heavens,
> That as men united against the old demon
> We shall not give up our historical right![36]

These new approaches to Dubrovnik still owed a great deal to the Illyrians. True, the symbol of national cultural worth was changed into the symbol of national liberty, but the spirit of Starčević's radicalism was ill adapted to veneration of any kind. Starčević thought nothing of debunking legends, however hallowed a place they held in Croat history.[37] Only Croat statehood was safe from his slings. This spirit was entirely missing in his followers' disposition to Ragusan themes. But the most radical of them all, the self-consciously iconoclastic Antun Gustav Matoš (1873-1914), more than made up for their, perhaps inadvertent, moderation.

Matoš's hatred of Austria was no less robust than Starčević's own. He deserted from the Austrian army in 1894 and fled to Serbia, where he fell in love with Serbian warmheartedness and democratic manner, but at the same time he learned to be wary of the Serbian appetite for expansion. This most homebred of Croat authors, whose bluntness was the very opposite of the dissembling niceties of discrimination that he pursued somewhat later as an expatriate in Paris, nevertheless succeeded in imbuing the forthcoming generation of Croat writers with the spirit of French modernism.

The influence of Latin Europe was also evident in the works of Ivo Vojnović, a native Ragusan and self-appointed guardian of Dubrovnik's traditions, who was for Matoš alternately the ideal of finesse and the favorite object of vituperation. It would not be fruitful to pause here to describe the nuances of this charged relationship. But it is important to remember that Vojnović was for Matoš the most immediate personification of the spirit of Dubrovnik, a city which he knew only from his extensive reading.

Matoš's contradictory attitude toward Dubrovnik was marked by a reverence for Gundulić and an ambivalence toward his contemporary Vojnović. Vojnović's writings were only an interpretation of the Ragusan "essence." The best example of his lofty style is his *Dubrovačka trilogija* (The Dubrovnik Trilogy, 1900), which is a drama of the republic's fall and funereal decay. As the philistine world of money and Habsburg insipidities destroys the harmony of the old republican order in which estates were interdependent, representatives of Dubrovnik's nobility struggle to maintain their aristocratic values and preserve the cult of old Dubrovnik, the desecration of which undermined their sense of terrestial equilibrium.

Lujo Vojnović (1864-1951), Ivo's historian brother and second self, described that desecration in 1909 as being of a sort in which all earthly powers appeared to conspire "to deprive the fatherland of Gundulić and Bošković of its charm and individuality and to transform it into an experimental field for the Viennese firms and rich repatriates from the Americas."[38] Most of all, he deplored the political profanation of Dubrovnik, which was manifest in the Croat-Serb conflict over its proprietorship. Dubrovnik's proper role was to act as a source of harmony, to be "an intermediary and unifier, guardian of beauty and broad lines of European civilization [for the benefit of] the vast, consanguineous, but rude, race" outside its walls.[39] And in the last part of his trilogy, Ivo Vojnović had his noble protagonist liken the Habsburg military presence in Dubrovnik to the sentry's thread of Roman guards at Christ's tomb, stationed there to restrain the scramble over the sacred remains on the part of self-appointed followers.[40]

It was this attitude that Matoš disliked. To be sure, he much admired both the proverbial liberty of Dubrovnik ("every blade of grass in Croatia, like Gundulić's *Dubravka,* sings of dear and sweet liberty") and Gundulić's aristocratic spirit.[41] If Croatia was the Spain of the Balkans, he declared, then Dubrovnik mixed the "dry, elegant and worm-eaten pride of Toledo with the wisdom of Salamanca, of course without the absolutist spleen of Escorial, with the sun of Andalusia, oleanders, and the modern free-thinking of Barcelona."[42] Gentility was innate in the Ragusans and among the Slavs only Dubrovnik and Polish nobility knew the highest level of sociableness.[43] And Ragusan refinement, far from being antithetical to the spirit of liberty, was, in fact, one of its strengths.[44] Even though moribund, aristocracy must remain the ideal of modern democratic individualism.[45] But with all that said, and though he fully recognized Vojnović's artistic genius ("Vojnović is our greatest, our only, writer")[46] Matoš still could not condone the failure to stand forthright on the side of Croat national radicalism. The tendency toward Ragusan "Hamletism" was apparent in the works of both Vojnović brothers. This attitude made Matoš recoil as much as the political activities of Frano Supilo, who outlived his earlier radical years as the editor of *Crvena Hrvatska* (Red Croatia), the Dubrovnik organ of Starčević's party, and crossed over to become the chief spokesman of the "New Course" of Croat-Serb reconciliation in opposition to Vienna.

Matoš's "skepticism toward the Dalmatians," to which he confessed in 1906,[47] led him to reevaluate Dubrovnik's record in liberty in light of the behavior of its present generation. Matoš's line of thinking was that since it was the ideal of liberty that led so many Ragusans into the Serb fold, they must have reasoned that though Serbianism "[was] not cultivated, gentlemanly, or Latin, it [was] nevertheless–free, and that therefore it could also free [them]."[48] It followed that there must be something lacking in Ragusan liberty if it could engender such epic conceits–Matoš said as much in 1907, putting his sentiments in the mouth of an allegorical Peacock (supposedly a representative of the aristocratic and decadent principle but undoubtedly voicing Matoš's own opinions).

A propos old Dubrovnik, I can say that. . . it was first of all an egotistical merchant and patrician nest, which applied the same craft to befool the Turk and the Venetian, the Croatian Ban and the Serbian Despot. Its inflated liberty could survive only at the cost of great imposture and mendacity, of great "diplomacy." As enthusiastic as I am about the incomplete culture of Dubrovnik, I do not enjoy the Jesuitical aspect of Ragusan lyricism and –more important–of Ragusan politics. It is but hypocrisy and empty phrases, artificiality and Tartuffism. The Illyrians revived that false spirit and left it as a bait for the satire of hyper-democratic Starčević. The Republic of Dubrovnik had no republicans; its classicism was but ascetic chants and unpaganlike arias of the selfish, self-satisfied, and Jesuitical aristocracy's Repentant Magdalenes [an allusion to an epic of Ivan Bunić Vučić, written in 1630] and Prodigal Sons [an allusion to Gundulić's canticle *Suze sina razmetnoga* (Tears of the Prodigal Son, 1622)]. There is not a trace of an Aretino, Rabelais, or Hutten in that grove [allusion to Dubrovnik; *dubrava* = grove], and Gundulić's Satyr is nothing but a disguised aristocratic cleric. Do not forget that [Petar] Hektorović [1487-1572], that popular, quite pagan, and robust figure, was an islander [from Hvar], and not an Argosine.[49]

Matoš's indictment was quite a handful in its own time. Though an odd Illyrian expressed regret that the "sun of fortune" shone upon Dubrovnik at the time when the Turks reduced the rest of the Croat lands to ashes,[50] the severity of Matoš's judgment was unprecedented, and its echo would not fade. In subsequent years, though Matoš still could refer to Dubrovnik as the "city of our soul," he saw it increasingly as representing the calculating and rationalist side of Croat emotions, whereas Zagreb was the city of love and heart.[51] Moreover, Dubrovnik and Dalmatia were not the schoolmasters of modern Croatia. Matoš's list of Croat nineteenth-century greats, headed by Starčević, Strossmayer, and Preradović (but curiously without any reference to Gaj), included almost no representatives of Dalmatia. Mihovil Pavlinović and Luka Botić were mentioned, although they were not placed in the front ranks. As for Dubrovnik, besides Vojnović, it produced only the genial Pucić, who, however, metamorphosed into a Serb.[52]

The denial of Croatia—in Matoš's terms, the denial of liberty—exposed all the weaknesses of Dubrovnik's fabled liberality. Judged against the standards of idealized Dubrovnik, this was indeed halfheartedness. Matoš even coined the term *"raguzirati"* (to Ragusate), which conveyed sitting on the sidelines, not taking any chances, and just plain opportunism. The term could be applied variously. The great sculptor Ivan Meštrović, for example (though he was not from Dubrovnik), "Ragusated" when "together with the other Dalmatiners [*sic*], he made the [artistic] Secession in the name of [supranational] Yugoslavism."[53]

The support that the Yugoslav unification enjoyed among Dubrovnik's intellectuals in one sense justified Matoš's harsh words. Though the realities of the interwar political situation soon dispelled most of the illusions that sustained integral Yugoslav nationalism, Dubrovnik produced its share of highly visible political conformists who lent credence to the suspicions that it was a den of soulless weather vanes. And since it is easier to believe the worst, the term *"settebandierism,"* a reference to the supposed seven flags (Venetian, Ottoman, Habsburg, Papal, Spanish, French, and Neapolitan) that the Ragusans allegedly flew with equal enthusiasm to protect their thriving commerce, became more believable a concept than the tradition of Dubrovnik's glorious past. This skeptical reappraisal was of course especially promising for the emerging political Left. Thus Matoš's rebellion against Dubrovnik's apparent aloofness from Croat national concerns, which began as a variation on the theme of liberty, assumed its penultimate contours in the work of Miroslav Krleža (b. 1893), the standard-bearer of Croatia's literary Left.

Krleža's views on Ragusan matters were rather similar to those of Matoš, about whom Krleža had mixed feelings. As early as 1916, Krleža characterized Supilo as a typical *"Raguseo"* and a *"settebandiere."*[54] But though he had occasion to change his mind on Supilo, who, in Krleža's hands ultimately became the most typical representative of the naïve Croat intelligentsia beguiled by dissembling Yugoslav unitarism, he did not change his mind on supposed Ragusan turpitude, at least as far as the city's historic upper classes were concerned. Moreover, unlike Matoš, whose main concern was the national liberty of the Croats, Krleža's Dubrovnik departed from the ideal of liberty in its pronounced subjugation of the city's lower orders. This magic city, white in morning dew, was only a stage prop for foreign tourists which hid the misery of its wretched people:

u sjeni kula jutro: slika bolesna i blatna
Tu nad Gradom, gdje Gondoline vile svadbuju
i Divjak skakuće niz Brgat s vijencem vinove loze,
u izbama sivim umiru djeca od gladi i tuberkuloze.

morning in the shadow of turrets: a sick and mired view
Here over the City, where Gondola's [Gundulić's] muses feast
and his Satyr hops from Brgat with a grapevine wreath,
in grey rooms children die of hunger and tuberculosis.[55]

Krleža's most passionate slurs against the Illyrian cult of Gundulić occur in his spectral *Planetarijom* from the cycle *Balade Petrice Kerempuha* (The Ballads of Petrica Kerempuh, 1936). This bitter attack on

Gundulić begins with a scathing ridicule of the "wheel of fortune" theme from *Osman.* Far from ever being humbled, Krleža says, the high and mighty always have the wheel of fortune rigged in their favor.[56] He derides Gundulić as a bewigged old woman, a mincing blueblood, and the idol of eunuchs, shopkeepers, and usurers, and offers a new hero, Supilo, the son of an ordinary mason, who died in emigration, "his heart crushed by the Croat wound":

> *Brez spomenika spi v preslavnoj Raguze,*
> *bogečke kaj nigdar ju pekle nisu suze.*

He sleeps without a monument in the most glorious Ragusa which was never scalded with beggarman's tears.[57]

Because of his outspoken defense of cultural and national pluralism in the late thirties, Krleža's ties with the Communist movement were strained after 1940 and were not restored until after 1945. Yugoslavia's new socialist regime did not fully rehabilitate him until after the break with the Soviet Union. Krleža's political setbacks in the immediate postwar period probably account for the renewed vigor he showed in his campaign against the reverential view of Dubrovnik's past. In 1948, after observing the annual Corpus Christi procession on Dubrovnik's main street, he wrote a venomously satirical account of the event in a rather lame imitation of the archaic style of old Ragusan poetry. He scorns it all:

> this city, where the abundant, honor-worthy, illustrious, and much esteemed Nobility never did anything except to render themselves obedient with the sundry shopkeepers' courtesies to the unbending Suleymans and the other Oriental, and by the Grace of God, Ottoman Gentlemen. . . .These worthy nobles, illustrious and exalted rectors of illustrious, exalted, worthy, and gentle blood, who sold Latin candles for the Ottoman gunpowder horns and who, humbly kissing the golden slipper of the Holy Roman Father, simultaneously clinked their bloody sequins; this foppish and glorious, blessed and honest Latin Republic, which, like a cancer, always moved backward.[58]

In one respect Krleža's opinions of Dubrovnik were undergoing a change: though his opinion of the old Ragusan elite hardly improved, he increasingly viewed the nobility as somewhat less villainous than the Catholic Church. His attitude was, however, more licentious than it was Leninist. In another essay, also written in 1948, Krleža, expanding on one of Matoš's earlier engrossments, argued that pagan gaiety and sensuality inspired the only genuinely wholesome literature and art, which were in any case superior to the best products of death-bearing Christian culture. Classical Ragusan literature could boast of a major writer who fitted Krleža's Rabelaisian bill. This was Marin Držić, Dubrovnik's principal Renaissance playwright, who was, alas, like Rabelais, a cleric. But since paganism, such as it was, was no more fashionable in 1948 than even the Church, Krleža made Držić out to be a playwright who was not only sociable but, even more, socially conscious.

The transformation of Držić had actually started in the 1930s. Ever since 1938, when Marko Fotez revived Držić's comedy *Dundo Maroje* (Uncle Maroje), the reputation of Dubrovnik's half-forgotten comic master had been steadily rising. Jean Dayre's discovery of four letters which Držić sent to Cosimo I de' Medici, the grand duke of Tuscany in 1566, revealed that this unassuming comic writer could be viewed as a revolutionist of sorts. In these letters Držić denounced the republican powerholders as "twenty armed and mad monstrosities" whose miserliness and ineptitude made their commune the laughingstock of Europe. He detailed their craven timidity and disloyalty to the Christian cause against the Turks and then requested that Florence intervene in Ragusan affairs to bring about a coequal representation of commoners and nobles in Dubrovnik's ruling councils.[59]

Držić's newly discovered insurrectionary credentials fitted the needs of the moment all too well. His moralistic tones and clerical station were brushed aside and he became a fixture in local socialist ideology. In Krleža's early version, Držić was lauded as the creator of a Slavic, indeed pagan, theater, who waged a relentless battle against clerical tutelage over Croatian literature. His was the "voice of a commoner, who rebelled against the nobility in the name of . . . democratic principles."[60] In addition, Držić was a poet of the "uncompromising, gay, freedom-loving Cinquecento, as opposed to the [latter-day] Jesuitical stage." With these credentials, Držić could indeed be viewed as a suitable antithesis of Jesuitical and aristocratic Gundulić. It was to be expected,

Krleža said, that Držić's work would be denigrated by those partisan critics who represented "unintelligent, ultramontane propaganda," and it was the responsibility of new socialist critics to see that Držić gained the place he deserved in the classical literature of Dubrovnik and in Croatian culture.[61]

The elevation of Držić was not without its contradictions. The closer his proximity to the ordinary people, the more he became Dum Marin, a Puckish curate with the sharp eye of a moralist. But though the proletarian cult of Držić, initiated by Krleža and expanded over the years by numerous other critics, did have some loose ends, it performed an admirable service by rehabilitating old Dubrovnik in its plebeian aspects. The aristocratic republic of letters could as a result swell with pride in its share of revolutionary predecessors.

From Illyrian romantic solemnity to contemporary irreverencies, each twist in the rendition of Dubrovnik's fabled story has served the changing needs of Croat society, in however, attenuated a form. As in so many similar situations, instrumentalization of history will stop only when a people ceases to be alienated from its past. It is possible, therefore, to envision new metamorphoses in the assessment of the old city's historical and moral worth. The bipolar Dubrovnik of Jesuitical Gundulić and plebeian Držić is already past its prime. The current handling of the Ragusan theme appears to have some of the same sort of eclecticism and demythifying that was evident in the Croat self-appraisals of the post-1966 period. One thinks especially of Ivan Kušan's satiric *Svrha od slobode* (The Reason for [The End of] Liberty, 1971), which adds a new twist to the old *settebandiere* theme. This time, after the whole city is auctioned off to foreign tourists and big Yugoslav firms, the figurehead Ragusan rector quiets the local chronicler with the words, "I permit the City historian to continue his silence."[62]

NOTES

1.   Grga Novak, *Prošlost Dalmacije: II. Od Kandijskog rata do Rapallskog ugovora* (Zagreb, 1944), p. 325.

2.   Ivan Stojanović, "Najnovija povjest Dubrovnika," in Christian von Engel, *Povjest Dubrovačke Republike* (Dubrovnik, 1903), p. 185.

3. For the most up-to-date exposition of the problem see Dalibor Brozović, "Hrvatski jezik, njegovo mjesto unutar južnoslavenskih i drugih slavenskih jezika, njegove povijesne mijene kao jezika hrvatske književnosti," in *Hrvatska književnot u evropskom kontekstu,* ed. Aleksandar Flaker and Krunoslav Pranjić (Zagreb, 1978), pp. 34-66.

4. Franjo Fancev, *Dokumenti za naše podrijetlo hrvatskoga preporoda (1790-1832)* (Zagreb, 1933), pp. xxxii-xxxiii.

5. Mihovil Kombol, *Povijest hrvatske književnosti do narodnog preporoda* (2d ed.; Zagreb, 1961), p. 399.

6. Petar Preradović, "Pjesma Dubrovniku," in *Pjesnička djela Petra Preradovića* (Zagreb, 1873), p. 125.

7. Ivan Tèrnski (Trnski), "Dopis iz Tèrsta," *Danica ilirska* (Zagreb), 5 (1839), no. 48: 193-94.

8. Mihovil Kombol, "Gundulić u hrvatskoj književnosti," in *Gundulićev zbornik,* ed. Blaž Jurišić (Zagreb, 1938), p. 10.

9. Ivo Frangeš, "Ivan Mažuranić," in vol. 32 of *Pet stoljeća hrvatske književnosti* (Zagreb, 1965), pp. 20-21.

10. Dimitrije Demeter, "Gundulić," *Danica ilirska,* 4 (1838), no. 50: 197-98.

11. "Dvěstolětna uspomena Ivana Gundulića," ibid., no. 51: 201.

12. Pavao Stoós, "Govor prigodom svetkovanja dvěstolětne uspomene Ivana Gundulića," ibid., no. 52: 205-8. Ferdinand II did take Croatian lessons from Marin Gundulić, the poet's Jesuit cousin. This inspired Gundulić to write a panegyric *Ferdinandu Drugomu od Toskane* (To Ferdinand II of Tuscany) on the occasion of the grand duke's wedding in 1637.

13. The term *matica* is notoriously difficult to translate precisely, but all its meanings—"mainstream," "womb," "queen bee"—suggest maternal protection. The building of the *matica* societies was a characteristic of early romantic nationalism among nearly all Slavic peoples. The Serbian Matica was the first (1826), followed by the Czech, Moravian, "Illyrian," and so on.

14. Frangeš, "Ivan Mažuranić," p. 21.

15. Ivica Kunčević, "Dubravka: radne bilješke," *Dubrovnik* (Dubrovnik), 2 (1973), no. 3: 84.

16. B., "Něšto o matematici," *Danica horvatska, slavonska i dalmatinska,* 12 (1846), no. 29: 117.

17. Ljudevit Gaj, "Proglas," ibid., 2 (1836), no. 49: 195.

18.   Pavle Ivić, *Srpski narod i njegov jezik* (Belgrade, 1971), pp. 186-87.

19.   Quoted in Zlatko Vince, *Putovima hrvatskoga književnog jezika* (Zagreb, 1978), p. 333.

20.   Quoted in Josip Horvat, *Ante Starčević* (Zagreb, 1940), p. 33.

21.   Ljudevit Gaj, "Odgovor," *Danica ilirska,* 4 (1838), no. 15: 60.

22.   Andrija Torkvat Brlić, "Književne viesti," ibid., 14 (1848), no. 7: 28.

23.   See Gaj's editorial note to Ivan Kukuljević-Sakcinski, "Něšto o iznenadnom pěsničtvu," ibid., 8 (1842), no. 20: 79.

24.   Ivan Kukuljević-Sakcinski, "Dopis iz Milana," ibid., 7 (1841), no. 14: 54.

25.   Preradović, "Pjesma Dubrovniku," p. 127.

26.   Antun Rocci, "Dopis iz Damacie," *Danica ilirska,* 5 (1839), no. 10: 39.

27.   Dimitrije Demeter, "Misli o našem književnom jeziku," ibid., 9 (1843), no. 3: 11.

28.   Σ. [Ante Starčević], "Dubrovnik cviet narodnoga književstva," *Narodne novine* (Zagreb), 17 (1851), no. 230: 662.

29.   Mirjana Gross, *Povijest pravaške ideologije* (Zagreb, 1973), p. 28.

30.   Matija Ban, "Osnova sveslavianskoga jezika," *Dubrovnik* (Dubrovnik), 1 (1849): 282.

31.   "Matija Ban (r. 16. decembra 1818 - † 14. marta 1903," *Srdj* (Dubrovnik), 2 (1903), no. 6: 286-87.

32.   The entire affair is described in Tijas Mortidjija, "Političko značenje otkrića Gundulićeva spomenika," in *Gundulićev zbornik,* pp. 117-21.

33.   Ferdo Šišić, ed., *Korespondencija Rački-Strossmayer,* vol. 4 (Zagreb, 1931), p. 376.

34.   August Harambašić, "Ivan Franjin Gundulić," in *Izabrane pjesme* (Zagreb, 1895), p. 169.

35.   Silvije Strahimir Kranjčević, *Sabrana djela,* vol. 3 (Zagreb, 1967), p. 377.

36.   Ibid., vol. 2 (Zagreb, 1958), p. 66.

37.   For example, Starčević denounced Nikola Zrinski, who died heriocally in 1566 defending the fortress of Szigetvár in southern Hungary against the Turks, as a traitor who sold out his homeland and protected

Croatia's enemies. And his nephew David Starčević inveighed against Ban Josip Jelačić, who defended Croatia against Kossuth's Hungarians in 1848-49, as an "Austrian hireling through and through." Cited in Vatroslav Jagić, *Spomeni mojego života,* vol. 2 (Belgrade, 1934), p. 334.

38.   Lujo Vojnović, *Književni časovi (1890-1905)* (Zagreb, 1912), p. 165.

39.   Ibid., p. 160.

40.   Ivo Vojnović, *Dubrovačka trilogija* (Zagreb, 1918), pp. 188-89.

41.   Antun Gustav Matoš, *Sabrana djela,* vol. 5 (Zagreb, 1973), p. 197.

42.   Ibid., vol. 7, pp. 102-3.

43.   Ibid., vol. 15, p. 52.

44.   Ibid., vol. 13, p. 149.

45.   Ibid., vol. 6, p. 191.

46.   Ibid., vol. 19, p. 375.

47.   Ibid., p. 401.

48.   Ibid., vol. 6, p. 189.

49.   Ibid., vol. 10, p. 73.

50.   See -k. [Bogoslav Šulek], "Junio Palmotić," *Danica horvatska, slavonska i dalmatinska,* 12 (1846), no. 16: 62.

51.   Matoš, *Sabrana djela,* vol. 7, p. 103.

52.   Ibid., vol. 6, p. 97.

53.   Ibid., vol. 13, p. 135.

54.   Miroslav Krleža, *Davni dani: Zapisi 1914-1921* (Zagreb, 1956), p. 203.

55.   Miroslav Krleža, "Dubrovačka kulisa," *Radio Zagreb,* 2 (1941), no. 9: 24.

56.   Miroslav Krleža, "Planetarijom," *Balade Petrice Kerempuha* (5th ed.; Zagreb, 1963), pp. 141-42.

57.   Ibid., pp. 148-49.

58.   Miroslav Krleža, "Brašančevo u Dubrovniku," *Knježevne novine* (Belgrade), 1 (1948), no. 24: 4.

59.   Jean Dayre, *Dubrovačke studije* (Zagreb, 1938), pp. 19-21.

60.   Miroslav Krleža, *O Marinu Držiću* (Belgrade, 1949), p. 9.

61.   Ibid., pp. 11-13.

62.   Ivan Kušan, "Svrha od slobode: Povijesna dražba s glumom i pjevanjem," *Prolog* (Zagreb), 4 (1971), no. 14: 66.

SOUTH SLAV ASPIRATIONS AND MAGYAR
NATIONALISM IN THE DUAL MONARCHY

Gabor P. Vermes
Rutgers University—Newark

> No country in Europe presents such a variety of complicated problems for solution as the Austro-Hungarian Monarchy; and among these, none is more important and more pressing than the Southern Slav Question.[1]

With these words, one of the foremost experts on the Monarchy, Robert W. Seton-Watson, introduced his book, *The Southern Slav Question,* published in 1911. Just three years later, the momentous event at Sarajevo powerfully confirmed the truth of Seton-Watson's statement, but in fact it has been fully valid in 1911; the South Slav question was already becoming the Monarchy's Achilles heel.

This vulnerability had first become apparent in 1903, when the austrophile Obrenović dynasty was overthrown in Serbia and the Karadjordjević dynasty's new regime embarked upon the gradual emancipation of Serbia from the Dual Monarchy's stifling economic and political tutelage. Unable to reverse or arrest this trend, the Monarchy sought to block further Serbian advances by annexing Bosnia-Hercegovina in 1908. This bold action proved counterproductive; the annexation inflamed Serbian nationalism and, in addition, Austria-Hungary incurred the wrath of Russia, Serbia's new protector. From that time forward, any collision between the Monarchy and Serbia had the potential to escalate into a major war.

When the Balkan Wars of 1912-13 further enhanced Serbia's power and prestige, frustration in Vienna reached a high plateau. A powerful and self-confident Serbia could, after all, provide the nucleus of either a Greater Serbia or a Yugoslav state. In either case, the future of the Monarchy's South Slav provinces and, with them, the Monarchy's very existence were

177

felt to be at stake. Nearly five million South Slavs, approximately 10 percent of the total population, were living in the Monarchy in 1910.[2] By the time of the Balkan Wars, Serbia was bound to attract not merely the Serbs of the Monarchy, but also, to a lesser degree, the Croats and the Slovenes. In the early twentieth century, as South Slav unity ceased to be the dream of poets and became a political program, it constituted a potential challenge to the territorial status quo of the Austro-Hungarian Monarchy.

The development of this political program provoked growing alarm in Vienna. Count Heinrich Clam-Martinic, an influential member of the Austrian Upper House and later to be prime minister, told his fellow Bohemian German Joseph Baernreither in November 1912:

> Either Serbia must fall to us, or our Serbo-Croats to the Serbs.
> One or the other is inevitable—there is no third possibility.[3]

At the 3 October 1913 meeting of the Council of Ministers for Joint Affairs, both the Austrian prime minister, Count Karl Stürgkh, and the minister of finance, Leon Bilinski, expressed strong concern over Serbia. The former claimed that a showdown humiliating to Serbia was vitally important to the Monarchy, while the latter predicted that such a test of strength was only a question of time, since the Serbs were waiting for the appropriate moment to take possession of the Monarchy's southern provinces. As usual, the chief of staff, General Franz Conrad von Hötzendorf, was the most aggressive of the imperial policymakers, suggesting the incorporation of Serbia into the Monarchy, peacefully if possible, by force if necessary.[4]

The Hungarian reaction to Serbia's new posture sounded several octaves below the shrill crescendo emanating from Vienna. Baernreither was appalled by the extent of Budapest's self-assurance, which revealed the Hungarians' confidence in the efficacy of the status quo. "Even now," Baernreither lamented on 13 November 1912, "after all that has happened in the Balkans, there is no conception in Hungary of the significance of the South Slav question.[5]

Among the leading Hungarian politicians, only Count István Tisza and Count Gyula Andrássy, Jr. attempted to instill a sense of awareness about foreign complications and the need for military preparedness. Yet Tisza and

Andrássy failed to integrate their concerns about foreign and military policies with a realistic appraisal of the nationality problems in Croatia and in southern Hungary. Even authors wholly sympathetic to Tisza have conceded his ignorance about the South Slav question, an ignorance that Tisza himself occasionally acknowledged.[6]

One major reason for the Hungarian elite's neglect of foreign policy questions in general and the South Slav issue in particular was the fact that, since nearly all Hungarians regarded their country as an independent state on an equal footing with Austria, they were engrossed with Austro-Hungarian relations. Still, this fixation on parity with Austria did not preclude Magyar politicians from imputing an expansive character to Slovak, Romanian, and German nationalism in Hungary. They labeled these nationalisms "Panslav," "Daco-Roman," and "Pan-German," respectively, implying that the far-reaching connections between certain minorities and their ethnic conationals abroad constituted a kind of international conspiracy aimed at Hungary's destruction. If the Hungarians had concentrated their concern on those minority-populated regions where the potential for outside support seemed most threatening, they would have accorded the South Slav territories increasingly high priority during the early twentieth century. These territories were, after all, close to the Balkans, an area of volatile national politics and the crossroads of Europe's Great Power rivalries. Instead, the Croats and Serbs of Hungary were perceived as living within a relatively static, self-contained framework, a view that accounts for the scant attention that the Hungarian elite paid to them and the concomitant ignorance about them. An attempt to unravel this apparent paradox sheds light both on the curious way that Hungarian nationalistic perceptions functioned and on the nature of the interaction between South Slav aspirations and Magyar nationalism.

Hungarian fears of a rising sense of solidarity among the Slavs date from the first half of the nineteenth century, when nascent Magyar nationalism collided not only with Vienna's bureaucratic centralism, but also with the burgeoning nationalism of Croats, Serbs, and Slovaks. Once the Hungarian reform movement combined its struggle for liberal goals in the social and political sphere with the centralizing tendencies inherent in nationalism, conflict between the Magyars and non-Magyars could not be avoided. The Croats presented a special case, for their historic right to self-government within the Kingdom of St. Stephen was acknowledged by the Hungarians. Lajos Kossuth, who by the 1840s had become the acknowledged leader of the Hungarian reform movement, insisted that, in Croatia's case, Hungary only wished to establish the Magyar language as the language of official intercourse between Magyars and Croats and that otherwise it would continue to respect Croatian autonomy. "The Croatian nation," Kossuth declared in a speech in 1842, "possesses constitutional foundations and historical precedents. The same cannot be said of Illyrism, which relates to a Panslav dream without a historical past and a lawful future."[7] The Illyrism to which Kossuth referred was the primarily linguistic and cultural movement initiated by Ljudevit Gaj in Croatia during the 1830s, a movement that had espoused South Slav unity. By the 1840s, Illyrism had acquired strong political overtones as the Croats resisted Magyar attempts to interfere with their autonomy.

The idea of Slav brotherhood grew naturally from a historic situation that left millions of Slavs fragmented, frustrated, and frequently oppressed by non-Slavs. It was no coincidence that this idea was adopted in Central and Eastern Europe by intellectuals who belonged to peoples without a truly independent national home, namely, Croats, as well as Slovaks and Czechs, who could not even boast of local autonomy. The ideal of Slavic unity offered a compensatory sense of strength and hope to individuals whose peoples were on the losing side of struggles for national autonomy or independence. Slavs oppressed by other Slavs, such as the Poles, understandably shied away from this ideal, whereas others, such as the Serbs, were generally indifferent because, despite their large numbers in Croatia, Dalmatia, Hungary, and the Ottoman Empire, they already had a state of their own, the principality of Serbia. Any hope for Serbian national regeneration could thus be linked to the expansion of something that already existed; indeed, the *Načertanije*, a national program expounded in Belgrade during the mid-1840s, was decisively Great Serbian, rather than Panslav. This distinction, as well as the difference between Illyrism and Panslavism, was overlooked by most Hungarians, who condemned as Panslavism any form of Slavic self-assertion.

From the Hungarian standpoint, Panslavism appeared threatening because the Magyars, for all their apparent self-assurance, were insecure, believing themselves to be surrounded by enemies on all sides. Exaggerated nationalistic rhetoric simultaneously boosted and undermined their morale. Their own extreme effusions about Magyar supremacy served as a welcome tonic in an uncertain world. On the other hand, bombastic phrases from their nationalistic adversaries heightened the insecurity of the Hungarians, precisely because they took their opponents's rhetoric at face value, just as they fervently believed in their own.

In this manner, Hungarians of the mid-nineteenth century regarded Pan-slavism as a monstrously evil force, particularly since they assumed that the mighty Russian Empire stood behind the movement. A liberal re-former and friend of Kossuth, Baron Miklós Wesselényi, saw dire impli-cations in the fact that the Magyars were stituated in the plains, for he was certain that in the surrounding mountains, the Slavs were readying themselves for the final attack. He compared Hungary to a small cottage at the foot of the mountain, constantly exposed to the danger of being buried by an avalanche, and maintained that Hungary was more fatally threatened by the Slavs than any other country in Europe. "My country, my country," he cried out, "your existence is at stake; wake up and act, or you will perish."[8]

Indeed, during the Hungarian War of Independence (1848-49), the Hun-garians' worst fears seemed to materialize. The Austrian troops fighting against Kossuth's soldiers were supported by a Croatian army, as well as Serbian and Slovak insurgents, and the short-lived Hungarian Republic was extinguished by the troops of Tsar Nicholas I. But only twenty years later, in an ironic twist of history, Hungary was elevated to equal status with Austria, while the Serbs, Slovaks and, to a lesser extent, the Croats were again subordinated to the Hungarian state.

To be sure, the Nationality Act of 1868 bestowed full legal equality on all citizens of Hungary, whatever their ethnic affiliation. Moreover, while asserting the unity of one Hungarian political nation, the act grant-ed certain autonomous rights to the non-Magyars, particularly in cultural and educational matters. Unfortunately, the idea of cultural pluralism under the leadership of Budapest—an idea advanced by Ferenc Deák and Baron József Eötvös, the moving spirits behind the Nationality Act—could not be sustained. On one hand, leaders of the national minorities regarded the Magyar concessions as insufficient; on the other hand, Hungarian public opinion and the political authorities, bitter about what they re-garded as past betrayal and current rejection of Hungarian overtures to the non-Magyars, pushed toward the creation of a Hungary based upon Magyar supremacy.

Within this rapidly shifting framework, the Croats retained their special position. Baron Eötvös had expressed the prevailing Hungarian view in 1865, stating that the difference of opinion between Croatia and Hungary centered on political questions that could be settled by a mutually satisfactory constitutional arrangement.[9] The *Nagodba* of 1868 was designed to fulfill that function. It granted autonomy to Croatia in matters of legislation, internal affairs, justice, and education, while retaining military, economic, and financial affairs under joint, and in reality Hungarian, control. In addition, the chief executive of the Croatian administration, the Ban, was to be appointed by the king, upon the recommendation of the Hungarian prime minister, and to be responsible to the Hungarian government.

In spite of superficial similarities, the *Nagodba* was not a replica of the 1867 *Ausgleich* between Austria and Hungary. The result in the first case was not parity between equals, but a compromise between the Hungarian unitary state and Croatian historic rights, a compromise heavily in favor of the dominant partner. This lack of balance caused subsequent Croatian political movements to strive for parity, while the Hungarians remained adamant in resisting any further extension of Croatian autonomy.

From the Hungarian point of view, any Croatian attempt to change the status quo stemmed from a desire to alter Croatia's constitutional status. Hungarian political tradition was permeated by an obsession with legal and constitutional matters, and this legalistic tone characterized the perennial grievances against Austria before and after 1867. Although these grievances were fueled by passionate nationalism, the very fact that they were circumscribed by precise legal language was thought to endow them with penetrating force and respectability. The political movements of all the national minorities in Hungary adopted this tradition and, consequently, their appeals, complaints, and petitions were equipped with meticulously phrased legal arguments. However, only the Croats, by virtue of their historic rights and political autonomy, had a chance to put forth arguments that, even if rejected in Budapest, were treated with some degree of respect.

This very emphasis on the legal and constitutional aspects of Hungarian-Croatian relations lay at the root of Magyar complacency toward Croatia:

the parameters of the relationship were well defined and the terms of the dialogue familiar. The *Nagodba,* a written, signed, and ratified agreement, could serve as the supreme yardstick, measuring loyalty to or deviation from the Hungarian national state at any given point.

This complacency would have been inconceivable had the Illyrian South Slav idea continued to thrive in Croatia, but it did not. After the 1867 *Ausgleich* and the 1871 collapse of the federalist Hohenwart cabinet in Vienna, there was no realistic hope for South Slav unity within the Monarchy, and even less hope outside it, though the idea, with rapidly diminishing appeal, was kept alive by eminent men like Bishop Strossmayer and Canon Franjo Rački. Apart from its impracticality, South Slav unity had run aground on the rocks of ethnic and religious hostility between Croats and Serbs, which flared up once the idea of unity had faded under the force of circumstances. The promotion of national self-interest, even if it did not obtain practical results, appeared at least to yield more dividends for national self-esteem. In this important sense, the Hungarians functioned not only as adversaries, but also as models.

Ante Starčević's "Party of Right" espoused virulent Croatian nationalism. Anti-Magyar, anti-Habsburg, and anti-Serb, it gained popularity as hopes for any radical modifications of the *Nagodba* dwindled and especially when the military frontiers, a territory inhabited by Serbian and Croatian military communities under the direct control of the Imperial Army, were incorporated into Croatia in 1881. This action considerably augmented the number of Serbs in Croatia and increased the frictions between the Croatian majority and the Serbian minority.

Stringent restrictions on the right to vote and manipulation of the suffrage kept the Party of Right in permanent opposition. Croatian nationalism did not cause alarm in Budapest, because Magyar politicians regarded it as a known quantity, fully within their control. Although its uncompromising exclusiveness was a source of annoyance to Hungarian governments, Croatian nationalism reassured the Magyars about the immense difficulties faced by any drive toward South Slav unity. Moreover, the Croat representatives in the Hungarian Parliament were, in general, carefully selected nonentities whose docility could easily lull their Hungarian colleagues into a state of bored unconcern. "Below the gallery, in separate sections," wrote Kálmán Mikszáth in his satirical portrayal of the Hungarian Parliament, "sit the belligerent Saxons and the Croats. What can we say about the latter? One Croat, two Croats, three Croats—forty Croats. It doesn't make any difference."[10]

Tension between Croatia and Hungary erupted in 1883, when the Hungarian government attempted to expand and strengthen its control in Croatia through certain magyarizing measures that clearly violated both the letter and the spirit of the *Nagodba*. Simultaneously with demonstrations in Zagreb, the Hungarian historian Frigyes Pesty lashed out virulently against the Croats, depicting them as the sworn enemies of the Magyars. In Pesty's judgment, Croatia should be fully integrated into Hungary, because "Hungary's independence will remain an empty slogan until the last bastion of this Croat federalism is abolished."[11]

But Pesty was apparently unable to influence the prevailing Hungarian attitude toward Croatia, described in an 1883 parliamentary speech by the Hungarian liberal leader, Dezső Szilágyi:

> Conditions in Croatia have been regarded in such a way that, as long as there is a facade of order and as long as the Croatian representatives in the Hungarian Parliament vote with the government, everything is all right in Croatia.[12]

The tension subsided upon the appointment of the new Ban, Count Károly Khuen-Héderváry, who succeeded in freezing the situation during his long tenure between 1883 and 1903. He rallied to his support all those who had some stake in the preservation of the status quo and skillfully employed the principle of "divide and conquer" by supporting the Serbs of Croatia against the Croats.

The two decades of Khuen-Héderváry's administration further lessened the Magyars' already meager interest in Croatia. To be sure, self-appointed advocates of constitutional purity continued to squabble over Croatia's status, an academic question in view of Croatia's total dependence on Hungary. Gusztáv Beksics, a prolific champion of late nineteenth-century Magyar nationalism, strongly asserted that Croatia did not constitute a state, but merely an autonomous province. Baron Viktor Thoroczkay went even further by decrying both the Act of Nationality and the *Nagodba* as products of "sentimental liberalism" and denying the constitutional validity of Croatian participation in all economic, financial, and military matters. However, this extreme point of view, reminiscent of the stand Pesty had taken, was the exception and not the rule. Even Baron Dezső Bánffy, the ultra-chauvinistic prime minister between 1895 and 1899, implicitly recognized Croatia's special status when he noted that Croatia was entitled to have a frontier separating it from Hungary proper, although Croatia would remain an integral part of the unitary Magyar state.[13]

Only a few Magyar commentators treated Hungary's relationship with Croatia separately from its constitutional aspects. Miklós Bartha, journalist and member of parliament, devoted only a few articles to Croatia in the otherwise bulky volume containing his collected articles about the problems of nationalities in Hungary. In one of his rare treatments of Croatia, written in 1902, Bartha used bitter words. "The more compromises we have with Croatia," he complained,

> the more hatred accumulates. . . . We have many ties to Croatia; still, Croatia does not belong to us. Neither the mail, nor the railways, nor the army has created a spiritual bond between us. . . . The distance separating us is so enormous that we are more Austrians than the Croats are Magyars.[14]

Another author who discussed the Croatian situation within a broader framework was Count Miklós Zay, a Hungarian landowner in Croatia who wrote a most revealing pamphlet in 1893. A devoted supporter of Khuen-Héderváry, he compared the Ban's administration to Hercules's destruction of the monsters and cleansing of the Augean stables. Zay enthusiastically endorsed Khuen's policy of alternating firmness and finesse. Taking the Croats' anti-Magyar sentiments for granted, Zag suggested "playing on the Croatian chessboard in a clever way, because the opponent is cunning and one should not generously return the captured pieces." Zay then condemned the Hungarian government's neglect of Croatia. "The control of navigable rivers," he wrote, "belongs to the sphere of governmental authority which, however, does as much about it in Croatia as it does on the moon." While Zay believed that Croatia should be ruled with a firm hand, he also thought that her poor economic conditions should be ameliorated. According to him, punitive measures were obsolete and should not be used again, particularly because our nation can rely more on Croatia than on the Romanians in some godforsaken region. The Croats are not gravitating outward. The Panslav idea could not take root beyond the river Drava. Strossmayer, the Southern Slav apostle, has lost the ground from beneath his feet. The followers of Starčević, those veritable Croatian chauvinists, stand as far from the Serbs, the Russians, and the Czechs as they do from the Papuans.[15]

As if to underline the deep cleavage between the Croatian and Serbian communities in Hungary, the history of the latter throughout the nineteenth century only intermittently coincided with developments in Croatia. The bulk of Hungary's Serbian population lived in southern Hungary, in the Vojvodina, which "was the center of Serbian religious and educational life, and it was the most economically and socially advanced Serbian community."[16] The Serbian National Congress of 1861 strongly expressed the collective self-assertion of the Vojvodina, demanding the full restoration of its autonomy, which had degenerated into a sham privilege by the time the king revoked it in 1860.

Under the leadership of Svetozar Miletić and Mihajlo Polit-Desančić, Serbian political activism carried over to the first years of the Dual Monarchy. In fact, the Serbian National Party, its organ *Zastava,* published in Novi Sad (Ujvidék), and a Serbian youth organization, the *Omladina,* together represented the most active and politically best-organized national minority at the time of the 1867 *Ausgleich.*[17] Miletić was in the forefront of those non-Magyar representatives, particularly Romanian and Serbian, who, while wishing to preserve Hungary's territorial integrity, fought for extensive linguistic and administrative autonomy within that unitary framework. The Serbian National Liberation Party was pursuing this goal in its 1869 Program of Veliki Bečkerek (Nagybecskerek), emphasizing the necessity of collaboration among Romanians, Slovaks, and Serbs and also expressing solidarity with Slavs in Austria and with Serbs still under Ottoman rule.[18]

In 1867, at the Panslav gathering in Moscow, Polit-Desančić was lavish in his praise of Russia, a potentially significant manifestation of Slav solidarity in a year when Austro-Hungarian dualism was born at the expense of Slavic pride and self-esteem. When insurrections broke out in Bosnia-Hercegovina in 1875, at the height of Russian-supported Panslav agitation in the Balkans, and during the subsequent, brief Serbo-Turkish war of 1876, "the Serbs of Vojvodina were full of enthusiasm but did practically nothing to help."[19] It is not difficult to identify the reason for their inaction; both the Austrian and Hungarian authorities were harshly enforcing their decision to keep the Monarchy's South Slav subjects isolated from the conflict. In 1876, Miletić was arrested (in violation of his parliamentary immunity), tried on charges of high treason, incitement, and the recruitment of volunteers on Serbia's behalf, and sentenced to five years' imprisonment.

The removal of Miletić from the political scene was not the Hungarian government's sole retaliatory measure. The municipal autonomy of Novi Sad had been curtailed by a government commissioner in 1868, even before the turmoil of the mid-1870s. Three years later, the government had disbanded the *Omladina,* and in 1872, a lieutenant general, dispatched to the south upon the Hungarian government's request, had dissolved the Serbian National Church Congress. The charges raised against various Serbian politicians and organizations were replete with assumptions and innuendos about their connections with Belgrade.

Yet, in comparison to the accusations directed against other national minorities, the tone of Hungarian anti-Serbian activities was relatively measured. Indeed, the damning epithet "Panslav" was applied almost exclusively to the Slovaks, and rarely to the Serbs. There was a considerable difference, both in the degree and general character of punitive actions, between the hysterical campaign conducted against Slovak cultural and educational institutions, such as the "Matica Slovenska" and Slovak high schools, and the comparative tolerance accorded their Serbian counterparts. Although the government cut off state aid from the Serbian high school in Novi Sad in 1872, it resolved to establish another Serbian school in Sombor, "where the correct selection of teachers and the education of Serbs in good [i.e., patriotic] spirit can be assured."[20] And the original Serbian high school managed to survive the loss of state aid. In contrast, three Slovak high schools were closed altogether in 1874-75, and the "Matica Slovenska" was dissolved in the latter year.

The harshness of the Hungarian measures is most surprising, for, in fact, the Slovak national movement was one of the weakest and least developed in Hungary. The Slovak middle class and intelligentsia were both small; among all the leading strata of the national minorities, they were most conspicuously susceptible to the pressures and temptations of assimilation to the Magyars.[21] Nor could any comparison be drawn between the diplomatic and military standstill along and beyond Hungary's northern frontier and the ferment in the Balkans. Panslav propaganda was naturally concentrated on the liberation of the Balkan Slavs from Turkish rule, and no particular attention was paid to the Slovaks. A voice of fatalistic resignation was struck by the Russophile Slovak poet, Svetozar Hurban-Vajansky, who wrote to a Russian friend that "if there is no chance for the Slovaks to live under Russian hegemony, then it would be better for them to vanish altogether."[22]

What, then, is the explanation for the apparent irrationality of Hungarian political behavior? It is clear that the Panslav threat was not rationally assessed, that matters of foreign policy were not considered in terms of their potential intersection with indigenous national trends. Instead, fear of a Slav onslaught varied according to local conditions and the perceptions of provincial Hungarian potentates, whose horizons were severely limited by their deeply ingrained insecurities and prejudices.

In several northern counties Slovaks vastly outnumbered the Hungarians. From the Hungarian standpoint, only a process of assimilation could redress this balance, and any manifestation of Slovak national consciousness, even in cultural and educational affairs, appeared to be threatening. In the Vojvodina, on the other hand, there was a relatively even distribution among Germans, Magyars, and Serbs. When the Magyar champion of equal rights for the national minorities, Lajos Mocsáry, arrived in Novi Sad in 1887, he was enthusiastically greeted by a mixed crowd comprised of these three groups. In no southern county did the Serbs constitute an absolute majority.[23] This situation accounted for the fact that no well-known Hungarian politician from the south wrote anything comparable to Béla Grünwald's *Felvidék* (Northern Hungary), published in 1878 and permeated with fright about the (to him) insidious growth of Panslavism.

In the end then, the crucial factor was less what non-Magyars said and did or what connections they did or did not have with their conationals abroad, but whether or not the Hungarians in particular localities felt threatened. Once certain fears had developed, corresponding rationalizations were formulated. For example, the very weakness of Slovak organizations gave them the appearance of a somewhat shadowy and indeterminate character, which already suspicious minds could easily interpret as the cover for more thoroughgoing subversive activities. It was tempting, then, to ascribe conspiratorial Panslav tendencies to inchoate Slovak manifestations. In the south, the more secure and consequently more tolerant Magyars learned to live with a certain level of Serbian militancy, and they were able to observe with satisfaction the growing antagonism between Serbs and Croats. Not surprisingly, these provincial attitudes strongly influenced the central government's policy toward different national minorities. After all, the government was in effect run by the gentry, whose roots were not in Budapest, but rather in the various regions of Hungary.

In addition, Hungarians perceived the Serbs as a people of brave fighters, very different from the stereotype of the Slovaks, who were usually considered meek and compliant unless aroused by "Panslav agitators."[24] József Székács, the Hungarian translator of Serbian folksongs, dedicated his work to the Serbs, "our brothers," in 1836.[25] Brotherly feelings soured quickly during the War of Independence, but General Mór Perczel, in command against Serbian insurgents, did not conceal his respect for his adversaries. "General Knićanin," he reported to Governor Lajos Kossuth on 2 May 1849, "is fighting against me with several thousand heroic soldiers who are prepared to defend themselves to the last man."[26]

Bertalan Szemere, who had been the last prime minister of the revolutionary Hungarian government, dedicated a poem that he wrote in Paris in 1854 to Sebő Vukovics, a man of Serbian descent who had been minister of justice in his government. Szemere claimed that the Hungarian nation proudly honored both Vukovics and General János Damjanics, another Serb by birth. In another poem, Szemere professed to feel pity for the Serbs, that "brave people," whom Austria had "rewarded" for their victory over the Hungarians by enslaving them.[27] In 1861, the onetime revolutionary, writer, journalist, and politician, Mór Jókai, traveled to Novi Sad to help celebrate a wealthy Serbian patron of the arts in a commemoration organized by the foremost Serbian cultural association, the "Matica Srpska." Jókai enjoyed himself thoroughly and expressed his hopes for friendly competition in the fields of education and culture and for mutual assistance, rather than combat, between "two kindred people," the Magyars and the Serbs.[28]

Apparently, then, the combination of regional familiarity among Hungarians and Serbs in southern Hungary and a reservoir of respect, perhaps even goodwill, on the part of the former toward the latter, spared the Serbs from the brunt of official harassments. In addition, specific political and economic conditions in the Vojvodina helped to sustain the relatively good relations between the two groups. Starting in the late 1870s, much of the energy of the politically active Serbian public was focused on the internecine struggle between the conservative clergy and liberal laymen and the squabbles among various Serbian factions and parties.[29] In 1881, the lord lieutenant of Novi Sad reported to Prime Minister Kálmán Tisza on a meeting of the "Matica Srpska." Although radical rather than moderate nationalists had been elected as officers of the organization, the lord lieutenant's report betrayed absolutely no sign of anxiety or panic.[30] Three years later, the moderates took control of the Liberal Party, prompting Polit-Desančić, still faithful to the Miletić line, to secede and to form his own party in 1885. Although the influence of the moderates declined, unity was not restored; Polit's liberals and a new grouping, the radicals, led by Jaša Tomić, continued to wage a venomous feud against each other.

Simultaneously, the favorable economic developments in the Vojvodina during the last two decades of the nineteenth century created conditions conducive to a "shift from national to economic matters."[31] The Serbian bourgeoisie and relatively affluent landed peasantry had a vested interest in not rocking the boat. While 48.3 percent of the purely Magyar regions consisted of arable land, the figure was 30 percent for the Romanian and 21.2 percent for the Ruthenian regions. The Vojvodina, on the other hand, was blessed by a 70 percent ratio, and consequently, the living standard of the Serbian peasantry was considerably higher than that of the Slovak, Romanian, or Ruthenian peasants.[32] The large Serbian agrarian proletariat, 33.7 percent of the adult male population in 1904, gained no appreciable benefits from this high living standard, but it concentrated on obtaining better working conditions, rather than fighting for Serbian national goals.[33]

These last two decades of the nineteenth century also coincided with Serbia's extreme dependence on the Monarchy, a situation that brought a concomitant loss of prestige and made it difficult to portray Serbia as a model and magnet for Serbs elsewhere. Not even the quickening of political activities during the 1890s, particularly among the Romanians, could reinvigorate the tired pace of nationalistic politics in Vojvodina, and it appeared as if Magyar complacency about the South Slavs were being repaid in kind. During the period between 1898 and 1906, only 4 Serbs were sentenced for political activities, while the corresponding number for Romanians was 210 during the period between 1897 and 1908 and, for Slovaks, 560 between 1896 and 1908.[34]

Two events in 1903 marked a sharp turn in the South Slav situation of the Monarchy. The change of dynasties in Serbia precipitated that country's determination to shake off the Monarchy's stifling patronage, while Khuen-Héderváry's departure from Croatia released forces that his manipulative regime had prevented from promoting either the Croatian or the South Slav cause.

Most of the spokesmen of the South Slav cause were young Croats, who joined with some Serbs in recognizing the futility of fratricidal rivalry and advocating a return to the abandoned, but never fully forgotten, idea of South Slav unity. The leading figures were two Croats from Dalmatia, Frano Supilo and Ante Trumbić, and a Serb from Croatia, Svetozar Pribićević. The formation of a Croatian-Serbian Coalition in 1905, with the signing of resolutions in Fiume (Rijeka) and Zára (Zadar) by Croatian and Serbian representatives respectively, signalled the beginning of a new chapter in the history of the South Slavs and in their relationship to both Austria and Hungary. The two resolutions endorsed the interdependence of the Hungarian and South Slav peoples, as well as the latter's support for the Magyar's current struggle with Vienna.

The groundwork for this fight had been laid in January 1905, when a coalition of Hungarian parties won a surprising victory over Count István Tisza's Liberals. This Coalition aimed at loosening Hungary's common ties to Austria, particularly in matters of joint defense and the economy, without abrogating the 1867 *Ausgleich*. Franz Joseph, rejecting the Coalition's demands, foisted an unconstitutional government upon the country. By the autumn of 1905, widespread bitterness against Austria and resistance to governmental arbitrariness had developed in Hungary. Some leaders of the embattled Coalition were eager to strike an alliance with the Croatian-Serbian Coalition. Ferenc Kossuth, chairman of the Hungarian Coalition's Steering Committee, sent a rousing telegram to Croatian representatives on 7 October 1905. He claimed that Hungarians had always shared their attained rights with the Croats, and ended by exclaiming: "We are waiting for you with hope and love."[35]

Turmoil in Hungary was severely testing the viability of dualism, and the South Slavs, delighted to find a source of renewed strength in mutual support, cleverly exploited the conflict. Serbia, struggling for her economic and political emancipation, was equally delighted with this turn of events, and widespread contacts between Belgrade and the leaders of the Croatian-Serbian Coalition developed during this period. The split between Austria and Hungary appeared to be serving their joint interests,[36] and in this manner, Serbia truly became the "Piedmont" of the South Slavs.[37]

Magyar motives for the alliance were a great deal less farsighted. To be sure, there is usually a short-range tactical advantage in any alliance. However, Kossuth, the mediocre son of a great leader, and his friends misread the situation. They sincerely believed that Hungary was not being treated as an equal by Austria, but "like Galicia or Dalmatia, regarded as a province which is only playing the role of a state."[38] Therefore, they thought, Hungarians could and should, along with the other oppressed peoples of the Monarchy, take up cudgels against Vienna. In fact, whatever the legitimacy of Hungarian grievances against Austria, they neither vitiated the substantial power and prestige that Hungary shared with her dualistic partner, nor concealed Magyar supremacy over the national minorities within Hungary itself. For the Hungarians to assume, then, that they could maintain the alliance between the two coalitions while simultaneously preserving Magyar supremacy, was yet another sign of their ignorance about the South Slavs. Even such a Magyar champion of friendship with the South Slavs as Count Tivadar Batthyány believed that all the national minorities, including the South Slavs, "can expect the fulfillment of their rights solely and exclusively through the Magyars."[39]

The hollowness of this idea was amply documented after the Hungarian Coalition finally assumed its constitutional right to govern Hungary in 1906. The following year, Minister of Trade Ference Kossuth introduced the obligatory knowledge of Magyar throughout the state railway system, including Croatia, an unnecessary affront to Croatian national sensitivities. The alliance collapsed, as Croatian members of the Hungarian Parliament retaliated by filibustering. In the same year, Minister for Religious and Educational Affairs Count Albert Apponyi, exacerbated tensions by introducing his educational bill. Although this legislation established the system of free public schools and raised the salaries of teachers, its emphasis on Magyarization and the enforcement of state control over this process in the schools of national minorities provoked strong resentment.

The annexation of Bosnia-Hercegovina in 1908, the Zagreb treason trial of Croatian-Serbian Coalition leaders in 1906 (both drawing international attention to the South Slav issue in the Monarchy), and, finally, the Balkan Wars of 1912-13, resulted in the very confluence of grave domestic concerns and foreign policy complications that leaders in Vienna had always hoped to prevent. In Budapest, however, deeply ingrained patterns of nationalistic perception precluded a similar recognition of these new realities. To be sure, as long as everyone from Oszkár Jászi, the Hungarian with the most comprehensive understanding of the national minorities, to Jenő Rákosi, the ultra-chauvinistic editor of the *Budapesti Hirlap,* agreed on the necessity of preserving Hungarian territorial integrity and even Magyar supremacy, albeit in widely differing forms, the question of ignorance versus expertise was essentially moot. Jászi advocated far-reaching autonomy for national minorities, while Rákosi argued for continuing outright Magyar domination. In the long run, either of these alternatives would have run counter to the dynamics of South Slav national aspirations. Even in the short run, the prevailing Hungarian ignorance and neglect of the South Slavs perpetuated a dangerous wishful thinking; the sudden confrontation with rapidly changing realities was bound to evoke confusion and despair.

In spite of warning signals, this confrontation did not take place before World War I as Hungarian politicians continued to take their traditional approach to the South Slav question. In 1910 the veteran Serbian leader Polit-Desančić could still infuriate his Magyar colleagues in the Hungarian Parliament, by characterizing the national minorities as political serfs,[40] but Polit and his Liberals were being overshadowed in any case by the Serbian Radical Party, which concentrated more on its fight against clerical influences and for universal suffrage than on a frontal attack against Magyar domination. In fact, the party kept close touch with Hungarian politicians who belonged to the ruling coalition and maintained those contacts after the coalition went into opposition again, following its resounding defeat at the polls in 1910. One of the coalition leaders, Count Tivadar Batthyány, defended the Serbian Radicals as loyal patriots in the parliament in 1911.[41]

It was the growing dissension in Serbian ranks that encouraged the Budapest government to suspend the autonomy of the Serbian Orthodox church in 1912. Instead of exacerbating the dissension, however, this step backfired totally, uniting all Serbian political parties. Their joint manifesto on 16 August 1912 "transcended the fight for national-church autonomy and became a preparatory stage for the declaration of struggle for South Slav unity."[42]

In the meantime, the government's inability to sustain a loyal regime in Croatia led to the introduction of dictatorial measures in 1908, which were continued intermittently until 1913. The prevailing Hungarian view of events in Croatia remained strictly legalistic and constitutional. Prime Minister László Lukács exemplified this attitude in his inaugural address, delivered in the parliament on 29 April 1912. "On this occasion," he stated,

> I wish to comment on the relationship between Hungary and Croatia, which is our own internal affair. Anyone who is discussing this relationship and wants to stay on legal grounds must stand on article XXX of the 1868 law, the *Nagodba,* which asserts that Croatia belongs to the Crown of St. Stephen both by right and in fact.[43]

The same fundamentally legalistic attitude was expressed, albeit with some degree of flexibility, by Lukács' successor, Prime Minister Count István Tisza, who restored constitutional rule in Croatia in November 1913, after making a pact with the Croatian-Serbian Coalition. Tisza agreed to remove the offensive language measures from the regulations of the state railways, while the Coalition consented to the continuation of the *Nagodba.* Tisza's reasons for concluding this pact included his desire to find a modus vivendi with the non-Magyars and, more specifically, his resolve to checkmate the renewed and growing strength of Croatian nationalists who, instead of collaboration with the Serbs, proposed the establishment of a Greater Croatia within the Monarchy (including Croatia proper, Dalmatia, the Slovene provinces, and Bosnia-Hercegovina) as an equal partner to Austria and Hungary.

To Tisza as to all Hungarians, such a "trialist" solution was anathema. Since the number of so-called unionist, "magyarone" Croats was dwindling to insignificance, Tisza decided to ally himself with the group that he considered the lesser of the two evils, the Croatian-Serbian Coalition. Although this move was clever from an immediate tactical standpoint, he failed to see that this alliance, at best, temporarily cured a symptom without getting to the root of the South Slav issue. To Tisza, an ardent believer in Magyar supremacy, concessions to national minorities were final, while to the minorities themselves, concessions were mere stepping stones toward far-reaching autonomy, a goal that deviated sharply from what Tisza had in mind.

These incongruities might have remained dormant for some time, had not the European war begun in 1914. After a brief period of *union sacrée* between both political and national opponents, prewar problems flared up amidst rapidly changing circumstances, in which the stakes of victory or defeat had become much higher.

In this new situation, Hungarian policymakers proved unable to transcend their prewar assumptions. When, in the Croatian *sabor* in June 1915, influential voices advocated unifying all Croatian lands in a separate state within the Monarchy,[44] Tisza tried to minimize the significance of these aspirations by calling them "isolated phenomena" and telling members of the parliament that "there is no need to raise the issue under current circumstances."[45]

The prime minister continued to hold this position when, in the spring of 1915, an Austrian officer of Croatian background, General Sarkotić, implored Tisza to do something about the South Slav question. Tisza answered that, during the war, there should be no tinkering with the Monarchy's structure. The general, sensitive to the growing impatience of the South Slavs, replied that waiting until the aftermath of the war would be too late. "There are many patriots among the South Slavs," the prime minister reported, "who understand that, during the war, the Monarchy cannot be reformed."[46]

Shortly after this conversation, in an astonishingly naïve letter to the Ban, Baron Iván Skerlecz, Tisza suggested creating a favorable atmosphere toward Hungary, as well as establishing a new party of reliable elements, in Croatia.[47] In fact, the Magyar protectorate was now unanimously resented in Croatia. Both the Croatian-Serb and the Croat nationalist camps contained dynamic potentials already in the process of tearing Croatia away from Hungary, in either the South Slav or Great Croat direction.

When the veteran Magyar politician Sándor Wekerle was appointed Hungary's prime minister in August 1917, three months after Tisza's resignation, he exhibited no greater understanding of the South Slav situation. He objected to the Austrian plan of uniting Croatia, Dalmatia, and Bosnia-Hercegovina within the Monarchy, recognizing that this would be a major step toward trialism. Obfuscating the real motive for his attitude, he told German Ambassador Count Botho von Wedel that "the Slav is particularistically motivated and loves to be on his own, and the division into small structures corresponds to the Slavic character."[48] He proceeded to connect his hypocritical concern for the Slav psyche with his desire to forward Hungarian expansion in a manner that would doom the Austrian plan. By advocating the annexation of Bosnia-Hercegovina as *corpus separatum* to Hungary, he hoped to accomplish this objective.

Both the Prime Minister and Tisza, now the influential leader of the opposition, stubbornly held to their positions on the South Slav issue until virtually the end of the war. Tisza did so, despite his experiences on a fact-finding tour through Croatia, Dalmatia, and Bosnia in September 1918. Ending his journey at Sarajevo, he dejectedly admitted to Sarkotić that he was bewildered by the confusion and disloyalty among people whom he had regarded as reliable.[49] Indeed, his bewilderment turned to rage the next day, when a delegation of South Slav-oriented Bosnian Serbs and Croats presented him with a memorandum, asserting the unity of all South Slavs and their right of self-determination.[50]

En route to Budapest, Tisza stopped at Osijek, where he had a conversation with Dr. A. Pinterović, a Croatian member of the *sabor*. Pinterović countered Tisza's repeated assertions that dualism must be maintained at all costs by stating that the unification of the South Slav lands could not be stopped. A decision superimposed upon the South Slavs would offer the Entente a welcome pretext for intervention, and Pinterović argued that this was an additional reason to reach a solution corresponding to the people's desires. "Thank God," Tisza replied, "we are not so far gone. We are, after all, not like Turkey at the Congress of Berlin!"[51]

Despite these brave words, the situation for the Central Powers in general and Hungary in particular turned from bad to worse during October, and Tisza himself announced in the Hungarian Parliament that "we have lost the war."[52] Yet, as late as 22 October, Prime Minister Wekerle consented to the unification of the South Slav territories only on condition that this unit would be attached to Hungary.[53] Tisza was wavering. On the same day, he told two Croatian nationalist leaders that his policy toward Croatia had been mistaken and that he now acknowledged the Croats' right to full independence.[54] But apparently Tisza did not hold to this new position, for only three days later a Hungarian diplomat in the Foreign Ministry, Count Lajos Ambrózy, reproached Tisza for insisting on the unification of the South Slav lands under St. Stephen's Crown, when, as Ambrózy argued, Croatia and Bosnia-Hercegovina were irrevocably lost to Hungary.[55]

Nothing could better illustrate the consistent Hungarian myopia about the South Slavs than the attitudes of Wekerle and Tisza during the last days of the war. A characteristic of the Hungarian political consciousness since the 1860s, this myopia shaped Hungarian views to the very end, weeks after the South Slav National Council had assumed the functions of a de facto government in Zagreb on 6 October 1918.

NOTES

1.   Robert W. Seton-Watson, *The Southern Slav Question* (London, 1911), p. vii.

2.   Tibor Erényi, Péter Hanák, and György Szabad, eds., *Magyarország Története 1849-1918* (Budapest, 1972), p. 620.

3.   Joseph M. Baernreither, *Fragments of a Political Diary* (London, 1930), p. 139.

4.   3 October 1913, Országos Levéltár, Filmtár. Közös Minisztertanács: Jegyzőkönyvek, 1912-1913; Feldmarschall Conrad, *Aus Meiner Dienstzeit* (Vienna, 1922), 3: 461.

5.   Baernreither, *Fragments*, p. 136.

6.   Gusztáv Grátz, *A Dualizmus Kora* (Budapest, 1934), 2: 325-27; Loránd Hegedűs, *Két Andrássyés Két Tisza* (Budapest, 1937); Tisza to Báró István Burián, 27 August 1914, *Gróf Tisza István Összes Művei* (Budapest, 1924), 2: 93; 24 October 1915, Thallóczy Napló, 10/5, Nr. 2744. Budapest, Országos Széchenyi Könyvtár, Kézirattár.

7.   Domokos Kosáry, "A Pesti Hirlap Nacionalizmusa 1841-1844," *Századok* 77, no. 7-10 (1943): 387.

8.   Báró Miklós Wesselényi, *Szózat. A Magyar és Szláv Nemzetiség Ügyében* (Lipcse, 1843), pp. 78, 99, 250.

9. Báro József Eötvös, *A Nemzetiségi Kérdés* (Pest, 1865), p. 44.
10. Kálmán Mikszáth, *A Tisztelt Ház* (Budapest, 1917), pp. 43-44.
11. Frigyes Pesty, *Száz Politikai és Történeti Levél Horvátországról* (Budapest, 1885), p. 119.
12. Quoted in László Katus, "A Tisza Kormány Horvát Politikája és az 1833 évi Horvátországi Népmozgalmak," *Századok* 92, no. 5-6 (1958): 670.
13. Gusztáv Beksics, *A Dualizmus Története, Közjogi Értelme és Nemzeti Törekvéseink* (Budapest, 1892), p. 248; Báró Viktor Thoroczkay, *A Magyar Állam és Nemzetiségei* (Budapest, 1896), pp. 116, 122; Báró Dezső Bánffy, *Magyar Nemzetiségi Politika* (Budapest, 1903), p. 212.
14. *Bartha Miklós Összegyűjtött Munkái* (Budapest, 1910), 3: 560-61.
15. Gróf Miklós Zay, *Croatiae Res (Zágrábi Levelek)* (Budapest, 1893), pp. 8, 9, 10, 36, 37, 40, 42.
16. Wayne S. Vucinich, "The Serbs in Austria-Hungary," *Austrian History Yearbook* 3, pt. 2 (1967): 4.
17. Erényi, Hanák and Szabad, *Magyarország Története*, p. 266.
18. Gábor K. Kemény, *A Magyar Nemzetiségi Kérdés Története* (Budapest, 1946), p. 114.
19. Alfred Fischel, *Der Panslavismus bis zum Weltkrieg* (Stuttgart, 1919), pp. 386-87; Michael Boro Petrovich, *A History of Modern Serbia 1804-1918* (New York, 1976), 2: 387.
20. Gábor K. Kemény, ed., *Iratok a Nemzetiségi Kérdés Történetéhez Magyarországon a Dualizmus Korában* (Budapest, 1952), 1: 294.
21. Erényi, Hanák and Szabad, *Magyarország Története*, p. 270.
22. Vladislav Stastny, ed., *Slovanstvi v Narodnim Zivote Cechu a Slovaku* (Prague, 1968), p. 328.
23. Kemény, *Iratok*, 1: 734-35. According to the statistical data published by the Hungarian government, in 1900, the population of Novi Sad was divided among 35.6% Hungarians, 21.8% Germans, and 33.9% Serbs, while in Sombor, the same ratio was 31.2%, 8.1%, and 40.8%. *Magyar Statisztikai Evkönyv* 17 (1910): 21.
24. I am grateful for this insight to Professor George Barany of the University of Denver, with whom I discussed the subject of this essay.
25. Sándor Hinóra, ed., *A Szomszéd Népekkel való Kapcsolataink Történetéből* (Budapest, 1962), p. 234. Cultural relations between Hungarians and Serbs were well established in the first half of the 19th

century. The home of the writer and poet Mihály Vitkovics was a frequent meeting place of such Hungarian literati as Kazinczy, Kőlcsey, Berzsenyi, Vörösmarty, and others. Ibid., p. 160. In addition, members of the Serbian intelligentsia, many of whom lived scattered in Hungary outside the Vojvodina, kept in touch with liberal Magyar politicians during the same period. Endre Kovács, *Magyar-Délszláv Megbékélési Törekvések 1848-49-ben* (Budapest, 1958), p. 12.

26. József Thim, *A Magyarországi 1848-49-iki Szerb Fölkelés Története* (Budapest, 1935), 3: 695.

27. Hinóra, *A Szomszéd Népekkel való Kaposolataink,* pp. 390-91.

28. Mór Jókai, *Emlékeim* (Budapest, 1875), 1: 45-46.

29. The Serbian Orthodox church played a complex role in the evolution of Serbian nationalism during the late nineteenth and early twentieth centuries. On one hand, the prelates were inclined to pursue a policy of accommodation with the Hungarian governments which, to their detractors, appeared as a policy of opportunism, if not betrayal. On the other hand, church autonomy proved to be an important safeguard in protecting a widespread educational chain which, by 1914, included several secondary and 356 elementary schools. Vucinich, "Serbs in Austria-Hungary," p. 42. "The still-existing church autonomy, although its influence on denominational elementary education was increasingly curtailed, distinguished the Serbian and Rumanian status from the even more inferior Slovak and Ruthenian position." Robert A. Kann, *The Multinational Empire: Nationalism and National Reform in the Habsburg Monarchy 1848-1918* (New York, 1964), 1: 287.

30. Kemény, *Iratok,* 1: 649-50.

31. Dimitrije Djordjević, "The Serbs as an Integrating and Disintegrating Factor," *Austrian History Yearbook* 3, pt. 2 (1967): 75.

32. Iván T. Berend and György Ránki, *Gazdaság és Társadalom* (Budapest, 1974), p. 72.

33. Lászlo Katus, "Über die Wirtschaftlichen und Gesellschaftlichen Grundlagen der Nationalitätenfrage in Ungarn vor dem Ersten Weltkrieg," *Die Nationalitätenfrage in der Österreichisch-Ungarischen Monarchie 1900-1918* (Budapest, 1966), pp. 183, 208.

34. Robert W. Seton-Watson, *Racial Problems in Hungary* (London, 1908), p. 466.

35. Kemény, *Iratok,* 4: 631.

36. Dimitrije Djordjević, "Tentatives de collaboration Serbo-Hongroise en 1906," *Acta Iugoslaviae Historica* 1 (1970): 118-20, 124-25.

37. Vucinich, "Serbs in Hungary," p. 20.

38. Károly Eötvös, A Habsburgok Politikája. Unpublished manuscript. Quart. Hung. 2048. Budapest, Országos Széchenyi Könyvtar, Levéltár.

39. Gróf Tivadar Batthyány, *Beszámolóm* (Budapest, n.d.), 1: 77.

40. Kemény, *Iratok,* 5: 321.

41. Ibid., p. 470.

42. Ibid., p. 561. Comment by the editor.

43. Ibid., p. 537.

44. Grátz, *A Dualizmus Kora,* 2: 326.

45. 26 January 1916. Hungary. *Országgyűlés Nyomtatványai. Képviselőház. Napló,* 28: 479.

46. Eduard Ritter von Steinitz, ed., *Erinnerungen an Franz Joseph I* (Berlin, 1931), p. 350.

47. 25 July 1915, Austria. Haus- Hof- und Staatsarchiv. Kabinett Kanzlei-Geheim Akten, K-28.

48. Wedel to Chancellor Hertling, 20 December 1917, Germany. Auswärtiges Amt. Abteilung A. 85-6, Nr. 379.

49. Sándor Tonelli, *Tisza István Utolsó Utja. Stefan Sarkotic Vozérezredes Naplója* (Szeged, 1941), pp. 94-95; Bogdan Krizman, "Die Politische Tournee Stephan Tiszas im Herbst 1918," *Der Donauraum* 13, no. 4 (1968): 226.

50. Details and an analysis of Tisza's factfinding tour are discussed in Gabor Vermes, *Count István Tisza.* Manuscript to be published by East European Quarterly Press.

51. Krizman, "Die Politische Tournee Stephan Tiszas," p. 231.

52. 17 October 1918, *Képviselőház. Napló,* 41: 292.

53. Miklós Komjáthy, ed., *Protokolle des Gemeinsamen Ministerrates des Österreich-Ungarischen Monarchie 1914-1918* (Budapest, 1966), p. 699.

54. Friedrich Funder, *Vom Gestern ins Heute* (Vienna, 1971), pp. 447-48; Hegedűs, *Két Andrássy,* p. 358; Prince Ludwig Windischgraetz, *My Memoirs* (London, 1921), p. 262.

55. Ambrózy to Tisza, 25 October 1918. Hungary. The Archive of the Hungarian Reformed Church. Tisza Iratok 20-41/16.

ENLIGHTENMENT AND NATIONAL CONSCIOUSNESS: THREE CZECH "POPULAR AWAKENERS"*

Hugh LeCaine Agnew
Queen's University, Ontario

In the historiography of the Czech National Revival, the term "awakeners" (*buditelé*) is usually applied to the patriots active in the early phase of the movement, roughly down to and including the generation of Josef Jungmann (1773-1847). Some of them are given the additional attribute "popular" (*lidový*, of or belonging to the people), since their origins, careers, or both link them with the common people. Thes popular awakeners—publicists, village clergy, and minor officials—are credited with playing an important role in transmitting the ideas of the Czech Revial to the masses.[1] Yet their works, especially in the early period, display an interesting dichotomy when viewed from the national standpoint: some clearly carry a national message, while others by the same authors reflect nothing but the desire, in the best Enlightenment tradition, to spread useful knowledge among the common people and to raise their living standard. Did the awakeners see these two fields of activity as separate or complementary? What sort of enlightenment, what sort of national consciousness were they spreading? With these questions in mind, the following discussion will concentrate on the careers of three leading popular awakeners active between 1780 and 1815: Václav Matěj Kramerius, František Jan Tomsa, and Jan Rulík.

Václav Matěj Kramerius (1753-1808) was born in Klatovy, southwest of Prague, and educated in the Jesuit gymnasium there.[2] After graduating in

---

* This study is based in part on research conducted in Prague in 1978-79 under the auspices of the International Research and Exchanges Board.

1773 he came to Prague to study philosophy; among his professors were Karl Heinrich Seibt, one of the leading representatives of the Catholic Enlightenment, and Stanislav Vydra, the patriotic mathematician and priest. Here Kramerius also made the acquaintance of Josef Dobrovský, who had been at the Klatovy gymnasium before him, and they became good friends.[3] Kramerius enrolled in law after completing his philosophical studies, but perhaps because, as a member of a large and not particularly well-to-do family, he had to support himself, he left university altogether about 1778. Shortly thereafter Dobrovský's recommendation enabled him to find employment in the service of Johann Franz Ritter von Neuberg (1743-84), who was a great supporter of learning and an enthusiastic collector of old Czech manuscripts and books.

Kramerius organized von Neuberg's extensive library, made copies of rare manuscripts, and helped edit and reprint some early Czech books on his patron's private printing press.[4] Thus he simultaneously gained a thorough knowledge of literary Czech at its fullest flowering, and valuable experience of the printer's trade. In addition, Kramerius attended von Neuberg's salon and there met with such leading figures of the Czech Revival as F. M. Pelcl, F. F. Procházka, F. J. Tomsa, and of course, Dobrovský. These influences helped point him in the direction of the literary career to which he devoted the remaining quarter-century of his life.[5]

František Jan Tomsa (1751-1814) was born in the village of Mokrý, near Turnov in northern Bohemia, and attented the Piarist gymnasium in Kosmonosy. He studied philosophy in Prague at the same time as Kramerius, obtained employment in 1777 as translator and corrector in the press and warehouse of the Prague Normal School, and remained with this institution, eventually serving as its director, until his death.[6]

Tomsa came from a Czech-speaking family, but it was his Piarist teachers in Kosmonosy who inspired in him the deep love for his mother tongue which was to give direction to his life. He later recalled that once, when his fellow students complained that so few Czech books were available, his professor had responded prophetically, "Tomsa will write them for you."[7] During his studies in Prague Tomsa was exposed to the ideals of the Enlightenment, which he warmly espoused. He could have made the acquaintance of Kramerius at this time; certainly they were both part of the group of patriotic and educated men around von Neuberg, and they became lifelong friends and associates.

The third member of this trio of popular awakeners, *Jan Rulík* (1744-1812), was a native of Žleby who came to Prague as a singer in the Jesuit seminary in the New Town. Here he completed his schooling in the humanities and philosophy preparatory to entering the priesthood, but he later changed his mind and devoted himself to literature and music. He made a living as a vocalist and musician in a series of Prague churches, ending in St. Vitus's Cathedral at the Prague Castle. How Rulík and Kramerius met is not clear, but there is no doubt that they eventually became close friends. Rulík was also acquainted with the other Prague patriots, including Tomsa, but it was Kramerius in particular on whom he patterned his own activities.[8]

The accession to power of Joseph II in 1780, the ambitious reform program upon which he immediately embarked, and the loosening of press censorship ushered in a period of considerable intellectual ferment in Bohemia as well as the rest of the Monarchy. Joseph's reforms, particularly the Patent of Toleration (1781) and other measures affecting the church, met with considerable suspicion and opposition not only among the clergy, but also among the common people.[9] Other sections of the population, however, welcomed them, and in the freer atmosphere of the time religion and the role of the clergy became frequent topics of discussion.[10]

The popular awakeners contributed to this discussion by publicizing the reforms in Czech. Their aim was to win first the parish priests, and through them the people, for the new trends. Tomsa worked to spread the ideas of the Catholic Enlightenment by translating K. H. Seibt's German prayer books; the first appearing as *Kniha katolická, obsahující v sobě naučení a modlitby* (Catholic book containing lessons and prayers) in 1780 and the second as *Vyučující a modlicí kniha pro mládež* (Instruction and prayer book for youth) in 1784. He continued in this vein after Joseph's death with his own *Modlitby pro křesťany katolické* (Prayers for Catholic Christians), published in 1803. It was Kramerius, however, who attacked intolerance and religious abuses most directly, beginning in 1782 with his translation of Bishop Johann Leopold Hay's pastoral letter urging his clergy to support toleration, *Cirkularní spis pána z Haje, biskupa královéhradeckého, no duchovenstvo osady jeho strany tolerancí* (Circular letter of Lord Hay, Bishop of Hradec Králové, to the clergy of his diocese regarding tolerance). The Czech edition sold quickly, receiving wide circulation in the countryside, where it was especially welcomed by the non-Catholics.[11]

Also in 1782 Kramerius published another work important for the country people's understanding of Joseph II's policies. His *Patentní ruční knížka pro měšťana i sedláka* (Patent handbook for townsman and peasant) was an attempt to put directly into the hands of the people an explanation of Joseph II's reform program, with extracts from the official patents of the first two years of his reign. A second edition appeared in 1787, at which time Kramerius wrote:

> Nothing more important or more useful for our dear Czech nation could thus far be published; . . . in this book the Czech people will find in their mother tongue all the patents and decrees . . . [explained] with such clarity that everyone can understand them right away.[12]

Even more popular was Kramerius's 1784 translation and adaptation of a book which had appeared in German in 1783, *Kniha Josefova* (The book of Joseph). He published it, as he wrote in his foreword, out of "nothing other than a love of truth," and to "eradicate from the minds of the common people prejudice, superstition, and error."[13] In language patterned after the Bible, *Kniha Josefova* described the reform policies of Joseph II, gave what it claimed to be the details of the future order of the reformed Catholic Church, and enthusiastically praised the monarch himself. It went through four editions by May 1784, and aroused both strong support and condemnation.[14] When its opponents forbade its reading or popular distribution, a proud Kramerius responded that *Kniha Josefova* helped to lead simple Catholics out of ignorance and thus "burns no less than salt in [the] eyes" of those priests who would prefer to keep the people in darkness.[15]

Kramerius continued his attack on religious ignorance and the intolerance of the clergy the following year with a Czech version of J. V. Eybel's *Christkatholische nützliche Hauspostile*. In addition to a foreword defending *Kniha Josefova* and Kramerius against their enemies, it contained a series of meditations in the spirit of reform on the Epistle and Gospel readings for the Sundays and holidays of the year. This *Křesťanská katolická užitečná domovní Postilla* (Christian Catholic useful house postilla) was also widely distributed among the people, and not only among the Catholics.[16] For the rest of his life Kramerius remained deeply committed to the idea of tolerance, and worked to spread it through his newspaper, and especially by means of the *Nový kalendář toleranci* (New calendar of tolerance), which he published yearly from 1787 to 1798. In addition to both Catholic and Protestant saints' days, the calendar included information on decrees affecting toleration and other material, both useful and entertaining.

Jan Rulík's attitude to Joseph's religious reforms was much cooler than that of Kramerius or Tomsa. Although he accepted the Patent of Toleration, he stressed that the Catholic Church retained precedence, and indicated that he was unhappy about the banning of certain ceremonies and the dissolution of the monasteries. He shared the emperor's wish (Court Decree of 17 April 1783) that "all his subjects would hold to the only-saving Catholic faith from their own conviction."[17] Rulík's own religious publications, catechisms and collections of sermons, date from the period following Joseph's death and belong to the traditional Catholic mainstream; nevertheless, Rulík was aware that good religious material in Czech must be circulated among the people.[8]

It is interesting that in their activities as direct publicists for Joseph II, the popular awakeners limited themselves almost exclusively to his religious reforms. It is true that in Kramerius's *Kniha Josefova* he mentions the Emancipation Patent, the school reforms, and the loosening of censorship, but the emphasis and language of the book are religious. Religious reform and the spreading of religious thought free from the superstition of the previous centuries were not, however, the only concerns of the popular awakeners. They also worked for the secular enlightenment of the people, hoping to raise their level of general knowledge and to improve their economic position.[19] Efforts in this direction enjoyed official encouragement and even direct sponsorship under Joseph II, as was the case with the periodical *Der Volkslehrer,* which was published by the Highest Burggrave, Prince Karl Egon Fürstenberg, from 1786 to 1788.[20] The task of preparing the Czech verion of this publication, *Učitel lidu* (The people's teacher), was given to František Tomsa. Like all the popular awakeners faced with a foreign work, he had to do more than make a literal translation; he needed to present the contents in a comprehensible language that would elicit the reader's active sympathy for the ideas involved.[21] This challenge must have appealed to Tomsa, for after a year he left *Učitel lidu* to begin his own monthly, *Měsíční spis k poučení a obveselení obecného lidu* (Monthly paper for the enlightenment and entertainment of the common people).[22] Directed against the harmful effects of some common superstitions, *Měsíční spis* gave clear, rational explanations of the physical origins of such phenomena as mist, fog, steam, fire, thunder, hail, and rings around the moon. Each monthly number also contained an illustration, fables, and moralistic anecdotes. *Měsíční spis* was greeted with enthusiasm by similarly minded patriots, such as Kramerius, who wrote:

> Mr. Tomsa's friends may clearly see from the contents that their wishes, when they wrote that Mr. Tomsa in his future monthly papers should explain especially physical matters, of which up to now the common people have had no understanding, are being completely and fully satisfied. . . . O! what an early enlightening of the mind can we expect among our Czech people, when they are acquainted with such knowledge, which had previously never occurred to them![23]

Kramerius also praised Tomsa's use of Czech, saying that he explained the most difficult topics in such clear language that "even the most simple man can understand them."[24] Due to the pressure of "other work," however, Tomsa ceased publication of *Měsíční spis* with the December 1787 issue, but he promised "to go on enlightening my fellow countrymen, if I am only given a bit quieter time for it."[25]

True to his word, Tomsa continued publishing similar enlightened-didactic works, though he never returned to the periodical form. Besides his translations of school textbooks for the Normal School, he translated several popular German works in the 1790s and the early part of the nineteenth century. These books contained advice, usually in the form of fables or short tales, on such aspects of life as: health, proper eating habits, animal and general husbandry, and especially the behavior of children and the proper methods of raising them.[26] Tomsa also maintained his interest in the physical and natural sciences, leaving behind him in manuscript a translation of Funk's *Naturgeschichte für Kinder,* parts of which appeared in Jan Nejedlý's *Hlasatel český* (Czech herald) from 1806 to 1818.[27]

Kramerius was also an active publisher of popular didactic literature. Typical of his work is *Večerní shromáždění dobrovické obce* (Evening gatherings of the community of Dobrovice), published in 1801. Cast in the conversation form so popular at the time, in this case a series of meetings between the members of a typical country village and their schoolmaster, the lessons stressed hard work, sobriety, and loyalty, while decrying drunkenness and ignorance. Kramerius also included certain patriotic passages, in one of which the teacher exclaims, "O if only you all would feel the same joy I do, when I hear or read something about our dear Czech fatherland!" When he considers what the ancient Czechs did for the fatherland and language, the teacher asks "if it is still possible that the present-day Czechs—or at least our descendants—will one day awake from their deep dream, and remembering who they are, value their country and mother tongue above all else, like all the other nations?"[28]

Similar themes are treated in Kramerius's *Dobrá rada v potřebě, anebo vypsání života Davida Opatrného* (Good counsel in need, or a description of the life of Careful David), which appeared first as a supplement to his *Vlastenské noviny* and then in book form in 1803, and his popular "encyclopedia," *Přítel lidu* (The people's friend), which was published in 1806-7. "In this work my main intention is, insofar as it is within the power of my intellect, to enlighten and amuse the common people," he wrote in *Přítel lidu.*[29] As before, however, he did not miss the opportunity to awaken patriotic feelings. He included a poem "In Praise of the Slavic Language," and excerpts from scholarly works (translated from the German) comparing the Slavs and Germans and pointing out the numerical superiority of Slavs to Germans in the Habsburg Monarchy.[30]

Like Tomsa, Kramerius also devoted his attention to didactic works for children. One of these, *Zrcadlo šlechetnosti pro mládež českou* (A mirror of nobility for Czech youth), he had originally written for his own four sons and subsequently published in 1805.[31] His most successful venture in this field, a free translation of a work by the German pedagogue Joachim Heinrich Campe, *Mladší Robinzon* (The younger Robinson), appeared in 1808. The story was based loosely on the novel by Daniel Defoe, but its moral message for young people had been given greater prominence.

Rulík, too, felt the need for good books in Czech for children, and had translated a book by Campe as early as 1792.[32] He followed this in 1794 with *Kastonova užitečná naučení o dobrém zvedení mládeže* (Kaston's useful lessons about the proper rearing of youth), and a sequel, *Kastonova kniha druhá* (Kaston's second book), which appeared the following year. As well as the usual lessons, Rulík placed a special emphasis on the virtue of loyalty to the authority of both church and state. "Be obedient to authority (*vrchnost*): and perform and render unto it what belongs to it. For there is no power, but from God."[33]

In addition to publishing these didactic works, intended to improve the peasant's living conditions, the popular awakeners worked to raise the economic position of the peasant. Beginning under Maria Theresia, the Habsburg government had concerned itself with this problem, supporting the establishment of the Society for Agriculture and the Free Arts in Bohemia, transformed in 1778 into the Imperial and Royal Patriotic-Economic Society. It was organized to spread new agrarian methods that would make Bohemian agriculture more efficient, and to popularize new crops or improved varieties of old ones. The Patriotic-Economic Society published pamphlets and books to this end, but almost always in German.[34] In order to reach the peasant who understood only Czech, the popular awakeners publicized these same discoveries and techniques. As editor of the *Schönfeldské císařské královské pražské noviny* (Schönfeld's imperial and royal Prague news) from 1786-89, Kramerius introduced a special rubric, "Naučení k domácímu hospodářství" (Lessons in home economics), in which he encouraged the use of new methods and crops. He later continued this trend in his own *Krameriusovy c. k. vlastenské noviny* (Kramerius's imperial and royal patriotic news), and in addition, an important section of his *Nový kalendář tolerancí* was devoted to these topics. Both Tomsa and Rulík also contributed to this effort with translations of German works concentrating on such practical subjects as: techniques of veterinary medicine, advice on raising livestock (especially sheep), and methods for growing fodder on otherwise unusable fields.[35]

Rulík paid particular attention to the life of the country-dweller. In 1798 he published a *Krátký spísek o stavu sedlském, aneb voráčském* (A short work about the peasant's or ploughman's estate), in which he wrote in idealistic terms about the value of the peasant to society:

> I do not know why many people are so retarded in understanding, that they consider the peasant's or ploughman's estate, which puts bread practically into the mouths of all the other estates, to be coarse and worthy of scorn. Of course only senseless people think this way. . . . This estate is the oldest in the world, the oldest work, practically as old as the human race. You therefore o farmers, when you cultivate your fields, also remember this; that you are called to work and produce bread not only for yourselves, but for the common good.[36]

Such sentiments can be interpreted merely as a cynical effort to keep the peasants happy in his miserable lot, but it could also be argued that the popular awakeners actually believed in the value of the peasant, who after all had maintained his Czech language through the dark years of the Counter-Reformation.[37] Rulík did link the peasant with the legendary Czech past through the popular figure of Přemysl, the plowman who was called by Libuše to be ruler, and he also emphasized the agricultural nature of "our ancestors the Slavs."[38]

Publicity on behalf of particular government policies and the interests of the state in general was not the only activity in which the popular awakeners were involved. They were also active in disseminating news of current events, whether of local or international significance, through newspapers, almanacs, and calendars. Mention has already been made of Kramerius's *Nový kalendář toleranci,* which was sold at such a low price that it was quite well circulated. Perhaps the crowning achievement of Kramerius's life, however, was his twenty-two years as a newspaper editor, first for the Prague publisher J. F. von Schönfeld, and from 1789 until his death for his own publication. Convinced that contemporary Czech newspapers were "nothing other than chronicles and tales of years, which are written for posterity to eternal memory,"[39] Kramerius was determined to use them to awaken patriotism and national consciousness among readers in the present generation. Although he never completely ignored these precepts, Kramerius fulfilled them most clearly during the early years of his newspaper, before the worsening economic situtation and the wars with France had taken their toll.

Kramerius seized on every occurrence that could illustrate his national message. Paying particular attention to the literary efforts of Czech patriots, he directed his readers' attention to plays, new books, and also political events that evoked the honor and glory of the Czech Kingdom. In the 1780s Kramerius detailed the fortunes of the Czech theater, giving advance notice of plays to be performed and reviewing those that had already been presented or published. He welcomed the establishment of a second company of actors to present Czech plays, writing that "this society of patriotic actors deserves support and help from every sincere fellow countryman all the more since in this way our dear language can improve and spread itself a great deal."[40] When these actors performed German as well as Czech plays, he criticized them by reprinting in translation these comments from a pamphlet about Prague that had appeared in German:

> The members of this patriotic theater called themselves a patriotic society, and actually, if they would stick to the patriotic plays, they would deserve all encouragement. But they should leave out the German plays which they mix in. . . . One can tell that they are more competent in their native tongue, and that every action suits them better in it.[41]

Part of the problem, of course, was that there were few Czech plays to be performed. Kramerius was aware of this, and tried his hand at translation for the theater in 1778 with the play *Albert a Lotte, aneb ctnost v největší nouzy* (Albert and Lotte, or virtue in greatest need). It was actually performed, as the first Czech play by the aforementioned second company of actors, but it did not have great success.[42] Notice of Czech plays gradually diminished in number, partly because of the increasing preponderance of war news, partly perhaps due to Kramerius's views on the linguistic "utraquism" of the theater companies.[43] Literature did not, however, disappear entirely from Kramerius's newspaper. New Czech books continued to be noted, and Kramerius frequently devoted an entire section, "Závěsek" (Supplement) or "Literální zpráva" (Literary report), to give notice of new and used books for sale or wanted by a buyer.

Current political events gave Kramerius another chance to emphasize national themes. When Joseph II died, his reform program was threatened:

Hungary was practically in open revolt, and the Estates in the Bohemian and Austrian lands were also restive. Leopold II, Joseph's brother and successor, called the Estates in all his possessions into session, so that they could present their suggestions and complaints, *Desideria,* before his government began shaping its policies.[44] At this time, the Bohemian nobles began to form a kind of tentative alliance with the patriotic intellectuals, especially on the question of the status of the Czech language; the patriot's dislike of the Germanization of schools and official life and the nobility's resistance to Joseph's centralizing policies had found a common issue in the language question.[45] Through his correspondents in Hungary, Kramerius kept his readers informed of the progress of the national demands of the Hungarians, and called upon their Bohemian counterparts to request similar concessions for Czech. What the patriots hoped to gain for Czech could in fact be presented as moderate in comparison with the Hungarian demands. After a report on yet another condition attached by the Hungarian Estates to their consent to Leopold's coronation, Kramerius wrote:

> As far as we Czechs, ever loyal to the House of Austria, are concerned, we would have no other or more humble request of his Royal Highness. . . than that he reintroduce into all our schools and government officies our mother tongue, for thus alone will our glorious nation again recover, and never demur at giving its life for our Monarch. O that this wish of thousands upon thousands of true patriots would be graciously fulfilled![46]

Hoping to inspire his compatriots to action, Kramerius would reprint his Budapest correspondent's glowing accounts of the popularity of the native tongue among all Hungarians and follow them with the pointed question: "What are the Bohemian Estates intending to do at present in the cause of the Czech language?"[47] "Who are we?" Kramerius asked rhetorically. "Are we not Czechs? What is our Kingdom? Is it not Czech7 And is it then fitting that we should unlearn our language?"[48]

In December 1791 Kramerius wrote that the joyous moment was arriving, in which Czech would again have all paths opened to it, for with the permission of the emperor, a chair of Czech would be established at the Prague university.[49] It was not until 1793, however, when František Martin Pelcl was finally appointed first holder of this chair, that

Kramerius could welcome this long-awaited sign that "the Czechs can be of good hope that their language, which in this century practically sank into oblivion, is slowly beginning to reach a higher level, and greater perfection and glory."[50] Leopold's coronation in Prague provided Kramerius with another opportunity to recall the bygone glories of the Czech Kingdom. The coronation involved the return of the Crown of St. Václav from Viennese exile, which was cause for rejoicing, and the favor that the Czechs found in the eyes of Leopold promised that perhaps the "golden age" was returning to them.[51] Kramerius also printed a Czech translation of Josef Dobrovsky's speech given on the occasion of the monarch's attendance at a meeting of the Royal Bohemian Society of Sciences. In this speech, "Über die Ergebenheit und Anhänglichkeit der Slavischen Völker an das Erzhaus Österreich," Dobrovsky stressed the importance of the Slavic inhabitants to the Monarchy, pointing out that they constituted a majority of the population, and had always been loyal to the ruling house.[52] Kramerius accorded the coronation of Franz II a similarly extensive coverage, paying particular attention to the "country celebration" put on by the Estates in the emperor's honor, at which representatives of each district of the kingdom were present in their native costumes. Again he stressed that all this was looked upon with favor by Franz, and thus did great honor to the Czech nation.[53]

In his *Kalendár historický*, Jan Rulík followed the lead of Kramerius and used political and other happenings as opportunities to deliver a national message. He also mentioned cultural events, noting in 1786 that "to the great delight of the Czech nation" Czech newspapers began to appear again, and Czech was heard on the stage.[54] Of the coronation of Leopold he wrote in enthusiastic terms:

> This is a memorable century, especially for the Czech nation and kingdom, in which our renowned Czech kingdom and nation enjoyed great fame, when they not only received back their priceless Crown of St. Václav from foreign lands, also also crowned their King. . . . It is fitting that we Czechs, together with our descendants, hold it in glorious memory forever.[55]

Both Rulík and Kramerius found their fellow patriots a further source of publicity for this national theme. The appearance of a new book, the appointment of a person to an official position, or the granting of a government honor—all constituted occasions to praise the living patriot and stress the glorious past. A sort of cult of the sincere patriot and the glorious ancestors grew up, and the litany of honored names was recounted at each appropriate moment. Tomsa, the brothers Thám, Rulík, Pelcl, Procházka, Dobrovský, and others were all celebrated in the pages of Kramerius's *Vlastenské noviny*, while Rulík dedicated volumes of his *Kalendář historický* to Antonín Strnad, Pelcl, Kramerius, and Jan Nejedlý (Pelcl's successor as professor of Czech Language and Literature at the Prague university), as well as occasional poems to both Pelcl and Nejedlý.[56] It was these men, and others like them, "who day by day [took] more pains and effort, that their language through their untiring work could achieve again the perfection which flourished during its golden age two hundred years ago."[57]

Rulík devoted several independent works to such themes. His *Velmi užitečná historie o slovutném národu českém* (A very useful history of the renowned Czech nation), published in 1793, was an account of the development and character of the nation from the earliest Slavic tribes to the present. He stressed the fact that the Czechs were a branch of the Slavs, and accused the Germans of folly when, because of this fact, they "turned their sharpened pens against us, ascribing to us excesses, unkindliness, insatiable robber's greed" (p. 6). The Czechs were never like that; on the contrary, they were honorable, loyal, and brave in battle. They were also intelligent and very talented in the arts, although in Rulík's day this talent was often wasted because Czech was no longer cultivated in the schools (p. 71). The Czechs were also blessed with a beautiful and richly endowed homeland that had produced many learned and holy men. "Therefore, my Czechs, true patriots," concluded Rulík, "let us also act the same; let us care about that name Czech, the nation and the language," so that "our descendants will also bless us for this zeal . . . as we now bless our dear ancestors of good memory" (p. 79).

Rulík's concern with national continuity was clearly manifested in his work. In order to preserve the memory of his contemporaries for coming generations, he dedicated to them his *Věnec pocty k poctivosti učených, výborných a statečných Čechu* (A wreath of honor in honor of learned, excellent, and valiant Czechs), published in 1795, and listed their names. He also included a bibliography of books published in Czech from 1782 to 1795, which he later extended down to 1804.[58] His *Učená Čechia* (Learned Czechia), three volumes of which appeared in 1807-8, and the five volumes of *Galerie, aneb vyobrazenost nejslovutnějších a nejvýznam-nějších osob země české* (Gallery, or a depiction of the most renowned and most significant persons of the Czech land) issued from 1803 to 1810, took a more historical view. Neither of these works is original,[59] but the material in them had previously appeared only in Latin or German, "so that many of our good Czechs, for whom speaking and reading Czech is the dearest and only thing, do not know anything about them."[60] *Učená Čechia* covered the entire history of learning in Bohemia, paying special attention to those members of the nobility who were famous for their knowledge, and those commoners whose learning had earned them noble status. After presenting these examples, Rulík called on his readers to remember that they came from a nation once the most renowned in Europe, both for its learning and its heroic deeds, and urged them to follow proudly in the footsteps of their ancestors. "Would that our descendants also will not be ashamed of us, when, remembering us, they say: that we are their ancestors and Czechs!"[61] *Galerie* consisted of a series of popularized biographies of famous personalities in Czech history, from the legendary Krok and Libuše to the eighteenth century.

During the Napoleonic wars the government found that it could put the example of these ancient Czechs to practical use. Especially in 1796, 1800, and 1809, when organizing local militias to protect Bohemia from invasion, the authorities appealed to the traditions of past heroes in order to excite the people's fighting spirit.[62] The proclamations of Archduke Karl and other official announcements were given space in both the *Vlastenské noviny* and *Kalendář historický,* and reports were made of the great patriotic response of the people.[63]

Rulík contributed personally to this war propaganda in 1808 with his one-act play, *Vlastenský mladý rekruta* (The patriotic young recruit). Though it is set in the time of the eleventh-century Czech prince Oldřich, the play was clearly intended to rally enthusiasm for the coming campaign against Napoleon. It tells the story of a young boy, rejected by the recruiters because of his age, who finally convinces the prince to let him join his forces as a drummer. Throughout the play the Czechs were depicted as loyal and willing to die for the prince. "Let others value their blood as they wish, sell it for what they wish," said one recruit who had just refused payment. "I come out of the simple love which I have for my lord."[64] In its appeals to the glories of the Czech past, the government clearly intended to serve only its own military needs, but the popular awakeners recognized that such propaganda could have much broader ramifications. Although they were as loyal as any other subjects, the popular awakeners were not unaware that in this case the govenment's interests coincided with their own.

Concern for the Czech language is the thread that unified practically all of the popular awakeners' work. They agitated for its spread, attempted to improve its condition, and used it in their own works. They worked to create a demand for Czech reading material in the countryside, and to make worthwhile books more available. Besides using Czech in their own works for the common people, the popular awakeners joined others in defending the language, stressing its historical excellence, and publishing again some of the monuments of its "golden age."

Rulík and Tomsa contributed directly to the genre of the "defense of the language," while Kramerius, in the pages of his newspaper and elsewhere, also stressed its value.[65] In 1792 Rulík published *Sláva a výbornost jazyka českého* (The glory and excellence of the Czech language), a work suffused with a love for language, that "gift of God and the priceless inheritance of each and every nation" (p. 35). Identifying Czech as one of the five main branches of the Slav language (which he claimed to be more widespread than any other European language[p.7]).Rulík argued that it was so rich in vocabulary that there was no need to borrow foreign words, a bad habit the Czechs had learned from the Germans, whose language contained more foreign words than Czech (p. 12). Rulík also assured his readers that since it contains all the sounds of the other European languages, a speaking knowledge of Czech would facilitate the pronunciation of other foreign languages (p. 17). He described the decline of the national language following the defeat at the White Mountain in 1620, and although he could not condone the rebellion, he did condemn the burning of Czech books during the Counter-Reformation (pp. 32-33). Insisting that every nation should cultivate its mother tongue, Rulík hailed the example of Hungary, where not only the common people, but also the highest nobles supported Hungarian (p. 38).

Tomsa's *Von den Vorzügen der čechischen Sprache*, published in 1812, stressed the long history of Czech as a cultivated language, its simplicity, pithiness of expression, and rich vocabulary. "And should it then not be worthwhile," he demanded, "to maintain and improve a . . . language such as Czech—the native language (*Landessprache*) of a not insignificant kingdom?"[66]

Kramerius also wrote about the importance of the language, arguing that one's mother tongue is such a rare jewel that even the barbarians do not value anything more highly, for language alone distinguishes nations from one another. "The Russians speak Russian, the French French, Italians Italian, and thus in the whole world each nation has its own language; why then should the Czechs alone have to betray and disown their mother tongue?"[67]

The relationship of Czech to the other Slavic languages frequently was cited as a reason for its importance. The popular awakeners, in fact, often identified Czech as a dialect of the single Slavic language, and the Czechs as only a branch of the Slavic nation. Rulík emphasized the Slavic ancestors of the Czechs in his *Velmi užitečná historie* and in *Sláva a výbornost jazyka českého*, and Kramerius dedicated his newspaper to "the Czech, Moravian, and glorious, widespread Slavic nation."[68] He begged his fellow countrymen to get rid of the obsolete antipathy that they had for their language, promising that they would then realize "that Russians, Poles, Pomeranians, Silesians, Moravians, Slovaks, Dalmatians, Bosnians, Moldavians, Serbs, Wends, Croats, and many other famous nations spread to all corners of the world are [their] brothers, and use the glorious Slavic language, with only slight differences."[69] Such proud affirmations did not blind the popular awakeners to the steep decline that had brought their language from its "golden age" in the sixteenth century to its present sorry condition. They knew all too well that many of its most precious monuments "were in part damaged and destroyed by coarse ignorance, in part given up to the flames by senseless zeal."[70] One way in which to improve the quality of the language and to make good at least part of the losses was to put those monuments of Czech literature which had survived back in the hands of the Czech reader.

In this activity the popular awakeners followed the example set by F. M. Pelcl, publisher in 1777 of *Příhody Václava Vratislava z Mitrovic* (The adventures of Václav Vratislav z Mitrovic), and F. F. Procházka, who during the 1780s published an entire series of works by the sixteenth-century Czech humanists and others.[71] Through Tomsa's efforts the auto-biography of Karel IV and Šimon Lomnický z Budče's *Tobolka zlatá* (The golden purse), a tract against the sin of greed, saw the light of day again in 1791. Kramerius published another work of Lomnický's in 1794, *Krátké naučení mladému hospodáři* (Short lessons for the young husbandman), which was written in verse and thus, Kramerius felt, could be used as a model by beginning Czech poets.[72] Kramerius also brought out a Czech version of the story of the Trojan War, which appeared in 1790, as well as translations of Aesop's fables (1791) and the fabulous travels of Sir John Mandeville (1795).[73] He continued to publish works from the Czech "golden age" into the nineteenth century, with *Krátká historie o válce židovské* (A short history of the Jewish war) in 1806, a re-issuing of Václav z Mitrovic's adventures in 1807, and *Xenofonta, mudrce athenského, život a skutkové Cyra staršiho* (The life and deeds of Cyrus the elder, by Xenophon, the Athenian philosopher) in 1809. Jan Rulík's 1800 translation of Jiří z Drachova's *Cesta z Moskvy do Činy* (A journey from Moscow to China) probably belongs with this group as well, although the original had been written in Latin.[74]

The popular awakeners anticipated that the publication of these books would spread good written Czech among the people and thereby promote the development of Czech literature. Kramerius boasted that although the Germans and others began to cultivate their languages seriously only in the eighteenth century, the Czechs had brought theirs two hundred years earlier to a level that was not only the equal of Latin and Greek, but surpassed every other language.[75] He and his colleagues expressed the hope that these books would remind their readers from whom they were descended, and teach them to respect their language and not to damage it further.[76] For, as Rulík vividly expressed it,

> Experience shows that there is no other way to the hope of pre-serving the purity of a language, and also that it cannot be better spread than by reading excellent books. Otherwise it would

become plucked and bare, like Aesop's magpie, from which all
the other birds (O! would that our native ones did not act that
way!), pulled the feathers.[77]

Although they revered the Czech of the "golden age," the popular
awakeners were more aware than others among their contemporaries that
the language could not be forced back into its sixteenth-century mold.
Their activities as translators and popularizers brought home to them the
difficulties of finding suitable Czech words for all topics, in spite of their
repeated assertions that Czech was lexically rich.[78] If the language were
to be a meaningful tool for spreading knowledge and stimulating national
consciousness, it must maintain its contact with the people who spoke
it daily.

Tomsa, who in addition to his work as a popular awakener was an
active philologist and lexicographer, emphasized this need to stay close
to the vernacular.[79] Especially when dealing with the terminology of
specialized fields, the translator or lexicographer must be willing to learn
from the person who performs the work, and if he is too proud to learn
Czech from a laborer, a peasant, or a servant, then he should give up
writing rather than become a corrupter of the language.[80] Tomsa did not,
however, recommend the uncritical acceptance of every word in the
spoken language. "A true Czech must not be ashamed to learn from all
Czechs, in order to comprehend the complete linguistic usage," he wrote;
"but he must test what he hears, in order to be able to teach true Czech."[81]

Intent on making their works comprehensible to the average Czech,
the popular awakeners did not hesitate to modify even the language of
the "golden age." Kramerius, for example, edited his version of Aesop's
fables to conform to contemporary spoken usage, pointing out that this
had been done in each of six previous editions.[82] When he translated
Cesta z Moskvy do Číny, Rulík's main concern was that everyone who
read it be able to understand everything "in their natural language."
Tomsa's edition of Karel IV's autobiography was also cast into a more
modern Czech, with the help of Procházka.[83] Despite the criticisms of
more traditionally minded patriots, who attacked Tomsa in particular for
his views, the popular awakeners persevered in their efforts.

Publishing these monuments of the "golden age" was only one aspect
of the popular awakeners' work on behalf of Czech literature. The number

of such classics was limited, and, in any case, the taste of the Czech reader was often not ready to appreciate them. The most popular form of reading, besides the saints' lives and "keys to heaven" (*nebekliče*), was the so-called knightly romance (*rytířský roman*), which was usually badly modeled on German tales and filled with witches, magic, enchanted princesses, and the like.[85] From the standpoint of both content and language these stories were very primitive, and the popular awakeners sought to replace them with readings on a similarly popular level, but in good Czech and with a more useful content.

During the last quarter of the eighteenth century, more and more Czech books were published in Bohemia. In addition to the press of the Normal School, the Prague publishers von Schönfeld, Diesbach, Herrl, and others all carried Czech books on their lists at one time or another. But for most of these publishers Czech books were only a sideline, since they also published works in German or other languages. It was only when Kramerius organized his Czech Expedition (Česká expedice) in 1790 that there existed a publishing house devoted exclusively to Czech literature.[86]

At first forced to publish works of approximately the same quality as those he hoped to replace, Kramerius gradually began to fulfill his aim that "the country people . . . get rid of many of that sort of tale, which indeed for its contemptibility deserves to be expunged completely from our Czech nation."[87] Through travelogues and historical tales set in far places, he acquainted his readers with foreign countries and customs. These works were usually in the dialogue form, and were more than simple lessons in geography, since they also covered economics, culture, and religion. Kramerius continued to praise reason and tolerance, as for example in *Historické vypsání, kterak. . . Amerika od Kolumbusa vynalezena byla* (A historical description of how America was discovered by Columbus), which appeared in 1803. In it he condemned the Spaniards' greed for gold and their behavior towards the natives, reminding his readers that "many Christians are much worse than those people who know nothing about our holy religion."[88] Kramerius also supported other Czech writers through the Czech Expedition, among them Prokop Šedivý, whose 1792 story *České amazonky* (The Czech amazons) he accompanied with a laudatory foreword. He stressed that it was an original Czech tale based on Czech sources (Hájek z Libočan's chronicle), and boasted that for a change it was being translated from Czech into German.[89]

Rulík was also interested in providing the people with entertaining but enlightening reading material. Of his 1799 story *Veselý Kubíček* (Merry Kubíček), he wrote that although it may be considered a made-up fable, "nevertheless it affords the benefit that everyone, having read it, not only amuses himself, but also sees how confused the human mind is by passion."[90] Its 1802 sequel, *Boženka, veselého Kubíčka manželka* (Boženka, merry Kubíček's wife), also has its moral, warning Czech girls to heed their elders' advice instead of trusting their own confused emotions.

Although they had little intrinsic literary worth, the works published by the Czech Expedition were important in that they began to raise the tastes of the common reader, and thus helped to spread a much higher standard of Czech into the countryside. Works such as Kramerius's travelogues and didactic "encyclopedias" such as *Přítel lidu* were crucial catalysts in the gradual enlightenment of the common people. As an organization dedicated solely to publishing in Czech for the Czechs, the Czech Expedition was also an important center of patriotic activity, as depicted in Alois Jirásek's novel about the National Revival, *F. L. Věk* (1887-1905).

Jan Rulík was the only one of these popular awakeners who specifically addressed himself to the question of what he thought "enlightenment" to be. In a work published in 1804, long after the period of enlightened absolutism in Bohemia had ended, he defined enlightenment as nothing other than making known something which had previously been unknown. From this it followed that there could be good and bad enlightenment; it was good when the new knowledge helped the community, bad when it harmed it. According to Rulík, a person who truly had the welfare of the people at heart "gives the rules, according to which [they] should maintain their health, . . . he teaches how children should be raised, and . . . he sincerely places in the hands of the husbandman what he should do to improve his husbandry."[91]

Rulík was probably the most conservative of the three, but since much of Kramerius's and Tomsa's lifework was dedicated to precisely the activities mentioned here, they probably would not disagree very much with Rulík's definition. The work of the popular awakeners went further than this, however. Tomsa and Kramerius, especially, tried to spread an enlightened religious outlook, and to free the common people from the superstition and intolerance of the preceding two centuries. Thus they began at least to prepare them to accept the changes which were to take place in their lives during the coming years. In this, the popular awakeners were motivated by a desire to serve, not so much the state, as their homeland (*vlast*) and nation. They believed that "the first and foremost duty of wise and truth-loving men in this century is to enlighten human understanding more and more each day; and the nation that gains the light of reason from their praiseworthy, resolute efforts cannot but be considered happy and truly blessed."[92] Their popular-enlightening activities were thus a part of their national activities. By helping to enlighten the Czech people, the popular awakeners were working to make it possible for their nation proudly to take its rightful place among the other enlightened nations of Europe.[93]

As we have seen above, the popular awakeners also worked to spread patriotism and Czech national consciousness among the people. Repeatedly they evoked the example of the early Czechs as a challenge to the present generation. Hailing the ancient heroes for their learning, their bravery in battle, and their love of their language, the awakeners implied that every Czech must strive to be worthy of such ancestors. Similar publicity was given to the activities of the awakeners' fellow patriots, and again the aim was to inspire the national pride of the common people. Above all the popular awakeners worked for the Czech language, encouraged its use in all areas of life, and stressed again and again that a true patriot would love it and try to improve and to spread it. These are all themes that would remain part of nineteenth-century nationalist thought; and in their identification of the Czech nation with the Czech language the popular awakeners left to the coming generation a fundamental belief, still part of the national consciousness of most peoples today. As Kramerius warned, "If we someday allow our language to be wiped out through our negligence, it will not be otherwise, than that we will cease to be that which we are, *the Czech nation,* and with time change into a completely different and foreign nation."[94] These words would not sound out of place in the mouth of any later nationalist.

NOTES

1. See Jan Novotný, "Příspěvek k otázce úlohy některých lidových buditelů v počátcích českého národního obrození," in *Československý časopis historický,* 2 (1954), 600-632.

2. Biographies of Kramerius include most recently Jan Novotný, *Matěj Václav Kramerius* (Prague, 1973); and also Václav Osvald, *Vychovatel lidu M. V. Kramerius* (Prague, 1943), and Antonín Rybička, *Přední křisitelé národu českého,* I (Prague, 1883), 9-39.

3. Novotný, *Kramerius,* p. 17.

4. Rybička, *Přední křisitelé,* I, 11; Novotný, *Kramerius,* p. 20.

5. On the von Neubergs and Prague intellectual life of the time see Josef Hanuš, *Národní museum a naše obrození,* I (Prague, 1921), 155-57.

6. Tomsa has not yet been the subject of a systematic study. For biographical details see the sketch by Hanuš in *Ottův slovník naučný,* 25 (Prague, 1906), 550-51, and L. Zeil, "Die Bedeutung des tschechischen Josefiners František Jan Tomsa (1751-1814) für die Entwicklung seiner Muttersprache," in *Zeitschrift für Slawistik,* 14 (1969), 596-608.

7. In his manuscript autobiography, now in the Literární archiv Památníku národního písemnictví (LA PNP), Prague, Dobrovský collection, sign. I 5/7.

8. Even less has been written about Rulík than about Tomsa; a biographical sketch by H. Máchal is in *Ottův slovník naučný,* 22 (Prague, 1902), 96-97.

9. Josef Kočí, *České národní obrození* (Prague, 1978).

10. See Hanuš, *František Faustin Procházka, český buditel a literární historik* [Rozpravy České akademie císaře František Josefa pro vědy, slovesnost, a umění, třída III, no. 39] (Prague, 1915), 21-48, where he discusses especially the magazine *Geissel der Prediger* and its supporters and opponents.

11. Novotný, *Kramerius,* p. 27.

12. *Schönfeldské císařské královské pražské noviny,* 11 August 1787.

13. V. M. Kramerius, *Kniha Josefova* (Prague, 1784), pp. 3-4.

14. Novotný, *Kramerius,* p. 36.

15. In his foreword to *Křesťanská katolická užitečná domovní Postilla* (Prague, 1785), unpaginated.

16. Novotný, *Kramerius*, pp. 38-39.

17. Jan Rulík, *Kalendář historický, obsahující krátké a summovní poznamenání všechněch promĕn, příbĕhů, válek, nejvyšších nařízení, a t. d. jak v slavném národu a království ceském, tak i na díle v jiných národech a zemích, zbĕhlých.* I (Prague, 1797), 41.

18. See his announcement of *Krátké katechetické kazání na nedĕle přes celý rok,* in *Krameriusovy c. k. vlastenské noviny,* 13 October 1799.

19. Novotný, "Příspĕvek," pp. 606, 611-19.

20. Miroslav Laiske, *Časopisectví v Čechách, 1650-1847* (Prague, 1959), pp. 126, 133.

21. See the discussion of this in Bedřich Slavík, *Od Dobnera k Dobrovskému* (Prague, 1975), pp. 169-70. Tomsa himself wrote of the problems of translation in his *Böhmische Sprachlehre* (Prague, 1782).

22. Josef Jungmann, *Historie literatury české,* 2d ed. (Prague, 1849), p. 417.

23. *Schönfeldské noviny,* 24 February 1787.

24. Ibid., 7 April 1787.

25. Tomsa, *Mĕsíční spis k poučení a obveselení obecného lidu,* I, no. 12 (December 1787).

26. They included *Pomoc v potřebĕ* (1791), *Nešťastné příhody k výstraze nezkušené mládeže* (1794, 2d ed. 1820), *Katechismus o zdraví pro chramy a školy* (1794), and *Knížka mravná, s 60 historiemi a providačkami pro dítky* (1810).

27. Jungmann, *Historie,* p. 474.

28. Kramerius, *Večerní shromáždĕní dobrovické obce* (Prague, 1801), pp. 143-44.

29. Kramerius, *Přítel lidu,* I (Prague, 1806), 4.

30. Ibid., pp. 5-6, 54-55.

31. Kramerius, *Zrcadlo šlechetnosti pro mládež českou* (Prague, 1805), pp. 3-4.

32. This was *Cvičení dítek jednohokaždého stavu* (Prague, 1792).

33. Rulík, *Kastonova užitečná naučení o dobrém zvedení mládeže* (Prague, 1794), p. 76.

34. Hanuš, *Národní museum a naše obrození,* I, 307; Mikulas Teich, "The Royal Bohemian Society of Sciences and the First Phase of Organized Scientific Advance in Bohemia," in *Historica,* 2 (1960), 161.

35. These included Tomsa's *Tejné rady Šubarta dobře míněné volání na všecky sedláky* (1785), *Laciný prostředek, jak i ze špatných a suchoparných polí živá a dobytku příjemná píce v hojnosti dostat se může* (1787), and *Způsob, jakby se vyplemenil všechen hmyz bez jedu* (1810); and Rulík's *Krátce obsahnutá pravidla k zprávě hospordářů* (1802), *Pravidla k zprávě hospodářů a polních mistrů o ovčím dobytku* (1802), and *Laciné, a v pravdě hojící dobytka lekářství* (1810).

36. Rulík, *Krátký spísek o stavu sedlském* (Prague, 1798), pp. 7-8.

37. Cf. Novotný, "Příspěvek," and Albert Pražák, *České obrození* (Prague, 1948), pp. 20-22.

38. Rulík, *Krátký spísek*, p. 9.

39. *Krameriusovy c. k. pražské poštovské noviny*, 1 July 1789.

40. *Schönfeldské noviny*, 12 April 1788.

41. Ibid., 5 May 1787.

42. Ibid., 3 May 1788.

43. Novotný, *Kramerius*, p. 91.

44. A still valuable treatment of this period is R. J. Kerner, *Bohemia in the Eighteenth Century* (New York, 1932).

45. Novotný, "Příspěvek," p. 609.

46. *Krameriusovy poštovské noviny*, 10 April 1790.

47. *Krameriusovy c. k. vlastenské noviny*, 7 May 1791.

48. *Krameriusovy poštovské noviny*, 27 March 1790.

49. *Krameriusovy vlastenské noviny*, 3 December 1791.

50. Ibid., 26 January 1793.

51. Ibid., 10 September 1791.

52. Ibid., 7 January 1792. The translation was by K. H. Thám.

53. Ibid., 18 August 1792.

54. Rulík, *Kalendář historický*, I, 41.

55. Ibid., p. 130.

56. The two poems were "Vlastenské plesání a díku činění nad slavném uvedením cís. král. profesora jazyka českého na učitelskou stolice v slavné pražské universí" (1793) and "Na den uvedení král. Profesora české literatury p. Jana Nejedlého na učitelskou stolici v slavné učené pražské universí léta 1801" (1801).

57. *Krameriusovy vlastenské noviny*, 4 April 1795.

58. In his *Vesnického faráře rozmlouvání se svými osadníky* (Prague, 1804), pp. 40-47.

59. *Učená Čechia* is basically a translation of M. A. Voigt's introductions to his *Effigies virorum eruditorum atque artificum Bohemiae et Moraviae* (1773-74), which also appeared in German with Pelcl's collaboration as *Abbildungen böhmischer und mährischer Gelehrten und Künstler* (1773-82); *Galerie* was a translation of a similary titled work by Josef Schiffner published in German.

60. Rulík, *Učená Čechia*, I (Prague, 1807), 5.

61. Ibid., II, 18.

62. See J. Kollman, "Obrana Čech v letech 1796 a 1800," in *Sborník archivních prací*, 1955, and Anton Ernstberger, *Böhmens freiwilliger Kreigseinsatz gegen Napoleon 1809* [Veröffentlichungen des Collegiums Carolinum XIV] (Munich, 1963).

63. E.g., *Kalendář historický*, 4 (Prague, 1803), 105; *Krameriusovy vlastenské noviny*, 1 November 1800.

64. Rulík, *Vlastenský mladý rekruta* (Prague, 1808), p. 3.

65. On the "defenses of the language" see expecially Pražák, *Národ se bránil* (Prague, 1945).

66. Tomsa, *Von den Vorzügen der čechischen Sprache, oder über die Billigkeit und den Nützen, die čechische Sprache zu erhalten, empor zu bringen, und über die Mittel dazu* (Prague, 1812), p. 38.

67. Kramerius, *Zrcadlo šlechetnosti pro mládež českou* (Prague, 1805), pp. 33, 78.

68. See for example his leaflet announcing the beginning of his own newspaper, *Obzvláštní zpráva veškerému národu českému moravskému a slovanském*, 6 June 1789.

69. *Krameriusovy poštovské noviny*, 2 January 1790

70. Kramerius, *Večerní shromáždění*, p. 153.

71. Hanuš, *František Martin Pelcl, český historik a buditel* [Rozpravy České akademie císaře Františka Josefa pro vědy, slovesnost a umění, třída III, no. 38] (Prague, 1914), 101-5; and his *Procházka*, pp. 106-19.

72. Kramerius, foreword to *Šimona Lomnického z Budče, Krátké naučení mladému hospodáři* (Prague, 1794), unpaginated.

73. *Letopisové trojanští* (Prague, 1790), *Ezopovy básně spolu s jeho životem* (Prague, 1791), and *Jana Mandivilly, znamenitého a vznešeného rytíře Cesta po světě* (Prague, 1795).

74. Rulík, foreword to *Cesta z Moskvy do Číny, kterouž s ruským vyslancem Isbrandem, skrze krajiny Ostiku, Siberii, Taursko, a Mogolskau*

Tartarii šťastně vykonal: Jiří z Drachova, Čech a rytíř vznešený Léta Páne *1693* (Prague, 1800), unpaginated.

75. Kramerius, foreword to *Letopisové trojanští*, unpaginated.

76. Tomsa, foreword to *Tobolka zlatá, aneb lakomá žádost peněz nenasycená* (Prague, 1791), unpaginated.

77. Rulík, foreword to *Cesta z Moskvy do Činy*, unpaginated.

78. See George Thomas, "The Role of Calques in the Early Czech Language Revival," in *Slavonic and East European Review*, LVI (1978), pp. 481-504.

79. For a discussion of this aspect of Tomsa's career, see Walter Schamschula, *Die Anfänge der tschechischen Erneuerung und das deutsche Geistesleben, 1740-1800* (Munich, 1973), pp. 238-43.

80. Tomsa, *Böhmische Sprachlehre*, p. 440.

81. Tomsa, *Über die Bedeutung, Abwandlung, und Gebrauch der čechischen Zeitworter* (Prague, 1804), 103n.

82. Kramerius, foreword to *Ezopovy básně*, unpaginated.

83. Rulík, foreword to *Cesta z Moskvy do Činy*, unpaginated; Tomsa, foreword to *Život Karla IV.* (Prague, 1791), unpaginated.

84. Schamschula, *Die Anfänge*, p. 240.

85. See *Dějiny české literatury. II. Literatura národního obrození* (Prague, 1960), pp. 88-90.

86. Jan Thon, "Vydávání českých knih v době Kramériusově," in *Slovesná věda*, 4 (1951-52), pp. 132-37.

87. In his announcement of *Maran a Onyra. Americký příběh*, in *Krameriusovy vlastenské noviny*, 31 December 1791.

88. Kramerius, *Historické vypsání, kterak čtvrtý díl světa, Amerika od Kolumbusa vynalezena byla* (Prague, 1803), p. 40.

89. *Krameriusovy vlastenské noviny*, 13 October 1792.

90. Rulík, foreword to *Veselý Kubíček, Aneb: v horách Kašparských zaklený dudák* (Prague, 1799), p. 4.

91. Rulík, *Vesnického faráře rozmulouvání*, pp. 13-14.

92. Kramerius, foreword to *Křesťanská kotolická užtečná domovní Postilla*, unpaginated.

93. Schamschula suggests this motivation for the critical historians of the period, but I believe it can apply as well to the popular awakeners. See his *Die Anfänge*, pp. 114-16.

94. Kramerius, foreword to *Večerní shromáždění*, p. 4.

NICHOLAS I AS REFORMER:
RUSSIAN ATTEMPTS TO CONQUER
THE CAUCASUS, 1825-1855

E. Willis Brooks
University of North Carolina

Almost without exception, historians have accepted the German historian Theodor Schiemann's classic evaluation of Nicholas I (1825-55) as "the most consistent of autocrats."[1] Perhaps such an epitaph explains why an emperor who introduced many changes into Russia is often portrayed as an inflexible despot whose awesome power flowed solely from harsh military "paradomania" and its civil equivalent, extraordinary bureaucratic regulation. But Russia's humiliating defeat in the Crimean War (1853-56) revealed, as Lenin and others have pointed out, "the rottenness and impotence of [the] serf Russia" Nicholas had ruled for thirty years.[2] Frequently used as a measuring rod for the reign of Nicholas I, the war in fact only partially demonstrates Russia's situation at mid-century and sheds no light on the processes at work in the generation since Russia had made a considerable contribution to the military defeat of the supposedly invincible Napoleon.

Moreover, the decisiveness and relative efficiency of the great changes that took place shortly after Nicholas's death raise important questions about the nature and legacy of his rule, suggesting that in spite of his attempts to impose uniformity throughout the empire, there were significant countervailing trends within the civil bureaucracy and the army. To be specific, immediately after the war, serfdom, a cornerstone of Nicholas's rule, was abolished by bureaucrats trained in Nicholas's reign, and with little resistance from the landowning gentry, loyal supporters of autocracy. Even more surprising, a nation that had just signed a peace treaty because of military incompetence and near bankruptcy in 1856 renewed costly military campaigns in the Caucasus, where nearly a half-century of attempts to conquer the mountain tribesmen (*gortsy*) had failed. The conquest was brought to a successful end early in the reign of Alexander II (1855-81) by officers and men who had served in the region under Nicholas I. Perhaps a study of military and administrative policies in a geographically restricted area such as the Caucasus can provide some insights about the Russian army and civil bureaucracy in the reign of Nicholas I—insights that may help us to clarify generalizations about the nature of Nicholas's rule as a whole.[3]

Although Russian expansion into the Caucasus can be traced back to the seventeenth century, the annexation of Georgia in 1801 formally established Russian power in the region, creating new Russian territorial boundaries, and raising unique political, legal, economic, military, and cultural problems.[4] In the manifesto that announced the unification of the Georgian Kingdom to Russia, Paul I proclaimed that the Georgian rulers had "taken refuge in Our patronage . . . seeing no other escape from ultimate ruin and conquest by their enemies." He added that Russia would preserve all "[previous] rights, privileges, and property" in addition to providing eternal protection to these new Russian subjects. When Paul also promised "to extend to Georgians all those rights, liberties, benefits, and privileges held by Russian citizens," however, he created a contradiction, for in other such situations this phraseology had become a euphemism for non-recognition of separate laws or customs.[5] Alexander I merely confirmed his father's edict and gave general instructions to introduce temporary administrative institutions. A Russian governor-general soon was established in Tiflis, capital of Georgia, and was assisted by a newly created Supreme Georgian Administration, charged with the management of domestic affairs. Russian bureaucrats, often military officers, headed each of the administration's four branches, but members of the Georgian nobility held important positions as councilors. Local institutions, including courts, city governments, and police, were organized on a parallel basis, that is, with close similarity to provincial rule within the Russian Empire.[6]

Russian law ruled in all cases involving Russians in Georgia, but the Code of Wakhtang VI, the Georgian law code, was acknowledged as supreme in civil litigation involving only Georgians (in cases where the code was unclear or silent, Russian civil laws would be applicable). Criminal cases would be handled according to Russian laws for all parties, but even here the practices of the local inhabitants were to be taken into consideration when a case involved only Georgians.

This pattern of mixed laws, often in practice administered by local and Russian officials ignorant of each other's system, was extended haphazardly as Russian political control spread throughout the Caucasus in the subsequent decade. The retention of and respect for local customs and laws often depended on the goodwill of local officials, but politically unsophisticated Russian officers not surprisingly understood their role only in terms of military discipline and resorted to punitive expeditions at the slightest pretext. Local aristocrats, used by the Russians as a bulwark of power both because of local tradition and because such a pattern coincided with Russian political and social organization, generally took advantage of the Russian presence to exact ever higher taxes and more labor from the lower classes.

General-lieutenant A. P. Ermolov commanded the Russian forces in the Caucasus between 1816 and 1827, and his policies typified the first quarter century of Russian rule in the region, exerting an important influence on subsequent events. During his rule, Georgians increasingly accommodated themselves to Russian rule, occasionally entering Russian civil and military service. Though thoroughly committed to the eventual Russification of all the Caucasian peoples, Ermolov claimed to recognize that the local customs of the *gortsy* would fade slowly, and only if Russian attempts to change them were gradual and unobtrusive.[7] Nevertheless, whenever the *gortsy* attempted to throw off the alien Russian occupier or, more often, plundered Russian-controlled regions, Ermolov dispatched retaliatory military columns to raze suspected villages and burn crops. When Alexander heard that Ermolov had attacked the *gortsy* without his advance knowledge, or that he had used excessive force, the tsar rebuked his commander, but without much success.[8] Indeed, Ermolov's brutality in dealing with the native peoples of the Caucasus was a major factor persuading them to abandon their own longstanding rivalries and to unite against the hated aliens. Many were easily attracted to the murids, an Islamic sect that emerged in the 1820s and preached a Holy War (*Ghazavat*) against the "infidel" Christian invaders.

While muridism's roots were deep and complex, the corruption of the Russian administration, as well as its harshness, undoubtedly contributed significantly to its growth and to the general resistance to Russian rule in the subsequent period.[9]

In sum, when Alexander I died in late 1825, Russia dominated the Caucasus, but in fact did not control it, and had no clear plan for doing so. Russia's power consisted of mountain roads extending between fortified points that were supported by a series of Cossack settlements with a similar pacifying purpose, all of which maintained the peace primarily through intimidation. One contemporary even reported, with evident pride, that the firing of several artillery rounds at twilight was sufficient to keep rampaging local tribesmen at bay for the night.[10] Rarely did Russians enter the mountain retreats of unconquered tribes without some destructive purpose, and the oppressed tribes in the valleys, visible evidence of the Russian idea of pacification, were reminders of the fate intended for all.

Phase one: Transition amid wars (1825-28)

The Decembrist uprising against Nicholas's accession at first preoccupied the new tsar, but wars against Persia and Turkey in 1826-28 soon turned his attention to the Caucasus. For a time, however, Nicholas's immersion in military operations precluded any direct response to the mounting domestic crises in the region. Moreover, the peace treaties ending those successful wars added further complexities in the form of new territories that had to be consolidated with Russia's former holdings.[11] The wars also revealed that the local administration was inept and corrupt, that communications were inadequate, basic hygiene lacking, and the economy primitive; illiteracy was almost universal and, most ominous of all, muridism was gaining in power. Not all of these problems were of equal concern to Nicholas, but in the first years of his reign he did recognize the need to resolve them sooner or later.

It is not surprising that in the wake of the Decembrist revolt, Nicholas quickly took steps to assure that the Caucasian command was headed by individuals whom he could trust. In August 1826, Nicholas sent Prince I.F. Paskevich and General-major D.V. Davydov, whose military competence and personal loyalty were assured, to assist Ermolov in organizing campaigns against the Persians and the Turks. In February 1827, while confirming the existing (and itself provisional) administration in Georgia and the Caucasus generally, he directed Ermolov to provide thorough data prior to the creation of a permanent administrative system. At the same time, he dispatched Count I.I. Dibich, chief of the Main Staff, to hasten the study's completion. Ermolov, who had not gotten along well with Paskevich, correctly interpreted Dibich's appointment as a sign of imperial disfavor, and immediately resigned. Ermolov's removal undoubtedly was influenced by his known contact and sympathy with the Decembrists, but Nicholas also could have justified replacing him because he had remained inactive militarily after war had erupted, and because he evidently had failed in the pacification of the *gortsy*, who had revolted the moment the Persians crossed the Russian frontier. Paskevich subsequently defeated both the Persians and the Turks with surprising efficiency, but in the process ignored civil affairs in the region, delegating them to a subordinate official.

Throughout his life Nicholas was known as a man with a passion for detail, so it was to be expected that he would examine the domestic situation in the Caucasus more closely than did his military commander, and with greater dispatch. For example, in addition to numerous requests to local officials for detailed information about Caucasian affairs, Nicholas in early 1826 began to send special emissaries to investigate similar or even identical matters, in order to compare data obtained by regular channels with his own specially selected sources.[12] By the time the foreign wars had been concluded, Nicholas possessed considerable information about the region, and was ready to begin its final conquest and integration into the Russian Empire.

Phase two: Paskevich as military commander
and civil reformer (1829-37)

Paskevich now assumed control of civil as well as military affairs in the Caucasus, and soon confirmed to Nicholas that "the external appearance of well-being only masked quite significant confusion and abuses, long since entrenched, the suppression of which the provincial administration to date had ignored."[13] Paskevich's somewhat self-serving report was the result of his own brief study, in which he acknowledged that some of his own aides in the civil administration had wasted state funds. He warned Nicholas that widespread corruption and mismanagement at all levels could have serious and immediate repercussions: "In a word," he wrote, "the local inhabitants have lost everything; disasters [from abuses by government officials, mostly, but also from the ravages of wars] have exceeded their powers of endurance but, fortunately, not their patience." Implying that resistance to Russian rule largely was the by-product of maladministration, Paskevich was optimistic that a substantive administrative reorganization would facilitate the establishment of permanent Russian rule in the region. He recommended that the Caucasian administration be simplified and standarized according to the administrative practices of the empire proper, and added that the purge of native officials from the bureaucracy was absolutely essential. He concluded by asking the emperor to send inspectors (*revizory*) to determine specific administrative measures and promised in the meantime to initiate wide-ranging reforms to preserve calm and to reestablish local trust in Russian rule.[14]

The work begun by Paskevich's committees attests to his recognition of the primitiveness of conditions in the Caucasus and to his own determination to introduce firm and permanent Russian rule. One committee continued a land survey barely begun by Ermolov some years earlier; another began the first census. A third committee examined current and future educational requirements, while still others prepared statutes to standardize the monetary system and to establish health safeguards, especially against epidemics. There were, however, ominous signs about how this general program would be realized. Although acknowledging a great need for competent officials, Paskevich opposed the creation of a cadet corps in the Caucasus, fearing that it would prolong parochialism. He eventually got his way, and only a single gymnasium was opened in Tiflis, plus several small district primary schools. In effect, while eliminating native inhabitants from position of governmental responsibility (he also began to investigate Georgian families' claims to noble status with a view to reducing the number of privileged non-Russian citizens), he made no provisions either for the future general educational needs of the region or for the cultivation of Russian manners, customs, and the like in local society.[15]

In similarly counterproductive fashion, Paskevich admitted that the region was economically backward but resisted the introduction of new business enterprises, in practice concerning himself with control in the narrowly political sense. Minister of Finances Count E.F. Kankrin, who had been commissioned in 1827 by Nicholas to study the economy of the Caucasus, supported Paskevich and opposed governmental investment in the region, on occasion even to the point of resisting certain military expenditures.[16] In 1831 Kankrin also raised the transit tariff for goods passing through the Caucasus, effectively curtailing one of the few successful economic endeavors in the region. Kankrin's resistance to industrial and commercial development was based on principles of parsimony, however, while Paskevich's attitude was principally patriotic.[17] And while the government occasionally did publicize some business opportunities for trade within the empire, as long as Paskevich influenced Russian policy individual entrepreneurs received little or no encouragement.[18] He personally rejected a proposal by the diplomat-dramatist A.S. Griboedov to exploit the region's natural resources. Griboedov had argued that the development of industry and trade in the Caucasus would boost the Russian economy, but Paskevich was fearful about competition with established Russian industry and commerce, and felt that only the state should benefit, not private enterprise.[19] Paskevich also ignored those who posited that economic penetration of the Caucasus would hasten and strengthen Russian political control, although on occasion he employed one of their proposed tactics by offering trade to certain mountain tribes as a privilege in return for obedience. In the near marginal tribal societies, however, the carrot-like prospect was hardly enticing, especially when the more familiar club remained a visible option likely to be used in any event.[20] In short, Paskevich's economic policy essentially was to support agriculture, less for anticipated governmental fiscal harvest than because it was a traditional occupation that would assure greater political stability in the region and also better fit the Russian pattern of landlord-serf society and economy.

In response to Paskevich's request for assistance, Nicholas quickly appointed two senators to undertake the civil-administrative inspection, but directed them (and Paskevich) to adapt general regulations for senatorial reviews "as much as possible to the peculiar circumstances of the region."[21] It was a cautionary note that would be ignored with dire results. In fact, Nicholas's own desire to settle affairs in the Caucasus as simply as possible led him to contradict his own advice, issuing a command a month later which directed Paskevich to proceed with the military conquest of the Caucasus as soon as possible:

> Having just completed one glorious enterprise [actually the defeat of both Persia and Turkey], I offer you another, in my eyes equally glorious; indeed, in terms of immediate value, of far greater importance—the permanent pacification of the mountain peoples or the annihilation of the unsubmissive (*istreblenie nepokornykh*). This matter does not demand immediacy; rather, decisive and mature execution after I receive your plan, which you may expect to fulfill for me.[22]

Nicholas implied that the conquest would be achieved quickly, however, when he added that "all troops temporarily under your command ... [would remain so for a brief time] in order that the blow might be the more decisive as well as sudden." In short, the Russian emperor himself now seemed to play down his predecessors' and his own promises to respect local customs when he bluntly ordered his civil-military commander to introduce orderly rule without regard for anything but the total subjugation of the local inhabitants.

In October 1829, Paskevich submitted the requested plan for military action but avoided a specific timetable and warned about possible difficulties in carrying it out. Nicholas approved the plan, but early the next spring, Minister of War Prince A.I. Chernyshev informed Paskevich that Nicholas was concerned that "the beginnings of military action against the hostile mountain tribes not be delayed in the least, so that in the course of this very summer and fall it will be possible to fulfill the whole plan of conquest of the mountain people."[23] The simplicity of Nicholas's optimistic injunction revealed the difficult situation facing Paskevich, and reasserted Nicholas's preference for military conquest as the means of establishing Russian rule in the Caucasus. Nicholas's low opinion of the local bureaucracy may have been a factor in giving such an order, but the military hardly deserved his confidence. In spite of Paskevich's warnings, then, Nicholas evidently saw the administrative reorganization under way only as a confirmation of results to be achieved by force, and not as a prerequisite for military success. Nevertheless, neither Nicholas nor Paskevich anticipated that Russian military expeditions could be resisted by primitive tribesmen nor, worse, that brutal attempts at subjugation would end by embarrassing the Russian army before Europe.

But Paskevich soon had to write Nicholas requesting a delay in military operations. Troop dislocations after the recent Turkish war were the major excuse cited for the immediate delay, but Paskevich had broader questions in mind when he rather candidly added that the *gortsy* seemed to have developed effective tactics to resist Russian military forces.[24] Once he felt that he had made the point that quick movement and imminent conquest were not feasible, Paskevich proceeded to propose two alternate strategies for Nicholas's consideration, frankly conceding that the first proposal, an all-out invasion of the Caucasus "in all directions," was doomed to failure. The second scheme, which Paskevich acknowledged was a long-term solution, called for a series of annual campaigns against the *gortsy,* beginning with Paskevich's own effort in 1830, which would be complemented by the construction of permanent fortresses and safe routes for communications. This long-term plan showed that Paskevich had a higher estimation of the *gortsy's* strengths than did Nicholas, and that both men now agreed to rely almost totally on military force to achieve conquest, employing civil measures only to consolidate the military victory.[25]

In many ways, this tactic was precisely what was attempted in the next decade. Instead of the immediate conquest Nicholas originally had commanded, a war of attrition set in. Annual Russian military expeditions invariably achieved their limited goals of temporary occupation of some mountaineers' strongholds before withdrawing to permanent garrisons for the winter, but the results were counterproductive. Russian officers and men became demoralized when no permanent gains were visible after great expenditures of energy and substantial casualties. Moreover, the *gortsy* could claim success because they had avoided military defeat and regained the lost territory as soon as the Russians retreated. Worst of all, those tribes that attempted to avoid involvement invariably were punished by the Russians for not aiding in the struggle against the murids, while the latter mercilessly taxed and kidnapped the same people, demonstrating both their prowess and the Russians' inability to protect even territories close by their forts from the murids' incursions. As a result, many previously pacified tribes joined the resistance as the lesser of two evils, while others closer to Russian military forces aided the murids in secret. With each passing year conquest seemed more distant.

In civil affairs, too, Nicholas's initial instructions were quickly swept aside. Less than two months after arriving in the Caucasus, the two senators, Count P.I. Kutaisov and E.I. Mechnikov, concluded, in close agreement with Paskevich's report of the previous year, that the introduction of the legal system that existed throughout the Russian Empire was necessary to eliminate existing administrative abuses and general disarray.[26] Paskevich and the senators concluded that only in especially primitive and inaccessible areas should native customs be preserved as the best means to ensure pacification, and this concession was only a tactic designed to avoid hostilities in regions where Russian forces were weak.[27]

Paskevich's arguments had merit. The difficulties of a mixed system of Russian and native laws and personnel were obvious to all parties, but while Ermolov had argued that the Russian administration of the Caucasus would fail without the prolonged use of local leaders, Paskevich concluded the opposite, that the administration could not succeed until local elements were purged from the bureaucracy. The final senatorial report in 1833 was explicit in endorsing Paskevich's ideas, urging the introduction of an administrative system that would force the native inhabitants to "speak, think, and feel Russian."[28]

The wholesale rejection of native customs and laws, and the belief that laws could change society radically and quickly suggest that more was at stake than a plan of conquest. In this period, Russia was entering a new phase of national self-appreciation, epitomized in Nicholas's official slogan, "Orthodoxy, Autocracy, and Nationality," and Paskevich was one of its most outspoken advocates. It was no accident that Nicholas chose Paskevich to suppress the Polish revolt in 1831; his zeal was grounded on the conviction that Russia was doing a favor to those he sought to bring under her sway. Paskevich's was an outlook common to many nineteenth-century European colonizers. And one of the most striking Russian reactions, again common to European overseas colonization, was an inability to understand the ingratitude of colonial populations, followed by an increased use of military force in response to all forms of resistance.[29]

Baron General G.V. Rozen, Paskevich's successor as commander-in-chief of military forces and overseer of the civil administration in the Caucasus, admitted that he knew little about the area, and was so baffled by the highly personal rule of his predecessor that he complained to the war minister that he did not see "general views on which might be based personal assumptions."[30] Chernyshev coolly replied that a general plan "had long been established: it consists of the assurance of safe boundaries from our Asian neighbors, and also of the means to great growth in public trade and industry."[31] The minister's concern for economic development must have surprised Rozen, but in any event he did not have to worry about personal initiatives. The annual military campaigns had been worked out in detail during the previous winter by Paskevich and Nicholas with little or no consultation with Rozen, whose orders thus boiled down to carrying out directives from St. Petersburg.

Far from achieving the final surrender that Nicholas continued to feel was imminent, Rosen soon realized that he was contributing little or nothing to the creation of permanent Russian rule in the Caucasus. Even clear Russian military victories at Ghimree in 1832 and in Northern Dagestan in 1834 produced only short-lived peace, and by 1836 a new murid leader, Shamil, had emerged as a powerful challenger to Russian rule. Rozen turned to a plan first drafted in 1830 by General I.A. Vel'iaminov (a veteran of many years in the Caucasus and critic of the current military strategy) and forwarded it to St. Petersburg along with his own negative evaluation of Paskevich's civil administrative system.[32] Vel'iaminov had likened the Caucasus to a "mighty fortress," and while acknowledging that Paskevich's strategy probably would work, he argued that it would take thirty years at the least and be extremely costly. To complete the subjugations more quickly and less expensively, Vel'iaminov asserted, it would be necessary to increase the military forces in the Caucasus substantially, grant considerable powers of individual initiative to the local commanders, and approach the mountainous strongholds more systematically. The gortsy, he emphasized, simply did not understand the potential strength of the Russian army, and only massive and dynamic military forces would convince the mountain people that resistance was impossible. Vel'iaminov also felt that the gortsy interpreted Russian "decency" (Vel'iaminov's euphemism for trade, cultural contacts, and respect for local customs) as evidence of Russian weakness. "In order to subdue the Caucasian peoples to rule by [Russian] law," he wrote, "first of all it is necessary to reduce them to obedience. This is only possible by military force .... Starvation seems to me the surest and easiest means of the conquest of the Caucasus." Vel'iaminov projected that after being subjected to five years of continuous military campaigns, and the razing of all of the mountaineers' agriculture, the starving native inhabitants would surrender all arms and accept total subjugation.

Vel'iaminov's ideas were presented to Nicholas, who decided to increase the size of military expeditions somewhat. He also restored to local commanders the limited initiative to mount brief campaigns to revenge mountaineers' raids. Nicholas was shielded from Rozen's many memoranda, which argued that Russian rejection of all local customs and laws aroused a greater will to resist Russian rule. After several years of bureaucratic debates in the capital, a series of special committees were about to submit Paskevich's "project" for final approval in 1835 when by accident Nicholas heard of Rozen's strong opposition to Paskevich's administrative reforms. Rozen was invited to testify before the State Council at the last minute, and somehow convinced that body, and subsequently the Committee of Ministers as well, that the proposed new reforms were ill advised, or at least premature.[33] The clash between Rozen and Paskevich was not over ends, for both agreed that the ultimate goal was full integration of the Caucasus into the Russian Empire. But Rozen advocated laws to fit the current reality, while Paskevich wanted to introduce laws to match the long-term ideal. For Paskevich, radical change was essential to end chaos, with the human cost a minor concern, while Rozen argued that evolutionary change would be more lasting and beneficial to all, and wanted to minimize the suffering and conflict. Finally, Rozen felt that civil administration must remain largely in the hands of local military commanders for the foreseeable future, while Paskevich wanted to transfer virtually all responsibilities immediately to civil authorities organized in a highly centralized system. In this last instance, Rozen undoubtedly struck a sensitive chord among ministers jealous of their individual powers, but Nicholas was not deterred as easily as his ministers in this classic confrontation. Brushing aside Vel'iaminov's pessimistic predictions and expensive solutions, and largely dismissing Rozen's arguments as rationalizations of failure, Nicholas in mid-1837 announced a renewed effort to end the bureaucratic squabbling and military stalemate when he established a powerful committee to draw up new administrative statutes. He also dramatically increased the military forces in the Caucasus in an attempt to achieve a decisive victory on the battlefield.

Phase three: Military and bureaucratic extremism (1837-40)

Nicholas's appointment of Baron P.V. Gan (Paul de Hahn), an undistinguished senator with no previous experience in Caucasian affairs, to the chairmanship of the new committee pointed up the emperor's impatience and extreme frustration at the lengthy delays and disagreements over what earlier had seemed relatively straightforward administrative questions.[34] And Gan's actions demonstrated how far a petty bureaucrat might take personal advantage from an emperor's whimsical move. From the outset he was far more sensitive to the delicate vibrations of court politics than to the hard data he was instructed to gather and evaluate in the Caucasus. When Nicholas sought to underscore the urgency he attached to resolving the problems in the Caucasus by paying a personal visit to the region later in 1837, Gan was emboldened. Soon he had maneuvered the ouster of Rozen, who continued to resist simple legalistic solutions. Gan then proceeded with ease to make Rozen's weak-willed successor, General E.A. Golovin, into a rubber stamp for his plans. Gan submitted the final report to his committee early in 1838, his haste surprising everyone, especially Nicholas. Actually, Gan's plan differed little from its predecessors, except in tone and degree: if Paskevich and the 1833 senatorial report had ignored or downplayed local laws and regional peculiarities, Gan simply denied their existence among "barbaric peoples." Leading governmental officials, notably Kankrin, Count P.D. Kiselev, and other ministers argued strongly against the plan, but Nicholas, obviously anxious to avoid added delays, overrode their objections: the new civil administrative system was enacted on 10 April 1840, and became effective 1 January 1841. Rejecting any attempt at legal or cultural differentiation of the region, the new system introduced a highly centralized bureaucratic system based "completely on the model of the internal provinces of Russia."[35]

Nicholas had a second reason to speed the administrative reform: the late 1830s had bought encouraging military victories. A powerful expedition penetrated deep into Shamil's mountainous strongholds in the

summer of 1838, and in the following August another large force successfully laid siege to Akhul'go, Shamil's headquarters, annihilating virtually
all of his followers.[36] At the time, Shamil's escape seemed of little significance, for resistance throughout the Northern Caucasus drastically declined. General-adjutant Count P.K. Grabbe, head of the Akhul'go
expedition, notified Chernyshev soon afterward that local deputations of
mountaineers already were promising loyalty to Russia, and that he was
ready to take "the necessary steps to stabilize the calm in the region."[37]
Chernyshev proposed an all-out invasion in 1840, his wording reminiscent
of Nicholas's command to Paskevich in 1829, though characteristically
he avoided projecting the date of success.[38] Golovin went so far as to
report to Nicholas that full pacification of the entire Caucasus was imminent.

Some observers were less bold in their predictions, however, and a few
were downright pessimistic. For example, General-lieutenant N.N.Raevskii,
Chief of the Black Sea Line forces and a strong advocate of trade ties,
the spread of education, and other "civilizing" measures as prerequisites
of lasting pacification, warned of aftereffects resulting when Russian
military "[often] took revenge on whole tribes for the guilt of a few
persons." His condemnation of the general strategy of pacification is
summarized in his statement that "[Russian] conduct in the Caucasus
resembles all the criminality of the original conquest of America by the
Spanish."[39] Another critic of tsarist colonial policies at this time, D.A.
Miliutin, a Guards General Staff captain and participant in the Akhul'go
expedition (and future war minister), was convinced that Russia would
never pacify the region without fundamental changes both in military
strategy and in civil administration.[40]

Raevskii was relieved from duty for his candor, in spite of prior
imperial support for his ideas of trade with the coastal tribes, and similar
memoranda by Miliutin and others were ignored.[41] Previous talk about
opportunities for governmental economic exploitation of the Caucasus was
squelched by governmental spokesmen who were now more anxious
to gain unequivocal support for their own narrowly bureaucratic and
military schemes.[42] In distant St. Petersburg, it appeared that final military victory was near, perfectly timed to coincide with the introduction
of the new civil administrative system. Reform of military strategy was
unthinkable after decisive victories; and after years without a clear

administrative scheme critics were not going to be allowed to interfere in an attempt to introduce what had worked for centuries within the Russian Empire. In spite of diverse and often powerful objections, Nicholas endorsed the extremist solutions—Gan's simplifications of complex administrative problems and the crude incremental reinforcement of already powerful military forces.

Phase four: The failure of extremism, and a new search for solutions (1840-45)

A few days after the new administrative law had been enacted, Nicholas created a temporary Caucasian Committee of his highest and most trusted officials to assist in its implementation,[43] dispatching Gan once more to the Caucasus to oversee the introduction of his creation. Soon, Gan was back in the capital, reporting in typically exaggerated language that the reform had been introduced "without the slightest shock and as if by magic." "I leave the region in complete quiet and calm; bureaucrats are working zealously and diligently; the number of crimes has declined visibly[!]; obligations are being fulfilled, taxes are being paid, and I am pleased to assure Your Imperial Highness that the new system completely meets the people's needs."[44] Gan concluded with the welcome claim that Russia soon would begin to harvest great dividends from its long and costly investment of men and money in the Caucasus.

But contrary to Gan's predictions, Russian rule in the region verged on collapse within months after the new civil system was introduced. Although the "Gan law" generally has been the scapegoat for the sudden deterioration of Russian rule in the Caucasus, military disasters in fact antedated that misguided edict and contributed to its failure. Less than six months after Akhul'go, Shamil had regained his former strength. Beginning in early February 1840, a series of raids along the Black Sea coast destroyed most of the Russian forts constructed there over the past decade. The war minister later acknowledged that many had been built without regard for basic rules of military fortifications, which undoubtedly was true, but such an admission does not explain why they lasted as long as they did. In fact, these successes by Shamil and his followers, at a time of an ever increasing Russian military commitment, underscored the heightening intensity of the struggle as well as Russian incompetence. The *gortsy* still could not risk open confrontation but while in the 1830s they were kept on the defensive most of the time, in the early 1840s Shamil's military organization was so ruthlessly efficient that he was able to arouse previously pacified tribes into open rebellion and to defeat isolated Russian units of moderate size.

Russian defeats helped to spark the flames of rebellion but there were other ways in which the Russians speeded their own decline. N. N. Murav'ev, a young but seasoned warrior in the Caucasus who later contributed significantly to Russia's expansion into Eastern Siberia, attributed Shamil's swift recovery entirely to an ill-advised ravaging of the village where Shamil had hidden after escape. Before the incident, Murav'ev noted, the natives were unwilling to feed or help Shamil "because of fear of the Russians. A few days afterward, all pacified Chechnia, outraged by the actions of Pullo [the Russian commander of the raid], invited Shamil to be their leader against the Russians." In fact, Murav'ev attributed Shamil's reemergence as a leader of the whole Caucasus almost solely to Russian mistakes in both civil and military affairs and to Shamil's uncanny ability to take advantage of them.[45] The impact of the new civil administration, then, closely paralleled that of the brutal and dimwitted military policy. Insultingly denying the existence of native culture, purging local inhabitants from governmental positions (and often expropriating their lands in the process), replacing them with often uncaring, incompetent, and corrupt Russian officials—all contributed to the will to resist of a population that had found a resourceful leader and tasted its first military victories.[46]

Reports of administrative chaos and local resistance soon reached Nicholas. Even Golovin became critical of the new law; and no amount of subterfuge could mask how badly the military situation had deteriorated. In early 1842 Nicholas decided once more to send aides to investigate civil and military affairs in the region. The powerful Chernyshev was chosen this time, along with M. P. Pozen, and instructed to examine the validity of the complaints, and to recommend changes in the military as well as in civil affairs. Nicholas was so concerned about the situation on this occasion that he gave the war minister extraordinary powers to revise the 1840 law on the spot when necessary to maintain civil order.[47] The Chernyshev-Pozen report concluded what Nicholas must have suspected all along: the 1840 law had not achieved "its desired fruits" because "the whole system, transferred here from Russian provinces, did not conform to the level of civic awareness (*grazhdanstvennost'*) of the local inhabitants, who have completely different concepts, beliefs, customs, and life habits."[48] The report also confirmed that the new administrative law had strangled the Caucasus with bureaucratic formalism (*pis'- movodstvo*); it recommended a number of procedural changes designed to clarify bureaucratic responsibilities and speed the flow of paperwork. In military affairs, Chernyshev made sure that only minor criticisms were noted in the final report: throughout the quarter century he served as war minister he managed to paint the rosiest possible picture in his own sphere while often finding fault in other ministries, and this occasion was no exception.[49] While in the Caucasus, Chernyshev had halted land confiscations, taken some measures to relieve incompetent administrators (often replacing them with military officers), acknowledged that some local laws and customs were legally binding, and reorganized several local administrative areas (mostly by restoring the military administration where it had been replaced by a civil administration).[50] Like Ermolov, Paskevich, and other Caucasian commanders, however, Chernyshev demanded obedience to Russian rule—"if not [Nicholas I] will annihilate your treasonable actions in a moment," he told one group of local leaders.[51] In sum, although Chernyshev eliminated some of the worst abuses in the region, local inhabitants not only refused to recognize him as a benefactor or reformer, but stiffened their resistance whenever the modifications seemed to signal Russian weakness.

As a result of Chernyshev's report, Nicholas angrily (and embarrassedly) dismissed Gan, on whom he had heaped laurels only months earlier, and apparently concluded that a new approach to reform was needed. This time, the emperor created another special committee and a new administrative body, a Sixth Section of His Imperial Chancery, to which he entrusted still another thorough study of the Caucasian civil structure. Nicholas repeated once more, as he had directed from the beginning of his reign, that any recommendations should "correspond to the conditions of the region and to the actual needs of the inhabitants."[52] Whereas earlier this directive had been taken as a formality, one which a nationalistic ruler could be talked out of, it now became the central concern of the Sixth Section, and of other bodies involved in Caucasian affairs. The tsar was not less imperial-minded; he was merely showing greater concern for domestic stability. Undoubtedly, however, Gan's dismissal was a better incentive for the bureaucrats to move in the new direction than any of the emperor's political rationalizations.[53]

Nicholas issued other edicts intended to alter Russian policy in the Caucasus, but these attempts to gain obedience from the local inhabitants foundered on their long-term distrust and, as usual, on the weaknesses of those who implemented them. For example, in late 1842 Nicholas issued a major decree that launched a reorganization of the civil administration: the long-range goal of complete integration, naturally, was unchanged, but the law explicitly declared that "unity of administrative forms" was no longer necessary. The upper classes, "who have influence over the common people," were to be strongly supported. Agriculture, cattle-raising, and even light industry were to be encouraged; the last if it did not challenge Russian products. Russian officials were directed to enter into close contact with local inhabitants in order to demonstrate the "value of obedience to the Russian state." Acts of patronage were also recommended, on a scale related to the "level of submissiveness."[54] But the law neither spelled out how certain levels of loyalty were to be measured, nor established many other necessary guidelines. For that matter, more precise directions may not have helped much, for many of the local officials were military officers, reluctant civil administrators at best, who much preferred to face the *gortsy* in combat than over a samovar. Orders to use bribes and other nonmilitary means to pacify fierce enemies were insults to such men: it was unthinkable to them to offer large sums of money, occasionally many times their own annual salaries, to their most bitter enemies to purchase a passivity that they had failed to win through combat. Such edicts generally were ignored and the next marching order against the *gortsy* embraced with added vengeance; but some residual anger was reserved for the callous, selfserving bureaucrats in far-off St. Petersburg.

In the meantime, Nicholas showed no similar inclination to compromise in military affairs. When even the toady Golovin blurted out in 1842 that peace could never be purchased, and that the Caucasus could not be subdued until Shamil had been killed, Nicholas replaced him with General A. I. Neidgardt. As Vel'iaminov and others had known long before Golovin, however, the *gortsy* understood bribes as indicators of Russian weakness, signs that further resistance might win full freedom from Russian rule. Nevertheless, Nicholas continued to pour more men and money into the Caucasus. Initially, Russian forces had to concentrate on regaining control of formerly pacified areas, but by late 1842 Neidgardt was able to resume another Winter Palace-planned expedition toward the *gortsy's* mountain hideouts.[55] Previous military strategy and tactics remained unaltered, then, whether because of Cheryshev's report, or Nicholas's persistence. All that changed were the commanding officers and the size of the Russian commitment, now approaching 150,000 troops.

For the next two years the bureaucrats studied and the generals periodically sallied forth into the mountains, but neither group made any visible progress. Indeed, to the military in the Caucasus the capital seemed no less blind to local conditions than earlier, and just as hostile to advice.[56] And the bureaucrats, with considerable justification, viewed the generals as more interested in promotions and medals than in conquest.[57]

Phase five: Vorontsov as viceroy (1845-53)

Nicholas's creation of a viceroy of the Caucasus in late 1844 was a dramatic departure from his handling of Caucasian affairs over the previous two decades; it marked his realization that generals and committees were getting nowhere and that he could not manage Caucasian affairs himself. In the first place, the initial viceroy Count M. S. Vorontsov, though holding a nominal military rank, was known primarily as an effective administrator. Historians frequently have noted Nicholas's preference for military figures in civilian affairs; for a "civilian" to command an area where combat was the order of the day was unprecedented.[58] Secondly, the title of viceroy for the first time united the direction of civil and military affairs in one person, thus eliminating the overlapping competencies that had been the source of frequent conflict among military and civilian officeholders in the Caucasus. The title of viceroy had been fairly common in earlier periods of Russian history, but there was only one other viceroy (in Poland) during Nicholas's reign. In short, the appointment denoted extraordinary imperial trust, and carried powers equal or greater than those of the ministers, including the enormously important right of direct access to the emperor.[59]

The appointment of Vorontsov produced surprise, but in fact he was a logical choice. He was from a powerful and wealthy family: unlike his predecessors in the Caucasus, personal gain was not apt to determine his policies. Moreover, Vorontsov's efficiency as governor-general of New Russia was unmatched in Russia's provincial administration, and his leading role in establishing Russian rule in Bessarabia in the 1820s and 1830s added experience that was relevant to his new assignment and expressed Vorontsov's attitudes toward non-Russian peoples.[60] Finally, Vorontsov was deeply loyal to the tsar and personally close to the throne. Others, most notably Paskevich, had wielded enormous influence in Caucasian affairs, but Paskevich's power, rooted solely in Nicholas's personal confidence, lacked the secure base Vorontsov was given. In addition, Nicholas gave Vorontsov, as regional commander on the spot, great freedom to work out his own strategy. Not even Paskevich had enjoyed such power.

It is not clear why Nicholas gave up so quickly on the highly personal approach of the Sixth Section, adopting instead a tactic that would restrict his own powers, and that would be interpreted generally as an admission of personal failure. Little time had elapsed since the creation of the Sixth Section, and Nicholas had attached great importance to the previous five sections of His Imperial Chancery. There was a precedent for the change, however; in 1836 Nicholas had established a Fifth Section, then reorganized it as a ministry (of State Domains) a short time afterward. Given Nicholas's life long record of personal involvement in even the most trifling affairs, he undoubtedly turned to the idea of a viceroy only after being convinced that no other alternative would achieve his goals. Once Nicholas had appointed Vorontsov, he reorganized the Caucasian Committee to act only as a liaison between himself, Vorontsov, and the various ministries. Vorontsov, of course, had to keep the ministries informed of his actions, but he was responsible to Nicholas alone.[61] Finally, Nicholas abolished the Sixth Section, cutting the last of so many bureaucratic strings that had made Caucasian commanders the mere puppets of St. Petersburg.[62]

Nicholas himself interfered only in Vorontsov's handling of military matters and, at that, only at the outset. Vorontsov frankly objected to Nicholas's previously planned military expedition to Dargo, Shamil's new stronghold, in the summer of 1845, and agreed to lead it only after having made clear that he believed the campaign ill advised in principle, and inappropriate in tactical conception. As Vorontsov predicted, Russian troops easily captured and occupied Dargo, which Shamil abandoned after only a token struggle. Soon, however, Vorontsov had to return to permanent garrison without having won any clear military victory over the elusive *gortsy*. As the Russian columns descended from the high mountains toward the valley floors, Shamil brilliantly surprised them in a densely forested area. The Russian advantage of superior numbers was nullified by the suddenness of the attack and by its concentration at a few points: over 3,800 Russian officers and men were killed or wounded, and greater losses were averted only by the extraordinary discipline of the Russian soldiers and by the tactical skill of their officers and rescuers.[63] Vorontsov's report after the expedition argued strongly for a new military plan of gradual conquest, to be implemented in conjunction with major civil reforms, and Nicholas had no choice but to support it. In the margin of Vorontsov's report Nicholas despaired: "I agree with everything; I completely share the opinion of Count Vorontsov, and I leave to him to act as he sees best."[64] For nearly a decade after 1845 Vorontsov was the master of Russia's fate in the Caucasus.

As events proved, the removal of St. Petersburg bureaucrats from direct involvement in Caucasian affairs was a critical step toward the final conquest, but Nicholas's own withdrawal worked as a mixed blessing. While Nicholas continued to ward off attempts in the capital to undermine Vorontsov's freedom of action, other matters that increasingly preoccupied the tsar made him less willing to devote more money and troops to Vorontsov's new projects in the Caucasus. As a result, Vorontsov had to be more cautious, especially in military affairs, than otherwise might have been the case. How important this factor was remains problematic, both because Vorontsov's record was one of considerable achievement in civil affairs and, less positively, because of significant weaknesses in his own military ideas.

Without detailing his policies, it is relevant to note that in some ways they closely paralleled projects advocated by his predecessors in the Caucasus. In civil affairs, Ermolov had taught that the local nobility were the key to the control of the general population. Rozen, Raevskii, and others had shown the merits of various non-military tactics which Vorontsov now adopted, including the establishment of trade ties, the cultivation of other economic endeavors appropriate to the diverse regions, construction of roads and bridges, elimination of corrupt and incompetent officials, expansion of educational opportunities for the local inhabitants, and the support of Christianity in predominantly Muslim areas.[65]

In military affairs, Vorontsov's policy closely resembled Paskevich's scheme of penetration and gradual conquest. Indeed, Vorontsov so resigned himself to Vel'iaminov's warning that such a system would take many years to succeed that he failed to map out any long-range strategy or even a timetable of expected progress. The cautious military advance avoided the disastrous defeats Shamil had inflicted whenever Russian expeditions penetrated deep into the mountains, but the slow advance exacerbated defeatism among officers and soldiers, the more so because promotions and medals could not be won while on garrison duty. Nor could careers be made while cutting forests to deny hiding places to Shamil—a situation that Leo Tolstoy, a young officer in the region at this time, vividly described in one of his stories.[66]

Vorontsov's failure to reorganize the military administration was a second critical mistake. In the 1830s and early 1840s, new units sent into the region had not been incorporated carefully into the overall military command structure. Instead, the military headquarters in Tiflis acted as the main link with each field unit and relayed orders from St. Petersburg in such peremptory fashion that local commanders rarely dared risk disfavor by proposing new ideas or by resisting or ignoring obviously poor or obsolete commands from distant and unknowledgeable supperiors. Centralization of military command in the Caucasus, then, meant an absence of effective communications between adjacent outlying commands, and Nicholas either never noticed the critical shortcoming or, more likely, never regarded it as such. In concrete terms, this situation meant that Shamil and his murid bands rarely had to worry about coordinated attacks by the Russian units.

In civil affairs, Vorontsov's specialty, he also ignored long-standing and widespread administrative weaknesses. Although he significantly reduced corruption and incompetence among bureaucratic officials, his own newly created committees were not integrated into an effective administrative system. For that matter, many of Vorontsov's new policies in the civil sphere emerged as piecemeal measures, occasionally even offsetting acts. Perhaps this was inevitable, for in attempting to guarantee respect for native customs, law, religions, and the like, while also introducing programs to modernize Caucasian society and economy, Vorontsov was attempting to reach contradictory goals. In addition, as has been shown, Nicholas himself reversed many of the provisions of the 1840 law between 1842 and 1845: in civil affairs Vorontsov in a number of ways merely continued along a path already outlined before his appointment. Some of those directions were even contrary to Vorontsov's prior record in Bessarabia and New Russia, suggesting not so much that his ideas had changed (though such change is possible) as that he accommodated himself to a job Nicholas had seen as necessary and empowered him to carry out.

When Vorontsov left the Caucasus in 1853 because of ill health, Nicholas appointed General-of-infantry N. N. Murav'ev as his successor.[67] The choice of an aging general with long-term experience in the Caucasus was not a reversion to Nicholas's former preference for passively compliant and loyal generals, for Murav'ev was extremely talented (as shown in part by his victory at the battle of Kars in 1855)—indeed, Nicholas had retired him for a time in the 1830s and 1840s because of his outspoken criticisms of the Russian army.[68] But the emperor did intervene once again in military affairs, personally planning most of Russia's military strategy in the Caucasus (and elsewhere) during Murav'ev's tenure—a tenure that was nearly coterminous with the Crimean War.[69] Nicholas substantially reinforced the Caucasian forces, anticipating an invasion of this exposed region, and he ordered Murav'ev to remain on the defensive wherever possible, keeping his troops ready for the expected attack. Shamil likewise waited for the Turks, and as a result the Caucasian front was quieter than it had been in years. The failure of the allies (and Shamil) to exploit Russia's weaknesses in the Caucasus was a gross strategic blunder, but it did not affect the outcome of the war or, at the time, Russia's efforts to complete the conquest. In 1855 the unsubjugated *gortsy* occupied basically the same territory they had held two decades earlier, and most contemporaries, including Murav'ev, agreed with Vorontsov that the end of the struggle lay beyond the foreseeable future.[70] When Nicholas died in February 1855, the Caucasus remained unconquered.

Russia's goals in the Caucasus in the first half of the nineteenth century were to make the region secure from foreign interference, and to integrate it into the Russian Empire. The former aim largely was achieved by Alexander I, though wars in the early years of the reign of Nicholas I confirmed previous treaties with Russia's neighbors and added significant territories to Russia's holdings. Success was so complete that even Russia's humiliating defeat in the Crimean War did not dislodge the gains of the previous half century. The second goal was not gained so easily, however, and when Nicholas died domestic stability had not yet been achieved.

From the outset of his reign, Nicholas I recognized the necessity of major changes in the Caucasus. As we have seen, he often changed his tactics as he attempted to learn what civil reforms were essential to the realization of his goals. In each case, Nicholas's support for the tactic of the moment was so strong that few dared to oppose the official policy. Those who did so were generally ignored, or effectively silenced by transfer, retirement, or other means, but most criticism only delayed matters and probably added pressure for a more extreme solution. In short, Nicholas decided everything, elevating those in control at a given moment to extraordinary power.

Nicholas employed a wide range of individuals as he pursued these diverse tactics. While he was not a man to tolerate disloyalty among his officials at any point in his reign, in the late 1820s and the 1830s he seemed to consider personal trust as virtually the only criterion for appointments to some of the positions affecting Caucasian affairs. After 1840, however, and especially after 1844, Nicholas reversed this pattern and placed far greater weight on competence. He gave his viceroy wide powers to select his own officials, thus further reducing the role played by personal loyalty in making appointments. Clearly, Nicholas had learned that his initial attempts to introduce an efficient administrative system in the Caucasus foundered precisely because his first bureaucratic commander in the region was selected without regard to his administrative expertise or knowledge of the region.

The utter failure of the 1840 law forced Nicholas to acknowledge fully that the Caucasus had to be treated as an area that required a highly individualized administrative system. In late 1844, after several years of half-measures, he appointed a viceroy to rule the area. This extraordinary precedent was primarily an acknowledgment that Nicholas's powers were inadequate to conquer the region or even to establish an effective administrative system; it did not represent any permanent surrender of the principle of uniform administrative rule. Moreover, the nature of the viceroy's powers revealed that Nicholas was aware that success depended as much on the Caucasian viceroy's ability to overcome deficiencies in the Russian bureaucracy as on his capacity to cope with the peculiarities of local problems. Winning the Caucasus meant not only a triumph over the *gortsy*, but a victory over civil officials in St. Petersburg.

Turning to military affairs, we see a similar inconsistency of policies as Nicholas tried to find a tactic that would force the *gortsy* to surrender. After persisting for two decades in the belief that a large military expedition was the key to victory, Nicholas allowed Vorontsov to adopt a strategy of less frequent and more limited forays—a strategy designed to reestablish firm Russian power in areas it already occupied. Beyond that generally passive strategy, the viceroy's main tactics were forest-cutting, road-building, and the use of bribes, trade privileges, and other peaceful means to pacify the region. In the late 1840s and early 1850s, the conquest was advanced more by axe and samovar than by guns, and Nicholas seemed resigned to that situation. Ironically, the prerequisites for future military conquest were firmly laid during this period.

Invested with full powers in military as well as civil affairs, Vorontsov was able to prevent Shamil from further success, and by the early 1850s the rebel leader's position among the *gortsy* had begun to erode, though this development was not yet visible to the Russians. Even more important, once Nicholas stopped issuing rigid and often irrelevant combat orders, local military commanders were able to contemplate alternative strategies and develop useful new ideas. But Nicholas made a more positive contribution to the future resolution of Caucasian strategy, as well. Beginning in the early 1830s, he ordered that guards general-staff officers should be sent regularly to the Caucasus to gain combat experience. Although there is no evidence that Nicholas utilized this cadre of officers in his own military planning, the insights developed by some of them were to play a crucial role in the subsequent conquest.[71] Russia's swift pacification of the Caucasus in the late 1850s was led by two men who had gained important experience during the earlier period: the new viceroy Prince A. I. Bariatinskii, and his chief of staff, D. A. Miliutin.[72] They were but two of many more who developed their ideas and competence during the Nicholaevian period. If Nicholas failed to conquer the Caucasus and adopted many fruitless policies, he still contributed significantly to the eventual pacification of the region, directly and indirectly, by making important changes in the military as well as the civil spheres.

More generally, while Nicholas would have been satisfied with Schiemann's appreciation of him as a "consistent" ruler, the present examination of Nicholas's policies in the Caucasus has revealed a rather different picture. Indeed, the only consistency revealed is that of the almost constant shifting of both military and civilian administrative tactics. Nicholas's ultimate goal of complete integration of the Caucasus within the empire may have remained unchanged, but after 1845, for all practical purposes, that goal functioned more as a vague aspiration than as a basis for real policy decisions. What we see throughout is a kind of flexibility— a greater responsiveness to changing conditions and particular situations than most accounts of the reign attribute to Nicholas. In the Caucasus, at least, "unsystematic," "ever-changing," "compromising," as well as "persistent," seem apt characterizations of Nicholas's activity—as does the term "reformist."

An explanation may be found in Nicholas's attempts to transform corrupt, incompetent, and self-protecting officials into an effective state instrument. As noted by the early twentieth century Russian historian Kizevetter and others, Nicholas had a low opinion of his bureaucracy and throughout his reign often tried to bypass it when it could not be made responsive to his demands.[73] This tactic was employed more often in the Caucasus than elsewhere in the empire, and with eventual success. Moreover, there were few other instances in Nicholas's long reign where so obscure an official was so suddenly awarded as much personal power as was Gan and there was no parallel to the creation of the viceroyalty. Both appointments smacked of imperial frustration at bureaucratic foot-dragging, but there were few problems that could be as threatening to Russia's international position as the exposure of weakness in the Caucasus. In any event, Nicholas effectively took control of the Caucasus away from the powerful St. Petersburg bureaucracy, and personally protected the viceroy's independence from ministerial politics. The decision to do that was difficult for Nicholas because the war minister, one of his favorites, was the most directly involved. Indeed, Chernyshev often chafed under this diminution of his powers, but Nicholas's support of the viceroy did not waver.[74] But the usurpation of power from St. Petersburg officials was only achieved by a unique arrangement after years of failures by other, less drastic solutions. Moreover, the lesson was not repeated elsewhere by Nicholas, or by any similar delegation of power or encouragement of local initiative within the Caucasus by Vorontsov.[75] Nicholas's appointment of a superbureaucrat showed that he considered a radical step necessary to overcome an enemy that in some ways was more elusive and more resistant to his will than the *gortsy*.

The full significance of Nicholas's handling of Caucasian affairs may be found by drawing a parallel. Historians often have noted that Nicholas's famous statement to the State Council in 1842 claiming that he would never touch serfdom, though it was "an evil, palpable and obvious to everyone," demonstrated his general resistance to the alteration of state institutions.[76] To be sure, serfdom was fundamental to the nature of the autocracy in ways the Caucasus never could be, and Nicholas generally did prefer the status quo. But Nicholas devoted far more time and national resources to the Caucasus than to the peasant question, suggesting that his attitude toward Caucasian affairs also is of great significance in evaluating his reign as a whole. In fact, a comparison of these two major questions reveals an important parallel, and a contrast. In the late 1830s and the 1840s, even as Nicholas directed Kiselev to plan and introduce reforms affecting the state peasants, he encouraged another appointment, the viceroy of the Caucasus to address important questions with new solutions.[77] Far from being a resister of change, Nicholas was supporing significant reforms in areas of critical importance to his empire well into the 1840s. And if after the European revolutions of 1848 Nicholas ended his support for peasant reform, there was no such break in Caucasian policy. Nicholas's last years, often called a stultifying "epoch of censorial terror," did not interrupt Vorontsov's activities until the outbreak of the Crimean War forced a total concentration on national defense. While the actual impact of Caucasian affairs on fiscal policy, general military affairs, relations with other nationalities, foreign affairs, and other important questions remains largely unaddressed here, it is clear that Nicholas's constant attention to the Caucasus and his use of powerful and costly military forces underscore the importance of studying this non-Russian region to gain an understanding of even the most fundamental issues in imperial Russia. This examination of Nicholas's administrative and military efforts to conquer the Caucasus, while confirming many of the shortcomings of Russia generally and of Nicholas I personally, has shown that Nicholas was more determined to reform and more flexible than previously acknowledged, and that his initiatives helped to lay the groundwork for future combat successes in the Caucasus, and for military reform throughout the empire.

NOTES

1. Theodor Schiemann, *Geschichte Russlands unter Kaiser Nikolaus I*, Band II (Berlin, 1908), p. xii; Nicholas V. Riasanovsky, *Nicholas I and Official Nationality in Russia, 1825-1855* (Berkeley and Los Angeles, 1959), pp. 184-85; *A Short History of the USSR* (Moscow, 1965), p. 201.

2. V. I. Lenin, *Sochineniia*, 4th ed. (Moscow, 1952), XVII, 95.

3. Many studies have examined the military campaigns in great detail, though few have treated the whole period of conquest. John F. Baddeley, *The Russian Conquest of the Caucasus* (London, 1908), is an exception. A lesser number of works have considered the administrative history of the Caucasus in this period, largely in isolation of military questions. Examples are: V.N. Ivanenko, *Grazhdanskoe upravlenie Zakavkaz'em ot prisoedinenniia Gruzii do namestnichestva Velikago kniazia Mikhaila Nikolaevicha: Istoricheskii ocherk* (Tiflis, 1901), and the recent dissertation of Laurens H. Rhinelander, Jr., "The Incorporation of the Caucasus into the Russian Empire: The case of Georgia, 1801-1854," Columbia University, 1972, and his article, "Russia's Imperial Policy: The Administration of the Caucasus in the First Half of the Nineteenth Century," *Canadian Slavonic Papers*, 17, 2 and 3 (1975).

4. The term "Caucasus" in this essay includes the territory bordered on the north by the Caucasian line, a defensive military cordon established in the late eighteenth century and manned by Cossacks from the Black Sea to the Caspian Sea (and east-west borders), and in the south by the Turkish and Persian frontiers. East and West Caucasus are the regions divided by the main Caucasian mountain chain.

5. *Polnoe sobranie zakonov rossiiskoi imperii* (hereafter cited as *PSZ*), first series, XXVI, No. 19,721., 18 January 1801. Precedent and subsequent parallels may be found in Peter the Great's treatment of the Baltic territories, and in many provisions included in Alexander I's manifesto joining Finland to Russian though, as has been shown, Russia's relations with regions conquered or annexed have differed widely. See Leonid I. Strakhovsky, "Constitutional Aspects of the Imperial Russian Government's

Policy Toward National Minorities," *Journal of Modern History*, 12, 4 (December 1941), 467-92.

6. *PSZ*, first series, XXVI, No. 19,770 , 6 March 1801, and No. 20,007, 12 September 1801. See Alexander's instructions to General K. F. Knorring, 12 September 1801, in *Akty, sobrannye Kavkazskoiu Arkheograficheskoiu komissieiu* (hereafter *AKAK*), 1 (Tiflis, 1866), 433-37.

7. Ivaneko, p. 90.

8. Alexander's naivete about Ermolov's brutality is evident in his letters to the latter. See *Zapiski Alekseia Petrovicha Ermolova* (Moscow, 1865), chast' 2, prilozheniia, especially 171,330. Various types of Russian misrule in the Ermolov period, and later, are spelled out in Kh. Kh. Ramazanov, *Kolonial'nia politika tsarizma v Dagestane v pervoi polovine XIX v.* (Makhachkala, 1956), and K. Sivkov, "Epizody iz istorii kolonial'nogo ogrableniia Kavkaza (XIX vek)," *Bor'ba klassov*, 8 (1936), 24-35.

9. A. Runovskii, "Muridizm i gazavat v Dagestane po ob"iasnenuiiu Shamilia," *Russkii vestnik*, 42 (1862), 680, is but one author who makes the preceding points, and also emphasizes that the Russian rule per se was actually soft in many instances compared to the preceding period. It was the use of the Russian "cannon and bayonets" in support of the local aristocracy (the former rulers) which was in the eyes of the common people "deceitful," for the Russians had seemed, on arrival, to be their saviors.

10. D. I. Romanovskii, *Kavkaz i kavkazskaia voina* (St. Petersburg, 1860), pp. 215-16.

11. Provisions of the Treaty of Turkmanchai with Persia, 10 February 1828, and the Treaty of Adrianople with Turkey, 2 September 1829, may be found in F. F. Martens, ed., *Sobranie traktatov i konventsii, zakliuchennykh Rossieiu s inostrannymi derzhavami* (St. Petersburg, 1874-1909).

12. See "Sekretnaia instruktsiia, dannaia Imperatorom Nikolaiem I polkovniku Bartolemeiu pered otpravleniem v Persiiu s rezoliutsiei Imperatora Nikolaia I otnositel'no Griboedova i donesenie polkovnika Bartolomeia," *Russkaia starina*, 142 (1910), 423-34.

13. Vespoddanneishii raport, 16 May 1829, No. 11, *AKAK*, 7 (1878), No. 35.

14. "Revizii," or inspections, immortalized in Gogol's play, "The Inspector General," date at least to the time of Peter the Great, but became rather common (and especially terrifying for the inspected) only in the

first half of the nineteenth century. See M. Polievktov, "Reviziia Zakavkazskogo kraia senatorami Kutaisovym i Mechnikovym i fond del etoi revizii v Istoricheskom arkhive v Leningrade," *Trudy Tbilisskogo gosudarstvennogo universiteta*, 15 (1940), 81-102; *Istoriia pravitel'stvuiushchogo senata za dvesti let 1711-1911 gg.* (St. Petersburg, 1911), III, 615-57.

15. See M. S. Lalaev, *Istoricheskii ocherk voenno-uchebnykh zavedenii* (St. Petersburg, 1880), chast' 2, 49-50, which also cites the relevant legislation. Small numbers were to be educated, but only in St. Petersburg, and even in these cases Paskevich's fears about regional allegiances were to be met by limiting the number eligible for study to those ten and under, and only with his personal approval. *PSZ*, second series, XI, No. 9130, 3 May 1836 and XIV, No. 12,082, 7 March 1839. See Mikhail Iablochkov, *Istoriia dvorianskogo sosloviia v Rossii* (St. Petersburg, 1876), pp. 617-18, concerning the status of the Caucasian nobility.

16. Kankrin's views of the Caucasus as a colony that should bring wealth to Russia, not drain Russia's economy, are already evident in the edict announcing the economic survey: *PSZ*, second series, II, No. 1019, 8 April 1827. The study was published as *Obozrenie rossiiskikh vladenii za Kavkazom, v statisticheskom, etnograficheskom, topograficheskom i finansovom otnosheniiakh, proizvedennoe i izdannoe po Vysochaishemu soizvoleniiu* (St. Petersburg, 1836), in four parts.

17. See especially Paskevich's memorandum to Kankrin, 5 October 1830, No. 342, published in *AKAK*, 7, No. 108.

18. A typical example of this kind of literature is P. Vysheslavtsov, "Vzgliad na Zakavkaze v khosiaistvennom i torgovom otnosheniiakh ego k Rossii," *Syn otechestva*, 166, 6(1834), 25-52.

19. Griboedov's proposal has been published in his *Sochineniia* (Moscow-Leningrad, 1959), pp. 471-95.

20. See, for example, *PSZ*, second series, II, No. 1064, 28 April 1827, offering the possibility for trade relations to the Cherkesses and Abazintsy at Kerch, while specifically denying other mountain tribes any right to trade there. Ironically, both of these tribes soon became fierce enemies of Russian rule. When they finally were conquered in the late 1850s, all were forcibly emigrated from their territory, either to interior Russian provinces or, in most cases, abroad to Turkey. The best example of those who believed that trade would abet the conquest is Count N. S. Mordvinov. See his 1816 memorandum, "O sposobakh, koimi Rossii

udobnee mozhno priviazat' k sebe postepenno kavkazskikh zhitelei," published, among other places, in Romanovskii, prilozheniia, pp. xxviii-xxxv. A. V. Fadeev, *Rossiia i Kavkaz pervoi treti XIX v.* (Moscow, 1960), pp. 365-69, also treats this subject, from a Soviet perspective.

21. Senate's ukaz to Count Paskevich, 23 August 1829, No. 52787, *AKAK*, 7, No. 39. See also, ibid., No. 45 and *PSZ*, second series, No. 3504, 25 February 1830.

22. Letter of Nicholas I to Paskevich, 25 September 1829, published in A. P. Shcherbatov, *General-fel'dmarshal kniaz' Paskevich: Ego zhizn' i deiatel'nost'* (St. Petersburg, 1891), III, 228-30.

23. Shcherbatov, III, 244, letter of 21 March 1830.

24. *Dvizhenie gortsev severo-vostochnogo Kavkaza v 20-50 gg. XIX veka: Sbornik dokumentov* (Makhachkala, 1959), pp. 68-72. Paskevich's report of 8 May 1830 was a response to Chernyshev's note of 21 March 1830, No. 9, to complete the conquest in the current summer and fall. Erroneously dated 6 May.

25. See *AKAK*, 7, Nos. 379 and 380, for Paskevich's proclamations to the Lezgins in February 1830 to accept "unconditional subjugation" and complete unification with Russia, and for the text of the initial administrative organization, which was approved by the Committee of Ministers and Nicholas, without change, as the model for local rule to be introduced wherever Russian arms succeeded.

26. *Kolonial'naia politika rossiiskogo tsarizma v Azerbaidzhane v 20-60-kh gg. XIX v.*, chast' 1 (Moscow-Leningrad, 1936), 230-35, Documents 16 and 17. The latter document refers approvingly to Paskevich's report of 16 May 1830. Paskevich's further thoughts on the subject are contained in his report of 24 April 1830, published in *AKAK*, 7, No. 47.

27. These and other points are spelled out more fully in *AKAK*, 7, No. 64, Paskevich's report of 28 April 1831, No. 1019, a draft project for the introduction of civil administration in the Transcaucasus.

28. *Kolonial'naia politika*, chast' 1, 280.

29. Without suggesting any close parallel between Paskevich and Nicholas I and the English statesman and historian, Thomas B. Macaulay, it is curious to note that in this same period Macaulay had similar ideas about how the Indians should be educated, hoping to create "a class of persons, Indian in blood and colour, but English in taste, in opinions, in morals, and in intellect." "Minute on Indian Education," 27 February

1835, as cited in T. B. Macaulay, *Selected Writings* (Chicago, 1972), p. 249. While Macaulay obviously could not be the source for the Russian report, considerable evidence points to close study of West European colonialism, especially their administrative tactics, by high Russian officials. See, for example, Chernyshev's memorandum about French rule in Algeria, published in part in *Kolonial'naia politika*, chast' 2, No. 27, 286-90.

30. Rozen's letter of 24 December 1831 is cited in F. Fon-Kliman, "Voina na vostochnom Kavkaze s 1824 po 1834 g. v sviazi s miuridizmon (prodolzhenie)," *Kavkazskii sbornik*, 15 (Tiflis, 1894), 516.

31. Ibid., pp. 517-18. Chernyshev's letter to Rozen is dated 11 January 1832.

32. One of Vel'iaminov's memoranda of this period, dated July 1832, is published in full in *Kavkazskii sbornik*, 7 (Tiflis, 1883), 78-144. Vel'- iaminov began to consider the Caucasus akin to a fortress at least as early as his memorandum of 30 May 1830, No. 155.

33. Shcherbatov, III, 306-7; "Zapiski barona M. A. Korfa," *Russkaia starina*, 101 (1900), 31-32.

34. Concerning Gan's earlier and subsequent career, see M. A. Dodolev, "Zapiski russkogo diplomata ob Italii (1816-1822 gg.)," *Istoriia SSSR*, 1976, No. 5, 157-64. Korf's devastating assessment of Gan is in *Zapiska Korfa*, pp. 31-33.

35. Kankrin's, and others', objections are cited in A. Sh. Mil'man, *Politicheskii stroi Azerbaidzhana v XIX-nachale XX vekov* (Baku, 1966), pp. 109-10. See also Korf, pages 35-39, for the political machinations. The law is printed in *PSZ*, second series, XV, No. 13,368.

36. The battles were costly to the Russians also. A. L. Gizetti, compiler, *Sbornik svedenii o poteriakh Kavkazskikh voisk vo vremia voin Kavkazsko-gorskoi, persidskikh, turetskikh i v Zakaspiiskom krae, 1801-1855 gg.* (Tiflis, 1901), p. 128, reports 4,821 as killed, wounded, or missing in 1839, three times the still sizeable casualties for the previous year. The Akhul'go campaign, one of the most famous of the entire Caucasian war, was described by a participant, the future war minister D. A. Miliutin, in his *Opisanie voennykh deistvii 1839 goda v Severnom Dagestane* (St. Petersburg, 1850).

37. Cited by V. G. Gadzhiev, *Rol' Rossii v istorii Dagestana* (Moscow, 1965), p. 219. See also Chernyshev's extract of another Grabbe report of

the same period in *Sbornik imperatorskogo russkogo istoricheskogo obshchestva*, (Henceforth SbIRIO), 122 (St. Petersburg, 1905), 292-93.

38. Chernyshev's memorandum, "Predpolozheniia po Kavkazskomu kraiu na 1840 g.," is published in ibid., pp. 414-23.

39. Several of Raevskii's related memoranda are published in *Arkhiv Raevskikh*, III (St. Petersburg, 1900); the quotes are from ibid., p. 339, and *AKAK*, 9 (1884), No. 434. For more material on Raevskii, see *Russkii biograficheskii slovar'*, XV (St. Petersburg, 1910), 402-4.

40. See K.V. Sivkov, "O proektakh okonchaniia Kavkazskoi voiny v seredine XIX v.," *Istoriia SSSR*, 1958, No. 3. 192-94.

41. Typically, Chernyshev's main accusation was Raevskii's flouting of "every kind of respect of rank."

42. Iu. A. Gagemeister, "O nadezhdakh Zakavkazskogo kraia, kak kolonii," *Biblioteka dlia chteniia*, 30 (1838), otdelenie IV, 1-6, is an example of the prevalent official tone in economic affairs at this time.

PSZ, second series, XV, No. 13,413 , 24 April 1840. Chernyshev was named chairman (as of so many committees dear to Nicholas I), joined by Kankrin and Kiselev (probably to force the latter to make it work), and other imperial favorites: Active Privy Councillors Count D.N. Bludov, and Count A.G. Stroganov, and State Secretaries Count V.N. Panin and M.P. Pozen. Pozen and Chernyshev had recommended Gan to Nicholas in the first place.

44. *AKAK*, 9 (1884), No. 33.

45. Ivan Barsukov, *Graf Nikolai Nikolaevich Murav'ev-Amurskii*, kniga 1 (Moscow, 1891), 140. The memorandum, "Zapiska o predlagaemykh voennyhk deistviiakh protiv Shamilia," January 1844, was forwarded to his brother Aleksander on 3 February 1844. It is published in ibid., kniga 2 (Moscow, 1891), 1-17.

46. Obviously it was not Nicholas's intent to appoint poor officials to these positions, but legislation which was enacted to attract many new civil servants to the Caucasus had this result.

47. *AKAK*, 9, Nos. 40 and 49; See also *SbIRIO*, 122, 255-74.

48. Cited by Korf, 41-46. Korf and others have suggested that a foreign traveler's account (Comte de Suzannet's "Les Provinces du Caucase sous la Domination russe," *Revue des deux mondes*, 4th series, 26 [April 1841], 50-106—subsequently published in expanded book form in 1846) played an important role in Nicholas's decision-making at this time. Korf

even claims that before Nicholas sent Chernyshev and Pozen to the Caucasus he almost went himself in an attempt to offset the embarrassment caused by Suzannet's strong criticism of Russian rule in the Caucasus. Certainly the threat of foreign interference in Caucasian affairs, which the Russians always considered domestic business, was frequently mentioned in official reports throughout Nicholas's reign, but there is no evidence proving a causal relationship between external factors and Nicholas's specific reform attempts in this period.

49. Perhaps Chernyshev's most visible whitewash is his report of military prowess delivered three years before the outbreak of the Crimean War. See "Istoricheskoe obozrenie voenno-sukhoputnogo upravleniia s 1825 po 1850 god," published in *SbIRIO*, 98 (1896), 299-447. The Caucasian war is evaluated on pp. 313-15.

50. See I.I. Surguladze, *Istoriia gosudarstva i prava Gruzii* (Tbilisi, 1968), p. 287.

51. *SbIRIO*, 122, 261.

52. *PSZ*, second series, XVII, No. 16,008, dated 30 August 1842.

53. Ibid. There were other unambiguous directions: Nicholas also closed the provisional committee established in 1840 to implement the "Gan law."

54. *PSZ*, second series, XVII, No. 16,205, 12 November 1842. See also N.A. Smirnov, *Miuridizm na Kavkaze* (Moscow, 1963), pages 184 ff.

55. See Nicholas's rescript to Neidgardt, 18 December 1843, No. 130, in A. Iurov, "1844-i god na Kavkaze," *Kavkazskii sbornik*, 7, 158. Variants of his document have been published in *Russkaia starina*, 48 (October 1885), 209-12 and in *Kavkazskii sbornik*, 6, 235-39.

56. As noted earlier, in 1844 Murav'ev went to the unusual length of sending a memorandum recommending a new military strategy in the Caucasus to his brother in St. Petersburg, admitting "I know that any attempt on my part [to forward the memorandum through normal channels] not only would likely remain without attention, but might even bring unpleasantness down on me." He pleaded that his brother "take this information to those who can have influence on the course of affairs—I really do not see any official way for my opinion to succeed." Murav'ev was not pressing for personal promotion, merely explaining the rigidity that continued to exist in the military-bureaucratic system, and trying harder than most to overcome it.

52.   Neidgardt's 1844 report to Nicholas added to the back-biting by reporting that self-seeking bureaucrats abounded in the Caucasus, undermining the military effort. The report is cited in part in Z.V. Anchabadze, *Ocherki ekonomicheskoi istorii Gruzii pervoi poloviny XIX veka* (Tbilisi, 1966), p. 34.

58.   Vorontsov held the rank of *General-ad'iutant,* but had not served in a military capacity for decades, though he had a distinguished combat record early in his career.

59.   *PSZ,* second series, XX, No. 18,679, 30 January 1845. In matters that exceeded Vorontsov's authority, he communicated with the chairman of the Caucasian Committee, revised in its functions since its creation in 1840.

60.   See George F. Jewsbury, *The Russian Annexation of Bessarabia: 1774-1828. A Study of Imperial Expansion* (Boulder, Colorado, 1976), chap. 8, especially p. 142. A.L. Zisserman, author of many works on the Russian conquest of the Caucasus, claimed that an 1836 memorandum by Vorontsov to Nicholas paved the way for his subsequent appointment by marking him as a knowledgeable person about both military and civil affairs in the Caucasus. The memorandum, plus a Chernyshev report of Nicholas's reaction, are published in "Vsepoddanneishii raport Novorossiiskogo general-gubernatora (26 avgust 1836 g.)," *Russkii arkhiv,* (1894), chast' 2, 215-35.

61.   *PSZ,* second series, XX, No. 18,702, 3 February 1845. See also No. 18,706, 5 February; and No. 19,230, 23 July 1845 for related administrative changes.

62.   *PSZ,* second series, XXI, No. 19,590, 6 January 1846; and No. 19,657, 25 January 1846.

63.   For purposes of comparison, this was 1,200 more casualties than Russia suffered in the entire two-year war with Persia in 1826-28, without counting losses by disease (estimated at at least one-third more). Gizetti, p. 128.

64.   Letter of 21 July 1845, cited in A.A. Zisserman, *Istoriia 80-go pekhotnogo kabardinskogo general-fel'dmarshala kniazia Bariatinskogo polka (1726-1880)* (St. Petersburg, 1881), II, 460. Nicholas elevated Vorontsov further by naming him a prince.

65.   Vorontsov's ideas on most of these subjects are treated in many published documents and a diverse monographic literature. Some of the

most significant documents include: *PSZ,* second series, especially XXI, Nos. 19,708, 20,672, and 20,699; and XXIII, No. 22,838, *Kolonial'naia, politika* chast' 2, *AKAK,* 10 (1885). Chapter 5 of Rhinelander's dissertation is especially good on cultural affairs in Georgia in this period; his conclusion that by 1853 there was a "thoroughly Russianized bureaucracy composed mainly of dedicated Caucasians" suggests a measure of Vorontsov's success in the process of assimilation in Georgia. Among the numerous Soviet Great Russian interpretations, see *Istoriia SSSR s drevneishikh vremen do nashikh dnei* (Moscow, 1967), IV 385-87. Interesting Soviet non-Great Russian interpretations are V. Rshtuni, *Krest'ianskaia reforma v Armenii v 1870 g.* (Erevan, 1947), pp. 100ff, and T. Kh. Kumykov, *Vovlechenie Severnogo Kavkaza vo vserossiiskii rynok v XIX v.* (Nal'chik, 1962), pp. 176-79. A highly sympathetic biography exists, M.P. Shcherbinin, *Biografiia general-fel'dmarshala kniazia Mikhaila Semenovicha Vorontsova* (St. Petersburg, 1858). The evaluation of Vorontsov by one of his successors is most enlightening: A.I. Bariatinskii, *Otchet namestnika kavkazskogo i glavnokomanduiushchago kavkazskoi armiei (1857, 1858, 1859)* (Tiflis, 1861), notably pages 279-81.

66.   Leo Tolstoy's "Rubka lesa. Rasskaz iunkera (1852-1854)," *Polnoe sobranie sochinenii* (Moscow, 1935), III, about forest-cutting, raids, etc., is completely accurate in its descriptions of military tactics and strategy at this time, and in its portrayal of the attitudes of those involved.

67.   To avoid confusion with a previously mentioned Murav'ev with the same full name, this Murav'ev soon came to be known as Murav'ev-Karsskii, while the former won honors in Siberia and gained the title of Murav'ev-Amurskii.

68.   The biographical sketch in the official *Stoletie voennogo ministerstva,* III, otdel 4, 233-61, is unusually full and accurate.

69.   Murav'ev was viceroy from November 1854 to July 1856, though he spent less than six months in Tiflis. Many of Nicholas's military orders related to the defense of Russia have been published. See, for example, "Zapiski ego [Nicholas I] ob ukreplenii Zapadnoi granitsy Rossii. 1843-1855 gg.," *Russkaia starina,* 42 (1884), 519-30.

70.   Murav'ev was of this opinion; so was Ermolov. See D.I. Romanovskii, "General-fel'dmarshal kniaz' A.I. Bariatinskii i Kavkazskaia voina, 1815-1879 gg.," *Russkaia starina,* 30 (1881), 247-318. M.I. Bogdanovich,

ed., *Istoricheskii ocherk deiatel'nosti voennogo upravleniia v Rossii (1855-1880)* (St. Petersburg, 1879), I, 365, expresses a similar official point of view a quarter century later.

71.   On the general staff in the Caucasus, 1832-1853, see N.P. Glinoetskii, *Istoriia russkogo general'nogo shtaba* (St. Petersburg, 1894), II, 200-66. The General Staff War Academy, supplier of these officers, was established by Nicholas I in 1832.

72.   Bariatinskii's general views are summarized in *Russkii biograficheskii slovar'*, II, 531-32. Miliutin's memoirs and memoranda on tsarist policy in the Caucasus in this period are treated in my dissertation, 'D.A. Miliutin: Life and Activity to 1856," chaps. 4 and 6.

73.   A.A. Kizevetter, "Imperator Nikolai I, kak konstitutsionnyi monarkh," in his *Istoricheskie ocherki* (Moscow, 1912), pp. 407-8.

74.   Two examples of Chernyshev's unhappiness may be extrapolated from the 1845 report on the French conquest of Algeria, in which Chernyshev emphasized that all powers were concentrated in the hands of the war minister, and from the previously cited quarter-century report of the war ministry's activities, in which Chernyshev tried to claim that the current (1850) policy in the Caucasus dated from 1842 (the time of his own trip there), not from Vorontsov's appointment.

75.   Raevskii's brief tenure as commander of the Black Sea forces may be regarded as imperial support for independent ideas on a lesser level, but Nicholas soon bowed to Chernyshev's complaints about Raevskii, and no one else was allowed similar independence of action.

76.   As translated in *A Source Book for Russian History From Early Times to 1917* (New Haven, Connecticut, 1972), II, 552.

77.   Implicit in Kiselev's study of state peasants was the thought that eventually similar reforms would be carried out for the serfs. As it turned out, the administrative reorganization begun with Vorontsov's appointment formed the basis for the organization of the Russian administration of Central Asia when that region was conquered in the 1860s-1870s.

Михаилъ Юрьевичъ Лермонтовъ и его произведенiе.

Княжна Мери.

Купецъ Калашниковъ.

Боярин Орша.

Литографія Т-ва И. Д. Сытина. Москва 1917г

NIKOLAI UTIN AND THE MARIENHAUSEN AFFAIR: LAND AND LIBERTY IN THE JANUARY REBELLION

Woodford Mc Clellan
University of Virginia

Even the happiest and most auspicious of anniversaries carries within itself the potential for trauma. Thus it was that the Russian revolutionary organization Land and Liberty (*Zemlia i volia*) looked forward apprehensively to 19 February 1863, the second anniversary of the Emancipation Proclamation and the date upon which the "temporarily obligated" status of the peasantry would end and—so the peasants believed—the "real" freedom would come. Land and Liberty struggled to define its mission and its role in the upheaval that would, its members anticipated, attend the rude awakening that awaited the *muzhik*. And at the same time the clandestine organization had to deal with another great problem which was always simmering but which since 1861 had been moving toward crisis proportions: Poland. It was the situation in Poland, and the reaction of Land and Liberty to developments there, that was to produce the mysterious Marienhausen Affair of early 1863, an affair that constitutes the subject of the present enquiry.[1]

Yet another rebellion was brewing in Poland and Land and Liberty was being drawn into the quickening current of events. This situation dismayed many of the organization's members who considered the Polish conspiracy unsound and thought an uprising to be premature. The Russians thought the Poles foolish to share the Russian peasantry's expectation of justice from the tsar. Indeed, in the late winter and spring of 1861 the massacre of several score demonstrators in Warsaw, Kraków, and other cities had destroyed the ill-conceived illusions and convinced many Poles that only force of arms could win independence for their tormented homeland.[2] (Given the balance of forces this view was as little grounded in reality as was the hope for fair treatment from Alexander II, but for the impatient among the Poles it had a powerful activist appeal.) The arrest of its leaders, N. G. Chernyshevskii and N. A. Serno-Solov'e-vich, severely crippled Land and Liberty in the late spring of 1862. These and other arrests, coming after a year of tension which was capped by a series of mysterious fires in St. Petersburg, weakened the organization and left it in the hands of second-level leaders, among them Nikolai Utin, Maksim Antonovich, and A. A. Sleptsov.[3]

One of Nikolai Utin's first acts after the spring arrests was to publish clandestinely his proclamation entitled "To the educated classes."[4] In this work Utin expressed horror at the execution in June 1862 of three Polish officers convicted of disseminating revolutionary propaganda in the First Army (stationed in Poland). Referring to this event as the "prologue to the bloody drama," by which he clearly meant an uprising in Poland, Utin spoke also of the "terrible uprising of the people which is drawing near" in *Russia.* The link was unspecific, but unmistakable.

In the autumn of 1862 it became imperative for the new leaders of Land and Liberty to meet with representatives of the Polish conspiracy. Those representatives were members of the misleadingly named Committee of Russian Officers in Poland. Among them were the Ruthenian Andrei Potebnia (a young officer of the Schlüsselberg Regiment of the First Army), Jarosław Dąbrowski, and Zygmunt Padlewski. All three of these men had studied at military academies in St. Petersburg and had many friends and acquaintances among the Russian revolutionaries.[5] It was Potebnia who had founded the committee in 1861 and who had worked out a plan calling for the First Army to rebel and thus spark a national uprising in Poland.[6] Even some of his closest friends regarded this as utterly impractical, but the scheme was attractive in its very simplicity, and behind it lay the awesome—if in this regard vague—precedent of the Decembrist Revolt. (Some of the Decembrists stationed in Poland had sought, with limited success, the make common cause with the Polish Patriotic Society.)

Before the authorities discovered its existence, the Potebnia group had subverted several units. In the spring of 1862 the infected outfits were disbanded and several officers were cashiered. Late in June Potebnia and some colleagues mounted an unsuccessful attempt on the life of the commander of the First Army. This action was designed as a protest against the executions that had also—as we have just seen—outraged Nikolai Utin; three men were arrested, but Potebnia escaped and went into hiding. His hopes for a military uprising dampened, he moved to implement an alternate plan that called for *concerted* revolutionary uprisings on the part of the Poles and the Russian revolutionaries. This was a new departure: Polish patriots had always insisted that *Polonia farà da sè*. But the goals of the Potebnia group and of Land and Liberty coincided. A peasant rebellion in Russia and a nationalist uprising in Poland would catalyze, reinforce, and augment each other.[7]

Potebnia and Padlewski went secretly to St. Petersburg in November 1862 to negotiate with Utin, Sleptsov, and others. Now Land and Liberty had never been an especially audacious organization (this is not to say that its members lacked courage, for they did not), and of course the arrest of its leaders had demoralized it. Thus it is not surprising to find Utin and Sleptsov cautioning the plotters from Poland that they had little to offer beyond sympathy and a couple of secret printing presses. Potebnia and Padlewski, heirs to a far more militant tradition, insisted upon more tangible support. The embarrassed Russians promised to try.[8]

In December of 1862 Nikolai Utin supervised the removal, by Mikhail Weide, of one of Land and Liberty's two secret presses to the village of Bolovsk in the Liutsin district of Vitebsk *guberniia*. This was done to make the press more readily accessible to the Poles, whose uprising was tentatively planned for the following spring. In the middle of February 1863, that is, after the January Rebellion had actually begun, the Russians moved the press to Marienhausen, the estate of the widow Alina Lippe-Lipska located a few *versts* from Bolovsk.[9]

The armed uprising had begun in Warsaw and other cities in mid-January, when Russian press-gangs began rounding up young Poles secretly selected by the authorities for conscription. This action had forced the hand of the Polish rebels, and their violent reaction ensured the triumph of the Polonophobes in St. Petersburg and Moscow. It became unpatriotic, not to say dangerous, to mention Poland and things Polish without adding a variety of more or less refined curses. The erstwhile liberal journalist M. N. Katkov, with all the vigor of the converted zealot, attacked the Poles, Roman Catholicism, and the West with reckless abandon, and his colleagues in the press followed his lead. Polish businesses were boycotted and occasionally sacked, Polish students in Russia were harassed and discriminated against, and countless public and private prayers were offered to the Orthodox God in the hope that divine vengeance would be visited upon Poland and its people. Anton Rubinstein did not sympathize with this madness, but he was forced to alter the winter program at the conservatory to eliminate the works of Chopin and other Polish composers. The mazurka was no longer danced at fancy balls or for that matter at the Salty Dog on the Nevsky, or anywhere else in Russia.

The explosive situation put enormous pressure upon the few score Russian revolutionaries of Land and Liberty. The Committee of Russian Officers in Poland (now known as the "Potebnians") called upon them to honor their commitment to the struggle against the Russian tsar.

Nikolai Utin assumed command of Land and Liberty's modest forces. His first act was to publish, at the press that remained near the capital, a broadsheet entitled "Polish blood is flowing, Russian blood is flowing." The author, Sleptsov, had chanced to be in Warsaw when the fighting began, and he sent his anguished, defiant statement back to his friends in St. Petersburg. Sleptsov called upon the Russian officers and men stationed in Poland not to "stain [your] hands with Polish blood" and to remember that the "liberation of Poland is closely linked with the freedom of our [own] long-suffering homeland." This echoed what Utin had said in "To the educated classes," and it reflected Chernyshevskii's general line with regard to Poland.[10]

The most important initiative undertaken by Utin and Land and Liberty to assist the Poles involved the violence that Russian revolutionaries had shunned since the Decembrist Revolt. In the most significant stockpiling of weapons and ammunition since that 1825 revolt, the Russian conspirators sought to create a base at Marienhausen. From that base they would try to launch a violent diversion to draw off troops fighting under General M. N. Murav'ev ("Hangman") in Lithuania and White Russia. Nikolai Utin directed this effort and helped to finance it with his own funds.

The Marienhausen Affair, as this episode of the January Rebellion came to be called, was designed to be part of a concerted armed attack on key military objectives. As such, it was linked to the better known "Kazan Conspiracy" and to the operations of the Polish rebels in the Northwest Territory.[11] The Marienhausen conspirators, operating in the densely forested northern part of the Vitebsk *guberniia,* had one monumentally crucial task: to cut the main St. Petersburg-Warsaw railway line and thus disrupt the flow of troops and matériel to the main theater of operations in the kingdom. The men of Land and Liberty had recruited supporters inside the Pskov Infantry Regiment and they were associated with a revolutionary circle in the Artillery Academy in St. Petersburg, a circle led by Peter Lavrov. All things considered, their position was not without its strong points: their financing was good and the Poles would provide some good field commanders. They needed only time, luck, and the goodwill of the local peasantry.[12]

The size of the cache at Marienhausen and nearby locations would seem at first glance rather modest. The conspirators had only about twenty hunting rifles; a few pistols; a couple of dozen sabers; three thousand cartridges; gunpowder and lead in considerable quantities; and victuals. It will not do, however, to disparage the effort on such grounds, for the Polish rebels were woefully deficient in arms in almost all sectors. They had only three hundred weapons for four thousand men in all the Podlasie, for example, and only one of Zygmunt Sierakowski's nine battalions was armed at all. The approximately three dozen men the Marienhausen conspirators hoped to put into the field could have made a significant (if hardly decisive) contribution to the rebel effort, especially if they had succeeded in disrupting traffic on the railway.[13]

At the end of February 1863, independent reports of suspicious activities at Marienhausen reached the authorities in Vitebsk and Pskov. The day after these reports, one of the "temporarily obligated" peasants on Alina Lippe-Lipska's estate told the police that as many as a hundred men were gathering at Marienhausen preparatory to joining the Polish insurrection. The governor of Pskov *guberniia* directed Major-General Count Pavel Andreevich Shuvalov to investigate these reports. Shuvalov was chief of staff of gendarmes, but since February 1 he had been—at the express order of the tsar—in charge of railway security between St. Petersburg and Vilna.[14] The full link between the capital and Warsaw had been completed only a few months earlier, and the government was extremely apprehensive that the new communications and transport system might be threatened. Shuvalov did not share the concern, but he obeyed orders and took four companies of men to investigate. His initial investigation at Marienhausen turned up part of the arms cache and led to a few arrests; this was not sufficient, in his view, to substantiate the reports of a sizable conspiracy and warrant further action. His superiors overruled him, however, not least because among the contraband was the *yarlyk* of the nearby railway station at the village of Pondery.[15]

Shuvalov broadened his search to the surrounding area, posted all four companies as sentries, and reported to General Murav'ev in Vitebsk. Murav'ev ordered the creation of a special investigative commission at the Dinaburg Fortress; the affair would be under military jurisdiction.[16]

Among those whom Shuvalov arrested at Marienhausen were Dmitri Stepanov, a noble from Kursk *guberniia,* and Ilya Zhukov, former staff officer of the Chernigov Infantry forced into retirement in 1862 for spreading anti-government propaganda among the enlisted ranks. Alina Lippe-Lipska was also arrested, as were her brother (the Polish rebel Antoni Ryk) and several others. More arrests in the northwest and in St. Petersburg were to follow.

The published and unpublished documents of the January Rebellion clearly reveal the enthusaiam of the "temporarily obligated" peasants for turning the quality over to the authorities. Both Polish and Russian revolutionaries neglected to cultivate the peasants, the former because they had neither the habit nor the inclination and the latter because they saw no need to consult the illiterate masses on whose behalf they professed to speak. In that part of Vitebsk *guberniia* the question was largely academic anyway, for the majority of the peasants were Latvian Catholic (there were some Russian Old Believers too), and the Latvians would not have trafficked with Land and Liberty under any circumstances at that time. The Russian authorities made use of peasant hostility toward the Polish and Russian gentry and in the savagery of 1863 frequently incited them to inform on and even rise up against their masters. The peasants were rewarded after the uprising was crushed with a relatively generous land settlement, although Alexander II and General Murav'ev put a high price on that: Russification. In any event, the failure of the rebels to win over the peasants anywhere has frequently been cited by Marxist historians as a major reason for the failure of the January Rebellion.[17]

Most of the people arrested at Marienhausen and in the vicinity were bound over to the military authorities in Vitebsk and Pskov, and a few were taken to the Dinaburg Fortress for interrogation. Stepanov and Zhukov, as alleged ringleaders, were taken to St. Petersburg, where the permanent investigative commission examined them in the spring and summer of 1863.[18] In the beginning, most of the suspects bore themselves courageously. On April 18, however, after five weeks of relentless pressure, Stepanov began to crack. He revealed that his mysterious associate "Briantsev" was Mikhail Weide. A week later he broke down—we do not know whether he was tortured—and revealed the identity of the central figure in the Marienhausen Affair, Nikolai Utin.[19]

The interrogators had established at the first session with Stepanov that he had lived in the capital with F. S. Sudakevich, leader of the "Petersburg Commune." This student circle was part of Land and Liberty, and Utin was a member of it.[20] The trap thus sprung on the hapless Stepanov, who inevitably followed his first revelations with others. Everyone he named was subjected to a *visite domiciliaire,* frequently followed by arrest. The Marienhausen case was broken, if not necessarily resolved.[21]

In February 1864, Stepanov, Zhukov, Weide, and five others were sent to hard labor in the mines for from eight to twenty years. Four of the forty-six people indicted in the Marienhausen conspiracy were freed, one died pending trial, and two—including Nikolai Utin—escaped and went into hiding. Alina Lippe-Lipska was sent into exile and the Marienhausen estate was sequestered. Stepanov received a full pardon in 1874, Zhukov in 1882. Weide's fate is unknown but presumably he died in the mines. General Murav'ev, who had dictated the sentences, did not survive to protest the pardons.[22]

None of the prominent figures in the January Rebellion who were associated with the Marienhausen Affair had to stand trial on that charge. Andrei Potebnia took to the field in the uprising and fought with Marian Langiewicz in the battle of Skała (near Kraków) on 5 March 1863. The Poles were victorious, but Potebnia lost his life and the cause of Polish liberation one of its most devoted champions. Zygmunt Padlewski was captured and executed by the Russians at Płock on May 15. Jarosław Dąbrowski, a party to the early negotiations with Land and Liberty, was arrested in August 1862 and did not actually fight in the rebellion though he did help plan strategy from his cell in the Warsaw Citadel. He escaped from a prison in Russia in December 1864, made his way to the West, and died on the barricades in 1871 as commander-in-chief of the armed forces of the Paris Commune.[23]

And what of Nikolai Utin, mastermind of the conspiracy? In May 1863 he fled to the West. The following year a court-martial issued a warrant for his arrest; when he did not present himself for trial within a year he was sentenced to death.[24] (No doubt he was not unwilling to suffer the punishment as it was awarded *in absentia*.) Because of Utin's escape it was impossible to bring the Marienhausen Affair to a conclusion, and the repercussions of his flight kept the matter festering.

Utin rarely receives more than brief and usually imprecise mention in Western studies of the Russian revolutionary movement, yet his career in the period 1861-72 found him at the center of important events in which he often played a critical role.[25] He was the son of Isaak Osipovich Utin, an uneducated entrepreneur who came out of the Finnish woods to make his first fortune as an *otkupshchik* (tax farmer) in spirits, his second as a financier. Jewish by birth, Isaak converted to Russian Orthodoxy and demonstrated his faith by providing funds to build the Uspensky Cathedral on Katajonokka Hill in Helsinki.[26] He and his wife raised five children; Nikolai was the third-born son. The Utins owned an imposing home on the English Embankment in St. Petersburg and a large dacha in Finland. Isaak Utin was an influential member of the capital's business community; he held the honorary title of *kommertsii sovetnik,* and Alexander II conferred the Order of St. Vladimir upon him.[27]

Isaak Utin valued education as only a person without one can. He sent his four sons to St. Petersburg University, and his daughter, Liubov', was one of the first women auditors there. Nikolai had a brilliant career in the philological faculty until he fell afoul of the police. In 1861 he won the gold medal in the faculty; Dmitri Pisarev was the keenly disappointed recipient of the silver.[28] For both winners scholarship gave way to political activism, and Utin was one of the ringleaders in the massive student movement of 1861. His name appears first, in a secret official history of the revolutionary movement, on a list of fourth-year students expelled from the university.[29] Remanded to the custody of his father, he continued his studies at home and earned a *kandidat* degree the following year.

It seems not to have been very difficult for Utin to evade the police and escape in May 1863 to Brussels.[30] His family, however, now found itself in an uncomfortable position, for passions ran extremely high during the Polish Rebellion. Suspicion fell upon Nikolai's father and brothers, and old Isaak Utin was kept under house arrest until the middle of September.[31] The St. Petersburg police were very much on the defensive, not least because they were denounced by both the military authorities (Marienhausen conspirators were court-martialed) and the Third Section. The *oberpolitseimeister* (I. V. Annenkov) complained that the fugitive had not been placed under regular police surveillance upon his expulsion from the university and that releasing him to his father's custody had been a mistake.[32]

Following Nikolai's escape, General Murav'ev (who had carte blanche in all matters under military jurisdiction in the Northwest Territory) decided to make Isaak Utin stand *in loco filii,* and the possibility existed that one or two of Nikolai's brothers would also be indicted.[33] The family turned to its protector, Prince A. A. Suvorov, governor-general of St. Petersburg, nephew of the great general and a close friend of Isaak Utin. Suvorov had frequently assisted the Utins in all manner of affairs, but in 1863 he had no choice but to establish a special commission under Major-General K. I. Ogar'ev to look into Nikolai's escape. The seriousness of the matter was reflected in Suvorov's public comment, in August 1864, that Isaak Utin would indeed probably have to stand trial. Privately, however, he was urging the Third Section to resist Murav'ev's demanded that Isaak Utin be court-martialed. He told the political police that Utin had "extensive commercial affairs [and] a large family," and that therefore, even though he had perhaps made a mistake, he should not be held responsible for his son's disappearance.[34]

What seems a ridiculous argument on Suvorov's part went in fact to the heart of the empire's financial stability, for Isaak Utin was an important if obscure member of that small band of entrepreneurs (D. E. Benardaki, V. A. Kokorev, S. I. Mamontov, E. G. Gintsburg, G. O. [E.] Gintsburg, and a few others) who were responsible—as Marxist historians have argued persuasively—for the "original accumulation" of capital in Russia during this period. Often these individuals made their original fortunes in mining, railroads, timber, or oil; Utin, like the more famous Kokorev, the Iakovlevs, and Zlobins, made his in spirits.[35] Vodka money (especially Jewish, however assimilated its possessor) was naturally regarded as the most unclean, and Isaak Utin and his fellow tax-farmers were frequently pilloried in the satirical magazine *Iskra.*[36]

The revenues raised through the *otkupshchiki* accounted for 40 percent of state receipts in the period 1859-63 (128 million rubles).[37] In 1863, in one of the reforms, the tax-farming system was abolished in favor of an excise tax on spirits, but the former *otkupshchiki* continued to play an important role in the financial affairs of the empire. Using their huge profits from tax-farming, many of them (including Isaak Utin) became bankers and financiers. Thus when Benardaki and others of Utin's associates told Prince Suvorov that their colleague's arrest would inevitably have an adverse effect upon the financial community, they spoke to the crux of the matter.[38]

Count F. F. Berg, now acting viceroy in Poland and no friend of Murav'ev, wrote to Suvorov in August 1864 to express satisfaction with the decision of the military authorities to permit a civilian court to deal with Isaak Utin. This is the first indication we have that General Murav'ev had changed his mind. Berg said that he was convinced that the "devout Orthodox Christian and devoted servant of the Fatherland" would never have helped his son escape. Without explaining why an innocent man should be punished at all, he suggested a fine as a way out of the dilemma.[39]

It would appear that General Murav'ev, deciding to bring Marienhausen to a tidy conclusion, had agreed to let the civilian courts have Isaak Utin. Now, however, enraged by the interference of Count Berg, who had no standing in the case and who did have the job Murav'ev coveted, and of Prince Suvorov, his sworn enemy, Murav'ev countermanded his order. He directed that Utin be bound over to the Dinaburg military-judicial commission. The state secretary V. P. Butkov pointed out that the emperor himself had seen the dossier on the case and had expressly sanctioned a civilian trial; a reversal would thus come to his attention.[40]

Murav'ev responded to the challenge to his authority with an apoplectic letter to Prince V. A. Dolgorukov (chief of gendarmes and head of the Third Section) expressing his anger that Dolgorukov's deputy (Mezentsov) had presumed to question his judgment. We might point out here that Mezentsov was Suvorov's nephew (and a grandson of the great general). Isaak Utin would stand trial by court-martial, Murav'ev declared, because the Marienhausen Affair was under military jurisdiction. The fact that Utin had not been involved in that affair was obviously immaterial. He himself was unwell, Murav'ev wrote, and had the strength only for the "fulfillment of the Sovereign Emperor's wishes, which are sacred to me." The St. Petersburg bureaucrats would henceforth, he declared, deal with him only after receiving the tsar's permission, for "I have neither the time nor the desire to fight with [them], the more so since that could only lead to the harming of the affair."[41]

A couple months after this exchange, Prince Suvorov refused to attend a reception for Murav'ev, declaring that he would have nothing to do with such a monster. Murav'ev returned this hostility in full measure.[42]

Not the least of old Isaak Utin's worries must have been the knowledge that he was thoroughly guilty. He had no role in the Marienhausen Affair itself, but he had, through his son Iakov, reimbursed Land and Liberty the three thousand rubles it had provided for Nikolai's escape. And Isaak Utin probably knew a great deal about the details of that escape. As soon as Nikolai reached Brussels he telegraphed his father for money, and we can assume—given the fine standard of living Nikolai maintained in the West—that money reached him without difficulty.[43]

All things considered, it was a minor miracle that Isaak Utin and three of his four sons (Evgenii was also involved in the escape) did not go to the gallows. Many people suffered the death penalty for lesser offenses in the brutal year of the January Rebellion.

But the Utins did not mount the scaffold, and General Murav'ev was denied a neat and soldierly resolution of the Marienhausen Affair. Unfortunately the historian does not fare markedly better, for Marienhausen did not so much die as quietly cease to exist as time and events gradually overtook the principals.[44]

The Utin family had a powerful ally—who was to fall in 1866 however—in Prince Suvorov.[45] The prince was in the capital, he saw the emperor and high-ranking officials (most of them inferior to him in rank) frequently, and he knew how to exploit the contempt in which many officials (Berg, for example) held General Murav'ev. And Suvorov made good use of the financial community's anxiety over Issak Utin's plight.

For his part, General Count Murav'ev (he held his title from September 1864) was indeed heavily burdened in the Northwest Territory, where from the late summer of 1863 he had been carrying out the thoroughgoing Russification he had recommended and the tsar had sanctioned.[46] And the last service he was to perform for the crown, one that consumed his energies when he was in the grip of a fatal illness, was to investigate the Karakozov attempt on Alexander's life in the spring of 1866. Murav'ev died shortly after completing the enquiry.

Thus Isaak Utin in a sense owed his deliverance to the failed regicide Karakozov. He lived on for another decade, unmolested by the state and restored to his prominent position in the financial community.[47]

As for Nikolai Utin, this central figure in the Marienhausen Affair arrived in the West a moderately celebrated revolutionary hero. He thought at first to collaborate with Herzen and Ogar'ev, but those two men were in their revolutionary dotage, and anyway Utin—true *shestidesiatnik*—was too abrasive to work with anyone his intellectual equal or superior. At the end of the 1860s he clashed with Michael Bakunin and seized control of an émigré newspaper in Geneva from him. With that base, he and some of his friends founded a Russian section of the First International and persuaded Karl Marx to represent them on the General Council.[48] Utin performed a significant service for Marx and the International in 1871-72 when he helped prepare a flimsy but successful case for expelling Bakunin from the organization. He remained close to Marx and indeed in 1876 Marx referred to him as "one of my best friends."[49]

In 1877, however, Marx's good friend begged the Russian authorities to allow him to return home. He denied having participated in the January Rebellion, blamed his bad reputation on some shady company he had kept as a callow youth, and said that "in this hour of test and trial [the Russo-Turkish War] for the beloved homeland every true son wants to serve tsar and country." He begged the tsar's mercy "not only for myself, but also for my whole family, which has the great happiness to be not unknown to Your Imperial Majesty for its devotion to you and the homeland."[50]

Having earned a diploma in civil engineering in England, Utin was then working with Baron S. S. Poliakov (a family friend) on the construction of the Bender-Galati railway in Romania. Poliakov endorsed his plea for a pardon.[51]

The letters from Bucharest naturally led to the reopening of the Marienhausen Affair. The Third Section initiated a search of the records on 2 November 1877, and in less than a week the military authorities in the Northwest Territory reported that Nikolai Utin was still under sentence of death for (1) not having presented himself for trial as ordered in 1864, and (2) having been a "direct and important" participant in the late rebellion in Poland.[52] This was naturally an ominous portent: always an important force in Russian society, the military was once again in a dominant position because the country was at war.

We still do not know why the Third Section decided to honor Utin's request and permit him to return hom. N. V. Mezentsov, chief of gendarmes and head of the Third Section, initialled a vague explanation that described not only Utin's role in the rebellion but also his not inconsiderable revolutionary activities abroad in the period 1863-72. So far as Marienhausen was concerned, the report noted that, because Stepanov, Zhukov, and the other conspirators had served their time and had been released (though not all had been pardoned), it was doubtful whether Utin should now be forced to suffer the supreme penalty demanded by the Dinaburg military-judicial commission in 1865. Utin had not had the opportunity to defend himself (*sic!*) and the evidence was "not without gaps." Utin could, therefore, return under "strict police surveillance."[53]

As his father had been saved by Prince Suvorov and the St. Petersburg financial community, so now was Nikolai Utin spared by the intervention of Suvorov's nephew, Mezentsov, and some of those same capitalists. He and his wife received their passports in Bucharest in January 1878 and returned to Russia. They were not disturbed by the authorities and indeed they left the country and returned without incident several times during the next few years. Nikolai worked as an engineer in the Urals and was involved in the construction of the first steel bridge across the Volga. He died in 1883.[54]

With Utin's death the Marienhausen Affair, an episode in the great January Rebellion, came to a close, a story without a concluding chapter. That chapter could only have been written by Nikolai Utin himself, and so far as we know he never undertook the task.[55] Marienhausen, like so many of Land and Liberty's projects in that period, was a failure, as was, in every conventional respect, the January Rebellion itself. Further, the great peasant uprising in Russia that was supposed to come on schedule in February 1863 did not materialize; it would be half a century before the Russian peasants finally decided they had had enough of tsarism.

The grandiose plans of the Russians and Poles who sought to topple the tsarist regime in the early 1860s had virtually no chance of success, and contemporaries must have sensed this even if they—especially the

Poles—refused to admit it. It might therefore seem perplexing that the various plans for a coordinated, "all-Russian" uprising proceeded as far as they did. But the important thing in the winter of 1863 was to keep the struggle against tsarism alive. This Land and Liberty and the Potebnians did.

NOTES

1. E. N. Kusheva first pointed out the obvious link between the second anniversary of the Emancipation Proclamation and events in Poland; see her "K istorii vzaimootnoshenii A. I. Gertsena i N. P. Ogar'eva s 'Zemlei i volei' 60-kh godov," *Literaturnoe nasledstvo,* vol. 41-42 (Moscow, 1941), 84. See also V. I. Neupokoev, "'Zemlia i volia' 60-kh godov po materialam dinaburgskogo protsessa," *Revoliutsionnaia situatsiia v Rossii v 1859-1861 gg.,* vol. 2 (Moscow, 1962), 317n-318n (cited hereafter as Neupokoev).

2. Franciszka Ramotowska, "Rząd rosyjski wobec manifestacji patriotycznych Królestwie Polskim (okres namiestnictwa M. Gorczakowa)," *Kwartalnik Historyczny,* 69, no. 4, 1962, 853-72. See also *Narodnoe delo* (Geneva), no. 2-3, October 1868, 35, for Nikolai Utin's assessment of the events of 1861-63.

3. M. A. Antonovich, "Arest N. G. Chernyshevskago," *Byloe* (St. Petersburg), 1, no. 3, March 1906, 90-94.

4. The text is in *Russko-pol'skie revoliutsionnye sviazi* (hereafter *RPRS*), vol. 1, Moscow, 1963, 175-77. See also L. F. Panteleev, *Vospominaniia* (Moscow, 1958), pp. 311-12 (cited hereafter as Panteleev).

5. General M. N. Murav'ev complained that the Poles who studied in Russia subverted Russian students; see *Russkii arkhiv,* 1885, no. 6, pp. 195-96.

6. Ludwik Kulczycki, *Rewolucja rosyjska od dekabristów do wędrówki w lud, 1825-1870,* vol. 1 (Lwów, 1909), 435-38; *Narodnoe delo,* no. 2-3, October 1868, 36.

7. The Ruthenian Potebnia was so thoroughly identified with the cause of Poland that many contemporaries simply overlooked the accident of his birth. Thus he is identified in this paper as an authentic spokesman for the Polish "Reds."

8. Panteleev, pp. 319-23; B. P. Koz'min, *Kazanskii zagovor 1863 goda* (Moscow, 1929), pp. 27-28; *Krasnyi arkhiv*, 1923, no. 4, 274.

9. Neupokoev, pp. 310-11. See also M. K. Lemke's editorial notes in A. I. Gertsen, *Polnoe sobranie sochinenii i pisem*, vol. 16 (Petersburg, 1920), p. 155, and see the map in V. M. Zaitsev, "Vozniknovenie mariengauzenskogo povstancheskogo tsentra i prichiny ego padeniia (k voprosu podgotovki vosstaniia na territorii Vitebskoi gubernii v 1863 g.)," in V. A. D'iakov et al., eds., *Revoliutsionnaia Rossiia i revoliutsionnaia Pol'sha (vtoraia polovina XIX v.)* (Moscow, 1967), p. 79 (cited hereafter as Zaitsev).

10. The text is in *RPRS*, vol. 2, 77-81. See M. N. Katkov's comment (from *Russkii vestnik*) on Sleptsov's work in *1863 goda* (Moscow, 1887), pp. 25ff.

11. See Koz'min, *Kazanskii zagovor*, and R. F. Leslie, *Reform and Insurrection in Russian Poland, 1856-1865* (London, 1963), p. 222n.

12. The best source on the mechanics of the Marienhausen operation is Zaitsev.

13. Zaitsev, pp. 86-91, 94, 96-97, 101.

14. Ibid., p. 90; *RPRS*, vol. 2, p. 206.

15. Zaitsev, pp. 91-92.

16. *Tsentral'nyi gosudarstvennyi arkhiv Oktiabrskoi revoliutsii* (hereafter *TsGAOR*), f. III otd., d. 407, no. 16100, S. Tatishchev, "Sotsial'norevoliutsionnoe dvizhenie v Rossii, 1861-1881. Istoricheskoe izsledovanie," *chast' 1, 1861-1871 gg.*, pp. 380-82, 384-89; Neupokoev, p. 323. Dinaburg (from the original German name, Dünaburg) was renamed Dvinsk in 1893, a not insignificant symbol of Alexander III's reorientation of Russian foreign policy away from Germany. It was and is a Latvian town; its name in that language is Daugavpils.

17. *RPRS*, vol. 2, pp. 209, 222-23, 229, 248. Katkov noted that the local peasants rushed to join the militia when Murav'ev issued the call; see *1853 god*, p. 253. The censor A. V. Nikitenko (*Zapiski i dnevnik [1804-1877 gg.]*, vol. 2 [St. Petersburg, 1905], 125), remarked about this phenomenon in the Dinaburg district. An excellent article on the background is V. I. Neupokoev, "Kontrreforma v gosudarstvennoi derevne Litvy (1857-1862 gg.)," *Revoliutsionnaia situatsiia v Rossii v 1859-1861 gg.*, vol. 5 (Moscow, 1970), 23-56. See finally Leslie, *Reform and Insurrection*, pp. 216-18, 225-26, 236-40.

18. *RPRS,* vol. 2, 214ff.

19. Ibid., pp. 243-44.

20. Panteleev, pp. 313, 318-19;*RPRS,* vol. 2, 214-15.

21. The day after he betrayed Utin, Stepanov recanted his testimony as an "infamous base slander." He had spent the night in his cell "in agony, wrestling with my conscience," and he told the investigator that he had made a false confession "for the sake of my mother" (*sic*). His was a classic crime-guilt-confession-sacrifice-redemption-salvation-syndrome, except that salvation did not come for a decade for Stepanov, See *RPRS,* vol. 2, 245-47.

22. Ibid., pp. 256-59; *TsGAOR,* Tatishchev, pp. 384-89; *TsGAOR,* f. III otd., 1 eksp., d. no. 97, "O vozmutitel'nykh vozzvaniiakh," *chast'* 90, "O byvshem studente Nikolae Utine, 1863 g.," *listy* 121-27, 6 December 1877, Third Section review of Utin's activities. Zaitsev (pp. 98-99) notes, apparently incorrectly, that only 34 people were involved, most of whom were under thirty years of age. For General Murav'ev's comments on the sentences in general in the Northwest Territory see "Graf M. N. Murav'ev: Zapiski ego ob upravlenii Severo-zapadnym kraem i ob usmirenim v nem miatezha, 1863-1866 gg.," *Russkaia starina,* March 1883, 615-30.

23. On Potebnia see Z. Młynarski and A. Ślisz, *Andrzej Potiebnia, bohater wspólnej sprawy,* Warsaw, 1955; V. R. Leikina-Svirskaia, "Adrei Potebnia," *Revoliutsionnaia situatsiia v Rossii v 1859-1861 gg.,* vol. 3 (Moscow, 1963), 83-114. On Padlewski see Krzysztof Dunin-Wąsowicz, "Zgymunt Padlewski," *Z dziejów współpracy polaków i rosjan w drugiej polowie XIX wieku* (Wrocław, 1956), pp. 71-131. On Dąbrowski see *Polski słownik biograficzny,* vol. 5 (Kraków, 1939-1946), 8-10; E. Przybyszewski, *Jarosław Dąbrowski i jego rola w organizacij narodowej, 1861-1862* (Warsaw, 1928); V. A. D'iakov, *Iaroslav Dombrovskii* (Moscow, 1969).

24. *TsGAOR,* Tatishchev, p. 388; *TsGAOR,* "O byvshem studente Nikolae Utine," *listy* 111-13, governor-general of Vilna-Kovno-Grodno to Third Section, 8 November 1877; Neupokoev, pp. 333-34.

25. The only extensive source on Utin in any Western language is, so far as I know, my *Revolutionary Exiles: The Russians in the First International and the Paris Commune* (London, 1979), passim. There is a considerable literature in Russian but no major monograph. A neglected Russian source is a work by a devout anti-Semite, General Vasilii Ratch:

Svedeniia o pol'skom miatezhe 1863 [goda] v severo-zapadnoi Rossii, vol. 1 (Vilna, 1867); a French-language version is B. Ratch, *La Question polonaise dans la Russie occidentale: Matériaux pour servir à l'histoire de l'insurrection de 1863* (Paris, 1868). Ratch notes on p. i of the Russian version that this work was commissioned by General Murav'ev in 1864. We can be certain, therefore, that the great importance Ratch ascribes to Utin's role in the planning of the January Rebellion reflects Murav'ev's own assessment.

26. *TsGAOR,* "O byvshem studente Nikolae Utine," *listy* 63-64, Count F. F. Berg in Warsaw to Prince Suvorov, 1 August 1864. The cathedral, designed by the Russian architect Aleksei Gornostaev, was built in the years 1862-68, and, as we shall see, Isaak Utin's generous piety was to be amply rewarded.

27. The title ("commercial counselor") was created in 1800 for deserving merchants who had spent twelve consecutive years in the First Guild; it was not part of the Table of Ranks. See *TsGAOR,* "O byvshem studente Nikolae Utine," *list* 104, Nikolai Utin to the tsar, 1 October 1877.

28. Panteleev, p. 313n., notes that several professors held the wholly unfounded suspicion that Utin won the gold only because his sister was married to M. M. Stasiulevich, who was until 1861 professor of history at the university (and who had for three years taught history to the tsesarevich; see Nikitenko, *Zapiski i dnevnki,* vol. 2, p. 231).

29. *TsGAOR,* Tatishchev, pp. 113-14.

30. It is possible that Prince A. A. Suvorov warned Utin to leave. He had earlier, in the crackdown on Land and Liberty, told him that he could not understand how he had escaped arrest. See *TsGAOR,* "O byvshem studente Nikolae Utine," *listy* 121-27, 6 December 1877, Third Section review of the Utin case.

31. Neupokoev, p. 331n. 126. Nikolai's lackey—the nouveau riche did not find revolutionism inconsistent with being gentlemen—was a police informant; see Panteleev, p. 291n.

32. *TsGAOR,* "O byvshem studente Nikolae Utine," *listy* 13-16, Annenkov report dated 9 July 1863. Nikolai Utin had been under "house surveillance." There was no provision for this in Russian law, and thus it was indeed difficult to determine where official responsibility lay for his escape. See ibid., *listy* 47-51, for a 16 October 1863, report of the special (Ogar'ev) commission on the escape.

33.   Panteleev, pp. 325-26.

34.   *TsGAOR*, "O byvshem studente Nikolae Utine," *listy* 59-60, Suvorov to Third Section, 19 August 1864. Ogar'ev was a member of the permanent investigating commission that had looked into the Marien-hausen Affair itself.

35.   I know of no definitive work, Marxist or otherwise, on the entre-preneurs of this type. See the articles "otkup" (vol. 10, cols. 687-88) and "vinnye otkupa" (vol. 3, col. 493) in the *Sovetskaia istoricheskaia entsik-lopediia*. See also the article "vinnye promysly" in *Evreiskaia entsiklo-pediia*, vol. 5, cols. 609-14. This latter study has much information on the Jews in the spirits trade in Russia.

36.   Panteleev, p. 326n., notes that Isaak Utin was called "Itsko Gusina" in *Iskra*, and he also notes rumors that he got rich by counter-feiting banknotes. On *Iskra* see Mikh[ail] Lemke, *Ocherki po istorii russ-koi tsenzury i zhurnalistiki XIX stoletiia* (St. Petersburg, 1904), pp. 31-142. There are caricatures of *otkupshchiki* on pages 39 and 73. *Iskra* was associated with Chernyshevskii's *Sovremennik*. Isaak Utin's shrewdness was not limited to business; he gave generously to the revolutionaries and was Peter Lavrov's patron in the early 1860s.

37.   *Sovetskaia istoricheskaia entsiklopediia*, vol. 3, col. 493.

38.   Panteleev, p. 325. On 29 August 1864, 17 leading St. Petersburg businessmen and financiers signed a petition addressed to Prince Suvorov requesting clemency for Isaak Utin. They stressed his important position in the business community and pointed out the difficulties his incarcera-tion would cause. See *TsGAOR*, "O byvshem studente Nikoale Utine," *list* 150. In this same source, at *listy* 148 and 152 (*sic*—the document has been misbound) is a letter (signature illegible) from the Fourth Section (charitable institutions under the protection of the Dowager Empress Mariia Fyodorovna) of His Majesty's Own Chancery requesting leniency for Isaak Utin; it is dated 21 August 1864.

39.   *TsGAOR*, "O byvshem studente Nikolae Utine," *listy* 63-64.

40.   Ibid., *listy* 65-66, undated and unsigned Third Section note; *listy* 69-71, Butkov to N. V. Mezentsov, 31 August 1864; *listy* 73-75, Mezen-tsov to Murav'ev, 2 September 1864; *listy* 76-85, miscellanea on the case.

41.   Ibid., *listy* 86-88, 25 September 1864.

42.   Nikitenko, *Zapiski i dnevnik*, vol. 2, 149. Nikitenko uses the word "cannibal" (*liudoed*), which is probably what Suvorov actually said;

the text, however, does not make this clear. On Murav'ev's hostility toward Suvorov see *Russkaia starina,* January 1883, 131-33, 152; March 1883, pp. 626-27.

43.   Panteleev, pp. 324-26. Panteleev (a close friend of the Utins and a member of Land and Liberty) notes that a special committee of the organization arranged Nikolai's escape. See V. I. Neupokoev's edition of Nikolai Utin's 5(17) July 1863, letter to his father in *Revoliutsionnaia situatsiia v Rossii v 1859-1861 gg.,* vol. 2 (Moscow, 1962), 573-82.

44.   The Soviet historians V. M. Zaitsev and V. I. Neupokoev, to whose excellent articles on Marienhausen this paper is indebted, have between them seen every conceivable piece of archival material on the affair. Neupokoev notes (p. 332) that the government's attempt to learn the secrets of Land and Liberty through the investigation of Utin's escape simply "fell through."

45.   In the wake of Dmitri Karakozov's attempt on the life of the tsar, Prince Suvorov lost his position as governor-general of the capital and became inspector-general of infantry, holding the latter post until his death in 1882.

46.   See Murav'ev's recommendations to the tsar (dated 14 May 1864) in *Russkii arkhiv,* 1885, no. 6, 186-97, 197-99.

47.   Count P. A. Valuev, minister of internal affairs, encountered Isaak Utin presiding at a dinner at the Commerce Club in St. Petersburg on 31 March 1866—even before Karakozov engaged first the tsar's, then Murav'ev's, attention; see Valuev's *Dnevnik,* vol. 2, *1865-1876 gg.* (Moscow, 1961), 113. Prince Suvorov and the American minister, Cassius Marcellus Clay, were also present.

48.   Nikolai Utin was under a very ineffective and inefficient surveillance during his years in exile. In the autumn of 1871, for example, an agent filed this report from Geneva: "One of the biggest figures in the International in general and in Geneva in particular is Nikolai Issakovich UTIN; if I am not mistaken he is, judging from his face, a member of the pure-blooded Jewish race. UTIN counts himself one of the émigrés . . . he really does have some unsettled accounts with the late Mikhail Nikolaevich MURAV'EV." The agent went on to note that Utin was preparing to go to Russia with a Swiss passport in the name of "W. Charlait." This report had no foundation in fact. See *TsGAOR,* f. III otd., 3 eksp., d. no. 514/1878, "Ob ustroistve v Moskve osoboi sekretnoi agentury," *listy*

149-56, undated (but autumn 1871) report from Geneva. This was probably the agent Appolon Młochowski, who served several other governments in addition to the Russian; on him see my *Revolutionary Exiles,* passim.

49.   Karl Marx and Friedrich Engels, *Werke,* vol. 34 (Berlin, 1966), 201.

50.   *TsGAOR,* "O byvshem studente Nikolae Utine," *list* 104, Utin letter dated Bucharest, 1 October 1877.

51.   Ibid., *list* 101, letter dated Bucharest, 5 October 1877. Utin himself wrote to Mezentsov (*listy* 105-6) on 1 October; his letter to the tsar was a mere formality. He did not appeal to Prince Suvorov, who had little influence after 1866.

52.   Ibid., *listy* 107, 111-13.

53.   Ibid., *listy* 121-27, 7 December 1877, "Spravka o politicheskom prestupnike Nikolae Utine." The *spravka* was endorsed by the governor-general of Vilna and was countersigned by Mezentsov.

54.   Ibid., *listy* 143, 144, 146. Nikolai Utin married Natal'ia Korsini, daughter of a well-known St. Petersburg architect, in Geneva in 1865. Natal'ia Utina ("N. A. Tal'") published "Zhizn' za zhizn'," a transparent account of émigré life in the 1860s and early 1870s, in Stasiulevich's *Vestnik Evropy* in 1885. She died in 1913.

55.   Utin did write an extremely important article on the revolutionary movement in *Narodnoe delo,* the Geneva newspaper he grabbed from Bakunin in the autumn of 1868. That article ("Propaganda i organizatsiia: Delo proshloe i delo nyneshnee," pp. 26-51), constitutes a valuable primary source for the history of the revolutionary movement in the 1860s; the Polish Rebellion is discussed on pp. 35-40. Utin had lavish praise for the Potebnians. (Another Russian who paid tribute to the Potebnia group was Sergei Nechaev; see *Narodnaia rasprava* [dated Moscow, but actually Geneva], Summer 1869, no. 1, 11.)

LUDWIK WARYŃSKI:
A REVOLUTIONARY CAREER

Norman M. Naimark
Boston University

Ludwik Waryński (1856-89), the founder of the Polish revolutionary party "Proletariat," was a romantic, but a romantic with sharp political instincts. As a student at the St. Petersburg Technological Institute in 1874-75, he fell under the utopian sway of Russian populism, but later modified his schoolboy views, turning to both the industrial workers of Warsaw and the works of Marx for revolutionary inspiration. Waryński's underground career was cut short by arrest and illness; but in his brief six years as a political activist, he succeeded in becoming the guiding force of the Polish socialist movement and in establishing the Proletariat, the first Marxist party in Poland, indeed the first Marxist party in the Russian Empire.[1] In addition, Waryński was the quintessential Polish internationalist—a role that won him the admiration of such prominent Russian revolutionaries as Plekhanov, Zasulich, Deich, and Figner but aroused the hostility of Polish patriots of diverse political persuasions.

Waryński's refusal to espouse the cause of Polish nationalism has sentenced him to historical obscurity. There are no Western-language biographies of Waryński. Even more striking, the ruling Polish Workers' Party in People's Poland has chosen not to publish scholarly works on the socialist leader's career. In its frantic search for legitimacy, the Polish party claims that it is at once the defender of the working class and the champion of the patriotic aspirations of all Poles, thus embracing the history of the patriotic movements and of Polish Marxism. Apparently, Waryński's synthesis of Marxism and antipatriotism presents the party with an insuperable problem, one that it is not yet prepared to resolve. Thus, Polish school children are taught half-fabricated stories reminiscent of the saints' lives, and Polish adults are given picture books and simplistic works of popular literature that reduce Waryński's life to a series of ideological clichés.[2] This essay surveys Waryński's short career in the hope that other scholars will decide to add to our knowledge of this man whose ideas and actions constitute a significant chapter in the history of East European socialism.

Waryński's Youth. The *kresy*, the western borderlands of European Russia, were the breeding grounds of a large number of men and women who became leaders of the Polish socialist movement in the 1870s and 1880s. Especially in the southwestern Ukrainian provinces of Podolia, Volhynia, and Kiev (the region of the *kresy* where Waryński spent his formative years), the Polish noble (*szlachta*) minority controlled the administrative and economic institutions. Magnates from the Poniatowski, Potocki, and Branicki families owned over 80 percent of the land in Kiev province, where, in the town of Martynówka, Ludwik Waryński was born on 24 September 1856.[3] His father, Seweryn Waryński, possessed only a tiny estate from his wife's dowry and, like many impoverished members of the *szlachta*, worked for one of the magnates; he had been hired by the owner of Martynówka, Dariusz Poniatowski, to supervise its small sugar-refining plant.[4] The elder Waryński sympathized with the 1863-64 uprising (and perhaps even played a minor role in it), read Mickiewicz and Słowacki to his six children, and contributed to the assistance fund for Poles sentenced to Siberia for their involvement in the uprising. He spent long hours in his home workshop, was fascinated with machinery, and certainly passed on to young Ludwik an ability to work with his hands.

Ludwik Waryński attended school and the gymnasium in nearby Biała Cerkiew (Belaia Tserkov), a central town whose population of fifteen thousand was nearly equally divided between Jews and Ukrainians. Although only several hundred Poles lived in the town, the middle schools were dominated by the offspring of the area's *szlachta*. Russification had begun in the gymnasium, the Polish library was closed down, and most class lectures were conducted in Russian rather than Polish. But, as Heironim Truszkowski recalled, a "liberal atmosphere" pervaded the school in spite of the autocratic interference, and relations between students and teachers were generally cordial.[5] There is little evidence that Waryński was swept into the radical movement during his gymnasium days. It is apparent from the memoirs of his schoolmates and later comrades, Edmund Brzeziński and the aforementioned Truszkowski, that Waryński came into contact with the gymnasium's patriotic circle and perhaps even with the Russian "to-the-people" movement in 1873-74, his last year at the gymnasium.[6] But in general, the evidence suggests that he studied hard, tutored younger students to earn money, and was undoubtedly a "young Pan" like most of his classmates.[7]

Upon graduating from the gymnasium of the *kresy*, Polish youngsters flocked to the technical schools, especially those of St. Petersburg. They generally avoided the schools in the Congress Kingdom of Poland, feeling that these were mediocre institutions that functioned as instruments of Russianization. The technical institutes were attractive because they prepared students for careers in industry, a field that seemed more promising than the increasingly anti-Polish bureaucracy. In the 1880s Poles constituted about 25 percent of the students in the half-dozen largest and most important technical schools in St. Petersburg.[8] Again, Waryński shared the experience of his generation. He graduated from the gymnasium in July 1874 and moved to St. Petersburg with the intention of enrolling at the Institute of Communications. Upon being denied entrance to the school of his choice, the lanky, blond-haired youth instead matriculated at the Institute of Technology, where he looked and acted the role of the typical "kresowiec."[9] Young Ludwik probably took a keen interest in his studies at the mechanics faculty of the institute, which required him to pay periodic visits to the city's factories and workshops.

Waryński's major interest, however, was the radical political activity that engulfed St. Petersburg students in 1874-75. Unfortunately, only the outlines of his involvement can be documented reliably. Of the dozens of Polish "self-education" circles that formed at the city's institutions of higher learning, Waryński joined the most radical. His circle included Aleksander Więckowski, Erazm Kobylański, and Edmund Brzeziński from the Institute of Technology, and Jan Hłasko and Bolesław Mondszajn from the Academy of Medical-Surgery.[10] Both Hłasko and Więckowski participated in the Russian movement and became members of the party "Land and Liberty." As a result, the circle's activities were heavily influenced by Russian populism, and Waryński and his friends read and discussed Herzen, Chernyshevskii, Lavrov, and Bakunin. It is probable that this St. Petersburg circle provided him with his first exposure to Marx's *Das Kapital.*

But it was primarily the utopian and romantic qualities of Russian populism that appealed to the Polish students, Waryński among them. In October and November 1875 the universities and technical schools of the capital witnessed repeated demonstrations and protests. Waryński was one of the hundreds of Russian and Polish students arrested and sent home for his participation in the disturbances. By administrative order, he was deprived of credit for his previous year at the institute and placed under police surveillance for a year. While in Krawiec (where his father now lived and worked as an administrator of a Branicki estate). Waryński maintained extensive contacts with the Kiev University radicals led by Kazimerz Dłuski and the Izbicki brothers.

The camaraderie of *kresy* Polish youth, based partly on familiarity with each other's families, made revolutionary unity both a natural goal and a genuine possibility. Waryński had already begun to command the respect of his peers and exercise leadership within the group. Partly it was his gentle good looks and "charm" that attracted them; partly it was his manner of speaking: noble manners and calm demeanor combined with an unpretentious and forceful style of argument.[11] Everyone believed in "the cause of equality, freedom, and brotherhood," wrote one memoirist, "but no one believed quite like Waryński, for his belief was strong, fervent, and arose from the depths of his soul."[12]

In the Congress Kingdom, 1876-78. Russian populism was so diffuse, fanciful, and inconsistent that historians find it impossible to deal with as an ideology. Polish populists (*narodniki*), Waryński among them, found themselves in a particularly confusing theoretical (and psychological) position. Their attachment to Polish culture and tradition—though not, it should be added, to the resurrection of Poland or to Polish patriotic movements—made it difficult for them to extol the Russian peasant commune as the key to the emergence of socialism. The *kresy*-born and Russian educated Polish students solved their personal and theoretical dilemmas by engaging in their own "to-the-people" movement. More and more, recalled Dłuski, "the notion spread that the ideas of socialism should be propagated by Poles not in Russia, but in their own country . . . in its capital—in Warsaw."[13]

Waryński moved to Warsaw at the end of December 1876 and immediately went to work as an apprentice at Lilpop, Rau, and Lowenstein, a hugh machine-building complex. The rapid industrialization of the Congress Kingdom between 1864 and 1876 had produced a sizable urban work force comprised of many individuals who had vivid memories of the uprising of 1863-64. In Warsaw itself, Polish workers had already formed rudimentary discussion circles and mutual-help groups. For Waryński, then, the problem of finding the elusive "people" was solved, but the marriage between the *kresy* activists (with Waryński at their head) and the Warsaw workers' circles was never to be an easy one. Waryński complained about worker ignorance and apathy, and the workers retaliated against the interference of intelligentsia activists by reporting them to the police. But Waryński understood instinctively that the workers would not be impressed by socialist slogans or elevated rhetoric; they would respond only to "agitation for economic demands."[14] With the aid of Henryk Dulęba, Hilary Gostkiewicz, and other worker-socialists, Waryński concentrated on building the defense treasuries (*kasy oporu*) to provide funds for those workers dismissed for agitational activities.[15] He also enlarged and combined the informal workers' circles, hoping to use the new organization as the basis for a mass workers' movement.

In the fall of 1877 a new group of *kresy* socialists, led by Kazimierz Hildt and Kazimierz Dłuski, arrived in Warsaw from Odessa, increasing to twenty the number of intelligentsia socialists.[16] During this same period, Waryński, threatened by conscription, enrolled in the School of Agronomy at Puławy. Although he organized a circle of Puławy students, his primary concern remained the Warsaw workers, and he traveled often to the capital on brief agitational trips. By April 1878 student life no longer suited Waryński, and he moved back to Warsaw under the assumed name of "Jan Buch." His return coincided with the arrival of some fifteen propagandists from St. Petersburg—a significant expansion of the local socialist intelligentsia. Dłuski and Hildt had also managed to convince some formerly patriotic groups from Warsaw University to join the movement.

With the police still convinced that Polish patriotism, not socialism, was the primary threat to Russian rule in the Congress Kingdom, Polish socialists in 1877-78 took bolder steps toward the all-encompassing social revolution that they believed to be imminent. Waryński was a frenetic agitator, impatient with the tedium of conducting revolutionary activity through several separate circles. Józef Uziembło, a follower of Lavrov, urged caution and careful propaganda among workers, criticizing Waryń-ski's "agitational" approach.[17] But Waryński moved ahead, holding larger meetings among workers to whip up enthusiasm for action against the exploitive policies of the factory owners. Under the leadership of both Uziembło and Waryński, the "Warsaw Social-Revolutionary Organization" —as the Polish socialists now called themselves—supervised the translation into Polish of seven German agitational pamphlets, most of them Lassallean in character. Kazimierz Hildt, Stanisław Mendelson, and Stanisław Waryń-ski (Ludwik's younger brother) arranged to print this literature in Leipzig. Once printed, the pamphlets were to be transported to Wrocław (Bres-lau) and Lwów. The dangerous mission of transporting the pamphlets, some six thousand in all, from Wrocław to Warsaw fell to Ludwik Waryń-ski.[18]

The circulation of illegal revolutionary literature, coupled in June 1878 with increasing reports of agitational meetings attended by twenty to forty workers, prompted the complacent judicial and police authorities to act. The officials were especially disturbed by descriptions of the per-suasive speeches made by one particular agitator (Waryński), known alternatively as "Jan Buch," the "tall one," and the "smooth-talker."[19] During the summer of 1878 the police began to arrest members of the extremely vulnerable organization. From the perspective of Polish socialists, there had been no need for caution. Seeing that the police were exclusively concerned with the patriotic movement and certain that the revolution would occur in a matter of months or at most a few years, the Warsaw Social-Revolutionary Organization had not felt it necessary to draw up a set of conspiratorial rules or tactics for self-defense. Such unbounded naiveté made the students and workers easy prey for the police, and by September 1878 the authorities held eighty members of the organization in jail. Szymon Diksztajn, Stanisław Mendelson, Dłuski, and Maria Jankowska fled to Switzerland in early October. Waryński es-caped to Galicia.

In Emigration. On the train to Galicia, Waryński wrote a threatening letter to Viachislav Pleve, who had led the judicial campaign against the Warsaw socialists. If the authorities continued to pursue the socialists, he warned, they would pay with their own blood.[20] Like most socialists of the period, Waryński's romantic attachment to the cause of social revolution had almost blinded him to the possibility of government repression; his response to the summer 1878 arrests was one of naive and violent indignation. He was shocked that the government had the audacity to interfere with the socialists' work among the people, but he was determined to fight force with force. From the time of the first arrests, Waryński was said to move about Warsaw "with a revolver in his pocket and a dagger in his belt." When a worker is harassed by the police, he told a group of socialists, "we should all join in! Don't be afraid of them! . . . Let them be afraid of us!"[21]

Guns, however, had no function in Galicia, where socialists and trade-unionists had openly organized workers' circles and published legal socialist newspapers for ten years. In October 1879 Waryński settled in the Galician city of Lwów, the home of Antoni Mańkowski, the head of the typesetters, and Bolesław Limanowski, the scholarly socialist patriot. He arrived only a few weeks before Limanowski's departure for Switzerland, but their few brief contacts were amiable. Limanowski remarked in his memoirs that the leader of Polish socialism "was a rather good-sized, articulate and handsome young man" who "left a pleasant impression." However, Limanowski also wrote of his displeasure that Waryński checked into the local hotel as man and wife with the lovely Maria Jankowska, who was married and had two children.[22] The more fundamental differences between Limanowski the patriot and Waryński the internationalist emerged only later. Even after the departure of Limanowski, Waryński found he could not operate among the Lwów artisan socialists. Their legalism frustrated him, and their trade-unionist goals fell far short of his immediate goal—international socialist revolution.[23]

Therefore, at the beginning of November 1878, Waryński left Lwów for Kraków, the Galician city dominated by loyalist conservatives and liberals. Three months later, shortly before his arrest, Waryński summarized his Kraków activities in a letter to his sister: "For this entire time I have been involved with agitation, with propaganda, in a word, with every kind of work which comes under the rubric of revolutionary activity . . . . Unremitting surveillance forces me to change names constantly."[24] He contacted underground circles, brought Mendelson and Jankowska to Kraków to help organize the city's intelligentsia, traveled to Vienna to organize a Polish socialist circle, and used Kraków as a base for transporting illegal brochures into the Congress Kingdom.

But a Kraków printer denounced Waryński to the police, and in mid-February 1880 Waryński and thirty-four of his confederates faced trial on charges of "disturbing the public peace."[25] The advocacy of socialism was not in itself a crime in Galicia; thus the Kraków authorities, spurred by Warsaw's cooperation in the investigation and indictment, attempted to portray Waryński and his group as a "nihilist" band determined to overthrow the legitimate Romanov and Habsburg monarchies. Since the trial was public, it became the subject of widespread political discussion and controversy. Kraków conservatives howled for a verdict of guilty, afraid that their limited political autonomy would be threatened if the Galician Poles advocated socialism. At the trial itself, all attention was focused on Waryński, the chief conspirator and spokesman for his group. "Socialism is a purely scientific matter," Waryński began his defense, and, as such, "socialists do not play with politics." Instead, he continued, his group advocated only that which was, in the end, a historical inevitability—economic revolution. Socialists do not make revolution, Waryński insisted, they prepare for it. Therefore, the charge that his group had attempted to overthrow governments was absurd. To be sure, the methods by which one prepares for revolution vary according to the political system, but, Waryński pointed out, the political system under which the Polish socialists were operating had led them to opt for a peaceful program of economic revolution, not a system of terror as advocated by the Russian revolutionaries.[26]

More important to the outcome of the verdict than Waryński's carefully constructed testimony was his calm, self-assured demeanor. His handsome, almost merry appearance provided an ironic contrast to the dark, evil, and "very dangerous" portrait of him painted by the conservatives. A writer for the Kraków newspaper *Czas* (Time) expressed this irony when he observed that Waryński's "lively physiognomy" did not "correspond at all" to his conception of a socialist.[27] The jury acquitted Waryński of the primary charge (a decision that the conservative newspaper regarded as "a social, political, and national defeat") and ordered the Austrian police to escort him to the Swiss border.[28] Upon arriving in Switzerland, the exile quickly made his way to the large Polish émigré community in Geneva.

By the fall of 1878, Limanowski, Diksztajn, Hildt, and Mendelson had formed a Geneva-based Polish socialist circle dedicated to the publication of socialist materials. In mid-October 1879 they began publishing *Równość* (Equality), and by the time of Waryński's arrival in February 1880, the *Równość* group had added Dłuski, Jankowska, and Witold Piekarski to its membership. It is apparent from the extensive memoirs of Lev Deich, who worked closely with the *Równość* group and was valued for his close ties to Plekhanov, that Waryński was frustrated by the confusion, inevitable in exile, of personal and theoretical politics.[29] He lived with Diksztajn, Dłuski, and Jankowska in a small commune in a village outside Geneva, but he bickered with Mendelson, who, as heir to a sizable banking fortune, used his financial position to influence the rules of the commune as well as the editorial policy of *Równość*. Jankowska, who also was quite wealthy and at this point lived with Mendelson, attracted the unwanted affections of Erazm Kobylański, one of Waryński's closest confederates. A duel between Kobylański and Mendelson was averted only by the "ruling" of an impartial tribunal headed by Plekhanov. And, to make matters worse, Limanowski's nerves were also raw; he felt jilted because the *Równość* group, inspired by Waryński, preferred the advice of the "Muscovites" to his own.[30]

Waryński left the commune in the summer of 1880 and somewhat impetuously moved into an apartment with Anna Sieroszewska, the eighteen-year-old sister of the Warsaw activist Wacław Sieroszewski. Though Anna bore him a son, the informal marriage between them, he later wrote, "did not bring [him] any joy."[31] At the same time, Waryński was forced to witness the tragic decline of Szymon Diksztajn, the author of the brilliant and later widely translated propaganda piece *Who Lives From What?* Entranced by Jankowska and frustrated by émigré politics, Dikstajn drank heavily and wrote increasingly incoherent love letters to Jankowska. In 1883, completely isolated from the émigré community, he committed suicide.[32]

Given this web of personal frustrations and romantic rivalry, Waryński's progress in welding the Polish socialist community into a major force in the international movement is all the more remarkable. Despite his personal frustrations, the Geneva period afforded Waryński a respite from police harassment and thrust him into a highly politicized environment in which the differences among socialists, muted during the active underground struggle, became the central concern. The polemics in which he engaged sharpened his mind, clarifying his thoughts on socialism and its application to the Polish question.

Like the other *Równość* socialists, Waryński arrived in Geneva a proponent of the "Brussels Program."[33] Formulated in Warsaw in September 1878, this program contained no plan of action, but did espouse a series of principles which could be described as Marxist in historical analysis, Lavrist in revolutionary strategy, and anarchist in social vision. Under the influence of the Lwów and Kraków trade unionists and the Swiss social democrats, Waryński slowly dropped the anarchist elements of the Brussels Program and became such a devoted convert to Marxism that Deich has given him partial credit for having set Plekhanov on his own road to Marxism.[34] But on one point Waryński never wavered; he remained a consistent supporter of the Brussels Program's opposition to the reconstruction of an independent Poland in the absence of an international socialist revolution.

On the fiftieth anniversary of the November 1830 uprising, *Równość* organized a conference in Geneva which attracted some four hundred European socialists. Waryński informed the assembly in unambiguous terms that Polish socialists had buried the slogan "Long Live Poland" and replaced it with "Proletarians of the World, Unite." He even chided Marx and Engels who, unable to attend the conference, ended their written greetings with the anathemized slogan, "Long Live Poland." The founders of scientific socialism do not understand, said Waryński, that "the slogan 'Long Live Poland' can also attract the bourgeoisie and the privileged classes. This worship of and sympathy for Poland, Poland the oppressed and the oppressor, shows that in the views of its defenders, the old political combinations still hold their meaning." But, Waryński insisted, Marx and Engels must understand that the "revolutionary fervor" of the independence movement's leaders with all "their hot desire for changes in social relations ... weakened and extinguished" when confronted with the need for real actions to improve the lives of the Polish people.[35] Before the shocked conference auditorium, Dłuski, Mendelson, and Diksztajn added their own voices to the litany of denunciations of Polish patriotism.

While the Russian radicals greeted Waryński's presentation with enthusiasm, radical-democratic Poles in Switzerland denounced the *Równość* group's stance as traitorous and severed further contact with them. Agaton Giller wrote to Limanowski, "*Równość* should be recognized as injurious to our cause and published in the interests of the enemies of Poland."[36]

Limanowski, who had already resigned from the editorial board of
Równość over the publication of Dłuski's virulently anti-nationalist
"What is Patriotism?" formed his own party, "Lud Polski" (Polish People).
The resurrection of an independent Poland, the program of Lud Polski
stated, was the precondition for the establishment of socialism on Polish
soil.[37] Waryński responded by attacking Lud Polski as "standing in total
opposition to the contemporary socialist movement in our country.[38]

When the Polish section of the conference of the International convened on 2 October 1881 at Chur, the meeting turned into a full-scale
clash between Waryński and Limanowski over the question of the independence movement. Limanowski wanted to form a three-partition
Polish socialist party allied with the patriotic movement and faithful
to the goal of Polish independence. Waryński totally rejected the notion
of a three-partition party, and added that the Polish socialists "cannot
extend their hands to the democratic bourgeoisie without the danger of
betraying their cardinal principles."[39] Frustrated and irritated by the
Polish arguments, the conference membership concluded only that "the
struggle for liberation is a class and not a national struggle."[40] Limanowski
later claimed with considerable bitterness that his defeat on this point
was the result of personal politics rather than theoretical wisdom.[41]

For Waryński, the Geneva and Chur Conferences resulted in a more
sympathetic attitude toward the Russians. Both camps of Russian socialism in emigration, Plekhanov's "Black Partition" and Tikhomirov's
"People's Will," had issued statements supporting Waryński's internationalist position and urging the Poles in the Congress Kingdom to ally
themselves with the Russian movement. For Russian radicals, Limanowski's plans for a single Polish socialist party dedicated to the attainment of
independence had seemed to be an expression of anti-Russian, Polish
chauvinism. The Western social democrats headed by Engels, on the other
hand, maintained that it was "unthinkable" for the Poles to make plans
for a socialist party before the resurrection of an independent Poland.[42]

Initially, Waryński was attracted to Black Partition and worked
especially closely with Lev Deich. His sympathies gradually shifted to the
more politically active People's Will, however, especially with the news of
the crescendo of assassinations that culminated in the 1 March 1881
killing of Alexander II. Partly in response to these assassinations and
partly out of pique with Marx and Engels, Waryński and Diksztajn sent

a note of greeting from *Równość* (July 1881) to the Conference of Anarchists in London, which was being boycotted by the European social democrats. But Mendelson, Jankowska, Dłuski, and Piekarski, irked at not having been consulted in the drafting of the letter and more closely tied in thinking to the social democrats, protested Waryński's gesture of "separatism" by resigning from *Równość* and founding a new periodical, *Przedświt* (Dawn).[43]

Waryński had no choice but to back down and apologize for his "mistake." Mendelson, Jankowska, and Dłuski controlled all the funds for *Równość,* and the newspaper could not continue without their support. Although he joined the new *Przedświt* board, Waryński, still smarting from the hostile reaction of his letter, decided to leave the distasteful world of émigré politics. During the fall 1881, while negotiations proceeded between Black Partition and the *Przedświt* Poles, Waryński began his preparations to return to the Congress Kingdom.

Although Plekhanov remained aloof, Deich, Aksel'rod, and Zasulich were determined to enlist the Poles in their efforts to reunite the Russian movement; they feared that if the two offshoots of Land and Liberty were not reunited, People's Will, the party credited with the successful assassination of Alexander II, would subsume and ultimately destroy their own party. The negotiations between the Poles and Black Partition resulted in a statement "To the Russian Comrades" calling for the establishment of a unified social-revolutionary party. Initially drafted by Mendelson and Dłuski as an address to the negotiators, the statement was refined by Deich and Plekhanov, who "added certain corrections and completions"; Waryński approved the document, and the final version was published on 3 November 1881.[44] The purpose of a unified social-revolutionary party, according to the document, was to struggle against the autocracy for the establishment of socialism and the guarantee of political freedom. Once socialism and political freedom had been established, there would be no more obstacles to prevent "the mass organization of the working class in Russia."[45] The appeal to People's Will, "To the Russian Comrades," approved terrorism as a means of political struggle and allowed the Russian and Polish peasantry a legitimate role in the revolutionary movement.

The discussions between *Przedświt* and Black Partition resulted in a definite plan of action: Waryński should return to the Congress Kingdom to win revolutionary groups over to the cause of party unity. Deich received funds to cover the cost of travel from I. Stefanovich in St. Petersburg, and Waryński left for Warsaw in late November 1881.

Waryński and the "Proletariat." "From the moment of Waryński's arrival in Warsaw," the Warsaw prosecutor later wrote, "social-revolutionary propaganda took on enormous proportions."[46] Although the prosecutor overstated his case, Waryński's activities undoubtedly hastened the process that united diverse workers' circles, intelligentsia groups, and Polish student organizations in Russian universities into a single party with common aims and methods. As he wrote in one of his few articles in *Równość,* "Do We have a Workers' Question?" the primary failing of the 1877-78 Warsaw movement was "disorganization," which had left the workers "apathetic" and deprived them of "a feeling of solidarity." Therefore, Waryński concluded, the "burning question" for Polish socialists was how to form an organization.[47]

Waryński's first plan of action—contacting the various socialist workers' circles in Warsaw—was made less taxing by the cooperation of his comrade Henryk Dulęba, who took him to each of the major industrial factories in the city.[48] After the Polish student Kazimierz Puchewicz had helped him make contacts with the socialist intelligentsia in the summer of 1882, Waryński had formed the nucleus of his party, the Proletariat.

The first proclamation issued by the party appeared on the streets of Warsaw in late July 1882. Entitled simply "Comrades," the proclamation expressed support for machinists at the Warsaw-Vienna railway workshop in their struggle against the management and summoned all workers to join in the socialist organizing efforts: "Unity and more unity, unity is all we need, and the future and happiness will belong to us."[49] On the first of September the "Workers' Committee" of the Proletariat issued its program, and from this point on the Workers' Committee assumed the leadership of the new party.

Between the summer of 1882 and the fall of 1883 (when he was arrested), Waryński carried out a tireless and spirited campaign of agitation among Warsaw's working class.[50] His message was simple and effective: the tsarist bureaucrats and the capitalist employers were conniving to keep workers' wages low, their hours long, and their hopes for a better life unfulfilled. Waryński's success as an agitator was reflected in his ability to attract workers to the ranks of the Proletariat; by the summer of 1883 he had succeeded in increasing the number of working-class members in his organization to three hundred.[50] But he also understood that the ultimate victory of the party depended on its ability to protect itself. Although no terrorist acts were carried out while Waryński was leading the Proletariat, he did fully support the terrorism of People's Will and later recommended that his party "pay attention to traitors, in order that they cause no further damage."[51]

With the 1882-83 arrival from St. Petersburg of Aleksander Dębski and Stanisław Kunicki, both of whom were deeply influenced by the heroic deeds of People's Will, the Proletariat became even more attuned to using terrorism, especially in "self-defense" against the police or in rooting government agents from its ranks. According to the police, Waryński himself was responsible for importing "ten revolvers of the bulldog type," and at one meeting he was reported to have said, "we will kill all spies and traitors."[52] Thus Waryński could not be dissociated from the major acts of party terrorism—the attacks on four alleged government agents—which occurred after his imprisonment. Indeed, he looked at terrorism not only as a legitimate means of party self-defense but also as a weapon of agitation. Polish socialists, he wrote, must struggle actively to gain the allegiance of the working people and must prove that they "are the enemies of the oppressors," "will not back down during the struggle," and "wish that the masses get everything that belongs to them."[53]

Waryński's views on the importance of the political struggle evolved out of a series of confrontations with fellow party leaders over the Proletariat's involvement in public issues. In the beginning of February 1883, the Warsaw authorities revived a health regulation that called for a twice-a-month medical examination for all female workers.[54] Since 1864-65, these regulations had applied only to prostitutes; thus the female workers refused to comply with the ordinance. Waryński sensed the agitational value of the issue and published a proclamation in support of the women. Calling the health examination order an "outrage," he urged the workers to hold fast. "Fight back," he wrote: "Death is better than disgrace! . . . If they want a fight—they shall have it."[55]

The government rescinded the order a week later, in part because the workers had demonstrated their anger but also because Minister of Interior D. Tolstoi had not approved the order in the first place. Waryński responded with a jubilant proclamation: the workers had scored a victory against the oppressors. In order to ensure futher successes, the workers should join with the party that "stood in [their] defense...that spoke for [them] in this question." In the necessary future confrontations between workers and government, Waryński added, "you can be sure of our help and sympathy."[56]

Waryński's determination to pursue the political struggle among workers provoked intense opposition from some party members and socialist allies. Kazimierz Puchewicz, the son of a Warsaw professor and devoted labor activist, tried to block Waryński's attempt to politicize the health order issue. In March and April 1883, when students at the Agronomy Institute in Puławy and at Warsaw University violently demonstrated against Curator of Schools A. Apukhtin's imposition of educational "counter-reform," Waryński again entered the fray, encouraging the party to issue leaflets in support of the students.[57] This, combined with Waryński's exhorations during the resistance to the health order, was too much for Puchewicz. He bolted from the party and formed his own group, "Solidarity."

The party veteran, Zgymunt Heryng, wrote that "Waryński and Puchewicz were like fire and water, the antithesis of revolutionary explosiveness and cold circumspection. Both aspired to the same goals, but with very different means."[58] Puchewicz's means consisted of organizing workers in broadly based federations in order to bargain with management for higher wages and better working conditions. The Solidarity group dismissed violence as counterproductive and focused on the peaceful strike as the only legitimate weapon of the socialist struggle. The revolution would occur, Puchewicz insisted, as the inevitable product of the development of capitalism. In the meantime, socialists should confine themselves to building a purely workers' organization based on improving the conditions of Polish labor.[59] Puchewicz agreed with Waryński's analysis of the negative influence of the national question, but this agreement meant little when set against Puchewicz's anger over Waryński's willingness to entertain the possibility of using terrorism.

In their private discussions, Waryński constantly argued with Puchewicz over the role of the Proletariat in bringing about revolution. "The activities of the party should be in public view," claimed Waryński, in order that the party exert an "influence on the future revolutionary government." The party must demonstrate its willingness to fight for the rights of workers and to defend its own existence by any means at hand, including terrorism. Otherwise, Waryński argued, the party could not expect either the allegiance or the active participation of its working-class membership.[60]

Waryński's own views on the importance of the political struggle, and specifically on the agitational value of party violence, became more clearly defined as a result of his confrontation with Puchewicz. Solidarity never seriously challenged the predominance of the Proletariat, and with Puchewicz's arrest in September 1883, the group disappeared. Its members rejoined the Proletariat, but the essence of Puchewicz's challenge—determinism on the matter of revolution and "economism" as a solution to the plight of the workers—remained alive in Waryński's second major battle over the political struggle, this time with the more formidable Krusiński circle.

Stanisław Krusiński was a talented Marxist philosopher and aesthetician who had gathered around him a group of brilliant Warsaw intellectuals including Ludwik Krzywicki, Poland's most prominent nineteenth-century sociologist, and Bronisław Białobłocki, an accomplished Marxist literary critic. The Krusiński group finished the translation of *Das Kapital,* a project begun by Szymon Diksztajn in 1877-78. They also made a valuable contribution to the legitimacy of socialism among the Polish intelligentsia by using the legal press to air their important challenge to the hegemony of liberalism.[61]

Throughout 1882 Waryński worked in tandem with Krusiński; the Proletariat concentrated on undergound activities while the Krusiński group propagandized for socialism in university circles and in the press. The schism between the two resulted, as in the case of Solidarity, from disagreements over the issue of the political struggle. Krusiński and his confederates analyzed the development of capitalism in the Congress Kingdom and concluded that neither the working class nor industrialization were sufficiently advanced to make a revolution possible. Engaging in illegal activities would only jeopardize the main task, which was the spread of socialist principles among the intelligentsia. The political struggle was foolhardy, indeed counter productive.

The actual break between Waryński and the Krusiński group was precipitated by a symbolic issue: Waryński's intention to fulfill the conditions of the Geneva "Letter to the Russian Comrades," which endorsed an all-empire social-revolutionary party. Puchewicz's and Krusiński's objections to combining the activities of Russian and Polish radicals were persuasive enough to prevent Waryński's plans from being included in the Proletariat's 1882 program, but the issue of an all-empire party was to resurface only a few months later at a meeting of Polish socialists held in Vilna in January 1883. At this conference, attended by a dozen socialists from various Polish centers of the empire, Krusiński attempted to defuse the growing movement toward centralization, terrorism, and political struggle by "heatedly debating with the defender of the latter —Waryński."[62] Krusiński did not oppose Waryński's internationalism, nor did he object to the conference's resolution that revolution must be viewed as "the unanimous uprising of the proletariat of the whole world, or at least of the whole of Europe."[63] But his opposition to the revolutionary role of the Proletariat fell on deaf ears. After Vilna, Krusiński ceased to participate in political activity and devoted himself exclusively to Marxist scholarship and journalism.

Waryński, on the other hand, received the near unanimous affirmation of his policies from the Vilan conferees. Seeking to parallel the organizational structure of People's Will, which was headed by an Executive Commitee, the Proletariat leaders elected a Central Committee of Waryński, Kunicki, Dębski, Dulęba, Płoski, and Rechniewski. Also elected was Aleksandra Jentysówna, a former schoolteacher who had lived with Waryński for a year and was involved in a torrid affair with him. Bolstered by the conferees' resolution that the Proletariat work toward participation in "a unified party, active within the borders of a Russian state," Waryński renewed his efforts to reach an agreement with the Executive Committee of People's Will.[64] His November 1882 meetings with Lev Tikhomirov, the head of the Executive Committee in emigration, had produced no results. Tikhomirov was a barely disguised Polonophobe who did not believe in Polish internationalism ("a Pole is always a Pole," he wrote), and, even more important, he was a man in the process of losing faith in the revolutionary movement.[65] In 1888 Tikhomirov recanted his radical past, returned to St. Petersburg, and became an apologist for the autocracy. Therefore, after the Vilna meeting, Waryński astutely turned to the branch of People's Will inside Russia rather than to the émigré group. His associates Rechniewski, Kunicki, and Dębski had already prepared the ground for negotiations by serving as liaisons to the Russian party, but Waryński took it upon himself to improve the chances for a favorable agreement. In the early spring of 1883 he traveled to St. Petersburg to drum up support for his all-empire approach to revolutionary politics.

Sergei Ivanov, a member of the Executive Committee of People's Will, remembered his meeting with Waryński in St. Petersburg as intense, but ultimately fruitless.[66] According to Ivanov, Waryński was willing to subordinate the Proletariat to the Russian organization in some areas if, in return, the Russians agreed to a common statement of purpose. But Ivanov rejected all but the most informal areas of cooperation. The Russian party was in shambles due to the still undetected work of the provocateur Sergei Degaev, and Ivanov was more interested in retaining the few remaining circles of People's Will than in what he called the "duplicity" of subordinating the stronger Polish to the weaker Russian organization.[67]

Thus, Waryński returned to Warsaw emptyhanded in the summer of 1883. He had irrevocably dismissed the possibility of a three-partition Polish revolutionary party and now could expect little help from the Russians. Having badly overestimated the strength of People's Will, Waryński now realized that the Proletariat would have to lead the way to revolution in the Russian Empire. As a result, he urged the Central and Workers' Committees of the party to extend their activities to the textile factory centers of Łódź, Zgierz, and Tomaszów. Sections of the party were also established, though with less success, in Białystok, Kalisz, Żyrardów, and Częstochowa. Waryński does "not recognize any territorial borders," the Warsaw prosecutor complained in response to the growth of Proletariat circles in Vilna, Kiev, St. Petersburg, Moscow, Odessa, and Dorpat.[68] Waryński even loaned Proletariat propagandists to the Workers' Section of People's Will in the hopes of drawing Russian workers' groups into the political struggle.[69]

Despite his need for allies, Waryński remained adamantly opposed to any concessions to either the Polish bourgeoisie, who were struggling for a constitution, or to the Polish patriots, who were demanding independence from the partitioning powers. His June 1883 proclamation on the coronation of Alexander III was his first speech addressed to "all Poles," but the text made it clear that participation in the Proletariat's political struggle was to be limited to the "millions of oppressed, the natural enemies of tsarism and capitalism."[70] In the newspaper *Proletariat*, Waryński analyzed the failure of the Paris Commune and reiterated his fundamental position that cooperation with the bourgeois enemies of the working class would be suicidal for the socialist cause; he rejected the prospect of "jousting with bourgeois parliaments."[71]

Waryński's only deviation from a classically Marxist approach to the political struggle was his conviction that the peasantry should be included in the socialist movement. The entire peasantry, with or without land, he wrote in his "Manifesto to the Workers on the Land," belonged to the exploited class. The struggle of peasant against landlord was the same as that of worker against factory owner; the gentry landowners, like the capitalists, were in league with the tsar. "Learn about us," Waryński told the peasants, "for we are the only ones who say: the land belongs to those who sow it, the factories to those who work in them."[72] Waryński was clearly in search of political allies, and realizing that the Polish peasantry was strongly patriotic, he refrained from any mention of internationalism in his "Manifesto." But despite his attempts to win over the peasantry (attempts which, it should be noted, Plekhanov, Marx, and Engels were not willing to make), the politically conservative and mostly illiterate Polish peasantry remained unmoved. "We must acknowledge," *Proletariat* wrote, "that unfortunately very little progress has been made [by our movement] among the people working on the land."[73]

Arrest and Imprisonment. During the summer of 1883, Waryński was at the height of his revolutionary career. The party included some four hundred active members and published three periodicals, one in Warsaw (*Proletariat*) and two in emigration (*Przedświt* and *Walka Klas*). Waryński had attracted many talented and dedicated Polish socialists to the Proletariat's Central Committee, among them Kunicki, Rechniewski, and Dębski. Perhaps most gratifying for Waryński was the strength of the workers' circles, which themselves included about three hundred members. With allies, associates, and party members actively engaged in revolutionary work in Paris, Zürich, Vienna, Poznań, and throughout the Russian Empire, Waryński had just cause for his ebullience, if not for his belief in the imminence of Europe-wide revolution. In addition, he was openly in love with Jentysówna, though he continued to live with both her and Anna Sieroszewska.

Part of Waryński's success can be attributed to the fact that the Russian police consistently misjudged the importance of Proletariat. Between March 1881 and the summer of 1883, the entire weight of the tsarist repressive organs fell on People's Will, the perpetrators of the assassination of Alexander II. Terrified of a renewed attempt on the life of Alexander III, the police and the Ministry of the Interior were convinced of the perfidy of student "nihilists" and discussion circles, groups that were for the most part politically innocuous. Meanwhile, the Polish section of the empire had been considered immune to the dangers of socialism; the patriotic movement was thought to be the only enemy to Russian autocratic rule in the Congress Kingdom. But by the summer of 1883, the police had found large quantities of Proletariat literature in Russian cities and realized that Poles in the ranks of People's Will had joined the Proletariat in Warsaw. Even the tsar and the Council of Ministers expressed their deep concern about the Proletariat when the reputable Justice of the Peace Petr Bardovskii was arrested in Warsaw and indicted for socialist activities.[74]

Awakened to the threat of Proletariat, the police were already on Waryński's trail when on 28 September 1883 he left a package filled with revolutionary materials in a shop in Warsaw. A suspicious store clerk opened the package, examined the contents, and, with some help, seized Waryński when he returned to fetch his package. The police moved quickly, searched Waryński's apartment, and found both an extensive list of Proletariat members and the addresses of party centers throughout the Congress Kingdom.[75] As a result, hundreds of Proletariat members and associates were arrested, and the original party organization was destroyed. Although the Proletariat was able to revive under the leadership of Kunicki and continue until the spring of 1886 under Maria Bohuszewiczówna and Marian Ulrych, Waryński's absence had a clearly negative impact on the functioning of the party. The Workers' and Central Committees,which had been united under Waryński's personal leadership, bickered and ceased to coordinate their activities. Terrorism rather than revolution dominated the party's thoughts and activities. Alleged police spies were too quickly tried and assassinated; the bourgeoning workers' movement was ignored, even chastised for its naiveté. The moral purity and sound political instincts that Waryński brought to the party quickly dissipated into intrigue, violent threats, and murder.

Immediately after his arrest, Waryński was locked up in the Tenth Pavilion of the Warsaw Citadel, the political prison of the Congress Kingdom since the 1830s. The government began its preparations for the trials of arrested Proletariat members in the fall of 1884. Finally, in July 1885, the Warsaw judicial district concluded its indictment in the so-called Question of the 190 and recommended that Waryński and twenty-eight other Proletariat leaders be tried by military tribunal.[76] The remaining 161 were to be sentenced by administrative order. During his nearly two and a half years of pre-trial detention in the Tenth Pavilion, Waryński continued to involve himself in the revolutionary movement despite his rapidly declining health. He wrote to Kunicki and Dębski, encouraging them to continue the struggle: "For us," he wrote in July 1884, "the greatest reward, the highest satisfaction, is the surety that the cause lives, that our work has not ceased, that it grows and develops."[77] He also propagandized and organized among his fellow inmates, earning the respect of prisoners and guards alike for his "ethical standards" and "democratic" outlook.[78]

In prison, Waryński was also determined to straighten out his personal life, which he saw an an integral part of the Proletariat's struggle. "I will never live with her [Sieroszewska]," he wrote to Kunicki and Dębski, "but long ago I gave her my word to marry, and I am ready at any time to stick to it. I must know whether she wants to marry, because if not, then it would be possible for me to marry Janka [Jentyszówna]. This matter is not only our own, for both [of them] belong to the cause and we will all serve it until death . . . ."[79] Sieroszewska apparently released Waryński from his vows, for in May 1885, Jentyszówna and Waryński petitioned the government to allow their marriage. But Governor-General Gurko denied the permission and allowed Waryński to see Jentyszówna for only a few minutes before she was sentenced by administrative order to five years exile in Siberia.

Finally, on 28 November 1885 the government brought twenty-nine leading members of the Proletariat before a military tribunal used since 1878 to try cases involving armed opposition to the authorities. The government based its case against Waryński and his comrades on their ties to People's Will and their involvement in assassination attempts that had occurred after Waryński's arrest. Typically, Waryński was the only defendant to refuse a lawyer and he was also the first defendant to speak

at the trial. Rather than presenting a personal defense, he defended the
ideas of the party and insured his own conviction by expressing "complete" solidarity with People's Will and with the terrorist actions of the
Proletariat. "I ask you not to separate my fate from that of my comrades," Waryński stated. "I was arrested earlier than all the comrades. But
that which was done by them, I myself would have done had I been in
their place." His speech before the military tribunal, like that at the
Kraków trial, emphasized the "scientific" foundations of his actions.

> We are not sectarians, nor are we dreamers divorced from real
> life. We organize the working class for the struggle with the con-
> temporary order. We do not organize a revolution but organize
> for a revolution. . . . We do not stand above history, we are
> subject to its laws. We look at the revolution to which we aspire
> as a result of historical development and social conditions.[80]

On December 22, the tribunal reached its unexpectedly harsh verdict.
Six members of the Proletariat were sentenced to hang.[81] Eighteen others,
including Waryński, Płeski, and Rechniewski, received the stiff sentences
of sixteen years hard labor. Rather than take the chance that Waryński
might escape his exile, the government transferred him to the Schlüsselburg fortress outside St. Petersburg in March 1886. According to the
accounts of his fellow inmates, he continued to assert the same kind of
moral authority that he had exhibited in the underground.[82] At the
same time, Waryński worried about the fate of the party he had so pain-
stakingly helped to organize. He told a prison comrade that there were
two basic threats to the Proletariat: parliamentarism, which involved
concessions to the liberals, and "patriotism," a force that was corroding
the party's unity and serving as a pretext for attacks from the enemies
of socialism.[83] Waryński's concerns were cut short by his declining health
in the extremely harsh conditions of Schlüsselburg. In and out of the
prison dispensary for nearly two years with a variety of lung diseases,
Waryński finally died on 2 March 1889.

Waryński did not live long enough to learn that his fears about Polish
patriotism's threat to the socialist movement were completely justified.
In the years following Waryński's death, Polish nationalism proved to be

the most powerful political force in the Congress Kingdom and it succeeded in fragmenting the socialist movement. Polish socialism split into two camps—the stronger Polish Socialist Party aligned with the patriotic movement and the weaker Social Democratic Party of the Kingdom of Poland and Lithuania, which can be considered the direct heir of the internationalist Proletariat. But with the formation of the Soviet Union and an independent Poland at the end of World War I, Polish internationalism suffered a severe setback. Perhaps the greatest irony of Polish internationalism is that its death was prompted by the establishment of a "socialist Poland" in 1945, and with its last sparks went all possibilities for dispassionate evaluations in Poland of Waryńsk's career.

Bred on *kresy* myths of the 1863-64 Polish uprising, inspired by Russian populism and the participation of valiant Polish generals in the Paris Commune, Waryński embodied all the characteristics of the romantic revolutionary. There was nothing disingenuous about him; his devotion to the cause was pure, and he willingly gave his life to it. Both his goals and methods blended in action—propagandizing among workers, agitating for the political struggle, defending his party at his trial. The only evidence we have of poor spirits or ill humor was his stay in Switzerland, when he clearly suffered from the lack of revolutionary involvement. Even in prison, Waryński seemed to relish the environment of martyrdom. That he saw his great love affair with Jentysówna as an integral part of the revolutionary struggle only reinforces the impression of a deeply romantic character. In fact, his internationalism was based on the ultimately romantic notion that Polish patriotic aspirations must be ignored, even vilified, in order for the Polish working class to achieve genuine liberation. Waryński did not and, given his personality, could not understand that the Polish political activist who ignored the struggle between the Poles and their partitioners could not ultimately be successful.

What distinguished Waryński from most romantic revolutionaries of the period was his sharp political intuition. Not only did he possess an extraordinary ability to move those around him, both workers and members of the intelligentsia, but he had a knack for moving with events, exploiting favorable situations, and outmanuevering those who challenged him. As an undergound political activist, he may well have no equals in revolutionary Russia. His Marxism was certainly not as sophisticated as that of Plekhanov, Martov, Luxemburg, or Lenin, but he did succeed in seizing Marx's fundamental points and in applying them with unrivaled tenacity and flexibility to an underground movement. Although Waryński's romantic internationalism led him to shun a cause that was to become the rallying point of Polish radicalism, his political acumen in organizing and directing the activities of the Proletariat presaged in many ways the successes of Russian social democracy. Waryński was the first Marxist in the Russian Empire to develop the techniques of agitation. He was the first to call for a union of the urban working class and peasantry in a class war against the gentry, the factory owners, and the autocracy. And he was the first to organize a Marxist party of workers and intelligentsia to bring about the socialist revolution.

NOTES

1.   The Proletariat is often referred to in historical literature as the "Wielki," or "Great Proletariat," to distinguish it from later, less significant Polish socialist parties of the same name. The best Polish work on the party is Leon Baumgarten's *Dzieje Wielkiego Proletariatu* (Warsaw, 1966). Some of the material for this essay has been drawn from my own monograph, *The History of the "Proletariat": The Emergence of Marxism in the Kingdom of Poland, 1870-1887* (Boulder, 1979). The most important archive collections that trace Waryński's career are located in Warsaw in the Main Historical Archives, Archiwum Główne Akt Dawnych (AGAD): Prokurator Warszawskiej Izby Sądowej (PWIS), 1878-88, and Warszawski Gubernialny Zarząd Żandarmeri (WGZZ), 1878-86. In addition the party archives in Warsaw, Archiwum Zakładu Historii Partii (AZHP), contain a complete collection of the Proletariat's proclamations, many written by Waryński.

2.   The best of the popular literature has been written by Jerzy Targalski: *Ludwik Waryński (Album)* (Warsaw, 1973); *Pierwsi buntownicy* (Warsaw, 1967); and *Ludwik Waryński: Próba życia* (Warsaw, 1976). See also L. Wudzki, *O Ludwiku Waryńskim* (Warsaw, 1956), and, from the turn of the century, B. A. Jędrzejowski, "Ludwik Waryński," *Światło*, no. 7 (1899).

3.   L. Krzywicki, *Wspomnienia*, vol. 2 (Warsaw 1957), 12, and L. Dejcz, "Pionerzy ruchu socjalistycznego w Królestwie Polskim," *Z pola walki*, no. 9-10 (1930), 37.

4. The best information on Waryński's family is contained in Targalski, *Ludwik Waryński: Próba życia*, pp. 9-13.

5. H. Truszkowski, "Z dalekiej przeszłości (Wspomnienia o Waryńskim)," *Kronika ruchu rewolucyjnego w Polsce*, no. 1 (5) (1936), 45.

6. Ibid., and E. Brzeziński, "Wspomnienia z mego życia," *Niepodległość*, vol. 4 (1931), 54.

7. Jędrzejowski, "Ludwik Waryński," p. 98.

8. Z. Łukawski, *Polacy w rosyjskim ruchu socjaldemokratycznym w latach 1883-1893* (Kraków, 1970), pp. 15-17.

9. Brzeziński, "Wspomnienia," p. 216.

10. For the history of this circle see E. Płoski, *Wspomnienia: Czasy uniwersyteckie* (Płock, 1938), p. 14; K. Dłuski, "Wspomnienia z trzech lat (1875-78)," *Niepodległość*, vol. 1 (1930), 222-33; Z. Heryng, "W zaraniu socjalizmu polskiego," *Niepodległość*, vol. 3 (1930), 52; AGAD, WGZŻ, no. 3, p. 95.

11. W. Sieroszewski, *Pamiętniki: Wspomnienia* (Kraków, 1959), p. 155.

12. "Na-Z", "Ludwik Waryński (Osobiste Wspomnienia)," *Z pola walki* (London, 1904), p. 46.

13. Dłuski, "Wspomnienia z trzech lat," p. 223.

14. Sieroszewski, *Pamiętniki*, p. 151.

15. M. Mazowiecki (L. Kulczycki), *Historia polskiego ruchu socjalistycznego w zaborze rosyjskim* (Kraków, 1903), p. 21; Dłuski, "Wspomnienia z trzech lat," p. 228; *Bohaterowie "Proletariatu"* (Warsaw, 1906), p. 5.

16. *Procesy polityczne w Królestwie Polskiem: Materiały do historii ruchu rewolucyjnego w Król. Polskiem.* Zeszyt 1: Rok 1878-1879 (Kraków, 1907), 12-13.

17. Ibid., p. 87; AGAD, PWIS, 1879, 349, p. 1; Amerykanin [Uziembło], "Wspomnienia," *Z pola walki* (London, 1904), pp. 58-62.

18. *Procesy polityczne*, pp. 81-82, 86-87. For a complete list of the publications see F. Perl (Res), *Dzieje ruchu socjalistycznego w zaborze rosyjskim: Do powstaniu PPS*, 3d ed. (Warsaw, 1958), pp. 66-70.

19. *Procesy polityczne*, p. 14; AGAD, PWIS, 1879, 345, 346.

20. The letter is quoted in full in Wudzki, *O Waryńskim*, pp. 66-67.

21. K. Dłuski, "Ludwik Waryński," *Z pola walki* (London, 1904), p. 47, and Sieroszewski, *Pamiętniki*, pp. 157-58.

22.   B. Limanowski, *Pamiętniki (1870-1907)*, vol. 2 (Warsaw, 1958), p. 181.

23.   J. Uziembło, "Wielki proces krakowski," *Z pola walki* (1904), p. 94, and E. Haecker, *Historia socjalizmu w Galicji i na Śląsku*, vol. 1 (Kraków, 1933), 164-65.

24.   Uziembło, "Wielki proces krakowski," p. 93.

25.   The conservative Kraków newspaper *Czas* carried a full report of the trial in a supplment (*dodatek*). This trial coverage is in AZHP, Materiały procesu krakowskiego, 1880, *Czas* dodatki, z. 1-5.

26.   AZHP, Materiały procesu krakowskiego, z. 2, pp. 63, 66-69.

27.   Ibid., pp. 2, 30.

28.   Ibid., z. 5, p. 293.

29.   L. Dejcz, "Pionerzy ruchu socjalistycznego," pp. 43-51.

30.   Limanowski, *Pamiętniki (1870-1907)*, pp. 255-56. Dejcz, "Pionerzy ruchu socjalistycznego," pp. 47-48.

31.   "Archiwum Bardowskiego," *Z pola walki*, no. 1 (9) (1960), p. 122.

32.   Krzywicki, *Wspomnienia*, vol. 2, 256-60.

33.   The best summation of the history of the program is in A. Molska, *Pierwsze pokolenie marksistów polskich*, 1878-1886, vol. 2 (Warsaw, 1962), n. 1, pp. 687-93.

34.   Dejcz, "Pionerzy ruchu socjalistycznego," p. 46, and L. Deich, "Pis'mo Plekhanovym," *Gruppa "Osvobozhdenie truda,"* ed. by V. I. Zasulich and L. G. Deich, vol. 2 (Leningrad, 1924), p. 218.

35.   *Sprawozdanie z międzynarodowego zebrania zwołanego w 50-letnią rocznicę listopadowego powstania przez redakcyję "Równości" w Genewie* (Geneva, 1881), pp. iii-iv, 50-52, 81-83.

36.   Limanowski, *Pamiętniki (1870-1907)*, pp. 256-57.

37.   The program was published in *Przedświt*, no. 3 (1881), 2. See Limanowski, *Pamiętniki (1870-1907)*, p. 268.

38.   "Z powodu odezwy stow. soc. 'Lud Polski,'" *Przedświt*, no. 3 (1881), 2-3.

39.   "Sprawozdanie delegowanych z krajów polskich," *Przedświt*, no. 5 (1881), 3.

40.   Ibid., p. 6.

41.   Limanowski, *Pamiętniki (1870-1907)*, pp. 271-72, 318.

42. See Engels's 7 February 1882 letter to Kautsky on the split in Polish socialism in J. Borejsza, *W kręgu wielkich wygnańców 1848-1895* (Warsaw, 1963), p. 160.

43. "Koniecznie wyjaśnienia," *Przedświt,* no. 1 (1881), 3; and F. Kon, *Narodziny wieku: Wspomnienia* (Warsaw, 1969), p. 142.

44. For the history of the document, see L. Deich, "Iz kariiskikh tetradei," *Gruppa "Osvobozhdenie truda,"* vol. 1, 139; "Pionerzy ruchu socjalistycznego," p. 554; and Mazowiecki (Kulczycki), *Historia,* p. 43.

45. The proclamation was published in *Przedświt,* no. 6-7 (1881), 1.

46. AGAD, PWIS, 1884, 977, p. 28.

47. "Czy jest u nas kwestia robotnicza," *Równość,* no. 8-9 (1880), 27.

48. AGAD, PWIS, 1884, 974, p. 86.

49. "Towarzysze," AZHP, 305/I, 1.

50. The police noted that Waryński was reported to have engaged in recruting activities in factories as well as in workers' apartments. AGAD, PWIS, 1884, 966, pp. 29-30.

51. AGAD, PWIS, 1884, 977, p. 32.

52. Ibid., pp. 31-32; AGAD, PWIS, 1884, 974, p. 89.

53. "My i burżuazja," *Proletariat,* no. 3 (1883), 31.

54. "Prikaz po varshavskoi politsii," AGAD, PWIS, 1884, 964, p. 19. For the background of the incident, see *Gazeta Narodowa* (Lwów), 8 March 1883, in ibid., pp. 59-60.

55. "Robotnicy Obywatele," AZHP, 305, I, 1.

56. "Robotnice!" AZHP, 305, I, 1. Also in *Przedświt,* no. 15 (1883), 1.

57. See J. Krzesławski, "Spoliczkowanie Apuchtina," *Kronika ruchu rewolucyjnego w Polsce,* no. 1 (1934), 5-10.

58. Z. Heryng, "X-ty Pawilon przed 50-ciu laty," *Niepodległość,* vol. 1 (1929-1930), 73.

59. For the program and a proclamation of Solidarity see AGAD, PWIS, 1884, 977, p. 15, and *Przedświt,* no. 24 (1883), 1-2. A short biography of Puchewicz is in *Walka klas,* no. 7 (1884), 9-10. See also Ż. Korman[owa], "Kazimierz Puchewicz i 'Solidarność'," *Niepodległość,* vol. 19 (1939).

60. AGAD, PWIS, 1884, 966, zapiska 5, p. 156. See also ibid., 974, pp. 71-72.

61. On the Krusiński circle, see T. Kowalik, "Wstęp," *Stanisław Krusiński: Pisma zebrane* (Warsaw, 1958); L. Baumgarten's review of the

Kowalik book, "'Odkrywczość' więćej niż wątpliwa," *Z pola walki,* no. 3 (1960), 60-69; and A. Molska, "Wstęp," *Pierwsze pokolenie,* vol. 1, p. xxvi.

62. Plokhotskii, L. (Wasilewski, L.), *Vzaimnyia otnosheniia pol'skikh i russkikh sotsialistov* (London, 1902), p. 6.

63. *Przedświt,* no. 17 (1883), 1.

64. Ibid.

65. L. Tikhomirov, *Vospominaniia L'va Tikhomirova* (Moscow, 1927), pp. 319-20. See also Tikhomirov's letter to M. Oshanina of 22 May 1883, in B. Sapir, ed., *Lavrov; Gody emigratsii,* vol. 2 (Dodrecht, Holland, 1974), 104.

66. V. Nevskii, "Iz narodovol'cheskikh vospominanii (pis'ma S. A. Ivanova k P. V. Karpovich)," *Narodovol'tsy 80-kh i 90-kh godov* (Moscow, 1929), pp. 45-46. On the negotiations see also I. I. Popov, "Revoliutsionnye organizatsii v Peterburge v 1882-1885 godakh," *Narodovol'tsy posle 1-go marta 1881 goda* (Moscow, 1928), p. 61, and A. Dębski, "Wspomnienia o Kunickim i Bardowskim," *Z pola walki* (1904), p. 86.

67. V. Nevskii, "Iz narodovol'cheskikh vospominanii," p. 46.

68. AGAD, PWIS, 1884, 977, p. 12.

69. I. I. Popov, "Revoliutsionnye organizatsii v Peterburge," pp. 59-60.

70. "Obywatele," AZHP, 305, I, 1.

71. "My i burżuazja," *Proletariat,* no. 3 (1883), 31.

72. "Manifest do pracujących na roli" (Warsaw, 1883), in AZHP, 305, I, 1.

73. "Ze wsi," *Proletariat,* no. 1 (1883), 9.

74. *Dnevnik gosudarstvennogo sekretaria A. A. Polovtsova,* vol. 1 (Moscow, 1966), p. 244.

75. The full account of Waryński's arrest and a list of the contents of his package are in AGAD, WGZŻ, no. 6, pp. 5-6, 8, and in AGAD, PWIS, 1884, 966, pp. 48-52.

76. Details of the correspondence between Warsaw and St. Petersburg on the best manner to try the arrested members of the Proletariat are ably recounted in Baumgarten, *Dzieje,* pp. 597-608.

77. "Archiwum Bardowskiego," *Z pola walki,* no. 1 (9) (1960), 120-21.

78. Z. Heryng, "X-ty Pawilon przed 50-ciu laty," pp. 74-75, and V. S. Pankratov, "Iz zhizni Varinskogo v Shlissel'burgskoi kreposti," *Katorga i ssylka,* no. 32 (1927), pp. 99-101.

79. "Archiwum Bardowskiego," p. 122.

80. For Waryński's speech at his trial, see "Sprawozdanie z procesu przeciwko 29 oskarżonym przed sądem wojennym w Warszawie," *Walka klas,* no. 8, 9, 10 (1886), 7-34. See also *Z pola walki* (Geneva, 1886), pp. 155-63, and *Z pola walki* (London, 1904), pp. 205-8.

81. Administrative action relieved Mikhail Luri and Józef Schmaus of their death sentences. On 27 January 1886 the Russians hanged Petr Bardovskii, Stanisław Kunicki, Jan Pietrusiński, and Michał Ossowski.

82. Pankratov, "Iz zhizni Varinskogo v Shlissel'burgskoi kreposti," pp. 99-101. (L. Janowicz), "Ze wspomnień szlisselburczyka," *Przedświt,* no. 1,2 (1901), reprinted in *Wspomnienia o "Proletariacie"* (Warsaw, 1953), pp. 187-205.

83. S. Valk, "Iz arkhiva V. Ia. Bogucharskogo: K biografii L. Varynskogo," *Katorga i ssylka,* no. 3 (1927), p. 101.

RUSSIAN NATIONALISM AND RUSSIAN LITERATURE: THE CANONIZATION OF THE CLASSICS

Jeffrey Brooks
University of Chicago

Among the changes that took place in late nineteenth- and early twentieth-century Russian cultural life was a shift in attitudes toward traditional symbols of Russian nationality, the tsar and the church. A new patriotism developed among the educated from the time of the critic Vissarion Belinskii, and allegiance was directed less toward church and state than to Russian culture, in particular the literature of the golden age, the Russian classics. After the emancipation, educated Russians of different political persuasions sought to communicate the social values they prized to the newly freed and increasingly literate common people, and to incorporate these new readers into a national culture based on the printed word. What the common people read was therefore a matter of great concern. Educated Russians involved in many different mass educational activities tried to create and distribute their own special literatures for the common people, but many soon concluded that the nineteenth-century literature they themselves so admired was also best suited for teaching the common people, and for drawing them into a unifed Russian culture. The works

* The author wishes to thank the National Endowment for the Humanities, The International Research and Exchanges Board, and the East European Center of the University of Illinois for their support and assistance. I am also grateful to Jean Hellie and Richard Hellie for their helpful comments. This essay was presented as a paper at the Sixth Annual Conference of the Study Group on the Russian Revolution, Jesus College, Oxford, 4-6 January 1980.

315

of Pushkin and Gogol, Lermontov and Turgenev, Dostoevsky and Tolstoy, Belinskii, Dobroliubov and others, already admired by educated Russians, were read, praised, and interpreted to the newly literate. The writers joined the pantheon of Russian national heroes with generals, tsars, and church fathers, and were celebrated and revered equally with their works. The church and state authorities were originally reluctant to sanction veneration of a group not formally identified with the Orthodox autocracy and in some respects hostile to it, but they eventually came to terms with the *fait accompli,* and sought to dispel the idea that writers were opposed to the state. Official patriotic interpretations of literary works added to the aura already forming around the classics. The idea of a hallowed literary tradition also gained force as a result of other intellectual and social developments. The advent of literary modernism served to define the earlier literature as a unified body of work, and the opposition to modernism accented the virtues of the classics for many educated Russians. Schoolteachers and others involved in mass education drew legitimacy in their dealings with the peasants from the sanctity of the culture they represented. When the Bolsheviks came to power and sought symbols of national unity independent of the church and the autocracy, they first hesitantly, and later with great enthusiasm, used Russian culture, and particularly the literature of the nineteenth century. All of these developments contributed to one of the most enduring trends of late nineteenth- and early twentieth-century Russian cultural life, the canonization of the classics.

The decision to bring nineteenth-century Russian literature to the common people was predicated on the idea that the people should share "the spiritual food" of the intelligentsia. This was the opinion of Belinskii, who blamed Russian writers for not reaching out to the people with good literature, but instead of forcing them to "slake their thirst," at the "dirty pools" of commercial chapbook literature (*lubochnaia literatura*).[1] This view was shared by A. F. Pogosskii, the pioneer publisher of people's books, and Dostoevsky. Pogosskii appealed unsuccessfully to chapbook publishers to publish Gogol and Turgenev and predicted that traditional tales would soon be driven from the market. "A year or two more," he wrote in 1863, "and every literate boy will laugh at the merchant who offers him some kind of frightful witch."[2] Dostoevsky urged intellectuals to take up bookselling and publishing, even if they had to begin by mimicking the chapbooks. He was sure the people would soon appreciate good literature; "The people will forget 'the beautiful Mohammedan'* for my books," he wrote at the time of the emancipation.[3] The question of whether the common reader, or "the reader from the people," in the contemporary Russian expression, could appreciate serious literature was answered definitively for many educators and intellectuals in the 1880s by the Kharkov Sunday schoolteacher Kh. D. Alchevskaia. Alchevskaia, together with a group of like-minded teachers, tested pupils' responses to various types of books in several schools in Kharkov and elsewhere. The result was a three-volume compendium titled *What to Read to the People?* which appeared in 1884, 1887, and 1906. The Kharkov teachers tried to demonstrate that the reader from the people could appreciate what was best in belles lettres, and that no special people's literature was necessary. Their initial concern was to test the suitability of specific books, but by the second volume, they became more concerned with revealing the taste and expectations of the readers themselves. Although Alchevskaia and her colleagues considered world literature suitable for the common reader, they preferred works by the authors of the nineteenth-century Russian classics. Alchevskaia's own reverence for these writers is revealed in the following note, written to Turgenev to arrange a meeting: "Do not take me for some kind of adventuress. I am a married woman, and if I want to see you, it is as an ideal embodied in a living person, an idol to which to bow down and pray."[4] When Dostoevsky died, she gave a special reading from his works for her students. By way of introduction, she explained: "Feodor Mikhailovich studied at an engineering school and could have been an engineer, earned much money, and lived comfortably for himself, but it seemed to him that he could be more useful to people if he would teach them through books, and he gave up the work and began to write."[5] For Alchevskaia and the many who shared her views, the classics contained what was best in the culture of educated Russia, and the writers personified an ideal of social service.

---

* He refers to *The Battle Between the Russians and the Karbardintsy or The Beautiful Mohammedan Dying on the Grave of Her Husband,* a popular chapbook.

Pedagogical journalists and educational policymakers expressed their enthusiasm for this view in articles with such titles as "Pushkin—the Mentor of Russian Youth" (1889)[6] and in statements such as: "The names of giants of native literature such as Gogol, Lermontov, Turgenev, and Dostoevsky ought to be households words for each really Russian person."[7]

Not all educated Russians shared this enthusiasm. Radical critics, such as Dobroliubov and Pisarev, questioned the relevance of Russian literature for the common people, and Lev Tolstoy advocated discarding Russian literature as class bound, irrelevant, and even harmful to the values and mores of the peasantry. Pushkin, Gogol, and Turgenev, "are not necessary for the people and do not bring them any benefit," Tolstoy wrote at the time of the emancipation.[8] He was even willing to accept the commercial chapbooks that had seemed so pernicious to Belinskii a few decades earlier. "If the people wish to read the English milord,"* he wrote, "then what right do we have to complain about that?"[9] Eventually, however, Tolstoy lost patience with the commercial publications, and in the 1880s he became actively involved in an attempt to create a special literature that would nurture the moral qualities distinguishing the peasantry from educated Russia. He called on all Russian writers to anwer the people's demand for "intellectual food worthy of you and of us."[10]

Tolstoy's views were shared by the populist critic N. K. Mikhailovskii and by the writer G. I. Uspenskii, both of whom saw the common people as a distinct group that should have its own literature. One of the most persistent advocates of this populist ideal of a special peasant literature was the critic and cultural activist S. A. Rappoport, who wrote under the pen name of An-skii. "With the exception of some ten works," he wrote in the early 1890s, "the literature of society is completely inaccessible to the peasant and it cannot be his literature in either language or content."[11] "The peasant now needs a book," he wrote, "that is written specially for him, in his spirit, in his language, and based on his life."[12]

---

* He refers to *The Story of the English Milord George and the Margravine Frederika Louisa,* a popular chapbook.

An-skii feared commercialization of the West. The evils of commercialization could be avoided, he argued as late as 1913, if the intelligentsia would step in and provide a people's literature.[13]

The argument about what the common people should read, the classics or a special literature, touched a fundamental question of Russian cultural development: should the common people be integrated into the culture and society of industrializing capitalistic Russia, or should they somehow be kept apart, either to serve as the raw material for a new and better society, or as a prop for the existing regime? Russian Marxists split on this issue in much the same way as had liberals like Alchevskaia and populists like An-skii. The Marxists had not inherited a consistent prescription for the literature of the future, or even for the literature to be read by the proletariat in the era of capitalism. Proletarian culture was expected to flourish after the proletarian revolution, but the nature of this culture, whether it would begin to develop in the period of capitalism, and whether its appearance would make the existing culture completely obsolete was unclear. Marx left his followers only a moderate bias in favor of a utilitarian approach to literature.[14] One might expect that the Mensheviks, who insisted on a proper bourgeois revolution, would have been likely to advocate gradual transformation of the working class and its absorption of capitalist culture, and that the Bolsheviks, guided by Lenin's suspicion of spontaneity and impatience with capitalism, would have been more suspicious of the acculturation of the proletariat to the literature and values of bourgeois Russia. The actuality, however, was simpler and less schematic: only a minority of Russian Marxists advocated the substitution of a purely proletarian culture for that of the bourgeoisie during the capitalist period.

G. V. Plekhanov was perhaps the first to urge the development of a purely proletarian literature that would superannuate the literature of nineteenth-century Russia. "You ought to have your own poetry, your own songs, your own verses," he wrote enthusiastically in a censored preface to an 1885 literary reader for workers.[15] Other ideologues and theorists developed this idea more fully. One of the most eloquent and extreme proponents of proletarian culture, more ready than Plekhanov to dispense with the heritage of educated Russia, was A. A. Bogdanov, a one-time Bolshevik who returned to the party after the October Revolution as a leading theorist of proletarian culture and activist in the

Proletkult movement. In a 1911 essay titled "The Cultural Tasks of Our Time," he called for the development of a new socialist literature to counter the individualistic ideals espoused by bourgeois writers; a literature to organize the collective consciousness and accelerate the victory of the proletariat.[16] Bogdanov's idea proved attractive to some Bolsheviks. A. V. Lunacharskii was drawn to it soon after the 1905 Revolution, but he subsequently changed his mind and defended the classics, first as a revolutionary and later as Soviet minister of culture.[17]

Lenin was conservative in his literary taste. He was not excited about the development of a totally new revolutionary art, but he was willing to pick and choose when dealing with Russia's nineteenth-century heritage. He expressed his ambivalence toward a part of the classical tradition in several articles about Tolstoy, written on the occasion of the writer's eightieth birthday in 1908 and his death in 1910. Tolstoy, Lenin argued in "Lev Tolstoy as a Mirror of the Russian Revolution" (1908), expressed the contradictions of the revolution: his pacificism helped to explain its failure, and the submission of the peasants to the authorities was "quite in the vein of Lev Tolstoy."[18] When Tolstoy died, however, Lenin's views softened, and he claimed Tolstoy for the proletariat as a great critic of capitalism. "The Russian proletariat will explain to the masses of the toilers and the exploited the meaning of Tolstoy's criticism of the state, the church, private property in land," Lenin wrote in 1910.[19] Although he returned to the idea that Tolstoy's thought was reactionary several times before the October Revolution, Lenin was hardly willing to urge the proletariat to jettison the classics. By 1914, a commentator in the Bolshevik magazine *Prosveshchenie* (Enlightenment) could ask what explains the sympathy of the proletariat for the classics, and answer that "this literature was the stormy petrel of the awakening third class...it sounds heroic themes," and touches the psyche of the proletariat.[20] Social Democrats, Bolsheviks, and Mensheviks alike increasingly contrasted this literary heritage with the contemporary modernist works. A critic in *Prosveshchenie* compared the classical literature of life and action with the "death and inaction" stressed in modernist works. A Menshevik journalist similarly juxtaposed the two literatures and observed that Chekhov was "the last master-teacher" of Russian literature.[21]

Trade unions joined in the enthusiasm for the nineteenth-century literary heritage, and labor journalists grouped a few contemporary progressive writers, such as Korolenko, together with the authors of the classics, as heroes of the working class. "The thinking workers will meet in the person of V. G. Korolenko," wrote a columnist in *Novoe pechatnoe delo* (New Printed Affairs), "the writer-citizen as a fighter for truth."[22] The metalworkers' paper *Nash put'* (Our Path) likewise hailed Tolstoy as "the defender of the oppressed," critic of inequality, idol of Russian workers.[23] Nineteenth-century social critics, such as Belinskii, received similar treatment, and their jubilees were front-page news.[24] Some trade unionists looked forward to a new art, but most conceived of the future proletarian literature as an extension of the classical heritage they idealized.

The increasing literacy of the common people and the efforts of many educated Russians to communicate to them their values and literary tastes forced the tsarist authorities to consider what the peasants and workers should be reading. The first official policy was essentially prophylactic: the loyalty and faith of the peasantry would be protected from the potentially harmful literature of the intelligentsia by minimizing exposure. The list of titles approved for public readings, a popular form of adult education in the late nineteenth century, was limited primarily to religious and patriotic works. Texts approved for St. Petersburg and its environs were published by the Standing Commission for Public Readings (1871-1917) and included only a few works of literature. Reviewing the list of permitted titles in 1873, one journalist complained that he had expected to recognize the names of leading writers, scholars, and scientists, but instead found those of people "completely unknown to us."[25] The list of titles permitted for public readings in the rest of Russia was no more lenient[26] with regard to Russian literature, and restrictions on the reading of nineteenth-century literary works were eased only at the turn of the century, when Russian officials began to treat these writers as patriotic figures.[27] The same hostility toward nineteenth-century literature is evident in the list of books permitted in libraries for the people. Church authorities were likewise wary of encouraging the reading of Russian literature, and were suspicious of secular works generally until the late 1890s. A commentator in a church-school magazine suggested in 1898 that it was possible to use belles lettres effectively for the moral education of children. Whenever the beauties of nature were described, reference should be made to the Supreme Artist, whenever high moral qualities were shown, to Christ, and in that way literature could "inspire love for humanity in general and the motherland in particular."[28]

Official hostility toward the classics abated at the end of the nineteenth century. When these writers had become widely recognized symbols of national pride, the authorities had cause to reconsider their earlier opposition. Moreover, the literature of the golden age and its creators threatened to become symbols of opposition to the autocracy. As a result, church and state policy was reversed, and a brief official romance with selected nineteenth-century writers began, lasting from the hundredth anniversary of Pushkin's birth in 1899 until Tolstoy's death in 1910. The decision to treat Pushkin's birthday as a holiday was attributed to the tsar himself. The writer was to be accorded a public celebration, with liturgies and requiems in churches, public readings throughout Russia, and the distribution of his picture in the greatest number of copies.[29] As nearly as possible, Pushkin was to be made into a bulwark of official Russia. On the birthday, the Petersburg metropolitan praised him in the Kazanskii Sobor as "a glorious son of the Russian land," and a Christian despite his stormy life.[30] A commentator in the church-school magazine hailed him as a fighter for "great Russian ideals" amid the atheism of the freethinking, French-dominated society of his time.[31] "Great national poets continue the work of Christ on earth," this commentator continued. "They are called to disperse the residue of darkness, falsehood, and delusion from the life of the peoples." There was even a survey of peasant attitudes toward Pushkin taken by the government people's newspaper, Sel'skii vestnik (Rural Herald).[32] The official appeal was greeted with great enthusiasm by some educators. A grateful pedagogical editorialist announced that Pushkin had now become a classical Russian poet, just as Belinskii had predicted: "That is why our Sovereign had commanded us to celebrate the hundred years from the birth of A. S. Pushkin; that is why everyone answers the summons of the Tsar so warmly."[33]

Gogol and the poet Zhukovskii were also selected for official praise. The Holy Synod issued instructions to parish teachers and others who wished to honor the two, suggesting that there should be liturgies and requiems and public readings of short selections from their works, accompanied by hymns and patriotic songs.[34] The officials of a semi-official Moscow enlightenment organization announced in their annual report for 1904: "The commission strives to support interest in the timeless untendentious artistic creations of the classical writers of the Russian land: Gogol, Pushkin, Tolstoy, Turgenev, and others."[35] Despite such efforts, the authorities did not succeed in identifying the classical writers with the autocracy. The literature of the golden age remained a symbol around which opponents of the regime could unite.

On the eve of his eightieth birthday, Lev Tolstoy personified the classical heritage that so many groups in Russian society tried to use for their own purposes, but the great *starik* seemed intent on alienating politically all but his most devoted followers. He had offended the church, with his personal religious teaching, and the government, which objected to his attacks on the death penalty. His condemnation of murder, in which he included revolutionary terror, disturbed some on the left, and his philosophy of pacifism worried liberal intellectuals and progressive educators. As one cultural activist complained, the message Tolstoy tried to communicate to the common people—"resign oneself, be humble, be patient, do not oppose evil, turn away from riches, prefer physical labor" —discouraged active involvement in life.[36] Yet as Tolstoy's birthday approached, liberal educators and politicians hurried to prepare a public celebration, and brushed aside Tolstoy's plea that his birthday be ignored. As the day approached the political atmosphere polarized. Liberals and the left, with some exceptions, lauded Tolstoy as an example of all that was good in the Russian intelligentsia, and state and church authorities moved to oppose the celebration. The minister of internal affairs instructed gendarmes and governors to be on the watch for anti-government agitation.[37] Pamphlets condemning Tolstoy were circulated by the authorities, and five days before the writer's birthday the Holy Synod barred the Orthodox from celebrating the birthday of "the heretic."[38] The press, meanwhile, was filled with tributes to the "great writer of the Russian land," and only a few conservative publications refused to join in. Lenin could hardly contain his disgust for the hypocrisy of the liberals, moderates, and conservatives, who hailed Tolstoy as "the voice of civilized mankind," despite their contempt for his ideas.[39] Although state authorities succeeded in preventing the celebration from becoming the "festival of Russian liberation" for which many had hoped, his birthday was celebrated widely, and Russians from all over the country sent congratulatory telegrams. The workers in a St. Petersburg factory even requested to be allowed to celebrate his birthday and work on an official holiday.[40]

Tolstoy's death on 7 November 1910, following his disappearance from his estate and flight as a wanderer, recreated the situation of two years earlier. Again the officials were isolated and found themselves condemning one of the most moving symbols of Russian nationality. While Tolstoy, in his final days, issued another appeal against the death penalty, the Holy Synod debated whether to pardon him and readmit him into the church. The answer was negative, as it had been to the question of whether the Orthodox would celebrate the writer's birthday. Lenin remarked jubilantly that the decision would be remembered "when the hour comes for the people to settle accounts with the officials in cassocks."[41] On Tolstoy's death the liberal press broke into a chorus of unrestrained praise. "Our country is poor and lawless," wrote Korolenko, "but she gave the world Tolstoy, whose death speaks so distinctly of eternal undying life."[42] So powerful a symbol had Tolstoy become that his death was an occasion for the first significant demonstrations since the suppression of the 1905 Revolution. Students took the lead, gathering in the streets of the capitals, demanding that the death penalty be abolished to honor Tolstoy's last wish. Liberal politicians, who wished to associate Tolstoy with the moderate opposition, tried to prevent a confrontation. They failed, however, and Russia was swept by student strikes, massive expulsions, and arrests.[43]

Russian educators, intellectuals, and activists of various perspectives sought to bring Russian literature to the people either by publishing their own inexpensive editions of works they favored or by purchasing this material from enterprising commercial publishers. These two types of subsidized literature began to appear soon after the emancipation. The non-commercial publishing ventures were more important in the nineteenth century than in the twentieth, when large commercial firms proved adept at satisfying the demands of the official and private educational systems. In the nineteenth century, belles lettres for the people was generally published by "society," as educated Russians of that time referred to themselves. The state and church issued primarily religious and patriotic texts, though in the period of official enthusiasm for the classics they published works of a few writers. More important, the classics were gradually permitted in the schools and people's libraries and reading rooms in the early twentieth century. In this way, the millions of inexpensive copies of Russian literature which were issued by philanthropic and cultural organizations, as well as commercial publishers, reached schoolteachers and other local intermediaries between educated Russia and the newly literate. Among the more active organizations that published for the common reader were the St. Petersburg Literacy Committee (1861-95), The Moscow Literacy Committee (1845-95), and the Kharkov Society for Spreading Literacy Among the People (1869-191?). The St. Petersburg Committee published nearly two million copies between 1880 and 1895, primarily works of belles lettres. Among the classical writers, they published Pushkin, Gogol, and Lermontov in the 1880s and Korolenko and other progressive writers in the early 1890s.[44] The Moscow committee began publishing in the 1870s,[45] and the Kharkov society issued nearly two million copies between 1891 and 1902.[46] Even some provincial self-government institutions began to publish literature, and one provincial *zemstvo* issued works by Pushkin, Lermontov, Gogol, and Korolenko at prices of one to five kopecks in the early twentieth century.[47]

Private individuals also made belles lettres available in cheap editions. Among the first was the Pskov landowner Fan-der-flit, who founded "The People's Library" at the beginning of the 1870s, and within a few years produced a series of ten booklets, including works by Gogol and Zhukovskii, as well as *Robinson Crusoe.*[48] Another pioneer in publishing for the people was V.N. Marakuev, who tried to provide the common reader with works that contained "a positive type," "a positive Russian idea."[49] A more commercial endeavor was that of A.S. Suvorin, the editor of a conservative Petersburg daily. By 1895 his "Inexpensive Library," which included works of Russian and foreign authors, had appeared in 3.8 million copies.[50]

A unique attempt to bring good books to the people was that of the firm Posrednik (Intermediary), founded in 1884 by Lev Tolstoy and V. Chertkov, in collaboration with the publisher I.D. Sytin, and operated from 1897 to 1917 by I.I. Gorbunov-Posadov. The Posrednik editors wished to create a special people's literature in accordance with Tolstoy's vision of the peasantry, but the association of Tolstoy with the project, the use of his works, and the tremendous success of the operation tended to encourage those who wished to bring Russian classical literature to the common people. Posrednik works were enthusiastically praised by educators such as Alchevskaia, who thought the people should read the classics and saw no contradiction in offering her pupils the series.

The importance of belles lettres in the educational system is indicated by figures on library holdings. Between 1905 and 1909 belles lettres comprised an approximately constant 80 percent of the holdings of twenty-three city libraries, but rose from 50 percent to 60 percent of the holdings of rural libraries in fourteen *uezdy*.[51] According to reports of twenty-five city libraries, the most popular authors in 1909 were: Lev Tolstoy, Jules Verne, the *Znaniia* miscellany (in which Leonid Andreev and Maxim Gorky frequently published), Nemirovich-Danchenko (who wrote adventure stories), Dostoevsky, and Turgenev. Similar observations about the importance of the classics were made by specialists who compiled publishing statistics during the 1890s and on the eve of the First World War.[52]

The rural primary schoolteachers were natural intermediaries between educated Russia and the common people, and in the late nineteenth and early twentieth centuries many of them shared the enthusiasm of intellectuals and educational policymakers for nineteenth-century literature. The schoolteachers' advocacy of the classics was pragmatic, as well as aesthetic. Whether conducting public readings, evening classes, Sunday-school courses, supervising libraries, or merely interacting with their communities, teachers had an interest in demonstrating the value of literacy, the usefulness of books, and their own authority over a kind of knowledge that many of their pupils' parents did not yet possess. Rural primary schoolteachers, dependent on the peasant community and responsible for enrollments and their pupils' performance on examinations, lived a precarious existence in which books could be very important. Although the private sale of books by teachers was illegal until 1904, a number did so anyway in order to satisfy their local communities. A teacher who had few books at hand described her predicament to A.S. Prugavin in a letter dated 1901:

> Our Iarinskaia school has an enormous need for books for extra-mural education. It is often necessary to refuse, not only the pupils, but also adult peasants, who come to the school for books to read in the evening. It is difficult and painful to look at the children leaving with disappointed faces, unsatisfied in the most legitimate demands of the heart and mind. It is painful and also

shameful to hear the conclusions expressed sometimes strongly by peasants after they are refused books; "Well, and here is the school, and I would like to read a bit. I thought there would be good reading at the school, but there is only 'The Little Humpbacked Horse.' "[53] *

"Many teachers, fulfilling the requests of pupils, adolescents, and adult peasants, have to buy books of their own choice during trips to the city," wrote a commentator in 1911.[54] "This phenomenon is observed not only in remote places," he continued, "but even in the comparatively cultured settlements near Moscow." Teachers who found themselves in this situation required books that would establish both their professional prestige and the legitimacy of the secular word, in contrast to the offerings of the parish priests. They needed a literature that could compete with the stories most familiar to the peasants, the traditional saints' lives. The Russian classics, in the form in which they reached the teachers, were well suited. The writers were praised as altruistic figures, and their biographies were presented as similar to the familiar saints' lives. When the hundredth anniversary of Pushkin's birthday was commemorated at the Burashevskaia School of Beekeeping, Horticulture, and Vegetable Gardening, and the Bavykinskaia Correctional Colony for Children, the school building was decorated with wreathed pictures of Pushkin and the tsar, as well as illustrations from Pushkin's works. One of the children from the correctional colony was asked why Pushkin was remembered, and the well-primed child replied: "He taught (people) to be good."[55] Similarly, a 1902 gathering in honor of Gogol at a church school began with a speech in which writers were compared to the clergy: "Talented writers also perform a great service to the people in the business of moral development; they awaken and develop in us the best feelings for truth, goodness, and beauty."[56] A colleague of Alchevskaia reported the following dialogue:

Teacher: "Why will the name of Pushkin never be forgotten in Russia?"

Pupil: "Because he loved Russia, defended her from the slanders of her enemies, and taught all to love the Russian people."[57]

---

* A popular fairy tale

Another colleague gave several writers' biographies to one of her pupils. The pupil was evidently astonished at the unexceptional quality of the writers' lives in contrast to those of the saints. When he returned the books, he announced that although he preferred the biographies to the writers' works, writers such as Pushkin and Lermontov "are already praised and extolled too much, and in their lives there is often nothing special."[58] The insulted teacher drew three conclusions from this encounter. First, the pupil was "not sensitive to perceiving artistic impressions"; second, "biographies are liked by the people"; and third, "the biographies selected ought to satisfy their search for truth and the ideal in the life of man, and therefore not every biography is appropriate; one must treat with special care the biographies of those people who are great on account of their literary works, but ordinary in their lives."

Nineteenth-century Russian literature and its creators were something more than a source of prestige and an educational tool for the teachers. Appreciation of literature was for schoolteachers an entreé into the collective national identity they felt they shared with those more privileged than they. Literature also served them as a cultural reference point in a rapidly changing society. With their few years of post-primary education, teachers were easily baffled by the difficult literature of Russian modernism; in the classics they found an intellectual and emotional anchor. The inspiration that teachers drew from writers is clear in the following passage from a story written by a teacher and awarded a prize by a pedagogical magazine:

> On the wall beside the violin hung a portrait of Gogol. Gogol looked seriously at the teacher, it seemed. Ivan Pavlovich thought a bit. Yes, it would be good to give the people complete literacy. Then the people themselves, without any prodding from above, would aspire to enlightenment and humanity, under the influence of "the world of laughter through tears that is (now) invisible to them."[59]

The same pedagogical journal reported that on the 20th of March 1909, "the name of N. V. Gogol was praised in every remote spot in Vologda Province which has a primary school."[60]

Did the efforts to bring literature to the common people have any concrete result? Studies of the books in the peasants' possession at the turn of the century show that some books intended for the people did reach them. According to a 1903 survey of over thirty thousand pupils and their families, almost 10 percent of the books in their possession were by well-known writers, primarily the nineteenth-century classics.[61] Other early twentieth-century surveys show a similar presence,[62] and a few works by classical authors appear in nineteenth-century investigations.[63]

Some of the classics most popular among educators also circulated in bowdlerized chapbook editions with flashy new titles and bright covers. Alchevskaia described a series of such works in the second volume of *What to Read to the People?* (1889). Turgenev's "Bezhin Meadow" became *The House Sprite Makes Mischief* (Moscow, 1886), Tolstoy's "What Men Live By," *The Secret Worker, or a Good Deed is Always Rewarded* (Moscow, 1886), and Gogol's "The Night Before Christmas," *Vakula the Smith, or a Pact With the Devil* (Moscow, 1884).[64] Poems by some nineteenth-century poets, including Nebrasov, occasionally adorned the prints (*lubki*) that were sold by colporteurs together with the chapbooks,[65] and their verses appeared in popular songbooks. "It is already the rare songbook that can do without the verses of Kol'tsov, Nekrasov, A. Tolstoi, and others," an official commentator on publishing observed in 1911.[66]

The halo that was forming around the classical writers was accepted and encouraged even in what was called the boulevard press. The most popular and cheapest of Russian newspapers, the *Gazeta kopeika* (The Kopeck Newspaper, St. Petersburg, 1908-1918), which was condemned by liberals and radicals alike as the urban equivalent of the vulgar chapbook, paid lavish tribute to the writers on their jubilees. Shevchenko was lauded as a critic of serfdom, Kol'tsov as the poet "who portrays the life of the common people as it is," and Chekhov as a writer noted for his great love of the common people.[67] "The great service of Gogol for Russian literature and the Russian people," wrote a journalist for this paper, was that "with his deathless creativity, he awakened the social conscience, mercilessly castigated evil, and promoted the self-consciousness of the people."[68] The 1911 anniversary of the emancipation of the serfs was greeted with quotes from Griboedov, Pushkin, Dostoevsky, Saltykov-Shchedrin, Nekrasov, and Korolenko on the evils of serfdom,[69] and the paper offered its readers two large pictures: Alexander II, the tsar-liberator, for fity kopecks and Tolstoy for forty-five. In 1912, subscribers to the Kopeika's weekly supplement were offered fifty-two books of "The

Classical Library," including the works of Pushkin, Gogol, Lermontov, and other well-known Russian writers.[70]

The names of the classical writers had entered into the rhetoric of a new language of national pride and self-awareness. In the 1913 almanac published by the government newspaper for the common people, *Sel'skii vestnik* (Rural Herald), writers figured prominently under the heading "Dates of noteworthy events and of the deaths of significant people," together with generals, tsars, and important battles, and comprised over 20 percent of the total.[71] Among the bonuses that the publishing magnate I. D. Sytin offered purchasers of his 1917 twenty-five kopeck *Universal Russian Almanac,* one of the most popular in Russia, was a print entitled "Mikhail Iur'evich Lermontov and His Work."[72] The iconography of the print matches that of the religious and patriotic *lubok* it closely resembles. The uniformed Lermontov surveys his creations from the heavens, flanked by an angel and a demon that signify his moral authority; beneath him are arrayed the symbols of poetic power: the lyre, the laurel wreath, the open book. This was the image of the classical writers educated Russians sought to convey to the common reader. For the 1916 Sytin almanac the creator of the Lermontov *lubok* also produced such hackneyed prints as "Home Again," showing a wounded hero in his village. Joining this rude company, Lermontov and his colleagues were enlisted in a cultural nationalism to which tsar and church were extraneous, and which outlasted the political and religious nationalism of the autocracy.

Mikhail Iur'evich Lermontov and His Work, from the Sytin *Universal Russian Almanac*, 1917.

NOTES

1. V. G. Belinskii, *Polnoe sobranie sochinenii* (Moscow, 1953), 3, p. 210.

2. Quoted in E. Nekrasova, *Narodnyia knigi dlia chteniia v. ikh 25-letnei bor'be s lubochnymi izdaniiami* (Viatka, 1902), pp. 14-15.

3. F. M. Dostoevskii, *Polnoe sobranie sochinenii* (St. Petersburg, 1891), 9, p. 138.

4. Kh. D. Alchevskaia, *Peredumannoe i perezhitoe* (Moscow, 1912), p. 94.

5. Ibid., p. 87.

6. *Russkii narodnyi uchitel'* (hereafter, RNU), 4 (1889), 1-20; 5 (1887), 217-24.

7. Iv. Shatalov, "Vospitatel'noe znachenie otechestvennykh pisatelei dlia nachal'noi shkoly," RNU, 4 (1884), 213.

8. L. N. Tolstoi, *Polnoe sobranie sochinenii* (Moscow, 1936), 8, p. 340.

9. Ibid., p. 364.

10. G. P. Danilevskii, "Poezdka v. Iasnuiu Polianu," *Istoricheskii vestnik,* 23 (1866), 539.

11. An-skii, *Ocherki narodnoi literatury* (St. Petersburg, 1894), pp. 130-31.

12. Ibid., p. 135.

13. An-skii, *Narod i kniga* (Moscow, 1913), p. 177.

14. Peter Demetz, *Marx, Engels, and the Poets* (Chicago: University of Chicago Press, 1967).

15. G. V. Plekhanov, *Iskusstvo i literatura* (Moscow, 1948), p. 485.

16. A. Bogdanov, *Kulturnyia zadachi nashego vremeni* (Moscow, 1911), p. 76.

17. A. V. Lunarcharskii, *Sobranie sochinenii* (Moscow, 1967), 7, pp. 167-92.

18. V. I. Lenin, *Collected Works* (Moscow, 1963), 15, pp. 204-209.

19. Ibid., 16, p. 327.

20. T. M., "Proletarskaia kul'tura v likvidatorskom oveshchenii," *Prosveshchenie,* 2 (1914), 95-96.

21. N. Abramovich' in *Novyi den',* 1 (20 July 1909), 3.

22. *Novoe pechatnoe delo,* 7 (18 July 1913).

23. *Nash put',* 10 (1910), 1-2.

24. Ibid., 18 (1911).

25. M. N. Popov, "Vred ili pol'za," *Delo,* 3 (1873), 56.

26. Vakhterov, "Narodnyia chteniia," *Russkaia shkola,* 11 (1896), 141-47, reprints the lists.

27. N. Tulupov, "Narodnyia chteniia v. gorodakh i selakh," *Russkaia mysl',* 4 (1902), 1-2.

28. M. Verzhbolovich', "Religioznoe vospitanie v. shkole," *Narodnoe obrazovanie,* 2 (1898), 19-20.

29. *Tserkovnyi vestnik,* 7 (1899), 269-70.

30. Ibid., 22 (1899), 809-11.

31. Ibid., 21 (1899), 799-82.

32. N. Etrinskii, "Pushkin i chitatel' iz naroda," *Obrazovanie,* 1 (1900), 79-95.

33. "Eshche o znachenii A.S. Pushkina," RNU, 5 (1899), 189.

34. *Tserkovnyi vestnik,* 7 (1902), 202.

35. *Popechitel'stva o narodnoi trezvosti v 1904 godu* (St. Petersburg, 1907), prilozhenie, p. 33.

36. Nekrasova, p. 72.

37. N. N. Gusev, *Letopis' zhizni i tvorchestva L. N. Tolstovo, 1891-1910* (Moscow, 1960), p. 616.

38. *Rech',* 24 August 1908.

39. Lenin, *Collected Works* (Moscow, 1963), 15, pp. 204-9.

40. P. I. Biriukov, *Biografiia L'va Nikolaevicha Tolstova* (Berlin, 1921), 4, pp. 154-66.

41. Lenin, *Collected Works* (Moscow, 1963), 16, p. 326.

42. *Rech',* 8 November 1910.

43. *Rech',* 30 July 1911.

44. D. D. Protopopov, *Istoriia S. Peterburgskago komiteta gramotnosti* (St. Petersburg, 1898), pp. 226-27.

45. Nekrasova, p. 15; *Ocherki istorii shkoly i pedagogicheskoi mysli narodov SSSR vtoraia polovina xix v.,* ed. A. I. Piskunov (Moscow, 1976), pp. 354-55.

46. "Programma izdanii dlia naroda Kharkovskago obshchestva," *Russkaia shkola,* 5-6 (1891), 287-88; "35-ti-letie Kharkovskago Obshchestva Rasprostravneniia v Narode Gramotnosti," *Obrazovanie,* 6 (1904), 86-87; *Ocherki istorii shkoly,* p. 356.

47. *Knizhnyi vestnik,* 15 (1904), 458.

48. Nekrasova, p. 18.

49. V. N. Marakuev, *Chto chital i chitaet russkii narod* (Moscow, 1886), pp. 1-4, 14-15.

50.   L. N. Pavlenkov, "Knizhnoe delo i periodicheskaia pechat' v Rossii v 1894 godu," *Istoricheskii vestnik,* 5-6 (1895), 868.

51.   P. Zhulev, "Sovremennyi chitatel' iz naroda," *Russkaia shkola,* 10 (1912), 28-29.

52.   *Knizhnyi vestnik,* 7 (1892), 315-16; *Vystavka proizvedenii pechati za 1909 god* (St. Petersburg, 1911), p. 16.

53.   Archive of N. A. Rubakin (f358) in the Manuscript Section of the Lenin Library, k. 6, ed. kh. 20, p. 1.

54.   *Shkola, zemstvo, i uchitel',* ed. E. A. Zviagintsev (Moscow, 1911), p. 90.

55.   "Khronika," *Vestnik vospitaniia,* no. 5 (1899), 146-53.

56.   "Izvestiia, soobshcheniia, i zemetki," *Narodnoe obrazovanie,* nos. 6-7 (1902), 85.

57.   Kh. D. Alchevskaia, *Chto chitat' narodu,* 1, 2d ed. (St. Petersburg, 1888), p. 661.

58.   Kh. D. Alchevskaia, *Chto chitat' narodu,* 3 (Moscow, 1906), p. 206.

59.   A. Cherniaev, "Ponial: rasskaz iz derevenskogo zhizni," RNU, 4, (1903), 15.

60.   "Dva shkol'nykh prazdnika," RNU, 6-7 (1910), 192-93.

61.   *Statisticheskii ezhegodnik poltavskago gubernskago zemstva na 1903 god* (Poltava, 1903), pp. 110-22.

62.   A. A. Nikolaev, "Kniga v sovremennoi russkoi derevne," *Vestnik znaniia,* 8 (1904), 172.

63.   Rubakin archive, f358, k. 5, ed. kh. 24; k. 5, ed. kh. 23; k. 6, ed. kh. 15.

64.   Kh. D. Alchevskaia, *Chto chitat' narodu,* 2 (Moscow, 1889), pp. 553-57.

65.   *Literaturnoe nasledstvo,* 53-54 (Moscow, 1949), 572.

66.   *Vystavka proizvedenii pechati za 1909 god* (St. Petersburg, 1911), p. 16.

67.   Nos. 219, 536, 432.

68.   No. 237 (1909).

69.   *Vsemirnaia panorama,* 95 (18 February 1911), supplement to *Kopeika.*

70.   No. 1979 (1914).

71.   My calculation from *Sel'skii vestnik kalendar spravochnaia knizhka* (St. Petersburg, 1913), pp. 3-25.

72.   This *lubok* is in the author's possession; I would like to thank Valery Kuharets for making it available to me.

IDEOLOGICAL AND POLITICAL EXTENSIONS
OF THE "NORMAN" CONTROVERSY

Alexander V. Riasanovsky
University of Pennsylvania

Perhaps the most volatile and persistent of all the controversies in Russian historiography centers on the so-called Norman theory, first advanced in the eighteenth century to explain the origins of the "first Russian state." Hundreds of scholars, representing a wide variety of disciplines, have since made contributions to the debate, and a comprehensive bibliography would easily exceed several thousand items.* The controversy over the "Norman" theory has not, however, remained the exclusive preserve of scholars. Indeed, almost from the beginning, the debate was invested with emotionally charged political and national considerations. As such, the history of the "Norman" controversy illustrates how partisanship, be it ideological, national, or personal, not only thwarts the pursuit of historical knowledge but also bends the available material to potentially destructive ends.

The "Norman" theory was first formulated by Th. S. Bayer, the noted German philologist who came to St. Petersburg at the invitation of the newly opened Imperial Russian Academy. While in Russia, he published two articles, "De Varagis" (1729) and "Origines Russicae" (1736), arguing that the "first Russian state" (more precisely, Kievan *Rus'*) was founded in the year 862 by three Varangian princes: the brothers Riurik, Sineus, and Truvor. In these articles, Bayer relied almost exclusively upon a single documentary source, the Kievan chronicle *Povest' vremennykh let*. His

---

* The interested reader can obtain some good leads towards an understanding of the main scholarly issues involved in the "Norman" controversy by consulting the selected bibliography offered in the Appendix to the present article.

interpretive reading of the text—for *Povest'* itself contains no such information—convinced him that the princely brothers were Swedes and that the "national" name *Rus'* stemmed from Scandinavia.

Bayer's writings on early Russian history not only stimulated interest in a relatively unexplored subject, but also provided a ready-made interpretive guide for future investigators. It was widely accepted that Scandinavians had founded "kingdoms" or "states" in Iceland, Denmark, England, Normandy, Sicily, and, according to Bayer, they had done the same in Russia. If this were true, then it seemed reasonable to draw analogies between Viking activities in the West and Varangian-Scandinavian activities in the East. Conceptions, generalizations, and patterns of data organization that had served so well in explicating the histories of several European countries could now be applied to Kievan *Rus'* by the simple process of extension. Thus, at least parts of the Russian *terra incognita* could be converted into *res cognitior*.

Bayer's "Normanist" formulations were adopted and amplified by Mueller, Strube, Stritter, Lehrberg, Thunman, Krug, Herman, Schloezer, and by other influential eighteenth- and nineteenth-century scholars. With such authoritative endorsements, the "Norman" theory became the generally accepted explanation of the origins of Kievan *Rus'* and, at least initially, no alternatives were advanced. Instead, new dimensions were added to "Normanism." Thus, it was argued that the Varangians-Scandinavians had not only founded the "first Russian state," but that they had also imported, established, and for centuries maintained all its major political, social, economic, military, and even religious institutions. It was claimed that the native Slavs possessed neither creative ability nor organizational skills. For example, describing Russia prior to the advent of the Varangian princes, the noted historian A. L. Schloezer wrote: "No doubt there were people there; God knows when they had come and from where, but people without government, living like birds and animals which filled the forests, excelling in nothing" (Nestor, 1 [1809], 419-20). All too often such pronouncements were accepted on authority, at face value, both in Russia and abroad.

Around the middle of the eighteenth century, however, a small but growing number of dissident voices began to question various "Normanist" contentions and to offer alternative interpretations of the evidence. Men such as I. N. Boltin, M. V. Lomonosov, and somewhat later, J. P. G. Ewers asked whether Riurik and his brothers were really Swedes and expressed reservations about the Scandinavian origins of the name *Rus'*. Lomonosov characterized as a gross oversimplification the central importance that "Normanist" scholars had assigned to the arrival of the Varangian princes and the year 862. He maintained that the origins of Kievan *Rus'* could not be reduced to a discrete event, or to the work of a single group of progenitors. An extended and vastly more complex process was involved.

So began the "Norman" controversy. It grew in scope and intensity during the closing decades of the eighteenth century, acquired further momentum in the nineteenth century, and has continued, unabated, to the present. But, as has already been suggested, the debate soon burst the bounds of scholarly discourse. All too quickly, notes of national pride and injury, of superiority and inferiority, crept into the arguments of both camps. Various "Normanist" and "anti-Normanist" statements were translated into the building blocks of vast ideological systems and, in time, racist themes further debased the debate. History was grievously misused, at great cost to both men and ideas.

The remainder of this essay concentrates on these political-ideological extensions of the "Norman" controversy. This is a subject with its own long-standing and involved history, and a thorough appraisal would fill several volumes. It is hoped, therefore, that the few examples discussed below, beginning with an eighteenth-century *cause célèbre,* will stimulate further scholary investigation.

In the 1740s, the brilliant but pugnacious Lomonosov precipitated a series of arguments with the German members of the Imperial Russian Academy. Although the real issue in these confrontations was control of the academy itself, the "Norman" theory also figured prominently. Heated public exchanges on that question led first to charges and counter-charges of scholarly fraud, then to national and personal insults (e.g., the *kukish* ["fig"] that Lomonosov allegedly displayed), and finally, even to physical violence. Incensed by the actions of the Russian "upstart," the German academicians complained to Empress Elizabeth, demanding the death penalty. Upon investigation, Lomonosov was officially accused of "interrupting academic sessions by indecent pranks" and of "rowdy conduct in the Department of Geography." He was fined and placed under house arrest.

After months of confinement, Lomonosov was forgiven by the empress, "owing to his most great erudition." Returning to the academy, the unrepentant Lomonosov wrote a systematic and, on the whole, scholarly rebuttal of the "Norman" theory. At the same time, however, he continued the political battle by warning his Russian compatriots that acceptance of "Normanism" meant recognition of German superiority.

Nothing so dramatic as the Lomonosov episode occurred during the nineteenth century, at least not within the ranks of the Russian academic community. While individual protagonists on both sides of the "Norman" controversy continued to trade thinly veiled insults, they maintained an outward semblance of decorum. Genuine attempts were made to conduct the dispute in a manner befitting scholars and gentlemen. S. A. Gedeonov, for example, allowed the manuscript of his lengthy "anti-Normanist" monograph, *Otryvki iz izsledovanii o variazhskom voprose,* to be sent to A. A. Kunik, the leading "Normanist" of the day. Subsequently, Gedeonov's work, together with Kunik's balanced appraisal and Gedeonov's brief rejoinder, were published by the Imperial Russian Academy as a set of "Supplements" to *Zapiski imperatorskoi akademii nauk,* 1862-63. The net impression was salutary. Despite occasional polemic flourishes, both authors demonstrated an overriding concern for the historical substance of the issues involved.

Another development took place in nineteenth-century Russia which, at first glance, may appear paradoxical. Eighteenth-century "anti-Normanism," at least in its more vocal manifestations, had seemed to go hand in hand with Russian "nationalism." In the first decades of the nineteenth century, however, "Normanist" arguments began to be used in attempts to define and to defend the ideology of a new, monarchy-centered Russian nationalism. The historian N. M. Karamzin was perhaps the earliest and certainly the most influential representative of this particular trend. His officially honored, staunchly patriotic, and immensely popular *Istoriia gosudarstva rossiiskago* (12 vols., 1804-26), taught generations of Russians to be proud of their national heritage, but, at the same time, advanced a very narrow concept of the elements constituting such a heritage.

Intellectually much closer to Montesquieu and Burke than to Herder and the German romantics, Karamzin praised the "nation," but defined it in terms of the ruler and not the ruled. In his *Istoriia,* which ended with the Time of Troubles (1605-13), and in the works that treated later periods, Karamzin portrayed Russia's past as a sequence of individual reigns. Inherent in the sequence he detected one basic process: the gradual articulation of those instruments of power and authority which culminated in the triumphant emergence of the centralized Russian state. In Karamzin's view, this was the end toward which the best of the Russian people had worked, fought, suffered, and sacrificed.

The "Norman" theory seemed to offer Karamzin a set of historically supportive and ideologically attractive arguments. The "Normanists" of his day continued to claim, *im Geiste Schloezers,* that Russian history began only with the arrival of the Varangian-Scandinavian princes. Moreover, these princes and their descendants—or so went the argument—were uniquely responsible for constructing the institutional edifice of Kievan *Rus',* the structure that, in turn, defined the life of the people. It could be claimed, therefore, that the emergent Russian nation itself had been shaped from above. Here, then, was the origin of that very process on the basis of which Karamzin sought to equate the Russian nation with its rulers and, in the final analysis, to justify monarchial absolutism.

But there was one important qualification to Karamzin's "Normanism." Perhaps he was too much a Russian nationalist or too careful a historian to accept the blanket assertion that all the institutions of Kievan *Rus'* were modeled on Norse prototypes. Indeed, although they were imposed from above, these institutions still had to reflect the particular needs of a Slavic milieu. Consequently, Karamzin argued that the Varangian-Scandinavian princes themselves were rapidly "Russified," becoming, thereby, the truly national rulers of the Russian people.

Like Karamzin, the nineteenth-century Russian Westernizers accepted the "Norman" theory as a valid explanation of the origins of the first Russian political institutions, but used it to serve very different ideological ends. A very heterogeneous group of thinkers, the Westernizers were linked by their conviction that Russia was generically a Western, or European, nation. They equated Westernization with progress and praised those "heroes of Russian enlightenment," like Peter the Great and Catherine II, who had initiated Westernizing policies. They characterized the contemporary Russian autocracy as an "Oriental despotism," condemned it for perpetuating a tradition-bound and iniquitous socioeconomic system, and called for drastic change to bring Russia closer to the West.

But what specific measures would achieve the desired transformation? The Westernizers themselves were divided on this issue. P. Ia. Chaadaev, for example, urged Russia's conversion to Roman Catholicism, and was officially designated a "madman" for his troubles. A. I. Herzen, on the other hand, opted for liberal reforms, while N. G. Chernyshevskii espoused communal ownership of the means of production. M. A. Bakunin pinned his hopes on an anarchist revolution. Yet, even while advocating diverse strategies of development, the Westernizers adhered to the concept of Westernization as the sanctioning principle of their thought, and marshaled the "Norman" theory in support of that ideological commitment.

Accordingly, the Varangian-Scandinavian princes were portrayed not only as the founders of the "first Russian state," but also as Russia's first Westernizers. Under their leadership—or so the Westernizers claimed—a series of crucial, indeed, decisive events had taken place. Emerging from the "darkness" of tribal barbarism, the Russian people achieved statehood, attained national unity, and through the instrumentality of imported, European-style institutions, began to acquire the rudiments of civilization. Maintaining that these had all been beneficial changes, the Westernizers drew the, to them, self-evident historical lesson that Westernization meant progress.

Such arguments failed to convince A. S. Khomiakov, the Kireevskii and Aksakov brothers, Iu. F. Samarin, and other nineteenth-century Russian Slavophiles. Like their Westernizer opponents, the Slavophiles also adopted the "Norman" theory, but used it for an entirely different purpose. The major aspects of their historical interpretation may be summarized as follows.

The Slavophiles agreed that the Varangian-Scandinavian princes had, in fact, founded the "first Russian state." In the process, however, they had imposed a set of "alien" institutions upon the Slavs, often supplanting native forms of social and political organization. Subsequently, force, intimidation, and guile were required to maintain these extrinsic institutions. As a result, the "state" was severed from the "nation," creating a dualism of ruler and ruled. The continued existence of this wound bred social, economic, political, and cultural strife that in turn precipitated a savage sequence of civil wars. When no common front could be erected against the Tatar invader, Kiev fell in 1240 and Kievan *Rus'* disintegrated into quarreling appanage princedoms. *Ex uno plures.* Such, then, was the Slavophile view of the tragic consequences of Westernization.

The Slavophiles extended this line of analysis to subsequent periods of Russian history, always likening Westernization to a disease that, by infecting those in power (for example, Peter the Great and Catherine II), caused the entire nation to suffer. They argued that Western-style reforms, especially when enforced from above, strengthened the hand of tyranny and thus facilitated the spiritual and physical debasement of the Russian people. From the Slavophile point of view, material gains had been purchased at a morally insupportable cost.

Although the Slavophiles regarded all forms of government per se with suspicion, they did not specifically reject the principles of monarchial absolutism. They did, however, condemn many of the specific policies and practices pursued by nineteenth-century Russian monarchs. Again, Westernization was at fault. The influence of Western ideas and the indiscriminate emulation of the Western example had converted the Russian monarchy into an artificial instrument of political power. Thoroughly bureaucratized and formalistic, it constantly interfered in the private lives of its citizens, while remaining indifferent to their real needs. In short, the Slavophiles felt that the "state" had become "Europeanized," while the "nation" lived apart, stubbornly true to its essential nature. Convinced that the gulf dividing the two was growing wider and deeper, the Slavophiles asked if contemporary Russia could long avoid the fate of Kievan *Rus'*.

According to the Slavophiles, Russia's salvation lay in a return to those ideals and principles that, unlike all officially conceived and enforced doctrines of "Russification," truly reflected the spirit of the people. That spirit manifested itself, first and foremost, in the Orthodox concept of *sobornost'*—the ideal of a Christian community bound together by voluntarily assumed ties of love, mutual respect, harmony, and peace. The same spirit found its historical expression in such institutions as the *veche*, the *Zemskii sobor* (in particular, the seventeenth-century *sobor*), the workers' *artel'*, and the peasant commune. The Slavophiles maintained that since these native and organic institutions had emerged in response to genuinely "national" needs, they could serve both the monarch and the people far better than swarns of ministries, bureaus, departments, and sub-departments created in the Western image. The emperor and autocrat who ruled on the basis of such moral and material foundations could indeed become, in the truest sense of these words, the Tsar of All Russia.

In nineteenth-century Russia, then, the "Norman" theory was integrated into three distinct historical interpretations and used to support their mutually contradictory ideological and political extensions. During this same period the general European reading public was both instructed and entertained by the numerous versions of the "Norman" theory which appeared in the popular literature about Russia. Thus, the British tourist who planned to visit Russia could purchase Josiah Conder's *The Modern Traveller* (London, 1825), in which he would learn that "the foundation of the present kingdom of Russia was laid by Ruric, a Scandinavian chief," that the Varangians were "corsairs of the Baltic," and that Riurik's "descendants held the sceptre above 700 years" (pp. 2-3). With time such accounts grew longer and more elaborate, as authors embellished supposed facts with their own often highly subjective value judgments.

Thus, according to Murray's handbook for *Travellers in Russia, Poland and Finland* (London, 1868):

> Europe was peopled by three great families of the human race, who emigrated westward . . . the last of these migrations was that of the Slavonians. . . . In the days of Herodotus their mode of life was exceedingly rude and barbarous; they had no houses, and lived a nomadic and pastoral life . . . . Their principal occupations were the rearing of cattle, the chase and the management of bees, while their chief characteristics seem to have been in a degree analogous to those of . . . the modern Russians:—they were hospitable, courageous, good-humored, contented, and immoderately fond of spirituous liquors; like most barbarous nations, however, the courage of the Slaves frequently degenerated into cruelty . . . . Their religion was idolatrous, and . . . resembled the gross and degrading forms of the ancient Druids; they not only offered their prisoners as a holocaust to their chief deity Perune . . . but would sometimes even immolate their children in his honour . . . . The tribal groups of the north began, about the middle of the 9th century, to feel a want of unity and of a system of government better adapted to the civilization which their intercourse with the Germans and Greeks was introducing . . . .

> The Slavonians sent a deputation to the Variags, or Normans, with the message and invitation, "Our land is great and bountiful, but there is no order in it; come and rule over us." In 864, Rurik, a Norman prince, took up his residence at Novgorod, and there founded the Russian monarchy, the sceptre of which continued to be held by his descendants for upwards of 700 years (pp. 1-2).

Such accounts, blending historical data with fiction and surmise, served to strengthen the impression, already held by some Europeans, that direct Western contributions had always played a "civilizing" role in Russian history. This line of reasoning sometimes culminated in blanket assertions that the West was, and had always been, inherently superior to Russia—culturally, politically, socially, and in every other respect.

The most bizarre use of the "Norman" theory for such purposes occurred in the twentieth century. A crude and simplistic form of "Normanism" was incorporated into that arrantly racist mythology that the Nazis devised as a substitute for historical scholarship and indeed, for reason itself. As Adolf Hitler wrote in *Mein Kampf*:

> The organization of a Russian state structure was not the result of Russian Slavdom's State-political capacity, but rather a wonderful example of the State-building activity of the German element in an inferior race. Thus innumerable mighty empires of the earth have been created. Inferior nations with German organizers and lords as leaders have more than once expanded into powerful State structures, and endured as long as the racial nucleus of the constructive State-race maintained itself. For centuries Russia drew nourishment from this Germanic nucleus of its superior strata of leaders (*Mein Kampf* [New York, 1940], p. 951).

As late as 1959, several Soviet students told me that they had listened to Nazi radio broadcasts that attempted to justify the invasion of the USSR on the following grounds: "Aryan Viking leaders" had founded the Russian "state" and had ruled it "for centuries"; the frontiers of "superior Western culture" were being expanded, therefore, over lands and territories that were "historically German." The same students who described these broadcasts denounced the "Norman" theory as a "murderous Hitlerite weapon."

A few years later, while attending an international conference, I took part in a discussion during which a Soviet medievalist accused "Western historians" of seeking "to conscript 'Normanism' for service in the Cold War." When asked to specify, he referred to Werner Keller's *Ost Minus West = Null* (Munich, 1960). Although some of those present, including myself, tried to argue that Keller's writings on Russian history were not, by any means, representative of current Western scholarship on the subject, nor of Western scholarly standards in general, the Soviet medievalist remained unimpressed. Apparently, he felt that a telling point had been made.

A useful insight into the spirit and substance of *Ost Minus West* is provided by Constantine FitzGibbon's Introduction to the English edition of the work (*Are the Russians Ten Feet Tall?* [London, 1961]):

> This book is part of the Cold War...for those of us who are interested and engaged it states an important thesis. Dr. Keller's argument...is that the Russians, coming late into the world of history, were still technologically in Western leading-strings when the Communists seized power. Imaginatively the Russians were, of course, our equals, as were pre-dynastic Egyptians and presumably Cro-Magnon man too....But whereas the arts are produced by individuals who may on rare occasions be uneducated, stupid or even mad, the sciences, and even more so the applied sciences, can only flourish well in a society...deeply imbued with skills and techniques which have been developed and passed on over the generations....Therefore the Russian method...was to import the technicians and copy their techniques....When Russian xenophobia won the day, and the foreigners were excluded or driven out, Russian technology fell badly behind that prevailing in more civilized lands....Russia was a mighty power in 1914, in 1815, in 1712. But as Dr Keller explains in such lavish detail...the West was and is the prime source of Russian power. And since Russia lacks the basic potential...it can never catch up on its own....If Russia can

now threaten us as she does, we have only ourselves to blame. We gave her the arms and the technical knowledge (pp. 7-10).

In order to emphasize the significance of early Western contributions to Russia, as well as their dangerous consequences, Keller employed a mixture of "Normanist" concepts and his own ideas. A few quotations, selected from the English edition of his book, indicate the direction of his argument:

The Eastern Slavs . . . had neither the ability nor the desire to combine politically and thus to create a state of their own. External teachers had to be called in before this could be achieved. When one examines the lives and customs of these Slavs. . . . it seems time for them stood still . . . they remained, as it were, rooted in prehistory, a strange contrast to the rest of the world . . . . All forms of political organization were unknown to them . . . . Temples and priests were both unknown . . . . Lightning-quick surprise attacks from ambush—such was their method of fighting. They could neither read nor write, were totally ignorant of astronomy and mathematics, medicine and engineering, were familiar neither with philosophical, moral nor religious teachings, had never seen a stone house, temple or palace. They knew nothing of seamanship nor the casting of iron—in fact they stepped upon the stage of history with empty hands. As Herder, after many years' study of the Slav people, wrote in the eighteenth century, "They take up more space on the map than they do in history." . . . The story of Rurik's call to the throne has been much embellished by myth and legend. One fact, however, is beyond dispute: Varangian overlords brought law and order to the Slavs. The birth of an eastern state coincides with the moment that their rule began. . . . The new empire of the Swedish rulers was rapidly expanded. . . . Thus with a few decades the Ruriki . . . had organized and unified the Slav peoples. . . . Scarcely had the Slavs acquired the status of a major power . . . before they embarked, quite characteristically, upon the first of a long series of aggressions against the West. . . . Without warning, a flotilla of two thousand boats, manned by fighting seamen, appeared off Byzantium (pp. 16-22).

In this fashion, then, Keller characterized Prince Oleg's 907 raid on Byzantium as "the first of a long series of aggressions against the West." According to Keller, these "aggressions," made possible only through the acquisition of superior Western organizational and technological skills, have remained a constant theme in Russian history.

When a comprehensive study of twentieth-century developments in Western historical thought is produced, Nazi and Cold War uses of the "Norman" theory will probably be mentioned only in passing, if at all. One tends to dismiss them as aberrant details, but on occasion, precisely such "details" have come to the attention of Soviet officialdom and, as a result, have been converted into ideological and political causes.

In Russia, immediately after the 1917 Revolution, historians continued to debate the scholarly issues involved in the "Norman" controversy. A. A. Shakhmatov, V. A. Brim, and P. S. Liashchenko, for example, tended to support the "Normanist" interpretation, while M. K. Liubavskii, D. I. Bagolei, and M. Hrushevskii championed the "anti-Normanist" side of the argument. B. D. Grekov, who later became the dean of Soviet medievalists, inclined towards "Normanism" in his early works.

During the 1920s, a single individual, M. N. Pokrovskii, came to dominate Soviet historical studies. Pokrovskii was not a medievalist, but his works, for example, *Russkaia istoriia v samom szhatom ocherke* (Moscow-Petrograd, 1923), did bear the stamp of political approval and thus tended to establish the interpretive pattern that other historians followed in discussing such controversial subjects as the origins of Kievan *Rus'*. In one significant respect, Pokrovskii was an "anti-Normanist." He heaped scorn upon the "un-Marxist" notion that the "first Russian state" had been imported by princes from beyond the sea, insisting instead that the process of state-formation was determined by economic and not political factors. On the other hand, he accepted the "Normanist" contention that the Varangian princes were Swedes and asserted that the philological evidence on the subject was complete and irrefutable. Finally, Pokrovskii's low estimate of the culture of the Eastern Slavs, and of Kievan *Rus'* in particular, also seemed to suggest common grounds with "Normanism."

In 1929, however, Pokrovskii's star had begun to wane, and by 1934, it was in total eclipse. Pokrovskii and his "school" were officially condemned as "sociologizers," as "vulgarizers of Marxism," as "Rickertain-Machists," and as "Trotskyite-Bukharinite hirelings of fascism," to quote only some of the epithets used. "Soviet patriotism" was now the order of the day, and under Stalin's supervision, Soviet historians were directed to praise Russian achievements, to glorify the Russian people, and to extol Russian "national heroes." As the threat from Nazi Germany grew, full political control was extended over Soviet academic affairs, creating conditions that doomed the "Norman" theory as a scholarly doctrine. Kievan *Rus'*, it was declared, was a "native, Russian creation," and must be portrayed as such by Soviet historians.

The most intense attacks on "Normanism," capped by its official proscription, occurred after World War II, at a time when "Normanism" was, for all practical purposes, a dead issue in Soviet scholarship. By that time most "Normanist" scholars of the older generation had either died or emigrated. Others had stopped publishing or, like B. D. Grekov, redefined their stand and admitted past "errors." The younger generation of Soviet medievalists had been trained in "anti-Normanism," especially cultural "anti-Normanism," from the start.

N. L. Rubinshtein's book *Russkaia istoriografiia* (Moscow, 1941) provided the occasion for exhuming the "Norman" question for its final condemnation and reburial. In this lengthy and, generally speaking, scholarly study of the main trends in pre-revolutionary Russian historical thought, Rubinshtein had touched only briefly on "Normanism." Ironically, however, *Russkaia istoriografiia* became the *bête noire* of the new, politically-charged "anti-Normanist" campaign. Perhaps the fact that no active Soviet "Normanist" could be found governed the choice of target.

The January 1948 issue of *Voprosy istorii* carried I. Mordvishin's report on a discussion of *Russkaia istoriografiia*. Mordvishin began by explaining that this work had achieved widespread circulation, but owing to wartime conditions, it had not yet passed the collective scrutiny of Soviet scholars. Mordvishin then quoted some of the remarks made by his colleagues censuring Rubinshtein's treatment of the "Norman" controversy. Rubinshtein was not accused of deliberate "Normanism"; instead, he was taken to task for being insufficiently "anti-Normanist." As one commentator put it, Rubinshtein had failed to subject to "scientific analysis" Bayer's "pernicious theory" that demeaned the "great Russian people" politically and spiritually. Critics also faulted Rubinshtein's assessment of the eighteenth-century debates: he had "praised" the German academicians, and not their Russian opponents.

In the next issue of *Voprosy istorii*, Rubinshtein answered some of the charges and admitted to certain "shortcomings," but the tide of criticism could not be stemmed. In the same issue of *Voprosy istorii*, the noted medievalist M. N. Tikhomirov continued the attack. He described the paragraph devoted to Bayer's activities in Russia as "the most incorrect . . . in Rubinshtein's entire book." Asserting that the origins of "Normanism" were rooted in a German political conspiracy. Tikhomirov argued that the Germans who occupied privileged positions in eighteenth-century Russia had sought an ideological justification of their position. Bayer and his colleagues had responded by conceiving the "Norman" theory. In so doing, Tikhomirov asserted, they had acted on orders from "highly placed German functionaries."

Writing in the April 1949 issue of the authoritative journal *Bol'shevik*, M. Morozov went even further. He accused Rubinshtein of fawning before German "racist" historians. According to Morozov, all manifestations of "Normanism," past as well as present, had but one purpose—the justification of Germany's eastward expansion. Similar views were expressed by other Soviet commentators. Thus, criticisms of *Russkaia istoriografiia*, centering on Rubinshtein's allegedly incorrect assessment of the early stages of the "Norman" controversy, were transformed into total and indiscriminate condemnations of the "Norman" theory as a politically motivated, racist, and inimical doctrine.

As a result, *Russkaia istoriografiia* was proscribed, at least ostensibly, because of its "Normanist" content. Other Soviet scholars were also affected, but, on the whole, less severely than Rubinshtein. Several prominent medievalists, including V. V. Mavrodin, were accused of displaying "Normanist" tendencies. The charge may have motivated Mavrodin to publish his tendentious "anti-Normanist" tract, *Bor'ba normanizmom v russkoi istoricheskoi nauke* (1949). Such details as the turn of a single sentence did not pass unnoticed. Thus, B. D. Grekov, who had been recently praised for "proving" that the *Rus'* people were Slavs (and not Scandinavians), apparently felt compelled to apologize in the March 1948 issue of *Voprosy istorii*. He had stated in a textbook that the "tendentious Norman theory" had lost its "scholarly significance." Grekov now admitted that he should have said that "Marxist science" had "completely demolished it."

In the midst of these developments, the November 1949 issue of *Voprosy istorii* published an unsigned, but clearly official, declaration announcing new "tasks" for Soviet medievalists. Their duty to the "Motherland" lay in an "active, unremitting struggle . . . against historical falsifications . . . and theories inimical to Marxism-Leninism," such as "the Indo-European theory of the origins of peoples, the Norman theory of the origin of the Russian state, fascist views on the alleged cultural role of the imaginary Goth 'state,' false and unfounded contentions concerning the lack of independent development on the part of the Russian people." Soviet medievalists were then told to combat manifestations of these views in foreign historical literature. This was clearly an order. It was also a signal for redoubled attacks on "bourgeois" scholarship in general, as well as on Western accounts of "Normanism" in particular.

Since the death of Stalin, Soviet historians have gained an appreciably greater freedom from direct political interference. The ban has been lifted on a number of works that had been proscribed under Stalin, and their authors have been partially or wholly "rehabilitated." Pokrovskii's writings, for example, are again receiving serious, and by no means entirely negative, attention from Soviet scholars. A balanced evaluation, tempering criticism with substantial praise, was given to Rubinshtein's *Russkaia istoriografiia* by the editors of *Istoriografiia istorii SSSR,* the first edition of which was published in 1961. Rubinshtein himself contributed several chapters to this collective work. Appraisals of Western and non-Marxist scholarship have become, on the whole, more judicious and objective. New avenues have opened up for meaningful academic discourse and cooperation with Soviet scholars.

But Soviet medieval studies remain basically "anti-Normanist" in orientation. Criticisms of the "Norman" theory, and in particular of cultural "Normanism," still seem to form an integral part of Soviet attempts to formulate "Marxist" explanations of the origins of Kievan *Rus'.* And "Normanism"—although less so today than in times past—still figures as a political issue in the Soviet Union.

APPENDIX

The following works were chosen primarily because they contain useful historiographical information on the "Norman" question. Both "Normanist" and "anti-Normanist" authors are represented.

Moshin, V. A. "Nachalo Rusi: Normany v vostochnoi evrope." *Byzantino-slavica* 3 (1931): 33-58, 285-306.

Paszkiewicz, H. *The Making of the Russian Nation.* London, 1963.

———. *The Origin of Russia.* London, 1954.

Riasanovsky, A. V. "The Varangian Question." *I normanni e la loro espansione in Europa nell' alto medioevo: Settimane di studio del Centro italiano di studi sull' alto medioevo* 16 (1969): 171-204.

Riasanovsky, N. V. "The Norman Theory of the Origin of the Russian State." *The Russian Review* 7 (Autumn, 1947): 96-110.

Riasanovsky, V. A. "Vopros o vliianii normannov na russkuiu kul'turu." *Obzor russkoi kul'tury* 1 (New York, 1947): 161-289.

Rybakov, B. A. "Predposylki obrazovaniia drevnerusskogo gosudarstva." In *Ocherki istorii SSSR: III-IX vv.,* ed. B. A. Rybakov. Moscow, 1958, pp. 733-878.

Shoskol'skii, I. P. *Normanskaia teoriia v sovremennoi burzhuaznoi nauke.* Moscow-Leningrad, 1965.

Shusharin, V. P. *Sovremennaia burzhuaznaia istoriografiia drevnei Rusi.* Moscow, 1964.

Vernadsky, G. V. *Ancient Russia.* New Haven, Conn., 1943.

———. *Kievan Russia.* New Haven, Conn., 1948.

Vucinich, A. "The First Russian State." In C. E. Black, ed., *Rewriting Russian History* 2d ed. New York, 1964, pp. 123-140.

The bibliographies offered in the two volumes by the prominent contemporary "Normanist" H. Paszkiewicz merit special attention. Although far from complete, these bibliographies, taken together, list over forty-five hundred relevant medieval documentary sources and secondary works.

THE VIEW FROM THE "KRAKOW ANTHILL": ONE SOURCE OF THE COMINTERN'S MISUNDERSTANDING OF EAST EUROPEAN NATIONALISM

James V. Hulse
University of Nevada

In the present era, it is widely recognized that the international Communist movement is as vulnerable to national and regional considerations as any other institution that draws its participants from various parts of the world. For many years, however, world Communist leaders disregarded the fact that nationalism was the most divisive factor with which they had to deal in their effort to create a unified proletarian organization dedicated to a Marxist world revolution. Historians of the Communist International, often studying that organization on its own terms, have failed to take into account the destructive work that nationalism performed upon it.

It is the thesis of this paper that the views on nationalism which were developed by Lenin and Stalin in the years immediately before and during World War I became Bolshevik dogma and in turn dictated the policy of the Communist International on nationalities during its founding period, 1919-21. These Leninist-Stalinist attitudes were shaped in the course of polemics with Otto Bauer, Rosa Luxemburg, and Kark Radek, among others, while Lenin was in Kraków. During this period, the question of Polish nationalism and its relationship to Bolshevik revolutionary aspirations was much on Lenin's mind, and therefore Polish issues had a greater influence than any other on Lenin's thinking on the nationality question. It also appears that Lenin—and as a consequence the later Communist International—was insensitive to or ignorant of the force of nationalism in other parts of Eastern Europe during and immediately after the war.

351

Lenin lived in Kraków in the last years before the outbreak of the war, the period of his definitive writings on the national question. During these prewar years, Lenin was especially annoyed by the writings of Otto Bauer, the prestigious Austrian Social Democrat, who had written a brilliant, long book on the subject of nationalism in 1907, and who in November 1918 would emerge as foreign minister of the new Austrian Republic.[1] In writing his 1907 work, Bauer had assumed that Austria-Hungary would survive and that socialists would therefore be wise to work toward a federal union of national groups, each of which would exercise a large measure of national-cultural autonomy. In Bauer's view, socialism and nationalism were compatible, and national differences would continue to grow even after the transition to socialism had been achieved. Bauer did not believe that nationalities would merge and disappear as economic development became more collectivist, and he argued that nationalist-socialist groups had the right to secede from a larger federal unit or empire.

These views stemmed from Bauer's concept of the nation, which was marked by the influence of Kant and Hegel. He regarded the nation as a community based upon a sense of a common historical destiny which had shaped the people's distinctive character. His understanding of this common destiny was not necessarily predicated on any sense of a shared class consciousness, nor did it even require that the people in question possess a common language. Clearly, Bauer was not rigidly Marxian in his analysis, and his national "communities" would admit of areas of common interest between the bourgeoisie and the proletariat.

Lenin was keenly aware in 1913, as he would be in 1919, that moderate socialism like that espoused by Bauer was one of the main obstacles to the Bolsheviks' plans for a revolutionary international proletariat. In particular, Lenin saw that Bauer's concept of nationalism was potentially harmful to the revolutionary cause, and that his ideas about "national-cultural autonomy" constituted a dangerous alternative for the Russian Social-Democratic Party. The Polish and Baltic sections of the Russian Social-Democratic Party had already attained a measure of autonomy, and, although Lenin recognized the rights of national groups to resist tsardom, too much autonomy within the party could diminish its international proletarian character and reduce its effectiveness. It was while living in Kraków and considering views such as Bauer's that Lenin in November 1912 met with Stalin and apparently assigned him the task of

writing a basic philosophical treatise on the relationship between nationalism and Marxism. Stalin had arrived in Kraków with a record of opposition
to Georgian nationalism and of loyalty to Lenin's brand of Marxism. He
seemed a logical candidate to formulate a definitive statement that would
answer Bauer and provide correct theoretical guidance for the revolutionary social democrats in Eastern Europe. We know that the young
Georgian revolutionary went to Vienna for several weeks to gather material with which to refute Bauer.[2]

At the outset, Stalin's primary mission was to discredit Bauer's theory
of nationalism, based on the view that a nation is an "aggregate of people
bound into a community by a common destiny." Rejecting this as an
unacceptable definition, Stalin proposed the following alternative:

> A nation is a historically constituted, stable community of
> people, formed on the basis of a common language, territory,
> economic life, and psychological make-up manifested in a com-
> mon culture.[3]

Bauer had regarded the Jews as a nation, but according to Stalin's
criteria this was incorrect; the Jews of Europe did not have a common
language, territory, or economic life—each of which was an essential
ingredient of a nation. The Leninist-Stalinist view, epitomized in Stalin's
statement, saw nationalism in Eastern Europe as inextricably related to
the development of bourgeois values. While the proletariat shared some
of the aspirations and interests of the various nations within which it lived,
it did not share the bourgeois patriotism toward the nation. Bauer's concepts of a "common culture" and a "common destiny" were not sufficiently explicit for Stalin; they implied an allegiance that he could not reconcile with revolutionary Marxism. In addition, Stalin could not accept the
assertion that "national autonomy" within a larger political federation
was an acceptable form of socialism. His own essay was intended as a
categorical refutation of Bauer's position:

> There is no need to mention the kind of "socialist principle
> of nationality" glorified by Bauer, which, in our opinion, sub-
> stitutes for the socialist principle of the *class struggle* the bour-
> geois *"principle of nationality."* If national autonomy is based

on such a dubious principle, it must be admitted that it can only cause harm to the working-class movement.[4]

Lenin's two statements on nationalism published in *Prosveshchenie* in late 1913 and early 1914 are essentially compatible with Stalin's article, although there are minor modifications. Lenin advocated a policy that would support nationalism as long as it was directed against autocracy and imperialism (as he felt it was in Russia), but he opposed those nationalist sentiments that threatened to divide the proletariat. In a crucial paragraph, composed late in 1913, he said:

> Marxism cannot be reconciled with nationalism, be it even of the "most just," "purest," most refined and civilized brand. In place of all forms of nationalism Marxism advances internationalism, the amalgamation of all nations in the higher unity, a unity that is growing before our eyes with every mile of railway line that is built, with every international trust, and every workers' association that is formed (an association that is international in its economic activities as well as in its ideas and aims).[5]

Where a unification of the proletariat already existed, decentralization or "federalism" was not to be tolerated. He opposed autonomy for the Bundist Jews and for the Ukrainians. He recognized the right of the Ukrainian proletariat to form a completely independent state, but he regarded it as the higher duty of the Great Russian and Ukrainian proletariats to cooperate against their common class enemies. For Lenin, nationalism was "progressive" so long as it served to undermine existing imperial or capitalistic regimes, but it was destructive if it obscured proletarian consciousness.[6]

Lenin's attitude toward the Polish question was similar, but in this case the matter was complicated by the fact that one of the most articulate Left Socialists of Europe, Rosa Luxemburg, was publicizing a contrary view—a view that manifested a proletarian internationalism more pure and more rigid than Lenin's. She was categorically opposed to nationalism and "self-determination" because she saw both of these concepts as tools of the bourgeoisie. She had published a well-formulated article at about the same time as Bauer's article had appeared—in 1908 and 1909—

and she repeated her basic position with sufficient frequency and force
that Lenin felt compelled to respond.[7] She had, among other things,
characterized the Leninist position on Polish nationalism as "metaphysi-
cal" and a "betrayal of the strictly class position which the [Russian
Social-Democratic] party has tried to observe in all points of its program."[8] Lenin regarded Polish nationalism as a potentially valuable
weapon against Great-Russian nationalism, which was the primary foe
of the proletariat throughout Eastern Europe. He was caustic about the
position of Luxemburg and in both his 1913 article and a 1914 sequel chided her for failing to look at the larger picture. In the latter statement, which
is a long polemic directed against her, he commented on "her inability
to see things from a viewpoint any deeper and broader than that of the
Cracow [Kraków] anthill."[9] He accused Luxemburg of trying to impose
"Kraków standards" on all nations and peoples inhabiting Russia and
he implied that it was her own provincialism that caused her to be short-
sighted on the question.

> Although Rosa Luxemburg's point of view could at first have
> been excused as being specifically Polish, "Kraków" narrow-
> mindedness, it is inexcusable today, when nationalism and,
> above all, governmental Great-Russian nationalism, has every-
> where gained ground, and when policy is being shaped by this
> *Great-Russian nationalism.*[10]

An examination of Lenin's writing on nationalism in this period leads
one to the conclusion that Lenin himself, as much as any of his associates
and adversaries of that period, was absorbed in the affairs of the "Kraków
anthill" to the extent that he overlooked or only superficially considered
the phenomenon of nationalism in other parts of Eastern Europe. He
seems to have been largely insensitive to the expressions of nationalism
which were activating Balkan governments and peoples during this period,
and his comments on the Balkan Wars in particular indicate that he was
either poorly informed or unconcerned about events there. For Lenin
nationalism was simply a manifestation of bourgeois development; a force
that was occasionally manipulated by the state, but not a force to be
reckoned with outside the context of the class struggle. That the bourgeoisie was not nearly as developed in the Balkan states as nationalistic

fervor might suggest is a fact that must have escaped his notice. It was axiomatic for Lenin that "not only the miniature Balkan states, but even nineteenth-century America was, economically, a colony of Europe, as Marx pointed out in *Capital.*"[11] Referring again to Luxemburg's views, Lenin then added that "the example of the Balkan states likewise contradicts her, for anyone can now see that the best conditions for the development of capitalism in the Balkans are created precisely in proportion to the creation of independent national states in that peninsula."[12] Lenin offers no examples or documentation to support his claim. If he knew anything of governmental policies or of Great Power financial interest in those countries, he did not reveal it—and it was not his method to possess examples and to fail to cite them.

Several times during his Kraków sojourn, Lenin was impelled to take up literary weapons against those of the left with whom he disagreed. No other national question occupied him more than the Polish problem, and a typical statement of his position was that composed in October 1915, "Das Revolutionäre Proletariat und das Selbstbestimmungsrecht der Nationen" (The Revolutionary Proletariat and the Right of Nations to Self-Determination). Here Lenin wielded his pen against one Parabellum, whom he knew to be Karl Radek, the one-time disciple of Rosa Luxemburg, who had recently published articles in the *Berner Tagwacht* on the nationality question. Radek's view was not much different from that of Luxemburg; he regarded nationalism as outmoded because capitalism had outgrown it and reasoned that most contemporary national problems were actually problems of imperialism. Radek believed that the idea of a resurrected fatherland had no place in the aspirations of a proletariat (such as the Polish) that found itself under foreign domination.[13]

In his counter-statement, Lenin denounced Radek as backward looking and as inconsiderate of the needs of those African and Asian peoples who suffered under imperialist rule. Near the end of his argument, Lenin referred directly to the Polish situation:

> Russia is a prison of peoples, not only because of the military-feudal character of tsarism and not only because the Great-Russian bourgeoisie support tsarism, but also because the Polish, etc. bourgeoisie have sacrificed the freedom of nations and democracy in general for the interests of capitalist expansion. The

Russian proletariat cannot march at the head of the people towards a victorious democratic revolution (which is its immediate task), or fight alongside its brothers, the proletarians of Europe, for a socialist revolution, without immediately demanding, fully and unreservedly (*rückhaltlos*) for all nations oppressed by tsarism, the freedom to secede from Russia. This we demand, not independently of our revolutionary struggle for socialism, but because this struggle will remain a hollow phrase if it is not linked up with a revolutionary approach to all questions of democracy, including the national question.[14]

Lenin regarded his demands for independence for Poland as comparable to Marx's demands in 1869 for the independence of Ireland. Marx had advocated separation for the Irish, "not for a split between Ireland and Britain, but for a subsequent free union between them, not so as to secure 'justice for Ireland,' but in the interests of the revolutionary struggle of the British proletariat."[15] In short, the Russian proletariat must demand independence for Poland not because of any rights of the Polish people but in order to frustrate the tsarist regime, the greatest enemy of the proletariat.

The common denominator of Lenin's opposition to the views of Bauer, Luxemburg, and Radek was his conviction that each was poorly designed for the struggle he was waging against tsardom. Bauer's theories set a bad example for the non-Russian proletarian peoples in Russia because they were not sufficiently supportive of the revolutionary mission that he envisioned for the Russian proletariat, while Luxemburg's ideas seemed to deny the service that one potentially powerful non-Russian nation could render to Lenin's main clients. Lenin wanted, above all, to use the nationalism of the minority nations in the Russian Empire to help destroy what he saw as a bourgeois-supported Romanov regime.

Lenin and his Bolshevik colleagues do not appear to have taken any meaningful notice of other political rumblings among the Poles during his stay in Kraków. The political activities of Roman Dmowski and Józef Piłsudski, which were to be of such importance in shaping a post-war Polish state, meant little to Lenin in this period, presumably because he did not regard their efforts as contributions to the proletarian cause. He certainly did not recognize the leadership ability of Piłduski, who was living in Kraków in the same prewar years when Lenin was there, and who was an ardent foe of Russian imperialism. Nor did he appreciate the intensity of Polish national sentiment which Piłsudski was to tap during and after the war.[16]

Lenin held rigidly to the attitude he had developed in Poland on the national question, and he imposed it on the Bolshevik party after his return to Russia in 1917. He regarded it as essential that the Bolsheviks insist upon the right of the Poles to secede as an example to the world's proletariat that the new revolutionary regime in Russia was breaking with the imperial past, but he frequently said, as he had done in 1914, that secession was only a preliminary to proletarian consolidation and cooperation.

The sequence of events that accompanied the end of the war on the Eastern front—the temporary triumph of the Central Powers in the East, the Treaty of Brest-Litovsk, and the proclamation of a Polish Republic—facilitated the separation of Poland from Russia and the other partition powers on terms that had nothing to do with Lenin's scenario. Poland had achieved her independence primarily as a result of the disability of her neighbors and the moral support of the victorious Entente, and not as the result of any upsurge by the proletariat. Nevertheless, Lenin, having worked out his ideas so decisively on the "Kraków anthill," was to hold to them tenaciously and to try to apply them to other parts of Eastern Europe.

Late in 1918 Lenin promoted his plan for a Third Communist International (Comintern) and, among the left-wing Socialists of Central Europe, it was Luxemburg who opposed the idea most vehemently. Although she had respected the Bolshevik's achievement in Russia, she was apprehensive about the possibility of a premature move to found a new International. Fearing that an International formed at that time under Russian leadership was likely to be Russian-dominated, she wanted the organization to be postponed until mass parties had been formed in several countries. The murder of Luxemburg following her arrest in the Spartacist uprising of January 1919 removed this obstacle to Lenin's proposal.[17]

The most significant statement to emerge from the First Comintern Congress of March 1919 was the *Manifesto,* which, while presumably originating with Trotsky, clearly reflected the now standard Bolshevik attitude toward the national question. "The national state, which has been given a mighty impulse by capitalist evolution, has become too narrow for the development of the powers of production."[18] According to the *Manifesto*, the appearance of independence in the various small states was merely illusory, and President Wilson's program of national self-determination was hypocritical. This statement crystallized the concept that the world was divided into two opposing orders, the international proletariat and the international bourgeoisie, and that the political or national units that composed the latter were entirely archaic and artificial. The Bolshevik-Comintern formulation did not recognize that the small countries of Eastern Europe could express a national consciousness independent of bourgeois institutions and unrelated to the stage of economic development.

This blindness to the power of nationalism was the main factor in the Bolshevik leaders' inability to understand the events that occurred in Hungary in the weeks immediately following the so-called First Congress of the Third International. When a coalition of Socialists and Communists assumed power in Budapest less than three weeks after the First Congress, Lenin and his colleagues in Moscow and Petrograd obviously did not recognize the extent to which national and historical conditions, rather than class-struggle considerations, contributed to the events. Count Mihály Károlyi, who had led Hungary out of the old Dual Monarchy late in 1918, hoped to maintain a republic in which Hungarian ethnic leadership would prevail, but both the separatist impulses of the non-Magyars within the old crownlands of St. Stephen and the policies of self-determination advanced by the Entente powers mitigated against this development. When Károlyi's efforts collapsed in March 1919, it was an upsurge of nationalism—not the rising of the proletariat—that brought a pro-Bolshevik coalition to power.[19]

Given the level of communications in Eastern Europe in the spring of 1919, it is not surprising that Moscow did not know the details of events in Hungary. But when Béla Kun, the Moscow-trained agitator, emerged as foreign minister and made his assurances to Lenin that the new regime in Budapest met all the Bolshevik criteria for a Soviet-style regime, the Comintern leaders jumped to the conclusion that revolutionary proletarian sentiments were in the ascendancy.[20]

Kun was as complete and reliable a convert to the Bolshevik cause as Lenin could have wanted in the last days of World War I. He had not only prepared propaganda in the Magyar language for publication, but he had also helped to operate schools for fellow Hungarian prisoners-of-war who were being wooed as revolutionists. When the Communists in Hungary had formed an alliance with the Social Democrats in March 1919, Lenin had been temporarily troubled about the nature of the union, but after Kun reassured him that ideological purity had been maintained, he said that the Hungarians may have surpassed the Russians in their ability to unite the workers within a truly revolutionary organization. Lenin wrote:

> Comrade Hungarian Workers, you have given the world an even better example than Soviet Russia in that you have immediately been able to unite all Socialists on a platform of true proletarian dictatorship.[21]

But a few weeks later, after the Hungarian Soviet Republic had collapsed, Lenin and the Comintern modified their position considerably, asserting that the Hungarian Communists had made a fatal error by affiliating with the Social Democrats.[22]

At no time during the short life of the Hungarian Soviet regime did Moscow recognize that Béla Kun, Tibor Szamuely, and the other Moscow-trained Communists were facing a rising wave of nationalism that could not be reconciled with pure Leninist ideology. Kun participated in some governmental decisions that were superficially similar to Bolshevik programs in Russia, but even these were modified in significant ways to accommodate Hungarian conditions. The government, for example, ordered the socialization of land on April 3, but limited this action to the socialization of medium and large tracts without precisely defining these categories, without removing most of the former estate managers, and without resolving the matter of land inheritance.[23] Obviously, the regime needed time to consider regional and national agrarian conditions before implementing one of the basic Bolshevik principles—collectivization.

Rudolf Tökés demonstrates that one of Kun's major errors was his "orthodox Marxist disregard for the revolutionary, and particularly the military potential of nationalism and patriotism."[24] Kun could not admit that the Hungarian working class might nurture legitimate national aspirations every bit as powerful as its proletarian sentiments. When the Soviet government was forced from power, Kun's immediate reaction was that the proletariat of Hungary had betrayed its cause; it had been insufficiently class-conscious and revolutionary.[25] It did not, apparently, occur to him that this was only one side of the matter—that a wave of nationalism had contributed to the party's success.

Turning to Yugoslavia during the same period, we see that the Comintern leadership proved as incapable of understanding the significance of nationalism for the South Slavs as for the Hungarians. Since Lenin's position had been worked out entirely with the Russian and Polish situations in mind, it was inapplicable to a situation such as that which emerged in the South Slav state that came into existence at the end of 1918. Among the left-wing socialists in Serbia and the neighboring provinces, there had been before and during the war a strong desire for a Balkan Socialist Federation, and Balkan Marxists had made several attempts to find a basis for unity. When the Yugoslav state had emerged around a Serbian nucleus at the end of the war, Serbian Left Marxist tended to support it as a workable substitute for—or perhaps as a forerunner of— a Communist federation.

Moscow vacillated greatly in its attitude toward the Yugoslav situation. At first, those South Slavs being trained in Moscow for revolutionary work in their native region argued against the idea of a Yugoslav state.[26] Their Moscow mentors had obviously encouraged them to oppose the idea of full Yugoslav unity, but once they returned to their homelands, they succumbed to the arguments of Filip Filipović (alias Bošković), the most articulate and influential of those who assumed leadership in Yugoslavia following the war and the man who became the first Communist party secretary.[27]

Throughout the founding period of the Comintern, 1919-21, its leaders in Moscow virtually ignored the nationalities problem in Yugoslavia, perhaps because it was seen as relatively unimportant, but probably also because they did not have sufficient information on which to base a policy. Moscow disapproved of the Kingdom of Serbs, Croats, and Slovenes on the ground that it was a creation of the imperialist powers that had dominated the Paris Peace Conference. At the same time, however, the existence of the unified monarchy facilitated the operation of a unified Communist party, and if the Comintern leadership had been more open-minded, it might have recognized that Yugoslav unity was advantageous to them.

Yugoslav socialists of both the moderate and the Bolshevik varieties did recognize that a unifed state was beneficial to their cause. The proto-Communist segment held a unity congress in Belgrade on 20-23 April 1919 and formed "The Socialist Workers' Party of Yugoslavia (Communist)," which included representatives from all the major national groups in the country. There was an impressive display of unity among these disparate elements, even though some serious differences of theory existed on agrarian questions and on tactical matters.[28] Lenin obviously did not recognize that the Yugoslav Communists, although confronted with a more complex and challenging situation than that faced by Béla Kun in Hungary, had moved closer to unity on a genuinely Bolshevik foundation than his disciples in Hungary.

The Yugoslav Communists' appeal to the electorate was quite effective in 1920, in large part because of the dual strategy by which the party presented itself: as a Yugoslav party when it wooed the Serbs and as a party opposed to Serbian hegemony when it courted the other peoples of the kingdom. "As a result of its support for the unitary state," Paul Shoup has observed, "the Party gained favor in Serbia and Montenegro, and by its unceasing attacks on the government, it attracted support in regions where national unrest was growing."[29] The Communists did surprisingly well in municipal elections in both Zagreb and Belgrade in the spring and summer of 1920, and in the autumn of that year they finished third, behind the ruling Democrats and Radicals, in the election of delegates to the Constituent Assembly. These results, coming in November 1920, revealed that the Communists had supporters in all parts of the country and had established themselves as a major political force in less than eighteen months of formal political existence. The Communists had won their biggest victories in Montenegro and Macedonia, the least industrialized regions in the new state, a fact that indicates that party leaders were doing quite well at exploiting rural and national discontent in the hinterland. It was because the Communist party was so successful in the legal political arena, of course, that the ruling parties took steps in 1921 to curtail its operation and eventually to drive it underground. The strikes that broke out in Slovenian coal mining villages, and the support announced for the strikers by the Communists, provided the rationale for the *Obznana* decree curtailing Communist party activities. In short order the government drove the Communist movement underground and ended its brief legal existence for a generation.

Moscow did not get around to taking a direct interest in the Yugoslav Communists' policy toward Yugoslav nationalities until three or four years later. During 1919 and 1920, the main spokesman for the Yugoslav Communists in Moscow was Ilija Milkić, a one-time salesman who had been associated with Serbian socialism for several years. He insisted —contrary to some opinions expressed by Zinoviev—that South Slavic Communists were neither opportunistic nor nationalistic. He painted a highly favorable picture of Bolshevik-proletarian activities in Yugoslavia, but the Comintern leadership apparently remained skeptical—or at least unusually reticent—about the achievements of the Comintern affiliate there.[30] It would appear that the Yugoslav Communists had been able to overcome national differences to a large extent and had been able to use national discontents against the established government in a manner consistent with Lenin's theories, but Moscow took virtually no notice of this accomplishment. It had become, once more, preoccupied with the Polish question.

The Bolshevik leadership received an emphatic object lesson in the strength of East European nationalism during the confrontation with Poland in 1920 and 1921. Józef Piłsudski was not only a Polish nationalist with dreams of assuring Poland a position of greatness, but at the time of his invasion of the Ukraine in April 1920, he also acted as a champion of Ukrainian nationalism, promising that Polish troops would withdraw from the Ukraine once a national government had been established there.[31]

Ukrainian nationalism was a reality, and the Bolsheviks tried to use it during their own counter-offensive against the Poles a few weeks later, playing on the fact that thousands of Ukrainians were at least as suspicious of Polish occupation as they were of a Great-Russian presence. The Soviets used this same occasion to stimulate Russian nationalism against the Poles in an attempt to rally their own forces.

When the Red Army undertook its counter-offensive and advanced to the edge of Warsaw in the summer of 1920, the Second Congress of the Comintern happened to be meeting in Moscow, and the appearance of victory produced a kind of euphoria among the Comintern delegates. It appeared that the Red Army might be able, after taking Warsaw, to cooperate with the revolutionary instincts of the proletariat in Germany and to continue pushing Communism westward. Julian Marchelewski, longtime friend and associate of Luxemburg but also one of the Bolsheviks' most trusted voices on Polish matters, had delivered a ringing report on prospects for revolution in Poland in the opening session of the Second Congress, and it had been followed by a resolution that on the one hand appealed for peace but on the other hand justified a continuation of the Red Army's offensive against the "clique of capitalist and Junker adventurers" in Poland.[32]

When Piłsudski launched his remarkable counter-attack on August 16, driving a decisive wedge between the two advancing Soviet armies and thereby throwing them into confusion and retreat, he was able to do so because of an upsurge of Polish patriotism. The "Government of National Defense" under Wincenty Witos and Ignacy Daszyński was able to mobilize some 80,000 men and the War Ministry mustered another 170,000 in the crucial weeks of the Bolshevik advance, and these forces were a crucial element in the Polish resurgence. Pleas to the Entente Powers had produced nothing; the much publicized presence and advice of General Weygand was of little consequence. The Bolsheviks have never acknowledged these facts, however, and have persistently regarded the events on the Polish front in 1920-21 as more evidence of an international imperialist conspiracy.

Just as Poland and the Polish national question had been important in shaping Lenin's attitude toward the nationalities problem in general in the years immediately before the war, so the developments in Poland in 1920 and 1921 had an impact on the Comintern and on Bolshevik thinking about the prospects of the revolution in that period. After the Polish victories in the summer of 1920, the Bolsheviks had to reconcile themselves to the fact that there were some parts of the former Russian Empire that had opted for national independence without the sequel that Leninist ideology anticipated. Poland, Finland, and the Baltic states had seceded, as according to Bolshevik theory they were entitled to do, but the secession had not led to a reunion under the banner of proletarian solidarity. The Bolsheviks could not admit to themselves in the 1920s that nationalistic and ethnic considerations had been stronger than so-called class consciousness in many parts of Eastern Europe, and it would appear that they still have trouble recognizing this in the present era.

NOTES

1. Otto Bauer, *Die Nationalitätenfrage und die Sozialdemokratie* (Vienna, 1907).

2. See the discussion of the relationship between Lenin and Stalin at this period in Robert C. Tucker, *Stalin as Revolutionary, 1879-1929: A Study in History and Personality* (New York, 1973), pp. 150-57.

3. J. V. Stalin, *Works* (Moscow, 1953), 2, p. 307. This essay was first published in *Prosveshchenie,* nos. 3, 4, 5, (March-May, 1913).

4. Stalin, *Works,* 2, p. 342.

5. V. I. Lenin, "Critical Remarks on the National Question," *Collected Works* (Moscow, 1954), 20, p. 34. This article appeared initially in three parts in *Prosveshchenie,* nos. 10, 11, 12 (October-December, 1913).

6. Ibid., pp. 32-33.

7. The article "Autonomy and the National Question" appeared as "Kwestia narodowościowa i autonomia," in *Przegląd Socjaldemokratyczny,* in several issues in 1908 and 1909. This and other relevant writings of Luxemburg have been assembled in *The National Question: Selected Writings by Rosa Luxemburg,* ed. Horace B. Davis (New York, 1976).

8. Luxemburg, *The National Question,* p. 153.

9. Lenin, "The Right of Nations to Self-Determination," *Collected Works,* 20, p. 426. The articles from which these phrases are taken first appeared in *Prosveshchenie,* nos. 4, 5, 6 (February-May, 1914).

10. Ibid., p. 452.

11. Ibid., p. 399.

12. Ibid., p. 400.

13. Radek's articles appeared in the *Berner Tagwacht,* no. 252 (28 October 1915) Beilage, 1, and no. 253 (29 October 1915), Beilage, 1.

14. Lenin's remarks in this instance do not appear to have been published immediately. They are reproduced in the *Collected Works,* (Moscow, 1964), 21, pp. 407-14. See p. 413.

15. Ibid., p. 414.

16. For useful discussions on the broader aspects of Russian-Polish relations, see Piotr S. Wandycz, *Soviet-Polish Relations: 1917-1921* (Cambridge, Mass., 1969); and Antony Polonsky, *Politics in Independent Poland: 1921-1939* (Oxford, 1972), pp. 45-79.

17.   For Luxemburg's attitudes on nationalism, see J. P. Nettl, *Rosa Luxemburg* 2 vols. (London, 1966), 2, pp. 842-62. See also pp. 782-83.

18.   *Der I. Kongress der Kommunistischen Internationale. Protokoll der Verhandlungen in Moskau vom 2. bis zum 19 Marz 1919* (Hamburg, 1921), p. 175. The entire *Manifesto* is at pp. 171-82.

19.   Informative discussions of the internal situation that contributed to the rise to power of the Hungarian Soviet government in March 1919, may be found in Robert A. Kann, *A History of the Habsburg Empire* (Berkeley and Los Angeles, 1974), pp. 494-520; and in Peter Pastor, *Hungary Between Wilson and Lenin: The Hungarian Revolution of 1918-1919 and the Big Three* (Boulder, 1976).

20.   An excellent brief summary of the events of the Hungarian Revolution of 1919 is available in Ervin Laszlo, *The Hungarian Ideology in Hungary* (Dordrecht, 1966), pp. 16-19. For a more thorough anlaysis of the events and of Kun's role in the revolution, see Rudolf L. Tökés, *Béla Kun and the Hungarian Soviet Republic,* published for the Hoover Institution on War, Revolution, and Peace (New York, 1967).

21.   *Kommunisticheskii internatsional,* no. 2 (1 June 1919), col. 155-58.

22.   *Pravda,* 6 August 1919, 1, 1-8.

23.   Tökés, *Béla Kun,* p. 186, and n. 17.

24.   Ibid., p. 210.

25.   Essential parts of Kun's remarks, from Vilmos Böhm, *Két Forradalom Tüzében* [In the Crossfire of Two Revolutions] (Vienna, 1923), are translated in Tökés, *Béla Kun,* pp. 203-4.

26.   The organ of the Yugoslav Bolsheviks in Moscow was *Svetska Revolucija.* Discussions of the complications of the Yugoslav Communist position may be found in Ivan Avakumović, *History of the Communist Party of Yugoslavia* (Aberdeen, 1964); and in Paul Shoup, *Communism and the Yugoslav National Question* (New York, 1968).

27.   Avakumović, p. 47, n. 73, and Shoup, p. 20.

28.   Avakumović, p. 29.

29.   Shoup, p. 20.

30.   For the most significant statement by Miklić, see "La Situation générale et le Mouvement communiste et revolutionnaire en Yougo-Slavie," in *Rapports sur le mouvement communiste international,* Présentés au Deuxième Congrès de l'Internationale Communiste, Moscou, 1920 (Petrograd, 1924), pp. 143-64. See Avakumović, p. 56, n. 105.

31. For the heart of Piłsudski's appeal to the Ukrainians, see M. Z. Dziewanowski, *Joseph Piłsudski: A European Federalist, 1918-1922* (Stanford, 1969), p. 284.

32. The Second Congress's views on Poland at the opening were summarized in "An die Proletarier und Proletarierinnen aller Länder!," *Der zweite Kongress der Kommunist. Internationale. Protokoll der Verhandlungen* (Hamburg, 1921), pp. 51-56.

THE POKROVSKII-TROTSKY DEBATE OF 1922

Roman Szporluk
University of Michigan

Although the Pokrovskii-Trotsky polemic of 1922 touched upon a broad variety of questions concerning Russia's historical development, its real significance lay in its concern, implied throughout, for the prospects of socialism in Soviet Russia. In the course of the debate, weaknesses became apparent in the historical conception of each of the protagonists. One might argue that the polemic, by undermining the authority of these two leading Marxist theorists, prepared the way for at least some Bolsheviks to accept the Stalinist interpretation of Russia's development and its practical consequences: the doctrine of "socialism in one country" and the rehabilitation of Russian nationalism.

The debate originated with Pokrovskii's summer 1922 review of Trotsky's book *The Year 1905 (1905 god)*. Here, Pokrovskii challenged Trotsky's statement (originally made in 1907 in a journal published abroad) that Russian autocracy, unlike West European monarchies, had grown on a "primitive economic base."[1] According to Trotsky, the Russian state had been forced by intense outside pressure to choose between surrender and the rapid development of its own economic power. Opting for the latter course, it had consumed a disproportionately large share of the nation's resources. The Russian state had successfully introduced industry and technology, but only by severely retarding the growth of the "rising privileged classes." Trotsky further argued that, whereas in the West an equilibrium between the propertied classes and the state had been established, in Russia the social weakness and political insignificance of social classes had produced a self-sufficient (*samodovleiushchuiu*) organization of the bureaucratic state.[2] This and similar statements convinced Pokrovskii that Trotsky had adopted the "supra-class" theory

369

of the state, a concept espoused by Paul Miliukov and other "bourgeois" historians, and thus, in Pokrovskii's view, a graver threat to the revolution than even the Orthodox church.

Pokrovskii pointed out that Trotsky failed to ask which *classes* the autocracy represented. He attacked Trotsky's suggestion that the state stood above the privileged classes, although he noted that at least his rival did not claim that it had been a "social monarchy," a state promoting the welfare of the workers.[3] Pokrovskii also admitted that Trotsky rejected the "banal interpretation" that the defense against "Eastern invaders" had caused the rise of the state. Trotsky instead emphasized the "pressure of Lithuania, Poland, and Sweden," an explanation Pokrovskii found no more convincing than the theory that identified the Tatar threat as the source of Russia's absolutist state.[4]

Pokrovskii noted that while he and Trotsky apparently concurred on "how the proletarian revolution was possible in Russia," they disagreed about the conclusion to be drawn from this: should one speak, in explaining the revolution, about Russia's "backwardness" and "slowness of development," or about her "catastrophically fast growth"?[5]

> The whole key to the secret of the possibility of a proletarian revolution in Russia lies in the solution of this controversy. I will speak, moreover, to the problem of the durability of its results. Is this revolution a new historical turning point [*sdvig*] of the type of Peter's "reform" (which is how the Kadets have found it convenient to debase the revolution of merchant capital) or the reforms . . . of the 1860s, only one immeasurably mightier —but in all respects a turning point after which it is impossible to go back and one is forced to go forward—or is it only a splash in the Russian sand-bank [*otmiel*] of a wave brought to us by a Western tide, but one which does not mark any dividing line in national history? The solution of this controversy depends in nine-tenths on the understanding of Russian historical development in general. Here is where the *practical* significance of our controversies lies—and this is why . . . to destroy *Kadet* fantasies in this matter is no less important than to conduct the struggle against religious superstitions.[6]

Pokrovskii stressed the importance of economic considerations in Russia's struggle for access to the Baltic from the sixteenth to the eighteenth century. A modern army had been needed to fight for trade routes, but Pokrovskii argued that the army had been established not because Russia was backward, but because Russia was a new power competing with well-established powers "for a place in the sun." To achieve this goal, it had been necessary for commercial capital to drain the country by imposing the "iron discipline" of a genuine dictatorship; "Muscovite autocracy was precisely an embodiment of this dictatorship of commercial capital."[7]

Trotsky responded that his original 1907 article had been written to provide historical and theoretical support for the proletariat's conquest of political power, in opposition to both the slogan that called for a "bourgeois-democratic republic" and Lenin's concept of a "democratic government of the proletariat and peasantry."[8] Trotsky conceded that his own position would appear to be a "monstrous departure from Marxism" to those who imagined that Marxism was confined to "historical mechanisms, formal analogies, converting historical epochs into a logical succession of inflexible social categories." However, an empirical appraisal of social forces had convinced Trotsky of the validity of his position. In order to adopt the correct policy, he first had to answer several questions: How could the proletariat of Russia, Europe's most backward country, face the task of capturing power? What was the nature of Russian backwardness? Did it consist merely of Russia's passing, in a rudimentary form, through the stages of Western Europe's historical development? Trotsky's conclusion was that "the indubitable and irrefutable belatedness" of Russia's development, "under influence and pressure from the more advanced culture of the West," had resulted not in "a simple repetition of the West European historical process, but in the creation of profound peculiarities demanding independent study."[9]

Trotsky granted that production was the basis of social life, that society was divided into classes, and that the state had a class character. In all these respects, Russian history was "subject to the same laws" that governed the development of France, England, and all other countries. He added, however, that although tsarism was an instrument of the possessing and exploiting classes, its relationship to them was not exactly the same as the analogous relationships between the West European autocracies and their possessing classes, the nobility and the bourgeoisie. In Trotsky's view it was the peculiarity of this power relationship between the various classes and the Russian state that had made possible the victory of the October Revolution before a proletarian revolution had begun in Europe.[10]

Turning his attention to the rise of the tsarist state, Trotsky observed that Russian history had not developed anything even remotely resembling Western Europe's medieval urban culture with its "craft-guild towns" and the struggle between these industrial centers and the feudal lords. Trotsky argued (in a manner that foreshadowed Stalin's later theory on the "relative independence of the superstructure") that tsarism had emerged as a "relatively independent state organization...not thanks to a struggle of powerful cities with powerful feudal lords, but in spite of the complete industrial feebleness of our towns and thanks to the feebleness of our feudal lords."[11] Russia's large area and sparse population allowed commercial capital to develop on a broad scale, but only so long as the more advanced West sent its goods and merchants to Russia, stimulating the commercial exchange which in Russia had an "extremely primitive, and in a certain measure, barbarian, economic basis."[12] Trotsky continued:

> Russian capitalism did not develop from handicraft through manufactories to factory, because European capital, first commercial capital, and then financial and industrial capital, poured down on us during that period when Russian handicraft had not in the mass separated itself from agriculture. Hence the appearance among us of the most modern capitalist industry in an environment of economic primitiveness: the Belgian or American factory, and round about it country roads, villages of thatch and wood, burning up every year, etc. The most primitive beginnings and the latest European endings. Hence the mighty role of West European capital in Russian economy; hence the political weakness of the Russian bourgeoisie; hence the ease with which we settled accounts with the Russian bourgeoisie; hence our further difficulties when the European bourgeoisie interfered.[13]

When this reply was published, Pokrovskii commented: "These are words under which I sign myself with both hands."[14] According to Pokrovskii, Trotsky's counterattack amounted to a virtual retreat to the orthodox Marxist position. He viewed Trotsky's statement as an admission that the West's pressure on Russia had been primarily economic, and felt that with this Trotsky had moved toward a materialist interpretation of Russian history, abandoning his earlier statement that the Russian national economy had a "natural," self-sufficient character that "guarded it from the influence of higher forms of production." Pokrovskii explained that he himself had previously written something very much like this. Russia represented an exceptionally valuable example, from the methodological point of view, of a country in which a capitalist society had developed rapidly on an unusually backward social-economic foundation. The "superstition" that Russian historical development had been very slow rested on a one-sided perception of the precapitalist period of Russian development. Pokrovskii agreed that owing primarily to geographic conditions, the growth of the surplus product and, along with it, primary accumulation, had proceeded very slowly. But, once Russian capitalism appeared and took advantage of the West's technological and managerial achievements, it had marched forward in "seven-mile shoes." It was producing new forms of economic life and new ideologies with remarkable speed, "until toward the beginning of the twentieth century Russia finally 'caught up' in this respect with Europe."[15]

According to Pokrovskii, this "partial coexistence, on the same territory and side-by-side (*vperemezhku*)," of two stages of capitalist development (commercial and industrial) contributed to the confusion as to exactly what was happening in Russia. In the "purely cultural sphere" this picture was further confused by "another coexistence"—that of the primitive foundation of capitalism with its advanced forms. A primitive peasant cabin stood by the side of a "wonderful model of European architecture," the lord's manor. The simplest methods of handicraft, which could find their counterparts "only in Central Africa or New Guinea," stood next to a factory run by electricity. Pokrovskii continued:

> This coexistence of "the primitives" and "latest word in science and technology" contributed strongly to reinforce the superstition concerning the "backwardness" and "slowness of development" of Russia in comparison to Western countries. . . . This was, on the contrary, one of the signs of the catastrophically fast development of the capitalist Russia which did not experience the

transitional stages characteristic of the older, advanced countries of the West.[16]

Thus, Pokrovskii was satisfied with the reply which, he thought, disclaimed Trotsky's previous viewpoint.[17] But if Trotsky had modified his language, so too had Pokrovskii. Qualifying his earlier statements, he now explained that he had always recognized that Muscovy had had no "Fuggers or Medici" and that Muscovite "primary accumulation" had lagged behind the West's. Pokrovskii emphasized that Muscovy had experienced phenomena analogous to those in the West, even if "in a more primitive form," and that any analysis of the rise of autocracy in Russia must therefore focus on these economic phenomena, rather than on the so-called natural, or self-sufficient character of the Russian economy.[18]

Pokrovskii also admitted that contact with Western Europe had strongly stimulated the development of Russian commercial capitalism. But, had there been no native accumulation before the initiation of contacts with the West, Russia would have become a purely colonial country, not even comparable to India, which did have an accumulation of her own, but to "central Africa." Pokrovskii believed—and identified this belief as one of his "heresies"—that Russia's development was "in its type, that of a colonial country," but he warned against pushing the analogy too far. "After all, Russia did not become a downright colony," as should have happened if Trotsky were right.[19] This statement, Trotsky replied in turn, proved that Pokrovskii's criticisms were misdirected. Trotsky said that he had always regarded Russia as "insufficiently primitive" to become a colony, yet sufficiently backward to require a "monstrous straining of the people's economic forces" for the rise of the state.[20]

It would seem that once the respective positions of Trotsky and Pokrovskii had been clarified and found to be very close if not identical, the debate would have ended. Three years later, however, Pokrovskii again attacked Trotsky, ascribing to him the view that Russian capitalism had been established by absolutism in a "supra-natural" way.[21] The significance of this new attack lies not in its critique of Trotsky's concepts but in its presumably unintentional exposure of the weaknesses of Pokrovskii's own position. Before examining this weakness, it may be useful to note a major flaw in Trotsky's theory of Russian history and world revolution.

Trotsky stressed the "peculiarities" of Russia's historical development, which he explained by reference to what he termed "the law of uneven development." Although these "peculiarities" reflected quite fundamental deviations from Western development, Trotsky refused to see them as a combination of features which might constitute an alternative type of historical development. He attributed the outbreak of the socialist revolution in Russia to these special Russian conditions, but failed to admit that the absence of such conditions in the West might prevent a revolution of the Russian type from breaking out there. In this sense, his "revolution in one country" was logically the antecedent of Stalin's "socialism in one country." Furthermore, since Russia was a backward country, as demonstrated by the survival of serfdom and "feudalism" until the modern age, its brand of socialism would necessarily differ significantly from the ideal upheld by West European Marxists.

To admit all this would have meant writing a death verdict for Trotsky's theory of permanent revolution, and Trotsky did not draw such "Stalinist" conclusions. To reconcile his theory of revolution with his view of Russian history, Trotsky had to insist that the "world economy in its entirety" was ripe for socialism, even if Russia or another country taken separately was not.[22] Trotsky wrote:

> Marxism proceeds from world economy, not as a sum of national parts, but as a mighty, independent reality, which is created by the international division of labor and the world market, and, in the present epoch, predominates over the national markets.[23]

It was from this "unitarian" standpoint[24] that Trotsky attacked Stalin's views on socialist construction in the USSR.[25] His critique of Stalinism was very persuasive, except for one disturbing circumstance: if world economy were indeed a "mighty, independent reality," and if, as Marxism teaches, "being (i.e., reality) determines consciousness," they why did the consciousness of Soviet Communists (surely among the world's most advanced) fail to develop as it was supposed to? Why did Trotsky lose and Stalin win?

In view of this weakness in Trotsky's argument, which staked everything on the worldwide unity of the proletariat, it becomes apparent why Pokrovskii was so insistent that the sociopolitical and economic development of old Russia had been essentially analogous to that of the West. In his later attack on Trotsky, however, he unwittingly modified this position. Pokrovskii launched his new offensive by isolating two features which he said were characteristic of Trotsky's scheme of history: the role of the city, and the role of the state, which in Trotsky's scheme had to "fill in" the vacuum that resulted from the absence of towns. But Pokrovskii questioned whether West European capitalism had really "come from town." Instead of presenting his own case against Trotsky, Pokrovskii quoted Marx at length, presumably intending to refute Trotsky:

> The prelude of the revolution that laid the foundations of the capitalist mode of production, was played in the last third of the fifteenth, and the first decade of the sixteenth century. A mass of free proletarians was hurled on the labour-market by the breaking-up of the bands of feudal retainers, who, as Sir James Steuart well ways, "everywhere uselessly filled house and castle." Although the royal power, itself a product of bourgeois development, in its strife after absolute sovereignty forcibly hastened the dissolution of these bands of retainers, it was by no means the sole cause of it. In insolent conflict with king and parliament, the great feudal lords created an incomparably larger proletariat by the forcible driving of the peasantry from the land, to which the latter had the same feudal right as the lord himself, and by the usurpation of the common lands.[26]

Pokrovskii pointed out that in contrast to Marx, who had recognized the critical role of the feudal lords, Trotsky consistently ignored "everything that extends beyond the limits of the town."[27] To demonstrate Trotsky's departure from Marx's position, Pokrovskii quoted another long passage from *Capital:*

> Although we come across the first beginnings of capitalist productions as early as the fourteenth and fifteenth century, sporadically, in certain towns of the Mediterranean, the capitalistic era dated from the sixteenth century. Wherever it appears, the abolition of serfdom has been long effected, and the highest development of the middle ages, *the existence of sovereign towns, has been long on the wane.*

In the history of primary accumulation, all revolutions are epoch-making that act as levers for the capitalist class in course of formation; but, above all, those moments when great masses of men are suddenly and forcibly torn from their means of subsistence, and hurled as free and "unattached" proletarians on the labour market. *The expropriation of the agricultural producer, of the peasant, from the soil, is the basis of the whole process.* The history of this expropriation, in different countries, assumes different aspects, and runs through its various phases in different orders of succession, and at different periods.[28]

Pokrovskii believed that with these quotes he had proved that from the Marxist viewpoint, his own interpretation was right, and Trotsky's was wrong. In fact Pokrovskii's selection of quotations undermined *his own* position. Marx had identified royal power as a product of bourgeois development, and then spoken about the lords' conflict with king and parliament: surely these developments did not occur in Russia, a point Trotsky had stressed in 1922. Pokrovskii admitted that medieval towns did not achieve the degree of development in Russia which they reached in the West, but he insisted that "*the type* of the old Russian town" was the same as in the West. The Russian town did not evolve fully because "commercial capital, which in Russia developed later than in the West, but which grew faster, killed our urban handicraft in the bud, transforming it into a system of domestic production."[29]

This statement amounted to an admission that the grand prince's or tsar's power was *not* a "product of bourgeois development," and that feudal lords in Russia did not find themselves in conflict with the king and (bourgeois) parliament simply because no such parliament existed.

There was another weakness in Pokrovskii's position: Marx had held that the expropriation of the peasantry was of fundamental importance for the development of capitalism, but in Russia the peasants had not been removed from the land and transformed into free proletarians. Pokrovskii did admit that East European peasants were enserfed at the same time that their Western counterparts were being expropriated, but he seems to have regarded this difference as secondary. He almost casually remarked that "there we have, indeed, a 'peculiarity of historical development'" not only of Russia, but of all Eastern Europe (Prussia, for example):

> This peculiarity was, of course, not indifferent for the *political* development of the affected countries. The unusual intensity and longevity of the Russian autocracy, as well as the fact that in Prussia a real monarchy, not a decorative one like that in England, existed as late as 1918, having survived by over a year even Russian autocracy, is explainable by the interests of that enserfment. Here one could speak of some . . . originality in the historical process; but as Trotsky did not notice precisely this variation, this does not save his theory to any degree.[30]

To declare that the different paths that Eastern and Western Europe followed were mere "variations" with exclusively political consequences was strange indeed. Did Pokrovskii not realize that Marx had stressed expropriation precisely because it converted ex-serfs into propertyless but legally *free* proletarians? If Russia's enslaved peasants became neither free nor proletarian, was this simply a political peculiarity? Pokrovskii must have realized that much more was involved, because he wrote in a footnote: "On the second edition of serfdom which should be distinguished from feudal bondage, see letters of Engels to Marx dated 15 and 16 December 1882."[31] Here is what Engels wrote in one of those letters which Pokrovskii did *not* quote:

> The general re-introduction of serfdom was one of the reasons why no industry could develop in Germany in the seventeenth and eighteenth centuries. . . . In England at this stage migration to the territory outside the guild took place, but in Germany this was prevented by the transformation of the country people and the inhabitants of the agricultural market towns into serfs.[32]

By minimizing the significance of serfdom's longevity in Russia, Pokrovskii was obscuring the crucial difference between "extra-economic" and "economic" coercion, a matter about which he had emphatically agreed with Marx. The problem at hand concerned not only scholars of Russian history, but also the Soviet state apparatus. Pokrovskii commented on the proletarian dictatorship's need to forestall the emergence of peasant capitalism in Russia, and to "train," "place. . . within the frame," and "combine" that peasant economy with the socialist system.

Pokrovskii's interpretation of the peculiarities of Russian history, as outlined in his debate with Trotsky, displays a striking similarity to Evgenii Preobrazhenskii's theory of "primitive socialist accumulation," a theory that Pokrovskii criticized in 1928. In his article Pokrovskii incorrectly attributed to Preobrazhenskii the view that "the only resources the socialist state can get are from the village, that is, only through beginning to exploit the peasantry in a new way." He accused Preobrazhenskii of a lack of faith in socialist construction and in the productive forces of socialist society.[33] Preobrazhenskii had actually argued that "primitive socialist accumulation" had to occur "simultaneously with the beginning of the transition of socialist production and with accumulation in the socialist complex itself."[34] There was in fact no question of getting the "means" only at the expense of the peasantry.

Preobrazhenskii's ideas in fact contradicted neither Pokrovskii's general interpretation of Russian history, nor his view of the Russian Revolution: Russian absolutism, as Pokrovskii had argued, corresponded to the age of primitive accumulation of capital, and this absolutist state managed to survive until 1917 because Russia had not yet become fully modernized. In Pokrovskii's terms, commercial capitalism, along with industrial capitalism, had continued to play an important part in Russia. Having admitted this, as well as the potential danger of a capitalist restoration, Pokrovskii might quite logically have concluded that the proletarian dictatorship had inherited from the old state the role of exploiter of the peasantry, albeit for different purposes.[35] Was Preobrazhenskii recommending anything different from what Pokrovskii had sought when he wanted to "train" and "combine" the peasantry?

It has been suggested that Trotsky resisted Preobrazhenskii's theory of "primitive socialist accumulation" because he sensed that Preobrazhenskii's view was not incompatible with Stalin's theory of "socialism in one country." Indeed, Preobrazhenskii's theory supported the view that "primitive socialist accumulation based on the peasantry represented the royal road for transforming a single, backward country into an industrially developed, socialist one."[36] The same conclusion can, however, be reached from Pokrovskii's assertion that Russia was primitive-capitalist up to the twentieth century, although Pokrovskii himself never explicitly drew this conclusion.

It might also be argued that the following formula derived by Preo-brazhenskii to describe the two historical paths of primary accumulation complements Pokrovskii's own attempt to formulate a theory of non-Western development:

> The celebrated "enclosure movement" [described by Marx] was not the typical method of primary accumulation for all coun-tries. The most typical methods were, first, plundering of the serf peasants by their lords and sharing of the plunder with merchant capital, and, second, crushing taxation of the peasantry by the state and transformation of part of the means so obtained into capital.[37]

Preobrazhenskii's formula resembles precisely Pokrovskii's characterization of the tsarist state as developed in his works on Russian history; Pokrov-skii's interpretation of Russia and its revolution can be seen as the counter-part in historical studies to the theory of "primitive socialist accumulation" in economics.[38]

Even though Pokrovskii firmly opposed Russian nationalism, the appli-cation of the concept of primary socialist accumulation bore certain dis-turbing implications for Russian/non-Russian relations within the USSR. There is no direct basis for drawing such inferences from Pokrovskii's own work, but they become quite clear when one pursues some of Preobrazhen-skii's arguments. When he contrasted the capitalist and socialist varieties of primitive accumulation, Preobrazhenskii declared that *national* exploitation under socialism, unlike capitalism, was out of the question. He nevertheless thought that taxation of "the pre-socialist economic forms" would inevit-ably play "a very great, a directly decisive role in peasant countries such as the Soviet Union."[39] In this way Preobrazhenskii asserted that the peasants would have to pay a large share of the cost of "socialist construction." Thus, although Preobrazhenskii formally rejected national exploitation and the "plundering of colonies" by more "advanced" nations under social-ism, his theory contained a built-in provision for national equality "at home." This was so because under Soviet conditions (and even more so in the eyes of the Moscow bureaucracy, socialist industry—"the socialist sector"—was identical with the Great Russian "centers," whereas the peasantry was largely non-Russian. There were, of course, many Russian peasants, but the non-Russian nationalities consisted, or were thought to consist, chiefly of peasants. The Russian (or Russified) bureaucracy which assumed control over the economy after the revolution tended to favor "the proletarian Center," the "all-state interests," at the expense of the "petty bourgeois" (and coincidentally also non-Russian) "provinces" or "borderlands."

Since the Soviet state in its industrialization policies in fact continued the historical mission of its tsarist predecessor, it was little wonder that under Stalin it soon became aware of, and recognized its affinity with, the state of Peter the Great and Ivan the Terrible. The rehabilitation of Russian history was an element in the ideological reassessment and "rearmament"; Pokrovskii, the "debunker" of tsarism, was found guilty of the "ideological disarmament" of the Russian people. This "transvaluation of values" in the sphere of history was of course never carried to its logical end: the Soviet Union continued to claim it was an "internationalist" state of all workers, and it was recognized as such by many.

Again, Pokrovskii never drew such inferences himself. But neither did he consistently speak about the future with the optimism which was so notable in "The Historical Importance of the October Revolution," the article he wrote for the tenth anniversary of the October coup.[40] On various occasions during the 1920s he warned of dangers which the Soviet regime would continue to face. There was the peasantry, that "peculiar embryo of Russian capitalism," which the Soviet regime needed to keep under control lest it bring a "restoration of capitalist economic relations." He also feared a revival of "defensism" (*oboronchestvo*), an attitude that placed the defence of the native land, and its welfare in general, above the class interests of the proletariat. He identified the highly skilled "technical-managerial intelligentsia," that is, the leading managing and technical personnel of Soviet industry, as the social stratum that might one day attempt to restore the old nationalist outlook, and by implication take over the state by abolishing the dictatorship of the proletariat. If the isolation of the socialist USSR in a capitalist encirclement continued, Pokrovskii feared, the danger of Russia's relapse to "defensism" might become quite real.[41]

Thus, following his own line of reasoning, Pokrovskii arrived at a conclusion that was almost as pessimistic about the prospects of socialism in

Russia as Trotsky's "statist" theory had been. Both Trotsky and Pokrovskii were led by the logic of their respective arguments to practical conclusions that implied one of two things: either "socialism in one country"
would be a socialism very different from what classical Marxism had
anticipated, or the Soviet regime would represent a new political system
that would include nationalism, a Russian statist nationalism,[42] as its
ideological foundation. Both men refused to accept these prospects.

NOTES

1. Pokrovskii's original attack, a review of *1905 god* (1st edition,
Moscow, 1922) appeared under the title "Pravda-li, chto v Rossii absoliu-
tizm 'sushchestvoval naperekor obshchestvennomu razvitiiu'?" *Krasnia
nov.*, no. 3, 1922, 144-51. Trotsky's long reply, "Ob osobennostiakh
istoricheskogo razvitiia Rossii," appeared in *Pravda* on 1 and 2 July 1922.
It was reprinted as an appendix in the second edition of *1905 god* (Moscow,
1922). Subsequently Pokrovskii wrote "Svoeobrazie russkogo istoricheskogo protsessa i pervaia bukva marksizma," *Pravda*, 5 July 1922; Trotsky
replied with an article entitled "Parokhod—ne parokhod, a barzha," *Pravda*,
7 July 1922; and the newspaper polemics ended with Pokrovskii's "Kon-
chaiu," *Pravda*, 13 July 1922. Pokrovskii's articles were reprinted in his
Istoricheskaia nauka i borba klassov (Moscow-Leningrad, 1933), vol. 1.
(Hereafter cited as *Ist. nauka*.) This posthumous edition omits all positive
references to Trotsky, as well as the title "Comrade" before his name,
and particularly the statements that indicate that Pokrovskii agreed with
Trotsky on some matters. In such cases references will be made to the
original articles. For references to the Pokrovskii-Trotsky debate, see
George M. Enteen, *The Soviet Scholar-Bureaucrat: M. N. Pokrovskii and
the Society of Marxist Historians* (University Park and London, 1978), pp.
28, 47-48, and O. D. Sokolov, *M. N. Pokrovskii i sovetskaia istoricheskaia
nauka* (Moscow, 1970), pp. 96-97. Baruch Knei-Paz, *The Social and Political Thought of Leon Trotsky* (Oxford, 1978), pp. 78-80 and passim,
makes extensive use of Trotsky's response to Pokrovskii in the second and
subsequent editions of *1905*, but does not address himself to any of
Pokrovskii's criticisms. For Knei-Paz's analysis of Trotsky's theory of the

state, especially with reference to Russian historical development, see *The Social and Political Thought,* pp. 62-107.

2. "Pravda-li. . . ?" *Ist. nauka,* 1, 133-34.

3. Ibid., pp. 134-35.

4. Ibid., pp. 136-37.

5. *Pravda,* 5 July 1922. (Omitted in *Ist. nauka,* 1, 149.)

6. *Pravda,* 5 July 1922. (Omitted in *Ist. nauka,* 1, 149.)

7. "Pravda-li?" *Ist. nauka,* 1, pp. 136-37, 141-42. Pokrovskii further argued that Muscovy had been a country with a fairly highly developed urban handicrafts and trade: "Precisely the testimonials of the foreigners who first came into contact with that economy, are capable of liquidating the superstition about the 'primitive economic foundation' upon which Muscovite autocracy had allegedly risen. As a matter of fact, the 'foundation' was no more 'primitive' than that on which the autocracy of the last direct descendents of Capet (thirteenth-fourteenth centuries) in France had risen" (Ibid., p. 140n.) Trotsky replied that to admit that the sixteenth-century Russian economy was no less primitive that that of France three hundred years earlier amounted to saying that sixteenth-century Russia was primitive and backward. For Trotsky never denied that Russia of the sixteenth century was more advanced than Russia of the preceding century (*Pravda,* 7 July 1922).

8. L. Trotsky, *1905 god* (2d edition, Moscow, 1922), p. 296, and in an abridged translation as "Appendix I", in *The History of the Russian Revolution* (Ann Arbor, 1957), 1, 464. Trotsky's article appears in full as chap. 27 of the English edition of *1905.* See Leon Trotsky, *1905,* tr. Anya Bostock (New York, 1971), pp. 327-47.

9. *1905 god,* p. 297, and *The History of the Russian Revolution,* 1, 464.

10. *1905 god,* p. 299, (*Hist. of Rus. Rev.,* 1, 465, contains this passage in somewhat abridged form).

11. *1905 god,* p. 303, *Hist. of Rus. Rev.,* p. 468.

12. *1905 god,* p. 301, *Hist. of Rus. Rev.,* p. 466.

13. *1905 god,* p. 304, *Hist. of Rus. Rev.,* p. 468. (I have not here followed the English translation precisely.)

14. *Ist. nauka,* 1, 148. See *Pravda,* 5 July 1922, for other statements indicating Pokrovskii's agreement with Trotsky. They were omitted in *Ist. nauka.*

15. *Ist. nauka,* 1, p. 147.

16. Ibid., pp. 148-49.

17. Ibid., p. 147. Cf. *Pravda,* 5 July 1922.

18. *Ist. nauka,* 1, 151.

19. Ibid., pp. 146-47.

20. *Pravda,* 7 July 1922; *1905 god* (1st edition, Moscow, 1922), p. 16; (2d edition, Moscow, 1922), p. 18. See also Trotsky's reflections on the "Peculiarities of Russia's Development" which form chap. 1 of his *History of the Russian Revolution,* 1, 3-15.

21. M. N. Pokrovskii, "Trotskizm i 'osobennosti istoricheskogo razvitiia Rossii'," *Kommunisticheskii Internatsional,* no. 3, 1925, 21-35; reprinted in *Ist. nauka,* 1, 152-66. Reference is on p. 158.

22. L. Trotsky, *The Permanent Revolution,* tr. Max Eastman (New York, 1931), p. 125.

23. Trotsky, "Introduction to the German Edition," ibid., pp. ix-x, and Leon Trotsky, *The Permanent Revolution and Results and Prospects* (New York, 1969), p. 146.

24. "To his last day," says Deutscher, "Trotsky believed that there was more reality in international communism, despite all its weakness, than in socialism in one country, despite all its achievements." See I. Deutscher, *Stalin,* 2d edition (New York, 1967), p. 393.

25. *The Permanent Revolution,* pp. xi-xii.

26. Karl Marx, *Capital,* 1, 789; "Trotskizm i 'osobennosti,'" *Ist. nauka,* 1, 159.

27. "Trotskizm i 'osobennosti,'" *Ist. nauka,* 1, 160.

28. Marx, *Capital,* 1, 787; *Ist. nauka,* 1, 160-61. (Pokrovskii's italics.)

29. *Ist. nauka,* 1, 156-57.

30. Ibid., p. 161.

31. Ibid., p. 161n.

32. Karl Marx and Friedrich Engels, *Correspondence 1846-1895,* tr. and ed. Dona Torr (New York, n. d.), pp. 407-8.

33. M. N. Pokrovskii, "Obshchestvennye nauki v SSSR za 10 let," *Vestnik kommunisticheskoi academii,* no. 2, 1928, 15.

34. E. Preobrazhenskii, *The New Economics,* tr. Brian Pearce (Oxford, 1965), p. 83; see also p. 84: "By *socialist* accumulation we mean the addition to the functioning means of production of a surplus product which has been created within the constituted socialist economy and

which does not find its way into supplementary distribution among the agents of socialist production and the socialist state, but serves for expanded reproduction. *Primitive socialist* accumulation, on the other hand, means accumulation in the hands of the state of material resources mainly or partly from sources lying outside the complex of state economy. This accumulation must play an extremely important part in a backward peasant country, hastening to a very great extent the arrival of the moment when the technical and scientific reconstruction of the state economy begins and when this economy at last achieves [clear] economic superiority over capitalism."

35.   See Preobrazhenskii, *New Economics,* pp. 232-33, for a statement of his own position: "The more successfully our state economy develops, the more vigorously it draws towards itself all the country's private economy, and the more successfully the process goes forward of subordinating the presocialist economic forms, adapting them to it, and eventually absorbing them into it. Naturally, for Russia this process will be incredibly prolonged and slow; it will take place at different rates and different periods, with breaks, with stoppages, with fresh advances."

36.   Alfred Evenitsky, "Preobrazhensky and the Political Economy of Backwardness," *Science and Society,* 30, no. 1 (Winter 1966), 60.

37.   Preobrazhenskii, *New Economics,* p. 85.

38.   Preobrazhenskii justifiably indicated the proximity of his own ideas to those of Pokrovskii, though he may have done so to associate Pokrovskii's name with his own position. In his article "The Basic Law of Socialist Accumulation" (published in *Vestnik kommunisticheskoi akademii* in 1924, and then as a part of *The New Economics,* his principal work) he referred to Pokrovskii's historical interpretation in the course of his own argument. After quoting Marx on the role of force in economic development during the age of merchant capital, Preobrazhenskii wrote: "The profound class analysis, full of concrete historical truth, to which M. N. Pokrovskii subjected the policy of the Muscovite tsars evokes a clear picture of this aspect of the period under consideration." See ibid., p. 87, and passim. For the original version see E. A. Preobrazhenskii, "Osnovnoi zakon sotsialisticheskogo nakopleniia," *Vestnik kommunisticheskoi akademii,* no. 8, 1924, 47-116.

39.   Preobrazhenskii, *New Economics,* p. 88.

40. "Istoricheskoe znachenie Oktiabr'skoi revoliutsii," *Kommun-isticheskaii revoliutsiia,* no. 20, 1927, 3-13, reprinted with major cuts in *Imperialistskaia voina* (Moscow, 1928), 2d ed., 1931, and in full in *Iz-brannye proizvedeniia* (Moscow, 1965-1967), vol. 4, 92-103. English translation in *Russia in World History,* ed. Roman Szporluk (Ann Arbor, 1970), pp. 203-17.

41. See Roman Szporluk, "Pokrovskii's View of the Russian Revolution," *Slavic Review,* 26, no. 1 (March 1967), 70-84, esp. 83-84.

42. For an attempt to define this type of nationalism in contradistinction from a "culturalist" nationalism, see Roman Szporluk, "History and Russian Ethnocentrism," in Edward Allworth, ed., *Ethnic Russia in the USSR: The Dilemma of Dominance* (New York and Oxford, 1980), pp. 41-54, and, more fully, "History and Russian Nationalism," *Survey,* 24, no. 3 (Summer 1979), 1-17.

FASCIST MYTHMAKING: THE ITALIAN
REGIME'S APPEAL TO YOUTH

Tracy H. Koon
University of Virginia

Political socialization is the process through which the young acquire attitudes, values, and beliefs about their political system. The goal of such socialization is to channel the behavior of the young into socially and politically acceptable forms and to produce loyalty and consensus— to give youth a feeling of belonging and community.[1] Political socialization takes place in all societies but for regimes with totalitarian aspirations it is of crucial importance. Such systems emphasize the total molding of the younger generation and socialization thus becomes indistinguishable from indoctrination: exorcising dangerous ideas and inculcating tenets of the new faith. The desire is not to train citizens to critical thinking but to train new priests for the ruling political cult.

For the Italian Fascists youth was both a propaganda device and a practical concern. The mystique of youth was a favorite propaganda theme in Fascist Italy though Mussolini was not the first to make such an appeal. Mazzini had pinned his hopes for the liberation of the peninsula on Young Italy. The daring and vitality of youth had also been an important element in the rhetoric of the early Italian nationalists and had figured prominently in the oratory of Gabriele D'Annunzio and the Futurists. Under Fascism, however, youth became a veritable obsession. Fascist Italy was depicted (with Corradinian echoes) as a young, virile nation struggling for her rightful heritage against the decadent and decrepit remnants of the great-power era. Fascism, the regime's propaganda repeatedly insisted, would bring a new order based on the spirit and idealism of youth.[2] But the regime was also concerned with youth for practical reasons. Italian young people were vital to the regime's continuity and stability. From among the younger generation the PNF (*Partito Nazionale Fascista*) hoped to find its "second wave" of new recruits.

Once in power the regime turned its attention almost immediately to its youth. One of Mussolini's first cabinet appointments was his nomination of the neo-idealist philosopher and educator Giovanni Gentile, who served as minister of public instruction from 1922 to 1924. Gentile, though much alarmed as the years passed by what he viewed as the progressive disfigurement of his school reform, had produced the philosophical underpinnings of an authoritarian and hierarchical education system —and the ideological justification for the Fascist socialization program.[3] Gentile's "ethical state" was to be realized by "developing new states of mind, new ideas, [by] forming new men and a new spirit."[4] The goal of Fascism was thus to create a new Italian: *l'uomo fascista*.

Mussolini referred to the 1923 legislation as the "most Fascist reform" but Gentile's handiwork was dissected and "retouched" in later years by those who found it lacking in true Fascist spirit.[5] If Gentile's main concern had been the role of the school as an instrument of moral indoctrination and cultural enrichment, his successors were more interested in using the school as an instrument of Fascist indoctrination.

The schools evidently had a critical role to play in the Fascist socialization program, but they were aided in this task by the regime's youth groups and by the youth-oriented media, especially the radio. Fascist youth groups—the *Opera Nazionale Balilla* established in 1926 and (after 1937) the *Gioventù Italiana del Littorio*—emphasized military and physical education, but with their sports activities and outings, members were also treated to large doses of propaganda and frequent political pep talks.[6] Fascist attempts to use the radio as a socialization tool had predictable results in the schools: in 1933 the regime began beaming weekly political broadcasts into Italian classrooms.[7]

In 1928 Ernesto Codignola, an early collaborator of Gentile's, spoke out against the direction of educational policy under the Fascists:

> He who has the illusion of imparting education with parades, demonstrations, with the continual distraction of pupils and teachers from their daily tasks, and worse yet, with the police state inquisition of the shrine of conscience. . .has nothing to do with Fascism.[8]

But by the late twenties both Gentile and Codignola were out of step with the martial cadence of Fascist Italy. By that time parades and oceanic rallies were the order of the day and the "historical climate" Mussolini had vowed to create had become increasingly militaristic and chauvinistic. The goal of education was no longer the Gentilian learn, think, and create but the Fascist "Believe, Obey, Fight." Schools, youth groups, and the media aimed at fulfilling goals forcefully articulated by the Duce:

> These youngsters must be educated in our religious faith. We must give to these young people a feeling of virility, of potency, of conquest; above all, we must inspire them with our faith and light in them the fire of our hopes.[9]

This study will be concerned not with the institutional aspects of Fascist socialization but rather with its rhetorical style and the content of its youth-directed propaganda: how the regime presented itself to Italian youth, what it wanted them to believe. It is impossible, given the limited length of this study, to deal with the entire range of Fascist youth propaganda. This article proposes, therefore, to treat the nature of myth-making in the Fascist state and then to evaluate the regime's specific appeal to youth through an examination of the state textbooks used in Italian elementary schools from 1938 to 1943.

Rhetoric was not mere window dressing in Fascist Italy but an essential function of the regime. Denis Mack Smith has said that Mussolini devoted more time to publicity than to policy.[10] It might rather be said that during the Fascist period, under the watchful eye of the Duce, publicity became policy. Mussolini's greatest talent was his ability to manufacture and communicate myths and slogans to capture the popular imagination. The regime made widespread and constant use of the media and educational institutions to propagate a series of myths that were, by virtue of repetition, probably more real to most Italians than the somewhat fuzzy musings of Fascism's purported ideologues. Mussolini, polemical journalist par excellence, was well aware of the power of the word. Much of his time each day was spent tending his public image: poring over foreign and domestic newspapers, writing articles, and composing the daily *veline*, or instructions, to the press which regulated in minute detail what could and could not be printed, what should be given great play, and what should be totally ignored in Italian papers.[11] The Duce sought to impose a certain linguistic style and the use of certain oratorical models, and an army of Fascist journalists and spokesmen took care to imitate Mussolinian rhetorical devices: the use of short, concise, affirmative (and often aggressive) phrases to communicate the regime's key propaganda themes.[12]

Mussolini was convinced that the masses would accept almost anything provided the appeal were clothed in the proper rhetorical garb. For him language was instrumental, a tool to mold opinion and organize consensus. Words were not passive but action-oriented. The function of Fascist rhetoric was, therefore, not really to communicate ideas or present coherent arguments but to elicit certain reactions: loyalty, belief, faith. Mussolini's use of what he termed action-words was an expression of his conviction that language had a magical power. "And why do I insist on proclaiming that October was historically a revolution?" he asked on one occasion. "Because words have their own tremendous magic."[13]

In his emphasis on the political potential of language Mussolini was much influenced by Gustave Le Bon and Georges Sorel, both of whom had suggested ways in which leaders might exploit the irrationalism of the masses to serve their own ends. In Le Bon's study of the crowd (which Mussolini claimed he had read with great interest) *les grands meneurs des foules* were able to harness and control the instinctual side of human nature and to tame the crowd by the use of "magic": myths that would have powerful mass appeal and provide the social cohesion and faith the leaders were seeking.[14] For Sorel, as well, a political appeal based on an evocative myth was not a rational and logical program but an incitement, a spur to action, a vital moving force of the masses.[15] As early as 1922, the Duce indicated his belief in the power of these political fictions. "Only myth," he said, "can give strength and energy to a people about to hammer out its own destiny."[16]

Also important influences on the development of Mussolini's particular notions of politics were Gaetano Mosca and Vilfredo Pareto. Both emphasized the role of belief systems in the political process: for Pareto individual or group decisions were governed by "non-logical fictions" while Mosca insisted on the importance of "political formulae."[17] The function of myth in both cases was to legitimize the claims of the political elite that was the real center of social control. The two necessary elements in the political life of a nation were, thus, some vivifying myths capable of mobilizing the masses and a ruling elite in whose service the myths were to be propagated.

Given the importance attached to the socialization of youth, it is logical that the Fascist regime placed special emphasis on the selection and propagation of myths certain to appeal to young people. In July 1931 Carlo Scorza, then secretary of the university Fascist groups (GUF), wrote a letter to Mussolini in which he pointed out that the youth of Italy, deprived of the heady experiences of war and revolution, needed such myths. "It is necessary," he said, "to give a Myth to youth, because youth needs to believe blindly in something."[18] These myths were supposed to produce a sense of identification with the symbols of party and nation, depriving the young of their own identity and forging a bond to the hero-leader and the group. Young people were to merge with the community, but only at the cost of eliminating their own critical faculties and replacing their personal judgments with ready-made answers and unreal stereotypes.

The state textbooks introduced in the first through fifth grades are perhaps the best sources for a detailed investigation of the process by which the regime propagated its key myths among the young. First used in 1930-31, these books were chosen by a ministerial commission delegated to see that they were "pedagogically sound and imbued with the true Fascist spirit."[19] The texts were revised on several occasions, primarily to bring them into line with the imperial theme and the racial policies of the late thirties. These *libri unici,* as they were called, included a primer and a religion text (approved by an ecclesiastical commission) for the first two grades. Combined texts on history, geography, arithmetic, and science were added for the three higher grades.[20] The first-grade texts concentrated primarily on phonics, but in textbooks for the four higher grades, there was a marked increase in the amount of space devoted to the Fascist regime, its achievements, and national themes. Children reading these textbooks were to be left with one overriding impression of incalculable propaganda value: the world revolves around Italy and Italy, in turn, revolves around Benito Mussolini and the Fascist Party.

The kernel of Fascist mythmaking for the young was undoubtedly this identification of the regime, symbolized by the *capo,* with the nation. Fascist propaganda unrelentingly hammered home the equations: love of country = faith in Fascism, fatherland = regime, Mussolini = Italy. Children sat in classrooms adorned with portraits of the King and Duce. and in their textbooks constantly contemplated a confusion of national and party symbols. The royal flag was intertwined with Fascist banners, and the national tricolors and black (for the ubiquitous Fascist uniforms) illustrated all stories. However revolutionary its propaganda, Italy under Fascism remained a dyarchy; the Fascist regime portrayed itself not as the destroyer of monarchial tradition but as the guarantor of national continuity. The texts made this central point very clearly: Fascists were Italians—the best Italians—and dedicated to the greatness of the nation against all who would threaten or deny it.

Deification of the leader in Fascist Italy did not take place overnight, but the transformation of Mussolini the Fascist into Mussolini the DUCE, the infallible political genius, was the main task of the regime's propaganda machinery. Textbooks and scores of books and pamphlets for the young emphasized the deprivations of Mussolini's early life, his humble beginnings as a man of the people, his simplicity and abstemious character. Perhaps the most important aspect of this myth was the constant emphasis on the Duce's physical courage and virility. Young Italians read again and again about his bravery and suffering during the war (though not about his flight to Switzerland to avoid military service) and the almost mystical effect he had on his men. By 1931, when the zealous *diciannovista* Achille Starace took over as secretary of the PNF, the ritualization of the charisma of the Duce had been a full-time business. Fascist authors outdid themselves in searching for the most appropriate adjectives: he (or rather He) was referred to variously as "the magnificent Duce," "the sublime Duce," or even as "the divine Duce." A flood of books was published analyzing the deep religious and philosophical significance of his thought. One of these, designed obviously to conjure up religious associations, was entitled *Imitazione di Mussolini.*[21] The hagiographic *Vita di Mussolini* by Giorgio Pini was distributed gratis to all students, and teachers were required to use the book in lessons. As Fascist cultural autarchy got into full swing, foreign authors were deleted from the school reading lists (so naturally were anti-Fascists such as Benedetto Croce and Jewish authors of the late 1930s) and replaced by readings from Mussolini. Special editions of his speeches were published and soon became compulsory reading in the schools.[22] After 1936 the Duce's

Dottrina del Fascismo, considered the apex of studies on philosophy and history, became required fare in all secondary schools.[23] The standard grammar book, *La grammatica degli italiani* by Ciro Trabalza and Ettore Allodoli, used Mussolini's speeches to illustrate points of grammar in addition to selections by more traditional authors such as Dante, Manzoni, and Machiavelli.[24]

The identification of the regime/leader and nation can be illustrated in a story from a first-grade primer. A grandmother is telling a group of fascinated children the life story of Mussolini; she ends her enthralling tale by saying:

> He loved his Fatherland ever more and wanted to make it strong-
> er and more powerful than all other lands . . . and because of his
> work Italy is strong and powerful. All good Italians love him and
> repeat his blessed name.[25]

In the second-grade reader *L'italiano nuovo,* Mussolini is depicted as a miracle worker. In a story called "The Yes of the Deafmute" we see little Giuliano immersed in a crowd cheering the Duce. He wants more than anything else to be able to call out in reply to the leader's questions. In the end, his eyes brimming with tears, he shouts "Yes! Du-ce! Du-ce!" The story concludes: "A star is watching from the heavens. It is the eye of God."[26]

A recurrent theme in these state textbooks was that of Mussolini as the savior of the nation. One second-grade reader begins the tale by saying that Italy was being ravaged by wolves, by "evil men who wanted to ruin the Fatherland." To save the day, "one Man rose up and put himself at the head of an army of courageous young men" who under-took a "glorious march during which the evildoers hid trembling with fear."[27] In another version of the same story, entitled "23 March 1919," Mussolini wages "war, war without pity on the sad betrayers of the Father-land," making "every sacrifice so that Italy may have her just place in the world." In the conclusion, "the squads become legions. The black stream, vigorous and cleansing, floods all the districts of Italy." The revolution is on the march.

In the same third-grade reader Mussolini is again portrayed as the far-seeing revolutionary. He is shown sitting at his desk at the *Popolo d'Italia,* his face

> lit by a superior intelligence and a great and passionate soul
> . . . . He sees the devotion of Italy: deserted fields, shuttered
> factories, public services in disorder. . . thefts and lootings
> . . . . He sees the Flag, bathed in the blood of martyrs, tram-
> pled. No, no! It must be saved. . . at all costs. And so he begins
> to write. . . words of warning to all Italians. . . to wake them
> to love for their outraged Mother.[28]

Even arithmetic could be made to serve the Mussolini myth. Third graders learned their numbers, for example, by writing: "The Duce proclaimed the Empire after 174 days of economic siege by 52 states against Italy."[29]

Mussolini was well aware that cultivation of his image and myth was of great value to his movement and for a time his propaganda had its desired effects. Ugoberto Alfassio Grimaldi, educated in the Fascist school system and later an outspoken anti-Fascist, commented on this almost physical bond between Mussolini and the young:

> Mussolini. . . was for all of us born in the Fascist climate an
> exceptional personality at whose altar we burned at least a bit
> of our youth. We never saw him as just any mortal. . . when
> we reached the conscious life he had already been *duce* for a
> while, a man infinitely higher than the others. The same criti-
> cisms of Fascism which we heard . . . and did not have difficulty
> sharing were criticisms of the men who surrounded him or of
> the altering of his ideas by others, very rarely of him or of his ideas.
> Of the various dogmas with which we had to break to get out
> from under Fascism, that of the infallibility of the *duce* was
> certainly the most resistant.[30]

The myth of Rome, or what De Felice calls the "myth of *Romanità*," also played an essential role in Fascist socialization of youth. Evocations of Roman imperial glories have been common rallying calls during many epochs of Italian history. Mazzini, Corradini, Oriani, Marinetti, D'Annunzio—these and many others have made the imperial past a potent rhetorical theme. But Mussolini and his followers were truly intoxicated by the heady fumes of Rome. In April 1922 Mussolini said: "Rome is our jumping-off point and our point of reference: it is our symbol or, if you will, our myth."[31] In his autobiography, he exclaimed: "I am desperately Italian! I believe in the function of Latinity."[32]

The "function" of this Roman myth was its appeal to wide segments of the Italian populace, especially to youth. The burden of Fascist propaganda in this context was to identify Fascism, and particularly its *capo*, with the glories of the past, to resurrect the greatness of the Empire in the new Caesar. Fascist Italy was frequently described as the Third Rome: "After the Rome of the Caesars, after that of the Popes, today there is a Rome, the Fascist Rome which . . . commands anew the admiration of the world."[33] Fascism thus represented a continuity, a fulfillment of the greatness of the past and a promise of greatness in the future. This unification of past, present, and future is clearly seen in one speech by Mussolini to the Fascist Militia: "Hail Goddess Roma! Hail for those who were, those who are, and who will be your sons ready to suffer and die for your power and your glory!"[34]

Obsession with the "function" of *Romanità* reached epic proportions during the tenure of Starace as Fascist Party Secretary. He insisted on the adoption of the virile Roman straight-armed salute, and the *passo romano* (suspiciously akin to the goose step) became the obligatory marching step of the Fascist troops. The Fascist lictor rods (symbolizing unity and strength) were a recurrent symbol: after 1937 the regime's youth group, for example, was called *Gioventù Italiana del Littorio,* and annual university competitions were known as *Littoriali.* Children were organized into paramilitary formations bearing Roman designations: maniples, cohorts, legions, centuria. Fascist fauna even served the myth; the Roman eagle was an ever-present symbol and the legendary she-wolf gave her name to the regime's groups for younger children, the *figli della lupa.* Socialist-tinged May Day celebrations were replaced by a new national holiday, the birthday of Rome celebrated on 21 April.

The young were, in fact, subjected to doses of the Roman myth more frequently than any other sector of the populace. In 1935 the minister of national education, Cesare Maria De Vecchi, whose reforms of the school have been referred to as "the expression in the field of education of the imperialist phase of Fascist policy," wrote in the ministry yearbook that "the destiny of Rome is a perennially imperial destiny. Rome is alive with all its wisdom, and all its power in the heart of the Italian school and culture."[35] From their earliest days in the schools and youth groups, the children were barraged with stirring justifications of Italian claims to *mare nostrum* and the *terre irredente*. Repeatedly, the regime's propaganda underlined the connections between Italy's Roman past, its Fascist present, and the imperial future.

In a training manual for ten-year old boys, the Roman myth was sold in dramatic terms:

> If you listen carefully. . .you may still hear the terrible tread of the Roman legions. . . .Caesar has come to life again in the Duce; he rides at the head of numberless cohorts, treading down all cowardice and all impurities to reestablish the culture and the new might of Rome. Step into the ranks of the army and be the best soldiers.[36]

Yet another manifestation of the imperial myth, here linked explicity with Mussolini's person, is this lyrical paean quoted from a fourth-grade textbook. Like Caesar, the children were told:

> [The Duce] has marched on Rome, not to sack or punish it, but to liberate it from incapable leaders. He, too, like Caesar had put an end to party struggles. He too has thought only of his people . . . .He too has conquered the world, breaking the siege of fifty-two nations and winning the war against a slave-trading empire . . . .He sees. . .whole regions to be colonized, countries waiting for law, people who want to work. He wants to see justice done, injustice set right. He sees there are wounds to heal, sadness to console, treason to punish and heroism to exalt.[37]

By the late thirties racial themes were also included in these state textbooks. Italians were descended, it was said, from the pure Italic race best exemplified by the ancient Romans. Schoolbooks mirrored this racial concern, particularly in the growing number of stories about Italy's civilizing mission in Ethiopia. One of the most interesting, and least subtle, is "The White Soul of Black John," a story in a second-grade reader. In this tale a missionary has returned from Africa with a young boy who is, as the priest explains black outside but white inside . . . he loves Italy which has taught him to know the lord. When he came to the missions he was little more than a beast: he went about nude and ate raw meat. Now he reads, writes, and wants to become a missionary like me to help his black brothers find their white souls.[38]

A different approach is evident in a geography book used by fifth graders:

The white race is the most civilized, that is the most capable of great ideas; to this group the Italic race belongs. The laws of Fascism forbid the citizens of the Italic race from contracting marriages with individuals of the colored race and with Jews; but aside from being prohibited by law it must also be forbidden by our own *amour-propre.*[39]

By the 1930s all school curricula, but most especially those at the elementary level, reflected the increasing chauvinism and militarism of PNF policies. Although virtually every subject taught at the elementary level had Fascism injected in one way or another, history and geography were the most deeply influenced by Fascist themes. Voltaire once said that history is a series of accumulated imaginative inventions and this certainly applies to the textbooks of the Fascist period. Teachers were urged to make the new spirit of imperial Italy the chief focal point of their history lessons so that all children might feel the pride of being "born between the Alps and the sea, on this soil bathed by so much blood, sanctified by so many martyrs, made powerful by His great genius."[40] Italy was the cradle of civilization (the contributions of the Greeks were almost ignored) and the conqueror of the Western world. The nineteenth century was usually taught as a mere prelude to the glories of Fascism, which had at last fulfilled the betrayed promise of the *Risorgimento.* Italian children were first introduced to history lessons in the third grade. Their introduction began:

The Italy of today has only one King Emperor Vittorio Emanuele III and only one government, the National Fascist government. The forty-five million Italians are one people—hardworking, frugal, disciplined—who, under the guidance of the DUCE, Benito

Mussolini, march on as one toward their secure future of glory and power. But it was not always like this.[41]

Given Mussolini's imperial preoccupations, it is not surprising that an emphasis on the beauty and social value of war constituted another major theme of this youth-oriented propaganda. In 1935 Mussolini said: "War alone brings up to its highest tension all human energy and puts the stamp of nobility upon the peoples who have the courage to meet it."[42] Instead of being viewed as an abnormality or a tragic necessity, war in Fascist propaganda became life's great test. The very name of the early movement, the *Fasci italiani di combattimento,* conjured up visions, albeit highly romanticized, of the heroism of the trenches and the camaraderie of the Great War. Mussolini clearly understood the importance of the war experience as a propaganda tool. His postwar appeals to the young men who represented the "aristocracy of the trenches" and the "nation in arms" found a ready audience. The first *squadristi* were really only demobilized versions of the *arditi*, the daredevil commandos of the World War. Adrift and without direction after the war, many of these young militants volunteered to serve with D'Annunzio in Fiume and many were present at the founding of the *Fasci* in 1919. They traded in their government issue weapons for the *santo manganello* and castor oil; they flaunted their motto *Me ne frego;* the *arditismo* of the war became the *squadrismo* of the first Fascist gangs.

The concern with militarism is clear in almost every story in the regime's textbooks. In these books the young children ardently desire one thing above all: to put on their uniforms and march around preparing for the day when they would become real soldiers in the Duce's army. They are fascinated by the strength and power of the Black Shirts and mesmerized by tales of the derring-do of the Fascist legions in Ethiopa, Spain, and Albania. Nationalism becomes chauvinism in these texts, especially in the frequent discussions of the African War, which is referred to repeatedly as "the war Italy was forced to fight." The Abyssinians are portrayed as bloodthirsty barbarians, and the highlight of such stories is always the bravery of the Italians who rally around their Duce in iron-willed opposition to the perfidy of the "fifty-two sanctionist nations." In one such story, the British and French are condemned for having forgotten "the generous Italian blood spilled for them; once again they forgot that the World War had been won, above all, by Italy." But the Italians will prevail, third graders are told, because "Italy is an immense legion on the march which no one can stop."[43]

In the second-grade text published in 1942, militarism and war take center stage. And so we read:

—For others the Mediterranean is a road, for us it is life.
—To die for the Fatherland is to live for glory.
—He who wears the Black Shirt wears a military uniform.
—Blessed are they who die for the Fatherland for theirs is the kingdom of heaven.[44]

The pervasive militarism of the regime's propaganda had one interesting corollary: the use of overtly sexual imagery to emphasize the virility and heroism essential to the Fascist soldier. The dashing Duce appeared in a succession of fast cars, airplanes, and motorcycles; he was photographed barechested skiing, reaping grain, draining the marshes. Photos of Mussolini jumping powerful horses, fencing, taming a lioness, and doing a thousand-and-one dangerous and manly things became familiar to all Italians.

The exaggerated machismo of this propaganda reflected Mussolini's oft-repeated conviction that war was a man's affair, as central to the male's life as "maternity is to a woman."[45] Mussolini's resolutely traditional attitude toward women was translated into educational policy, and it was made clear that women would be accorded the same secondary role in the schools and youth groups which they played in society at large. Mussolini specifically ridiculed the notion of giving women the vote and extolled the virtues of the ideal Fascist woman, who was ample-bosomed, wide-hipped, and apple-cheeked—a young, healthy specimen valued for her procreative capacities and not her brain.[46] As one Fascist commentator put it, a girl should be educated "according to the Italian traditions of femininity and sweetness, keeping in mind that she is destined primarily to become the queen of the domestic hearth, soul of the healthy Italian family, on whom the regime counts for the fortunes of the race."[47] Education for girls, therefore, was clearly to serve a purpose different from that for boys. It was not to arouse "silly notions of knowledge, but to guide the students to become good wives and mothers."[48] It was to train not brave citizen-soldiers but prolific citizen-mothers.

Yet another propaganda theme favored by the regime was the identification of Fascism with religion and the constant use of religious-oriented language and symbols. Portrayed in this context, the party acquired a chiliastic character; it was a cult with its own priests, its own liturgy, and its own body of inviolable truths. Fascist rhetoric was replete with words that conveyed some religious meaning: martyr, redemption, sacrifice, mission, rite, faith, commandment. Ceremonies, festivals, and parades —the liturgical expressions of this secular religion—were exploited to draw the young into worship of the nation. Mussolini's many orchestrated speeches were a type of religious communion between leader and people which replaced the mediating institutions of democratic governments with a personal bond. The Duce behaved not as a political leader communicating with his citizens, but as a charismatic leader with his faithful following. His calculated use of rhetorical questions in speeches (a practice borrowed from D'Annunzio) was intended to elicit ritual responses from the crowd: "To whom the future? To whom Italy? . . . To us! Eia, eia, alalà!"

One example from the state texts will suffice to illustrate the party/ regime's attempt to win support among the young by playing on religious themes. The most popular fifth-grade reader was *Il balilla Vittorio* by Roberto Forges Davanzati. Millions of Italian children read with fascination about Vittorio's adventures: his meeting with Mussolini, his trip to the new Fascist-built cities, his enthusiasm for the Ethiopian War. In one scene Vittorio goes with his uncle to Assisi where he meets a Franciscan monk whose monastery has just been returned by order of the Duce. The story takes pains to show the close relationship between party and church. Vittorio is told by the friar: "We Franciscans pray every day for the Duce's well-being which is, after all, the well-being of Italy." He compares the words of the Duce to those of God and adds that Italians are of a new order "which is Fascism, of a new Italy which after centuries of slavery . . . is today the Italy of the Italians."[49]

This identification of Fascism with religion is presented in an incredibly unsubtle manner in one of the regime's youth-group training manuals:

> Fascism, O *Balilla,* is a second religion which demands from the young and the old good and just things like the Christian religion does. . . Fascism is a Faith which commands the love . . .

of this great and glorious Fatherland which God has given us
. . . the nation which in every age has taught civilization to all
others. . . . Fascism is a blessing of God sent to our Fatherland
so that it will be ever more powerful.[50]

Those who point to Fascism's lack of ideological consistency as one of
its failures overlook the fact that, at least for a time, it was the dynamic
aspects of Fascism which were most attractive to the young. Fascism did
not claim doctrinal coherence but it did claim therapeutic value. For many
young Italians the essence of Fascism was in the myths that they heard
repeated all around them: in the frenzy of reconstruction, the new cities,
social programs for the poor, land reclamation and public works, waving
fields of grain—all of these linked to Mussolini who was (or so it seemed)
determined to see that Italy looked forward and not backward. For the
young educated in the new style, Fascism was enthusiasm, building, cooperation in the grand plan for the future. It seemed to open a world of
struggles, passions, and idealism which exerted a powerful pull on many.
Davide Lajolo, active after the fall of the regime in the PCI, expressed
this youthful response to the rhetoric of the regime:

They put a fez on our heads and they told us tales of *Balilla*
. . . they spoke to us of glory, of justice, of the greatness of the
Fatherland. We heard no other voices. We had to make Italy a
great country. Get rid of the rich, do away with the cowards
. . . go to the people. With a lively will to do, to battle . . . how
could we not listen to those calls? What youth with blood in his
veins does not love to see justice where there is injustice, who
does not feel love for his country, who does not feel himself
shiver with pride if he is called to make history? These great,
immense words: history, fatherland, justice—they filled us with
enthusiasm.[51]

Many of the young did not realize for some time that they were Fascist only inasmuch as they believed Fascism to be something other than
it was. It was in this context that the fundamental contradictions of
Fascism, and the delusions of the young, began to emerge. To attract
the young the Fascists had used the lure of real social change and promises

of participation by the younger generations in the ongoing revolution. But the social change promised by the regime was in profound contrast to a set of goals that were in reality reactionary: preservation of the existing social and economic system and demobilization of the lower classes. When it became clear that the future was not going to fulfill their hopes, many young Italians began what Ruggero Zangrandi has called the "long journey through Fascism" to the other side.[52] For some that meant only passive resistance or psychological distance; for others it meant open resistance outside and against the regime.

External events also served to belie the Fascist myths. The great enthusiasm of the Ethiopian War—the epoch of *il bel fascismo* as Zangrandi called it—had made many believe that Italy was finally a great military power, the Italy of *otto milioni di baionette.* But it also had some serious long-term effects that we have seen illustrated in the state textbooks. It established an unbridgeable distance between regime and people, putting Mussolini on a pedestal by camouflaging the reality of the situation behind the myth of the Duce and the imperial destiny of Italy. By the end of that war the panorama was complete: Italy was supposed to be a powerful military nation, but in fact it was being run by a regime and party ever more characterized by obtuse Staracian conformity, ever more reliant on exterior manifestations of might and power to cover up basic weakness and corruption. An enormous propaganda machine constructed dreams of universal empire bit by bit out of words and illusions. The contrast between reality and rhetoric, between what seemed to be and what was, began to be striking—and obvious to an ever-growing number of Italians, both young and old.

World War II made the breach a chasm. Fascist mythmaking aside, the regime had not produced its new warrior caste. It could not make many young men fight in a war for which they were unprepared, for an alliance that they scorned. The war turned myths to dust as the moral and political bankruptcy of the regime was displayed for all to see. Mussolini, it appeared, was not always right. The reforming zeal that myth and propaganda had tried to portray as one of the chief virtues of Fascism degenerated into facile platitudes as the defeats multiplied and the promised greatness failed to materialize. In the end it was clear that many young men called up to fight simply did not believe any longer. The regime branded these young men traitors for refusing to accept Nazi domination and useless carnage, but, in the words of one contemporary:

Those young men betrayed nothing and no one. The truth is that, faced with the naked reality, they realized that no voice inside spoke to them seriously. Those presumed ideals. . . by which they had believed themselves dominated were not ideals clarified and meditated upon in the intimacy of their consciences . . . but rather words repeated because they had been heard so often, names without objects. For those they could not die.[53]

Carlo Scorza, the last secretary of the PNF, was appointed in April 1943. His reaction to that appointment indicated the desperate situation of party and regime. "I feel," he said, "as if I've been called to the bedside of a dying man."[54] In a letter to Mussolini dated 7 June 1943, Scorza analyzed the ills and failures of the party. Of the youth he said:

The youth have a somewhat limited belief in Fascsim for various reasons by now well known. But the vast majority of the young can be recaptured as soon (only a few months more, Duce!) as we have changed the climate of the party.[55]

In another letter dated 23 June 1943 Scorza was even more adamant on the subject of the young: "We will win the young back only if we convince them that we can renew ourselves and keep faith with the principles of the Revolution."[56] Scorza was quite correct about the defection of the young from Fascism but he was overly optimistic about the ability of the regime to renew itself and to win back its younger generations. The climate of the party was not to change. The myth of the Duce's infallibility no longer struck a responsive chord; it could no longer serve to keep a seriously flawed system from cracking apart under the strain.

In his unguarded moments Mussolini himself realized that all the propaganda and publicity had produced little in the way of a lasting influence on the Italians whom "a tenacious therapy of twenty years had succeeded in modifying only superficially."[57]

After twenty years the new political elite trained under Fascism should have been stepping onto center stage. But no such "second wave" ever materialized. The tools used by the Fascists in their attempt to socialize the youth of Italy proved inadequate to the task. The myths, used at first with such effect by the regime's propaganda machine, no longer sufficed to mask the less-than-glorious reality of Italy under Fascism. The PNF failed to mass-produce its new Fascist man. The program to socialize and indoctrinate Italian youth had called for an immense outlay of financial and human resources, but the party never reaped the intended benefits of this expenditure and effort. The long journey was complete for many young Italians when they realized that Fascism had given them nothing to believe in, no one to obey, and nothing for which to fight. In that sense, the events of 25 July 1943 were anticlimactic.

NOTES

1.   The theory of political socialization has been discussed by many social scientists. See for example: Herbert H. Hyman, *Political Socialization* (New York: Free Press, 1959); Robert LeVine, "Political Socialization and Culture Change," *Old Societies and New States,* ed. Clifford Geertz (Glencoe, N.Y.: Free Press, 1963); Robert D. Hess and Judith V. Torney, *The Development of Political Attitudes in Children* (Chicago: Aldine Publishing Co., 1967); David Easton and Robert D. Hess, "Youth and the Political System," *Culture and Social Character: The Work of David Riesman Reviewed,* eds. Seymour Martin Lipset and Leo Lowenthal (Glencoe, N.Y.: Free Press, 1961); Richard E. Dawson and Kenneth Prewitt, *Political Socialization* (Boston: Little, Brown and Co., 1969). For cross-cultural studies of political socialization see: Urie Bronfenbrenner, *Two Worlds of Childhood: U.S. and U.S.S.R.* (New York: Russell Sage Foundation, 1970) and James S. Coleman, *Education and Political Development* (Princeton, N.J.: Princeton University Press, 1965), pp. 225-72.

2.   The question of the political role of youth under Fascism became a familiar theme in the Fascist press in the 1930s, especially in the pages of Giuseppe Bottai's journal *Critica Fascista.* For a recent treatment of the question, and Bottai's role in the debate, see: Luisa Mangoni, *L'interventismo della cultura: Intellettuali e riviste del fascismo* (Rome: Laterza, 1974), pp. 197-205.

3.   Until his death in 1944 Gentile remained personally loyal to Mussolini though he frequently expressed his disillusion with the "retouchings" of his reform. See, for example, his letter to Mussolini dated

4 August 1927 in the Archivio Centrale dello Stato, *Segretaria Particolare del Duce, Carteggio Riservato*, Busta 7/R, Sottofascicolo 6.

4.   Giovanni Gentile, *Che cosa è il fascismo* (Florence: Vallecchi, 1925), p. 38.

5.   The literature on the Gentile reform and subsequent reforms of education under Fascism is vast. Several especially valuable works should be mentioned, however: Merritt Moore Thompson, *The Educational Philosophy of Giovanni Gentile* (Los Angeles: USC Press, 1934); H. S. Harris, *The Social Philosophy of Giovanni Gentile* (Urbana: University of Illinois Press, 1966); Lamberto Borghi, *Educazione e autorità nell'Italia moderna* (Florence: La Nuova Italia, 1951); Luigi Minio-Paluello, *Education in Fascist Italy* (London: Oxford University Press, 1946); Sotto-commissione dell'Educazione della Commissione Alleata in Italia, *La politica e la legislazione scolastica in Italia dal 1922 al 1943* (Rome: Garzanti, 1946). Two more recent studies on the question are: Teresa Maria Mazzatosta, *Il regime fascista tra educazione e propaganda 1935-1943* (Bologna: Cappelli Editore, 1978) and Giorgio Canestri and Giuseppe Ricuperati, *La scuola in Italia dalla legge Casati a oggi* (Turin: Loescher Editore, 1976).

6.   The major provisions regarding the development of the ONB until 1937 can be found in Archivio Centrale dello Stato, *Presidenza del Consiglio dei Ministri, Gabinetto, Atti, (1931-1933),* Fasc. 1.1.15, No. 3500, Sottofasc. 1-11. On the youth groups see also: Pietro Caporilli, *L'educazione giovanile nello stato fascista* (Rome: Edizioni Sapientia, 1930); Renato Marzolo, *L'Opera balilla e la leva fascista* (Rome: Reale Accademia die Lincei, 1937); D. S. Piccoli, *Le organizzazioni giovanili in Italia* (Rome: Novissima, 1936); Partito Nazionale Fascista, *Venti anni* (Rome, 1942).

7.   On the use of the radio in Fascist education see: Alessandro Galante Garrone, "L'aedo senza fili," *Il Ponte* 8 (October 1952): 1401-24 and in the same issue of that journal, Marcella Olschki, "Ricordi di scuola," pp. 1485-93. Three more detailed studies on the same topic are: Franco Monteleone, *La radio italiana nel periodo fascista: Studio e documenti, 1922-1945* (Venice: Marsilio Editore, 1976); Antonia Papa, *Storia politica della radio in Italia,* 2 vols. (Naples: Guida Editore, 1978); Alberto Monticone, *Il fascismo al microfono: Radio e politica in Italia, 1924-1945* (Rome: Edizioni Studium, 1978).

8.   Quoted in Renzo De Felice, *Mussolini il duce: Gli anni del consenso, 1929-1936* (Turin: Einaudi, 1974), p. 188.

9.   G. B. Marziali, *I giovani di Mussolini* (Palermo: Trimarchi, 1935), pp. 17-18.

10.   Denis Mack Smith, "Mussolini, Artist in Propaganda: The Downfall of Fascism," *History Today* 9 (April 1959), 224.

11.   For compilations and comments on these daily *veline* see: Francesco Flora, *Stampa dell'era fascista: Le note di servizio* (Rome: Mondadori, 1945) and Claudio Matteini, *Ordini alla stampa* (Rome: Editrice Polilibraria Italiana, 1945).

12.   There is currently a great deal of scholarly interest in the rhetorical and linguistic aspects of Fascsim. See especially: Augusto Simonini, *Il linguaggio di Mussolini* (Milan: Bompiani, 1978) and Erasmo Leso, Michele A. Cortelazzo, et. al., *La lingua italiana e il fascismo* (Bologna: Consorzio Provinciale Pubblica Lettura, 1978).

13.   Benito Mussolini, *Opera Omnia*, eds. Edoardo Susmel and Duilio Susmel, 36 vols. (Florence: La Fenice, 1951-63), 20:207.

14.   Gustave Le Bon, *The Crowd: A Study of the Popular Mind* (London, Ernest Benn, Ltd., 1930), pp. 47-48, 163.

15.   For a discussion of the influence of Sorel on Mussolini see: Jack J. Roth, "The Roots of Italian Fascism: Sorel and Sorelismo," *Journal of Modern History* 39 (March 1967), 30-45.

16.   A. Gatti, "Abbozzo per un ritratto di B. Mussolini," *Il Popolo d'Italia*, 27 March 1938, quoted in Simonini, *Linguaggio di Mussolini*, p. 37.

17.   Gaetano Mosca, *Ruling Class* (New York: McGraw-Hill, 1939), p. 71. See also William Ebenstein, *Fascist Italy* (New York: American Book Co., 1939) and Simonini, *Linguaggio di Mussolini*, pp. 101-4.

18.   Archivio Centrale dello Stato, *Segretaria Particolare del Duce, Carteggio Riservato*, Busta 31, Fasc. 242/R, "Riunione del Direttorio del 14 luglio 1931," Sottofasc. 2.

19.   Mussolini took a personal interest in the choice of authors for these textbooks. See Archivio Centrale dello Stato, *Presidenza del Consiglio dei Ministri, Gabinetto, Atti (1931-1933)*, Busta 678, Fasc. 3-5/4-23.

20.   The texts used in this study were used in the schools from 1938 to 1943. They are available in a special collection at the Hoover Institution at Stanford University. Another analysis of the texts used during the

period is available in the Collection of Constantine M. Panunzio, Box 5, "School Books During the Fascist Regime," also at Hoover, Special Collections. An indictment of the content and approach of these state texts can be found in Francesco Flora, *Ritratto di un ventennio* (Bologna: Edizioni Bologna, 1965), pp. 48-53. An article on the same theme by a young woman educated in the Fascist schools is Anna Garofalo, "Veleno sui banchi di scuola," *Il Ponte* 8 (October 1952), 1430-38.

21.   Edgardo Sulis, *Imitazione di Mussolini* (Milan: Casa Editrice Novecentesca, 1934). For an illustration of the content of this adulatory literature see: Armando Carlini, *Filosofia e religione ne pensiero di Mussolini* (Rome: Instituto Nazionale di Cultura Fascista, 1934); Paolo Orano, *Mussolini di fronte della storia* (Rome: Pinciana, 1941); *Mussolini da vicino* (Rome: Pinciana, 1928); and *Mussolini fondatore dell'impero* (Rome: Pinciana, 1936).

22.   The regime published a great amount of literature on Mussolini especially for the young. See, for example: Arnaldo Mussolini, *Ammonimenti ai giovani e al popolo* (Rome: Libreria del Littorio, 1931); Benito Mussolini, *Diuturna-Scritti scelti e annotati per la gioventù* (Milan: Edizioni Alpes, 1929); G. B. Marziali, *I giovani di Mussolini;* Vio Perroni, *Il Duce ai balilla* (Rome: Libreria del Littorio, 1930).

23.   Minio-Paluello, *Education in Fascist Italy,* p. 170.

24.   Simonini, *Linguaggio di Mussolini,* p. 196.

25.   Vera Cottarelli Gaiba and Nerina Oddi, *Il libro della prima classe* (Rome: Libreria dello Stato, 1942), p. 133.

26.   Alfredo Petrucci, *L'italiano nuovo: Letture della seconda classe elementare* (Rome: Libreria dello Stato, 1938), pp. 57-58.

27.   Eros Belloni, *Il libro per la seconda classe dei centri rurali* (Rome: Libreria dello Stato, 1942), p. 22.

28.   Adele Zanetti and Maria Zanetti, *Patria: Il libro di lettura per la terza classe dei centri urbani* (Rome: Libreria dello Stato, 1940), pp. 111-14, 122-28.

29.   *Il libro della terza classe: Religione, grammatica, storia, geografia, aritmetica* (Rome: Libreria dello Stato, 1942), p. 191.

30.   Testimony of Ugoberto Alfassio Grimaldi, *Autobiografie dei giovani del tempo fascista* (Brescia: Morcelliana, 1947), pp. 68-69.

31.   Mussolini, *Opera omnia,* 2:278.

32.   Benito Mussolini, *My Autobiography* (London: Paternoster Library, 1928), p. 37.

33. Mussolini, *Opera omnia*, 26:136.

34. From Benito Mussolini, *Scritti e discorsi*, 4:94, cited in Leso and Cortelazzo, *La lingua italiana*, p. 39.

35. The comment about De Vecchi is by Borghi, *Educazione e autorità*, p. 297. De Vecchi's statement can be found in Ministero dell'Educazione Nazionale, *Annuario 1935* (Rome: Provveditorato Generale dello Stato, 1936), p. 13.

36. Partito Nazionale Fascista, Gioventù Italiana del Littorio, *Il capo centuria* (Rome: Pizzi e Pizio, 1938), p. 245.

37. Piero Bargellini, *Il libro della quarta classe: Letture* (Rome: Libreria dello Stato, 1942), pp. 171-74.

38. Pina Ballario, *Quartiere Corridoni: Letture par la seconda classe dei centri urbani* (Rome: Libreria dello Stato, 1942), p. 76.

39. *Il libro della quinta classe elementare: Aritmetica, geografia, scienze* (Rome: Libreria dello Stato, 1942), p. 141.

40. See the notes of a conference held in May 1938 under the auspices of the Royal Superintendent of Education at Bari in Rosa Jannelli Caravella, *Considerazioni sull'educazione fascista nella scuola elementare* (Trani: n.p., 1938), p. 36.

41. *Il libro della terza classe* (1942), p. 116.

42. Benito Mussolini, "The Political and Social Doctrine of Fascism," *International Conciliation*, 306 (January 1935), pp. 6-7.

43. Zanetti, *Patria*, pp. 38-41.

44. Ballario, *Quartiere Corridoni*, passim.

45. Mussolini, *Opera omnia*, 26:259.

46. Mussolini's conversations with the German journalist Emil Ludwig, quoted in Emilio Ludwig, *Colloqui con Mussolini* (Verona: A. Mondadori, 1932), p. 168.

47. Renato Marzolo, *L'Opera balilla e la leva fascista*, p. 9. Two interesting and more recent studies of the role of women under Fascism are: Piero Meldini, *Sposa e madre exemplare* (Rimini: Guaraldi, 1975) and Maria Antonietta Macciocchi, *La donna "nera": "Consenso" femminile e fascismo* (Milan: Feltrinelli, 1976).

48. Luigi Collino, "Le organizzazioni giovanili," *La civiltà fascista* ed. Giuseppe Luigi Pomba (Turin: Editrice Torinese, 1928), pp. 605-6.

49. Roberto Forges Davanzati, *Il balilla Vittorio* (Rome: Libreria dello Stato, 1930), p. 55.

50. Vincenzo Meletti, *Il libro fascista del balilla* (Florence: La Nuova Italia, 1936), p. 11.

51. Davide Lajolo, *Classe 1912* (Rome: Edizioni di Cultura Sociale, 1953), p. 13.

52. Ruggero Zangrandi, *Il lungo viaggio attraverso il fascismo: Contributo alla storia di una generazione* (Milan: Garzanti, 1971).

53. Testimony of G. C., *Autobiografie di giovani del tempo fascista*, pp. 16-17.

54. Attilio Tamaro, *Venti anni di storia, 1922-1943*, 3 vols. (Rome: Editrice Tiber, 1953), 3:468.

55. The text of this letter is available in the Archivio Centrale dello Stato, *Segretaria Particolare del Duce, Carteggio Riservato*, Busta 45, Fasc. 242/R, "Carlo Scorza."

56. Ibid., Busta 22, Fasc. 242/R, "Riunioni del Direttorio."

57. Ottavio Dinale, *Quarant'anni di colloqui con lui* (Milan: Editrice Ciarrocca, 1962), p. 181.

RESISTANCE AND THE NATIONAL QUESTION IN THE VENEZIA GIULIA AND FRIULI, 1943-1945

Eric R. Terzuolo
Gustavus Adolphus College

Disputes over the Italo-Yugoslav frontier have been a persistent and often highly significant feature of European diplomatic life during the twentieth century. Indeed, a seemingly final settlement of the vexed question of Trieste came only in 1975. The extended process of achieving that settlement was necessitated by the particular constellation of events in the region during the Second World War, the last major armed conflict in which the Italo-Yugoslav frontier was at stake. The events of that time have done much to shape the character of present-day life in the region and, as such, have drawn, and seem to merit, continued attention.

Of particular interest is the period between Mussolini's downfall on 25 July 1943 and the end of the Yugoslav occupation of Trieste on 12 June 1945. During this time, three main forces contended for the succession to Nazi-Fascist rule in the Venezia Giulia and Friuli: the non-Communist parties represented in the local National Liberation Councils (CLNs—*Comitati di Liberazione Nazionale*); the Italian Communist Party (PCI—*Partito Comunista Italiano*); and the Liberation Front (OF—*Osvobodilna Fronta*), the political arm of the Slovene National Liberation Movement. All three worked to undermine the position of the German authorities, yet each maintained separate military formations and held distinct opinions concerning the ideal nature and goals of the Resistance. The differences led to sharp conflict, the results of which proved especially tragic for representatives of the Italian parties, both Communist and non-Communist.

It was perhaps inevitable that national and territorial questions were the roots of discord; these issues had been the focal point of political debate in the region for decades. The tension between Marxist and nationalist goals was sharply marked within both the PCI-led forces and the OF, although they ultimately arrived at very different resolutions of that tension. On the other hand, the non-communists of the CLNs (especially in Trieste) did not face up to such a choice, and continued to pose the territorial question in essentially nationalistic terms.

The contest was never schematically three-sided, however. The PCI played a rather pivotal role, in the sense that it was originally part of the CLNs in the disputed territory (as it was throughout Italy), but at the same time tried to negotiate and maintain fraternal relations with the Yugoslav Communists who dominated the OF and the National Liberation Movement in Yugoslavia. The PCI had some success for a time, but Gestapo arrests of outstanding local leaders and the absence of others —drawn away from the major urban centers (Trieste in particular) to take charge of partisan formations—had serious consequences for the party. In those areas where the contest became one between the non-Communists of the CLNs and the OF, the former, with their limited popular support and organizational strength, were bound to lose. In the end, only Allied occupation of Trieste "saved" the city for Italy. Yet it seems reasonable to ask whether nationality policies that aimed at "saving" the Venezia Giulia and Friuli for one nation or another were necessarily what the situation required.

The OF, founded at Ljubljana on 27 April 1941, was the first of the forces under consideration to organize in the disputed region and adopt a precisely defined nationality policy. Various political currents were represented in the OF, including progressive nationalist and leftist intellectuals, Christian Socialists, the left wing of the Sokol movement, and the Communist Party of Slovenia (KPS–*Komunistična Partija Slovenije*). In relatively industrialized Slovenia, however, the Communists could count on substantial worker support, which, coupled with a superior organizational structure, allowed the KPS quickly to assume predominace over the other elements represented in the Front. In fact, the first OF representative in Trieste, Oskar Kovačič (who arrived in August 1941), soon formed something resembling a KPS Regional Committee.[1]

OF and KPS representatives in the Venezia Giulia could rely on certain important precedents in formulating their nationality policy. The crucial reference point for Communists favoring a Slovene solution was the work of Pino Tomažič (Tomasi). Expelled from his university Fascist Group in 1932 for Communist activity, he joined the KPS in 1934. At a February 1939 meeting in Opicina (a suburb of Trieste), he laid out a program for resolving the national question in a progressive manner. Tomažič's program was based on a recognition of the fact that Trieste, finding itself in compactly Slovene territory, necessarily belonged to the Slovene nation. At the same time, however, Tomažič did not deny the essentially Italian character of the city, but instead foresaw granting the broadest possible cultural, political, and economic autonomy to the Italian population.[2] Still, the assertion of the primacy of the hinterland in determining to which nation a port or coastal region belonged was the crucial element of Tomažič's conception, and has remained a prominent point in Yugoslav writings on the Trieste question.

That conception represented a rather dramatic break with the Comintern-inspired thesis found in a joint declaration of the Yugoslav, Italian, and Austrian Communists dating from April 1934. This declaration asserted that the Slovene question could become a lever of revolution, in that the proletariat of the three nations involved had interests coinciding with those of the oppressed Slovenes. The parties declared themselves in favor of the right of self-determination.[3] Yugoslav scholars, most notably Metod Mikuž, have tended to present this statement as a call for the construction of an integral Slovenia within a broader Yugoslav framework and a promise on the part of the Italian and Austrian Communists to aid their Slovene counterparts in the struggle to achieve this aim.[4] Yet shortly after the statement was published, Ivan Regent, probably the leading Slovene Communist of his day, warned that to treat the Venezia Giulia as an organic Slovene whole, without permitting the large non-Slovene population to exercise the right of self-determination, would represent a return to an essentially imperialistic policy, serving the interests of the Slovene nationalist bourgeoisie.[5]

It seems likely, in fact, that for quite some time KPS leaders remained hesitant to call for annexation of cities and areas with an Italian majority.[6] What, then, finally drove the OF's Executive Committee in October 1942 to issue a call for the reunification of all the Slovenes, from Spielfeld to

Trieste? Italian Communists have often argued that the ranks of their Yugoslav counterparts had been penetrated by nationalistic and chauvinistic elements. A report from the Trieste PCI federation, dated January 1944, mentions the presence of an extremely powerful anti-Italian spirit among certain Slovene elements, which made it difficult to believe that they were actually Communists.[7] Given the advantages that accrued to the KPS as a result of remaining within a broad front of democratic parties (providing easier legitimacy in the eyes of the Allies), certain concessions to more strongly nationalistic bourgeois elements within the OF could be expected. One should also bear in mind the demonstrated effectiveness of nationalistic revindications in winning popular support for the National Liberation Movement. Admittedly, most of those being drawn into the movement by such appeals were peasants and others whose orientation was not particularly proletarian, yet the interests of social revolution were clearly being served (in Yugoslav eyes) if nationalist propaganda furthered the overall struggle.[8] Finally, one should remember that our mental categories sometimes become unduly rigid when discussing heavily ideological movements such as Communism. Most "Western" definitions of Communism include a stress on internationalism. Yet it seems unwise to exclude the possibility that individuals sincerely devoted to a Marxist socioeconomic program may demonstrate a latent nationalism. Thus we should question whether all the nationalistic elements in the program of the National Liberation Movement in fact represented "concessions" to bourgeois allies.

Whatever the weight of each of the above factors, however, it seems clear that well before the outbreak of armed resistance in Italy the anti-Axis forces of Yugoslavia and, in particular, the OF had worked out a concrete policy regarding the national and territorial questions in the disputed Venezia Giulia. As early as May 1942 a Kardelj report to the Central Committee of the KPS emphasized the importance of strengthening Partisan penetration in the direction of Trieste.[9] A bit over a year later, the instructions were beginning to assume a more precise form. In his instructions to the Central Committee's members on 12 August 1943, Kardelj called on them to organize strikes and demonstrations in all parts of Slovenia still occupied by the Italian army. He ordered that a particular effort be made in Trieste to popularize the notion of a Yugoslav liberation of the Slovene Littoral (*Slovensko Primorje*): "Keep in mind that you will have to be in the vicinty of Trieste!"[10] At about the same time, the OF's Executive Committee was ordering all its local committees to stress the call for the unification of the entire Slovene land, including the Littoral and Trieste.[11]

With the Italian capitulation of 8 September 1943, ultimate Partisan victory began to seem more likely and it became imperative to formulate more precise territorial demands, launching an aggressive campaign to propagandize those demands. Perhaps the two most important statements came in September 1944. In an article in *Nova Jugoslavija,* Josip Smodlaka, foreign minister of the AVNOJ government, denounced the Treaty of Rapallo (1920) and demanded for Yugoslavia all of the Venezia Giulia up to the Isonzo River. Italy of course had to pay off its debts in connection with the war and its prewar persecution of Slavs, but the fundamental consideration was that the Venezia Giulia *belonged* to Yugoslavia as a consequence of ethnic, geographic, and economic factors. The Italian "minority" in the urban centers would be granted a measure of autonomy and have its national rights (primarily language and culture) respected. Tito's 15 September speech in honor of the anniversary of the Second Dalmatian Brigade included a simpler and less detailed exposition of the ideas that Smodlaka had expressed. The South Slavs of Istria, the Littoral, and Carinthia had to be liberated so that they might live "in their fatherland with their own brothers." The point of the speech lay in the rather catchy slogan "Tudje nećemo, svoje ne damo." ("We don't want what belongs to others, but will give up nothing of our own.")[12] These demands were put forth in language typical of traditional nationalists and tended to recapitulate the arguments long used by dominant Yugoslav political parties in debates with their Italian counterparts.

The essential elements in the National Liberation Movement's position was the desire to see the entire Venezia Giulia incorporated into the new Yugoslav state. This emphasis on the state and the firm conviction that the disputed territory genuinely *belonged* to Yugoslavia was evident in many aspects of OF and Partisan conduct. On 16 September 1943, only a matter of days after Italy's capitulation and long before any resolution of the military situation seemed imminent, the Supreme Plenum of the OF proclaimed the annexation of the Slovene Littoral to united Slovenia and Democratic Yugoslavia. Already on the same day, the OF's Executive

Committee had passed a resolution giving the power of public administration in the Littoral to the National Liberation Council headed by
Jože Vilfan, France Bevk, and Aleš Bebler. On 30 November 1943,
AVNOJ confirmed the OF's declaration as part of its own "Decision on
the Annexation of the Slovene Littoral, Venetian Slovenia, Istria, and the
Croatian Adriatic Islands to Yugoslavia."[13] With this, the Yugoslavs came
to regard the fate of the Venezia Giulia as an issue beyond dispute, already settled.

For some time, however, the OF's conduct vis-à-vis the National Liberation Committee of Upper Italy (CLNAI–*Comitato di Liberazione
Nazionale dell Alta Italia*), the supreme organ of the Italian Resistance,
tended to belie such a view. At the urging of Giuseppe Dozza, the PCI
delegate, the CLNAI decided in February 1944 to establish relations with
the Slovene and Croat National Liberation Councils. The aim was to foster
mutual support, coordinate the armed struggle, and arrive at a settlement between the various peoples. The success of negotiations between
Yugoslav and Italian Communists for conclusion of pacts between their
respective partisan formations helped create an atmosphere of cooperation. A mission composed of Anton Vratuša and Franc Štoka came to
Milan in order to negotiate with the CLNAI on behalf of the OF and
KPS. At a meeting on 8 June 1944, Vratuša argued that Slovene national
unity and independence had to be regarded as a fait accompli, although
he recognized that discussions on zones of mixed population and precise
delimitation of borders should be postponed until the common victory.
This was sufficient to permit CLNAI approval on 10 June of a manifesto
entitled "To the Italian Population of the Venezia Giulia." It included
an appeal to join Italian units fighting under overall Yugoslav command,
to aid the partisans in every way, and to promote formation of local
CLNs and Italo-Slovene or Italo-Croat anti-Fascist committees.[14] At a
second meeting on 16 July, Vratuša pressed for immediate CLNAI recognition of the annexations that AVNOJ had decreed, although he did
not discuss precise territorial limits. Despite the problems this caused,
the second meeting was probably the high point of Italo-Slovene collaboration. A committee composed of representatives from the CLNAI and
the Trieste CLN, as well as Vratuša himself, began work on a draft accord
with the Slovene government. The document that eventually resulted,

however, called for delaying the territorial settlement until the end of hostilities, and when Vratuša returned to Milan on 4 September he brought
with him the Slovene government's refusal to ascribe to any agreement that
did not recognize as final the AVNOJ decisions on territorial matters.[15]

At the practical level, the OF and KPS worked to undermine all instruments of Italian influence in the disputed territory. This effort was by no
means limited to attacks on supporters of Fascist rule, but included
assaults on the parties of the Italian Resistance, most significantly the
PCI. Not only did the OF treat the Venezia Giulia as already incorporated
into the new Yugoslav state, but the KPS regarded the region as its exclusive sphere of jurisdiction. This insistence, along with the disagreements
over the meaning and implementation of "self-determination," was a
major source of friction between Slovene and Italian Communists. Already
in 1942, Umberto Massola, the leading PCI organizer in Italy at the time,
had opposed KPS plans to create a single, Slovene-run Communist party
organization in Trieste and the Littoral. Massola contended that both the
KPS and the PCI should be able to maintain organizations there.[16] Pietro
Secchia, another extremely important PCI organizer, also notes persistent
Yugoslav rejection of the idea that the Italian Communists should be
allowed their own organization in areas of mixed population. He repro-
duces a report from the Friuli dating from autumn 1944, which suggests
that in Gorizia the KPS had set up a dummy PCI Federation Committee
of its own to take over from an already functioning Federation Committee.[17] The KPS conducted extensive work among the Italian workers
of Trieste and the other coastal cities, in part via creation of mixed Italo-
Slovene organizations or of parallel organizations among the Italian and
Slovene populations—organizations that invariably ended up under complete KPS control.[18] These KPS initiatives represented a serious attempt
to erode the mass base or potential mass base of the PCI, an intrusion
on a supposedly fraternal party's legitimate sphere of operations.

The tendency of the OF and KPS to act early on as governing parties
in the Venezia Giulia and Friuli is further reflected in their dispositions
regarding Italian partisan formations fighting in the area. This is a complex
problem, one that deserves more extensive and detailed discussion than
is possible here. Suffice to say that the non-Communist Italian Resistance
forces met overt hostility on the part of the Slovenes and that the OF

regarded collaboration with them as impossible.[19] The Yugoslavs were more ready to accept the Communist-inspired Italian formations, but the price was rather steep. The "Trieste" Battalion in Istria, for example, suffered poor treatment at the hands of its Slovene counterparts, who demanded political subordination and hindered communication with the PCI Federation.[20] This was a generalized pattern. One should perhaps expect a certain necessary measure of subordination, as the Italians took to arms only in mid-1943 and their formations were small and weak compared to those of the Yugoslavs, especially in the early stages. Yet the OF was intent on eliminating the Italian formations as possible points of support for Italian ambitions in the Julian region. An April 1944 accord between the General Command of the Garibaldi Brigades (PCI-controlled) and the 9th Corps of the National Liberation Army of Yugoslavia (operating in the Venezia Giulia) had stipulated only that Garibaldi Brigades operating on the 9th Corps' territory would be under parenthetical command of the two parties to the agreement.[21] But when the "Natisone" Division, as a result of German pressure and disputes with non-Communist formations, found itself forced to accept operational dependence upon the 9th Corps, it was also forced to accept a long and costly march into the interior of Slovenia. Furthermore, the Division was reorganized to suit the regular army structure of the Corps and efforts were made to wipe out Italian sentiment within its ranks.[22] The point of these Yugoslav dispositions regarding Italian units was to assure that no strong Italian formations were in the vinicity of Trieste when the fall of the city was imminent. In this, the Yugoslavs were extremely successful.

A final bit of evidence indicating that the OF and KPS were concerned primarily with incorporating all of the Venezia Giulia into the new Yugoslavia, rather than with stringent application of self-determination, can be found by examining their conduct during the occupation of Trieste (beginning of May to mid-June 1945). Already in the aftermath of the Italian surrender, Yugoslav forces had temporarily occupied the Julian region and launched a campaign of reprisals against the Italian population which claimed 400-500 lives. Although Vratuša would later blame irresponsible local elements, a conscious desire to destroy the area's largely Italian or Italianized ruling class and create a power vacuum figures as another likely motivating factor.[23] When the National Liberation Army returned to Venezia Giulia in May 1945, the Italian elites again had good reason to fear, whether they had supported Fascist rule or opposed it. On the evening of 2 May, for instance, Yugoslav troops appeared at the Trieste town hall and arrested 6 members of the CLN. It is estimated that, during the occupation, about 950 people were deported from Trieste alone; approximately 600 never returned and are presumed to have perished. Of the latter, about 160 were followers of the CLN or members of the Civic Guard (an organization heavily infiltrated by the CLN).[24] OF front organizations such as the Italo-Slovene Anti-Fascist Union charged the CLN with collaboration with the Fascists, but at that point in time "Fascist" meant anyone who opposed the Yugoslav solution for Trieste.[25] The speed with which a governmental structure was created was impressive. On 13 May, control of the city was vested in the Liberation Council of Trieste, an outgrowth of the Italo-Slovene Anti-Fascist Executive Committee that had sat side-by-side with the Yugoslav military government since the first days of the occupation. It ruled the city as a district within the new Slovene Littoral region of Yugoslavia, and claims of ample autonomy for the Italian population proved to be of no substance.[26]

In essence, Trieste had been conquered not in the name of social revolution, but in the name of the new Yugoslav state. Expecting a genuine liberation that cut across ethnic boundaries, the Italian workers of the San Giacomo quarter had put out their red banners, but "withdrew their flag because the occupiers, who yet proclaimed themselves Yugoslav Communists and spoke of abolishing all nationalisms, entered not with the red flag, as expected, but with the white, red, and blue."[27]

The Italian Communist Party's position on the national and territorial questions in the Venezia Giulia has drawn fire from both Yugoslav commentators and authors aligned with the non-Communist parties of the Trieste CLN. The latter cite the PCI's failure to uphold the *italianità* of the entire region, while the KPS and KPJ have emphasized their struggle against "opportunism and chauvinism in the ranks of the PCI."[28] A persistent Yugoslav claim has been that the PCI leadership hesitated to undertake armed struggle and call on its supporters to collaborate with the OF, and that the Italian Communist organization was weak and inefficient.[29] These charges are justified to a certain degree, yet should be evaluated in light of the fact that the PCI had been illegal in Italy since 1926 and suffered severe persecution at Fascist hands. As a result, virtually all of the most talented leaders and cadres were in prison or exile until some time after Mussolini's fall on 25 July 1943. In its aftermath, we see a dramatic increase in PCI activity all over Italy. The Venezia Giulia, in fact, saw more activity than many other provinces, thanks to the efforts of such unusually talented individuals as Giordano Pratolongo, Vincenzo Gigante, Natale Colarich (Božo Kolarič) and, most particularly, Luigi Frausin.[30]

Talented as they were, however, these men had been isolated from conditions in the Julian region for some time and were not well acquainted with the development and prospects of the Yugoslav National Liberation Struggle; both circumstances had important implications. While the KPS and KPJ had been driven by the needs of the struggle to accept the primacy of practice over theory, PCI organizers entered the Venezia Giulia with a mind-set in which theoretical constructs tended to predominate over pragmatic considerations. The antecedents of the PCI position lay in discussions among Julian exiles on the Fascist prison island of Ventotene, and the Party's statements sometimes had the "abstract flavor appropriate to political formulae prepared in exile."[31] As a result, the PCI tended to cling to Comintern directives on the national question and the nature of the war. This was the tone of the first instructions that Togliatti sent to Massola in late 1940, when the latter was stationed in Yugoslavia with the task of trying to rebuild a PCI directorate within Italy. Also, PCI operatives continued to promote the Comintern-inspired positions detailed in the 1934 agreement with the Communist Parties of Austria and Yugoslavia, and in a 1936 agreement with a major Slovene nationalist organization.[32]

Yet despite a tendency toward abstraction, the PCI's position regarding the Venezia Giulia did take into account certain considerations that its Yugoslav counterpart and/or the non-Communists of the Julian CLNs did not. First, the PCI apparently recognized that a new international order was emerging as a result of the war and that the Venezia Giulia would have some importance within the context of that new order's consolidation. Second, the PCI looked to a policy that would take into account Italy's national interest, without abandoning Marxism's essentially negative view of nationalism. Finally, the PCI recognized that Italy would have to pay off some of the debts that Fascism had incurred, but that this debt could not be used to justify all the actions that those people who had suffered under Fascist rule might now be prepared to take. As Luigi Longo put it in his discussion of Fascist persecution of the Slavs: "These facts gave birth to. . .not simply national, but chauvinistic revindications on the part of the Slavic populations of our country's eastern border. Yugoslav leaders made these chauvinistic revindications a weapon of struggle against the national rights of the Italian population of these lands."[33]

The PCI's position on the Venezia Giulia was, simply stated, to post-pone any decision on territorial questions until the end of hostilities, to oppose any unilateral action in this matter, and to reject either a return to the *status quo ante bellum* or outright Yugoslav annexation without according the Italian population the right of self-determination. In a letter of 6 October 1943 to the Central Committee of the Croatian Communist Party, the PCI Directorate for Northern Italy stated:

> We are of the opinion that our original position, self-determina-
> tion up to the right of secession, is absolutely sufficient for the
> needs of the struggle. Of course we hold. . .that the program
> of a "Free and United Slovenia" is also correct. But frankly we
> do not see at this time any need for you to support absolutely
> the annexation of Trieste. The principle of self-determination
> holds for the *triestini* as well, and for the moment a more con-
> crete program seems premature.

The Directorate went on to suggest that annexation of Trieste would prevent or seriously hinder Italian collaboration in the Yugoslav struggle. It is not surprising that such a stance should have led to discord between the two parties. A meeting of KPJ and PCI members in late November 1943 came to naught when the Italians rejected a Yugoslav demand that they recognize Yugoslavia's rights over Trieste and that all Italian partisan formations in the area pass to the National Liberation Army and adopt Yugoslav insignia.[34]

A report by Giordano Pratolongo is perhaps the best of the published Italian sources on the situation in the Venezia Giulia as of the beginning of 1944. He comments at length on the problem of national minorities and PCI relations with the Slovene comrades. The PCI organization in Trieste demanded *recognition* of the right of self-determination, pure and simple, to be put into effect according to conditions arising at the end of hostilities. No radical or simple solution was possible; the rights of the small minorities inevitably left on either side of the eventual frontier would have to be guaranteed. Actions carried out during the brief Yugoslav occupation in September 1943—immediate incorporation decreed by conferences "that represented nothing serious," armed imposition of governments that took no account of the will of the Italian-speaking population, prohibitions from exhibiting Italian flags or red flags with tricolor ribbons—represented a clear statement of position on the settlement. Pratolongo and others saw this position to be in clear contradiction to the spirit of the Liberation Fronts, to the principles of Communism, and to the principles upon which the Soviet Union was basing its own struggle. A final consideration was that the OF's public statements gave the PCI's Fascist and reactionary enemies the possibility of launching propaganda campaigns based on a supposed Slavic peril or threat to the *italianità* of Trieste. Such statements also drove the non-Communist parties of the CLNs to strengthen their stand in favor of the Venezia Giulia's continued union with Italy.[35]

Pratolongo's is perhaps the most acutely critical PCI comment on the OF's conduct, yet we find some of its essential points reiterated even in the generally accommodating and pro-Yugoslav instructions that Togliatti gave to Vincenzo Bianco, the PCI Directorate's man in Trieste, in October 1944. Togliatti termed eventual Yugoslav occupation of the Venezia Giulia a "positive" event, in that it would prevent a British occupation or the resurgence of a reactionary Italian regime. He also argued that the PCI should collaborate with its Yugoslav comrades in creating organs of popular power in the Italian-inhabited zones occupied by Tito's troops, opposing all those who would sow discord among the peoples. Such collaboration was seen as particularly important in the case of Trieste, although Togliatti rejected the possibility of beginning discussions on the fate of the city at that point in time, feeling that such discussions would inevitably breed conflict between Italians and Slavs. The PCI leader also called on Bianco to recruit widely among Italian workers, peasants, and intellectuals for partisan formations that, though part of Tito's army, would maintain "their national character." He instructed the Party to conduct throughout liberated Italy a campaign in favor of solidarity and collaboration with the Yugoslav peoples and the new power they were creating. As far as the future was concerned, Togliatti stressed the importance of pressing the point that this line of political collaboration would create conditions in which all the questions that might arise between Italy and Yugoslavia could be resolved in conformity to the interests of the two states. This document was the outgrowth of a meeting that Togliatti had at Bari with Kardelj and two other Yugoslav leaders —a meeting that perhaps explains the exceptionally positive and agreeable tone. But Yugoslav insistence on annexation was such that on 29 January 1945, the PCI Directorate sent a rather crisply worded letter to the KPJ Central Committee, indicating that approval of Yugoslav occupation did not imply that the problem of Trieste's future had already been resolved and annexation of the Venezia Giulia recognized.[36]

When in April 1945 a fairly detailed plan for the disposition of the disputed territory appeared in *Rinascita,* the major PCI journal, it sought a position between the Yugoslav annexationist and Italian nationalist theses. The proposal called for creation of an autonomous Venezia Giulia that would eventually became an independent state under Italian or international protection. Within this body, wide municipal autonomy would protect local customs and languages. Economic questions would be under the control of a commission representing the six nations who shared an economic interest in Trieste.[37]

This statement is in many respects a logical extension of the position that the PCI had held since the beginnings of the Resistance. Two essential needs were being balanced: (1) the need to defend the rights of the Italian population of the disputed territory from the OF's aggressive nationality policy; (2) the need to recognize the just claims of the Yugoslavs in the territory, thus helping to eliminate potential sources of tension with the National Liberation Movement, which was a full-fledged *ally* of the USSR and the Anglo-Americans and could expect to have a comparatively strong position in the final settlement. One should also consider a certain natural PCI sympathy for the Yugoslavs, determined not just by ideological considerations, but by the fact that both had suffered from Fascist oppression. For the PCI, the Yugoslavs had never really been an enemy, as they had been for the non-Communist parties of the Trieste CLN, but an important, though in certain respects misguided, friend.

The difficulties in pursuing such a course become apparent as soon as one begins to examine the wartime history of the PCI organizations in the Julian region, most particularly in Trieste. The outstanding PCI leader in the zone of Italo-Yugoslav contention was undoubtedly Luigi Frausin. He could hardly be accused of anti-Slavic feeling, having devoted much of his effort during the interwar period to fostering Italo-Slav cooperation within the PCI. Furthermore, he was the only member of the Trieste CLN to approve the CLNAI's June 1944 manifesto to the Italians of the Venezia Giulia. He argued that the language of the appeal would help ease tension in the region.[38] The fact that he does not come in for direct attack in *Trieste nella lotta per la democrazia,* published by an OF front organization, is also highly significant. At the same time, Frausin retained a staunchly critical attitude vis-à-vis the Yugoslav movement. For example, he approved an article in the Action Party organ *Il Risorgimento* attacking excesses during the September 1943 occupation.[39] As the leading figure in the Trieste PCI Federation, he undoubtedly left his imprint on a letter of 7 January 1944, criticizing the Yugoslav failure to take into account the needs of the Italian population of Istria. On 5 February 1944, the Trieste Federation sent a letter to the commissar of the "Trieste" partisan battalion, arguing that it was essential for the success of the PCI's course that its Slovene and Croat comrades be made to understand that they must not set borders that included groups of one nationality within the territory of another nationality. The Slavs also had to recognize that certain anti-Fascist forces were collaborating with the PCI to throw out the invaders, but would lose fighting spirit if they saw that Italian zones were being joined to Yugoslavia.[40] Frausin often found himself at odds with representatives of the other parties in the Trieste CLN, but his was always a loyal opposition. He was the driving force behind the foundation, in spring 1944, of the "Alma Vivoda" Battalion. Largely composed of Italian Communists from Istria and the Venezia Giulia, this battalion operated on the border between the two provinces; its *raison d'être* lay in a sense of the need for a strong *Italian* partisan presence on that crucial spot.[41]

It may have been precisely Frausin's loyalty to the interests of the Italians of the frontier region which led to his arrest by the Gestapo in late August 1944 and subsequent death. Various authors have noted the rather suspicious circumstances under which anti-annexationist PCI leaders disappeared.[42] In any case, after Frausin's departure the Trieste PCI was led to withdraw from the CLN and soon passed under complete OF control.[43]

A certain tension between loyalty to their Yugoslav comrades within the context of united anti-Fascist struggle and a desire to defend the interests of the Italians of the frontier region is evident also in the conduct of PCI-led partisan formations. In summer 1944, the Garibaldi brigades of the Friuli had joined with the non-Communist Osoppo brigades to form the so-called Friuli and Carnia Free Zones. This marked a temporary shift to a territorial concept of resistance. Yet attitudes toward the Slovene partisans became a major point of contention. Although it was not necessarily easy to impress an attitude favorable to Tito and the Yugoslavs on newly recruited *garibaldini,* the prospects for reorienting members of the Osoppo brigades invariably seemed far dimmer.[44] Yet the PCI formations were themselves rather hesitant to undertake full-fledged collaboration with Yugoslav units. As noted above, the "Natisone" Division did pass to effective operational dependence upon the 9th Corps in November 1944, but it did so under the pressure of circumstances. A PCI report from Udine dated 15 October 1944 reviewed the possibilities open to the "Natisone" after the collapse of the Friuli Free Zone, in light of the fact that its primary duty was to conduct an energetic fight against the Nazis and Fascists. The best prospect (indeed the only realistic one) lay in fighting alongside the 9th Corps as an autonomous unit. The report argued that it was desirable to consolidate friendship with the Yugoslavs via mixed committees, pacts, and other such joint arrangements, yet it noted the uncertainity and hostility on the part of many *garibaldini* and insisted that the integrity of the unit would have to be respected.[45] Giovanni Padoan, commissar of the "Natisone," hoped that at war's end the Yugoslavs would have to take into account the fact that Italians had fought alongside them even in the interior of the country. Their having fought as part of the forces of a full-fledged *ally* could also help Italy pay back the debts it had incurred in the minds of the Allies and provide stronger grounds for resisting eventual unjust Slovene territorial demands. Padoan's account of his various dealings with the OF reveals a desire to believe that its essence was progressive, coupled with wariness of its nationalistic and dictatorial side.[46]

In sum, the PCI tended to look toward a settlement of the Venezia Giulia question within the context of a great international reckoning in which physical possession of a piece of territory would not necessarily decide its final disposition. Much of its work was designed to contribute to conditions under which fruitful Italo-Yugoslav negotiations might be undertaken. As far as precise territorial delimitation was concerned, PCI representatives were on the whole prepared to cede the compactly Slavic areas of the Venezia Giulia, which the Fascists had included under the rubric of *terre italianissime*. Yet outright Yugoslav annexation of the entire region was in clear contradiction to the principle of self-determination. The PCI's conception of the Italian national interest was such that it tended to downplay the *amount* of territory held in favor of *solid and just claims* to that territory and its populations. It implied an attempt to minimize possible sources of tension with a new Yugoslavia, which, for a whole complex of reasons, the Italian Communists viewed in an essentially positive light.

Whereas the PCI and, to a lesser extent, the OF seem to have represented relatively discrete bodies, one might expect the non-Communist parties of the Julian CLNs—Action Party, Christian Democrats, Liberals, and Socialists—to have presented a picture of greater heterogeneity, yet many authors treat them as a discrete block of forces. The qualified condemnation of the PCI which we find in Yugoslav sources becomes a blanket condemnation when they deal with the other Italian parties. Alongside the legitimate and not necessarily negative observation that the Trieste CLN wanted to be the only representative of Italian Trieste, we find the charge that the CLN's conduct during the National Liberation Struggle was "dirty" and that it remained tied to leading Fascists and collaborationists. Failure to organize any actions against the occupiers and refusal to collaborate with progressive forces are also cited.[47] These particular claims have little or, at most, limited validity. The Trieste CLN's concept of the struggle was simply very different from that of the OF, yet the linking of the four non-Communist parties per se seems justified. Their approaches to the national question did have important common traits, distinguishing them both from the PCI and from their own central organizations as represented in the CLNAI.

These parties tended to view the problem of the succession to Fascist rule in terms of political programs dominant in the Venezia Giulia long before Fascism's advent. The fact that since 1941 the entire Balkan peninsula had been the scene of a violent anti-Italian insurrection and the implications of that insurrection seem to have escaped these politicians almost entirely. As of mid-1943 the proposals of the Liberals were limited to improvement of the local political and administrative situation, coupled with collection of documents testifying to the Italian nature of the Venezia Giulia. The Catholic program emphasized the need to overcome the moral collapse that Fascism had signified, although some of the clergy in the Friuli would later adopt a more activist approach. Even the more strongly democratic elements tended to cast their policy in terms of traditional demands for the Julian Alps as Italy's natural frontier. Thus, the first civic anti-Fascist committees that these parties organized on the whole resembled those that had blossomed in 1918 for irredentist purposes.[48]

The Julian Resistance saw itself as having a function distinct from that of the resistance elsewhere in Italy. As Dennison Rusinow points out: "The particular function of the Julian Committees of National Liberation (CLN) was to reinsert Italy into the Julian situation, and to prepare the basis for a post-war Italian claim to those parts of the district with an Italian majority."[49] Yet while this statement is applicable to many of the local CLNs along the Italo-Yugoslav frontier, it is not strictly appropriate to the Trieste CLN. Perhaps because that city was obviously such a key point of contention, its political life had always been especially intense and the stances that its inhabitants adopted particularly radical. Thus when the CLNAI issued its 10 June 1944 "Manifesto to the Italian Population of the Venezia Giulia," the Trieste CLN (with the exception of Luigi Frausin) was the only CLN in the Julian region which did not accept it. The majority of the Trieste CLN did not hold to the ethnic principle and did not recognize the right of the Yugoslavs to annex compactly Slav areas. The entire Venezia Giulia, they thought, must remain united to Italy, and they reserved the right to sever connections to the CLNAI if it was prepared to recognize the divisibility of the province.[50]

One should bear in mind that the non-Communist party organizations in Trieste tended to assume less politically advanced positions than their central leaderships represented in the CLNAI. Whereas in the rest of Italy the Action Party was characterized by an attempt to fuse the best aspects of liberal democracy with a socialistic program in the socio economic field, the older generation of Action Party leaders in Trieste retained an essentially traditional, irredentist outlook. The arrest of Gabriele

Foschiatti in December 1943 meant the loss of the potentially most progressive figure in the local organization.[51] Furthermore, while the Socialist Party was linked to the PCI in a unity of action pact, the Socialist organization in Trieste and its leader, Carlo Schiffrer, remained well to the right of the positions Socialists were adopting in the rest of Italy and closely tied to the irredentist tradition.

The non-Communists of the Trieste CLN also displayed a generalized anti-Slavic sentiment that tended to damage their relations with both the OF and CLNAI. It often seemed that they regarded the Slavs as the most important enemy, perhaps in the conviction that the Germans were bound for defeat in any case. As one figure closely tied to the CLN remarked: "I can't express the sense of total annihilation which I experience at the thought of the Slavs being in Trieste."[52] Quarantotti-Gambini stresses the fact that Slavic was not spoken in Trieste, without any inkling that the urban / rural dichotomy this suggests may have been at the root of certain justifiable complaints on the part of the Slavic population. To the irredentist mentality, the Slavs remained something primitive, indeed almost barbarous.[53]

A certain fundamental anti-Communism was also associated with this irredentist world view. The Fascist policy of repressing Communism had been coupled with an effort to denationalize the Slovene and Croat communities of the Julian region, with the result that Slav and Communist had become synonymous in the minds of many, including those who were by no means friends of Fascism.[54]

The combination of the above factors resulted in a tendency on the part of the non-Communist forces of the CLN to seek alliance with legitimate forces of order. This tendency took the form, among other things, of memoranda and appeals to the Badoglio government that had succeeded Mussolini. These appeals generally contained recommendations to the effect that concessions to the Slovenes would actually aid the Italian cause of the Venezia Giulia. Specifically, the memoranda called on Badoglio et al. to prove that they rejected the Fascist policy of national repression by releasing Slovene political prisoners, abrogating the decree annexing the so-called Provincia de Lubiana, and providing restitution for damages that the Fascists had caused.[55]

The concept of armed resistance taken up by these elements reflected the same tendency to seek the support of traditional authorities and the same underlying structure of motivations. The Osoppo Brigades, which began to form after 8 September and acquired organized status at the beginning of 1944, were the only important non-Communist partisan formations to function in the disputed territory. Many of the *osovani* had been members of the Italian army prior to capitulation, and their basic driving force was an essentially apolitical *ribellismo,* directed against the Nazi occupiers. From the beginning, the brigades were homogenous neither in terms of origin nor in terms of ideological orientation. Precisely for this reason, they proved relatively easy to manipulate and became a tool of the rising forces of Christian Democracy and of the local ecclesiastical hierarchy. The chaplains of the Osoppo Brigades exercised a function not unlike that of the commissars among the *garibaldini;* their propaganda tended to link anti-Communism and anti-Slavism.

> Thus an accent was placed on the perils of Marxism and of Communist methods, on the Slovene threat, etc. With the passage of time and the growth of tension between the *osovani* and *Garibaldini* in connection with the Slovene question, not only the military but also the political importance of the Osovan contribution [came to be emphasized] —today vis-à-vis the Germans, tomorrow vis-à-vis the "orientals."

As far as the final territorial settlement was concerned, the commanders of the Osoppo looked to diplomatic negotiations between the Italian government and the supreme Allied command.[56]

A similar tendency to work for a final solution under Allied auspices can be seen among the non-Communists of the Trieste CLN, who delayed concentrated armed action against the Germans until the very last minute. Their call to insurrection had two purposes: (1) to encourage the Western Allies to speed up their advance toward Trieste; (2) to beat the OF to the punch and occupy as much of the city as possible before the Allies did appear.[57] The successes of the insurrection of 28-30 April 1945 were perhaps sufficient to absolve the non-Communists of CLN from a charge of total inactivity, yet could not make up for almost twenty months of playing a waiting game in the face of German occupation.

The positions that these parties adopted were very similar to those of middle-class resistance movements in other European countries, opposed to the occupiers, yet at the same time fearful of upsetting the *status quo ante bellum*. They feared the Slavs at least as much as they feared the Germans. This concern with the national question, anti-Communism, social conservatism, as well as the tendency to rely on the Anglo-Americans reminds one of Chetnik ideology. Unlike the Chetniks, however, the non-Communist parties of the Julian CLNs were not collaborationists, and remained true to their idealistic, if often hopelessly anachronistic, conception of the struggle for the *italianità* of the Venezia Giulia.

The debate over the Italo-Yugoslav frontier has been long indeed, yet if it has a distinguishing factor, it is precisely the sameness of the arguments brought to bear. Although ethnic, geographic, economic, and all varieties of historical arguments have been used, each of the parties to the dispute has found a way to exploit them for the benefit of its own case. The basic goal has almost always been that of bringing the *entire* disputed region into either the Italian or Yugoslav state. Thus the approaches that the OF and the non-Communists of the CLNs (especially in Trieste) took with respect to the national question followed in a long, if not necessarily honored, tradition. Neither force was prepared to cede an inch of territory. In this respect, the policy adopted by the PCI Directorate for Northern Italy and local leaders like Frausin represented a new possibility. Admittedly this policy had it antecedents in formulations of the interwar period which did not necessarily consider the specific conditions in the Venezia Giulia. Still, Axis defeat created precisely the sort of fluid conditions under which one could discard traditional regional boundaries as criteria on which to base the territorial settlement and proceed to apply self-determination with some rigor. The outstanding feature of the PCI's policy was that it alone recognized that *both* Italians and Slavs had strong claims in the zone and that *both* these claims had to be taken into account and satisfied to a reasonable extent if the frontier was not to remain a perennial apple of discord. The OF and CLN proposals tended to leave the essential points of dispute in the same terms they had taken on during the Fascist period. Italian territorial voracity and desire for total control had stimulated the growth of similar sentiments among the Slavs. Although Fascism had fallen, the OF often acted as if it were dealing with Mussolini's Italy, while many of the CLN parties simply forgot that the fact of Fascism's existence tainted their traditional territorial program.

Admittedly, the concept of self-determination has a certain abstract quality and is difficult to apply in satisfying fashion. Perhaps the OF acted as the most pragmatic of the groups we have considered, in the sense that it had all the military force necessary to take what it wanted. Yet this proved a rather short-sighted approach. The Trieste question became a crucial one within the context of the new bipolar world order that emerged at war's end. Unreasonable Yugoslav acquisitiveness infuriated a broad spectrum of Italian opinion and helped to drive the country even further into the arms of the Western Bloc. Furthermore, the OF's conduct during the war helped alienate the PCI and gave it an added impetus to join in the Cominform assult on Yugoslavia after the Tito-Stalin split. Reflections of the arbitrary manner in which the Yugoslavs annexed the Venezia Giulia could be seen in the eventual arbitrary division of the disputed territory—the Morgan Line—which permitted self-determination for no one. Finally, it is questionable to what extent the Yugoslavs should have expected to be able to hold Trieste, a large, compactly Italian city. The desire for the city helped create a wound which festered for nine years, bringing Yugoslavia few advantages and costing it dearly. One should at least consider the possibility that Yugoslavia could have gained many of the benefits it did, while avoiding such serious long-term conflicts, had the OF and its associates from the beginning shown more willingness to recognize the rights of *all* the peoples of the frontier region.

NOTES

1. Elio Apih, *Italia, fascismo e antifascismo nella Venezia Giulia (1918-1943)* (Bari, 1966), pp. 395-96; *Istra i Slovensko Primorje* (Belgrade, 1952), p. 521. The KPS may be considered essentially a branch of the Communist Party of Yugoslavia (KPJ—*Komunistička Partija Jugoslavije*).

2. Elio Apih, *Dal regime alla resistenza: Venezia Giulia 1922-43* (Udine, 1960), p. 75, and Comitato Cittadino dell U.A.I.S., *Trieste nella lotta per la democrazia* (Trieste, 1945), p. 38.

3. Apih, *Dal regime alla resistenza,* p. 47.

4. Metod Mikuž, "Boji Komunistične Partije Jugoslavije za zahodne meje (od 1941 do 1945)," *Zgodovinski Časopis* 12-13 (1958-59), 7, 8, 9, 49-50; Vjekoslav Bratulić, "Medjunacionalni odnosi i razvitak socijalistickog pokreta u Istri," in *Prikjučenje Istre Federalnoj Državi Hrvatskoj u Demokratskoj Federativnoj Jugoslaviji 1943-1968* (Rijeka, 1968), p. 31.

5. Apih, *Dal regime alla resistenza*, pp. 47-48.

6. Apih, *Italia, fascismo e antifascismo*, pp. 402-3.

7. Luigi Longo, "I communisti hanno sempre difeso l'italianità di Trieste," *Rinascita* 10 (December 1953), 652. See Pietro Secchia, *Il Partito comunista italiano e la guerra di Liberazione 1943-1945: Ricordi, documenti inediti e testimonianze* (Milan, 1973), p. 169. This collection was published as volume 13 of the *Annali* of the Istituto Giangiacomo Feltrinelli.

8. See the discussions of this point in Elio Apih's two books cited above.

9. Vojonoistoriski Institut, *Zbornik dokumenata i podataka o narodnooslobadilačkom ratu jugoslovenskih naroda*, vol. 2, bk. 4, 161.

10. *Zbornik*, vol. 2, bk. 10, 193, 196.

11. Mikuž, p. 9.

12. Galliano Fogar, *Sotto l'occupazione nazista nelle provincie orientali* (Udine, 1961), pp. 70-73; *Istra i Slovensko Primorje*, p. 528. See alo the comments in Carlo Ventura, *La stampa a Trieste 1943-1945* (Udine, 1958), pp. 114-17.

13. *Priključenje Istre*, pp. 209-10, 232.

14. Secchia, pp. 354-55, 264-66; Fogar, *Sotto l'occupazione nazista*, pp. 116-21; *Istra i Slovensko Primorje*, p. 527; Mikuž, pp. 28-29.

15. Dennison Rusinow, *Italy's Austrian Heritage* (Oxford, 1969), pp. 351-52; Fogar, *Sotto l'occupazione nazista*, pp. 143-45, 165-68. Cf. Mikuž, pp. 30-32.

16. Paolo Sema, *La lotta in Istria, 1890-1945* (Trieste, 1971), pp. 236-37.

17. Secchia, pp. 352-519.

18. See *Istra i Slovensko Primorje*, pp. 521 ff.; *Trieste nella lotta per la democrazia*, pp. 45 ff.

19. Galliano Fogar, "Le Brigate Osoppo—Friuli," in *Fascismo, Guerra, Resistenza* (Trieste, 1969), p. 353; *Istra i Slovensko Primorje*, p. 485.

20. Secchia, p. 163.

21.   Ibid., p. 361.

22.   Giovanni Padoan, *Abbiamo lottato insieme* (Udine, 1965), pp. 210 ff.; *Istra i Slovensko Primorje*, pp. 485-86.

23.   See Fogar, *Sotto l'occupazione nazista*, pp. 61-62, 67.

24.   Geoffrey Cox, *The Road to Trieste* (London, 1947), p. 196, and Ennio Maserati, *L'occupazione jugoslava di Trieste (maggio-giugno 1945)* (Udine, 1963), pp. 122-24.

25.   *Trieste nella lotta*, p. 82; Cox, p. 228.

26.   Cox, pp. 226-27. For more details see Maserati, pp. 55-132, and *Trieste nella lotta*, pp. 91 ff.

27.   P. A. Quarantotti-Gambini, *Primavera a Trieste* (Verona, 1951), p. 132.

28.   *Istra i Slovensko Primorje*, p. 519.

29.   Ibid.; Mikuž, p. 15; *Trieste nella lotta*, pp. 43-52.

30.   Secchia, p. 154.

31.   Apih, *Italia, fascismo e antifascismo*, p. 455.

32.   Umberto P. Massola, *Memorie 1939-1941* (Rome, 1972), pp. 92-93. See also Sema, Appendix n. 22, pp. 341-43.

33.   Longo, p. 651.

34.   Ibid., p. 654; Secchia, pp. 359-60.

35.   Secchia, pp. 166-68.

36.   Paolo Spriano, *Storia del Partito comunista italiano*, vol. 5, *La Resistenza: Togliatti e il partito nuovo* (Turin, 1975), pp. 436-38.

37.   Tergestinus, "Relazione sul problema della Venezia Giulia," *Rinascita* 2 (April 1945), 102-5.

38.   Fogar, *Sotto l'occupazione nazista*, p. 122; Sema, pp. 180 ff.

39.   Ventura, p. 92.

40.   Longo, p. 654; Secchia, p. 360.

41.   Sema, p. 247.

42.   See for example, Giorgio Bocca, *Palmiro Togliatti* (Bari, 1973), p. 497 and Vittorio Vidali, "Sul Titismo," special edition of *Il Lavatore* (Trieste), 9 October 1950, p. 10.

43.   Fogar, *Sotto l'occupazione nazista*, pp. 169 ff.

44.   Ibid., pp. 174-75; Secchia, p. 617.

45.   Secchia, p. 611.

46.   Padoan, pp. 17, 210, 225, 247.

47. *Istra i Slovensko Primorje,* pp. 518, 533-34, and *Trieste nello lotta,* p. 82.

48.   Apih, *Italia, fascismo e antifascismo,* pp. 457-60.

49.   Rusinow, p. 329.

50.   Bogdan C. Novak, *Trieste 1941-1954* (Chicago, 1970), p. 115.

51.   Leo Valiani, *Tutte le strade conducono a Roma* (Firenze, 1947), pp. 188-89, and Fogar, *Sotto l'occupazione nazista,* pp. 102-3.

52.   Quarantotti-Gambini, p. 59.

53.   Ibid., pp. 65, 159.

54.   Maserati, p. 18.

55.   Apih, *Italia, fascismo e antifascismo,* pp. 461-63.

56.   Fogar, "Le Brigate Osoppo-Friuli," pp. 339, 347.

57.   Maserati, pp. 36-54.

ISLAMIC FUNDAMENTALISM AS AN ALTERNATIVE TO NATIONALISM

Caesar E. Farah
University of Minnesota-Minneapolis

The recent surge of Islamic activism in the Middle East appears to signal the reemergence of a politicized Islam as a dynamic factor in national and international affairs, a development that some feel has ominous implications for the United States and the Soviet Union. The most dramatic manifestation of this resurgence, the revolt versus the shah in Iran and subsequent holding of American hostages, has been widely misunderstood—at least in part because of the American tendency to treat these developments as a "media event." Clearly, we have only begun to understand the role Islamic activism has played in the upheavals in Iran and Afghanistan, and the challenge it poses to both the material values of the West and its political ascendancy.

The political activism that attends the Islamic revival is fueled by the activation of Islamic fundamentalism, and it aims to serve Islam's puritanical ideals—ideals that call for the reestablishment of the model Muslim state first organized by the Prophet Muḥammad after his emigration to Medina in 622. A crucial motivating factor in this revival is the conviction that the ideals embodied in the first Muslim political entity are still valid today and that their espousal in no way represents a retrogressive movement.

It has been a full century since the secular modernists of the world of Islam undertook the struggle to establish viable democratic institutions that were inspired by Graeco-Roman principles of government and refined by the political philosophers of the Age of Enlightenment. Almost without exception, their efforts have come to naught. All the known nationalisms of the Middle East—Arab, Turkish, and Iranian—have failed to deliver on the promises of internal unity, social and economic betterment, justice, and egalitarianism. Persistent internal struggles in Turkey, Iran, and Egypt itself, the leading Arab state, all seem to belie the promises held forth by the secularizing and modernizing campaigns of recent nationalists like Nasser, Ataturk, and the Pahlavi dynasty.

In the wake of Ayatollah Khomeini's ending of 2,500 years of monarchic rule in Iran, several important questions confront us: are we about to see the scales of political determination tipped in favor of the Islamic alternative as propounded a century ago by Jamāl al-Dīn al-Afghānī, himself of Iranian birth? Are the mullas and ulema now to take charge of their people's political and social aspirations for a just and equitable society? In other words, does this signify the triumph of Islamic nationalism over secular nationalism?

Were we to review the record of the two types of nationalism over the past one hundred years, we would discover that the recent upheaval in Iran, as well as similar events that threaten in Afghanistan and possibily Turkey, does not represent merely an isolated historical event. Nor are such manifestations of Islamic activism recent phenomena; indeed, they represent a continuing process. This process had not attracted attention until recently because the preponderant concern has been with secular nationalism. Enlightened liberals in the West have held to their strong conviction that modernization and progress can be achieved only by the espousal of purely secular ideologies. Freedom, equality, and justice were considered unattainable outside the framework of democratically chosen representative institutions. Muslims educated in Western institutions and saturated with secular values were convinced that if they could transplant and nurture the Western experience, it would flourish in Islamic soil. They had come to equate modernism and Westernization, with the latter's stress on the separation of church and state.

This Westward-looking element in Islamic society branded the traditionalists as reactionaries for looking to the past rather than to the future in search of guidance. The Westernizers argued that revolution, not reformed traditionalism, was needed to transform dormant Islamic societies into dynamic entities whose quest for development and progress would emulate the Western model. These Westernizers, also known as modernists and secularists, were not prepared to concede that a reinvigorated Islamic reformism could effect the revolutionary changes required to propel Islamic societies rapidly into the present age.

Those who looked askance upon a passionately revived traditionalism, as manifested in the Wahhābī militancy of eighteenth-century Arabia, or the violent Mahdi movement in eastern Sudan in the latter part of the nineteenth century, were not prepared to admit that such expressions of Islam could constitute the basis of a revitalized Islamic community wherein faith and state would once again march hand in hand. The skepticism of Westernized Muslims was reinforced by a suspicious West, which saw Islamic revivalism as a threat to its own interests in the Islamic world. The time of the reformed traditionalists, or fundamentalists, had not yet come, and it was instead the secular nationalists who (until very recently) occupied center stage in the immediate post-colonial decades.

Despite their secular emphasis, these nationalists were not oblivious in the role of religion as a vehicle for progress. In the words of one authority, "many political, economic and social problems in this part of the world are interwoven with religion. The force of Islam is still much greater than the force of politico-secular nationalism. This basic truth should neither be ignored nor underestimated."[1]

Historically, Islam was aware of the need for periodic rejuvenation. The record of Abū Ḥāmid al-Ghazālī (d. 1111), the leading theologian of his age, is a good case in point. He served as reviver and unifier of Islamic views in the midst of shattering controversies engendered by the arguments of Muslim philosophers and scholastics. He preached reform by a return to the fundamentals of Islam, unencumbered by theological or philosophical wranglings.

Reformers today are sounding the same call, convinced that properly interpreted and applied, Islam can minister effectively to the needs of Islamic peoples everywhere, cure the ailments besetting their societies, and place them upon the path of progress and social betterment. This conviction is grounded in the belief, firmly held by all fundamentalist reformers, that to separate religion from the state constitutes heresy and detracts from the authority of Islam. The two—government and faith—are seen as mutually dependent. These reformers point to the role of the Prophet Muḥammad himself, who not only preached the new religion of Islam but also reordered tribal loyalties (the mark of citizenship in pagan Arabia) to conform with the basic Islamic precept that all believers constitute one nation (*umma*) governed by the law of God—a law that applies equally both to faith and social behavior. The Šarīᶜa is thus at once the constitution of Islam and the law of Muslim lands. Faith sustains government and government upholds faith. The two are intertwined, mutually interdependent, and a necessary corollary of social solidarity and just rule.[2]

Muḥammad al-Ghazālī, a contemporary thinker who espoused Islamic revivalism based on the return to fundamentals, has stated that the ruler in Islam combines in his person spiritual and temporal authority and is at once military commander, judge, and spiritual exemplar. Were it not for Western cultural imperialism, he argued, the spiritual and temporal components of Islam would not have been separated in the thinking of modern Muslims.[3] To him the modern secularist nation-state constitutes a reversion to the *Jāhilīya* (pre-Islamic pagan Arabia), a form of regression that accounts for the disintegration of the Islamic political unity that was once symbolized in the caliphate.

The first important step in reestablishing the model Islamic state as organized by the Prophet Muḥammad is to replace secular governments with states that conform to Islamic decrees governing both the organization and conduct of the state and those selected by true Muslims to lead them. The underlying assumption is that the ties established by the common faith of Islam transcend all ethnic or racial separatism. In this instance faith is stronger than blood, for a state that coheres by virtue of the laws of God, the true ruler and judge of the community of believers, is a state joined by much firmer bonds than those polities based on common nationality.

Modern expressions of nationalism based on ethnic or cultural distinctions are abhorrent to Islamic purists. But since World War I Muslim reformers have been willing to cooperate with Muslim nationalists to combat Western intrusion, influence, and domination over Muslim lands. Such cooperation and resistance was deemed both patriotic and Islamic. Christians shared this sentiment with Muslims and worked together with them to achieve independence.[4] But the resistance of Muslim nationalists was fueled more by a devotion to Islam than a sense of patriotism stemming from allegiance to a particular secular state. The late ᶜAbd al-Raḥmān ᶜAzzām, architect and first secretary-general of a secular organization known today as the League of Arab States, wrote that "in its modern form, nationalism (secular) is a new evil, and racism is worse still." He claimed that until the triumph of Western-style secular nationalism, Muslims had not argued over the racial and nationality questions that have plagued the modern world and given rise to notions of superiority based on ethnic and racial considerations. Islam alone, he argued, can assure the world a triumph of the spirit and lead it away from divisive ideologies arising from material quests, because Islam, in his view, asserts the primacy of humanity over nationality.[5] To him, "the fatherland of the Muslim admits of no geographic delimitations . . . it is a spiritual fatherland, just as religion is a spiritual matter."[6] ᶜAzzām disavowed the European brand of nationalism, blamed it for much of the world's turmoil, and argued that only Islamic universalism, reinforced by its strong spiritualism, could guide the secular arm of society and guarantee it stability and tranquility.

Unlike Muslim secular reformers, Ḥasam al-Bannā, a discontented school teacher who in 1928 founded the Society of Muslim Brethren, insisted that Islam constitutes both religion and state, inseparable. In this view, the whole Muslim world is one indivisible entity, the fatherland of each and every Muslim regardless of ethnic or racial background. To combat present political divisions, Muslim nations were entreated to establish a league of Muslim states, similar in structure to the League of Arab States. Arab unity was to constitute only a preliminary step toward achieving the broader, and more desired, Islamic unity. Non-Muslim citizens were to be treated in accordance with the laws of Islam governing non-Muslim but God-worshipping peoples (*dhimmis*). Al-Bannā was convinced that all the necessary remedies for a "sick" Muslim society can be obtained from the Qurʾān, the ultimate arbiter in Islam.[7]

The linking of political decline with moral and religious decline gave the Islamic reform movement the character of both a political renaissance and a religious rebirth. Fear of and resentment for the West fueled the movement's activism, which aimed at strengthening the ideological defences of Islam after centuries of neglect—a neglect that had caused Islam to drift away from "the reign of reason, from the egalitarianism and individual freedom natural to it," and to "become mired in the less salutary varieties of innovation (*bidᶜah*) and imitation (*taqlīd*)."[8]

Such a reform program presupposes that the disagreements within the ranks of Islamic leaders will disappear and that all will cooperate to bring about the pristine state willed in the Qurʾān and announced as an attainable ideal by the teachings and record of the Prophet Muḥammad. Sunnite-Šiᶜite mistrust in Iran and Iraq, Šafiᶜite-Zaydite strife in Yemen, the mutual distrust of secularist and Islamist, conservative and liberal reformer, and the so-called "internal crisis"[9] of Islam will presumably all be overcome. Simultaneously, the skepticism that has characterized a generation of non-practicing Muslims will disappear with the triumph of the principles preached by an ᶜAbd al-Wahhāb in Arabia over two centuries ago or by an Ayatollah Khomeini in Iran at the end of the 1970s.

If we are to understand the present and future courses of this Islamic activism, we must first consider the historical factors that led to the emergence of conceptual differences concerning Islam's role in faith and society. These conceptions have supported very different notions of the remedy that Islam can provide for a stagnant body politic, deficient in both ethics and morality.

As mentioned above, Ghazālī had apparently provided the remedy in the twelfth century when he reconciled seemingly conflicting views within the body of Islam concerning state and faith, ethics and politics, and the orthodox and non-orthodox interpretations of Islam. But centuries of economic impoverishment, social disintegration, and foreign domination opened a wide gap between the ideals of Islam and the practices of those charged to fulfill its destiny. The latter understood little if anything of Islam's fundamental precepts and their application. Secure under the umbrella of the Ottoman imperium, Muslin and non-Muslim alike were content to endure without much questioning the authority of the caliph-sultan, at least until a few decades before the demise of the empire. The fate of Arab Islam was in the hands of Ottoman sultans who had reduced the caliphate to a mere title and rarely asserted the spiritual leadership inherent in it to the pious. The fact that the empire was more Turkish than Muslim mattered little to Muslims as long as the sultan safeguarded their security. National and sectarian differences did not come into conflict until the last century of the empire's existence. Indeed, even Europeans were inclined to describe all Muslims of the empire as "Turk." The term "Arab" was invariably reserved for the bedouin.

When, due to centuries of benevolent neglect on the part of the Ottoman and other rulers of Muslim peoples, cultural development was arrested and devotional obligations became slack, self-righteous Muslims and non-Muslims alike laid the blame at the doorsteps of the caliph-sultan. Doing so, they made no reference to the anarchic trends generated by their own endless, petty dissensions, tribal feuds, self-serving factionalism, dynastic rivalries, greed, and selfishness. The critics themselves could not agree on methods to solve such problems. Some cried for reform and freedom within the Ottoman framework; others, despairing of such change, demanded complete indpendence. Yet during the most heated phase of the debate, the question of Islam's role was rarely challenged. Admirer and detractor alike still looked to the sultan as defender of *din ve devlet* (faith and state), the premise upon which the fabric of Ottoman rule had rested for over four hundred years. "For the Ottoman, his Empire was Islam itself. In the Ottoman chronicles, the territories of the Empire are referred to as 'the lands of Islam,' its armies as 'Soldiers of Islam,' its religious head as the 'Sheikh of Islam.' Its people thought of themselves first and foremost as Muslims. 'Ottoman' was a dynastic name like Umayyad and Abbasid, which only acquired a national significance in the nineteenth century under the influence of European liberalism."[10]

To the extent that the Ottoman state was able to uphold its protective image, the majority of Muslims, apolitical though they may have been, were prepared to tolerate the seemingly seditious ramblings of critics and reformist liberals. But when several decades of pleading yielded only further deprivation of their liberties and freedom of expression, exasperated Arab Muslims launched a movement to divorce Islam's leadership from the Ottomans. Among the leaders of the movement were ᶜAbd al-Raḥmān al-Kawākibī (1849-1902), Rafīq al-ᶜAẓm (1867-1925), Qāsim Amīn (1863-1908), and Muḥammad Rashīd Riḍa (1865-1935). They attacked the trend toward secular nationalism manifested by the Young Turks, whom they accused of detracting from the unity of Islam, and began to argue for an Arabian leadership based on a reinvigorated and active Islamism. These men and others like them were convinced that only Arab Muslims could now shore up the ideological defences of Islam against an aggressive West. "Islamic reformism saw the Muslim world engaged in a decisive struggle with Europe. Sometimes consciously, sometimes unconsciously, it sought to base its leadership on a foundation of political power."[11]

The stage was now set for the emergence of an Arabic component within the trend toward Islamic activism, and for the ulema, acknowledged spokesmen of the faith, to assume a position of leadership therein. Social and political decline were deemed a malaise of the Muslim community which resulted from the weakening of the individual Muslim and not from any fault intrinsic to Islam itself. Islamic doctrine was deemed sound, requiring only that it be properly understood and applied. The increasing publication of key Islamic works that for centuries had been inaccessible to Islamic readership merely strengthened this conviction.

As the removal of the crust of medieval accretions revealed the workings of the faith in a purer form, moralists pointed the finger of blame for centuries of abuse at their leaders, enjoining them to cease imitating Western ways and to return to the pure teachings of early Islam. Fundamentalists were convinced that the teachings of the Qurᶜān, interpreted rationally, could supply the wherewithal of reform and infuse Islamic society with the vigor necessary to catch up technologically with the more advanced nations of the world.

The arguments put forth by Islamic reformers seemed logical and cogent in their emphasis on the religious approach to overall reform. As the history of the Middle Eastern societies demonstrates, family ties, social relationships, and group loyalties have been conditioned by religious and denominational affiliations. One is a Sunni or Šiᶜite Muslim, a Maronite, Orthodox, or Coptic Christian before he is an Arab, Lebanese, or Persian. Religion often has superseded ethnic affinity in competing for the partaker's loyalty. It would be difficult, therefore, to attempt a radical transformation of values and practices without first assessing both the hold of religion over the individual and denominationalism as a force conditioning his behavior.

Nineteenth-century preachers of reform, both Muslim and Christian, were optimists laboring to upgrade Ottoman principles of rule, which for centuries had allowed denominationalism to govern in the form of the millet system. Indeed, from the administrative beginnings of the Ottoman Empire, the millet, with its stress on religious separatism as the criterion for citizenship, had served as the basis of social and political affiliation. Reformers now envisioned a new Ottomanism that stressed loyalty to state and ruler over loyalty to the millet and its priest-administrator. Muslim reformers believed that Islam could supply that common denominator, without regard, of course, to the sensitivities of non-Muslim Ottoman subjects.[12] To the reformers there was no contradiction, for Islam was simultaneously faith and state.

Thus, early Muslim preachers of reform aimed at the enlightening of established government, headed in the case of the Ottomans by the caliph-sultan. They reminded those who controlled their political and social affairs that it was incumbent upon them by the teachings of fundamental Islam to honor their obligations as rulers and respect the rights of citizens, that is Muslims. They applied logic to put across their arguments. Muḥammad ᶜAbduh (1849-1905), rector of the Azhar University, the leading institution of higher learning in the world of Islam, and a disciple of al-Afghānī, used rational arguments in calling upon Muslims to cease imitating uncritically the ways of their predecessors, a practice that in fact spelled blind conformity to distortions of Islam. Without restoring the role that reason played in the shaping of the pure Islamic polity, Islam could not undergo in the twentieth century the transformation needed to cope with the exigencies of a rapidly changing world. He called for a holistic approach to Islam,[13] and in his polemical treatises[14] set forth those premises that he considered relevant to a viable reformation of Islam. He expected that through the application of reason his fellow ulema would distinguish between the true and the false in the legal practices that they had inherited from predecessors who had long since lost contact with the realities of Islam. He stressed the role of science and education as essential to this reform.

Al-Afghānī had preached the rejection of the West's materialism[15] and the strengthening of the political bonds of Islam to withstand the encroachments of Europe. Both ᶜAbduh and his disciple Riḍā recognized that the political independence, unity, and strength advocated by al-Afghānī could be achieved only if religious reformers joined hands with political reformers.[16] This alliance alone could guarantee "the most firm bond (al-ᶜurwa al-wuthqa), which they advocated for the entire Islamic world.

The Salafīya group endeavored to prove that modernization was compatible with a reformed traditionalism and that modernism was by no means alien to the basic teachings of Islam in its purer stage of evolution, that is, in the days of the Prophet Muḥammad and his companions. They called on the sultan in his capacity as caliph to respect his obligations as titular head of the Muslims and to safeguard the rights of all Muslim subjects. In doing so, they pointed to the exemplary conduct of the first four, or righteous, caliphs of Islam (632-61). Riḍā called for the reestablishment of the institution of šawra (consultation) and close adherence to the provisions of the Šarīᶜa. He criticized those Muslims who sought solutions in a blind emulation of Western ways rather than by following in the footsteps of the righteous caliphs. Strength, he argued, lay in re-affirmation of the spiritual resources of Islam, not in the adoption of Western-style ideologies.[17]

A colleague of Riḍā and a friend, Rafīq al-ʿAẓm, drew attention to the great personalities of Islam in his work *Ašhar mašāhīr al-Islām* (The most famous personalities of Islam).[18] Here he not only stressed their progressive contributions and exemplary conduct, but also accounted for the arrestation in Islam and advanced his views as to how the Islamic world could be set in forward motion again. He turned to Arabo-Islamic revivalism after losing hope in reforming Ottomanism and at a moment when the Young Turks were preaching ethnic Turkish nationalism as a substitute for Ottoman universalism. His immediate concern was the Arabs, and how they could resume leadership of an Islam weakened by Ottoman dependence on the West. As organizer of the Consultative Committee that was intended to decentralize Ottoman government and expose the anti-Arab orientation of the Young Turks, al-ʿAẓm already had close working relations with such leading Arab Muslims as: ʿAbduh, Riḍā, Qāsim Amīn, Fatḥī Zaghlūl, and Ḥasan ʿĀṣim.[19] He now favored an Islamic universalism led by Arabs and branded the policies of the Young Turks as irrational and disastrous to Islam. Reform cannot be achieved by the edge of the sword, he reminded them, nor by conspiracy and alienation of the Arabs.[20] The fact that most of the leaders of the Young Turks were of Jewish or ethnic Balkan background only served to intensify the suspicions of the Muslim Arab Ottomanists concerning this element's regard for Islam.[21]

Although al-ʿAẓm and his colleagues gravitated toward Pan-Islamism to counter the orientation of the centralists toward Pan-Turanism, a movement that purported to unify all Turkish-speaking ethnic groups from Central Asia to Istanbul under the banner of secular nationalism, he nevertheless argued that ties based on ethnic affinities and a common homeland are stronger, more natural, and more enduring than those engendered by the political accidents of history and fleeting common interests.[22] He respected Arabism but did not accept the arguments of those who claimed that nationalist ties are stronger than the Islamic and, like al-Afghānī, he urged all Muslims to unite in order to resist the extension of European culture, which he considered a threat to the Islamic way of life. He refused to equate progress with the emulation of European ways, and he reminded those Muslims affected by Western cultural norms that a revitalized Islam, not European civilization, would guarantee what they sought—freedom, human rights, and egalitarian justice—because these concepts were integral to the fundamental precepts of Islam.[23]

Though their approach was Islamic, non-ulema Muslim reformists were moved more by secular Arab than by Islamic ideals. In treating Islam as a motivating force for change, one must cope with more than one Islamic outlook. In theory Islam may not be subject to varied interpretations, but the existing realities of Islamic societies gave proof of differing views. The modernist, or Western-educated Muslim's outlook differed from that of the ulema, as did the conception of the uneducated masses who, under the influence of Sufi organizations, had given in to much superstition and saint worship, converting their practice of faith into some sort of folk religion. And to a younger generation of educated Muslims, "Islam has become less of a personal faith and more of a national heritage, a product of Arab genius. Traditional Islamic piety, with its elaborate systems of erudition and scholarship, has receded more and more into the small circles of ulema."[24] This latter element took as much pride in its Arabian an in its Islamic heritage and was inclined to support Arabism as an expression of its quest for national identity and progress.

It was al-Kawākibī who first undertook seriously to demonstrate the integral relation of Islam to Arabism as a means of strengthening the Arab Muslim determination to assume leadership of Islam. History was on his side, for it took little effort to show that Islam was at the foundation of Arab society and culture. Secular nationalists, particularly non-Muslims, had hoped to separate these two elements out of fear and mistrust and later for ideological convenience.

The interrelationship of Arabism and Islam did not escape notice by enlightened Christian intellectuals, who were in fact rather proud to announce this reality. Qunsṭanṭīn Zurayq wrote that Arab nationalism "can on no account contradict true religion," and he urged every Arab to "study it, understand its true nature and sanctify the memory of the great prophet (Muḥammad), to whom Islam was revealed."[25] Salīm Sarkīs (1876-1926),[26] a Christian firebrand known for his irreligion, addressed his fellow Syrians from his sanctuary in Egypt with an appeal to "unite with the Muslims and be prepared to gain your freedom from the aggressors [Sultan Abdülhamid's officials] . . . unite with one heart with your Muslim brethern as the source of your interests is one." He called for unity of purpose and unity of action to free the Arab nation from "Turkish oppression," chiding the sultan's government for "bartering the Arab homeland for worldly gain" and predicting a quick demise for it.[27]

Fleeing what he termed Ottoman oppression, al-Kawākibī made a point of touring Arabia, heartland of Islam, where he talked to Arabs of all shades of life, and then recorded his observations and conclusions under the title *Umm al-Qura*.[28] In this widely read work and a later study (in which he expounded the meaning and social impact of tyrannical rule),[29] al-Kawākibī proposed a solution for the Islamic dilemma and a future course for Islam under Arab leadership. An Islamist as well as an Arab nationalist, al-Kawākibī differentiated between Arab and non-Arab Muslims, but made it clear that he strongly criticized Ottoman officials not because they were non-Arab but because they did not behave as good Muslims. He maintained that because Arabs were the original propagators of Islam and had a greater historical and moral commitment to it, it was proper that they should regain the caliphate and thereby the leadership of Islam.[30]

The renaissance of Islam and ultimate unity of all Muslims could occur only with the restoration of Islamic morality and ethics: this is how Muslims had distinguished themselves in the past, argued al-Kawākibī, and it remains the sine qua non of unity in the present and future. By strengthening Islamic ethics and morality, Muslims would be able to withstand the onslaught of the Christian world, not that he doubted the Muslim's ability to head off Christianizing attempts given the deep divisions within Christianity itself.

Al-Kawākibī felt that the Arabs would play the leading role in the resurgence of Islam because they alone of all Muslims were committed by their historical mission to uphold the primacy of faith.[31] He lashed out against oppression, arguing that it led to both religious suppression and the deprivation of political freedom.[32] He advocated a system of checks and balances, institutionalized in a consultative body that would insure the responsible exercise of authority on the part of the ruler[33] and prevent government from sliding into tyranny. The public must be educated and politicized in order to insure the surveillance necessary to help keep rulers in check.[34]

Both Muslim and Christian activists advocated the return of the caliphate to Arab control because, in their eyes, the sultan's government had contravened the Islamic principles of rule with its deprivation of rights and generally suppressive policies. Moreover, Ottoman leaders had discriminated among Muslims on the basis of ethnic differences, where as the Qu ʾ ān teaches that all Muslims constitute one fraternity.[35]

Christian by birth, the Buchnerian Darwinist Šiblī Šumayyil supported an Arab caliphate, arguing that the Arabs not only have a legitmate historical claim to repossessing it, but that they also have a more perfect understanding of the workings of Islam than do the Turks. The latter, Šiblī Šumayyil argued, had gone through the mechanics of memorizing the Qurʾān in Arabic without appreciating its regulatory effect on their conduct, hence the absence of justice, humanity, and culture in their dealings.[36] Riḍā was equally skeptical of the Turks' ability to undergo the changes necessary to insure the extensive reform needed for the reestablishment of enlightened rule and justice. He saw in Ottoman officials "atheists and infidels" who did not understand religion's relevance to nationalism.[37] ᶜAbd al-Raḥmān Bazzāz also upheld the Arabs' claim to the leadership of Islam, maintaining that they were not only its founders, but also the potential saviors both of Islam and, through this reinvigorated faith, of the world as well.

This emphasis on the centrality of the Arabs' role in reform stimulated a consciousness that could be shared by Muslim and non-Muslim alike. While Bazzāz continued to preach nationalist rule, he saw no contradiction between Arabism and Islamism. Similarly, Zurayq insisted that religion and nationalism stem from the same source and argued that "if nationalism is opposed to anything, it is not to religious spirituality, but to the disruptive partisanship which places communal solidarity above the bonds of nationality."[38]

Modernization in a Western civilizational context was not rejected out of hand by these reformers. Riḍā himself conceded that "it is the product of certain intellectual attitudes and social habits which Muslims had lost and in which Westerners came to excel."[39] Progress is in the essence of Islam, and it can be reinstituted as a motivating principle once it has attained a truer understanding of this essence as it had been understood and applied by the Prophet's companions. The companions were open-minded men and women who consulted openly and achieved consensus of opinion (ijmāᶜ) over policy matters. Only by returning to the practice of consultation and consensus, argued Riḍā, could Muslims become progressive. Only by observing the common good (al-maṣlaḥa al-ᶜāmma) could Muslims of varying sectarian differences understand the workings of the Šarīᶜa and achieve progress. Riḍā maintained that the ulema of Islam, Šiᶜite and Sunnite, have a responsibility to unite in one voice in rendering the proper interpretation of the sacred law of Islam, whose guardians they are, so as to promote the general welfare of the Islamic community. "Riḍā combined the concepts of consultation (al-shura) with consensus in order to demonstrate that representative government is feasible under the Islamic system."[40]

Riḍā deferred to the role of the Arabs in the formulation of Islam and the establishment of its hegemony. He insisted, however, that Islam and its laws must be integral to the national polities that they seek to establish. Indeed, he even envisioned a modern caliphate presiding over the legislative and law-enforcement functions of such polities with the ulema serving as overseers. The mullas of Iran have been serving in such a capacity ever since the establishment of the Islamic republic. There and elsewhere the ulema have been active in efforts to reconcile theory and practice in Islam in spite of the opposition of secularist modernists who, like Kemal Ataturk before them, are not convinced that such reconciliation is relevant to a government based on reason and not on religious law. Moreover, and as Sharabi has noted, "reformist thought was, from a methodological standpoint, too ill-equipped to achieve a rational and focused consciousness of social reality. . . . It lacked the basic precondition for such consciousness—the capacity for self-corrective criticism."[41] Al-Afghānī, ᶜAbduh, Riḍā, and other like-minded advocates of Islamic reform in recent times have admitted to no alternative to change and progress, insisting that it can be achieved in steps: first, liberate the mind from the fetters of imitative reasoning, second, revert to basics, undercutting thereby the authority of all but the reforming ulema, and finally, depend on the rational interpretation of religious truth.

Muslim advocates of secular reform were reluctant to accept this formula for reasserting progress in Islam even though many of the early modernists had been disciples of ᶜAbduh (albeit more liberal than he in their willingness to avail themselves of the experiences of the West).

Christian Arab liberals trained in western schools identified with this element in supporting a stance that they held in common, namely that religion should be relegated to the background of political life. They were prepared to accept from the West that which would enable them to strengthen Arab society and to eliminate elements that had weakened it. They were convinced that secular government was necessary to the reform, education, and democratization of their societies. Salvation, they argued, lies in an educated and enlightened populace that can control the conduct of its rulers through representative institutions.

These arguments did not comport with Islam's notions of political authority and its exercise. First, Islam recognized no separation of temporal and spiritual functions; second, orthodox Islam stressed the primacy of the collectivity (al-jamāᶜa) over individual effort. Communal solidarity not individual initiative assures responsiveness at the highest level of government in guaranteeing the rights of citizens. This concept of authority is not a matter of an implicit contract between governor and governed, for it views sovereignty as residing not in the people but in God. God entrusts this sovereignty to those in charge of the faithful's worldly affairs. He makes no reference to the means by which this authority was acquired provided the provisions of the Šarīᶜa are not violated in the discharge of this authority.

In the latter part of the eighteenth century, the Wahhābis of Arabia, in alliance with the house of Saud, became the first to activate Islam for the purpose of accomplishing religio-political objectives. They were followed by the Mahdi movement in the Sudan in the latter part of the nineteenth century, and to a considerable extent by the Grand Sanusi, who sought to establish a theocratic state in equatorial Africa and Cyrenaica. Similarly, the Ottoman reformers known as the Young Turks embarked on a policy of politicizing Islam under the heading of "Pan-Islamism," particularly after the Ottoman state's failure to contain the national upheavals in its Balkan territories. At a congress held in Salonika in 1911, Ahmed Riza, first president of the Ottoman Chamber of Deputies, said that Islam was the only force capable of uniting the disparate elements of the empire.[42] In its first bulletin, published in Geneva in 1913, the Society for the Progress of Islam (Encumeni Terekkiyi Islam) promised to work towards achieving an Islamic unity of purpose to improve the status and strength of the Muslims, and called on all Muslims in and out of the empire to support the Ottoman caliphate as the "last refuge of Islam."[43]

It was too late. Secular Arab nationalists almost simultaneously called for independence and unity under Arab leadership at their own 1913 congress in Paris.[44] The Young Turks responded by launching a secularist movement of their own: Turanism and Pan-Turanism, which purported to work for unity and progress on behalf of all Turkish-speaking peoples within and outside the empire, namely in Central Asia. World War I set the stage for the Arab revolt. Aware of the interdependence of "Islamic and Arab interests," nationalists rallied around the banner of Sherif Hussein of Mecca in 1917. Hussein's speeches between March and June of that year demonstrated that the Islamic emphasis was just as strong as the Arab component in his revolt.[45] His son Abdallah stated that the distinction and greatness of the Arabs derived from Islam and from the traditions of the Prophet, and that history had shown that when the Arabs were weak so was Islam. Attempts by Young Turks to kill Arabic as a language of instruction were deemed a blow to Islam in that the Qurʾān identifies Arabic as the sacred text of the faith, ordained by God's will.

Proclaiming that "we cannot leave our religious and national existence in the hands of the Unionists (C.U.P.),"[46] Hussein rendered the revolt a religious as well as a patriotic obligation. Young Turk leadership was now dubbed a heresy and a defiance of the Šarīʿa. It became incumbent upon righteous Muslims everywhere to strip the Young Turks of their role as arbiters of Islamic destiny because they were held to have violated the moral and religious duties enjoined by Islam. Hussein thus can be considered a pioneer of Islamic activism in this century.[47] Not only did he invoke Islam in the name of Arabism, he simultaneously undermined the Young Turks' attempts to appropriate it for accomplishing their own political ends.

Even such Islamic revivalists as ʿAbduh, al-Kawākibī, Riḍā, and others realized that an Arabic revival was the sine qua non of an Islamic revival. As Dawn noted, "the theory of Arab nationalism. . . grew out of the modernist diagnosis of Moslem decline and presciption for Moslem revival."[48] Religious and secular activists alike refused to concede a position of inferiority to the West and interpreted their current stagnation as the result of a loss of contact with the traditional norms of

Arabo-Islamic civilization. Thus the activist policy espoused by those who favored an Arabic and an Islamic reform came to embrace both culture and politics as well as religion.

Some Christian Arab activists felt more comfortable in separating religion from politics. Ibrāhīm al-Yāzijī (1847-1906) was allegedly the first to call upon all Arabs to awaken and assert their nationalism. But in this call al-Yāzijī preferred to accentuate Arabism as a secular ideal, and not call attention to its Islamic roots. He gloried in the Arabic language and its great cultural legacy. Other Christians like Adīb Isḥāq (1856-85), a disciple of al-Afghānī and an associate of ᶜAbduh but a secular nationalist by disposition, still saw a revived and active Islam as an uplifting force in the life of the East. He attributed decline and weakness in the body politic of the Muslim world to the casting aside of the *Sarīᶜa* and to shameful innovations.[49] In still stronger language, the Lebanese Christian Nadra Muṭrān referred to Islam as "one of the glories of the Arab nation." Because of Islam's Arab character, he saw no advantage in both Christain and Muslim Arabs submitting to Islamic rule. Arabism and Islamism converged in Muṭrān's thinking and philosophy.

But some modernists, even among Muslims, were insisting on separating the religious and secular dimensions of Islam for the purpose of achieving progress in a twentieth-century context. Sāmī Šawqat argued that this is an age of nationalisms not religion.[50] In 1913 Luṭfī al-Sayyid took issue with the Pan-Islamists, who argued that the whole world of Islam constituted the homeland (*waṭan*); he alleged that, on the contrary, there was no alternative but to replace political Islam with nationalism in a secular context (*waṭanīya*).[51] As hard as he tried to identify Arabism and Islamism in the hope of inculcating a unity of purpose in the partisans of both, a leading nationalist of his age, Sāṭiᶜ al-Ḥuṣrī (1880-1968),[52] still could not escape the conclusion that Islam must serve as the instrument of Arab fulfillment before all else.[53]

There were doubts concerning the efficacy of an Arab caliphate even among the ulema themselves. ᶜAlī ᶜAbd al-Rāziq preferred to concentrate on strengthening the spiritual resources of Islam rather than to activate it to accomplish political ends. He saw no reason why secularists could not emulate their counterparts in the West, who for centuries had managed to make progress without wedding religion to politics.[54] He was excommunicated by his fellow ulema and voted out of the judgeship he occupied in Islamic courts.

Muslim secularists supported the principles of Arab nationalism and worked to eliminate Western domination of Arab lands, although Muṣ-ṭafā al-Marāghī, rector of the Azhar, bastion of Islamic learning, had condemned Arab nationalism outright in 1938. Influential Muslim Arab intellectuals were not distracted by such opposition, nor were the Muslim political leaders of the interwar period less inclined to concentrate first on achieving Arab nationalist ends. Some like Aḥamad Ḥasan al-Zayyāt, editor of the important publication al-Risāla (the Message), cooperated with them on the understanding that Arab unity and independence were to serve as the basis of a broader Islamic unity.[55]

European domination of Arab and non-Arab Muslim lands enabled secular principles of government and society to assert themselves and tended to curb Islamic activist trends. The triumphs of Mustafa Kemal in Turkey and of Riza Pahlavi in Iran, the French mandate over Syria-Lebanon, and the British political ascendancy in Egypt, Jordan, and Iraq all served to intensify nationalist secular trends and to dampen Islamic activism in the interwar period. Nationalist activities were channeled towards regaining independence from the French and the British and, in the case of Indonesia, from the Dutch. Meanwhile, foreign domination mangaged to dilute nationalist thought, which no longer concentrated on achieving Pan-Arab or Pan-Islamic unity in the first instance, but independence for countries that became known as Iraq, Jordan, Syria, Lebanon, Libya, Tunisia, Algeria, and Morocco.[56] Foreign occupation had succeeded also in fostering local and denominational nationalisms: Phoenicianism, Pharoahism, Maronitism, Kurdism, and so on, which were in turn countered by such regional movements as the Greater Syria, unified Nile valley, and Magreb unity schemes.

By 1960 all of the above countries had regained their independence but the second component of the Arab secularist dream, a united states of Arabia, has continued to meet with frustration and is able to show only a list of failures: Nasser's attempt to unite Egypt, Syria, and Yemen in 1958-59, the countering paper-unity scheme of the Hashemite-dominated states of Iraq and Jordan, and more recently, the Libyan-sponsored movement to unite Egypt, Syria, and Libya (with only Syria agreeing to unification with Libya). Quite clearly, Arab nationalism was in the throes of a dilemma that Arab leadership could not transcend.[57]

Muslim activists, on the other hand, did bring about the final triumph of the Wahhābī ideal in what became known during the interwar period as Saudi Arabia; the first Islamic polity in over half a millennium. At the end of World War II Pakistan was born. It too was heralded as another Islamic state, although it has failed to make the Šerīᶜa the law of the state as in Saudi Arabia.

Though largely subdued during the period of Western political ascendance in Muslim lands, Islamic activism yielded some concrete results with the formation in 1927 of the Young Men's Muslim Association which, like its Christian counterpart, concentrated on matters of religion and society and avoided political agitation. Its members were educated young men and intellectuals who sought to apply Islamic ethics and morality in their daily lives. Founded in Egypt, the association soon had branch operations in Palestine, Syria, and Iraq. As one authority put it, "The emphasis on religious morality and avoidance of polemical discussion of doctrines insured the association a continuing appeal to young men who would otherwise have fallen under agnostic and secular influences."[58]

The Ikhwān al-Muslimūn (Muslim Brotherhood), founded by Ḥasan al-Bannā at Ismailiya, Egypt, in 1928, represented a concrete attempt to realize reformist Muslim ideas, as preached by Riḍā, in practice. He taught that Muslims should observe the strict teachings of the Qurᵓān in their daily lives. His immediate audience consisted of underprivileged Muslims who believed they could have their share of economic betterment and justice through the restoration of the classical Islamic state.[59] Sayyid Quṭb, a leading member of the brotherhood who was later executed by Nasser's regime, summed up the methods for reducing the essence of Islam to a formula applicable to contemporary Muslim society in his widely read treatise, Social Justice in Islam.[60] In it he stated that Islam represents the unity of worship and social relations, of spiritual and material values in this world and the next, and of all obligations— social, political, and legal—controlled by the sacred law of Islam.[61]

Al-Bannā had stressed the need for Arab unity, but only as a precondition for reuniting the world of Islam and reestablishing the Islamic state. After his assassination in 1949, his philosophy concerning religion and the state was continued by al-Ḥudaybī and ᶜUda, both of whom warned that for secularists to suspend the Šarīᶜa as a font of secular as well as religious law is tantamount to the suspension of Islam itself.[62]

In his *Principles of Government in Islam,*[63] al-Sammān calls Islam "a vital factor in the formation of the state." Arguing that "Islam takes into consideration only the sovereignty of the people and looks upon the state as the servant of the people," he urges Muslims to understand that "their fatherland is a part of their creed, that they are its guardian and responsible for its freedom."[64] He denounces the League of Arab States and calls for an Islamic League instead. While grudgingly conceding that a Muslim might have to acknowledge a "smaller fatherland," one of birth and immediate citizenship, and to defend it and be loyal to it, he maintains that still the "Muslim has a greater fatherland: this is the Muslim state towards which he is attracted by a creed anchored in the depths of his soul." Al-Sammān concludes with the observation that "Muslim peoples will not have a corporate existence unless they are ruled in the true Muslim way and thereby attain internal stability and unless they have an Islamic union strong enough to provide them with power and a voice which counts in the world."[65]

The continuation of the Islamic activist ideal was assured by the strong sympathy it elicited from both known nationalists and those with ambivalent feelings—men like ᶜAzzām who, although a founder of the secular League of Arab States, persisted in his conviction that there is no contradiction between Islamism and Arabism.[66] Al-Bazzāz also argues that the two are complementary, for when "the Muslim Arab . . . exalts his heroes, [he] partakes of two emotions, that of the pious Muslim and that of the proud nationalist."[67] Even Christians, like Khalīl Qubrusī in 1931, called on fellow Christians to accept Islam. He argued that the West had succeeded in corrupting the essence of Christian teachings, rendering it a less viable route to salvation than Islam, which, he asserted, was not only a product of Arab genius, but had remained incorrupt and more egalitarian, benevolent, and democratic than Christianity.[68]

Islamism received an additional boost from an unexpected quarter in the post-World War II era, when it profited from the ideological conflict between the forces representing Godliness and democracy on the one hand, and communistic atheism on the other. The arbiters of American foreign policy in the 1950s deemed it only logical that the seemingly natural antithesis of ideological Islam to communism should be accentuated and strengthened as a foreign policy option in their attempt to contain communist expansion. Through funds made available to respectable educational foundations, the works of leading modern Muslim thinkers were translated into English and became available for study, assessment, and adaptation. The West now had an interest in shoring up the defenses of Islam and Islamic countries.

This maneuver served only to sharpen the differences between advocates of a secular Arab nationalism, like Nasser, and promulgators of Islamic nationalism, like the Muslim Brethern. While not ruling out the role of Islam in providing the basis of Arab socialism, the exigencies of Nasser's confrontational policies with Israel and with Arab rulers dependent for survival on the West dictated his closer political relations with the communist world. This in turn necessitated Nasser's suppression of Muslim activists who opposed dealings with "the atheists." But the Islamists received a boost from Colonel Qadhdhāfī, the ideological successor of Nasser, who believes that the Arabs have a special role to play as promulgators of Islam's political ideals. Thus to the extent that the objectives of Arab nationalism and Islamic nationalism converge, Qadhdhāfī sees no contradiction in espousing both. Indeed, he has followed in the footsteps of Nasser by embracing military and political support from the communist countries. In accepting such support, Qadhdhāfī in no way compromises his Islamic beliefs and policy objectives.

Both Nasser and Qadhdhāfī have sought to undercut one of the communist bloc's most potent weapons, social and economic egalitarianism, by pointing out that this concept is also central to Islam and one of its great strengths. All the reformers have stressed this principle, and al-Bannā has declared in his teachings that Islamic socialism will triumph once discrepancies in material possessions are eliminated and social justice prevails. Al-Bannā did not condemn private ownership, nor did he frown on wealth; he simply insisted that accumulated wealth be used to promote the productivity and welfare of the entire community. He demonstrated that Islam also stressed the work ethic and frowned upon withdrawal from participation in society. Nasser likewise, even after suppressing the Muslim Brethren and imprisoning its leaders, emphasized the socialistic character of Islam and talked about an Arab socialism, which is a euphemism for Islamic socialism.

Whereas the diffuse populist movement fostered by Nasser's emotional appeal to Arab masses everywhere lost momentum with his death, the Arab Resurrectionist Socialist Party based in Syria and neighboring Iraq

came forth to uphold the banner of Pan-Arabism and to blunt communism's sword with its own brand of utopian socialism. Because the party's
membership is multi-sectarian, embracing Christians, Muslims, Druzes,
Armenians, and other minority groups, the party believes it can transcend
religious and ethnic partisanship only by stressing the secular features
of nationalism. It has labored to provide the Arab portions of the Islamic
world with an alternative to the Islamic ideology by appealing to Arabs
on cultural rather than religious bases. Its cofounder and chief ideologue,
Michel ᶜAflaq, who hails from Damascus but now lives in Iraq, has called
on Arabs of all shades of belief to see that politics and faith will play
complementary roles in a united Arab state. By deemphasizing the role
of religion, ᶜAflaq hopes to slow down and eventually eliminate the centrifugal trends of confessional politics. He also hopes to quiet the fear of
non-Muslims who see an activist Islamic movement as an attempt to
smother them with the blanket of Islam. ᶜAflaq does not deny the historic
role of Islam in shaping a distinct Arabic culture that today serves as the
fuel for Arab nationalism and its secular orientation. Indeed, he openly
acknowledges this role, pays deference to Islam as a builder of Arabic
civilization, but prefers that it leave the political destiny of the Arabs to
secular nationalism. He acknowledges that in the days of the Prophet
Muḥammad a political activism was a necessary role for Islam. But at
the same time, the Prophet was an Arab, and the Islam that burst out
of Arabia in the seventh century was led by Arabs. To ᶜAflaq, Islam is
a product of Arab genius, a religion of the Arabs, and the cornerstone
of Pan-Arabism. He sees in Islam "a faithful picture, a complete and true
symbol of the nature of the Arab soul" and not merely an incident of
history; it constitutes to him "a permanent tendency within the Arab
nation." That which "represents the Arab soul in its absolute reality,
cannot be known by the intellect but only by living experience"[69] –
hence the argument that Islam must abandon politics to secular agencies.

From the pronouncements of activists, be they secularist or non-secu-
larist nationalists, Arab Muslim or non-Arab Muslim, traditionalist or
modernist, we might tentatively conclude that Islam is the basis of their
motivation. It would appear that to work for the triumph of a nationalist
ideal divorced from Islam, as religion, ideology, or all-embracing way of
life, will end in frustration. Religion and nationality are difficult to separate in the lives of Middle Easterners, be they Muslim, Christian, or Jew.

For the Arab Muslim, Islam represents both the embodiment of his faith and his cultural assertion; for the non-Muslim Arab it constitutes his heritage, source of pride, and an indivisible part of the nation to which he belongs.

A commonly shared view among modern ideologues is that some form of Islam will remain at the foundation of Arab and non-Arab Muslim societies and will continue to govern their religious, socio-economic, and political development. We have a recent reminder of this assertion in the mullas' assuming the reins of state and society in Iran and in the continuing clash between partisans of an Islamic state and a nationalist secular system in neighboring Turkey and Afghanistan. In Saudi Arabia, a state governed by Islam in its purer form, rapid development towards modernization with full use of the latest technology seems to belie the customary view of secularist modernists that such progress cannot be achieved without separating church and state. For the moment, Islamic activism appears to be moving to center stage in its continuing drive to assert the primacy of religion in state and society.

NOTES

1.   Zeine Zeine, *The Emergence of Arab Nationalism* (Beirut, 1966), p. 142.

2.   For further details see E. I. J. Rosenthal, *Political Thought in Medieval Islam* (Cambridge, 1962), pp. 97-102; see also his *Ibn Khalduns Gedanken über den Staat* (Munich, 1932), pp. 50-60.

3.   See al-Ghazālī's *Min huna na^clam* [From here we know] (Cairo, n.d.), p. 55.

4. Makram ^cUbayd, then minister of finance in Egypt, told Marcel Colombe, author of *L'évolution de l'Egypte* (Paris, 1951), p. 146: "I am a Christian, it is true, through my religion, but through my fatherland, I am a Muslim," which applies to other Christians.

5.   See my translated edition of ^cAzzām's *The Eternal Message of Muḥammad* (New York, 1964), pp. 241-43.

6.   Ibid., p. 240.

7.   Muḥammad al-Maḥzūmī, *Khāṭirāt Jamāl al-Dīn al-Afghānī al-Ḥusaynī* [Memoirs of . . .] (Beriut, 1931), p. 88.

8.   Robert Haddad, *Syrian Christians in Muslim Society* (Princeton, N.J., 1970), p. 89.

9.   For a detailed analysis of this statement see H. Sharabi, *Nationalism and Revolution in the Arab World* (Princeton, N.J., 1966), pp. 6-7.

10.   Bernard Lewis, "Islamic Revival in Turkey," *International Affairs*, 28/1 (January, 1952), 47.

11.   Hisham Sharabi, *Arab Intellectuals and the West* (Baltimore, 1970), p. 27.

12.   Evidence of this type of argument is seen in *al-Manār* [The Lighthouse] of Riḍā, a publication dedicated to Islamic reform and rejuvenation. See vol. 1 (1897), and subsequent issues.

13.   Detailed in his *Risālat al-tawḥīd* [The Epistle of Unicity] (Cairo, 1315/1897); French translation by B. Michel & M. Abdel Razik (Paris, 1925); English translation by I. Musaᶜad & K. Cragg (London, 1966).

14.   See his *al-Islām wa 'l-radd ᶜala muntaquidīh* [Response to the Critics of Islam], which appeared for the first time in *al-Muᵓayyad*, vanguard of Islamic newspapers, published in Cairo (1327/1929) and translated into French by M. T. Harb, *L'Europe et l'Islam* (Cario, 1950).

15.   Elaborated upon his treatise *al-Radd ᶜala al-dahriyīn* [Refutation of the Materialists], translated from Persian by ᵓAbduh himself (2d ed. (Cairo, 1955); and in his memoirs edited by M. Makhzūmī.

16.   See the introduction of ᶜAbduh's biography by Ridā, *Taᵓrīkh al-Ustādh al-Imām Muḥammad ᶜAbduh* (Cairo, 1931), 2 vols.

17.   See his *al-Khilāfa aw al-imāma al-ᶜuẓma* [The caliphate or the greatest leadership], which first appeared in vols. 23 and 24 of *al-Manār*, then separately in 1341/1921.

18.   Published in Cairo, 1344/1925.

19.   See *Majallat al-Majmaᶜ al-ᶜIlmī al-ᶜArabī* (Damascus), 12/5 (December, 1925), pp. 561-65 for further detail.

20.   See "Rafīq Beg al-ᶜAẓm, 1282-1342 [1865-1924]," in *al-Zahrā* (Baghdad), 3/4 (R II, 1344/1925), a biographical account; also ᶜUthmān al-ᶜAzm, *Majmūᶜat Āthār* [Collection of Rafīq's works] (Cairo, 1344/1925), pp. 125-26.

21.   For more on their backgrounds, see R. W. Seton-Watson, *The Rise of Nationality in the Balkans* (London, 1917), pp. 134-36.

22.   See his *al-Jāmiᶜa al-Islāmīya wa Urūbba* [The Islamic commonwealth and Europe] (Cairo, 1344/1925), p. 49.

23.   *al-Jāmiᶜa al-Islāmīya*, pp. 52-54.

24.   Hisham Sharabi, *Nationalism and Revolution in the Arab World* (Princeton, N.J., 1966), p. 6.

25.   From his *al-Islām wa 'l-qawmīya al-ᶜArabīya* [Islam and Arab nationalism] (Baghdad, 1952); cited in Sylvia Haim's translation in *Die Welt des Islams*, n.s. 4 (1954), 207.

26.   For a brief biographical note see Jurjī Bāz, *Salīm Sarkīs* (Beriut, 1926).

27.   See his "Bayānnāmé al-umma al-ᶜArabīya," dated 17 R 1298 and published in his newspaper *al-Mušīr,* issue of 29 May 1895.

28.   "The mother of towns," a term ascribed to Mecca as the first city of Islam.

29.   Titled *Tabāᵓiᶜ al-istibdād wa maṣāriᶜ al-istiᶜbād,* published anonymously at first (1903) in a number of issues of *al-Muᵓayyad;* see back ground information in I. S. Najjār's biography of him in *al-hadīth,* year 25, 2 (February, 1951), 111-21.

30.   This is the central theme of his *Umm al-Qura;* other tracts were written for the purpose of asserting Arab primacy in Islam, notably *Ṣaḥāᵓif Qurayš,* sent to the sultan after the author's death; but most of his treatises were confiscated. See Sāmī al-Kayyālī, "Dhikra 'l-Kawākibī," *al-Ḥadīth,* year 26, issues 9 and 10 (September-October, 1952, commemorating the 50th year of his death), 537-41.

31.   For more details see his *Umm al-Qura,* pp. 212-16; also Nobert Tapiero, *Les idées réformists d'al Kawâkibi. . .* (Paris, 1956), pp. 98-102.

32.   His *Ṭabāᵓiᵓ al-istibdād* [The moods of tyranny] is dedicated to the study of oppression and its impact on society.

33.   He had read Montesquieu's works, as well as those of Alfieri Vittoria (1749-1803). See Aḥmad Amīn's "Zuᶜamāᵓ al-islāh al-Islāmī fī 'l-ᶜaṣr al-ḥadīth: al-Sayyid ᶜAbd al-Raḥmān al-Kawākibī" [Champions of Islamic reform in the modern age . . .], in *al-Thaqāfa,* no. 303 (issue of 30 L 1363/17 October 1944), 5-7.

34.   From his *Ṭabā ᵓiᶜ al-istibdād;* see also "Ṣafaḥāt lam tunšar min kitāb Taba iᶜ al-istibdād," in *al-Ḥadīth,* year 26, issue of Sept.-Oct., 1952; also *al-Thaqāfa,* year 6, issues 304-06 (ZI 1363/ Oct. 1944) for more details on tyranny's impact; also Raᵓīf Khūrī, *Maᶜālim al-waᶜī al-qawmī* (Beriut, 1941), pp. 204-12.

35. For more see Rafīq al-ᶜAzm, *al-Jāmiᶜa al-ᶜUthmānīya wa 'l-ᶜasabīya al-Turkīya aw al-taᵒlīf bayn al-Turk wa 'l-ᶜArab* [Ottoman unity and Turkish fanaticism or reconciling Turk with Arab] (Cairo, 1344/1925).

36. Published in *Lisān al-ᶜArab,* which he edited; issue of 27 January 1896 (no. 447).

37. Cited in Charles Adams, *Islam and Modernism in Egypt* (London, 1933), p. 181.

38. Cited by Hazem Nusseibeh in his *Ideas of Arab Nationalism* (Ithaca, N.Y., 1956), p. 92. Nusseibeh made much of the basic inter-relatedness of Islamic and Arab nationalism in their mutual dependence and sharing of ideals: freedom, unity, and justice for Arab and non-Arab Muslims as well.

39. Majid Khadduri, *Political Trends in the Arab World* (Baltimore, 1972), p. 67.

40. Ibid., p. 69.

41. Sharabi, *Arab Intellectuals,* p. 35.

42. Great Britain. *Foreign Office Handbooks,* 96a (*The Rise of Islam and the Caliphate*) and 96b (*The Pan-Islamic Movement*) (London, 1919), pp. 68-69.

43. Full text in Bibliothèque nationale (Paris), 80 2g/779, cited by Zeine, *Emergence,* p. 89.

44. See Negib Azoury's *Réveil de la nation arab dans l'Asie Turque* (Paris, 1905) for the views of both Christian and Muslim Arabs on na-tionalism.

45. For texts of Hussein's speeches on the subject, both in Arabic and French, see "Textes historiques sur le réveil arabe au Hedjaz," *Revue du Monde Musulman* (henceforth *RMM*), 46 (1921); also in Amīn Saᶜīd's collection entitled *al-Thawra al-ᶜArabīya al-kubra,* 3 vols. (Cairo, n.d. [1943?]).

46. *RMM,* 46 (1921), 21.

47. For a cogent analysis of Hussein's attitude see Ernest Dawn, *From Ottomanism to Arabism* (Urbana, 1973), pp. 77-86.

48. Ibid., p. 140.

49. For details see his *al-Durar* [ed. by his brother ᶜAwnī] (Beriut, 1909), pp. 202-3.

50.   Former minister of education in Iraq. See Haim, *Die Welt des Islams* (1956), pp. 136-41 for details of his views.

51.   E. I. J. Rosenthal, *Islam in the Modern National State* (Cambridge, 1968), p. 122.

52.   For a full analysis of his career and thinking see W. L. Cleveland, *The Making of an Arab Nationalist. . . Sati^c al-Husri* (Princeton, N.J., 1971).

53.   See his "Hawla 'l-wahda al-^cArabīya" in *al-Risāla* (Cairo, issue 315 [1939]) addressed to Taha Hussien; also "Bayna 'l-wahda al-Islāmīya wa 'l-wahda al-^cArabīya" [Between Islamic unity and Arab unity], ibid., no. 328 (1939).

54.   From his treatise *al-Islām wa usūl al-hukm* [Islam and the foundations of government] (Cairo, 1925).

55.   See Nabīh Fāris, *Ghuyūm ^cArabīya* [Arab clouds] (Beriut, 1951), p. 91.

56.   See my "Impact of the West on Ideological Conflicts in the Arab World," *Islamic Culture*, 35/2 (1961), 100-14, for an analysis of the centrifugal tendencies generated by Western involvement.

57.   For a full treatment of this problem see my article, "The Dilemma of Arab Nationalism," *Die Welt des Islams*, n.s. 8/3 (1963), 140-64.

58.   Khadduri, *Political Trends*, p. 72.

59.   See his *Da^cwatuna fī tawr jadīd* [Our mission is a new phase] (Cairo, n.d.) for his views on the brotherhood's mission.

60.   *Al-^cAdāla at-ijtimā^cīya fī 'l-Islām* (Cairo, ca. 1945); translated for ACLS by J. B. Hardie (Washington, D.C., 1953).

61.   *Al-^cAdāla*, p. 28.

62.   Citations by Rosenthal, *Islam*, p. 124.

63.   Usus al-hukm fī'l-Islām (Cairo, 1953).

64.   From a translation by S. G. Haim, quoted by Rosenthal, *Islam*, p. 115.

65.   Ibid., pp. 115-16.

66.   For details S. G. Haim, ed., *Arab Nationalism: An Anthology* (Berkeley, 1976), pp. 154-66.

67.   Ibid., p. 56; for the full text of the speech see selection 15 in ibid., pp. 172-88; and for details of his views, his *Min rūh al-Islām* [From the spirit of Islam] (Baghdad, 1959).

68. See his *Da^cwat naṣāra al-^cArab ila 'l-dukhūl fī 'l-Islām* [A call to Christian Arabs to convert to Islam] (Cairo, 1931).

69. Cited by Haim, *Arab Nationalism*, p. 62.

AHMAD KASRAVI AND THE "PURIFICATION" OF PERSIAN: A STUDY IN NATIONALIST MOTIVATION

Amin Banani
University of California, Los Angeles

Common to all the diverse efforts which have been made for "purification" of Persian since the last quarter of the nineteenth century—be they the caprices or crusades of individuals, arbitrary promulgations of self-appointed associations, or the officially sponsored and enforced decisions of the *Farhangestan*[1] —is an ill-defined but unmistakable hostility to Arab influence on Persia. The present essay is concerned not with the linguistic aspects of these arbitrary manipulations of a language, but instead approaches them as a tangible index for the understanding and analysis of nationalism. Openly avowed or tacitly implied in the arguments of all such advocates of "purification" of language—from the ludicrous de-Latinizers of English, to Adamantios Korais and his pleas for the *katharevousa,* to his counterparts among virtually every Balkan nationality in the Ottoman realm, to the "Yeni Turan" and its organ, the *Turk Yurdu,* and to the Nazis and their predecessors in Germany— is an assertion or evocation of a sense of national superiority. "Purification" of language is not only motivated by nationalism, but it is also one of the more definable symptoms of that complex ideology.

The study of the relation of movements for the "purification" of language to nationalism is particularly instructive as it permits one to deal with an actual historical phenomenon, and also allows one both to gain insight into a crucial phase in the genesis of nationalism and to understand the characteristics of one of its components. In such a study one must carefully distinguish between the sense of cultural attachment and pride which is attendant on and perhaps resultant from philological studies

463

and literary revivals, and the impassioned endeavors to "purify" a language by eliminating alien words and influences and replacing them with unfamiliar or synthetic words from a purportedly superior past. This distinction is, in fact, central to any analysis of the origins, the stages of development, and the distinguishing properties of nationalism.

The growth of nationalism in Persian is generally corroborated by comparative examples, particularly by those drawn from central and southeastern Europe and from the Turkish and Arab parts of the Ottoman Empire. Indeed, Istanbul, and to a lesser extent Beirut and Cairo, often provided direct stimuli for developments in Persia. Early literary revivals preceded and gave a considerable impetus to the emergence of nationalism. But the efforts for "purification" of language crystallized later, and from the start were symptomatic of the newly emerging modern nationalism. In their open hostility to Arab influences and their thinly veiled ambivalence toward Islam, in their evocation of a glorified past and their assertions of superiority over all neighbors, these efforts displayed some of the insoluble tensions and pernicious tendencies that have characterized modern nationalism.

When the historian subjects the totality of nationalism to analysis he is tempted to begin, and perhaps to remain, on broad plans of generalization. This approach also entails a dangerous conceptual and methodological pitfall, for it tends to elevate the ideology of nationalism above its concrete historical context, and to endow it with a life of its own. But in fact, the very considerations that are paramount for analysis of the genesis of nationalism, a grasp of the pragmatic, temporal, and existential context of ideological change, do not lend themselves to purely intellectual abstractions. These factors can be fruitfully examined in the study of a particular event or a historical movement, and still more revealingly, in the analysis of the interactions between such movements and the men who are responsible for shaping, leading, or transforming them. A sensitive pursuit of the growing resonance between the man and the movement, the idea and the event, then, is a suitable conceptual framework for historical inquiry into the origins, nature, and development of nationalism.

The life and labors of Ahmad Kasravi, and his impact upon the modern Persian scene are by no means limited to the category of nationalism. Nor are his views on reform of the Persian language exclusively "purificatory" and therefore, related only to nationalism. But his growing concern with "purification," and the course of his struggles for that cause, as well as the considerable response that he evoked, provide us with a remarkable opportunity to inquire into the forces and ideas that affected the birth and development of modern Persian nationalism. Kasravi is the more eligible for such a scrutiny as he was no mere intellectual critic and theoretician, but an intense and courageous activist. His relatively short life embraced the full range of collective and cumulative experiences that had evolved through the lives of three generations of Persian intellectuals and political activists, from liberal awakeners to revolutionary nationalists. In the end he was struck down in the struggle against a milieu that had refused to keep pace with him.

We are afforded a vivid panorama of this encompassing experience in Kasravi's labors on behalf of the Persian language. His initial steps were self-taught and random forays into some of the dialects of Persia, studies that display a precise temperament and a surprising degree of scholarly merit. There followed a relatively mild phase of interest in "purification" and a tenaciously self-sustained campaign to reform Persian by battling the high degree of imprecision, inexpressiveness, and sterile verbosity of the contemporary language. And finally, he embarked upon a self-righteous crusade for "purifying " Persian, or eliminating from it all traces of Arabic. The three phases of Kasravi's career were nearly synchronous with the 1920s, 1930s, and the first half of the 1940s.

Nationalistic tendencies and motives are increasingly present and perhaps paramount in all three phases of Kasravi's preoccupation with the Persian language. We must consider the personal experiences, the external influences, and the pragmatic circumstances that surrounded periods of gradual or abrupt change in Kasravi's development if we are to learn anything about the nature and influence of nationalism, and the interaction of events and ideas.

Ahmad Kasravi was born in the Hokmavar section of Tabriz, a poor area of urban lower class and farm laborers, on the first of October 1890. He was the first surviving son in a family of *mullas*. His father, although he had received the education of a *mulla* and was very devout and pious, had forsaken the ancestral calling and lived as a merchant. Family tradition, however, survived this solitary lapse, and everyone, including the father, awaited a son to continue the tradition of religious learning and to resume the family birthright to the spiritual leadership of Hokmavar. Ahmad grew up with a conscious sense of destiny and even as a young boy he felt the deference and the expectations reserved for a man of religious learning.[2]

His future views on language were influenced by the traditional education required for a person of his social calling, as well as by his Azarbaijani identity. A recurrent theme of bitter and discouraging school experiences runs throughout his gloomy recollections of childhood. He recalled that in the *maktab*[3] "after the *Qur'an* we had to read the *Golestan, Jam-e Abbasi, Nisab, Tarrasul, Abwab al-Janan,* . . . and other similar texts. These were our school primers. Books that were not written for classroom use by children, and some of which were replete with very difficult Arabic words and phrases, were put in the hands of children. I, who knew neither Persian nor Arabic, had to struggle with these books. And as the *akhund* was also ignorant of Persian, I had to learn to read these books at home with the help of my father or other relatives."[4]

Kasravi's Azarbaijani provenance must also be sensitively considered in any analysis of the views that bear upon his contribution to the formulation of Persian nationalism, and nowhere is this consideration more germane than in the elaboration of his views on the Persian language. A discussion of the contributions that Azarbaijanis have made to Persian letters is outside the purview of this study. Nevertheless, the quality and quantity of these contributions, both in creative belles lettres and critical scholarship, particularly in the nineteenth and early twentieth centuries, has been a potent issue in the volatile complex of mutual attitudes developed by Turkish-speaking Azarbaijanis and Persians. Among these sometime facetious and often acrimonius attitudes characteristic of educated Azarbaijanis and Persians, a feeling that the Persian language is superior to the Turkish constitutes at once the sharpest weapon in the armory of the Persian and the most vulnerable spot in the defense of the Azarbaijani. Not until late in the nineteenth century did any of the Azarbaijani in Persia respond to this challenge with a concerted effort to place Turkish on an equal literary footing with Persian. When they did, their response echoed voices in Baku, Tiflis, and Istanbul, and was far from the representative response of the educated Azarbaijanis of Persia. The latter's usual reaction to the taunts of the Persians was to point to the vast company of Azarbaijanis who had added luster to the Persian language.

Ahmad Kasravi was hardly a typical man, but in his views on the relative merits of Persian and Azari Turkish he was more akin to the traditional Azarbaijani than to the new "separatist" Azarbaijani literati. Both in the intellectual development of his position on Persian language, and through the experiences surrounding and affecting that development, there runs a thread of modern Persian nationalistic motivation—a motivation that, far from submerging his Azarbaijani identity, often produced a fascinating and revealing paradox of reactions. He left no doubt of his love for the Persian language and his conviction of its superior merits: "Persian is one of the best languages. Of the seven or eight languages with which I am familiar Persian is the most beautiful and the least complicated. I do not say this thoughtlessly, nor out of patriotic fervor."[5] On occasions he went even further, advocating an active campaign to eradicate the various dialects in Persia,[6] including his own mother tongue, Azarbaijani Turkish,[7] as a necessary step for removing elements of disunity in the nation.

Indeed, the occasion that marked the first prominent involvement of Ahmad Kasravi in the political arena was precipitated largely by his adamant stance on the use of Persian in Azarbaijan. At a meeting of the leaders of the Democratic Party in Tabriz in 1918, Kasravi, then twenty-eight, led a successful protest against the dubious patriotism of certain fellow Democrats. The Party also approved two resolutions chiefly as result of Kasravi's persuasion: (1) that "Mirza Taqi Khan, who had gone to the Ottoman camp, had published a newspaper in Turkish and in the Ottoman interests, had composed a Turkish panegyric to Khalil Pasha and recited it at the ceremony for the arrival of the Ottoman commander in the Tabriz railway station, be expelled from the Party for his hypocrisy;" (2) that "all the proceedings and speeches at the meetings of the Party be in Persian; and the Party accept as its policy the growth and dissemination of Persian in Azarbaijan."[8] His success on that day led to a bitter rivalry with Shaikh Mohammad Khiyabani, the leader of the Democratic Party, and eventually resulted in the formation of a faction known as *tanqidiyyun* (The Critics), galvanized and led by Kasravi.[9]

Still, Kasravi frequently voiced indications of the characteristic Azarbaijani contempt for the lethargy and indolence of the Persians. These attitudes emerged clearly when he condemned the Persians for the debasement of their own language. It was as though he, an Azarbaijani, galled by the linguistic snobbery of the Persians, condescended to save their language: "So far research in the history and language of Persia has been the preserve of a band of European orientalists, and Persians have come to believe that only Europeans are capable of such work. . . . This conviction of the Persians. . . is based on nothing but ineptitude. . . . I take pity on this miserable helplessness of Persians and wish to tear up this veil of cowardice and inferiority."[10] So wrote Kasravi in 1928-29, a year of fundamental crisis and profound change in his outlook, in the preface to a small volume on toponymy. He was also apt to point to the comparative explicitness and precision of Turkish, thereby demonstrating the absence of those qualities in Persian.[11] But there was never a tinge of Pan-Turanism in Kasravi and he constantly disparaged Mongol and Tatar impacts on Persia. The immediate seed of his nationalist motives, however, must have been the natural and traditional anti-Ottomanism of the *shi^cih* Azarbaijani.

Kasravi's professional career, marked as it was by his crusading effort, was a mosaic of intense conflicts with the human and institutional frailties that surrounded him. The immediate irritations and the specific incidents that led to these struggles were often precipitated by his own unbending independence, his headstrong integrity, and his willful and temperamental pursuit of reason and action. Indeed, to ignore his highly personal sense of the moral categorical imperative[12] would be seriously to misrepresent Kasravi; it was the chief facet of his personality. Nevertheless, underlying many of these clashes was a strong current of nationalist motivation, and many of them stemmed from his preoccupation with language.

A brief and unhappy stint as the *mulla* of Hokmavar, a year as teacher of Arabic in the American Presbyterian mission school in Tabriz, and a period of restless inactivity during the final year of the Great War, were followed in 1919 by Kasravi's inadvertent entry into the Ministry of Justice. He spent nearly eleven fitful and contentious years in that Ministry. Brief periods of high responsibility, uncommon accomplishment, and personal satisfaction interrupted an otherwise continuous record of clashes—clashes with jealous and vindictive *ulama* whose hold over the administration of justice was being challenged by the Ministry, conflicts with local magnates, feuds with ubiquitous rivals for his authority, wranglings with colleagues, and bitter frustrations suffered at the hands of his superiors. He left the service of the Ministry in 1930 after a courageous stand against pressure from the royal court in a case involving expropriation of land. Kasravi never accepted another official post.

His tenure in the Ministry of Justice was characterized by frequent reassignments which took him to virtually every corner of Persia, and by periodic resignations or dismissals which afforded him ample time for developing his avocations. His professional peregrinations profoundly influenced the development of his views on language and nationality. Two interrelated fields of activity, both of them related to nationalistic motivations, constituted the pragmatic setting for his formative ideological period: (1) an avid interest in the various Iranian dialects which he encountered at his numerous posts, and (2) his personal response to the Pan-Turkist claims concerning Azabaijan and the Arab assertions regarding Khuzestan (which until 1924 was known as Arabestan). He studied dialects in Azarbaijan, Mazanderan, Khuzestan, and Lorestan with the aid of indigenous speakers as well as historical, literary, philological, lexicographic, and geographical sources.

Kasravi's first work (in what was to be an amazing torrent of publications) appeared in 1925. It was an investigation into the Azari dialect, the pre-Turkish language of Azarbaijan. He explicitly said that the furor created by Pan-Turkist claims and Persian counterclaims over the identity of Azarbaijanis had led him to make his study.[13] Evidence of an Iranian dialect superseded by Turkish in relatively recent centuries was a significant catalyst in the development of Kasravi's nationalistic ideology. The implications of this objective knowledge were heightened by a subjective experience of achievement and self-importance, for it was this first publication that brought him a measure of international recognition and respect, earned him membership in the British and American Oriental Societies, and enlisted the patronage of Teimurtash, the powerful court minister of Reza Shah.[14]

He had spent a tenuous year (1924) as the chief of judiciary in Khuzestan, where actual control by the Arab Shaikh of Muhammara (*Khiz^{c}il*) rendered Kasravi virtually impotent, and where his daring attempts at exercise of authority actually endangered his life. Out of this period of personal frustration came his studies in local history and the Iranian dialects of Khuzestan.

It is doubtful that Kasravi had an integrated and far-reaching nation-alistic ideology while he was engaged in these linguistic and historical enterprises. Recalling these labors in his autobiography, written in 1944, two years before his death, however, he was explicit on the need to eradicate all these dialects as a step toward national unity.[15]

Our focus on the interactions between Kasravi's experiences and the development of his ideas should not deflect us from the monumental event of his generation, this is, the apparently radical change in the concrete historical situation of Persia occasioned by the accession of Reza Shah Pahlavi. On the surface it appears that there should have been a basic harmony between Kasravi and the emerging ideological tone of Reza Shah's regime. The intense patriotic fervor, the appeal to national pride, the evocation of a glorified ancient history, the growing secularism, the officially promoted language "purification," and above all, the activism that characterized the new regime—all appeared to be in harmony with the ideas of Kasravi. More concretely, it was to extend the power of Reza Shah's government to Khuzestan that Kasravi was assigned to that province in 1924; and it was Reza Shah's "conquest" of Khuzestan which delivered Kasravi from probable death. Later, the patronage of Teimurtash, Reza Shah's closest adviser, kept Kasravi's enemies at bay and procured him high office in the Ministry of Justice. No doubt the experience of Reza Shah's regime constituted the overwhelming existential context of Kasravi's ideological development.

Yet, Kasravi's was a dissonant and dissatisfied voice in that era of the "savior of the nation." His dissatisfaction sprang from a series of personally disillusioning and frustrating experiences, but the dissonance was due to a deeper sense of rebellion against the basic moral void and ideological vapidity of that tinsel period in the modern history of Persia. Soon after the establishment of Reza Shah's power in Khuzestan, Kasravi clashed with the rapacious and omnipotent officers of military government and was brushed aside. There followed three years of forced retirement (1925-28) with severe material hardship and privation. During his final two years on the bench (1929-30), he succeeded thoroughly in making himself a persona non grata by refusing to bend before the gathering force of Reza Shah's despotism.

It was in those three years, 1925 to 1928, that Kasravi began his prolific literary output. He launched his first serious attempt to learn a pre-Islamic Iranian language (he began studying Pahlavi with E. Herzfeld) in 1927, a year that marked the nadir of his career with both the bitterness of apparent professional failure and poverty pressing upon him.[16] The year 1928, both by Kasravi's own assertion and by the external evidence of his changing style and focus (from scholarly works to social and ideological themes), was the year of a sudden and intense psychological metastasis. His own references to this phenomenon are elliptical and uninformative: "It was in this year [1928] that a severe upheaval appeared in my mind; and when I journeyed to Gilan that upheaval became ever so stronger."[17] One thing is certain: this transformation, which ushered in the less rational and more expansive phase of his ideological development, took place under adverse subjective circumstances. Clues revealing the nature and direction of this soul-searching are to be found in abundance in *A 'iyn,* a short book that Kasravi published in 1932. It had taken the quick-writing Kasravi three years to shed his scholarly reserve and to gather his psychic energies for this passionate commentary on the predicament of modern man. It is a quixotic assault on "Western" civilization and its soul, the machine. It is a ringing, Jeremiah-like warning to the "East" to preserve its soul and its ways, and to triumph over the forces of materialism by the power of religion. (At the end of the book it turns out that his notion of religion is a peculiarly Western blend of deism and humanism.) *A 'iyn* took many Persians by surprise, and it proved a great source of embarrassment to the regime. Although it seemed to echo the xenophobic official mood, it was in fact a clear condemnation of the haphazard westernization and Kemalist imitations characteristic of Reza Shah's regime.

In 1933 Kasravi founded the monthly periodical *Peyman,* which served as the organ of his personal crusade to invest the sterile atmosphere of Reza Shah's Persia with an ideology and a sense of moral conviction. Although there was no conscious rapport between Kasravi and the arbiters of the regime, the latter sensed the need to fill the gaping ideological void, and partly tolerated this persistent and courageous gadfly.

From the start *Peyman* was written in a "semi-purified" Persian which while consciously avoiding Arabic words, was still comprehensible and even graceful. The barbarous *zaban-e pak* (the pure language) of the 1940s was yet to appear, but from its first issue *Peyman* served as Kasravi's platform for the exposition and dissemination of "purification" of Persian.

Kasravi entered upon the stage of language "purification" not as a pioneer but as a reformer; he was to leave as a law-giving prophet. Sporadic attempts at writing "pure" Persian, that is, free from Arabic words, are encountered throughout the history of the Persian language. Sometimes such reform is a worthy effort to endow Persian with technical and philosophical terminology, such as in Ibn Sina's *Daneshaname-ye Ala'i* (10th century A. D.). Often the purification is the caprice of a poet or a scribe, and sometimes it is carried out in the spirit of "Iranism." Such is the case with the *Dasatir*, an allegedly ancient text, actually forged in India by a group of parsee zealots in the 17th century; it has served as the inspiration of many a "purifier" in the nineteenth and twentieth centuries. The so-called literary renaissance of the early Qajar period (1820s to 1850s), with its emphasis on writing simpler prose, was not so much a result of novel social and ideological forces, as a consequence of the inevitable and staggering collapse of basic communication —a mere stylistic detour, necessitated by the sheer impasse of the old style. Simplification also meant avoidance of unassimilated and obscure Arabic words, but the link with the patriotic caprices of the late nineteenth-century "purifiers" was only fortuitous. The Revolution of 1906 gave an impetus to the development of modern Persian nationalism, and "purification" of Persian found new exponents.

The chief external influences upon the Persian "purifiers" of the Constitutional era (1905-11) came from Istanbul, where many Persians were quick to absorb and reflect the example of the "Yeni Turan" ideologists (and where Persian language newspapers such as *Akhtar* carried these reflections back to Persia), and from the relatively recent parsee emigres in India. In 1922 a certain Abol-Qasem Azad of Maraghe returned from a sojourn of several years in India and founded a periodical dedicated to the cause of "Parsi sareh." He was both a native Persian, and a Muslim, which meant that he could denigrate the Islamic heritage of Persian with greater impunity. The advent of Reza Shah with his frequent emulations of Kemalist programs prepared the ground for the disease of "purification."

Compared with the ludicrous views and activities of the self-appointed "purifiers" of the 1920s, Kasravi's articles in *Peyman* appear temperate and well reasoned. He exorcises his contemporaries for their unscientific

approach, for their anarchic word-coinages, and even for their nationalistic bias and their anti-Islamism.[18] The temperate appearance of Kasravi's
articles, however, does not conceal their rank contradictions, the faulty
logic of the arguments, the fanciful linguistic theories, and the arbitrary
historical constructions, which may be understood only in terms of
nationalistic motivation: "When a language is formed it must achieve independence and maintain its separateness. It must do this by closing its
gates on words from other languages even if they be from its own mother
language . . . . The language which does not shut its doors in the face of
foreign words loses its independence very much as the nation which does
not guard against foreigners loses her independence."[19] "It is a scientific
fact that every language must have words of its own, otherwise it loses its
independence; as our Persian has lost its independence."[20] Already a
peculiar and deep-rooted facet of modern nationalism in the Near East
is apparent: the yearning for an inviolate and transcendent symbol. Language is not a permutating tool of human communication. It is endowed
with organic life of its own. The purpose of that life is to symbolize
national independence.

Kasravi explains that the influx of Arabic words into Persian was the
work of pretentious writers who did not know Arabic well and wished to
conceal that fact by the profuse and indiscriminate use of Arabic words
in Persian.[21] (He took pride in his own thorough knowledge of Arabic.)
Kasravi, the meticulous historian of only recent times, now ignores historical proof and is satisfied with this intuitive behavioral supposition.
He passes scathing judgment on such well-known works of Persian prose
as *Kalila va Dimna, Tarikh-i-Vassaf,* and *Tarikh-i-Juvaini,* remarking that
"those who have pride of Iranism should read these works and sigh in
grief. . . . This is the language which a handful of ignorant scribes have
bequeathed to Persia, a language that may be condemned as the vilest
and the most tortuous of languages. . . and which is absolutely not fit
to be used by a people like the Persians."[22] Earlier in the same article
Kasravi had criticized the nationalistic bias of other "purifiers."

Grappling more directly with the issue at hand, Kasravi argues that
the border between Arabic and Persian must be guarded, "otherwise the
Persian language will not exist, as it does not exist today."[23] But this
vigilance is to be retroactive. It is not enough to bar the entry of new
aliens; old, settled, and naturalized ones must be uprooted and driven

out. "The only solution is to reverse the course that has brought us to this impasse and return the language to its state of a thousand years ago."[24] Still, all is not obduracy and rampant autonomy in the writings of Kasravi of the mid-1930s. He concedes the need to keep a certain number of "familiar" Arabic words "whose Persian equivalents have disappeared." He warns the young to follow the example of recognized authorities. He cautions against haste. And, most ironic of all, he denounces the synthesizing of words.[25] Instead, he directs the "purifier" to glean beautiful but abandoned Persian words from such classics as the *Golestan* and *Asrar al-Tauhid,* which abound in Arabic vocabulary.[26] Furthermore, he recognizes the need for coordination of efforts and exercise of central and final authority by the Ministry of Education.[27]

The *Peyman* articles drew the criticism of several prominent members of the scholarly "establishment," among them: Mohammad Qazvini, Mohammad ᶜAli Forughi, and Siyyid Hasan Taqizadeh. These men were exponents of tradition in Persian letters, and they were deeply offended by "purification." Kasravi's sense of single-handed messianic combat was enhanced by the fact that his opponents were ranking members of the government and close advisers of the Shah. But the Shah seldom took the advice of his scholar-ministers, and the chauvinism of the regime gave official sanction to the mania for "purification." In 1935 the *Farhangestan* was created. Its members included most of the reluctant traditionalist opponents of Kasravi, but he himself was snubbed. From its inception Kasravi clashed with the new institution. The disagreements were based on philological differences of opinion. The *Farhangestan* tried to use its official authority to compel Kasravi to abandon his own "purified" vocabulary and use its official adoptions. Numerous directives from the *Farhangestan,* the Ministry of Education, and the Office of the Prime Minister were sent to Kasravi to force his compliance. Kasravi responded with a long and defiant letter to Mahmud Jam, the prime minister at the time, protesting his higher loyalty to "science."[28] In the late 1930s nearly all publications were censored before going to press. Often the censor would make deletions and insert *Farhangestan*-approved words in Kasravi's manuscripts, only to have him cross out the censor's emendations and print the original version.[29] (There is perhaps an inherent measure of comic laxity in the grimmest of Near Eastern totalitarianisms.)

The second half of the 1930s were for Kasravi thankless years of working at odds, but for the same goals, with an increasingly despotic regime. In this period he turned more to the purely linguistic aspects of reforming Persian. His studies and proposals for more precise use of verbs, prefixes, suffixes, and tenses constitute the more positive and valuable side of his efforts on behalf of the Persian language. Yet even here the nationalistic impulse is not hard to detect. In the prologue of an essay on Persian verbs and ways of rendering them more precise, Kasravi says: "Often we read in European books that oriental languages are elastic and vague. They are so adamant on this issue that for centuries they have forced us to recognize as valid only the Western-language version of our mutual treaties when disputes arise. Their pretext is that oriental languages are inadequate. This is a humiliation for every oriental. But what answer can we give? What is true must be accepted. Having accepted, we must act to put our language in order, as I have been doing."[30]

The end of Reza Shah's twenty-five dictatorship in 1941 was sudden but not violent. The actual circumstances were ludicrous and anticlimatic; but the shock to the psyche of many Persians was of the first magnitude. The exposed moral sham and ideological shallowness of that regime was to many a national humiliation. As the rapid breakdown of political and economic order set in, there were many who sought the strength of a conviction, and so, competing ideological lines were drawn. The tinsel chauvinism of the Reza Shah period was now a debased commodity. The social concern and the "internationalism" of the left vied with the opportunism and the pragmatic defense of the vested interests on the right. Both the political left and the right were at once assisted and handicapped by real and apparent foreign support. But it was the unfulfilled nationalism of some concerned civil servants, university students, teachers, and a revealingly large number of young army officers which suddenly found its focus in Ahmad Kasravi. He had always enjoyed the devoted loyalty of a small coterie, but the aura of dissidence about him in the time of Reza Shah had kept many more away. Now he experienced an exhilirating sense of vindication, and a strong urge to action. A sterile and unresponsive official nationalism had, in fact, brought about the downfall of the nation; now was the moment to labor for its redemption. It was this spark of nationalism which provided Kasravi with an ardent following and imbued his authoritarian personality with the attributes of a charismatic leader.

He quickly molded his devotees into an organized and active movement known as *Bahmad-e Azadegan* (The Society of the Free). The experience of leading an actual movement, the entrancing resonance between the leader and his followers, and the tantalizing vision of power and actual significance radically affected Ahmad Kasravi. The intensification of his "purification" mania resulted in a self-wrought Persian that is well-nigh incomprehensible to the uninitiated. In place of the defunct *Peyman,* he published *Parcham* as the organ of *Bahmad-e Azadegan.* In it he advocated and practiced a headlong "purification" that grossly violated every condition that he had earlier established for this task in *Peyman.* Between 1941 and 1945 he published more than thirty large and small volumes of books essays, polemics, and speeches which elaborated his creed and its relation to the exigent problems of the day. His quasi-philosophical or "scriptural" works carry the cult of the *zaban-e pak* to enigmatic extreme. "Purification" had evolved from being a symptom of nationalism to becoming the symbol of its exclusiveness.

In 1945 Ahmad Kasravi was struck down by a Muslim zealot in a courtroom, as he was defending himself against charges of heresy. His movement survives, small but tenacious; galvanized and sustained by the catalyst of nationalism; and active in pursuit of language "purification." Its badge of identity and symbol of mystic communion is the *zaban-e pak.* Perversely, Kasravi's urgent concern for the unity and independence of the nation through the unity and purity of the language has succeeded in creating yet another insular and embattled core of loyalty, kept apart from the rest of the nation by a vritual language barrier. *Zaban-e pak* defeats its own highest nationalist motives, for it acts as a divisive force within Persia, and widens the chasm between the Persians and the Persian-speaking peoples beyond the country's borders.

NOTES

1.   A body appointed by the Council of Ministers in 1935, vaguely conceived along the lines of the French *Academie,* but concerned exclusively with purging the Arabic element from the Persian language and

decreeing "pure Persian" vocabulary to take its place. Like many similar enterprises of the Reza Shah regime it dissolved informally in 1941. It was resuscitated in 1962 with broader but vaguer intent, and it has not resumed either its "purificatory" functions or the manufacture of words.

2. Cf. Ahmad Kasravi, *Zendegani-ye man* (Tehran, 1944), pp. 5-6.

3. The term *maktab* has a specific meaning in the Persia of the 19th and the 20th centuries. It is the primary educational institution where teaching is done by a religious functionary—an *akhund,* or *mulla.* For further information see my *The Modernization of Iran* (Stanford, 1961), pp. 86-87.

4. Kasravi, *Zendegani,* p. 9.

5. Ahmad Kasravi, *Zaban-e Farsi,* collated and reprinted from vols. 1-4 of *Peyman* (Tehran, 1933-37), by Yahya Zoka' (Tehran, 1955), p. 26.

6. Cf. Kasravi, *Zendegani,* pp. 136, 205.

7. Cf. Kasravi, *Zaban-e Farsi,* p. 37.

8. Kasravi, *Zendegani,* pp. 87-88.

9. Cf. ibid., pp. 88-95.

10. Ahmad Kasravi, *Namha-ye shahrha va deyhha-ye Iran,* third edition (Tehran, 1956), pp. 4-5.

11. Cf. Kasravi, *Zaben-e Farsi,* p. 37.

12. The temptation to call it almost neo-Kantian is great. But Kasravi, characteristically, seldom acknowledged his intellectual creditors. That he was an avid follower of European intellectual trends—albeit in their pale and often distorted reflections in Turkish and Arabic journals—is frequently attested in his autobiography (*Zendegani-ye man,* pp. 43, passim). The western language he knew best and used most often was English. In his quasi-philosophical work, *Varjavand-e Bonyad* (first published in Tehran in 1943), he reveals a naive Newtonian mechanistic view of the universe, an almost deistic notion of religion, and a rigid humanistic basis of morality.

13. Cf. Kasravi, *Zendegani,* pp. 244-45.

14. Teimurtash had no interest in linguistics but was very sensitive to Persia's prestige abroad. Sir Dennison Ross's abridged translation of Kasravi's booklet, and the recognition of the Royal Asiatic Society alerted Teimurtash and caused him to seek out and bestow his patronage upon Kasravi.

15.   Kasravi, as has been noted, seldom identified individual sources of his ideas. It may well be that the watershed for his radical views on unity of language and the nation is to be found in a little event during his last year in the Ministry of Justice. In the winter of 1930 he was sent by the Ministry to western Persia as a member of a mission of general inspection. (Cf. Kasravi, *Zendegani*, pp. 311-12). In 1933 a collection of Persian essays and speeches of Siyyid Jamal al-Din Afghani were published in Tehran under the title, *Maqalat-e Jamaliyeh*. The editor of this volume was one Sefatollah Jamali (the first name, as well as names of his brothers, give a decided indication of Babi persuasion), son of Lotfollah Jamali who claimed to be the nephew of Jamal al-Din, as well as his emanuensis during both of his Persian visits. In a footnote on page 172 of this volume the editor states that Ahmad Kasravi, while he was in Asadabad with the Commission of Inspection in the winter of 1930, spent an evening in his house in order to peruse the manuscripts of Afghani which constitute the contents of the same volume published three and a half years later. The same footnote contains a translation by Kasravi of a verse of al-Ma^{c}ari cited in one of the papers of Afghani, and written by Kasravi on its margin in the course of that nocturnal visit. On pages 75-87 of this volume there is an essay entitled, "The Philosophy of Unity of Nationality and Unity of Language." In it Afghani argues that the only index of national unity is the unity of language, that in fact the two are identical, that unity of language is the prerequisite of national independence, and that unity of language is more meaningful and more enduring than unity of religion. Kasravi in his brief account of the inspection trip of 1930 does not mention his visit to the house of Jamali. Nor should this possible source of influence obscure the obvious influences of Mirza Aqa Khan Kermani, Mirza Ahmad Khan Sur-e Esrafil, Abol-Qasem Azad, and other assorted and occasional heirs of the spurious *Dasatir* tradition and advocates of *Parsi sareh* (straight Persian) upon Kasravi's notions of "purifying" Persian.

16.   Cf. Kasravi, *Zendegani*, pp. 231ff.

17.   Ibid., p. 275.

18.   Cf. Kasravi, *Zaban-e Farsi*, pp. 1-3, reprinted from vol. 1 (1933) of *Peyman*.

19.   Ibid., pp. 8-9.

20.   Ibid., p. 3.
21.   Cf. ibid., p. 12.
22.   Ibid., pp. 24, 29.
23.   Ibid., p. 9.
24.   Ibid., p. 14.
25.   Cf. ibid., p. 15.
26.   Cf. ibid., p. 18.
27.   Cf. ibid., p. 5.
28.   Cf. ibid., p. vi. (the editor's introduction).
29.   Cf. ibid., p. vi.
30.   Ibid., p. 33. Reprinted from vol. 3 (1936) of *Peyman.*
31.   Cf. Yahya Zoka', *Farhang-e Kasravi* (Tehran, 1957), p. 12.

EAST EUROPEAN MONOGRAPHS

The *East European Monographs* comprise scholarly books on the history and civilization of Eastern Europe. They are published by the *East European Quarterly* in the belief that these studies contribute substantially to the knowledge of the area and serve to stimulate scholarship and research.

Political Ideas and the Enlightenment in the Romanian Principalities, 1750-1831. By Vlad Georgescu. 1971.

America, Italy and the Birth of Yugoslavia, 1917-1919. By Dragan R. Zivjinovic. 1972.

Jewish Nobles and Geniuses in Modern Hungary. By William O. McCagg, Jr. 1972.

Mixail Soloxov in Yugoslavia: Reception and Literary Impact. By Robert F. Price. 1973.

The Historical and National Thought of Nicolae Iorga. By William O. Oldson. 1973.

Guide to Polish Libraries and Archives. By Richard C. Lewanski. 1974.

Vienna Broadcasts to Slovakia, 1938-1939: A Case Study in Subversion. By Henry Delfiner. 1974.

The 1917 Revolution in Latvia. By Andrew Ezergailis. 1974.

The Ukraine in the United Nations Organization: A Study in Soviet Foreign Policy. 1944-1950. By Konstantin Sawczuk. 1975.

The Bosnian Church: A New Interpretation. By John V. A. Fine, Jr., 1975.

Intellectual and Social Developments in the Habsburg Empire from Maria Theresa to World War I. Edited by Stanley B. Winters and Joseph Held. 1975.

Ljudevit Gaj and the Illyrian Movement. By Elinor Murray Despalatovic. 1975.

Tolerance and Movements of Religious Dissent in Eastern Europe. Edited by Bela K. Kiraly. 1975.

The Parish Republic: Hlinka's Slovak People's Party, 1939-1945. By Yeshayahu Jelinek. 1976.

The Russian Annexation of Bessarabia, 1774-1828. By George F. Jewsbury. 1976.

Modern Hungarian Historiography. By Steven Bela Vardy. 1976.

Values and Community in Multi-National Yugoslavia. By Gary K. Bertsch. 1976.

The Greek Socialist Movement and the First World War: The Road to Unity. By George B. Leon. 1976.

The Radical Left in the Hungarian Revolution of 1848. By Laszlo Deme. 1976.

Hungary between Wilson and Lenin: The Hungarian Revolution of 1918-1919 and the Big Three. By Peter Pastor. 1976.

The Crises of France's East-Central European Diplomacy, 1933-1938. By Anthony J. Komjathy. 1976.

Polish Politics and National Reform, 1775-1788. By Daniel Stone. 1976.

The Habsburg Empire in World War I. Robert A. Kann, Bela K. Kiraly, and Paula S. Fichtner, eds. 1977.

The Slovenes and Yugoslavism, 1890-1914. By Carole Rogel. 1977.

German-Hungarian Relations and the Swabian Problem. By Thomas Spira. 1977.

The Metamorphosis of a Social Class in Hungary During the Reign of Young Franz Joseph. By Peter I. Hidas. 1977.

Tax Reform in Eighteenth Century Lombardy. By Daniel M. Klang. 1977.

Tradition versus Revolution: Russia and the Balkans in 1917. By Robert H. Johnston. 1977.

Winter into Spring: The Czechoslovak Press and the Reform Movement 1963-1968. By Frank L. Kaplan. 1977.

The Catholic Church and the Soviet Government, 1939-1949. By Dennis J. Dunn. 1977.

The Hungarian Labor Service System, 1939-1945. By Randolph L Braham. 1977.

Consciousness and History: Nationalist Critics of Greek Society 1897-1914. By Gerasimos Augustinos. 1977.

Emigration in Polish Social and Political Thought, 1870-1914. By Benjamin P. Murdzek. 1977.

Serbian Poetry and Milutin Bojic. By Mihailo Dordevic. 1977.

The Baranya Dispute: Diplomacy in the Vortex of Ideologies, 1918-1921. By Leslie C. Tihany. 1978.

The United States in Prague, 1945-1948. By Walter Ullmann. 1978.

Rush to the Alps: The Evolution of Vacationing in Switzerland. By Paul P. Bernard. 1978.

Transportation in Eastern Europe: Empirical Findings. By Bogdan Mieczkowski. 1978.

The Polish Underground State: A Guide to the Underground, 1939-1945. By Stefan Korbonski. 1978.

The Hungarian Revolution of 1956 in Retrospect. Edited by Bela K. Kiraly and Paul Jonas. 1978.

Boleslaw Limanowski (1835-1935): A Study in Socialism and Nationalism. By Kazimiera Janina Cottam. 1978.

The Lingering Shadow of Nazism: The Austrian Independent Party Movement Since 1945. By Max E. Riedlsperger. 1978.

Britain and the War for Yugoslavia, 1940-1943. By Mark C. Wheeler. 1980.

The Turn to the Right: The Ideological Origins and Development of Ukrainian Nationalism, 1919-1929. By Alexander J. Motyl. 1980.

The Maple Leaf and the White Eagle: Canadian-Polish Relations, 1918-1978. By Aloysius Balawyder. 1980.

Antecedents of Revolution: Alexander I and the Polish Congress Kingdom, 1815-1825. By Frank W. Thackeray. 1980.

Blood Libel at Tiszaeszlar. By Andrew Handler. 1980.

Democratic Centralism in Romania: A Study of Local Communist Politics. By Daniel N. Nelson. 1980.

The Challenge of Communist Education: A Look at the German Democratic Republic. By Margrete Siebert Klein. 1980.

The Fortifications and Defense of Constantinople. By Byron C.P. Tsangadas. 1980.

Balkan Cultural Studies. By Stavro Skendi. 1980.

Studies in Ethnicity: The East European Experience in America. Edited by Charles A. Ward, Philip Shahshko, and Donald E. Pienkos. 1980.

The Logic of "Normalization:" The Soviet Intervention in Czechoslovakia and the Czechoslovak Response. By Fred Eidlin. 1980.

Red Cross. Black Eagle: A Biography of Albania's American Schol. By Joan Fultz Kontos. 1981.

Nationalism in Contemporary Europe. By Franjo Tudjman. 1981.

Great Power Rivalry at the Turkish Straits: The Montreux Conference and Convention of 1936. By Anthony R. DeLuca. 1981.

Islam Under the Double Eagle: The Muslims of Bosnia and Hercegovina, 1878-1914. By Robert J. Donia. 1981.

Five Eleventh Century Hungarian Kings: Their Policies and Their Relations with Rome. By Z.J. Kosztolnyik. 1981.

Prelude to Appeasement: East European Central Diplomacy in the Early 1930's. By Lisanne Radice. 1981.

The Soviet Regime in Czechoslovakia. By Zdenek Krystufek. 1981.

School Strikes in Prussian Poland, 1901-1907: The Struggle Over Bilingual Education. By John J. Kulczycki. 1981.

Romantic Nationalism and Liberalism: Joachim Lelewel and the Polish National Idea. By Joan S. Skurnowicz. 1981.

The "Thaw" In Bulgarian Literature. By Atanas Slavov. 1981.

The Political Thought of Thomas G. Masaryk. By roman Szporluk. 1981.

Prussian Poland in the German Empire, 1871-1900. By Richard Blanke. 1981.

The Mazepists: Ukrainian Separatism in the Early Eighteenth Century. By Orest Subtelny. 1981.

The Battle for the Marchlands: The Russo-Polish Campaign of 1920. By Adam Zamoyski. 1981.

Milovan Djilas: A Revolutionary as a Writer. By Dennis Reinhartz. 1981.